Banach Algebras

WALL, H. S. — Analytic Theory of Continued Fractions

HALMOS, PAUL R. — Measure Theory

JACOBSON, NATHAN — Lectures in Abstract Algebra

Vol. I — Basic Concepts

Vol. II — Linear Algebra

KLEENE, S. C. — Introduction to Metamathematics

LOOMIS, LYNN H. — An Introduction to Abstract Harmonic Analysis

LOÈVE, MICHEL — Probability Theory, 2nd Edition

KELLEY, JOHN L. — General Topology

ZARISKI, OSCAR, and SAMUEL, PIERRE — Commutative Algebra, Vols. I and II

GILLMAN, LEONARD, and JERISON, MEYER — Rings of Continuous Functions

RICKART, CHARLES E. — General Theory of Banach Algebras

A series of advanced text and reference books in pure and applied mathematics. Additional titles will be listed and announced as published.

General Theory of Banach Algebras

by

CHARLES E. RICKART
Professor of Mathematics
Yale University

D. VAN NOSTRAND COMPANY, INC.
PRINCETON, NEW JERSEY
TORONTO LONDON
NEW YORK

D. VAN NOSTRAND COMPANY, INC.
120 Alexander St., Princeton, New Jersey (*Principal office*)
24 West 40 Street, New York 18, New York

D. Van Nostrand Company, Ltd.
358, Kensington High Street, London, W.14, England

D. Van Nostrand Company (Canada), Ltd.
25 Hollinger Road, Toronto 16, Canada

Published simultaneously in Canada by
D. Van Nostrand Company (Canada), Ltd.

Library of Congress Catalogue Card No. 60–14788

PRINTED IN THE UNITED STATES OF AMERICA

PREFACE

A Banach algebra is a linear associative algebra which, as a vector space, is a Banach space with norm satisfying the multiplicative inequality $\| xy \| \leq \| x \| \, \| y \|$. Many of the Banach spaces which occur in analysis are at the same time Banach algebras under a multiplication operation which is itself important for the analysis. A good example is the space of absolutely integrable functions on the infinite real line under convolution as multiplication. In spite of the fact that examples from analysis have always provided the main impetus to the study of Banach spaces, a comparable interest in Banach algebras was rather late in coming. Some of the reason lies no doubt in the absence of appropriate algebraic tools, since a large part of the earlier work in algebra was based on finiteness conditions which rule out the most interesting examples from analysis. There were, of course, a number of early papers in which some of the additional structure given in a Banach space by an operation of multiplication was exploited, a few of the authors being Nagumo [1] and Yosida [1] (metric rings), von Neumann [1] and Murray and von Neumann [1] (rings of operators), and Stone [1]. Also, Wiener [1] and Beurling [1], although not explicitly drawing attention to the algebraic methods they were using, made systematic use of the algebraic properties of convolution in establishing certain deep theorems in analysis. However, it remained for Gelfand to lay the foundation for a general theory of Banach algebras in his now classical paper [4] on normed rings which was announced in 1939 [1] and appeared in 1941. Gelfand's innovation was a systematic use of elementary ideal theory coupled with the Mazur-Gelfand theorem which states that a normed division algebra (over the complex field) must be isomorphic with the complex field. His fundamental result was that a semi-simple commutative Banach algebra with an identity element is isomorphic to an algebra of continuous functions on a compact Hausdorff space. At the same time, Gelfand [7] used his theory to give an elegant proof of the well-known Wiener lemma that the reciprocal of a non-vanishing absolutely convergent Fourier series is also an absolutely convergent Fourier series. This proof attracted a great deal of attention to Banach algebras.

Since the appearance of Gelfand's 1941 papers, there has been a rapid growth of interest in Banach algebras. The resulting development of the subject has brought the theory to a point where it is no longer just a promising tool in analysis but is an important field of research in its own right. Standing, as it were, between analysis and algebra (or perhaps more accurately, with feet in analysis and head in algebra), the theory of Banach algebras has developed roughly along two main lines representing respectively the analytic and algebraic influences. The analytic emphasis has been on the study of certain special Banach algebras, along with some generalizations of these algebras, and on extending certain portions of function theory and harmonic analysis to the more general situations offered by Banach algebras. On the other hand, the algebraic emphasis has naturally been on various aspects of structure theory. Of great importance here has been the growing interest of algebraists in algebras without finiteness restrictions. This development, which has been much stimulated by the study of Banach algebras, has supplied important new algebraic methods which are profitably applied to Banach algebras. It becomes increasingly evident that, in spite of the deep and continuing influence of analysis on the theory of Banach algebras, the essence of the subject as an independent discipline is to be found in its algebraic development.

There is already an impressive literature concerning Banach algebras, so that it is obviously no longer possible to give a complete coverage of the subject in a single volume. Therefore, as the title indicates, this book is devoted primarily to an exposition of the general theory. Needless to say, an algebraic point of view has dominated strongly the selection and organization of material. Many of the applications to analysis have been omitted completely since they can be found in their proper context in works such as Hille-Phillips [1], Loomis [1], and Dunford-Schwartz [1]. A word is also in order here concerning rings of operators (or von Neumann Algebras). The theory of this important class of Banach algebras, which preceded and has since developed more or less independently of the general theory, is systematically covered in a recent book by Dixmier [15]. The original plan was to include an introduction to rings of operators which would place the theory of these algebras properly into the general theory, but limitations of both time and space have prevented this.

The main body of this book is divided into four chapters: I Fundamentals, II The radical, semi-simplicity and the structure spaces, III Commutative Banach algebras, and IV Algebras with an involution. In addition to the main text, there is a substantial Appendix devoted primarily to examples. It consists of three sections: Algebras of operators, Algebras of functions, and Group algebras. Finally, there is a Bibliography in which an attempt has been made to include every reference concerned at least in part with Banach algebras. It should go without saying that most of the many items in the Bibliography are not even mentioned in the text.

The many references scattered throughout the text are included primarily for the convenience of the reader. In other words, no attempt is made to give a specific reference for every result mentioned or to give priority credits in every case. On the other hand, at the end of most of the sections will be found remarks directed to the literature involving related results and applications or further development of the material covered in the section.

Section references are written in the form § 1.3, which means § 3 of Chapter I. Also, Corollary (3.2.3) and Theorem (3.2.4) are respectively the third and fourth numbered items in § 2 of Chapter III. Similarly, § A.1 means § 1 of the Appendix, and A.1.3 refers to the third numbered item in § 1 of the Appendix.

In general, the material covered here is rather closely integrated and was intended to be read in its entirety. However, the reader whose interests are less algebraic could perhaps skip the following sections: § 1.3, § 2.7, § 2.8, §§ 3.4–3.7. He might also omit most of the material scattered throughout the text which is primarily concerned with real algebras or algebras without an identity element. Finally, anyone who is only interested in commutative algebras could, without too much trouble, pass directly from Chapter I to Chapter III. Familiarity with the basic results from the theory of Banach spaces and Hilbert spaces as well as the elements of modern algebra is assumed. The ring theory which is required is sketched in Chapter II.

In the preparation of this book, I have profited greatly from suggestions and criticisms offered by many friends, especially by my colleagues and students at Yale. In particular, I have had the benefit of many valuable conversations with S. Kakutani and F. Quigley. P. C. Curtis and R. B. Smith did much of the work on the Bibliography. A. B. Willcox read carefully the final manuscript. Because of his efforts there are substantially fewer errors and obscurities in the text. T. Jenkins and N. McShane did much of the proof reading and preparation of an index. My deepest thanks go to my wife who with great patience and skill typed most of the manuscript. I also wish to acknowledge the financial support which was given at various stages of the writing by the Office of Ordnance Research (Contracts DA-19-059-ORD-2049 and DA-19-059-ORD-2300), the National Science Foundation (Grant NSF-G3017) and

Yale University. Finally, I wish to express my appreciation to Van Nostrand for their most efficient and understanding role in bringing this book to its completion.

C. E. R.

New Haven, Conn.
June, 1960

CONTENTS

Chapter I: FUNDAMENTALS

Chapter II: THE RADICAL, SEMI-SIMPLICITY AND THE STRUCTURE SPACES

Chapter III: COMMUTATIVE BANACH ALGEBRAS

I. FUNDAMENTALS

Introduction. This chapter contains a variety of topics which in one way or another are basic for everything which follows. The first section contains a few introductory definitions, including the definitions of real and complex Banach algebras. This section also contains the standard construction by which an identity element can be adjoined to a Banach algebra. In § 2, the regular representations are introduced and discussed briefly. (Representations in general are not taken up until the next chapter.) In § 3, the "complexification" of a real Banach algebra is introduced. This construction permits reduction of the study of many properties of a real Banach algebra to the complex case, which is usually somewhat more manageable. In § 4, the multiplicative group of regular elements in an algebra with an identity element is examined in some detail. This group, which forms a substantial portion of a Banach algebra, holds an important place in the theory. When the algebra does not possess an identity element, the group of regular elements is not defined and its role is taken over by the group of quasi-regular elements. In § 5, we study the topological divisors of zero in a Banach algebra. These elements are, in a sense, the most "singular" of the elements in the algebra as opposed to the regular elements discussed in § 4. They turn up at many points in the pages which follow. In § 6, the concept of the spectrum of an element in a Banach algebra is considered in detail. This is an extremely important notion for Banach algebras and is involved in a large part of the theory. Elementary proofs of the existence of the spectrum, the spectral radius formula and a variety of other properties of the spectrum are obtained in § 6. Finally, in § 7 the Mazur–Gelfand theorem which was mentioned in the preface is proved.

§ 1. Definitions. Let $\mathfrak{A}$ be a linear associative algebra with either the real or complex numbers as its field $\mathscr{F}$ of scalars.

The algebra $\mathfrak{A}$ is called a NORMED ALGEBRA provided there is associated with each element x a real number $\|x\|$, the NORM of x, with the properties:

(i) $\|x\| \geqslant 0$, and $\|x\| = 0$ if and only if $x = 0$.

(ii) $\|x+y\| \leqslant \|x\|+\|y\|$.

(iii) $\|\alpha x\| = |\alpha|\,\|x\|$, α a scalar.

(iv) $\|xy\| \leqslant \|x\|\,\|y\|$.

(v) If $\mathfrak{A}$ has an identity element 1, then $\|1\| = 1$.

Thus, as a vector space, $\mathfrak{A}$ is a normed linear space, and condition (iv), which is called the MULTIPLICATIVE CONDITION, forces continuity of multiplication in the norm topology of $\mathfrak{A}$. If $\mathfrak{A}$ is complete with respect to the norm (i.e. if $\mathfrak{A}$ is a Banach space), then it is called a BANACH ALGEBRA. Every normed algebra can be completed in the usual way to become a Banach algebra. The algebra is said to be REAL or COMPLEX according as $\mathscr{F}$ is the real or complex numbers.

Normed algebras constitute a subclass of a much wider class of objects known as TOPOLOGICAL RINGS. These are rings $\mathfrak{R}$ which carry a Hausdorff topology such that the mappings $(x, y) \rightarrow x-y$ and $(x, y) \rightarrow xy$, from the product space $\mathfrak{R}\times\mathfrak{R}$ into $\mathfrak{R}$, are continuous. A number of results obtained originally for Banach algebras have been extended to certain topological algebras by E. A. Michael [1]. Since virtually all of our attention will be directed toward normed algebras (and especially toward Banach algebras), we forego any discussion of general topological rings.

Many of the most important Banach algebras, for example the general case of a group algebra, do not possess an identity element. For this reason it is desirable to develop as much of the theory as possible without assumption of an identity. On the other hand, certain parts of the theory assume a more natural and better motivated form when an identity element is present. This dilemma is alleviated somewhat, though not resolved completely, by the fact that any normed algebra can be isometrically embedded in another normed algebra which does possess an identity element. To show this, let $\mathfrak{A}_1$ denote the vector space direct sum of $\mathfrak{A}$ with the field of scalars $\mathscr{F}$. Then elements of $\mathfrak{A}_1$ are pairs (x, α), where $x \in \mathfrak{A}$ and $\alpha \in \mathscr{F}$. With norm defined by the relation $\|(x, \alpha)\| = \|x\|+|\alpha|$, $\mathfrak{A}_1$ is a normed linear space and is a Banach space if and only if $\mathfrak{A}$ is a Banach space. If mulitiplication is defined by the relation $(x, \alpha)(y, \beta) = (\alpha y+\beta x+xy, \alpha\beta)$, then it is easy to see that $\mathfrak{A}_1$ becomes a normed algebra with identity element $(0, 1)$. The mapping $x \to (x, 0)$ establishes a norm preserving isomorphism of the algebra $\mathfrak{A}$ with a maximal closed 2-sided ideal in $\mathfrak{A}_1$. By this construction, the study of general Banach algebras can, with no loss of generality though perhaps with some loss of elegance, be reduced to consideration of Banach algebras with identity. The algebra $\mathfrak{A}_1$ will be referred to as the algebra obtained by adjunction of an identity to $\mathfrak{A}$. Notice that if $\mathfrak{A}$ already has an identity element, then that element is no longer an identity in $\mathfrak{A}_1$.

Even when $\mathfrak{A}$ does not possess an identity element, it will be convenient in computations to use the formal sum $\alpha+x$, where $\alpha \in \mathscr{F}$ and $x \in \mathfrak{A}$, in spite of the fact that it can be regarded as an element of $\mathfrak{A}$ only if $\alpha = 0$. For example, if $a \in \mathfrak{A}$, then $(\alpha+x)a$ means the element $\alpha a+xa$ of $\mathfrak{A}$. With this convention, it is easy to see that any algebraic computations performed on such formal sums are valid in $\mathfrak{A}$ provided everything is multiplied by an element of $\mathfrak{A}$.

A collection $\{e_\lambda : \lambda \in \Lambda\}$ of elements of $\mathfrak{A}$, where the index set Λ is a directed set, is called an APPROXIMATE IDENTITY for $\mathfrak{A}$ if the following two conditions are satisfied: $\|e_\lambda\| \leqq 1$, for each λ, and $\lim_\lambda e_\lambda x = \lim_\lambda xe_\lambda = x$, for each $x \in \mathfrak{A}$. (Segal [3].) Certain properties of algebras with an identity element extend easily to algebras with only an approximate identity. Important classes of Banach algebras which may not possess identity elements but always contain approximate identities are the L_1 group algebras (Appendix, § 3) and all $B^\star$-algebras (Theorem 4.8.14)).

As a general rule, our discussion of an abstract algebra will not presuppose the existence of an identity element unless an explicit statement is made to the contrary.

Banach algebras have been called METRIC RINGS by Nagumo [1] and Yosida [1]. They were called NORMED RINGS by Gelfand [1] and, more recently, BANACH RINGS by Naĭmark [7]. The terminology BANACH ALGEBRA, which has become rather common in the last few years, seems to have been used first by Ambrose [1].

§ 2. **The regular representations.** Let $\mathfrak{A}$ be any algebra over a field $\mathscr{F}$. Let $\mathfrak{X}$ be a linear vector space over the same field $\mathscr{F}$ and denote by $\mathfrak{L}(\mathfrak{X})$ the algebra of all linear transformations of $\mathfrak{X}$ into itself. Then any homomorphism of $\mathfrak{A}$ into the algebra $\mathfrak{L}(\mathfrak{X})$ is called a REPRESENTATION OF $\mathfrak{A}$ IN $\mathfrak{L}(\mathfrak{X})$ or ON $\mathfrak{X}$. The representation is called FAITHFUL if the homomorphism is an isomorphism. If $\mathscr{F}$ is either the reals or complexes and $\mathfrak{X}$ is a normed linear space, then a homomorphism of $\mathfrak{A}$ into the algebra $\mathscr{B}(\mathfrak{X})$ of all bounded linear transformations of $\mathfrak{X}$ into itself is called a NORMED REPRESENTATION. For the case of a normed algebra the term "representation" will, unless otherwise indicated, mean "normed representation". A representation $a \to T_a$ of a normed algebra $\mathfrak{A}$ on $\mathfrak{X}$ is said to be (uniformly) CONTINUOUS or BOUNDED provided there exists a constant β such that $\|T_a\| \leqslant \beta\|a\|$ for all $a \in \mathfrak{A}$. It is said to be STRONGLY CONTINUOUS provided for each $x \in \mathfrak{X}$ there exists a constant β_x such that $\|T_a x\| \leqslant \beta_x\|a\|$ for all $a \in \mathfrak{A}$. By the uniform boundedness theorem, any strongly continuous representation on a Banach space is continuous.

Among the representations of an algebra $\mathfrak{A}$ there is the so-called LEFT REGULAR representation on the vector space of $\mathfrak{A}$ obtained by taking for each $a \in \mathfrak{A}$ the linear transformation A_a defined by $A_a x = ax$. It is obvious that the mapping $a \to A_a$ so defined is a representation. Moreover, if $\mathfrak{A}$ is a normed algebra, then $\|A_a x\| = \|ax\| \leqslant \|a\|\,\|x\|$, so that A_a is bounded with $\|A_a\| \leqslant \|a\|$. Thus $a \to A_a$ is a continuous normed representation of $\mathfrak{A}$. Note that this representation will be faithful if and only if zero is the left annihilator of $\mathfrak{A}$. If $\mathfrak{A}$ has an approximate identity, then $\|ae_\lambda\| \to \|a\|$ and hence $\|A_a\| = \|a\|$, so that the regular representation is not only faithful but is norm preserving. A weaker condition giving the same result is that $\|a\| = \sup\,(\|ax\|/\|x\|)$, which says directly that $\|A_a\| = \|a\|$. When this condition is satisfied, a more "natural" adjunction of an identity element to $\mathfrak{A}$ can be obtained as follows. Identify $\mathfrak{A}$ with its image in $\mathscr{B}(\mathfrak{A})$ and let $\mathfrak{A}_1$ be the smallest subalgebra of $\mathscr{B}(\mathfrak{A})$ which contains $\mathfrak{A}$ and the identity of $\mathscr{B}(\mathfrak{A})$. In this case, if $\mathfrak{A}$ already has an identity, then $\mathfrak{A}_1 = \mathfrak{A}$.

We can always obtain a faithful norm preserving representation. For example, consider the representation of $\mathfrak{A}$ induced by the left regular representation of the algebra $\mathfrak{A}_1$ formed by adjunction of an identity element. It is convenient to refer to this representation as the EXTENDED LEFT REGULAR REPRESENTATION of $\mathfrak{A}$. In an analogous way, using right instead of left multiplication, we can define a RIGHT REGULAR and an EXTENDED RIGHT REGULAR REPRESENTATION of $\mathfrak{A}$. However in this case we have to do with anti-homomorphisms rather than homomorphisms. Denote by $\mathfrak{A}^{(l)}$ and $\mathfrak{A}^{(r)}$ the images of $\mathfrak{A}$ in $\mathscr{B}(\mathfrak{A}_1)$ under the extended left and extended right regular representations respectively. Also denote by $\mathfrak{J}$ the right ideal in $\mathscr{B}(\mathfrak{A}_1)$ consisting of all $T \in \mathscr{B}(\mathfrak{A}_1)$ such that $T(\mathfrak{A}_1) \subseteq \mathfrak{A}$. It is obvious that both $\mathfrak{A}^{(l)}$ and $\mathfrak{A}^{(r)}$ are contained in $\mathfrak{J}$. It is easy to verify that in order for an element T in $\mathfrak{J}$ to belong to $\mathfrak{A}^{(l)}$ (to $\mathfrak{A}^{(r)}$) it is necessary and sufficient that it commute with each element of $\mathfrak{A}^{(r)}$ (of $\mathfrak{A}^{(l)}$), in which case $T = A_a$ where $a = T(0, 1)$. We note in passing that a corollary of this observation is that the sets $\mathfrak{A}^{(l)}$ and $\mathfrak{A}^{(r)}$ are closed in $\mathscr{B}(\mathfrak{A}_1)$ with respect to the strong neighborhood topology for operators. If $\mathfrak{A}$ has an identity element, then analogous statements hold for the regular representations, with, of course, $\mathfrak{J} = \mathscr{B}(\mathfrak{A})$ and $T = A_a$, $a = T1$. (See Gelfand [4].)

It has already been observed that the multiplicative condition on the norm in a normed algebra has the effect of making the product xy a continuous function of x and y. Conversely, if $\mathfrak{A}$ is an algebra, which as a vector space is a Banach space such that the product xy is a continuous function of x for fixed y and of y for fixed x, then an equivalent norm can be introduced into $\mathfrak{A}$ for which the multiplicative condition is satisfied. (See Gelfand [4].) To prove this consider the extended left regular representation $a \to A_a$ on the vector space direct sum $\mathfrak{A}_1 = \mathfrak{A} \oplus \mathscr{F}$. It is defined by $A_a(x, \alpha) = (ax + \alpha a, 0)$. Note that $\mathfrak{A}_1$ is a Banach space under the norm $\|(x, \alpha)\| = \|x\| + |\alpha|$, where $\|x\|$ is the given norm in $\mathfrak{A}$. Since ax is continuous in x for fixed a, it follows that A_a is continuous with respect to the norm $\|(x, \alpha)\|$, so that A_a is bounded. In other words the representation $a \to A_a$ is normed. Now define in $\mathfrak{A}$ the new norm $\|a\|' = \|A_a\|$, which does have the multiplicative property. It only remains to prove that $\|a\|$ and $\|a\|'$ are equivalent. Since $\|A_a(0, 1)\| = \|(a, 0)\| = \|a\|$ and $\|(0, 1)\| = 1$, we have immediately that $\|a\| \leqslant \|a\|'$. On the other hand, if we define $F(a; x, \alpha) = \|ax + \alpha a\|/\|a\|$, then, since ax is a continuous function of a for fixed x, it follows that F is a bounded function of $a \neq 0$ for fixed x and α. It follows by the uniform boundedness theorem that

$$\frac{\|a\|'}{\|a\|} = \sup_{x,\alpha} F(a; x, \alpha) \leqslant \beta, \quad \|x\| + |\alpha| = 1,$$

where β is a constant independent of a. Therefore $\|a\| \leqslant \|a\|' \leqslant \beta\|a\|$ and thus the two norms are equivalent.

§ 3. Complexification of a real normed algebra. Most of the theory of Banach algebras is concerned with algebras over the complex field. However, algebras over the real field (which, of course, include the complex algebras) are of interest not only for their own sake but also because they throw some light on the complex case. Somewhat analogously to the case of algebras without an identity, the study of real algebras can be reduced to a study of complex algebras. This is done by embedding the given real algebra $\mathfrak{A}$ isometrically and (real) isomorphically in a certain complex normed algebra. The strictly algebraic portion of this problem is easy. In fact, let $\mathfrak{A}_C$ denote the cartesian product $\mathfrak{A} \times \mathfrak{A}$ in which algebraic operations are so defined that (x, y) behaves like $x+iy$. More precisely, define $(x, y)+(u, v) = (x+u, y+v)$, $(\alpha+\beta i)(x, y) = (\alpha x-\beta y, \alpha y+\beta x)$, and $(x, y)(u, v) = (xu-yv, xv+yu)$. Then it is readily verified that $\mathfrak{A}_C$ is a complex algebra and that the mapping $x \to (x, 0)$ is a (real) isomorphism of $\mathfrak{A}$ into $\mathfrak{A}_C$. The algebra $\mathfrak{A}_C$ is called the COMPLEXIFICATION of $\mathfrak{A}$. The main difficulty here is with the norm, the problem being to norm $\mathfrak{A}_C$ as a complex algebra in such a way that the isomorphism $x \to (x, 0)$ is an isometry. If we drop the requirement that $x \to (x, 0)$ be an isometry and ask only that it be a homeomorphism, then the problem is much easier (Kaplansky [5]). In fact, let $|(x, y)| = \|x\|+\|y\|$ and define $\|(x, y)\| = \sup_\theta |e^{i\theta}(x, y)|$. Then $\mathfrak{A}_C$ is a complex normed algebra with $\|(x, y)\|$ as norm and $\|(x, 0)\| = \sqrt{2}\|x\|$, so that $x \to (x, 0)$ is a homeomorphism but not an isometry. Also, if $\mathfrak{A}$ has an identity element 1 (of norm 1), then $(1,0)$ is an identity for $\mathfrak{A}_C$ but $\|(1, 0)\| = \sqrt{2}$. The problem of obtaining a norm in $\mathfrak{A}_C$ for which $x \to (x, 0)$ is an isometry is a bit more subtle than might at first be expected. Actually we find it convenient to deal first with a slightly different problem which, however, is interesting in itself.

THEOREM (1.3.1). *Let $\mathfrak{X}_C$ be the complexification of an arbitrary real normed linear space $\mathfrak{X}$. Then $\mathfrak{X}_C$ can be given a norm $\|(x, y)\|$ so that it is a complex normed linear space with the following properties:*

(i) *The isomorphism $x \to (x, 0)$ of $\mathfrak{X}$ into $\mathfrak{X}_C$ is an isometry.*

(ii) *$\mathfrak{X}_C$ is a Banach space if and only if $\mathfrak{X}$ is a Banach space.*

(iii) *Let T belong to $\mathscr{B}(\mathfrak{X})$ and define $T'(x, y) = (Tx, Ty)$ for (x, y) in $\mathfrak{X}_C$. Then the mapping $T \to T'$ is an isometric (real) isomorphism of the algebra $\mathscr{B}(\mathfrak{X})$ into $\mathscr{B}(\mathfrak{X}_C)$.*

PROOF. Note that $\mathfrak{X}_C$ is equal to the cartesian product $\mathfrak{X} \times \mathfrak{X}$ in which the operations of addition and multiplication by complex scalars are defined by the relations $(x, y)+(u, v) = (x+u, y+v)$ and $(\alpha+i\beta)(x, y) = (\alpha x-\beta y, \alpha y+\beta x)$. Now define $|(x, y)| = \|x\|+\|y\|$. Then $\mathfrak{X}_C$ becomes a *real* normed linear space with $|(x, y)|$ as norm. Observe that $\mathfrak{X}_C$ will be complete with respect to the norm $|(x, y)|$ if and only if $\mathfrak{X}$ is complete in its norm. Now define

$$\begin{aligned}\|(x,y)\| &= \frac{1}{\sqrt{2}} \sup_\theta |e^{i\theta}(x,y)| \\ &= \frac{1}{\sqrt{2}} \sup_\theta (\|x \cos \theta - y \sin \theta\| + \|x \sin \theta + y \cos \theta\|).\end{aligned}$$

It is readily verified that $\mathfrak{X}_C$ is a complex normed linear space under $\|(x, y)\|$ as norm. Also, since $\|x\| = |(x, 0)| = \|(x, 0)\|$, the embedding $x \to (x, 0)$ of $\mathfrak{X}$ in $\mathfrak{X}_C$ is an isometry. Moreover,

$$\frac{1}{\sqrt{2}} |(x, y)| \leqslant \|(x, y)\| \leqslant |(x, y)|,$$

so that the norms $|(x, y)|$ and $\|(x, y)\|$ are equivalent. In particular, $\mathfrak{X}_C$ will be a Banach space under $\|(x, y)\|$ if and only if $\mathfrak{X}$ is a Banach space. This establishes properties (i) and (ii).

For the proof of (iii), it is straightforward to check that T' is complex linear on $\mathfrak{X}_C$ and that $T \to T'$ is a real isomorphism of $\mathscr{B}(\mathfrak{X})$ into the algebra of complex linear transformations on $\mathfrak{X}_C$. Denote by $\|T\|$ the bound of T relative to $\|x\|$, and by $|T'|$ and $\|T'\|$ the bounds of T' relative to $|(x, y)|$ and $\|(x, y)\|$ respectively. Now

$$\|T\| = \sup_x \frac{\|Tx\|}{\|x\|} \leqslant \sup_{x,y} \frac{\|Tx\| + \|Ty\|}{\|x\| + \|y\|} \leqslant \|T\|.$$

Since

$$|T'| = \sup_{x,y} \frac{|T'(x, y)|}{|(x, y)|} = \sup_{x,y} \frac{\|Tx\| + \|Ty\|}{\|x\| + \|y\|},$$

we obtain that $\|T\| = |T'|$. Furthermore,

$$\begin{aligned}\|T'(x, y)\| &= \frac{1}{\sqrt{2}} \sup_\theta |e^{i\theta} T'(x, y)| = \frac{1}{\sqrt{2}} \sup_\theta |T'(e^{i\theta}(x, y))| \\ &\leqslant \frac{|T'|}{\sqrt{2}} \sup_\theta |e^{i\theta}(x, y)| = \|T\| \, \|(x, y)\|.\end{aligned}$$

Hence $\|T'\| \leqslant \|T\|$. On the other hand, $\|Tx\| = \|T'(x, 0)\| \leqslant \|T'\| \, \|x\|$, so that $\|T\| \leqslant \|T'\|$. Therefore $\|T\| = \|T'\|$ and the theorem is proved.

By the above theorem, if $a \to T_a$ is a normed representation of a real algebra $\mathfrak{A}$ in $\mathscr{B}(\mathfrak{X})$, then $a \to T'_a$ is a representation of $\mathfrak{A}$ in $\mathscr{B}(\mathfrak{X}_C)$. Moreover, the original representation is a norm-preserving restriction of the representation $a \to T'_a$. In this sense, the study of representations of a real algebra could be reduced to a study of representations of that algebra on a complex linear space.

We return now to the problem of norming $\mathfrak{A}_C$, where $\mathfrak{A}$ is a real normed algebra. The desired result is given in the next theorem.

THEOREM (1.3.2). *The complexification $\mathfrak{A}_C$ of any real normed algebra $\mathfrak{A}$ can be given a norm $\|(x, y)\|$ so that it becomes a complex normed algebra with the following properties:*

(i) *The isomorphism $x \to (x, 0)$ of $\mathfrak{A}$ into $\mathfrak{A}_C$ is an isometry.*

(ii) *$\mathfrak{A}_C$ is a Banach algebra if and only if $\mathfrak{A}$ is a Banach algebra.*

(iii) *If $\mathfrak{A}$ is a Banach algebra, then all norms under which $\mathfrak{A}_C$ is a complex Banach algebra and which satisfy* (i) *are equivalent.*

PROOF. Let $a \to T_a$ denote any norm-preserving representation of $\mathfrak{A}$ on a real normed linear space $\mathfrak{X}$ (in particular, $a \to T_a$ might be the extended left regular representation of $\mathfrak{A}$). By the preceding theorem, $a \to T'_a$ is a norm-preserving representation of $\mathfrak{A}$ in $\mathscr{B}(\mathfrak{X}_C)$. Notice that the mapping $(a, b) \to T'_a + iT'_b$ is an isomorphism of $\mathfrak{A}_C$ into $\mathscr{B}(\mathfrak{X}_C)$. Now define $\|(a, b)\| = \|T'_a + iT'_b\|$. Then $\mathfrak{A}_C$ is obviously a complex normed algebra under $\|(a, b)\|$, and $\|(a, 0)\| = \|a\|$ for all $a \in \mathfrak{A}$. This proves the first part of (i).

In order to establish (ii), we let $|(a, b)| = \|a\| + \|b\|$, as in the proof of the preceding theorem. Then

$$\|(a, b)\| = \|T'_a + iT'_b\| \leqslant \|T'_a\| + \|T'_b\| = |(a, b)|$$

and

$$\begin{aligned} \|T_a x\| + \|T_b x\| &= |(T'_a + iT'_b)(x, 0)| \leqslant \sqrt{2}\|(T'_a + iT'_b)(x, 0)\| \\ &\leqslant \sqrt{2}\|T'_a + iT'_b\| \, \|x\| = \sqrt{2}\|(a, b)\| \, \|x\|. \end{aligned}$$

Since $\|a\| = \|T_a\|$, it follows that $\|a\| \leqslant \sqrt{2}\|(a, b)\|$. Similarly, $\|b\| \leqslant \sqrt{2}\|(a, b)\|$ and therefore

$$|(a, b)| \leqslant 2\sqrt{2}\|(a, b)\| \leqslant 2\sqrt{2}|(a, b)|.$$

This proves that the two norms $|(a, b)|$ and $\|(a, b)\|$ are equivalent in $\mathfrak{A}_C$. It is obvious that $\mathfrak{A}_C$ is complete relative to $|(a, b)|$ if and only if

$\mathfrak{A}$ is complete. Therefore (ii) follows. Observe finally that any norm $\|(a, b)\|'$ in $\mathfrak{A}_C$ which satisfies (i) is such that

$$\|(a, b)\|' \leqslant \|a\| + \|b\| = |(a, b)|.$$

Therefore, if $\mathfrak{A}_C$ is complete with respect to each of these norms, then the two norms are equivalent by the closed graph theorem. Property (iii) follows from this and completes the proof of the theorem.

We close this section with a result suggested by the above discussion. (See Kaplansky [5].)

THEOREM (1.3.3). *Let $\mathfrak{A}$ be a complex algebra which is a real normed algebra under a given norm $|x|$. Also assume the mapping $x \to ix$ to be continuous relative to $|x|$. Then there exists a second norm $\|x\|$ in $\mathfrak{A}$ which is equivalent to the first and for which $\mathfrak{A}$ becomes a complex normed algebra.*

PROOF. Define $\|x\| = \sup_\theta |e^{i\theta}x|$. Then $\mathfrak{A}$ is a complex normed algebra under $\|x\|$ except that the identity element, if it exists in $\mathfrak{A}$, may not have norm equal to 1. This defect can easily be removed and will be ignored. That $\|x\|$ is equivalent to $|x|$ is proved as follows. Since $x \to ix$ is continuous, there exists a constant $\beta > 0$ such that $|ix| \leqslant \beta|x|$ for all x. Therefore

$$|x| \leqslant \|x\| = \sup_\theta |x \cos \theta + ix \sin \theta| \leqslant (1+\beta)|x|$$

and the two norms are equivalent.

§ 4. **The groups of regular and quasi-regular elements.** Let $\mathfrak{A}$ be a real or complex normed algebra with an identity. An element $r \in \mathfrak{A}$ is said to be LEFT (RIGHT) REGULAR provided there exists $s \in \mathfrak{A}$ such that $sr = 1$ ($rs = 1$). The element s is called a LEFT (RIGHT) INVERSE for r. An element which is both left and right regular is called REGULAR. In this case, all left and right inverses coincide in a unique element r^{-1} called the INVERSE of r. The set of all left regular elements will be denoted by G^l and the set of all right regular elements by G^r. The set $G^l \cap G^r$ of all regular elements will be denoted by G. Observe that G is a group under multiplication. If an element is not (left, right) regular then it is called (LEFT, RIGHT) SINGULAR and the set of all such elements is denoted by (S^l, S^r) S. Note that $S = S^l \cup S^r$. It is not difficult to verify that an element of $\mathfrak{A}$ is regular in $\mathfrak{A}$ if and only if it is regular in the complexification of $\mathfrak{A}$. As will be seen below, a Banach algebra is well supplied with regular elements. However, before proving this it is desirable to establish an important property of the norm in any normed algebra.

THEOREM (1.4.1). *The limit* $\nu(x) = \lim \|x^n\|^{1/n}$ *exists for each* $x \in \mathfrak{A}$ *and has the following properties:*

(i) $\nu(x) = \inf_n \|x^n\|^{1/n}$.

(ii) $0 \leqslant \nu(x) \leqslant \|x\|$.

(iii) $\nu(\alpha x) = |\alpha|\nu(x)$.

(iv) $\nu(xy) = \nu(yx)$ *and* $\nu(x^k) = \nu(x)^k$, $k = 1, 2, \cdots$.

(v) *If* $xy = yx$, *then* $\nu(xy) \leqslant \nu(x)\nu(y)$ *and* $\nu(x+y) \leqslant \nu(x)+\nu(y)$.

PROOF. We note in advance that the existence of the limit and property (i) depend only on the multiplicative property of the norm and, in fact, are consequences of a well-known elementary result for sequences of real numbers. (See Polya–Szego [1], vol. I, Prob. 98, p. 171.) A proof is included here for completeness.

Let $\nu = \inf \|x^n\|^{1/n}$. It is required to show that $\nu = \lim \|x^n\|^{1/n}$. For $\epsilon > 0$, choose m such that $\|x^m\|^{1/m} \leqslant \nu+\epsilon$. For arbitrary n, write $n = pm+q$, where $0 \leqslant q \leqslant m-1$. Then

$$\|x^n\|^{1/n} \leqslant \|x^m\|^{p/n}\|x\|^{q/n} \leqslant (\nu+\epsilon)^{pm/n}\|x\|^{q/n}.$$

Obviously $pm/n \to 1$ and $q/n \to 0$ as $n \to \infty$. Therefore

$$\limsup_{n\to\infty} \|x^n\|^{1/n} \leqslant \nu+\epsilon.$$

Since this holds for all $\epsilon > 0$ and $\nu \leqslant \|x^n\|^{1/n}$ for all n, the desired limit follows. Properties (ii), (iii), (iv) and the first part of (v) are quite easy. The second part of (v) is more difficult and will now be proved. (See Riesz and Sz.-Nagy [1, p. 426].)

Let x, y commute and choose real numbers α, β such that $\alpha > \nu(x)$ and $\beta > \nu(y)$. Set $a = \alpha^{-1}x$ and $b = \beta^{-1}y$. Then

$$\|(x+y)^n\|^{1/n} = \left\|\sum_{k=0}^{n} \binom{n}{k} x^k y^{n-k}\right\|^{1/n}$$

$$\leqslant \left[\sum_{k=0}^{n} \binom{n}{k} \alpha^k\beta^{n-k}\|a^k\|\,\|b^{n-k}\|\right]^{1/n}.$$

For each n, choose integers n' and n'' such that $n'+n'' = n$ and

$$\|a^{n'}\|\,\|b^{n''}\| = \max_{0\leqslant k\leqslant n} \|a^k\|\,\|b^{n-k}\|.$$

Then

$$\nu(x+y) \leqslant (\alpha+\beta)\|a^{n'}\|^{1/n}\|b^{n''}\|^{1/n}.$$

Now choose a sequence $\{n_m\}$ such that

$$\delta = \lim_{m\to\infty} \frac{n'_m}{n_m}$$

exists. Note that $0 \leqslant \delta \leqslant 1$ and that

$$\lim_{m\to\infty} \frac{n''_m}{n_m} = 1-\delta.$$

If $\delta \neq 0$, then necessarily $n'_m \to \infty$ and we have

$$\lim_{m\to\infty} \|a^{n'_m}\|^{1/n_m} = \lim_{m\to\infty} (\|a^{n'_m}\|^{1/n'_m})^{n'_m/n_m} = \nu(a)^\delta \leqslant 1.$$

If $\delta = 0$, then

$$\limsup_{m\to\infty} \|a^{n'_m}\|^{1/n_m} \leqslant \lim_{m\to\infty} \|a\|^{n'_m/n_m} = 1.$$

Thus, in either case,

$$\limsup_{m\to\infty} \|a^{n'_m}\|^{1/n_m} \leqslant 1.$$

Similarly we obtain

$$\limsup_{m\to\infty} \|b^{n''_m}\|^{1/n_m} \leqslant 1.$$

It follows that $\nu(x+y) \leqslant \alpha+\beta$. Since this holds for all $\alpha > \nu(x)$ and $\beta > \nu(y)$, we have $\nu(x+y) \leqslant \nu(x)+\nu(y)$. This completes the proof.

The above theorem shows that, if $\mathfrak{A}$ is commutative, then $\nu(x)$ is a pseudo-norm in $\mathfrak{A}$. In other words, $\nu(x)$ has all the properties of a norm with the possible exception that $\nu(x)$ may be zero for non-zero x. An important special situation is that for which $\nu(x)$ and $\|x\|$ coincide. The following lemma shows when this happens.

LEMMA (1.4.2). *In order for $\nu(x)$ to coincide with $\|x\|$ in $\mathfrak{A}$, it is necessary and sufficient that $\|x^2\| = \|x\|^2$ for every x in $\mathfrak{A}$.*

PROOF. If $\nu(x) = \|x\|$, then $\|x^2\| = \|x\|^2$, since $\nu(x^2) = \nu(x)^2$, by part (iv) of the above theorem. Hence the condition is necessary. Now assume that $\|x^2\| = \|x\|^2$, for all x. Then, by iteration, we obtain $\|x^{2^k}\| = \|x\|^{2^k}$ for all k. Therefore

$$\nu(x) = \lim_{k\to\infty} \|x^{2^k}\|^{1/2^k} = \|x\|,$$

and the sufficiency is proved.

DEFINITION (1.4.3). *An element x in a normed algebra such that $\nu(x) = 0$ is called* TOPOLOGICALLY NILPOTENT. *The set of all topologically nilpotent elements is denoted by N.*

Returning to the study of regular elements, we assume until further notice that $\mathfrak{A}$ has an identity element.

LEMMA (1.4.4). *If $\mathfrak{A}$ is a Banach algebra, then every element $r \in \mathfrak{A}$, such that $\nu(1-r) < 1$, is regular and its inverse is given by the series*

$$r^{-1} = 1+\sum_{n=1}^{\infty} (1-r)^n.$$

PROOF. Since $\nu(1-r) < 1$ and $\mathfrak{A}$ is complete, the above infinite series converges absolutely to an element r^{-1} of $\mathfrak{A}$. By continuity of multiplication and elementary properties of absolutely convergent series in a Banach space

$$rr^{-1} = r+\sum_{n=1}^{\infty} r(1-r)^n = r+\sum_{n=1}^{\infty} (r-1)(1-r)^n+\sum_{n=1}^{\infty} (1-r)^n$$

$$= r-\sum_{n=1}^{\infty} (1-r)^{n+1}+\sum_{n=1}^{\infty} (1-r)^n = r+(1-r) = 1.$$

Similarly, $r^{-1}r = 1$, so that r is regular with inverse r^{-1}.

COROLLARY (1.4.5). *If $\|1-r\| < 1$, then r is regular.*

THEOREM (1.4.6). *If $\mathfrak{A}$ is a Banach algebra and r is left (right) regular with s as a left (right) inverse, then any element $x \in \mathfrak{A}$ such that $\|r-x\| < \|s\|^{-1}$ is also left (right) regular. Therefore each of the sets G^l, G^r and G is open.*

PROOF. Since $\|1-sx\| = \|s(r-x)\| \leqslant \|s\| \, \|r-x\|$, the condition $\|r-x\| < \|s\|^{-1}$ implies $\|1-sx\| < 1$, so that sx is regular. But regularity of sx implies left regularity of x and the theorem is proved.

THEOREM (1.4.7). *Let $\mathfrak{A}$ be a Banach algebra and $\{r_n\}$ a sequence of left (right) regular elements of $\mathfrak{A}$ which converges to an element $r \in \mathfrak{A}$. If s_n is a left (right) inverse for r_n and if $\{s_n\}$ is a bounded sequence, then r is also left (right) regular.*

PROOF. Since $1-s_nr = s_n(r_n-r)$, boundedness of $\{s_n\}$ and the fact that $r_n \to r$ implies $\|1-s_nr\| < 1$ for large n. Therefore s_nr is regular for large n. But regularity of $s_n r$ implies left regularity of r and the theorem follows.

THEOREM (1.4.8). *For any normed algebra with identity, the mapping* $r \to r^{-1}$ *is a homeomorphism of* G *onto* G.

PROOF. It will be sufficient to prove that the mapping $r \to r^{-1}$ is continuous. Suppose that $r, r+h \in G$ and set $(r+h)^{-1} = r^{-1}+k$. The problem is to show that if $\|h\|$ is small then $\|k\|$ is small. Since

$$1 = (r^{-1}+k)(r+h) = 1+r^{-1}h+kr+kh,$$

it follows that $r^{-1}h+kr+kh = 0$. Multiplying this equation on the right by r^{-1}, we obtain $r^{-1}hr^{-1}+k+khr^{-1} = 0$ and hence $k = -r^{-1}hr^{-1}-khr^{-1}$. Therefore $\|k\| \leqslant \|r^{-1}\|^2\|h\|+\|k\|\,\|h\|\,\|r^{-1}\|$ and, if $\|h\|\,\|r^{-1}\| < 1$, then

$$\|k\| \leqslant \frac{\|r^{-1}\|^2}{1-\|h\|\,\|r^{-1}\|}\|h\|.$$

For ϵ such that $0 < \epsilon < \|r^{-1}\|$, choose $\delta = (2\|r^{-1}\|^2)^{-1}\epsilon$. Then, for $\|h\| < \delta$, we have $\|h\|\,\|r^{-1}\| < \delta\|r^{-1}\| < \frac{1}{2}$ and hence

$$\|k\| < 2\|r^{-1}\|^2\|h\| < 2\|r^{-1}\|^2\delta = \epsilon.$$

This proves the theorem.

DEFINITION (1.4.9). *That component of the group* G *which contains the identity element is called the* PRINCIPAL COMPONENT *and is denoted by* G_1.

At this point it is desirable to define the exponential and logarithmic functions for elements of a Banach algebra $\mathfrak{A}$. We need only the most elementary properties of these functions and refer the reader to Hille–Phillips [1, § 5.4] and Hille [3] for a complete discussion. For x an element of $\mathfrak{A}$, define

$$\exp x = 1+\sum_{n=1}^{\infty}\frac{x^n}{n!}.$$

The series converges absolutely for all x. Thus, if x and y commute, then it is straightforward to prove the addition formula

$$\exp(x+y) = \exp x \exp y.$$

In particular, $\exp(-x) = (\exp x)^{-1}$, so that $x \to \exp x$ is a mapping of $\mathfrak{A}$ into the group G.

A logarithm of an element $x \in \mathfrak{A}$ is defined to be any solution $y \in \mathfrak{A}$ of the equation $\exp y = x$. In other words an element has a logarithm if and only if it belongs to the range of the exponential function. Thus a necessary (but not sufficient) condition for the logarithm to exist is that the element in question be regular. A sufficient (but not necessary) condition is that $\nu(1-x) < 1$. In fact, set

$$\log x = -\sum_{n=1}^{\infty} \frac{1}{n}(1-x)^n.$$

Then the series converges absolutely for $\nu(1-x) < 1$ and defines a solution $y = \log x$ of the equation $\exp y = x$.

THEOREM (1.4.10). *Let E denote the set of all those elements of G which have logarithms. Then the subgroup of G generated by E coincides with the principal component G_1.*

PROOF. Let $\exp v = u$ and consider the set

$$H_u = \{\exp(\xi v) : -\infty < \xi < \infty\}.$$

It is obvious that H_u is an abelian subgroup of G which contains u. Moreover, since

$$\begin{aligned} \|\exp(\xi v) - \exp(\xi_0 v)\| &\leqslant \|\exp(\xi_0 v)\| \, \|\exp(\xi-\xi_0)v - 1\| \\ &\leqslant \|\exp(\xi_0 v)\| \, |\exp(|\xi-\xi_0| \, \|v\|) - 1|, \end{aligned}$$

the mapping $\xi \to \exp(\xi v)$ is continuous. It follows that H_u is connected and hence $E \subseteq G_1$. Therefore the subgroup G_0 of G generated by E is contained in G_1. Observe that G_0 consists of all finite products of elements from E. We prove that G_0 exhausts G_1 by showing that G_0 is both open and closed in G. First let $\{u_n\}$ be a sequence of elements of G_0 which converges to an element u of G. Then $u_n^{-1}u \to 1$ and hence $u_n^{-1}u \in E$ for large n. Since $u = u_n(u_n^{-1}u)$, it follows that $u \in G_0$. In other words, G_0 is closed in G. Next let u_0 be any element of G_0. If u is any element of G such that $\|u-u_0\| < \|u_0^{-1}\|^{-1}$, then $\|u_0^{-1}u - 1\| \leqslant \|u_0^{-1}\| \, \|u-u_0\| < 1$. Hence $u_0^{-1}u \in E$ and again we obtain $u \in G_0$. This shows that G_0 is open in G and completes the proof that $G_0 = G_1$.

COROLLARY (1.4.11). *In order for every element of G_1 to have a logarithm (that is, $E = G_1$), it is necessary and sufficient that E be a group. In particular, if $\mathfrak{A}$ is commutative, then $E = G_1$.*

The following theorem is due to Nagumo [1].

THEOREM (1.4.12). *In order for an element of $\mathfrak{A}$ to have a logarithm,* *it is necessary and sufficient that it be contained in a connected abelian subgroup of* G.

PROOF. The necessity was established in the proof of the above theorem. For the sufficiency we have only to show that every connected abelian subgroup H is contained in E. Let $\mathfrak{C}$ denote any closed commutative subalgebra of $\mathfrak{A}$ which contains H. By the above corollary, every element of the principal component of the group of regular elements in $\mathfrak{C}$ has a logarithm. Since H is a connected group in $\mathfrak{C}$, it is contained in the principal component. Therefore every element of H has a logarithm in $\mathfrak{C}$ and hence in $\mathfrak{A}$.

LEMMA (1.4.13). *If* $\mathfrak{A}$ *is a complex Banach algebra and* r *is an element of* G *with finite order, then* $r \in G_1$.

PROOF. Since r is of finite order, there exists an integer m such that $r^m = 1$. Let λ be any complex number and define

$$u_\lambda = \sum_{k=0}^{m-1} (\lambda - 1)^k (\lambda r)^{m-k-1}.$$

Then, since $\lambda^m - (\lambda - 1)^m = (\lambda r)^m - (\lambda - 1)^m$, we have

$$\lambda^m - (\lambda - 1)^m = (\lambda r + 1 - \lambda) u_\lambda = u_\lambda (\lambda r + 1 - \lambda).$$

Hence, if $\lambda^m - (\lambda - 1)^m \neq 0$, then the element $\lambda r + 1 - \lambda$ is regular. It follows that $\lambda r + 1 - \lambda$ is regular for all but a finite number of values of λ and, in particular, the set of those λ for which $\lambda r + 1 - \lambda$ is regular is a connected set. Since $\lambda \to \lambda r + 1 - \lambda$ is a continuous mapping of the complex plane into $\mathfrak{A}$, we conclude that regular elements of the form $\lambda r + 1 - \lambda$ constitute a connected subset of G. Finally, $\lambda = 0$ gives the identity element and $\lambda = 1$ gives r. Therefore $r \in G_1$.

We can now prove the next theorem which is due to Lorch [1].

THEOREM (1.4.14). *Let* $\mathfrak{A}$ *be a complex commutative Banach algebra. Then the group* G *is either connected or has an infinite number of components.*

PROOF. The proof consists in showing that, if r is an element of G not in G_1, then the various powers of r lie in distinct components of G. Suppose, on the contrary, that there exist integers $k < l$ such that r^k and r^l lie in the same component of G. If $m = l - k$, then $r^m \in G_1$. By Corollary (1.4.11), there exists $v \in \mathfrak{A}$ such that $\exp v = r^m$. Define $u = \exp(1/m)v$. Then $u^m = r^m$ and hence $(u^{-1}r)^m = 1$. By the preceding lemma, this implies $u^{-1}r \in G_1$. Since $u \in G_1$ and $r = u(u^{-1}r)$, it follows that $r \in G_1$. This contradicts the assumption that $r \notin G_1$ and completes the proof.

Examples show that the number of components in G can be either countably or uncountably infinite. (See Examples A.2.1 and A.2.10.)

We turn attention now to an algebra $\mathfrak{A}$ which does not possess an identity element, so that the above definitions of regularity do not apply. One could, of course, apply the above discussion to the algebra obtained by adjunction of an identity to $\mathfrak{A}$ and then interpret the results back in the original algebra. However it is easier and more instructive to give a discussion which is intrinsic to the given algebra. In order to do this, it is necessary to consider a new operation in $\mathfrak{A}$, called the CIRCLE OPERATION, defined by the equation

$$x \circ y = x+y-xy.$$

This operation is clearly associative and has the zero element of $\mathfrak{A}$ as an identity element. If $\mathfrak{A}$ happens already to possess an identity element (for multiplication), then the relationship between the circle operation and multiplication is shown by the identity

$$(1-x)(1-y) = 1-(x \circ y).$$

Thus the mapping $x \rightarrow x^q = 1-x$ of $\mathfrak{A}$ onto itself has the property $(x \circ y)^q = x^q y^q$. In other words, it transforms the circle operation into the operation of multiplication. The importance of the circle operation in a sense derives from this relationship to multiplication, but for obvious reasons it is more difficult to manipulate than is multiplication. Even when $\mathfrak{A}$ does not possess an identity element, the formal identity $(1-x)(1-y) = 1-(x \circ y)$ provides a convenient guide to computation.

An element of $\mathfrak{A}$ which has a left (right) inverse relative to the circle operation is said to be LEFT (RIGHT) QUASI-REGULAR and the inverse is called a LEFT (RIGHT) QUASI-INVERSE. If r is both left and right quasi-regular then it is called QUASI-REGULAR, in which case all left and right quasi-inverses coincide in a unique QUASI-INVERSE r° for r. An element which is not (left, right) quasi-regular is called (LEFT, RIGHT) QUASI-SINGULAR. It is convenient to denote the various sets of quasi-regular and quasi-singular elements by the same symbols used to denote the sets of regular and singular elements but with a superscript q added. Thus the set of all left-quasi-regular elements will be denoted by G^{lq}, etc. The set G^q of all quasi-regular elements is obviously a group under the circle operation. If $\mathfrak{A}$ has an identity element, then G^{lq}, for example, is actually the image of the set G^l under the mapping

$x \to x^q = 1-x$. In particular, this mapping takes isomorphically the group G onto the group G^q and the group G^q onto the group G.

It is not difficult to verify that an element r is (left, right) quasi-regular in $\mathfrak{A}$ if and only if it is (left, right) quasi-regular in the complexification of $\mathfrak{A}$. Also, if $\mathfrak{A}_1$ is the algebra obtained from $\mathfrak{A}$ by adjunction of an identity element 1, then an element $r \in \mathfrak{A}$ is (left, right) quasi-regular in $\mathfrak{A}$ if and only if r is (left, right) quasi-regular, and hence $1-r$ is (left, right) regular, in $\mathfrak{A}_1$.

Theorem (1.4.15). *If the representation $a \to A_a$ on $\mathfrak{X}$ is either the left regular or extended left regular representation of $\mathfrak{A}$, according as $\mathfrak{A}$ has or does not have an identity, then an element $r \in \mathfrak{A}$ is quasi-regular in $\mathfrak{A}$ if and only if A_r is quasi-regular in $\mathscr{B}(\mathfrak{X})$.*

Proof. We make the proof for the extended left regular representation. It is obvious that quasi-regularity of r implies quasi-regularity of A_r. Therefore let A_r have a quasi-inverse A_r° in $\mathscr{B}(\mathfrak{X})$. Since $A_r^\circ = A_rA_r^\circ - A_r$, it is obvious that A_r° belongs to the right ideal of elements in $\mathscr{B}(\mathfrak{X})$ which map $\mathfrak{X} = \mathfrak{A} \oplus \mathscr{F}$ into $\mathfrak{A}$. Therefore we have only to show that A_r° commutes with each element of $\mathscr{B}(\mathfrak{X})$ in the image of the extended right regular representation of $\mathfrak{A}$. This comes down to showing that $A_r^\circ((x, \alpha)y) = (A_r^\circ(x, \alpha))y$ for all $x, y \in \mathfrak{A}$ and $\alpha \in \mathscr{F}$. Since

$$\begin{aligned}(A_r^\circ(x, \alpha))y &= (I-A_r^\circ)(I-A_r)((A_r^\circ(x, \alpha))y)\\ &= (I-A_r^\circ)(((A_r^\circ-A_rA_r^\circ)(x, \alpha))y)\\ &= (I-A_r^\circ)(((-A_r)(x, \alpha))y)\\ &= (-A_r+A_r^\circ A_r)((x, \alpha)y) = A_r^\circ((x, \alpha)y),\end{aligned}$$

the proof is complete.

Corollary (1.4.16). *Let $\mathfrak{A}$ have an identity element and let $a \to A_a$ be the left regular representation of $\mathfrak{A}$. Then an element $r \in \mathfrak{A}$ is regular in $\mathfrak{A}$ if and only if A_r is regular in $\mathscr{B}(\mathfrak{A})$.*

Lemma (1.4.17).

(i) *For all x and y, $(x \circ y)(1-x) = (1-x)(y \circ x)$.*

(ii) *If $s \circ r = 0$, then $(x-s)(1-r) = x \circ r$ and $(1-s)(x-r) = s \circ x$ for all x.*

(iii) *Left (right) quasi-regularity for $(\alpha+x)y$ is equivalent to left (right) quasi-regularity for $y(\alpha+x)$.*

PROOF. The first two statements may be verified by direct calculation. For the proof of (iii) write $\bar{x} = \alpha + x$ and, for s any element of $\mathfrak{A}$, set $t = y(s-1)\bar{x}$. Then $(y\bar{x}) \circ t = y((\bar{x}y) \circ s)\bar{x}$ and $t \circ (y\bar{x}) = y(s \circ (\bar{x}y))\bar{x}$. Hence, if s is a left (right) quasi-inverse for $\bar{x}y$, then t is a left (right) quasi-inverse for $y\bar{x}$. This proves one-half the equivalence. The other half is obtained by interchanging $\bar{x}$ and y in the above argument.

We obtain now a sequence of properties of quasi-regularity which parallels the properties already obtained for regularity.

LEMMA (1.4.18). *If $\mathfrak{A}$ is a Banach algebra, then every element $r \in \mathfrak{A}$ such that $\nu(r) < 1$ is quasi-regular with quasi-inverse*

$$r^{\circ} = -\sum_{n=1}^{\infty} r^n.$$

PROOF. Since $\nu(r) < 1$ and $\mathfrak{A}$ is complete, the series converges in $\mathfrak{A}$, so that r° is defined. Moreover

$$r \circ r^{\circ} = r - \sum_{n=1}^{\infty} r^n + \sum_{n=1}^{\infty} r^{n+1} = 0.$$

Similarly $r^{\circ} \circ r = 0$, and r is quasi-regular.

COROLLARY (1.4.19). *If $\|r\| < 1$, then r is quasi-regular in $\mathfrak{A}$.*

THEOREM (1.4.20). *If $\mathfrak{A}$ is a Banach algebra and r is a left (right) quasi-regular element with s as a left (right) quasi-inverse, then $\|x-r\| < (1+\|s\|)^{-1}$ implies that x is left (right) quasi-regular. Therefore the sets G^{lq}, G^{rq} and G^{q} are open.*

PROOF. Since $s \circ x = (1-s)(x-r)$, we have $\|s \circ x\| \leqslant (1+\|s\|)\|x-r\|$. Now, if $\|x-r\| < (1+\|s\|)^{-1}$, then $\|s \circ x\| < 1$, so that $s \circ x$ is quasi-regular. This implies that x is left quasi-regular and completes the proof.

THEOREM (1.4.21). *Let $\mathfrak{A}$ be a Banach algebra and $\{r_n\}$ a sequence of left (right) quasi-regular elements of $\mathfrak{A}$ which converges to an element r. If s_n is a left (right) quasi-inverse for r_n and if $\{s_n\}$ is a bounded sequence, then r is left (right) quasi-regular.*

PROOF. By Lemma (1.4.17), $s_n \circ r = (1-s_n)(r-r_n)$. Therefore $\|s_n \circ r\| \leqslant (1+\|s_n\|)\|r-r_n\|$. If $\{s_n\}$ is bounded, then, since $\|r-r_n\| \to 0$, $s_n \circ r$ will be quasi-regular for large n. Since quasi-regularity of $s_n \circ r$ implies left quasi-regularity of r, the desired result follows.

THEOREM (1.4.22). *For any normed algebra, the quasi-inverse mapping $r \to r^\circ$, is a homeomorphism of G^q onto G^q.*

PROOF. Let $r, r+h \in G^q$ and set $(r+h)^\circ = r^\circ + k$. By Lemma (1.4.17) (ii) (with $x = r+h$ and $s = r^\circ$), $(1-r^\circ)h = r^\circ \circ (r+h)$. Hence $((1-r^\circ)h) \circ (r^\circ + k) = r^\circ$ or $(1-h+r^\circ h)k = (1-r^\circ)h(r^\circ - 1)$. Therefore $\|k\| - (1+\|r^\circ\|)\|h\|\,\|k\| \leqslant (1+\|r^\circ\|)^2\|h\|$, so that, if $(1+\|r^\circ\|)\|h\| < 1$, then

$$\|k\| \leqslant \frac{(1+\|r^\circ\|)^2\|h\|}{1-(1+\|r^\circ\|)\|h\|}.$$

For arbitrary ϵ such that $0 < \epsilon < 1$, let $\delta = \frac{1}{2}\epsilon(1+\|r^\circ\|)^{-2}$. Then $\|h\| < \delta$ implies $\|k\| < \epsilon$, which proves the theorem.

We close this section with the following sharpening of Theorems (1.4.7) and (1.4.21) in a special case needed later.

THEOREM (1.4.23). *Let $\mathfrak{A}$ be a Banach algebra and $\{r_n\}$ a sequence of regular (quasi-regular) elements of $\mathfrak{A}$ which converges to an element $r \in \mathfrak{A}$ such that $rr_n = r_n r$ for each n. If s_n is an inverse (quasi-inverse) for r_n and if $\{\nu(s_n)\}$ is a bounded sequence, then r is also regular (quasi-regular).*

PROOF. In the regular case, as in the proof of Theorem (1.4.7), we have $1-s_n r = s_n(r_n - r)$. Since the elements which appear in this relation commute, we can apply Theorem (1.4.1)(v) to obtain $\nu(1-s_n r) \leqslant \nu(s_n)\nu(r_n - r) \leqslant \nu(s_n)\|r_n - r\|$. Therefore $\nu(1-s_n r) \to 0$, so that $s_n r$ is regular for large n. It follows that r is regular. A similar modification of the proof of Theorem (1.4.21) gives the quasi-regular case.

The "circle" notation "$x \circ y$" was introduced by Kaplansky [1] to denote the operation $x+y+xy$, which has been used by a number of writers (for example, Perlis [1] and Jacobson [2]). More recently, the notation $x \circ y$ has been used for the operation $x+y-xy$, which is preferable to $x+y+xy$ for technical reasons. (See Jacobson [5] and Rickart [3].) Hille [2, Sec. 22.6] used the notation $x \times y$ for $x+y-xy$ and called the inverse of an element with respect to this operation the REVERSE of the element. Segal [2] also uses this operation and calls the inverse element an ADVERSE. We have followed Perlis and Jacobson in the use of the prefix "quasi-" to distinguish concepts associated with the circle operation from the corresponding notions for multiplication. The proof of Theorem (1.4.8) is due to Arens [3]. The fundamental group of the principal component G_1 of G has been studied by E. K. Blum [1].

§ 5. Topological divisors of zero.

Let $\mathfrak{A}$ be a normed algebra. An element $z \in \mathfrak{A}$ is called a LEFT (RIGHT) TOPOLOGICAL DIVISOR OF ZERO provided there exists a sequence $\{z_n\}$ in $\mathfrak{A}$ such that $\|z_n\| = 1$ for all n and $zz_n \to 0$ ($z_n z \to 0$). An element which is either a left or a right topological divisor of zero is called simply a TOPOLOGICAL DIVISOR OF ZERO. If it is both a left and a right topological divisor of zero, then it is called a 2-SIDED TOPOLOGICAL DIVISOR OF ZERO. Any divisor of zero is obviously a topological divisor of zero. Also, it is not difficult to verify that z is a topological divisor of zero in $\mathfrak{A}$ if and only if it is a topological divisor of zero in the complexification of $\mathfrak{A}$. Any element which is a (left, right) topological divisor of zero is automatically (left, right) singular. In fact, if $wz = 1$, then $wzz_n = z_n$, so that $zz_n \to 0$ implies $z_n \to 0$. More generally, a (left, right) topological divisor of zero is PERMANENTLY (left, right) SINGULAR in the sense that it will be (left, right) singular in any normed algebra which contains $\mathfrak{A}$ topologically as a subalgebra.

The set of all topological divisors of zero in $\mathfrak{A}$ will be denoted by Z. The sets of left and of right topological divisors of zero will be denoted by Z^l and Z^r respectively. Note that $Z = Z^l \cup Z^r$. The complements of these sets in $\mathfrak{A}$ will be denoted by H^l, H^r and H respectively. From the above remarks we obtain the following inclusions when $\mathfrak{A}$ has an identity: $Z^l \subseteq S^l$, $Z^r \subseteq S^r$ and $Z \subseteq S$, so that $G^l \subseteq H^l$, $G^r \subseteq H^r$ and $G \subseteq H$. An element which is left (right) regular but right (left) singular is necessarily a right (left) divisor of zero. For, if $wz = 1$ and $zw \neq 1$, then $1 - zw \neq 0$ and $(1-zw)z = 0$. Therefore we also have the inclusions $G^l \cap S^r \subseteq Z^r$ and $G^r \cap S^l \subseteq Z^l$. It follows easily that $G = G^l \cap H^r = G^r \cap H^l$.

It is convenient to introduce the functions

$$\lambda(x) = \inf_y \frac{\|xy\|}{\|y\|}, \qquad \rho(x) = \inf_y \frac{\|yx\|}{\|y\|}.$$

Obviously $\lambda(z) = 0$ if and only if $z \in Z^l$ and $\rho(z) = 0$ if and only if $z \in Z^r$. (See Rickart [2].)

LEMMA (1.5.1). *The functions* λ, ρ *have the properties*

(i) $|\lambda(x) - \lambda(y)| \leqslant \|x-y\|$, $|\rho(x) - \rho(y)| \leqslant \|x-y\|$.

(ii) $\lambda(x)\lambda(y) \leqslant \lambda(xy) \leqslant \|x\|\lambda(y)$, $\rho(x)\rho(y) \leqslant \rho(xy) \leqslant \rho(x)\|y\|$.

PROOF. It will be sufficient to consider only λ. For all z,

$$\lambda(x) \leqslant \frac{\|xz\|}{\|z\|} = \frac{\|(x-y)z + yz\|}{\|z\|} \leqslant \|x-y\| + \frac{\|yz\|}{\|z\|}.$$

Therefore $\lambda(x) \leqslant \|x-y\| + \lambda(y)$, so that $\lambda(x) - \lambda(y) \leqslant \|x-y\|$. By symmetry, $\lambda(y) - \lambda(x) \leqslant \|x-y\|$ and hence (i) follows.

Next we have

$$\inf_z \frac{\|xz\|}{\|z\|} \inf_z \frac{\|yz\|}{\|z\|} \leqslant \inf_z \frac{\|xyz\|}{\|yz\|} \inf_z \frac{\|yz\|}{\|z\|}$$

$$\leqslant \inf_z \frac{\|xyz\|}{\|z\|} \leqslant \|x\| \inf_z \frac{\|yz\|}{\|z\|}.$$

In other words $\lambda(x)\lambda(y) \leqslant \lambda(xy) \leqslant \|x\|\lambda(y)$, which proves (ii).

This lemma shows that the functions λ, ρ are continuous. Also, $\mathfrak{A}Z^l \subset Z^l$ and if $xy \in Z^l$ then either $x \in Z^l$ or $y \in Z^l$. Similar statements hold for Z^r. A consequence of the continuity is that the sets Z^l, Z^r and Z are closed, so that the complementary sets H^l, H^r and H are open. In fact, if $y \in H^l$, then H^l contains the sphere of all elements x such that $\|x-y\| < \lambda(y)$. This follows from the inequality $\lambda(y) - \|x-y\| \leqslant \lambda(x)$. Similar statements hold for H^r and H.

Lemma (1.5.2). *If h is not a left divisor of zero in $\mathfrak{A}$, then in order for $h \in H^l$ it is necessary and sufficient that the principal ideal $h\mathfrak{A}$ be closed.*

Proof. Since h is not a left divisor of zero, the linear transformation $A_h : a \to ha$ of $\mathfrak{A}$ onto $h\mathfrak{A}$ is one-to-one. Therefore A_h^{-1} exists as a linear transformation of $h\mathfrak{A}$ onto $\mathfrak{A}$. Moreover

$$\|A_h^{-1}\| = \sup_{x \in h\mathfrak{A}} \frac{\|A_h^{-1}x\|}{\|x\|} = \sup_{a \in \mathfrak{A}} \frac{\|a\|}{\|ha\|} = \frac{1}{\lambda(h)}.$$

Therefore A_h^{-1} is bounded if and only if $h \in H^l$. Now, if $h \in H^l$, and $ha_n \to k$, then $\|a_m - a_n\| \leqslant \|A_h^{-1}\| \|ha_m - ha_n\|$, so that $\{a_n\}$ converges to an element $b \in \mathfrak{A}$. It follows that $ha_n \to hb$. Hence, $k = hb$ and $h\mathfrak{A}$ is closed. On the other hand, assume $h\mathfrak{A}$ closed. Then A_h is a bounded linear transformation of one Banach space onto another, so that A_h^{-1} must be bounded and hence $h \in H^l$. This completes the proof.

Theorem (1.5.3). *Let $h \in H^l$. Then $(h\mathfrak{A}) \cap H^l = hH^l$ and hH^l is closed relative to H^l. A similar statement holds for H^r.*

Proof. Let $ha \in H^l$. Since $\lambda(ha) \leqslant \|h\|\lambda(a)$, it follows that $a \in H^l$, and so $h\mathfrak{A} \cap H^l \subseteq hH^l$. Since $\lambda(hk) \geqslant \lambda(h)\lambda(k)$, we have $hH^l \subseteq H^l$, so that $hH^l = hH^l \cap H^l \subseteq h\mathfrak{A} \cap H^l$. Therefore $h\mathfrak{A} \cap H^l = hH^l$. Since $h\mathfrak{A}$ is closed, we conclude that hH^l is closed relative to H^l, by definition.

THEOREM (1.5.4). *If $\mathfrak{A}$ is any Banach algebra with an identity, then*

(i) $S \cap \overline{G^l} \subseteq Z^r$.

(ii) $S \cap \overline{G^r} \subseteq Z^l$.

(iii) $S \cap \overline{G} \subseteq Z^l \cap Z^r$.

PROOF. Since $G = G^l \cap G^r$, property (iii) follows from (i) and (ii). Because of symmetry, we have only to prove (i). Since $S \cap G^l = S^r \cap G^l \subseteq Z^r$, it will be sufficient to show that Z^r contains all limit points of G^l which are in S^l. Let z be such a point and let $\{r_n\}$ be a sequence of elements of G^l which converges to z. If w_n is a left inverse of r_n for each n, then, by Theorem (1.4.7), $\lim_{n\to\infty} \|w_n\| = \infty$; for otherwise $z \in G^l$. Since

$$\rho(r_n) \leqslant \frac{\|w_n r_n\|}{\|w_n\|} = \frac{1}{\|w_n\|},$$

it follows that $\rho(r_n) \to 0$. But ρ is continuous and $r_n \to z$; therefore $\rho(z) = 0$ and $z \in Z^r$.

THEOREM (1.5.5). *In any Banach algebra with an identity, the set H^l is the union of the disjoint open sets G and $S^r \cap H^l$; and H^r is the union of G and $S^l \cap H^r$. Also, H is the union of the disjoint open sets G and $S \cap H$.*

PROOF. Since $G = G^r \cap H^l$, the complement of G in H^l is equal to $S^r \cap H^l$. Similarly, the complement of G in H^r is equal to $S^l \cap H^r$. Also, it is obvious that the complement of G in H is equal to $S \cap H$. Since G is open, it only remains to show that the complementary sets are open. Now the complement of $S^r \cap H^l$ in $\mathfrak{A}$ is equal to the set $G^r \cup Z^l$. Since Z^l is closed and $\overline{G^r} \subseteq G^r \cup Z^l$, we have

$$\overline{G^r \cup Z^l} = \overline{G_r} \cup Z^l \subseteq (G^r \cup Z^l) \cup Z^l = G^r \cup Z^l.$$

Hence $G^r \cup Z^l$ is closed, so that $S^r \cap H^l$ is open. Similar proofs hold for the other sets.

COROLLARY (1.5.6). *Every component of H is either a component of G or consists entirely of singular elements.*

THEOREM (1.5.7). *Let $\mathfrak{A}'$ be a second Banach algebra which contains the Banach algebra $\mathfrak{A}$ as a closed subalgebra with the same norm and identity element. Let S' be the set of singular elements of $\mathfrak{A}'$. Then $\mathfrak{A} \cap S' \subseteq S$ while* bdry $S \subseteq$ bdry $(\mathfrak{A} \cap S')$.

PROOF. It is obvious that $\mathfrak{A} \cap S' \subseteq S$. On the other hand, let z be any point on the boundary of S. Then $z \in Z$, so that z cannot be regular in $\mathfrak{A}'$ and hence $z \in \mathfrak{A} \cap S'$. But since $\mathfrak{A} \cap S' \subseteq S$, if a boundary point of S belongs to $\mathfrak{A} \cap S'$, then it must also be a boundary point of $\mathfrak{A} \cap S'$. This completes the proof.

The following corollary contains a result of Nagumo [1].

COROLLARY (1.5.8). *Let G' be the group of regular elements of $\mathfrak{A}'$. Then every component of $G' \cap \mathfrak{A}$ in $\mathfrak{A}$ is a component of H. In particular, the component of $G' \cap \mathfrak{A}$ which contains the identity element must coincide with the principal component of G.*

The disc algebra of all functions which are continuous on the closed unit disc $\Delta = \{\zeta : |\zeta| \leqslant 1\}$ of the complex plane and which are holomorphic in the interior of the disc, has the property that Z is a proper subset of S. In particular, the set S has interior points. (See Appendix, A.2.6.) The Banach algebra of all bounded complex-valued functions on an abstract set has the property that its group of regular elements is dense in the algebra. (See Appendix, A.2.1 and Blum [2].) Therefore in this case $Z = S$. The algebra $\mathscr{B}(\mathfrak{X})$ of all bounded operators on a Banach space $\mathfrak{X}$ also has the property that $Z = S$. However, for certain $\mathfrak{X}$, the set S has interior points. This is true in particular for $\mathfrak{X}$ an infinite dimensional Hilbert space. (See Appendix, A.1.1, and Yood [1].)

When $\mathfrak{A}$ does not possess an identity element, the above results relating topological divisors of zero to regular elements cannot, of course, be stated. In order to obtain similar results in the general case, it is necessary to extend the notion of topological divisor of zero. This extension is based on the observation that the limit $(z+\zeta)z_n \to 0$, for example, is meaningful for $z \in \mathfrak{A}$ and ζ a scalar whether or not $\mathfrak{A}$ has an identity. Therefore the notion of (left, right) topological divisor of zero can be applied to the formal sum $z+\zeta$. Note that any element z such that $1-z$ is a (left, right) topological divisor of zero is necessarily (left, right) quasi-singular. In fact, if $w \circ z = 0$, then $(1-w)(1-z)z_n = z_n$, so that $(1-z)z_n \to 0$ implies $z_n \to 0$. Following the notational convention introduced in the preceding section, we denote by Z^{lq} the set of all z in $\mathfrak{A}$ such that $1-z$ is a left topological divisor of zero. The set Z^{rq} is similarly defined and Z^q is the union of the two sets Z^{lq} and Z^{rq}. The complements of these sets are denoted by H^{lq}, H^{rq} and H^q respectively. A discussion of the sets defined here and their relations to the sets G^{lq}, G^{rq} and G^q paralleling that given above can be carried through with only minor changes. We limit further attention to only those properties which will be needed below. Define the functions,

$$\lambda^q(x) = \inf_y \frac{\|y - xy\|}{\|y\|}, \qquad \rho^q(x) = \inf_y \frac{\|y - yx\|}{\|y\|}.$$

Then $\lambda^q(z) = 0$ if and only if $z \in Z^{lq}$, and $\rho^q(z) = 0$ if and only if $z \in Z^{rq}$. The same method employed in the proof of Lemma (1.5.1) can be used to obtain the following properties of the functions λ^q and ρ^q:

(1) $|\lambda^q(x) - \lambda^q(y)| \leqslant \|x-y\|, \quad |\rho^q(x) - \rho^q(y)| \leqslant \|x-y\|.$

(2) $\lambda^q(x)\lambda^q(y) \leqslant \lambda^q(x \circ y) \leqslant (1+\|x\|)\lambda^q(y),$
$\rho^q(x)\rho^q(y) \leqslant \rho^q(x \circ y) \leqslant \rho^q(x)(1+\|y\|).$

Therefore both functions are continuous.

THEOREM (1.5.9). *Let $\mathfrak{A}$ be a Banach algebra with or without an identity element. Then the following statements are true:*

(i) *$\mathfrak{A} \circ Z^{lq} \subseteq Z^{lq}$ and, if $x \circ y \in Z^{lq}$, then either $x \in Z^{lq}$ or $y \in Z^{lq}$. Similar statements hold for Z^{rq}.*

(ii) *$\overline{G^q} \cap S^q \subseteq Z^{lq} \cap Z^{rq}$.*

(iii) *If ζz is quasi-regular for scalars with arbitrarily large modulus, then either z is a (left, right) topological divisor of zero or there exists in $\mathfrak{A}$ a (left, right) identity element e such that $e\mathfrak{A}e$ contains z as a regular element.*

PROOF. The properties in (i) follow immediately from the properties noted above for the functions λ^q and ρ^q. For the proof of (ii), let $\{r_n\}$ be a sequence of quasi-regular elements which converges to a quasi-singular element z. By Theorem (1.4.21), $\|r_n^\circ\| \to \infty$. Since

$$\lambda^q(r_n) \leqslant \frac{\|r_n^\circ - r_n r_n^\circ\|}{\|r_n^\circ\|} = \frac{\|r_n\|}{\|r_n^\circ\|},$$

it follows that

$$\lambda^q(z) = \lim_{n\to\infty} \lambda^q(r_n) = 0.$$

Therefore $z \in Z^{lq}$. Similarly, $z \in Z^{rq}$ and (ii) is proved.

Now assume ζz quasi-regular for arbitrarily large scalars ζ and choose $\{\zeta_n\}$ such that $\zeta_n z$ is quasi-regular and $|\zeta_n| \geqslant n$ for each n. Let

u_n denote the quasi-inverse of $\zeta_n z$ and suppose that z is not a left topological divisor of zero. Since

$$\frac{zu_n}{\|u_n\|} = \frac{z}{\|u_n\|} + \frac{u_n}{\zeta_n\|u_n\|},$$

it is immediate that $\{u_n\}$ must be bounded in order for z not to be a left topological divisor of zero. Therefore, since $zu_n = z+\zeta_n^{-1}u_n$, it follows that

$$\lim_{n\to\infty} zu_n = z.$$

This means that z belongs to the closure of the principal ideal $z\mathfrak{A}$. However, by Lemma (1.5.2) the fact that z is not a left topological divisor of zero implies that $z\mathfrak{A}$ is closed. Therefore there exists $e \in \mathfrak{A}$ such that $z = ze$. Notice that $z(ex-x) = 0$, so that $ex-x = 0$; that is, e is a left identity for $\mathfrak{A}$ and so is, in particular, an idempotent. Since $z(u_n-e) \to 0$, it follows that $u_n-e \to 0$. Otherwise z would be a left topological divisor of zero. From the relation $u_n z = z+\zeta_n^{-1}u_n$, we conclude that

$$\lim_{n\to\infty} u_n z = z,$$

which gives $ez = z$. Hence the element e is both a left and a right identity for z. If it is known that z is not a right divisor of zero, then, since $(xe-x)z = 0$, we conclude that e is actually an identity for $\mathfrak{A}$. In the general case we drop down to the subalgebra $e\mathfrak{A}e$ which contains each u_n, as well as z, and has e as an identity. The elements $\zeta_n^{-1}e-z$ are regular in $e\mathfrak{A}e$ and converge to $-z$ as $n \to \infty$. Thus z, being a limit of regular elements, is either regular or is a 2-sided topological divisor of zero in $e\mathfrak{A}e$. Since the last possibility is ruled out by hypothesis, we conclude that z is regular in $e\mathfrak{A}e$. This completes the proof.

COROLLARY (1.5.10). *If ζz is quasi-regular for arbitrarily large scalars ζ and if z is not a topological divisor of zero, then $\mathfrak{A}$ must have an identity element and z is regular.*

It is interesting to note that, by an appropriate extension of a Banach algebra $\mathfrak{A}$, all of its topological divisors of zero can be converted into divisors of zero. This extension, which was first pointed out to us by F. Quigley, will now be described. Consider first the class $\mathfrak{A}^\infty$ of all sequences $\{x_n\}$ of elements of $\mathfrak{A}$ such that

$$\limsup_{n\to\infty} \|x_n\| < \infty.$$

Two such sequences $\{x_n\}$ and $\{y_n\}$ are defined to be equivalent if $\lim \|x_n - y_n\| = 0$. This notion of equivalence is actually an equivalence relation and thus decomposes $\mathfrak{A}^\infty$ into equivalence classes. Denote by $[\mathfrak{A}^\infty]$ this collection of equivalence classes and denote by $[x_n]$ the equivalence class which contains $\{x_n\}$. It is not difficult to check that $[\mathfrak{A}^\infty]$ is a Banach algebra under the algebraic operations $[x_n]+[y_n] = [x_n+y_n]$, $\alpha[x_n] = [\alpha x_n]$, $[x_n][y_n] = [x_n y_n]$, and norm $\|[x_n]\| = \limsup \|x_n\|$. For each $x \in \mathfrak{A}$, denote by $\{x\}$ the constant sequence each of whose elements is equal to x. Then it is obvious that $x \to [x]$ is an isometric isomorphism of $\mathfrak{A}$ onto a closed subalgebra of $[\mathfrak{A}^\infty]$. We can now formulate the extension result mentioned above.

THEOREM (1.5.11). *Every (left, right) topological divisor of zero in* $[\mathfrak{A}^\infty]$ *is a (left, right) divisor of zero and an element* $x \in \mathfrak{A}$ *is a (left, right) topological divisor of zero in* $\mathfrak{A}$ *if and only if* $[x]$ *is a (left, right) divisor of zero in* $[\mathfrak{A}^\infty]$. *An element* $x \in \mathfrak{A}$ *is (left, right) quasi-regular in* $\mathfrak{A}$ *if and only if* $[x]$ *is (left, right) quasi-regular in* $[\mathfrak{A}^\infty]$.

PROOF. Let $[z_n]$ be a right topological divisor of zero in $[\mathfrak{A}^\infty]$. Then there exists a sequence $[x_n^{(k)}]$ $(k = 1, 2, \cdots)$ in $[\mathfrak{A}^\infty]$ such that $\|[x_n^{(k)}]\| = 1$ and $\|[x_n^{(k)} z_n]\| < k^{-1}$ for each k. Now, for each k, there exists n_k such that $\|x_{n_k}^{(k)}\| \geqslant 2^{-1}$ and $\|x_{n_k}^{(k)} z_{n_k}\| < k^{-1}$. Next define $y_n = x_{n_k}^{(k)}$, for $n = n_k$, and $y_n = 0$ otherwise. Then $[y_n] \neq 0$ while $\|y_n z_n\| < k^{-1}$, for $n \geqslant n_k$, so that $[y_n z_n] = 0$. In other words, $[z_n]$ is a right divisor of zero in $[\mathfrak{A}^\infty]$. A similar proof holds for a left topological divisor of zero.

If an element $x \in \mathfrak{A}$ is a (left, right) topological divisor of zero, then it is obvious that $[x]$ is a (left, right) topological divisor of zero and hence a (left, right) divisor of zero in $[\mathfrak{A}^\infty]$. On the other hand, suppose that $[x]$ is a right divisor of zero in $[\mathfrak{A}^\infty]$, with $[z_n x] = 0$, where $[z_n] \neq 0$. Then $\|z_n x\| \to 0$, while $\limsup \|z_n\| \neq 0$. This clearly implies that x is a topological divisor of zero in $\mathfrak{A}$.

Finally let $[x]$ be left quasi-regular in $[\mathfrak{A}^\infty]$ with $[r_n]$ as its left quasi-inverse. Then $[r_n \circ x] = 0$ and hence $\|r_n \circ x\| \to 0$. Therefore $r_n \circ x$ is quasi-regular for large n. This implies that x is left quasi-regular. Similarly, if $[x]$ is right quasi-regular, then so is x. This completes the proof of the theorem.

Since every Banach algebra $\mathfrak{A}$ admits a faithful norm and inverse preserving representation in an algebra $\mathscr{B}(\mathfrak{X})$ (see Theorem (1.4.15)), and since $Z = S$ in $\mathscr{B}(\mathfrak{X})$, an application of the above theorem to

$\mathscr{B}(\mathfrak{X})$ yields the following corollary. For the sake of simplicity we consider only the case in which $\mathfrak{A}$ has an identity element.

COROLLARY (1.5.12). *There exists a Banach algebra $\mathfrak{B}$ and a norm-preserving isomorphism of $\mathfrak{A}$ into $\mathfrak{B}$ such that an element x in $\mathfrak{A}$ is singular in $\mathfrak{A}$ if and only if its image in $\mathfrak{B}$ is a divisor of zero. Also, $\mathfrak{B}$ has the property that each of its singular elements is a divisor of zero.*

Using some of the ideas developed in the next chapter, we can describe the algebra $[\mathfrak{A}^\infty]$ in another way. First let $\mathscr{S}_\mathfrak{A}$ denote the class of all bounded sequences of elements from $\mathfrak{A}$. Then $\mathscr{S}_\mathfrak{A}$ is a Banach algebra under the algebra operations $\{x_n\}+\{y_n\} = \{x_n+y_n\}$, $\alpha\{x_n\} = \{\alpha x_n\}$, $\{x_n\}\{y_n\} = \{x_n y_n\}$, and norm $\|\{x_n\}\| = \sup \|x_n\|$. Next let $\mathfrak{N}$ denote the subset of $\mathscr{S}_\mathfrak{A}$ consisting of all those sequences $\{x_n\}$ such that $\lim \|x_n\| = 0$. Then $\mathfrak{N}$ is obviously a closed 2-sided ideal in $\mathscr{S}_\mathfrak{A}$. Therefore the difference algebra $\mathscr{S}_\mathfrak{A}/\mathfrak{N}$ is defined and is a Banach algebra under the norm

$$\|\{x_n\}'\| = \inf \|\{x_n+z_n\}\|, \qquad \{z_n\} \in \mathfrak{N},$$

where $\{x_n\}' = \{x_n\}+\mathfrak{N}$. (See §1, Chapter II.) Now it is not difficult to show that

$$\|\{x_n\}'\| = \limsup \|x_n\|.$$

Therefore, it follows that the mapping $\{x_n\}' \to [x_n]$ is an isometric isomorphism of $\mathscr{S}_\mathfrak{A}/\mathfrak{N}$ onto $[\mathfrak{A}^\infty]$.

The notion of a topological divisor of zero was introduced by Šilov [3] who used the terminology GENERALIZED DIVISOR OF ZERO. The notion of PERMANENT SINGULARITY is due essentially to Lorch [1]. The results in Theorems (1.5.4) and (1.5.5), which were proved by the author [2], have been generalized to transformations between two Banach spaces by Yood [1]. The extensions to algebras without an identity element were made by Kaplansky [5]. The result in Corollary (1.5.10) was also proved by the author [3].

§ 6. **The Spectrum.** In this section we consider what is perhaps the most important notion in the theory of Banach algebras, namely, the spectrum of an element. If $\mathfrak{A}$ is a complex Banach algebra with an identity, then the spectrum of an element x in $\mathfrak{A}$ is usually defined as the set of all complex numbers ξ such that $\xi - x$ is a singular element of $\mathfrak{A}$. If $\xi \neq 0$, then the relation $1-\xi^{-1}x = \xi^{-1}(\xi-x)$ shows that ξ will be in the spectrum of x if and only if $\xi^{-1}x$ is quasi-singular. Also, zero will be in the spectrum if and only if x is singular. We are thus led to a definition of the spectrum which is meaningful whether or not $\mathfrak{A}$ has an identity element, provided we agree in the latter case to regard all elements as singular.

DEFINITION (1.6.1). *Let $\mathfrak{A}$ be a complex algebra and let x be any element of $\mathfrak{A}$. Then the* SPECTRUM OF x IN $\mathfrak{A}$ *is the set $Sp_{\mathfrak{A}}(x)$ of all complex numbers ξ such that $\xi^{-1}x$ is quasi-singular, plus zero if x is singular.*

This definition of spectrum can obviously be applied to an algebra over an arbitrary field of scalars. Unfortunately, however, it turns out that the general notion of spectrum so obtained is not sharp enough to be of much use. For example, this spectrum can be empty even for a real normed algebra. On the other hand, in the case of complex normed algebras, the spectrum is never empty and has properties which make it an especially useful concept. For this reason, the above definition is reserved for complex algebras. In order to deal with real algebras, we pass to the complexification.

DEFINITION (1.6.2). *Let $\mathfrak{A}$ be a real algebra and let x be any element of $\mathfrak{A}$. Then the* SPECTRUM $Sp_{\mathfrak{A}}(x)$ OF x IN $\mathfrak{A}$ *is defined to be equal to the spectrum of x as an element of the complexification $\mathfrak{A}_C$ of $\mathfrak{A}$.*

With this definition, the spectrum of an element need not be real and so may not be contained in the field of scalars of the algebra. Note, however, that a non-zero real number ξ will belong to $Sp_{\mathfrak{A}}(x)$ if and only if $\xi^{-1}x$ is quasi-singular. (See Corollary (1.6.7).) In other words, the real portion of $Sp_{\mathfrak{A}}(x)$ coincides with the general "spectrum" obtained by application of the definition for complex algebras to the real case.

We shall frequently write $Sp(x)$ in place of $Sp_{\mathfrak{A}}(x)$ for the spectrum of an element x in $\mathfrak{A}$ wherever it is clearly understood what algebra is involved.

The next theorem shows that the spectrum is never empty for elements of a normed algebra.

THEOREM (1.6.3). *Let x be an element of an arbitrary normed algebra $\mathfrak{A}$. Then there exists in $Sp(x)$ a complex number α such that $\nu(x) \leqslant |\alpha|$.*

PROOF. Recall that $\nu(x) = \lim \|x^n\|^{1/n}$. (See Theorem (1.4.1).) Also, in view of the definition of spectrum and the fact that a real algebra is isometrically embedded in its complexification, it is obviously sufficient to consider complex algebras. Note first that, if $0 \notin Sp(x)$, then $\mathfrak{A}$ has an identity element and x has an inverse x^{-1}. Since $xx^{-1} = x^{-1}x = 1$ and $\nu(1) = 1$, it follows by Theorem (1.4.1)(v) that $1 \leqslant \nu(x)\nu(x^{-1})$.

Therefore $\nu(x) = 0$ implies $0 \in Sp(x)$, and the theorem is proved for this case.

Now assume $\nu(x) = \nu > 0$, and suppose the theorem false in this case. Then the function $f(\zeta) = (\zeta^{-1}x)^\circ$ is defined and continuous for $|\zeta| \geqslant \nu$. Moreover, since $\zeta^{-1}x \to 0$ as $\zeta \to \infty$, continuity of the quasi-inverse gives $(\zeta^{-1}x)^\circ \to 0$ as $\zeta \to \infty$. Therefore f is uniformly continuous for $|\zeta| \geqslant \nu$. In the remainder of this proof ζ will always denote a complex number with $|\zeta| \geqslant \nu$.

Let $\omega_1, \cdots \omega_n$ be the nth roots of unity and, if λ is any complex number, write $\lambda_j = \lambda\omega_j$ $(j = 1, \cdots, n)$. Then the polynomial $1-\zeta^{-n}\xi^n$ can be factored in the form

$$1-\zeta^{-n}\xi^n = (1-\zeta_1^{-1}\xi)(1-\zeta_2^{-1}\xi)\cdots(1-\zeta_n^{-1}\xi).$$

Writing this relation in terms of the circle operation and substituting x for ξ, we obtain

$$\zeta^{-n}x^n = (\zeta_1^{-1}x)\circ(\zeta_2^{-1}x)\circ\cdots\circ(\zeta_n^{-1}x).$$

It follows that $\zeta^{-n}x^n$ is quasi-regular for each n. Next let $R_j = -(\zeta_j^{-1}x+\zeta_j^{-2}x^2+\cdots+\zeta_j^{-n+1}x^{n-1})$ and observe that $\zeta^{-n}x^n = (\zeta_j^{-1}x)\circ R_j$. Since $\zeta^{-n}x^n$ and $\zeta_j^{-1}x$ are quasi-regular, this can be rewritten in the form

$$f(\zeta_j) = R_j \circ (\zeta^{-n}x^n)^\circ. \tag{1}$$

Now each term of R_j is of the form $\omega_j^{-k}\zeta^{-k}x^k$ where $1 \leqslant k \leqslant n-1$. Therefore $R_1+R_2+\cdots+R_n = 0$ and summation of (1) for $j = 1, \cdots, n$ gives

$$\frac{1}{n}\sum_{j=1}^{n} f(\zeta_j) = (\zeta^{-n}x^n)^\circ. \tag{2}$$

Since f is uniformly continuous, there exists for arbitrary $\epsilon > 0$ a μ (independent of n) such that $\nu < \mu$ and $\|f(\nu_j)-f(\mu_j)\| < \epsilon$ for $j = 1, 2, \cdots, n$. Using equation (2), we obtain at once

$$\|(\nu^{-n}x^n)^\circ-(\mu^{-n}x^n)^\circ\| < \epsilon, \tag{3}$$

for all n. On the other hand, since $\nu < \mu$, it follows that $\mu^{-n}x^n \to 0$, so that $(\mu^{-n}x^n)^\circ \to 0$ as $n \to \infty$. Therefore (3) implies that $\|(\nu^{-n}x^n)^\circ\| < \epsilon$ for sufficiently large n. In other words, $(\nu^{-n}x^n)^\circ \to 0$ and hence $\nu^{-n}x^n \to 0$ as $n \to \infty$. However, this is impossible since $\|\nu^{-n}x^n\| \geqslant 1$ for all n. Therefore the supposition that $Sp(x)$ does not contain an α with $|\alpha| \geqslant \nu$ is false and the theorem is proved.

THEOREM (1.6.4). *Let $\mathfrak{A}$ be any Banach algebra. Then for every $x \in \mathfrak{A}$ the spectrum $Sp(x)$ is a non-vacuous bounded closed set such that* $\max_{\xi \in Sp(x)} |\xi| = \nu(x)$.

PROOF. By the preceding theorem, $Sp(x)$ is non-vacuous and $\nu(x) \leqslant \sup |\xi|$, for $\xi \in Sp(x)$. It remains only to prove the reverse inequality and that $Sp(x)$ is closed. Again we can restrict attention to the complex case. If $\nu(x) < |\xi|$, then $\nu(\xi^{-1}x) < 1$, and hence $\xi^{-1}x$ is quasi-regular by Lemma (1.4.18). This proves the reverse inequality. Since the quasi-regular elements of a Banach algebra constitute an open set, it is immediate that the complement of $Sp(x)$ plus zero is open. Moreover, if $0 \notin Sp(x)$, then $\mathfrak{A}$ must have an identity element and x is regular. Since the set of regular elements is open, $\xi - x$ will be regular, and thus $\xi^{-1}x$ will be quasi-regular, for small ξ. Therefore $Sp(x)$ must be closed and the proof is complete.

DEFINITION (1.6.5). *The number $\nu_{\mathfrak{A}}(x)$, which is given algebraically by* $\max |\xi|$, *for $\xi \in Sp_{\mathfrak{A}}(x)$, and topologically by* $\lim \|x^n\|^{1/n}$, *is called the* SPECTRAL RADIUS *of x.*

Although our main interest is in complex algebras, we digress briefly to obtain a few elementary results for the real case. The first theorem gives a characterization of $Sp_{\mathfrak{A}}(x)$ intrinsic to $\mathfrak{A}$. (See Kaplansky [5].)

THEOREM (1.6.6). *Let x be an element of a real algebra $\mathfrak{A}$ and consider the complex number $\xi = \alpha + \beta i$, where α and β are real. If $\xi = 0$, then $\xi \in Sp_{\mathfrak{A}}(x)$ if and only if x is singular in $\mathfrak{A}$. If $\xi \neq 0$, then $\xi \in Sp_{\mathfrak{A}}(x)$ if and only if $|\xi|^{-2}(2\alpha x - x^2)$ is quasi-singular in $\mathfrak{A}$.*

PROOF. Recall that $\mathfrak{A}_C$ has an identity if and only if $\mathfrak{A}$ has one and that an element of $\mathfrak{A}$ will be regular in $\mathfrak{A}$ if and only if it is regular in $\mathfrak{A}_C$. Therefore, the statement about $\xi = 0$ follows. Now any element of $\mathfrak{A}_C$ can be written uniquely in the form $u + iv$ with $u, v \in \mathfrak{A}$. Let $\overline{u+iv} = u - iv$. Then it is readily verified that $u + iv$ is quasi-regular if and only if $\overline{u+iv}$ is quasi-regular. Since $x \in \mathfrak{A}$, $\overline{\xi^{-1}x} = \bar{\xi}^{-1} x$, so that $\xi^{-1}x$ is quasi-regular in $\mathfrak{A}_C$ if and only if $\bar{\xi}^{-1}x$ is quasi-regular in $\mathfrak{A}_C$. By direct computation, we obtain the relation

$$(\xi^{-1}x) \circ (\bar{\xi}^{-1}x) = (\bar{\xi}^{-1}x) \circ (\xi^{-1}x) = |\xi|^{-2}(2\alpha x - x^2).$$

Therefore $\xi^{-1}x$ is quasi-regular in $\mathfrak{A}_C$ if and only if $|\xi|^{-2}(2\alpha x - x^2)$, which belongs to $\mathfrak{A}$, is quasi-regular in $\mathfrak{A}_C$ and hence in $\mathfrak{A}$.

COROLLARY (1.6.7). *If $\mathfrak{A}$ is a real algebra, then $Sp_{\mathfrak{A}}(x)$ is self-conjugate;*

that is, $\xi \in Sp_{\mathfrak{A}}(x)$ *if and only if* $\bar{\xi} \in Sp_{\mathfrak{A}}(x)$. *If* ξ *is real and non-zero, then* $\xi \in Sp_{\mathfrak{A}}(x)$ *if and only if* $\xi^{-1}x$ *is quasi-singular.*

If $\mathfrak{A}$ is a complex algebra, then it can also be regarded as a real algebra. Therefore the definition of spectrum is ambiguous in this case. This ambiguity will always be resolved in favor of the complex algebras. In any case, the two spectra are closely related, as the following theorem shows.

THEOREM (1.6.8). *Let* x *be an element of the complex algebra* $\mathfrak{A}$. *Denote the spectrum of* x *in* $\mathfrak{A}$, *as a complex algebra, by* $Sp_{\mathfrak{A}}(x)$ *and, as a real algebra, by* $Sp_{\mathfrak{A}}{}^{r}(x)$. *Then* $Sp_{\mathfrak{A}}{}^{r}(x)$ *is equal to the union of* $Sp_{\mathfrak{A}}(x)$ *with its complex conjugate.*

PROOF. Since it is immediate from the definition that $0 \in Sp^{r}(x)$ if and only if $0 \in Sp(x)$, we can assume $\xi \neq 0$. Before continuing, we must emphasize that multiplication of elements of $\mathfrak{A}$ by complex scalars means one thing in $\mathfrak{A}$ and something quite different in $\mathfrak{A}_C$. Therefore, in order to avoid confusion, we write $\mathfrak{A}_C$ as a cartesian product $\mathfrak{A} \times \mathfrak{A}$ with the appropriate definition of algebraic operations (see § 3) and embed $\mathfrak{A}$ in $\mathfrak{A}_C$ *via* the mapping $x \to (x, 0)$. Now, if $\xi = \alpha + \beta i$ where α, β are real, then $\xi x \to (\xi x, 0)$ while $\xi(x, 0) = (\alpha x, \beta x)$. If $\xi(x, 0)$ is quasi-regular in $\mathfrak{A}_C$, then there exists $(u, v) \in \mathfrak{A}_C$ such that $(\alpha x, \beta x) \circ (u, v) = 0$. This means that $\alpha x + u - \alpha x u + \beta x v = 0$ and $\beta x + v - \beta x u - \alpha x v = 0$. If we take $w = u + iv$ in $\mathfrak{A}$, then it follows that $(\xi x) \circ w = 0$. Similarly, $w \circ (\xi x) = 0$, so that ξx is quasi-regular in $\mathfrak{A}$. Thus $Sp^{r}(x)$ contains $Sp(x)$ and, being self-conjugate, also contains the conjugate of $Sp(x)$. Next assume that both ξx and $\bar{\xi} x$ are quasi-regular in $\mathfrak{A}$. Define the elements

$$u = \frac{(\xi x)^{\circ} + (\bar{\xi} x)^{\circ}}{2}, \qquad v = \frac{(\xi x)^{\circ} - (\bar{\xi} x)^{\circ}}{2i}.$$

These are elements of $\mathfrak{A}$ and it is readily checked that

$$(\alpha x, \beta x) \circ (u, v) = (u, v) \circ (\alpha x, \beta x) = 0.$$

Therefore $\xi(x, 0)$ is quasi-regular in $\mathfrak{A}_C$. It follows that $Sp^{r}(x)$ is contained in the union of $Sp(x)$ with its complex conjugate, which completes the proof.

We return now to the general situation in which the algebra can be either real or complex.

THEOREM (1.6.9). *Let $\mathfrak{A}$ be any real or complex algebra.*

(i) *If $\mathfrak{A}$ does not possess an identity and $\mathfrak{A}_1$ is the algebra obtained in the usual way by adjunction of an identity to $\mathfrak{A}$, then $Sp_{\mathfrak{A}}(a) = Sp_{\mathfrak{A}_1}(a)$ for every $a \in \mathfrak{A}$.*

(ii) *Let $a \to T_a$ be a representation of $\mathfrak{A}$ on $\mathfrak{X}$ which is either the left regular or extended left regular representation according as $\mathfrak{A}$ does or does not possess an identity element. Then $Sp_{\mathfrak{A}}(a) = Sp_{\mathscr{B}(\mathfrak{X})}(T_a)$.*

PROOF. Since an element of $\mathfrak{A}$ is quasi-regular in $\mathfrak{A}$ if and only if it is quasi-regular in $\mathfrak{A}_1$, the first statement follows from the definition for complex algebras and from Theorem (1.6.6) for real algebras. The second statement follows from Theorem (1.4.15) and Corollary (1.4.16) plus Theorem (1.6.6), for real algebras.

THEOREM (1.6.10). *Let $\mathfrak{A}$ be a real or complex algebra and let $P(\xi)$ be any polynomial with coefficients in the field of scalars of $\mathfrak{A}$ and with constant term zero in case $\mathfrak{A}$ does not have an identity. Then, for every $a \in \mathfrak{A}$, $P(a) \in \mathfrak{A}$ and $P(Sp(a)) = Sp(P(a))$.*

PROOF. Assume first that $\mathfrak{A}$ is complex and let β be any complex number. Consider the polynomial $\beta - P(\xi)$. If $\alpha_1, \cdots \alpha_n$ are the roots of this polynomial, then $P(\alpha_j) = \beta$ for each j and we can write

$$\beta - P(a) = \gamma \prod_{j=1}^{n} (\alpha_j - a),$$

where γ is a scalar.

Observe that if $\mathfrak{A}$ has an identity element, then the element $\beta - P(a)$ will be regular if and only if each of the factors $\alpha_j - a$ is regular. Thus, if $\beta \in Sp(P(a))$, then $\alpha_j \in Sp(a)$ for some j. Since $P(\alpha_j) = \beta$, it follows that $Sp(P(a)) \subseteq P(Sp(a))$. On the other hand, if $\alpha \in Sp(a)$, let $\beta = P(\alpha)$ and note that α is one of the α_j. Therefore $\beta \in Sp(P(a))$ and we conclude that $Sp(P(a)) = P(Sp(a))$ when $\mathfrak{A}$ has an identity. If $\mathfrak{A}$ does not have an identity, then zero is in all spectra. Also $P(0) = 0$, and so, if $\beta \neq 0$, then $\alpha_j \neq 0$ for each j. Therefore, if $\beta \neq 0$, then

$$1 - \beta^{-1}P(\xi) = \prod_{j=1}^{n} (1 - \alpha_j^{-1}\xi)$$

and hence

$$\beta^{-1}P(a) = (\alpha_1^{-1}a) \circ (\alpha_2^{-1}a) \circ \cdots \circ (\alpha_n^{-1}a).$$

Thus $\beta^{-1}P(a)$ is quasi-regular if and only if each of the factors $\alpha_j^{-1}a$

is quasi-regular. Therefore we obtain again $Sp(P(a)) = P(Sp(a))$. The real case follows from the complex since a real algebra is embedded in its complexification *via* a real algebra isomorphism and the spectrum is defined in terms of the complexification.

As will be seen later (Theorem (3.5.1)), the above theorem, in the case of a Banach algebra, is a special instance of a more general "spectral mapping theorem" in which the polynomials are replaced by a wider class of functions. It is convenient to include here another special instance of that theorem.

THEOREM (1.6.11). *Let r be an element of the real or complex algebra $\mathfrak{A}$. If r is regular, then*

$$Sp(r^{-1}) = \{\lambda^{-1} : \lambda \in Sp(r)\}.$$

If r is quasi-regular, then

$$Sp(r^{\circ}) = \left\{\frac{\lambda}{\lambda - 1} : \lambda \in Sp(r)\right\}.$$

PROOF. It will be sufficient to make the proof for the complex case. If r is regular, then the desired result follows immediately from the relation

$$\lambda^{-1} - r^{-1} = -\lambda^{-1}r^{-1}(\lambda - r).$$

If r is quasi-regular, then the desired result follows from the relation

$$\frac{\lambda - 1}{\lambda} r^{\circ} = r^{\circ} \circ (\lambda^{-1}r).$$

Observe also that $r^{\circ} = r(r-1)^{-1}$ and $r = r^{\circ}(r^{\circ}-1)^{-1}$, so that r° is regular if and only if r is regular. This disposes of $\lambda = 0$ and completes the proof.

The following theorem is obviously related to Theorem (1.5.7).

THEOREM (1.6.12). *Let $\mathfrak{B}$ denote a closed subalgebra of the Banach algebra $\mathfrak{A}$. Then, for every $b \in \mathfrak{B}$, $Sp_{\mathfrak{A}}(b) \subseteq Sp_{\mathfrak{B}}(b) \cup (0)$ while* bdry $Sp_{\mathfrak{B}}(b) \subseteq$ bdry $Sp_{\mathfrak{A}}(b)$.

PROOF. The first inclusion is immediate from the fact that $\mathfrak{B}$ is a subalgebra of $\mathfrak{A}$. In order to prove the second inclusion it is sufficient to obtain bdry $Sp_{\mathfrak{B}}(b) \subseteq Sp_{\mathfrak{A}}(b)$. Let ζ be any point on the boundary of $Sp_{\mathfrak{B}}(b)$ and let $\zeta = \alpha + \beta i$ with α, β real. If $\mathfrak{A}$ is complex, then by Theorem (1.5.4) or Theorem (1.5.9), $\zeta - b$ is a topological divisor of zero in $\mathfrak{B}$ and hence in $\mathfrak{A}$. It follows that $\zeta \in Sp_{\mathfrak{A}}(b)$. On the other hand, if $\mathfrak{A}$ is real, then $|\zeta|^2 - 2\alpha b + b^2$ is a topological divisor of zero in $\mathfrak{B}$ by the same theorems cited above. Therefore it is a topological divisor of zero in $\mathfrak{A}$ and again $\zeta \in Sp_{\mathfrak{A}}(b)$. The inclusion of zero in the right hand side of the first inclusion is necessitated by the fact that $\mathfrak{B}$ can have an identity element which is not an identity for $\mathfrak{A}$.

THEOREM (1.6.13). *Let a be any fixed element of the Banach algebra* $\mathfrak{A}$. *Then in order that* $Sp_{\mathfrak{A}}(a) = Sp_{\mathfrak{B}}(a)$ *for every closed subalgebra* $\mathfrak{B}$ in $\mathfrak{A}$, *which contains a along with the identity element of* $\mathfrak{A}$ *if one exists, it is necessary and sufficient that* $Sp_{\mathfrak{A}}(a)$ *fail to separate the plane.*

PROOF. The sufficiency is an immediate consequence of the preceding theorem. For the necessity consider the subalgebra $\mathfrak{B}$ which consists of all limits in $\mathfrak{A}$ of sequences $\{P_n(a)\}$ of polynomials in a with coefficients in the scalar field of $\mathfrak{A}$. Note that if $\mathfrak{A}$ does not possess an identity element, then $P_n(a)$ must have constant term zero. By Theorem (1.6.10), if P is any polynomial such that $P(a) \in \mathfrak{A}$, then $P(Sp_{\mathfrak{A}}(a)) = Sp_{\mathfrak{A}}(P(a))$. Therefore $\max |P(\alpha)| \leqslant \|P(a)\|$ for $\alpha \in Sp_{\mathfrak{A}}(a)$. In fact, if Γ is the unbounded component of the complement of $Sp_{\mathfrak{A}}(a)$, then, by the maximum modulus theorem applied to the polynomial P, we even have

$$\max_{\alpha \notin \Gamma} |P(\alpha)| \leqslant \|P(a)\|.$$

Next let ζ denote any complex number not in $Sp_{\mathfrak{B}}(a)$ and assume $\zeta = \alpha + \beta i$ with α, β real. Also let $Z(\xi)$ denote either the polynomial $\zeta^{-1}\xi$ or $|\zeta|^{-2}(2\alpha\xi - \xi^2)$ according as $\mathfrak{A}$ is or is not complex. Then $Z(a)$ is quasi-regular in $\mathfrak{B}$. If $\{P_n(a)\}$ is a sequence of polynomials in a such that $P_n(a)$ converges to the quasi-inverse of $Z(a)$ and if $Q_n(a)$ is the polynomial $Z(a) \circ P_n(a)$, then $\|Q_n(a)\| \to 0$ as $n \to \infty$. It follows that $Q_n(\alpha) \to 0$ for every $\alpha \notin \Gamma$. On the other hand, $Z(\zeta) = 1$ and hence $Q_n(\zeta) = 1$ for all n. Therefore it follows that $\zeta \in \Gamma$. Now, if $Sp_{\mathfrak{A}}(a) = Sp_{\mathfrak{B}}(a)$, we conclude that Γ exhausts the complement of $Sp_{\mathfrak{A}}(a)$, which means that $Sp_{\mathfrak{A}}(a)$ does not separate the plane. This completes the proof.

Consider next a subset A of the Banach algebra $\mathfrak{A}$ and assume that A is COMMUTATIVE in the sense that every pair of its elements commute. By Zorn's lemma there will exist a maximal commutative subset of $\mathfrak{A}$ which contains A. Such maximal commutative sets automatically have algebraic and topological properties which we summarize in the following theorem.

THEOREM (1.6.14). *Every maximal commutative subset* $\mathfrak{C}$ *of a normed algebra* $\mathfrak{A}$ *is a closed commutative subalgebra of* $\mathfrak{A}$ *such that* $Sp_{\mathfrak{C}}(c) = Sp_{\mathfrak{A}}(c)$ *for every* $c \in \mathfrak{C}$. *The center of the algebra* $\mathfrak{A}$ *is equal to the intersection of all maximal commutative subsets of* $\mathfrak{A}$.

PROOF. It is almost immediate that $\mathfrak{C}$ is a closed subalgebra of $\mathfrak{A}$ and that the center of $\mathfrak{A}$ is equal to the intersection of all such subsets. Furthermore, $\mathfrak{C}$ obviously will contain the identity element if one exists in $\mathfrak{A}$. Now let c be any element of $\mathfrak{C}$ and suppose that c is quasi-regular in $\mathfrak{A}$. If x is any element of $\mathfrak{A}$ which commutes with c, then also $x \circ c = c \circ x$ and we have

$$c^{\circ} \circ x = c^{\circ} \circ x \circ c \circ c^{\circ} = c^{\circ} \circ c \circ x \circ c^{\circ} = x \circ c^{\circ},$$

so that c° also commutes with x. It follows that c° commutes with every element of $\mathfrak{C}$ and therefore must belong to $\mathfrak{C}$. Similarly, if an element of $\mathfrak{C}$ is regular in $\mathfrak{A}$, then it must be regular in $\mathfrak{C}$ and we conclude that $Sp_{\mathfrak{C}}(c) = Sp_{\mathfrak{A}}(c)$.

THEOREM (1.6.15). *Let* $\mathfrak{A}$ *be a Banach algebra and let* e *be a proper idempotent in* $\mathfrak{A}$ (*that is*, $e \neq 0, 1$ *and* $e^2 = e$). *Then* $e\mathfrak{A}e$ *is a closed subalgebra of* $\mathfrak{A}$ *with* e *as an identity element and, for every* $e \in e\mathfrak{A}e$, $Sp_{\mathfrak{A}}(a) = Sp_{e\mathfrak{A}e}(a) \cup (0)$.

PROOF. That $e\mathfrak{A}e$ is a subalgebra is obvious and that $e\mathfrak{A}e$ is closed follows from the fact that $ex_ne \to x$ implies $e^2x_ne^2 \to exe$, and so $x = exe$. Since $eae = a$ for elements of $e\mathfrak{A}e$, the fact that e is proper forces a to be singular in $\mathfrak{A}$. In other words $0 \in Sp_{\mathfrak{A}}(a)$ and we have only to check the non-zero portions of the two spectra. That $Sp_{\mathfrak{A}}(a) \subseteq Sp_{e\mathfrak{A}e}(a) \cup (0)$ is immediate since $e\mathfrak{A}e$ is a subalgebra of $\mathfrak{A}$. On the other hand, let r be any element of $e\mathfrak{A}e$ which is quasi-regular in $\mathfrak{A}$. Then since $er = re = r$,

$$(er^{\circ}e) \circ r = er^{\circ}e + r - er^{\circ}er = e(r^{\circ} + r - r^{\circ}r)e = 0.$$

Similarly $r \circ (er^{\circ}e) = 0$, so that $er^{\circ}e = r^{\circ}$ and hence $r^{\circ} \in e\mathfrak{A}e$. In other words $e\mathfrak{A}e$ contains quasi-inverses of its elements which are quasi-regular in $\mathfrak{A}$. This implies $Sp_{e\mathfrak{A}e}(a) \subseteq Sp_{\mathfrak{A}}(a)$ and completes the proof.

We consider briefly some continuity properties of $Sp(x)$ as a function of x.

THEOREM (1.6.16). *Let* x *be an element of the Banach algebra* $\mathfrak{A}$ *and let* V *be any neighborhood of zero in the complex plane. Then there exists* $\delta > 0$ *such that* $\|y-x\| < \delta$ *implies* $Sp(y) \subseteq Sp(x)+V$.

PROOF. It is obviously sufficient to make the proof for the complex case. Suppose the theorem false and set $U = Sp(x)+V$. Then there exists for each n an element z_n and a scalar ζ_n such that $\|z_n - x\| < n^{-1}$, $\zeta_n \in Sp(z_n)$ and $\zeta_n \notin U$. Since $\|z_n\| \leqslant \|x\| + n^{-1}$, the sequence $\{\zeta_n\}$ is bounded. Therefore, by passing to a subsequence if necessary, we can obtain ξ such that $\lim \zeta_n = \xi$. Note that $\xi \notin U$, so that $\xi \notin Sp(x)$. If $\xi = 0$, then $\mathfrak{A}$ has an identity element and x is regular. Moreover, $\lim (\zeta_n - z_n) = x$ and it follows that $\zeta_n - z_n$ must be regular for large n. This contradicts the assumption that $\zeta_n \in Sp(z_n)$ and shows that $\xi \neq 0$. Since $\xi^{-1}x$ is quasi-regular and $\lim (\zeta_n^{-1} z_n) = \xi^{-1}x$, it follows that $\zeta_n^{-1} z_n$ is quasi-regular for large n. This also contradicts the assumption that $\zeta_n \in Sp(z_n)$ and completes the proof of the theorem.

The above theorem asserts that the spectrum $Sp(x)$ in a Banach algebra is always an upper semi-continuous function of x. Without further conditions, this is the sharpest continuity property that can be obtained. This is shown in A.1.1 of the Appendix where we obtain a sequence of nilpotent operators in $\mathfrak{B}(\mathfrak{H})$ which converges to an operator which is not topologically nilpotent. Thus, a sequence of elements whose spectra contain only zero can converge to an element whose spectrum contains non-zero values. On the other hand, by the next theorem, we see that commutativity forces the spectrum to be continuous.

THEOREM (1.6.17). *Let x be an element of the Banach algebra $\mathfrak{A}$ and let V be a neighborhood of zero in the complex plane. Then there exists $\delta > 0$ such that $\|x - y\| < \delta$ and $xy = yx$ imply*

$$Sp(y) \subseteq Sp(x) + V, \qquad Sp(x) \subseteq Sp(y) + V.$$

PROOF. Since the first inclusion is given by the preceding theorem, it remains to prove the second. Again we can restrict attention to the complex case. We can also assume that V is a circular disc of radius $2\epsilon > 0$ with center at zero. Now suppose the theorem to be false. Then there exists a sequence $\{z_n\}$ such that $\lim z_n = x$, $z_n x = x z_n$ and $Sp(x) \nsubseteq Sp(z_n) + V$ for every n. By using the compactness of $Sp(x)$ and passing to a subsequence if necessary, we can obtain $\xi_0 \in Sp(x)$ such that $|\xi_0 - \zeta| > \epsilon$ for every $\zeta \in Sp(z_n)$ and every n. Consider the case $\xi_0 = 0$. Then, since $\xi_0 \notin Sp(z_n)$, $\mathfrak{A}$ has an identity element and z_n is regular. Moreover, by Theorem (1.6.11), $Sp(z_n^{-1}) = \{\zeta^{-1} : \zeta \in Sp(z_n)\}$, so that $\nu(z_n^{-1}) < \epsilon^{-1}$. Thus $\{\nu(z_n^{-1})\}$ is bounded and it follows that x must be regular, by Theorem (1.4.23). This contradicts the assumption $\xi_0 \in Sp(x)$ and disposes of the case $\xi_0 = 0$.

Now assume $\xi_0 \neq 0$. Then $\xi_0^{-1}z_n$ is quasi-regular for each n and $\lim \xi_0^{-1}z_n = \xi_0^{-1}x$. By Theorem (1.6.11), the spectrum of $(\xi_0^{-1}z_n)^\circ$ consists of all scalars $\zeta(\zeta-1)^{-1}$ such that $\zeta \in Sp(\xi_0^{-1}z_n)$. Since $\zeta \in Sp(\xi_0^{-1}z_n)$ if and only if $\zeta\xi_0 \in Sp(z_n)$, and $|\zeta\xi_0-\xi_0| > \epsilon$ for $\zeta\xi_0 \in Sp(z_n)$, we have

$$\left|\frac{\zeta}{\zeta-1}\right| = \left|\frac{\zeta\xi_0}{\zeta\xi_0-\xi_0}\right| \leqslant \|z_n\|\epsilon^{-1},$$

for all $\zeta \in Sp(\xi_0^{-1}z_n)$. It follows that $\{\nu((\xi_0^{-1}z_n)^\circ)\}$ is bounded and again, by Theorem (1.4.23), that $\xi_0^{-1}x$ is quasi-regular. This contradicts the assumption that $\xi_0 \in Sp(x)$ and completes the proof of the theorem.

By the above theorem the spectrum, as a function restricted to the centralizer of x, is continuous at the point x. Therefore the spectrum is continuous at each point of the center of $\mathfrak{A}$ and, in particular, will be continuous at every point of $\mathfrak{A}$ if $\mathfrak{A}$ is commutative. An examination of the proof of the theorem reveals that commutativity of z_n with x was used only at the end to obtain a contradiction *via* Theorem (1.4.23). Therefore, failure of continuity implies the existence of a sequence $\{y_n\}$ of quasi-regular elements which converge to a quasi-singular element y in such a way that $\{\nu(y_n^\circ)\}$ is bounded. On the other hand, by Theorem (1.4.21), the sequence $\{\|y_n^\circ\|\}$ must be unbounded. The elements y_n and y are given by $y_n = 1-z_n$ and $y = 1-x$, if $\xi_0 = 0$, and by $y_n = \xi_0^{-1}z_n$ and $y = \xi_0^{-1}x$, if $\xi_0 \neq 0$. If it happens that boundedness of $\{\nu(y_n^\circ)\}$ implies boundedness of $\{\|y_n^\circ\|\}$, then we again have a contradiction and continuity follows. From this observation we see that the spectrum is a continuous function when restricted to the set of normal elements in a B*-algebra (see Chapter IV), since in this case $\nu(x) = \|x\|$. This result is proved by Newburgh [1] who also proved that, if a sequence $\{x_n\}$ converges in a Banach algebra to an element x, then $Sp(x_n)$ ultimately has points in the neighborhood of each component of $Sp(x)$. In particular, if each of the sets $Sp(x_n)$ is connected, then $Sp(x)$ is connected. It also follows that the spectrum is continuous at every point x whose spectrum is totally disconnected.

In closing this section on the spectrum, it is desirable to call attention to some elementary results which are important for the analytic side of the theory. In the interests of simplicity, we limit attention to a complex Banach algebra $\mathfrak{A}$ with an identity element. For $x \in \mathfrak{A}$ and $\zeta \notin Sp_{\mathfrak{A}}(x)$, define

$$R(\zeta, x) = (\zeta - x)^{-1}.$$

Then $R(\zeta, x)$, regarded as a function of ζ, is called the RESOLVENT of x. It is not difficult to verify that $R(\zeta, x)$ satisfies the following equation:

$$R(\xi, x) - R(\eta, x) = (\eta - \xi)R(\xi, x)R(\eta, x),$$

for $\xi, \eta \notin Sp(x)$. This equation is called the FIRST RESOLVENT EQUATION (Hille [2, Sec. 5.9]). Making use of the fact that the inverse is a continuous function, we have

$$\lim_{\eta \to \xi} \frac{R(\xi, x) - R(\eta, x)}{\xi - \eta} = -R(\xi, x)^2.$$

This shows that $R(\zeta, x)$ is a holomorphic vector-valued function in each component of the complement of $Sp(x)$. The SECOND RESOLVENT EQUATION (Hille [2, Sec. 5.16]), which follows, concerns $R(\zeta, x)$ as a function of x and is also not difficult to obtain:

$$R(\zeta, x) - R(\zeta, y) = R(\zeta, x)(x - y)R(\zeta, y),$$

for $\zeta \notin Sp(x)$ and $\zeta \notin Sp(y)$. When $\mathfrak{A}$ does not have an identity element, analogous equations hold for the function $(\zeta^{-1}x)^\circ$, $\zeta \notin Sp(x)$. (See Hille [2, Sec. 22.8].)

A cursory examination of Hille [2] or Hille–Phillips [1] will show the fundamental role which these equations play in the analytic theory. On the other hand, they are of only secondary importance for us.

For some purposes, it is desirable to deal differently with zero in defining the spectrum of an element, at least when the algebra does not possess an identity element. Hille [2, Sec. 22.7], for example, includes zero in the spectrum of x except when there exists a subalgebra which has an identity and contains x as a regular element. With his definition, zero need not belong to the spectrum even when $\mathfrak{A}$ fails to possess an identity element. With only superficial changes, all of the properties obtained above for the spectrum can also be established for the Hille spectrum. Hille's more subtle treatment of zero becomes important in certain analysis questions, but is not needed for our discussion. Kaplansky [2, 5] uses the characterization in Theorem (1.6.6) as a definition of the spectrum in real algebras.

The "spectral radius formula" of Theorem (1.6.4), which was proved by Gelfand [4] in the general case of a Banach algebra, was proved for the algebra of absolutely convergent trigonometric series by Beurling [1]. The usual proof uses complex function theory. The elementary proof given here is due to the author [6].

§ 7. Normed division algebras.

We are in a position now to obtain the important Mazur–Gelfand theorem on normed division algebras. The complex case is particularly easy at this stage.

THEOREM (1.7.1). *Every complex normed division algebra is isomorphic to the field of complex numbers.*

PROOF. Let $\mathfrak{A}$ denote a complex normed division algebra. By hypothesis, $\mathfrak{A}$ has an identity element and every non-zero element is regular.

This means that $Sp(x)$ does not contain zero for any non-zero element $x \in \mathfrak{A}$. On the other hand, $Sp(x)$ is non-vacuous by Theorem (1.6.4) and so will contain at least one complex number ξ. But then $\xi - x$ is singular in $\mathfrak{A}$ and must therefore be equal to zero. In other words $x = \xi$, a complex multiple of the identity. It is immediate that $\mathfrak{A}$ is isomorphic to the complex field.

Corollary (1.7.2). *A complex Banach algebra with identity and with no topological divisors of zero except zero is isomorphic to the field of complex numbers.*

Corollary (1.7.3). *If $\mathfrak{A}$ is a complex normed algebra with identity, whose norm satisfies the condition $\|x\| \, \|y\| \leqslant \beta \|xy\|$, β constant, then $\mathfrak{A}$ is isomorphic to the field of complex numbers.*

Theorem (1.7.4). *Let $\mathfrak{A}$ be any real normed division algebra. If $x^2 + y^2 = 0$ implies $x = y = 0$ in $\mathfrak{A}$, then $\mathfrak{A}$ is isomorphic with the field of real numbers.*

Proof. Let a be an arbitrary element of $\mathfrak{A}$ and consider a maximal commutative subalgebra of $\mathfrak{A}$ which contains a; call it $\mathfrak{C}$. Then $\mathfrak{C}$ is evidently a commutative real normed division algebra. Let $x + iy$ be any non-zero element in the complexification $\mathfrak{C}_C$ of $\mathfrak{C}$. Then $x \neq 0$ or $y \neq 0$, so that $x^2 + y^2 \neq 0$. Since $\mathfrak{C}$ is commutative, we have $(x+iy)(x-iy)(x^2+y^2)^{-1} = 1$, so that $\mathfrak{C}_C$ is also a division algebra. Therefore, by the preceding theorem, elements of $\mathfrak{C}_C$ are complex multiples of the identity. From the definition of the algebra $\mathfrak{C}_C$, it is clear that elements of $\mathfrak{C}$ must be real multiples of the identity. In particular, a is a real multiple of the identity so the proof is complete.

Theorem (1.7.5). *Let $\mathfrak{A}$ be any commutative real normed division algebra. Then $\mathfrak{A}$ is isomorphic to either the field of real numbers or the field of complex numbers.*

Proof. If the condition in the previous theorem is satisfied then $\mathfrak{A}$ is isomorphic with the reals. Therefore assume the existence of $u, v \in \mathfrak{A}$ such that either $u \neq 0$ or $v \neq 0$ and $u^2 + v^2 = 0$. Since $\mathfrak{A}$ is a division algebra it follows that both $u \neq 0$ and $v \neq 0$. Define $j = uv^{-1}$. Then $j^2 = -1$. Let $\alpha + \beta i$ be any complex number and, for $x \in \mathfrak{A}$, define $(\alpha + \beta i)x = (\alpha + \beta j)x$. With this definition of multiplication by complex scalars, $\mathfrak{A}$ becomes a complex algebra. Since $\|ix\| = \|jx\| \leqslant \|j\| \, \|x\|$, the mapping $x \to ix$ is continuous in the given norm of $\mathfrak{A}$. Therefore, by Theorem (1.3.3), $\mathfrak{A}$ can be renormed as a complex normed algebra. Again, by Theorem (1.7.1), $\mathfrak{A}$ is isomorphic to the complex field and the proof is complete.

THEOREM (1.7.6). *Let* $\mathfrak{A}$ *be any real normed division algebra. Then* $\mathfrak{A}$ *is isomorphic to either the reals, complexes or quaternions.*

PROOF. The commutative case is covered by the preceding theorem. In the general case, let x be any element of $\mathfrak{A}$. Since $\mathfrak{A}$ has an identity and $Sp(x)$ is non-vacuous, there exists a complex number $\xi = \alpha+\beta i$ such that $|\xi|^2-(2\alpha x-x^2)$ is singular. Therefore $|\xi|^2-(2\alpha x-x^2) = 0$, which shows that every element of $\mathfrak{A}$ satisfies a quadratic equation with real coefficients. In other words, $\mathfrak{A}$ is algebraic of bounded degree (equal to two). This implies finite dimensionality (Jacobson [6, p. 704]), so that the desired conclusion is given immediately by the classical Frobenius theorem, which asserts that any finite dimensional division algebra over the reals is isomorphic to either the reals, the complexes, or the quaternions.

The Mazur–Gelfand theorem (1.7.1) was announced without proof by Mazur [1]. The first published proof, by Gelfand [4], is based on a generalization of the Liouville Theorem to vector-valued functions. Arens [3] extended this proof to cover a more general situation. Elementary proofs which avoid the function theory have been given by Kametani [1], Rickart [6], Stone [7], and Tornheim [1].

II. THE RADICAL, SEMI-SIMPLICITY AND THE STRUCTURE SPACES

Introduction. This chapter is primarily concerned with general structure properties of Banach algebras. As might be expected from ring theory, the notion of a radical and the associated notion of semi-simplicity are of fundamental importance in these matters. It turns out that the radical introduced by N. Jacobson for arbitrary rings is, for most purposes, exactly the radical which is needed for the study of Banach algebras. In fact, for these algebras, the Jacobson radical is characterized by a property which is a most natural generalization of the classical definition of radical for finite dimensional algebras.

In the first two sections of the chapter we discuss some of the properties of ideals and representations for Banach algebras. The next section (§ 3) is devoted to a study of primitive algebras. These are special algebras which arise in the general structure theorem for semi-simple algebras. The radical is discussed in § 4. In § 5 some uniqueness properties of the norm topology of certain semi-simple Banach algebras are obtained and the fundamental isomorphism theorem for primitive Banach algebras with minimal ideals is proved. The next section (§ 6) contains the general structure theorem for semi-simple Banach algebras and the definition of the structure spaces. The last two sections (§§ 7, 8) of the chapter deal with the structure of some general classes of Banach algebras.

§ 1. Ideals and difference algebras. A subset $\mathfrak{J}$ of an algebra $\mathfrak{A}$ is called a LEFT IDEAL of $\mathfrak{A}$ provided it is a linear subspace of $\mathfrak{A}$ such that $xy \in \mathfrak{J}$ for all $x \in \mathfrak{A}$ and $y \in \mathfrak{J}$. It is a RIGHT IDEAL if the latter condition is replaced by $xy \in \mathfrak{J}$ for all $x \in \mathfrak{J}$ and $y \in \mathfrak{A}$. If $\mathfrak{J}$ is both a left and a right ideal, then it is called a 2-SIDED IDEAL. Any ideal different from $\mathfrak{A}$ is called PROPER. An ideal $\mathfrak{J}$ is called MINIMAL if it is different from (0) and does not contain properly any ideal of the same type other than (0).   It is called MAXIMAL if it is different from $\mathfrak{A}$ and is not properly contained in any ideal of the same type other than $\mathfrak{A}$.

An ideal is said to be QUASI-REGULAR provided each of its elements is quasi-regular.   A left ideal $\mathfrak{I}$ each of whose elements is left quasi-regular is a quasi-regular ideal.   In fact, let $m \in \mathfrak{I}$ and choose n such that $n \circ m = 0$.   Then $n = nm - m$, so that $n \in \mathfrak{I}$.   Hence n is left quasi-regular.   But m is already a right quasi-inverse for n.   Therefore $n \circ m = m \circ n = 0$.   This also implies that m is quasi-regular and proves that the ideal $\mathfrak{I}$ is quasi-regular.   A similar statement holds for right ideals.   In § 3, when we discuss the radical, quasi-regular ideals will be considered again.

A left ideal $\mathfrak{I}$ is said to be MODULAR if there exists $e \in \mathfrak{A}$ such that $\mathfrak{A}(1-e) \subseteq \mathfrak{I}$.   In other words, the element e is a right identity for $\mathfrak{A}$ modulo $\mathfrak{I}$.   Similarly, a right ideal is modular if there exists a left identity for $\mathfrak{A}$ modulo the ideal.   Note that if e is a right (left) identity for $\mathfrak{A}$ modulo the left (right) ideal $\mathfrak{I}$, then the same is true for the elements $e + m$, for $m \in \mathfrak{I}$, and e^k, k an integer.   A 2-sided ideal $\mathfrak{I}$ is defined to be modular if it is modular both as a left and as a right ideal. In this case there is an element e which is at the same time both a right and a left identity for $\mathfrak{A}$ modulo $\mathfrak{I}$.   In fact, if e_1 is a right identity and e_2 is a left identity modulo $\mathfrak{I}$, then $e_1 - e_2 e_1 \in \mathfrak{I}$ and $e_2 - e_2 e_1 \in \mathfrak{I}$, so that $e_2 - e_1 \in \mathfrak{I}$.   Therefore either one of e_1 or e_2 will serve as both a right and left identity modulo $\mathfrak{I}$.   If $\mathfrak{A}$ has an identity element, then all ideals are obviously modular.   If e is any element of $\mathfrak{A}$, then $\mathfrak{A}(1-e)$ is clearly a modular left ideal with e as a right identity for $\mathfrak{A}$ modulo the ideal.   This ideal is proper if and only if e is left quasi-singular.   In fact left quasi-regularity of e is equivalent to $e \in \mathfrak{A}(1-e)$ and this is equivalent to $\mathfrak{A}(1-e) = \mathfrak{A}$.   More generally, if $\mathfrak{I}$ is any modular left ideal with e as a right identity modulo $\mathfrak{I}$, then $e \in \mathfrak{I}$ implies $\mathfrak{I} = \mathfrak{A}$ and, in particular, if e is left quasi-regular then $e \in \mathfrak{I}$ so that $\mathfrak{I} = \mathfrak{A}$.

THEOREM (2.1.1).

(i) *Every proper modular ideal is contained in a maximal ideal of the same type.*

(ii) *If $\mathfrak{I}_1$, $\mathfrak{I}_2$ are modular and if $\mathfrak{I}_2$ is 2-sided, then $\mathfrak{I}_1 \cap \mathfrak{I}_2$ is a modular ideal of the same type as $\mathfrak{I}_1$.*

PROOF.   Let $\mathfrak{I}$ be a modular left ideal and e a right identity modulo $\mathfrak{I}$. A simple application of Zorn's lemma gives a left ideal $\mathfrak{L}$ which is maximal with respect to the properties of $\mathfrak{I} \subseteq \mathfrak{L}$ and $e \notin \mathfrak{L}$.   It is obvious that $\mathfrak{L}$ is a maximal left ideal and e is a right identity modulo $\mathfrak{L}$. Thus (i) is proved. For the proof of (ii), let $\mathfrak{I}_1$ be a left ideal and let e_1, e_2 be right identities modulo $\mathfrak{I}_1$ and $\mathfrak{I}_2$ respectively. Set $e = e_2 \circ e_1$. Then

$$\mathfrak{A}(1-e) = \mathfrak{A}(1-e_2)(1-e_1) \subseteq \mathfrak{A}(1-e_1) \subset \mathfrak{I}_1.$$

Similarly $\mathfrak{A}(1-e) \subseteq \mathfrak{I}_2(1-e_1) \subset \mathfrak{I}_2$, so that $\mathfrak{A}(1-e) \subseteq \mathfrak{I}_1 \cap \mathfrak{I}_2$. This proves (ii).

COROLLARY (2.1.2). *If $\mathfrak{A}$ is an algebra with an identity element, then, in order for an element $a \in \mathfrak{A}$ to be regular, it is necessary and sufficient that no maximal (right or left) ideal in $\mathfrak{A}$ shall contain a.*

The above definitions and remarks apply to arbitrary algebras. If $\mathfrak{A}$ is a normed algebra, then it is immediate from continuity of the algebraic operations that the closure of an ideal is also an ideal of the same kind. A proper closed ideal in $\mathfrak{A}$ is said to be MINIMAL-CLOSED if it does not contain properly any closed ideal of the same type other than (0). Similarly, a proper ideal is said to be MAXIMAL-CLOSED if it is not contained properly in any closed ideal of the same type other than $\mathfrak{A}$. It can happen that a proper ideal is dense in $\mathfrak{A}$ so that the closure of a proper ideal may not be proper. (See Corollary (4.2.6).) On the other hand, this cannot happen for modular ideals in a Banach algebra.

THEOREM (2.1.3). *Let $\mathfrak{I}$ be a proper modular ideal in a Banach algebra $\mathfrak{A}$ and let e be an identity modulo $\mathfrak{I}$. Then $\mathfrak{I}$ will not intersect the neighborhood of e consisting of all $x \in \mathfrak{A}$ such that* $\|e-x\| < 1$.

PROOF. We make the proof for a left ideal. By Corollary (1.4.19), if $\|e-x\| < 1$, then $e-x$ is quasi-regular in $\mathfrak{A}$. Let $u = (e-x)^\circ$; then $e = (1-u)x-u(1-e)$. It is always true that $u(1-e) \in \mathfrak{I}$ and, if $x \in \mathfrak{I}$, then also $(1-u)x \in \mathfrak{I}$. But this gives $e \in \mathfrak{I}$ which is impossible if $\mathfrak{I}$ is proper.

COROLLARY (2.1.4). *If $\mathfrak{A}$ is a Banach algebra, then the closure of every proper modular ideal is also proper. In particular, maximal modular ideals in $\mathfrak{A}$ are closed.*

Consider, for the moment, an arbitrary linear space $\mathfrak{X}$ and a linear subspace $\mathfrak{M}$ of $\mathfrak{X}$. For each x in $\mathfrak{X}$, define $x' = x+\mathfrak{M}$. The collection of all such cosets becomes a linear space under the algebraic operations defined by the relations $x'+y' = (x+y)'$ and $\alpha x' = (\alpha x)'$.

We call this linear space the DIFFERENCE SPACE MODULO $\mathfrak{M}$ and denote it by $\mathfrak{X}-\mathfrak{M}$. The mapping $x \to x'$ is a linear transformation and is called the NATURAL HOMOMORPHISM of $\mathfrak{X}$ onto $\mathfrak{X}-\mathfrak{M}$. If $\mathfrak{X}$ also has a norm $\|x\|$, we define

$$\|x'\| = \inf_m \|x+m\|, \quad m \in \mathfrak{M}.$$

If $\mathfrak{M}$ is closed in $\mathfrak{X}$ with respect to the norm $\|x\|$, then $\|x'\|$ is a norm in $\mathfrak{X}-\mathfrak{M}$. Also, since $\|x'\| \leqslant \|x\|$, the natural homomorphism $x \to x'$ is continuous. Furthermore, let $\{x'_n\}$ be a sequence of elements in $\mathfrak{X}-\mathfrak{M}$ such that $\|x'_n - x'_{n+1}\| < 2^{-n}$, for each n. Then the elements x_n can be chosen successively in $\mathfrak{X}$ from the corresponding cosets x'_n such that $\|x_n - x_{n+1}\| \leqslant 2^{-n}$, for each n. If $\mathfrak{X}$ is a Banach space, then this observation shows that the natural homomorphism takes closed sets F, with the property $F+\mathfrak{M} = F$, into closed sets and, in particular, that $\mathfrak{X}-\mathfrak{M}$ is also a Banach space.

We return now to an algebra $\mathfrak{A}$ and let $\mathfrak{I}$ denote a 2-sided ideal in $\mathfrak{A}$. Define the linear space $\mathfrak{A}-\mathfrak{I}$ as above and, for $x', y' \in \mathfrak{A}-\mathfrak{I}$, define $x'y' = (xy)'$. This product, which is well-defined since $\mathfrak{I}$ is an ideal, evidently converts $\mathfrak{A}-\mathfrak{I}$ into an algebra. We denote this algebra by $\mathfrak{A}/\mathfrak{I}$ and note that the natural homomorphism $x \to x'$ is now an algebra homomorphism of $\mathfrak{A}$ onto $\mathfrak{A}/\mathfrak{I}$. Next let $\mathfrak{A}$ be a normed algebra under a norm $\|x\|$ and assume that $\mathfrak{I}$ is a closed 2-sided ideal in $\mathfrak{A}$. Then $\mathfrak{A}/\mathfrak{I}$ is also a normed algebra under the infimum norm $\|x'\|$. In fact,

$$\|x'y'\| = \inf_{m \in \mathfrak{I}} \|xy+m\| \leqslant \inf_{m,n \in \mathfrak{I}} \|(x+m)(y+n)\|$$

$$\leqslant \inf_{m \in \mathfrak{I}} \|x+m\| \inf_{n \in \mathfrak{I}} \|y+n\| = \|x'\|\,\|y'\|.$$

Furthermore, if $\mathfrak{I}$ is modular and e is an identity element for $\mathfrak{A}$ modulo $\mathfrak{I}$ with norm equal to one, then

$$1 = \frac{\|e'^2\|}{\|e'\|} \leqslant \frac{\|e'\|^2}{\|e'\|} = \|e'\| \leqslant \|e\| = 1,$$

so that $\|e'\| = 1$. In particular, if $\mathfrak{A}$ is a normed algebra with identity element, then so is $\mathfrak{A}/\mathfrak{I}$. Also, if $\mathfrak{A}$ is a Banach algebra, then $\mathfrak{A}/\mathfrak{I}$ is a Banach algebra.

Notice that the kernel of any continuous homomorphism of a normed algebra $\mathfrak{A}$ into a second normed algebra is a closed 2-sided ideal $\mathfrak{I}$ in $\mathfrak{A}$. The image of $\mathfrak{A}$ under this homomorphism is, of course, isomorphic as an algebra to $\mathfrak{A}/\mathfrak{J}$. However, the norms obviously need not be equivalent.

We discuss next a few properties of minimal ideals, most of which are well-known from ring theory (Jacobson [4, 5]). We limit attention to left ideals with the remark that similar properties hold for right ideals.

LEMMA (2.1.5). *Let $\mathfrak{A}$ be an arbitrary algebra and $\mathfrak{L}$ a minimal left ideal in $\mathfrak{A}$ such that $\mathfrak{L}^2 \neq (0)$. Then there exists an idempotent e in $\mathfrak{A}$ such that $\mathfrak{L} = \mathfrak{A}e$ and $e\mathfrak{A}e$ is a division algebra with identity element e.*

PROOF. Since $\mathfrak{L}^2 \neq (0)$, there exists $u \in \mathfrak{L}$ such that $\mathfrak{L}u \neq (0)$. Now $\mathfrak{L}u$ is a non-zero left ideal contained in the minimal ideal $\mathfrak{L}$. Therefore $\mathfrak{L}u = \mathfrak{L}$. In particular, there exists $e \in \mathfrak{L}$ such that $eu = u$. Again, $\mathfrak{L}(e-1)$ is a left ideal contained in $\mathfrak{L}$, so that either $\mathfrak{L}(e-1) = (0)$ or $\mathfrak{L}(e-1) = \mathfrak{L}$. In the latter case there exists $v \in \mathfrak{L}$ such that $ve - v = e$. Hence $u = eu = veu - vu = 0$, contrary to the assumption $\mathfrak{L}u \neq (0)$. Therefore, $\mathfrak{L}(e-1) = (0)$ and, in particular, $e^2 = e$ and $\mathfrak{A}e \neq (0)$. Since $\mathfrak{A}e \subseteq \mathfrak{L}$, it follows that $\mathfrak{A}e = \mathfrak{L}$. Next let eae be any non-zero element of $e\mathfrak{A}e$. Then $\mathfrak{A}eae = \mathfrak{A}e$, and so there exists $ebe \in e\mathfrak{A}e$ such that $(ebe)(eae) = e$. In other words, eae is left regular in $e\mathfrak{A}e$. Since every non-zero element of $e\mathfrak{A}e$ is left regular, it follows that $e\mathfrak{A}e$ is a division algebra.

COROLLARY (2.1.6). *If $\mathfrak{A}$ is also a Banach algebra, then $e\mathfrak{A}e$ is isomorphic to the reals, quaternions or complexes. In particular, if $\mathfrak{A}$ is a complex Banach algebra, then $e\mathfrak{A}e$ consists of scalar multiples of e.*

DEFINITION (2.1.7). *An idempotent e such that $e\mathfrak{A}e$ is a division algebra is said to be* MINIMAL. *Two idempotents e_1 and e_2 such that $e_1e_2 = e_2e_1 = 0$ are said to be* ORTHOGONAL.

LEMMA (2.1.8). *Let (0) be the only (left or right) ideal in $\mathfrak{A}$ with square equal to zero. If e is a minimal idempotent in $\mathfrak{A}$ and u is any element of $\mathfrak{A}$ such that $eu \neq 0$ (or $ue \neq 0$), then the ideal $\mathfrak{A}eu$ (or $ue\mathfrak{A}$) is minimal.*

PROOF. Let $\mathfrak{L}$ be any non-zero left ideal contained in $\mathfrak{A}eu$. Since $\mathfrak{L}^2 \neq (0)$, there exist elements aeu and beu in $\mathfrak{L}$ such that $aeubeu \neq 0$. In particular, $eube \neq 0$ and there exists $c \in e\mathfrak{A}e$ such that $ceube = e$. Hence

$$\mathfrak{A}eu \supseteq \mathfrak{L} \supseteq \mathfrak{A}beu \supseteq \mathfrak{A}ceubeu = \mathfrak{A}eu.$$

Therefore, $\mathfrak{L} = \mathfrak{A}eu$ and it follows that $\mathfrak{A}eu$ is a minimal left ideal.

COROLLARY (2.1.9). *If e is a minimal idempotent, then* $\mathfrak{A}e$ *is a minimal left ideal and* $e\mathfrak{A}$ *is a minimal right ideal.*

LEMMA (2.1.10). *Let* $\mathfrak{A}$ *be a Banach algebra and e any idempotent in* $\mathfrak{A}$. *Then the left ideal* $\mathfrak{A}e$ *is closed. If* $\mathfrak{A}e$ *is a minimal-closed ideal, then it is minimal.*

PROOF. If $a_n e \to a$, then, since $a_n e = a_n e^2$, it follows that $ae = a$. Therefore, $\mathfrak{A}e$ is closed. Now let $\mathfrak{L}$ be any non-zero left ideal contained in $\mathfrak{A}e$. If $\mathfrak{A}e$ is minimal-closed, then $\bar{\mathfrak{L}} = \mathfrak{A}e$. In particular, there exists $\{a_n\} \subset \mathfrak{L}$ such that $a_n \to e$. Also $ea_n e \to e$. Since $e\mathfrak{A}e$ is a Banach algebra with e as identity element, it follows that $ea_n e$ is regular in $e\mathfrak{A}e$ for large n. Hence $e \in \mathfrak{L}$ and we obtain $\mathfrak{L} = \mathfrak{A}e$. This completes the proof.

Let $\{\mathfrak{J}_\lambda : \lambda \in \Lambda\}$ be a family of (left, right) ideals in an algebra $\mathfrak{A}$. Then the smallest (left, right) ideal in $\mathfrak{A}$ which contains every $\mathfrak{J}_\lambda$ is called the SUM of the ideals $\mathfrak{J}_\lambda$. If the intersection of each $\mathfrak{J}_\lambda$ with the sum of the remaining ideals contains only zero, then the sum is called a DIRECT SUM. If $\mathfrak{A}$ is a topological algebra, then the closure of the sum of the ideals $\mathfrak{J}_\lambda$ is called their TOPOLOGICAL SUM. If each $\mathfrak{J}_\lambda$ is closed and intersects the topological sum of the remaining ideals in the zero element, then the topological sum is called a DIRECT TOPOLOGICAL SUM. The sum of the ideals $\mathfrak{J}_\lambda$ evidently consists of all finite sums of elements from the ideals $\mathfrak{J}_\lambda$. The sum of all minimal left (right) ideals in $\mathfrak{A}$ is called the LEFT (RIGHT) SOCLE of $\mathfrak{A}$. The left (right) socle exists if and only if $\mathfrak{A}$ contains minimal left (right) ideals. If the left and right socles exist and are equal, then the resulting 2-sided ideal is called simply the SOCLE of $\mathfrak{A}$. We denote the socle, when it exists, by $\mathfrak{F}$. (See Dieudonné [1] and Jacobson [5, p. 64].)

LEMMA (2.1.11). *If the left (right) socle exists, then it is a non-zero 2-sided ideal in* $\mathfrak{A}$.

PROOF. Let $\mathfrak{L}$ be any minimal left ideal in $\mathfrak{A}$ and let u be an arbitrary element of $\mathfrak{A}$. Then $\mathfrak{L}u$ is a left ideal in $\mathfrak{A}$. If $\mathfrak{L}u \neq (0)$, choose any $v \in \mathfrak{L}$ such that $vu \neq 0$. Since $\mathfrak{L}$ is minimal, the smallest left ideal which contains v must equal $\mathfrak{L}$. Therefore the smallest left ideal which contains vu must equal $\mathfrak{L}u$. In other words, $\mathfrak{L}u$ is either zero or is a minimal left ideal in $\mathfrak{A}$. It follows immediately that the left (and, by symmetry, the right) socle of $\mathfrak{A}$ is a 2-sided ideal.

LEMMA (2.1.12). *If* $\mathfrak{A}$ *contains minimal one-sided ideals (right or left) and if* (0) *is the only ideal with square equal to zero, then the socle of* $\mathfrak{A}$ *is defined.*

PROOF. It follows from Lemma (2.1.5) and Corollary (2.1.9) that the left and right socles are both generated by the minimal idempotents and therefore coincide, defining the socle.

In general, we have more to do with maximal ideals than with minimal ideals since the former exist in abundance in most Banach algebras while the latter are usually conspicuous by their absence.

Modular ideals were first considered by Segal [2] who called them "regular ideals" and obtained their fundamental properties. The term "modular ideal" was introduced by Jacobson [5].

§ **2. Representations.** At this point, a more detailed examination of representations is needed. The discussion follows more-or-less standard algebraic lines with the usual topological overtones when there is a norm. Recall, from Chapter I, § 2, that a representation of an algebra $\mathfrak{A}$ on a linear space $\mathfrak{X}$ is any homomorphism of $\mathfrak{A}$ into the algebra of all linear operators on $\mathfrak{X}$. Two such representations, $a \to T_a^{(1)}$ and $a \to T_a^{(2)}$, on $\mathfrak{X}^{(1)}$ and $\mathfrak{X}^{(2)}$ respectively are said to be ALGEBRAICALLY EQUIVALENT provided there exists a one-to-one linear transformation U mapping $\mathfrak{X}^{(2)}$ onto $\mathfrak{X}^{(1)}$ such that $T_a^{(1)}U = UT_a^{(2)}$ for every $a \in \mathfrak{A}$. If we have to do with normed representations and if U is a homeomorphism between the normed linear spaces $\mathfrak{X}^{(2)}$ and $\mathfrak{X}^{(1)}$, then the two representations are said to be TOPOLOGICALLY EQUIVALENT. When there is no chance of confusion, the term EQUIVALENCE will be used to refer to either algebraic or topological equivalence. In general, we are interested in representations only up to an equivalence.

Let $\mathfrak{B}$ be a subalgebra of the algebra of all linear operators on the linear space $\mathfrak{X}$. A linear subspace $\mathfrak{M}$ of $\mathfrak{X}$ is said to be INVARIANT WITH RESPECT TO $\mathfrak{B}$ if $T(\mathfrak{M}) \subseteq \mathfrak{M}$ for every $T \in \mathfrak{B}$. If $\mathfrak{X}$ is normed and $\mathfrak{B}$ consists of bounded operators, then it is evident that the closure of an invariant subspace is also invariant. Let z be a fixed vector in $\mathfrak{X}$ and denote by $\mathfrak{X}_z$ the set of all Tz for $T \in \mathfrak{B}$. Then $\mathfrak{X}_z$ is clearly an invariant subspace of $\mathfrak{X}$ with respect to $\mathfrak{B}$. If there exists z such that $\mathfrak{X}_z = \mathfrak{X}$, then $\mathfrak{B}$ is said to be STRICTLY CYCLIC and, if $\bar{\mathfrak{X}}_z = \mathfrak{X}$ in the normed case, then $\mathfrak{B}$ is said to be TOPOLOGICALLY CYCLIC. In the first case z is called a STRICTLY CYCLIC VECTOR and in the second a TOPOLOGICALLY CYCLIC VECTOR. The algebra $\mathfrak{B}$ is said to be

STRICTLY IRREDUCIBLE provided (0) and $\mathfrak{X}$ are the only invariant subspaces and is said to be TOPOLOGICALLY IRREDUCIBLE in the normed case provided these are the only closed invariant subspaces. It follows immediately that $\mathfrak{B}$ will be strictly (topologically) irreducible if and only if every non-zero vector in $\mathfrak{X}$ is strictly (topologically) cyclic. A representation will be said to possess one of the properties defined above for an algebra $\mathfrak{B}$ provided its range has the property in question. Again, when there is no possibility of confusion, we will drop the qualifying terms "strictly" and "topologically".

Let $a \to T_a$ be a representation of an algebra $\mathfrak{A}$ on $\mathfrak{X}$ and let $\mathfrak{M}$ be a linear subspace of $\mathfrak{X}$ which is invariant with respect to the representation. The invariance of $\mathfrak{M}$ implies that the restriction of each T_a to $\mathfrak{M}$ is a linear operator $T_a^{\mathfrak{M}}$ on $\mathfrak{M}$. It is obvious that $a \to T_a^{\mathfrak{M}}$ is a representation of $\mathfrak{A}$ on $\mathfrak{M}$. This representation is called the RESTRICTION of the given representation to $\mathfrak{M}$. If $a \to T_a$ is normed with respect to a norm in $\mathfrak{X}$, then the restriction $a \to T_a^{\mathfrak{M}}$ is also normed with respect to the same norm in $\mathfrak{M}$ and $|T_a^{\mathfrak{M}}| \leqslant |T_a|$.

The representation $a \to T_a$ also defines a representation $a \to T_a^{\mathfrak{X}-\mathfrak{M}}$ of $\mathfrak{A}$ on the difference space $\mathfrak{X}-\mathfrak{M}$, where $T_a^{\mathfrak{X}-\mathfrak{M}}$ is defined by the relation

$$T_a^{\mathfrak{X}-\mathfrak{M}}x' = (T_a x)', \quad x' \in \mathfrak{X}-\mathfrak{M}.$$

That $T_a^{\mathfrak{X}-\mathfrak{M}}$ is well defined is a consequence of the invariance of $\mathfrak{M}$. It is obvious that $a \to T_a^{\mathfrak{X}-\mathfrak{M}}$ is a representation of $\mathfrak{A}$ on $\mathfrak{X}-\mathfrak{M}$. This representation is called the REDUCTION of the given representation to $\mathfrak{X}-\mathfrak{M}$. If $a \to T_a$ is a normed representation and $\mathfrak{M}$ is closed in $\mathfrak{X}$, then $a \to T_a^{\mathfrak{X}-\mathfrak{M}}$ is also normed. In fact,

$$\inf_{m \in \mathfrak{M}} |T_a x + m| \leqslant \inf_{m \in \mathfrak{M}} |T_a(x+m)| \leqslant |T_a| \inf_{m \in \mathfrak{M}} |x+m|,$$

where $|T_a|$ is the bound of T_a relative to the norm in $\mathfrak{X}$. Therefore, if $|T_a^{\mathfrak{X}-\mathfrak{M}}|$ is the bound of $T_a^{\mathfrak{X}-\mathfrak{M}}$ relative to the norm in $\mathfrak{X}-\mathfrak{M}$, then $|T_a^{\mathfrak{X}-\mathfrak{M}}| \leqslant |T_a|$, so that the reduced representation $a \to T_a^{\mathfrak{X}-\mathfrak{M}}$ is indeed normed.

If the representation $a \to T_a$ is normed and continuous, then it is easily seen that both the restriction and the reduction representations associated with an invariant subspace $\mathfrak{M}$ are also continuous. Furthermore, if $a \to T_a$ is strongly continuous, then both of the representations $a \to T_a^{\mathfrak{M}}$ and $a \to T_a^{\mathfrak{X}-\mathfrak{M}}$ are also strongly continuous. It is, of course, understood in these statements that $\mathfrak{M}$ is closed in the case of the reduced representation.

The kernel $\mathfrak{K}_1$ of the representation $a \to T_a^{\mathfrak{M}}$ consists of all elements $k \in \mathfrak{A}$ such that $T_k\mathfrak{M} = (0)$. It is obviously a 2-sided ideal and, if $a \to T_a$ is a strongly continuous normed representation, is automatically closed. Similarly, the kernel $\mathfrak{K}_2$ of $a \to T_a^{\mathfrak{X}-\mathfrak{M}}$ consists of all $k \in \mathfrak{A}$ such that $T_k\mathfrak{X} \subseteq \mathfrak{M}$. Again $\mathfrak{K}_2$ is a 2-sided ideal and, in the normed case, is closed if $\mathfrak{M}$ is closed and $a \to T_a$ is strongly continuous.

If $a \to T_a$ is any strongly continuous representation of the normed algebra $\mathfrak{A}$ on $\mathfrak{X}$ then, as has been observed, the kernel $\mathfrak{K}$ of the representation is a closed 2-sided ideal in $\mathfrak{A}$. Therefore the image of $\mathfrak{A}$ under the representation, being isomorphic with $\mathfrak{A}/\mathfrak{K}$, carries the norm $\|T_a\| = \inf_{k \in \mathfrak{K}} \|a+k\|$ in addition to the operator bound $|T_a|$. If the representation is continuous, say $|T_a| \leqslant \beta\|a\|$, then, since $T_{a+k} = T_a$ for $k \in \mathfrak{K}$, we have $|T_a| \leqslant \beta\|a+k\|$, for all $k \in \mathfrak{K}$, and so it follows that $|T_a| \leqslant \beta\|T_a\| \leqslant \beta\|a\|$. If $\mathfrak{A}$ is a Banach algebra, then the image of $\mathfrak{A}$ in $\mathscr{B}(\mathfrak{X})$ is complete under $\|T_a\|$ while it may or may not be complete under the norm $|T_a|$.

We now examine some special representations of an algebra which are associated with its left ideals. These representations are derived from the left regular representation and result from the fact that the left ideals are precisely those linear subspaces of the algebra which are invariant with respect to this representation. A parallel discussion could of course be carried through for right ideals.

Let $\mathfrak{L}$ be a left ideal in the algebra $\mathfrak{A}$ and consider the representation $a \to A_a^{\mathfrak{L}}$ of $\mathfrak{A}$ obtained by restricting to the ideal $\mathfrak{L}$ the left regular representation $a \to A_a$ of $\mathfrak{A}$. This representation is called the LEFT REGULAR REPRESENTATION ON $\mathfrak{L}$. An element $u \in \mathfrak{L}$ will be strictly cyclic for the representation $a \to A_a^{\mathfrak{L}}$ if and only if $\mathfrak{L} = \mathfrak{A}u$; that is, provided $\mathfrak{L}$ is the principal left ideal generated by u. The representation $a \to A_a^{\mathfrak{L}}$ will be strictly irreducible if and only if $\mathfrak{L}$ is minimal. In the normed case, $a \to A_a^{\mathfrak{L}}$ is normed and continuous, since $|A_a^{\mathfrak{L}}| \leqslant |A_a| \leqslant \|a\|$ for all $a \in \mathfrak{A}$. The element $u \in \mathfrak{L}$ will be topologically cyclic for $a \to A_a^{\mathfrak{L}}$ if and only if $\mathfrak{L}$ is equal to the closure of the principal ideal $\mathfrak{A}u$. The representation $a \to A_a^{\mathfrak{L}}$ will be topologically irreducible provided (0) and $\mathfrak{L}$ are the only left ideals contained in and relatively closed in $\mathfrak{L}$ or, in case $\mathfrak{L}$ is closed, provided $\mathfrak{L}$ is minimal-closed. The kernel $\mathfrak{K}$ of the representation $a \to A_a^{\mathfrak{L}}$ is a 2-sided ideal equal to the left annihilator of $\mathfrak{L}$ in $\mathfrak{M}$. In the normed case, $\mathfrak{K}$ is automatically closed since the representation $a \to A_a^{\mathfrak{L}}$ is continuous.

We turn now to the representation $a \to A_a^{\mathfrak{A}-\mathfrak{L}}$, which is induced on the space $\mathfrak{A}-\mathfrak{L}$ by the left regular representation of $\mathfrak{A}$. This representation is called the LEFT REGULAR REPRESENTATION ON $\mathfrak{A}-\mathfrak{L}$. The kernel of the representation consists of all $k \in \mathfrak{A}$ such that $k\mathfrak{A} \subseteq \mathfrak{L}$. This 2-sided ideal is called the QUOTIENT of the ideal $\mathfrak{L}$ and is denoted by $\mathfrak{L} : \mathfrak{A}$. (Jacobson [2].) Similarly, the quotient of a right ideal consists of all $k \in \mathfrak{A}$ such that $\mathfrak{A}k$ is contained in the ideal. If $\mathfrak{L}$ is modular, then it is easily verified that $\mathfrak{L} : \mathfrak{A} \subseteq \mathfrak{L}$. Modularity of $\mathfrak{L}$ also implies that $a \to A_a^{\mathfrak{A}-\mathfrak{L}}$ is strictly cyclic, a cyclic vector being $e' = e+\mathfrak{L}$ where e is a right identity modulo $\mathfrak{L}$. This follows from the fact that $A_a e' = a'$ for every $a \in \mathfrak{A}$. The vector e' also has the property that $A_a e' = 0$ implies $a \in \mathfrak{L}$. Conversely, if u' is a vector in $\mathfrak{A}-\mathfrak{L}$, which is strictly cyclic for $a \to A_a^{\mathfrak{A}-\mathfrak{L}}$ and which has the property that $A_a u' = 0$ implies $a \in \mathfrak{L}$, then $\mathfrak{L}$ is modular. In fact, choose $e \in \mathfrak{A}$ such that $A_e u' = u'$, then $A_{a-ae}u' = 0$ for every $a \in \mathfrak{A}$, so that $\mathfrak{A}(1-e) \subseteq \mathfrak{L}$ and $\mathfrak{L}$ is modular. If $\mathfrak{A}$ is normed and $\mathfrak{L}$ is closed, then the quotient ideal $\mathfrak{L} : \mathfrak{A}$ is obviously closed. Furthermore, since

$$|A_a^{\mathfrak{A}-\mathfrak{L}}x'| = |(ax)'| = \inf_{m \in \mathfrak{L}} \|ax+m\| \leqslant \inf_{m \in \mathfrak{L}} \|a(x+m)\| \leqslant \|a\| \, \|x'\|,$$

$|A_a^{\mathfrak{A}-\mathfrak{L}}| \leqslant \|a\|$, so that the representation $a \to A_a^{\mathfrak{A}-\mathfrak{L}}$ is continuous. It follows that, if $\|A_a^{\mathfrak{A}-\mathfrak{L}}\| = \inf_{k\mathfrak{A} \subseteq \mathfrak{L}} \|a+k\|$, then $|A_a^{\mathfrak{A}-\mathfrak{L}}| \leqslant \|A_a^{\mathfrak{A}-\mathfrak{L}}\| \leqslant \|a\|$, for all $a \in \mathfrak{A}$.

THEOREM (2.2.1). *The representation $a \to A_a^{\mathfrak{A}-\mathfrak{L}}$ will be strictly irreducible if and only if $\mathfrak{L}$ is a maximal ideal. If $\mathfrak{A}$ is a Banach algebra and $\mathfrak{L}$ is closed, then this representation will be topologically irreducible if and only if $\mathfrak{L}$ is maximal-closed. In particular, if $\mathfrak{L}$ is modular, then strict and topological irreducibility are equivalent.*

PROOF. Let $\mathfrak{L}_1$ be any left ideal in $\mathfrak{A}$ which contains the ideal $\mathfrak{L}$ and denote by $\mathfrak{L}'_1$ its image in $\mathfrak{A}-\mathfrak{L}$. Since $\mathfrak{L}_1$ is a left ideal, $\mathfrak{L}'_1$ is clearly an invariant subspace of $\mathfrak{A}-\mathfrak{L}$ with respect to the representation $a \to A_a^{\mathfrak{A}-\mathfrak{L}}$. Note also that, since $\mathfrak{L} \subseteq \mathfrak{L}_1$, $\mathfrak{L}_1 = \{x : x' \in \mathfrak{L}'_1\}$ and hence the correspondence $\mathfrak{L}_1 \leftrightarrow \mathfrak{L}'_1$ is one-to-one. Furthermore, if $\mathfrak{M}$ is any linear subspace of $\mathfrak{A}-\mathfrak{L}$ which is invariant with respect to the representation $a \to A_a^{\mathfrak{A}-\mathfrak{L}}$ and if $\mathfrak{L}_1 = \{x : x' \in \mathfrak{M}\}$, then $\mathfrak{L}_1$ is a left ideal in $\mathfrak{A}$ which contains $\mathfrak{L}$. This shows that the above correspondence is one-to-one between all left ideals containing $\mathfrak{L}$ and all invariant subspaces of $\mathfrak{A}-\mathfrak{L}$. It is immediate from this observation that $a \to A_a^{\mathfrak{A}-\mathfrak{L}}$ will be strictly irreducible if and only if $\mathfrak{L}$ is maximal.

Now let $\mathfrak{A}$ be a Banach algebra and assume $\mathfrak{L}$ closed. In order to prove that topological irreducibility of the representation $a \to A_a^{\mathfrak{A}-\mathfrak{L}}$ is equivalent to maximality of $\mathfrak{L}$ among closed left ideals, we have only to show that a left ideal $\mathfrak{L}_1$ which contains $\mathfrak{L}$ is closed in $\mathfrak{A}$ if and only if its image $\mathfrak{L}'_1$ is closed in $\mathfrak{A}-\mathfrak{L}$. If $\mathfrak{L}'_1$ is closed in $\mathfrak{A}-\mathfrak{L}$, then it is an immediate consequence of the continuity of the mapping $x \to x'$ of $\mathfrak{A}$ into $\mathfrak{A}-\mathfrak{L}$ that $\mathfrak{L}_1$ will be closed in $\mathfrak{A}$, and this does not depend on completeness of $\mathfrak{A}$. In the presence of completeness, the mapping $x \to x'$ (as was observed in § 1) takes closed sets F, with the property $F+\mathfrak{L} = F$, into closed sets, so that $\mathfrak{L}_1$ closed implies $\mathfrak{L}'_1$ closed. Finally, if $\mathfrak{L}$ is modular, then every left ideal which contains $\mathfrak{L}$ is modular. Since in a Banach algebra the closure of a proper modular ideal is proper, it follows in this case that $\mathfrak{L}$ maximal among closed ideals is equivalent to simply $\mathfrak{L}$ maximal. In other words strict and topological irreducibility are equivalent.

THEOREM (2.2.2). *Let $a \to T_a$ be a strictly cyclic representation of an algebra $\mathfrak{A}$ on the linear space $\mathfrak{X}$. Then there exists a modular left ideal $\mathfrak{L}$ in $\mathfrak{A}$ such that the representation $a \to T_a$ is algebraically equivalent to the representation $a \to A_a^{\mathfrak{A}-\mathfrak{L}}$. If $\mathfrak{A}$ and $\mathfrak{X}$ are normed and $a \to T_a$ is also a strongly continuous normed representation, then the ideal $\mathfrak{L}$ can be assumed closed. If in addition $\mathfrak{A}$ is a Banach algebra and $\mathfrak{X}$ is a Banach space, then the equivalence is topological.*

PROOF. Let u be a vector in $\mathfrak{X}$ which is cyclic with respect to the given representation $a \to T_a$ and let $\mathfrak{L}$ be the set of all $a \in \mathfrak{A}$ such that $T_a u = 0$. It is obvious that $\mathfrak{L}$ is a left ideal in $\mathfrak{A}$ and that $\mathfrak{L}$ will be closed if the representation is normed and strongly continuous. Since u is a cyclic vector, there exists $e \in \mathfrak{A}$ such that $T_e u = u$. Since $T_{a(1-e)} u = 0$ for every $a \in \mathfrak{A}$, it follows that $\mathfrak{A}(1-e) \subseteq \mathfrak{L}$, so that $\mathfrak{L}$ is modular. Now, for $x' = x+\mathfrak{L}$ in $\mathfrak{A}-\mathfrak{L}$, define $Ux' = T_x u$. Since $x_1 - x_2 \in \mathfrak{L}$ implies $T_{x_1} u = T_{x_2} u$, the mapping $x' \to Ux'$ of $\mathfrak{A}-\mathfrak{L}$ into $\mathfrak{X}$ is well-defined and is also one-to-one. It is readily verified that U is linear and, u being a cyclic vector, the range of U will be all of $\mathfrak{X}$. Since

$$UA_a^{\mathfrak{A}-\mathfrak{L}} x' = U(ax)' = T_{ax} u = T_a T_x u = T_a U x',$$

we obtain $UA_a^{\mathfrak{A}-\mathfrak{L}} = T_a U$ for all $a \in \mathfrak{A}$, which means that U implements an algebraic equivalence between the two representations, $a \to T_a$ and $a \to A_a^{\mathfrak{A}-\mathfrak{L}}$. If $a \to T_a$ is normed and strongly continuous, then, for $m \in \mathfrak{L}$,

$$|Ux'| = T_x u| = |T_{x+m} u| \leqslant \beta |x+m|,$$

where β is a constant and the last inequality is given by the strong continuity. Therefore $|Ux'| \leqslant \beta|x'|$, which says that the mapping $x' \to Ux'$ is continuous. If $\mathfrak{A}$ is a Banach algebra, then $\mathfrak{A}-\mathfrak{L}$ is a Banach space. Therefore, if $\mathfrak{X}$ is also a Banach space, the inverse of U must be continuous (by the interior mapping theorem) and we have a topological equivalence.

THEOREM (2.2.3). *Let $a \to T_a$ be a non-trivial strictly irreducible representation of the algebra $\mathfrak{A}$ on the linear space $\mathfrak{X}$. Then there exists a maximal modular left ideal $\mathfrak{L}$ in $\mathfrak{A}$ such that the representation $a \to T_a$ is algebraically equivalent to $a \to A_a^{\mathfrak{A}-\mathfrak{L}}$.*

PROOF. Since an irreducible representation is automatically cyclic, the preceding theorem plus Theorem (2.2.1) gives the desired result.

COROLLARY (2.2.4). *If $\mathfrak{L}$ is any maximal left ideal in the algebra $\mathfrak{A}$, then there exists a maximal modular left ideal $\mathfrak{L}_1$ in $\mathfrak{A}$ such that the two representations $a \to A_a^{\mathfrak{A}-\mathfrak{L}}$ and $a \to A_a^{\mathfrak{A}-\mathfrak{L}_1}$ are algebraically equivalent. If $\mathfrak{A}$ is a Banach algebra and $\mathfrak{L}$ is closed, then the equivalence is topological.*

COROLLARY (2.2.5). *Let $\mathfrak{L}$ be a maximal left ideal in $\mathfrak{A}$. Then there exists a maximal modular left ideal $\mathfrak{L}_1$ in $\mathfrak{A}$ such that $\mathfrak{L} : \mathfrak{A} = \mathfrak{L}_1 : \mathfrak{A}$.*

The following two theorems show that an irreducible Banach algebra of linear operators induces an essentially unique Banach space topology in the vector space on which it operates. (See Rickart [3, 4].)

THEOREM (2.2.6). *Let $\mathfrak{B}$ denote a strictly irreducible Banach algebra of linear operators on a vector space $\mathfrak{X}$. Let u be any fixed non-zero element of $\mathfrak{X}$ and, for each x in $\mathfrak{X}$, define*

$$|x| = \inf \|T\|, \quad Tu = x, \quad T \in \mathfrak{B},$$

where $\|T\|$ is the given norm in $\mathfrak{B}$. Then $\mathfrak{X}$ is a Banach space with $|x|$ as norm such that each operator T in $\mathfrak{B}$ is bounded relative to $|x|$ with bound $|T| \leqslant \|T\|$.

PROOF. Denote by $\mathfrak{L}$ the set of all T in $\mathfrak{B}$ such that $Tu = 0$. Then, as in the proof of Theorem (2.2.2), $\mathfrak{L}$ is a modular left ideal in $\mathfrak{B}$. Furthermore, if U is any element of $\mathfrak{B}$ not in $\mathfrak{L}$, then $Uu \neq 0$. Hence, for any $T \in \mathfrak{B}$, there exists $S \in \mathfrak{B}$ such that $SUu = Tu$. Since $T = SU+(T-SU)$ and $T-SU \in \mathfrak{L}$, it follows that $\mathfrak{L}$ is a maximal left ideal in $\mathfrak{B}$. This, with the assumption that $\mathfrak{B}$ is a Banach algebra, implies that $\mathfrak{L}$ is closed and that $\mathfrak{B}-\mathfrak{L}$ is a Banach space. Observe that the mapping $T' \to Tu$, where $T' = T+\mathfrak{L}$, is a linear isomorphism of $\mathfrak{B}-\mathfrak{L}$ with $\mathfrak{X}$. Now it is obvious that the norm $|x|$ is precisely the norm of $\mathfrak{B}-\mathfrak{L}$ transferred to $\mathfrak{X}$ *via* this isomorphism. Hence $\mathfrak{X}$ is a Banach space under $|x|$. Moreover,

$$|Tx| = \inf_{Su=Tx} \|S\| \leqslant \inf_{Su=x} \|TS\| \leqslant \|T\||x|.$$

Therefore $|T| \leqslant \|T\|$ and the theorem is proved.

A given norm $\|x\|$ in a vector space is said to MAJORIZE a second norm $\|x\|'$ if there exists a constant β such that $\|x\|' \leqslant \beta\|x\|$ for all x. Take $\mathfrak{B}$ as in the above theorem and call any norm $|x|'$ in $\mathfrak{X}$ a $\mathfrak{B}$-ADMISSIBLE NORM if each operator in $\mathfrak{B}$ is bounded with respect to $|x|'$ and the bound $|T|'$ is majorized by the given norm $\|T\|$ in $\mathfrak{B}$. Thus the norm

$$|x| = \inf \|T\|, \quad Tu = x, \quad T \in \mathfrak{B}$$

is $\mathfrak{B}$-admissible.

THEOREM (2.2.7.) *Every $\mathfrak{B}$-admissible norm in $\mathfrak{X}$ is majorized by $|x|$ and every complete $\mathfrak{B}$-admissible norm in $\mathfrak{X}$ is equivalent to $|x|$.*

PROOF. If $Tu = x$ and $T \in \mathfrak{B}$, then

$$|x|' = |Tu|' \leqslant |T|'|u|' \leqslant \beta\|T\||u|'.$$

Taking the infimum over all such T, we obtain $|x|' \leqslant \beta|u|'|x|$. In other words, $|x|$ majorizes $|x|'$. If $|x|'$ is also complete, then, since $|x|$ is complete, the closed graph theorem implies that $|x|$ and $|x|'$ are equivalent. This proves the theorem.

We conclude this section with a brief discussion of a class of ideals which are of fundamental importance in the structure theory. (See Jacobson [3; 5, p. 4].)

DEFINITION (2.2.8). *A 2-sided ideal is called* PRIMITIVE *if it is the quotient of a maximal modular left ideal.*

Recall that the quotient of a left ideal $\mathfrak{L}$ in an algebra $\mathfrak{A}$ is the 2-sided ideal $\mathfrak{L} : \mathfrak{A}$ consisting of all $a \in \mathfrak{A}$ such that $a\mathfrak{A} \subseteq \mathfrak{L}$. It is also equal to the kernel of the left regular representation of $\mathfrak{A}$ on the difference space $\mathfrak{A}-\mathfrak{L}$. If $\mathfrak{L}$ is modular, then $\mathfrak{L} : \mathfrak{A} \subseteq \mathfrak{L}$, so that primitive ideals are necessarily proper. Since maximal modular ideals are closed in a Banach algebra, it follows that primitive ideals are closed in these algebras. In the following theorem we summarize a few well-known properties of primitive ideals in a general algebra $\mathfrak{A}$.

THEOREM (2.2.9).

(i) *A 2-sided ideal is primitive if and only if it is the kernel of a strictly irreducible representation.*

(ii) *Any maximal modular 2-sided ideal is primitive.*

(iii) *Every modular 2-sided ideal is contained in a primitive ideal.*

(iv) *If* $\mathfrak{P}$ *is primitive and* $\mathfrak{L}_1$, $\mathfrak{L}_2$ *are left ideals such that* $\mathfrak{L}_1\mathfrak{L}_2 \subseteq \mathfrak{P}$, *then either* $\mathfrak{L}_1 \subseteq \mathfrak{P}$ *or* $\mathfrak{L}_2 \subseteq \mathfrak{P}$.

(v) *If* r *is an element of* $\mathfrak{A}$ *which is quasi-regular modulo every primitive ideal* $\mathfrak{P}$, *then* r *is quasi-regular.*

PROOF. Statement (i) is a consequence of Theorem (2.2.1) and Theorem (2.2.3). Next let $\mathfrak{M}$ be a maximal modular 2-sided ideal in $\mathfrak{A}$. Then there exists a maximal modular left ideal $\mathfrak{L}$ which contains $\mathfrak{M}$. Since $\mathfrak{M}\mathfrak{A} \subseteq \mathfrak{M} \subseteq \mathfrak{L}$, it follows that $\mathfrak{M} \subseteq \mathfrak{L} : \mathfrak{A}$. Therefore $\mathfrak{M} = \mathfrak{L} : \mathfrak{A}$ and $\mathfrak{M}$ is primitive. This proves (ii), and statement (iii) follows immediately from (ii), since every modular 2-sided ideal is contained in a maximal modular 2-sided ideal. Now let $\mathfrak{P}$ be any primitive ideal with $\mathfrak{P} = \mathfrak{L} : \mathfrak{A}$, where $\mathfrak{L}$ is a maximal modular left ideal in $\mathfrak{A}$. If $\mathfrak{L}_1$, $\mathfrak{L}_2$ are left ideals such that $\mathfrak{L}_1\mathfrak{L}_2 \subseteq \mathfrak{P}$ and if $\mathfrak{L}_2 \nsubseteq \mathfrak{P}$, then $\mathfrak{L}_2\mathfrak{A} \nsubseteq \mathfrak{L}$. Since $\mathfrak{L}_2\mathfrak{A}+\mathfrak{L}$ is a left ideal containing $\mathfrak{L}$ and $\mathfrak{L}$ is maximal, we have $\mathfrak{L}_2\mathfrak{A}+\mathfrak{L} = \mathfrak{A}$. Therefore

$$\mathfrak{L}_1\mathfrak{A} \subseteq \mathfrak{L}_1\mathfrak{L}_2\mathfrak{A}+\mathfrak{L}_1\mathfrak{L} \subseteq \mathfrak{P}+\mathfrak{L} \subseteq \mathfrak{L},$$

and hence $\mathfrak{L}_1 \subseteq \mathfrak{P}$. This proves (iv). Finally, let r be an element of $\mathfrak{A}$ which is quasi-regular modulo every primitive ideal. Suppose first that r were left quasi-singular. Then $\mathfrak{A}(1-r)$ is a modular left ideal and so is contained in a maximal modular left ideal $\mathfrak{L}$. Set $\mathfrak{P} = \mathfrak{L} : \mathfrak{A}$. Then $\mathfrak{P}$ is a primitive ideal and is contained in $\mathfrak{L}$. Since r is quasi-regular modulo $\mathfrak{P}$, there exists $s \in \mathfrak{A}$ such that $r+s-sr \in \mathfrak{P}$. This, along with the fact that $s(1-r) \in \mathfrak{L}$, implies $r \in \mathfrak{L}$, which is impossible and proves that r is left quasi-regular. Now let s be a left quasi-inverse for r. Then the image of s in each of the algebras $\mathfrak{A}/\mathfrak{P}$ must coincide with the quasi-inverse of the image of r in $\mathfrak{A}/\mathfrak{P}$. Therefore, by the above argument, s is left quasi-regular and it follows immediately that r is quasi-regular. This completes the proof.

If $\mathfrak{A}$ is commutative, then every ideal $\mathfrak{L}$ has the property $\mathfrak{L}\mathfrak{A} \subseteq \mathfrak{L}$ so that $\mathfrak{L} \subseteq \mathfrak{L} : \mathfrak{A}$. Therefore, if $\mathfrak{L}$ is maximal modular, then $\mathfrak{L} = \mathfrak{L} : \mathfrak{A}$ and we obtain the following corollary.

COROLLARY (2.2.10). *If* $\mathfrak{A}$ *is commutative, then an ideal is primitive if and only if it is maximal modular.*

§ 3. The radical. The notion of radical which is used here coincides with that introduced by N. Jacobson [2; 5, p. 4] for arbitrary rings. We sketch briefly some of the well-known general properties of the radical and examine in more detail those properties which are special for Banach algebras. There are several equivalent ways of defining the radical. We prefer the definition in terms of irreducible representations.

DEFINITION (2.3.1). *The* RADICAL $\mathfrak{R}$ *of an algebra* $\mathfrak{A}$ *is equal to the intersection of the kernels of all (strictly) irreducible representations of* $\mathfrak{A}$. *If* $\mathfrak{R} = (0)$, *then* $\mathfrak{A}$ *is said to be* SEMI-SIMPLE *and, if* $\mathfrak{R} = \mathfrak{A}$, *then* $\mathfrak{A}$ *is called a* RADICAL ALGEBRA.

It is immediate from the definition that the radical is a 2-sided ideal in $\mathfrak{A}$. Note that $\mathfrak{A}$ will be a radical algebra if and only if the trivial representation, which maps every element of $\mathfrak{A}$ into zero, is the only irreducible representation.

The following theorem contains four different characterizations of the radical, each of which is useful in certain situations.

THEOREM (2.3.2).

(i) *If* $\mathfrak{A}$ *is not a radical algebra, then* $\mathfrak{R}$ *is equal to the intersection of all primitive ideals in* $\mathfrak{A}$.

(ii) *If* $\mathfrak{A}$ *is not a radical algebra, then* $\mathfrak{R}$ *is equal to the intersection of all maximal modular left (or right) ideals in* $\mathfrak{A}$.

(iii) $\mathfrak{R}$ *is equal to the sum of all quasi-regular left (or right) ideals in* $\mathfrak{A}$.

(iv) $\mathfrak{R}$ *consists of all elements* q *such that* $(\xi+x)q$ *(or* $q(\xi+x)$*) is quasi-regular for every scalar* ξ *and* $x \in \mathfrak{A}$.

PROOF. Statement (i) follows immediately from Theorem (2.2.9) (i). Now, by Lemma (1.4.17) (iii), the element $(\xi+x)q$ is quasi-regular if and only if $q(\xi+x)$ is quasi-regular. Hence, it is sufficient to prove statement (iv) for $(\xi+x)q$. This fact, plus a symmetry argument, shows that we have only to establish the "left" statements in parts (ii)–(iii).

If $\mathfrak{L}$ is a modular left ideal, then $\mathfrak{L} : \mathfrak{A} \subseteq \mathfrak{L}$. Therefore it follows from (i) that $\mathfrak{R}$ is contained in the intersection of all maximal modular left ideals. On the other hand, if $r \notin \mathfrak{R}$, then there exists an irreducible representation $a \to T_a$ on a vector space $\mathfrak{X}$ with $T_r \neq 0$. Choose any $u \in \mathfrak{X}$ such that $T_r u \neq 0$ and set $\mathfrak{L} = \{a : T_a u = 0\}$. Then $\mathfrak{L}$ is a maximal modular left ideal in $\mathfrak{A}$ and $r \notin \mathfrak{L}$. This proves (ii) for left ideals.

Let s be any left quasi-singular element of $\mathfrak{A}$. Then $\mathfrak{A}(1-s)$ is a proper modular left ideal and so is contained in a maximal modular left ideal $\mathfrak{L}$. Since $s \notin \mathfrak{L}$ and $\mathfrak{R} \subseteq \mathfrak{L}$, this proves that every element of $\mathfrak{R}$ is left quasi-regular. Therefore $\mathfrak{R}$ is a quasi-regular ideal (§ 1). Next consider $r \notin \mathfrak{R}$ and let $a \to T_a$ be an irreducible representation such that $T_r \neq 0$. Again choose a vector u such that $T_r u \neq 0$. Since $a \to T_a$ is irreducible, there exists $b \in \mathfrak{A}$ such that $T_{br}u = u$. Then, for arbitrary $a \in \mathfrak{A}$, $T_{a\circ(br)}u = u$. Therefore $a \circ (br)$ cannot equal zero, so that br cannot be quasi-regular. It follows from this observation that $\mathfrak{R}$ contains every quasi-regular left ideal in $\mathfrak{A}$. This means that $\mathfrak{R}$ is the sum of such ideals and proves statement (iii) for left ideals.

Since $\mathfrak{R}$ is quasi-regular, $(\xi+x)q$ will be quasi-regular for each scalar ξ, $x \in \mathfrak{A}$ and $q \in \mathfrak{R}$. On the other hand, if q is an element such that $(\xi+x)q$ is always quasi-regular, then the set of all elements $(\xi+x)q$ is a quasi-regular left ideal which contains q. Therefore $q \in \mathfrak{R}$, by statement (iii). This completes the proof of the theorem.

The radical contains any nilideal (each element nilpotent). This follows from the above theorem since any nilpotent is quasi-regular. (If $a^m = 0$, then $a^0 = -a-a^2- \cdots - a^{m-1}$. In particular, the radical contains the left and right annihilator ideals of the algebra. Therefore semi-simplicity guarantees that the regular representations are faithful.

Notice that zero is the only idempotent which is quasi-regular. In fact, if $e^2 = e$ and $e+u-eu = 0$, then we have $e = e^2+eu-eu = e(e+u-eu) = 0$. It follows that zero is the only idempotent in the radical of any algebra.

Observe that the algebra $\mathfrak{A}/\mathfrak{R}$ is semi-simple. This is immediate since the natural homomorphism $a \to a+\mathfrak{R}$ which maps $\mathfrak{A}$ onto $\mathfrak{A}/\mathfrak{R}$ takes each maximal modular left ideal of $\mathfrak{A}$ into an ideal of the same kind in $\mathfrak{A}/\mathfrak{R}$. It is also easy to see that, if $\mathfrak{J}$ is any 2-sided ideal in $\mathfrak{A}$ such that $\mathfrak{A}/\mathfrak{J}$ is semi-simple, then $\mathfrak{R} \subseteq \mathfrak{J}$.

We specialize now to normed algebras.

Definition (2.3.3). *An ideal in a normed algebra is called a* topologically nil ideal *provided it is contained in the set N of topologically nilpotent elements.*

Theorem (2.3.4). *The radical of any normed algebra is a topologically nil ideal.*

PROOF. Let $\mathfrak{A}$ be a normed algebra (real or complex) and consider an element $q \in \mathfrak{R}$. If $\zeta = \alpha + \beta i$ (α, β real) is any non-zero complex number, then $|\zeta|^{-2}(2\alpha q - q^2)$ also belongs to $\mathfrak{R}$, and is therefore quasi-regular. It follows that the spectrum of q in $\mathfrak{A}$, as a real algebra, is equal to zero. By theorem (1.6.8), this shows that $Sp(q) = (0)$ whether $\mathfrak{A}$ is real or complex. An application of Theorem (1.6.3) completes the proof.

THEOREM (2.3.5). *The radical $\mathfrak{R}$ of a Banach algebra $\mathfrak{A}$ has the following properties.*

(i) *$\mathfrak{R}$ is a closed 2-sided ideal.*

(ii) *$\mathfrak{R}$ is a topologically nil ideal equal to the sum of all topologically nil left (or right) ideals.*

(iii) *Each element of $\mathfrak{R}$ is a 2-sided topological divisor of zero.*

PROOF. Property (i) follows from the fact that $\mathfrak{R}$ is the intersection of maximal modular left ideals which, in a Banach algebra, are automatically closed. That $\mathfrak{R}$ is a topologically nil ideal is given by the preceding theorem. For the proof that $\mathfrak{R}$ contains all such ideals, let $\mathfrak{I}$ be any topologically nil ideal in $\mathfrak{A}$. Then $Sp(q) = (0)$ for each $q \in \mathfrak{I}$. This implies that q is quasi-regular for each $q \in \mathfrak{I}$. Therefore $\mathfrak{I}$ is a quasi-regular ideal and so is contained in $\mathfrak{R}$. This completes the proof of (ii). Since $Sp(q) = (0)$ for every $q \in \mathfrak{R}$, it follows by Theorem (1.5.9) (iii) that q must be a 2-sided topological divisor of zero. For example, if q were not a left topological divisor of zero, then there would exist a left identity e in $\mathfrak{A}$ such that q is regular in $e\mathfrak{A}e$. But this implies that $\mathfrak{R}$ contains the idempotent e, which is impossible and completes the proof of (iii).

COROLLARY (2.3.6). *If the set N of topologically nilpotent elements in a Banach algebra is an ideal, then $\mathfrak{R} = N$. In particular, if the algebra is commutative, then $\mathfrak{R} = N$.*

The result in this corollary plus Theorem (2.3.4) gives the following corollary.

COROLLARY (2.3.7). *Any subalgebra, closed or not, of a semi-simple commutative algebra is semi-simple.*

We have already noted that zero is the only idempotent in the radical of any algebra. Banach algebras have another important property relative to idempotents, in that any element which is idempotent modulo the radical is equal modulo the radical to an idempotent. Rings with this property have been called, by Kaplansky, SBI-rings (abbreviation for "suitable for building idempotents". See Jacobson [5, p. 53]). The key to this property lies in the following lemma which asserts that certain quadratic equations can be solved in the radical.

LEMMA (2.3.8). *Let $\mathfrak{A}$ be a Banach algebra with radical $\mathfrak{R}$ and q_0 any element of $\mathfrak{R}$. Then the equation $x^2 - x + q_0 = 0$ has a solution in $\mathfrak{R}$ with the property that it commutes with every element of $\mathfrak{A}$ which commutes with q_0.*

PROOF. Consider the infinite series

$$-\frac{1}{2}\sum_{k=1}^{\infty}\binom{1/2}{k}(-4q_0)^k,$$

where the coefficients are binomial coefficients. Since q_0 is in the radical, $\nu(-4q_0) = 0$. Therefore the series converges absolutely to an element q_1, which moreover belongs to $\mathfrak{R}$ since the radical is closed. Furthermore we have the formal relation $1 - \sqrt{1-4q_0} = 2q_1$, which leads to $q_1^2 - q_1 + q_0 = 0$. This equation can, of course, be verified directly since the series for q_1 converges absolutely and hence can be manipulated just as in the case of a numerical series. That q_1 commutes with every element of $\mathfrak{A}$ which commutes with q_0 follows directly from the definition of q_1 in terms of q_0.

THEOREM (2.3.9). *Let u be an element of the Banach algebra $\mathfrak{A}$ which is idempotent modulo the radical. Then there exists in $\mathfrak{A}$ an idempotent e which is equal, modulo the radical, to u.*

PROOF. Since u is idempotent modulo the radical, there exists $q \in \mathfrak{R}$ such that $u^2 = u - q$. The problem here is to obtain a solution z of the equation $(u+z)^2 = u+z$ in the radical. If we insist on a solution which commutes with u, this equation reduces to $z^2 + (2u-1)z - q = 0$. The substitution $z = (2u-1)x$ gives $(2u-1)^2(x^2-x) - q = 0$. Furthermore $(2u-1)^2 = 1-4q$, so that the equation can be written

$$x^2 - x - q(1-4q)^{-1} = 0,$$

where $q(1-4q)^{-1} = q(1-(4q)^{\circ})$, and $(4q)^{\circ}$ exists since $q \in \mathfrak{R}$. The element $q(1-4q)^{-1}$ belongs to $\mathfrak{R}$. Therefore, by the preceding lemma, there exists an element $q_1 \in \mathfrak{R}$, which commutes with u (notice that u commutes with q and hence with $q(1-4q)^{-1}$) and for which $q_1^2 - q_1 - q(1-4q)^{-1} = 0$. It follows that $z = (2u-1)q_1$ is a solution of

$(u+z)^2 = u+z$. Therefore the desired idempotent is $e = u+(2u-1)q_1$.

We close this section with the definition of another radical which is important for certain special algebras. (See Brown and McCoy [1].)

DEFINITION (2.3.10). *The* STRONG RADICAL $\mathfrak{R}_{\mathscr{S}}$ *of an algebra* $\mathfrak{A}$ *is the intersection of all maximal modular 2-sided ideals of* $\mathfrak{A}$ *unless there are no such ideals, in which case* $\mathfrak{R}_{\mathscr{S}} = \mathfrak{A}$. *If* $\mathfrak{R}_{\mathscr{S}} = (0)$, *then* $\mathfrak{A}$ *is said to be* STRONGLY SEMI-SIMPLE.

THEOREM (2.3.11). *The strong radical always contains the radical.*

PROOF. Since the radical is equal to the intersection of all primitive ideals, this theorem follows from Theorem (2.2.9) (ii), which says that maximal modular 2-sided ideals are primitive.

The two radicals $\mathfrak{R}$ and $\mathfrak{R}_{\mathscr{S}}$ are in general different. For example, the algebra $\mathfrak{B}(\mathfrak{X})$ of all bounded operators on an infinite dimensional Banach space is semi-simple but not strongly semi-simple (see Appendix, A.1.1). This is also an example of a semi-simple Banach algebra for which $N \neq (0)$.

If $\mathfrak{M}$ is any modular 2-sided ideal in $\mathfrak{A}$, then $\mathfrak{A}/\mathfrak{M}$ is an algebra with an identity. If $\mathfrak{M}$ is maximal, then $\mathfrak{A}/\mathfrak{M}$ contains no 2-sided ideals other than (0) and $\mathfrak{A}/\mathfrak{M}$; that is, it is a simple algebra with an identity. Conversely, the kernel of any homomorphism of $\mathfrak{A}$ into a simple algebra with identity is a maximal modular 2-sided ideal in $\mathfrak{A}$, so that $\mathfrak{R}_{\mathscr{S}}$ is the intersection of all such kernels. In particular, if $\mathfrak{A}$ is simple and possesses an identity element, then $\mathfrak{A}$ is strongly semi-simple. Finally, we observe that, if $\mathfrak{A}$ is a Banach algebra, then $\mathfrak{R}_{\mathscr{S}}$ is a closed 2-sided ideal of $\mathfrak{A}$.

Hille and Zorn (See Hille [2, Sec. 22.13] or Hille–Phillips [1, Sec. 24.8],) defined the radical using property (iv) of Theorem (2.3.2). The characterization of the radical of a normed algebra given in Theorem (2.3.5) (ii), was obtained by Jacobson [2]. Segal [2] uses the terms "radical", "semi-simplicity" and "weak semi-simplicity", respectively, in place of our "strong radical", "strong semi-simplicity" and "semi-simplicity".

If $\mathfrak{A}$ is any finite dimensional algebra with radical $\mathfrak{R}$, then there exists a subalgebra $\mathfrak{A}_1$ of $\mathfrak{A}$ isomorphic with $\mathfrak{A}/\mathfrak{R}$ such that $\mathfrak{A} = \mathfrak{A}_1 \oplus \mathfrak{R}$, where the sum is a vector space direct sum. This is the first principal Wedderburn structure theorem. The generalization of this theorem to (infinite dimensional) Banach algebras should carry the additional condition that $\mathfrak{A}_1$ be homeomorphic with $\mathfrak{A}/\mathfrak{R}$. In this form the theorem is not true in general. This is shown by an example due to C. Feldman [1] (see A.2.2. of the Appendix) in which $\mathfrak{A}$ is even commutative and $\mathfrak{R}$ is one-dimensional. On the other hand, Feldman is able to prove the theorem for a variety of special Banach algebras. The theorem also holds for certain algebras associated with spectral operators. (See Dunford [4] and A.1.6 of the Appendix.) Bade and Curtis [2] have also obtained some results along these lines.

§ 4. **Primitive Banach algebras.** In this section we consider a very important class of semi-simple Banach algebras which arise in the general structure theory for semi-simple algebras. (See Jacobson [2; 4; 5, p. 4].)

DEFINITION (2.4.1). *The algebra $\mathfrak{A}$ is said to be* PRIMITIVE *in case the zero ideal is a primitive ideal.*

In other words, primitivity for $\mathfrak{A}$ means that there exists a maximal modular left ideal $\mathfrak{L}$ such that $\mathfrak{L} : \mathfrak{A} = (0)$. Also, $\mathfrak{A}$ will be primitive if and only if there exists for it a faithful irreducible representation. Thus, the study of primitive algebras reduces to a study of irreducible algebras of linear operators and, in the case of Banach algebras (see Theorem (2.2.6)), to the study of irreducible algebras of bounded linear operators on a Banach space where the algebra is also a Banach algebra under a norm which is not less than the operator bound. In particular, primitive algebras are semi-simple. Also, if $\mathfrak{A}$ is any algebra and $\mathfrak{P}$ is a primitive ideal in $\mathfrak{A}$, then $\mathfrak{A}/\mathfrak{P}$ is a primitive algebra. Before specializing to Banach algebras, we consider briefly the general case. In the following, $\mathfrak{X}$ will be any linear vector space over a field $\mathscr{F}$, and $\mathfrak{B}$ will be an algebra of linear operators on $\mathfrak{X}$.

DEFINITION (2.4.2). *The algebra $\mathfrak{B}$ is said to be k-*FOLD TRANSITIVE ON $\mathfrak{X}$ *if, for arbitrary vectors $x_1, \cdots, x_k$ and $y_1, \cdots, y_k$ where $x_1, \cdots, x_k$ are linearly independent, there exists $T \in \mathfrak{B}$ such that $Tx_i = y_i$ $(i = 1, \cdots, k)$. If $\mathfrak{B}$ is k-fold transitive for every k, then $\mathfrak{B}$ is said to be* STRICTLY DENSE ON $\mathfrak{X}$.

Notice that 1-fold transitivity is equivalent to irreducibility. In the following lemma we see that 2-fold transitivity already implies density. (Jacobson [1].)

LEMMA (2.4.3). *If $\mathfrak{B}$ is 2-fold transitive on $\mathfrak{X}$, then it is strictly dense on $\mathfrak{X}$.*

PROOF. The proof is by induction. Assume k-fold transitivity and let $x_1, \cdots, x_{k+1}$ be any linearly independent set of $k+1$ vectors in $\mathfrak{X}$. In order to prove $(k+1)$-fold transitivity it will be sufficient to prove that for each i, with $1 \leqslant i \leqslant k+1$, there exists $T_i \in \mathfrak{B}$ such that $T_i x_i \neq 0$ while $T_i x_j = 0$ for $i \neq j$. In fact, if $y_1, \cdots, y_{k+1}$ are arbitrary vectors in $\mathfrak{X}$, we can choose $T'_i \in \mathfrak{B}$ such that $T'_i T_i x_i = y_i$ and, if $T = T'_1 T_1 + \cdots + T'_{k+1} T_{k+1}$, then $Tx_i = y_i$ for $i = 1, \cdots, k+1$. It is clearly sufficient to consider the case $i = k+1$. By k-fold transitivity, choose $T' \in \mathfrak{B}$ such that $T'x_i = 0$ for $i = 1, \cdots, k-1$ and $T'x_{k+1} \neq 0$.

If $T'x_k = 0$, then T' is the desired element of $\mathfrak{B}$. Also, if $T'x_k$ and $T'x_{k+1}$ are linearly independent, by 2-fold transitivity choose $S \in \mathfrak{B}$ such that $ST'x_k = 0$ while $ST'x_{k+1} \neq 0$. Then ST' is the desired element of $\mathfrak{B}$. Therefore suppose $T'x_{k+1} = \alpha T'x_k$. Since $x_1, \cdots, x_{k-1}, x_{k+1} - \alpha x_k$ are linearly independent, there exists $T'' \in \mathfrak{B}$ such that $T''x_i = 0$ for $i = 1, \cdots, k-1$ and $T''(x_{k+1} - \alpha x_k) \neq 0$. Again, if $T''x_k = 0$, T'' has the desired property and, if $T''x_k$, $T''x_{k+1}$ are linearly independent, choose $U \in \mathfrak{B}$ such that $UT''x_k = 0$ and $UT''x_{k+1} \neq 0$. Then UT'' has the desired property. Therefore suppose $T''x_{k+1} = \beta T''x_k$. Then $\alpha \neq \beta$. Finally choose $T''' \in \mathfrak{B}$ such that $T'''T''x_k = T'x_k$ and let $T = T' - T'''T''$. Then $Tx_i = 0$ for $i = 1, \cdots, k$ and $Tx_{k+1} = (\alpha - \beta)T'x_k \neq 0$. This completes the proof.

In general, 1-fold transitivity (that is, strict irreducibility) does not imply strict density. In fact, the image of the algebra of quaternions under its left regular representation is obviously strictly irreducible but not strictly dense. In this example we even have to do with a real Banach algebra. On the other hand, for complex Banach algebras strict irreducibility does imply strict density. We need first another lemma.

LEMMA (2.4.4). *Let $\mathfrak{B}$ be a strictly irreducible Banach algebra of linear operators on a vector space $\mathfrak{X}$ and let $\mathfrak{D}$ be the set of all endomorphisms of the additive group of $\mathfrak{X}$ which commute with each element of $\mathfrak{B}$. Then $\mathfrak{D}$ is isomorphic with either the reals, complexes or quaternions. If $\mathfrak{B}$ is complex $\mathfrak{D}$ reduces to the complex field.*

PROOF. By Theorem (2.2.6) a norm $|x|$ can be introduced into $\mathfrak{X}$ so that $\mathfrak{X}$ becomes a Banach space and each $T \in \mathfrak{B}$ is bounded with bound $|T|$ satisfying the inequality $|T| \leqslant \|T\|$, where $\|T\|$ is the given norm in $\mathfrak{B}$. In fact, if u is any non-zero vector in $\mathfrak{X}$, set $|x| = \inf \|X\|$, $Xu = x$. Let D be any element of $\mathfrak{D}$ and choose any $X \in \mathfrak{B}$ such that $Xu = x$. Then $Dx = XDu$. For a scalar α, $(\alpha X)u = \alpha x$; hence $D(\alpha x) = \alpha Dx$, so that D is linear. Furthermore, $|Dx| = |XDu| \leqslant |X||Du|$, for X such that $Xu = x$. Therefore $|Dx| \leqslant |x||Du|$. In other words, D is bounded with respect to $|x|$. Now, by Schur's lemma, the irreducibility of $\mathfrak{B}$ implies that $\mathfrak{D}$ is a real or complex division algebra according as $\mathfrak{B}$ is real or complex. Since $\mathfrak{D}$ is normed, the desired conclusion follows by Theorems (1.7.1) and (1.7.6).

COROLLARY (2.4.5). *The center of a primitive Banach algebra is either equal to* (0) *or is isomorphic to the real or complex field.*

The following theorem was proved by the author [3] and by Yood [2]

THEOREM (2.4.6). *Let $\mathfrak{B}$ be a strictly irreducible complex Banach algebra of linear operators on a complex vector space $\mathfrak{X}$. Then $\mathfrak{B}$ is strictly dense on $\mathfrak{X}$.*

PROOF. By Lemma (2.4.3) we have only to prove that $\mathfrak{B}$ is 2-fold transitive. For this it will be sufficient to prove that for any pair v, w of linearly independent vectors there exists $T \in \mathfrak{B}$ such that $Tv = 0$ and $Tw \neq 0$. Suppose on the contrary that $Tv = 0$ implies $Tw = 0$. For any x choose $X \in \mathfrak{B}$ such that $Xv = x$ and define $Dx = Xw$. Note that $X_1v = X_2v$ implies $X_1w = X_2w$, so that Dx is independent of the choice of X. Moreover, for any $T \in \mathfrak{B}$, $TDx = TXw$, where $Xv = x$. Since $(TX)v = Tx$ we have $D(Tx) = TXw$. In other words, $TD = DT$. If $Xv = x$ and $Yv = y$, then $(X+Y)v = x+y$. Therefore $D(x+y) = (X+Y)w = Xw+Yw = Dx+Dy$, so that D is additive. Thus $D \in \mathfrak{D}$ and so must reduce to a complex scalar δ times the identity operator. Therefore $Tw = \delta Tv$ or $T(w-\delta v) = 0$ for each $T \in \mathfrak{B}$. But this implies $w-\delta v = 0$ and contradicts the linear independence of v and w. Therefore T must exist in $\mathfrak{B}$ such that $Tv = 0$ while $Tw \neq 0$.

COROLLARY (2.4.7). *A complex Banach algebra is primitive if and only if it has a faithful continuous strictly dense representation on a Banach space.*

We turn our attention now to primitive Banach algebras which possess minimal (one-sided) ideals. For this discussion it is convenient to introduce the notion of dual vector spaces. We restrict attention to the real or complex case. (See Jacobson [4; 5, p. 69].)

DEFINITION (2.4.8). *Two (real or complex) vector spaces $\mathfrak{X}$ and $\mathfrak{Y}$ are said to be* DUAL *provided there exists a function defined on $\mathfrak{X} \times \mathfrak{Y}$ to the field of scalars, whose value on a pair x, y will be denoted by (x, y), which satisfies the following two conditions:*

(i) $(x, y) = 0$ *for every x implies $y = 0$ and $(x, y) = 0$ for every y implies $x = 0$.*

(ii) (x, y) *is linear in x for fixed y and in y for fixed x.*

If the two spaces $\mathfrak{X}$ and $\mathfrak{Y}$ are normed, then they are said to be NORMED DUAL *provided, in addition to conditions* (i) *and* (ii), *there exists a constant β, called the* BOUND *of (x, y), such that*

(iii) $|(x, y)| \leqslant \beta|x||y|, \quad x \in \mathfrak{X}, \quad y \in \mathfrak{Y}$.

Property (i) is called NON-DEGENERACY and property (ii) is called BILINEARITY. Hence, (x, y) is called a non-degenerate bilinear FORM.

Property (iii) is, of course, continuity of the form in both variables simultaneously. Notice that either of the spaces $\mathfrak{X}$ or $\mathfrak{Y}$ can be regarded (*via* the bilinear form) as a linear subspace of all (in the normed case, bounded) linear functionals on the other. An example of a pair of normed dual spaces is given by any normed vector space $\mathfrak{X}$ and its conjugate space $\mathfrak{X}'$ of all bounded linear functionals. The bilinear functional which implements the duality is given by the definition:

$$(x, f) = f(x), \quad x \in \mathfrak{X}, \quad f \in \mathfrak{X}'.$$

The following lemma contains a basic property of dual vector spaces.

LEMMA (2.4.9). *Let $\mathfrak{X}$, $\mathfrak{Y}$ be dual vector spaces with bilinear form (x, y). If $y_1, \cdots, y_n$ are any n linearly independent elements of $\mathfrak{Y}$, then there exist elements $x_1, \cdots, x_n$ in $\mathfrak{X}$ such that $(x_i, y_j) = \delta_{ij}$, $i, j = 1, 2, \cdots, n$.*

PROOF. The proof is by induction. It is obvious that there exists, for any $y \neq 0$, an $x \in \mathfrak{X}$ such that $(x, y) = 1$, so that the lemma is true for $n = 1$. Now assume the existence of $x_1, \cdots, x_{k-1}$ such that $(x_i, y_j) = \delta_{ij}$, for $i, j = 1, 2, \cdots, k-1$, where $k \leqslant n$. For arbitrary $x \in \mathfrak{X}$, set

$$u = x - \sum_{i=1}^{k-1} (x, y_i)x_i.$$

Then $(u, y_j) = 0$ for $j = 1, \cdots, k-1$. Also

$$(u, y_k) = \left(x, y_k - \sum_{i=1}^{k-1} (x_i, y_k)y_i\right).$$

Therefore, by the non-degeneracy of the bilinear form and the linear independence of $y_1, \cdots, y_n$, it follows that x can be chosen such that $(u, y_k) \neq 0$. If we define $x_k = (u, y_k)^{-1}u$, then $(x_i, y_j) = \delta_{ij}$ for $i, j = 1, 2, \cdots, k$ and the proof is complete.

DEFINITION (2.4.10). *Let T be a linear operator on $\mathfrak{X}$, where $\mathfrak{X}$, $\mathfrak{Y}$ are dual vector spaces. Then a linear operator T' on $\mathfrak{Y}$, such that*

$$(Tx, y) = (x, T'y), \quad x \in \mathfrak{X}, \quad y \in \mathfrak{Y},$$

is called the ADJOINT *of T with respect to the bilinear form (x, y).*

Observe that non-degeneracy of the bilinear form ensures the uniqueness of T' if it exists. Furthermore, if T' exists, then $(T')'$ exists (as an operator on $\mathfrak{X}$) and is equal to T. The collection of all T such that

T' exists is clearly a subalgebra of all linear operators on $\mathfrak{X}$. It is readily verified that $T \leftrightarrow T'$ is an anti-isomorphism between the algebra of all linear operators on $\mathfrak{X}$ with adjoints (on $\mathfrak{Y}$) and the algebra of all linear operators on $\mathfrak{Y}$ with adjoints (on $\mathfrak{X}$).

If $u \in \mathfrak{X}$ and $v \in \mathfrak{Y}$, we denote by $u \otimes v$ the linear operator on $\mathfrak{X}$ defined by the relation

$$(u \otimes v)x = (x, v)u, \quad x \in \mathfrak{X}.$$

Observe that $(u \otimes v)'$ exists and is given by

$$(u \otimes v)'y = (u, y)v, \quad y \in \mathfrak{Y}.$$

The RANK of an operator is defined to be the dimension (finite or infinite) of the range of the operator. It is easily shown that an operator T of finite rank n can be written in the form

$$Tx = \sum_{i=1}^{n} f_i(x)u_i,$$

where $u_1, \cdots, u_n$ are linearly independent vectors in $\mathfrak{X}$ and $f_1, \cdots, f_n$ are linear functionals on $\mathfrak{X}$. Suppose that T' exists. Then

$$(x, T'y) = \sum_{i=1}^{n} f_i(x)(u_i, y).$$

By Lemma (2.4.9), there exist vectors $y_1, \cdots, y_n$ in $\mathfrak{Y}$ such that $(u_i, y_j) = \delta_{ij}$. Therefore we obtain

$$f_j(x) = (x, T'y_j), \quad j = 1, \cdots, n.$$

Set $v_i = T'y_i$. Then T can be written in the form $T = \Sigma\, u_i \otimes v_i$. This characterizes the operators on $\mathfrak{X}$ which have adjoints on $\mathfrak{Y}$ and finite rank.

The way is now clear for a study of primitive Banach algebras with minimal ideals. We restrict attention to the complex case and so, by Corollary (2.4.6), have to do with a Banach space $\mathfrak{X}$ and a strictly dense subalgebra $\mathfrak{B}$ of $\mathscr{B}(\mathfrak{X})$ which is a Banach algebra under some given norm $\|T\|$ which majorizes the operator bound $|T|$. As usual, the purely algebraic portions of the following results are valid in a much more general situation. (See Jacobson [4].)

In preparation for the discussion of the above Banach algebras, it is desirable to make a few general algebraic remarks. Hence, for the moment, let $\mathfrak{X}$ be an arbitrary linear vector space and let $\mathfrak{B}$ be any strictly dense algebra of operators on $\mathfrak{X}$. For any two non-zero elements T_1 and T_2 in $\mathfrak{B}$, choose vectors x_1 and x_2 such that $T_1x_1 \neq 0$ and $T_2x_2 \neq 0$. Since $\mathfrak{B}$ is irreducible, there exists $T \in \mathfrak{B}$ such that $TT_2x_2 = x_1$. Thus $T_1TT_2 \neq 0$, and it is an immediate consequence that (0) is the only ideal in $\mathfrak{B}$ with square equal to (0). Therefore, by Lemma (2.1.12), if $\mathfrak{B}$ contains minimal one-sided ideals, then its left and right socles coincide and so define the socle. If $\mathfrak{L}$ is a minimal left ideal in $\mathfrak{B}$, then $\mathfrak{L} = \mathfrak{B}E$, where $E^2 = E$. We prove that E has rank one. Suppose on the contrary that Ex_1 and Ex_2 were linearly independent, and choose $T \in \mathfrak{B}$ such that $TEx_1 = Ex_1$ and $TEx_2 = 0$. Since $ETE \neq 0$, we have $\mathfrak{B}TE = \mathfrak{B}E$. In particular, there exists $S \in \mathfrak{B}$ such that $STE = E$. But then $Ex_2 = STEx_2 = 0$, a contradiction. Thus E, and hence every non-zero element of $\mathfrak{L}$, has rank equal to one. Furthermore, if A is any element of $\mathfrak{B}$ with rank one, then it is easy to verify that $\mathfrak{B}A$ is a minimal left ideal in $\mathfrak{B}$. In other words, a left ideal in $\mathfrak{B}$ is minimal if and only if it consists of elements of rank one. Note also that if A is of rank one, then $A \in \mathfrak{B}A$. It follows that the socle of $\mathfrak{B}$ consists of operators of finite rank. (Dieudonné [1].) On the other hand, if T is any element of $\mathfrak{B}$ with finite rank, then there exist linearly independent vectors $u_1, \cdots, u_n$ in $\mathfrak{X}$ and linear functionals $f_1, \cdots, f_n$ on $\mathfrak{X}$ such that $T = u_1 \otimes f_1 + \cdots + u_n \otimes f_n$. Choose elements $U_i \in \mathfrak{B}$ such that $U_iu_j = \delta_{ij}u_i\ (i, j = 1, \cdots, n)$. Then $U_iT = u_i \otimes f_i$, so that $T = U_1T + \cdots + U_nT$. Since the operators U_iT are of rank one and belong to $\mathfrak{B}$, it follows that the socle of $\mathfrak{B}$ coincides with the set of all operators in $\mathfrak{B}$ with finite rank. It is also easy to see that the socle is a minimal 2-sided ideal which is contained in every 2-sided ideal of $\mathfrak{B}$.

Next let f be any linear functional on $\mathfrak{X}$ such that $u \otimes f \in \mathfrak{B}$ for some non-zero $u \in \mathfrak{X}$. Then, since $\mathfrak{B}$ is irreducible and $T(u \otimes f) = Tu \otimes f$, it follows that $x \otimes f \in \mathfrak{B}$ for every $x \in \mathfrak{X}$. Now denote by $\mathfrak{X}^{\mathfrak{B}}$ the collection of all linear functionals f on $\mathfrak{X}$ such that $u \otimes f \in \mathfrak{B}$ for some (and hence any) non-zero $u \in \mathfrak{X}$. It is obvious that $\mathfrak{X}^{\mathfrak{B}}$ is a linear subspace of the space of all linear functionals on $\mathfrak{X}$. For any $f \in \mathfrak{X}^{\mathfrak{B}}$ and $T \in \mathfrak{B}$, define $f^T(x) = f(Tx)$. Then f^T is a linear functional on $\mathfrak{X}$. Furthermore, since $(u \otimes f)T = u \otimes f^T$, it follows that $f^T \in \mathfrak{X}^{\mathfrak{B}}$. Define

$$(x, f) = f(x), \quad x \in \mathfrak{X}, \quad f \in \mathfrak{X}^{\mathfrak{B}}.$$

Then (x, f) is a bilinear form. We prove that (x, f) is also non-degenerate. In the first place, if $(x, f) = 0$ for every $x \in \mathfrak{X}$, then $f = 0$

by definition. On the other hand, fix a non-zero element $h \in \mathfrak{X}^{\mathfrak{B}}$ and choose $z \in \mathfrak{X}$ such that $(z, h) \neq 0$. Now if $x \neq 0$, choose $T \in \mathfrak{B}$ such that $Tx = z$. Then $(x, h^T) = (z, h) \neq 0$. Therefore, $(x, f) = 0$ for every $f \in \mathfrak{X}^{\mathfrak{B}}$ implies $x = 0$. We now have that $\mathfrak{X}$ and $\mathfrak{X}^{\mathfrak{B}}$ are dual under the bilinear form (x, f). Observe that, for any $T \in \mathfrak{B}$,

$$(Tx, f) = (x, f^T), \quad x \in \mathfrak{X}, \quad f \in \mathfrak{X}^{\mathfrak{B}}.$$

Therefore the adjoint T' exists and $T'f = f^T$. We denote by $\mathfrak{B}'$ the algebra of all T' for $T \in \mathfrak{B}$ and notice that $T \leftrightarrow T'$ is an anti-isomorphism between $\mathfrak{B}$ and $\mathfrak{B}'$. Finally, let $f_1, \cdots, f_n, g_1, \cdots, g_n$ be arbitrary elements of $\mathfrak{X}^{\mathfrak{B}}$ with $f_1, \cdots, f_n$ linearly independent. By Lemma (2.4.8), there exist elements $u_1, \cdots, u_n$ in $\mathfrak{X}$ such that $(u_j, f_i) = \delta_{ij}$ $(i, j = 1, \cdots, n)$. Define

$$T = \sum_{i=1}^{n} u_i \otimes g_i.$$

Then $T'f_i = g_i$, for $i = 1, \cdots, n$. In other words, $\mathfrak{B}'$ is strictly dense on $\mathfrak{X}^{\mathfrak{B}}$.

We now add the assumption that $\mathfrak{B}$ is a Banach algebra under a norm $\|T\|$. Observe that the adjoint algebra $\mathfrak{B}'$ is also a Banach algebra under the norm $\|T'\| = \|T\|$.

LEMMA (2.4.11). *Assume that $\mathfrak{B}$ is a Banach algebra under a norm $\|T\|$. Let u be a fixed non-zero element of $\mathfrak{X}$ and h a fixed non-zero element of $\mathfrak{X}^{\mathfrak{B}}$. For $x \in \mathfrak{X}$ and $f \in \mathfrak{X}^{\mathfrak{B}}$, define*

$$|x| = \inf_{Tu=x} \|T\|, \qquad |f| = \inf_{T'h=f} \|T\|.$$

Then, under $|x|$ and $|f|$ as norms, $\mathfrak{X}$ and $\mathfrak{X}^{\mathfrak{B}}$ are Banach spaces and are normed dual relative to the bilinear form (x, f).

PROOF. That $\mathfrak{X}$ and $\mathfrak{X}^{\mathfrak{B}}$ are Banach spaces under the norms $|x|$ and $|f|$ is given by Theorem (2.2.6) applied to the algebras $\mathfrak{B}$ and $\mathfrak{B}'$. Observe next that $(x \otimes f)^2 = (x, f)(x \otimes f)$. Therefore

$$|(x, f)| \|x \otimes f\| = \|(x \otimes f)^2\| \leqslant \|x \otimes f\|^2,$$

so that we have $|(x, f)| \leqslant \|x \otimes f\|$. Now let T and S be any elements of $\mathfrak{B}$ such that $Tu = x$ and $S'h = f$. Then $x \otimes f = T(u \otimes h)S$ and hence $\|x \otimes f\| \leqslant \|u \otimes h\| \, \|T\| \, \|S\|$. Taking the infinum over all such T and S, we obtain $\|x \otimes f\| \leqslant \|u \otimes h\| \, |x| \, |f|$. It follows that $|(x, f)| \leqslant \|u \otimes h\| \, |x| \, |f|$, which completes the proof.

THEOREM (2.4.12). *Let $\mathfrak{A}$ be any primitive complex Banach algebra which contains minimal one-sided ideals. Then there exists a pair of normed dual Banach spaces $\mathfrak{X}$ and $\mathfrak{Y}$ and a continuous isomorphism $a \to T_a$ of $\mathfrak{A}$ into $\mathscr{B}(\mathfrak{X})$ such that each T_a admits an adjoint T'_a on $\mathfrak{Y}$ and the socle of $\mathfrak{A}$ maps onto the subalgebra of $\mathscr{B}(\mathfrak{X})$ generated by all operators of the form $x \otimes y$, where x ranges over $\mathfrak{X}$ and y over $\mathfrak{Y}$.*

PROOF. By Corollary (2.4.7), $\mathfrak{A}$ is isomorphic with an algebra $\mathfrak{B}$ of the type involved in the preceding discussion. Therefore it only remains for us to note that each T in $\mathfrak{B}$ is bounded relative to the norm $|x|$, introduced into $\mathfrak{X}$ in the preceding lemma, and that its bound $|T|$ relative to $|x|$ satisfies the inequality $|T| \leqslant \|T\|$. Since this is provided by Theorem (2.2.6) the proof is complete.

We close this section with some miscellaneous results which will be needed later. Consider the algebra $\mathfrak{B}$ and the two spaces $\mathfrak{X}$ and $\mathfrak{X}^{\mathfrak{B}}$ normed as in Lemma (2.4.11). Let z, g be fixed non-zero elements of $\mathfrak{X}$, $\mathfrak{X}^{\mathfrak{B}}$ respectively. Denote by $\mathfrak{L}$ the set of all operators in $\mathfrak{B}$ of the form $x \otimes g$, $x \in \mathfrak{X}$, and by $\mathfrak{R}$ the set of all operators in $\mathfrak{B}$ of the form $z \otimes f$, $f \in \mathfrak{X}^{\mathfrak{B}}$. Then $\mathfrak{L}$ is a minimal left ideal and $\mathfrak{R}$ is a minimal right ideal in $\mathfrak{B}$. Since minimal ideals in $\mathfrak{B}$ are automatically closed (Lemma (2.1.10)), the ideals $\mathfrak{L}$ and $\mathfrak{R}$ are Banach spaces relative to the given norm in $\mathfrak{B}$. We can now state the next lemma which, for the case $\mathfrak{B} = \mathscr{B}(\mathfrak{X})$, was proved by Kawada [7].

LEMMA (2.4.13). *The mapping $x \otimes g \to x$ defines an equivalence between the Banach spaces $\mathfrak{L}$ and $\mathfrak{X}$, while $z \otimes f \to f$ defines an equivalence between $\mathfrak{R}$ and $\mathfrak{X}^{\mathfrak{B}}$.*

PROOF. It will be sufficient to make the proof for $\mathfrak{L}$ and $\mathfrak{X}$. That the mapping $x \otimes g \to x$ is a linear space isomorphism is obvious. Hence we have only to show equivalence of the norms $|x|$ and $\|x \otimes g\|$. Let T be any element of $\mathfrak{B}$ such that $Tu = x$. Then

$$\|x \otimes g\| = \|T(u \otimes g)\| \leqslant \|T\| \, \|u \otimes g\|.$$

Therefore $\|x \otimes g\| \leqslant |x| \|u \otimes g\|$. On the other hand, $x \otimes g$ defines an operator on $\mathfrak{X}$ which is bounded relative to $|x|$, and moreover its bound is equal to $|x||g|_0$ where $|g|_0$ is the bound of the functional g relative to $|x|$. Since $|x \otimes g| \leqslant \|x \otimes g\|$, we obtain $|x||g|_0 \leqslant \|x \otimes g\| \leqslant |x| \|u \otimes g\|$, which provides the desired equivalence.

If $\mathfrak{B}$ is a strictly dense Banach algebra of linear operators on a vector space $\mathfrak{X}$, then it is always true (Theorem (2.2.6)) that $\mathfrak{B}$ induces a complete norm in $\mathfrak{X}$ so that $\mathfrak{B} \subseteq \mathscr{B}(\mathfrak{X})$. The next theorem shows that if $\mathfrak{B}$ also contains minimal one-sided ideals, then any complete norm in $\mathfrak{X}$ for which $\mathfrak{B} \subseteq \mathscr{B}(\mathfrak{X})$ is already equivalent to the induced norm. (See Rickart [4].)

THEOREM (2.4.14). *Assume that $\mathfrak{X}$ is a Banach space and $\mathfrak{B}$ is a strictly dense subalgebra of $\mathscr{B}(\mathfrak{X})$ which contains minimal one-sided ideals. Then any Banach algebra norm $\|T\|$ in $\mathfrak{B}$ necessarily majorizes the operator bound $|T|$ and the associated norm induced into $\mathfrak{X}$ is equivalent to the given one.*

PROOF. In view of Theorem (2.2.7), we have only to prove that $\|T\|$ majorizes $|T|$. This is equivalent to showing that the injection mapping of $\mathfrak{B}$, as a Banach space under $\|T\|$, into the Banach space $\mathscr{B}(\mathfrak{X})$ is continuous. The closed graph theorem reduces the problem further to showing that, if B is an element of $\mathscr{B}(\mathfrak{X})$ for which there exists $\{B_n\} \subseteq \mathfrak{B}$ such that $\|B_n\| \to 0$ and $|B_n - B| \to 0$, then $B = 0$. For arbitrary $x \in \mathfrak{X}$ and $f \in \mathfrak{X}^{\mathfrak{B}}$, set $E = x \otimes f$ and observe that since $E \in \mathscr{B}(\mathfrak{X})$ the linear functional f is bounded relative to the given norm in $\mathfrak{X}$. Now, for any $T \in \mathscr{B}(\mathfrak{X})$, we have $(TE)^2 = f(Tx)TE$, so that $|f(Tx)| \leqslant \|T\|\,\|E\|$. In particular, taking $T = B_n$ and then letting $n \to \infty$, we obtain $f(Bx) = 0$. Since this holds for all $x \in \mathfrak{X}$ and $f \in \mathfrak{X}^{\mathfrak{B}}$ and these spaces are dual, it follows that $B = 0$. This completes the proof.

Using Lemma (2.4.13), we can state the following corollary.

COROLLARY (2.4.15). *The left regular representation of $\mathfrak{B}$ on any minimal left ideal in $\mathfrak{B}$ is topologically equivalent to the given representation of $\mathfrak{B}$ on $\mathfrak{X}$.*

Another version of the preceding corollary can be formulated as follows:

COROLLARY (2.4.16). *Let $\mathfrak{A}$ be a primitive complex Banach algebra and let $\mathfrak{L}$ be a minimal left ideal in $\mathfrak{A}$. Then the regular representation of $\mathfrak{A}$ on $\mathfrak{L}$ is a faithful, continuous, strictly dense representation on $\mathfrak{L}$ as a Banach space.*

By strengthening somewhat the minimal ideal condition in Theorem (2.4.14), we can improve the first part of the conclusion. The result is due essentially to Bonsall [1].

THEOREM (2.4.17). *Let $\mathfrak{X}$, $\mathfrak{Y}$ be a pair of dual Banach spaces with bilinear form (x, y) such that*

$$\sup |(x, y)| = |x|, \quad \text{for} \quad |y| = 1,$$

where $|x|$, $|y|$ are the norms in $\mathfrak{X}$, $\mathfrak{Y}$ respectively. Also let $\mathfrak{B}$ denote any subalgebra of $\mathscr{B}(\mathfrak{X})$ which contains all operators of the form $x \otimes y$. Then any norm $\|T\|$ under which $\mathfrak{B}$ is a normed algebra majorizes the operator bound $|T|$.

PROOF. Note that $\mathfrak{B}$ is not assumed to be complete under $\|T\|$. Consider the Banach space direct sum $\mathfrak{X} \oplus \mathfrak{Y}$ with norm $|x+y| = \max(|x|, |y|)$. Then, for any $T \in \mathscr{B}(\mathfrak{X})$, we obviously have,

$$\sup |(Tx, y)| = |T|, \quad \text{for } |x+y| = 1.$$

If $T \in \mathfrak{B}$, then, as in the proof of Theorem (2.4.14), we also have

$$|(Tx, y)| \leqslant \|T\| \, \|x \otimes y\|,$$

for all $x \in \mathfrak{X}$ and $y \in \mathfrak{Y}$. For each $T \in \mathfrak{B}$ with $\|T\| \leqslant 1$, regard (Tx, y) as a function in $\mathfrak{X} \otimes \mathfrak{Y}$. Applying the uniform boundedness theorem to this class of functions, we conclude that a constant β exists such that $|T| \leqslant \beta\|T\|$, for all $T \in \mathfrak{B}$, and so the theorem is proved.

The next theorem gives some information concerning the closed ideals in $\mathfrak{B}$.

THEOREM (2.4.18). *Let $\mathfrak{R}$ be a closed right ideal in $\mathfrak{B}$ and let $\mathfrak{M}$ be the smallest closed linear subspace of $\mathfrak{X}$ which contains the range of each operator in $\mathfrak{R}$. Then $\mathfrak{R}$ contains every element of $\mathfrak{B}$ with finite rank whose range is contained in $\mathfrak{M}$.*

PROOF. Since $\mathfrak{R}$ is a right ideal and $\mathfrak{B}$ is irreducible, it is readily verified that $\mathfrak{M}$ is equal to the closure in $\mathfrak{X}$ of the set $\{Tu : T \in \mathfrak{R}\}$. Now let T be any element of $\mathfrak{B}$ with finite rank n. Then $T = \Sigma v_i \otimes f_i$, where $f_1, \cdots, f_n$ can be assumed to be linearly independent elements of $\mathfrak{X}^{\mathfrak{B}}$. By Lemma (2.4.9), there exist elements $x_1, \cdots, x_n$ in $\mathfrak{X}$ such that $(x_i, f_j) = \delta_{ij}$ $(i, j = 1, \cdots, n)$. Hence $Tx_i = v_i$ $(i = 1, \cdots, n)$, and it follows that $T(\mathfrak{X}) \subseteq \mathfrak{M}$ implies $v_1, \cdots, v_n \in \mathfrak{M}$. Thus we have only to prove that $\mathfrak{R}$ contains every operator of the form $v \otimes f$ with $v \in \mathfrak{M}$. Now $v \in \mathfrak{M}$ implies the existence of a sequence $\{T_n\} \subset \mathfrak{R}$ such that $\lim T_n u = v$ relative to the norm in $\mathfrak{X}$. By Lemma (2.4.13), convergence of the sequence $\{T_n u\}$ in $\mathfrak{X}$ implies convergence of the sequence $\{T_n u \otimes f\}$ in $\mathfrak{B}$. Furthermore, by the same lemma, the latter sequence converges in $\mathfrak{B}$ to the operator $v \otimes f$. Finally, since $T_n \in \mathfrak{R}$

and $T_n u \otimes f = T_n(u \otimes f)$, it follows that $T_n u \otimes f \in \mathfrak{K}$ and therefore, by the closure of $\mathfrak{K}$, $v \otimes f \in \mathfrak{K}$.

If $\mathfrak{L}$ is a closed left ideal in $\mathfrak{B}$, then $\mathfrak{L}'$ is a closed right ideal in $\mathfrak{B}'$. Therefore an application of the theorem yields the following corollary.

COROLLARY (2.4.19). *Let $\mathfrak{L}$ be a closed left ideal in $\mathfrak{B}$ and denote by $\mathfrak{M}'$ the smallest closed subspace of $\mathfrak{X}^{\mathfrak{B}}$ which contains the range of each operator T' with $T \in \mathfrak{L}$. Then $\mathfrak{L}$ contains every element of $\mathfrak{B}$ with finite rank and the range of whose adjoint is contained in $\mathfrak{M}'$.*

§ 5. Uniqueness of the norm topology and the fundamental isomorphism theorem. As will be shown below, the norm topology in certain Banach algebras is uniquely determined in the sense that any two norms under which the algebra is a Banach algebra are automatically equivalent. It is obviously too much to expect this situation to hold in general, since we can make any Banach space into a Banach algebra by defining all products of elements to be equal to zero. On the other hand, these algebras are radical algebras and so can be elminated by an assumption of semi-simplicity. It is thus natural to ask whether or not the norm topology in any semi-simple Banach algebra is uniquely determined. This question, which is still open, will be discussed in some detail in the present section. Further results along these lines for certain algebras with an involution will be found in Chapter IV, § 1.

Let $\|x\|_1$ and $\|x\|_2$ be two norms with respect to which a given algebra $\mathfrak{A}$ is a normed algebra. These norms are equivalent, that is, determine the same norm topology in $\mathfrak{A}$, if and only if there exist constants α, β such that $\|x\|_1 \leqslant \alpha\|x\|_2 \leqslant \beta\|x\|_1$ for all $x \in \mathfrak{A}$. In the presence of completeness, the closed graph theorem shows that the two norms will be equivalent if and only if $\|x_n\|_1 \to 0$ and $\|s - x_n\|_2 \to 0$ imply $s = 0$. This observation suggests the following definition.

DEFINITION (2.5.1). *For each $s \in \mathfrak{A}$, let*

$$\Delta(s) = \inf_{x \in \mathfrak{A}} (\|x\|_1 + \|s - x\|_2).$$

Then Δ is called the SEPARATING FUNCTION *for the two norms and, if $\Delta(s) = 0$, then s is called a* SEPARATING ELEMENT. *The set of all separating elements is denoted by $\mathfrak{S}$.*

The function Δ could also have been defined as

$$\Delta(s) = \inf (\|s-x\|_1 + \|x\|_2),$$

which shows that the norms are involved symmetrically. The following properties of $\Delta(s)$ are not difficult to establish:

(1) $$\Delta(s+t) \leqslant \Delta(s)+\Delta(t).$$

(2) $$\Delta(\alpha s) = |\alpha|\Delta(s).$$

(3) $$\Delta(s) \leqslant \min (\|s\|_1, \|s\|_2).$$

(4) $$\Delta(st) \leqslant \begin{cases} \Delta(s)(\|t\|_1 + \|t\|_2) \\ (\|s\|_1 + \|s\|_2)\Delta(t). \end{cases}$$

By properties (1) and (2), $\Delta(s)$ is a pseudo-norm for $\mathfrak{A}$. These properties along with (3) and (4) show that $\mathfrak{S}$ is a 2-sided ideal in $\mathfrak{A}$ which is closed relative to each norm. This ideal will be called the SEPARATING IDEAL for the two norms. If $\mathfrak{A}$ is complete with respect to both norms, then the condition $\mathfrak{S} = (0)$ is necessary and sufficient for the norms to be equivalent.

THEOREM (2.5.2). *Let $\mathfrak{A}$ be a Banach algebra under each of the norms $\|x\|_1$, $\|x\|_2$ and let $\Delta(s)$ be the separating function for these norms. If c is any element in the center of $\mathfrak{A}$, then $\nu_{\mathfrak{A}}(c) \leqslant \Delta(c)$.*

PROOF. Since $\mathfrak{A}$ is a Banach algebra with respect to both norms, we have $\nu_{\mathfrak{A}}(x) \leqslant \|x\|_1$ and $\nu_{\mathfrak{A}}(x) \leqslant \|x\|_2$ for all $x \in \mathfrak{A}$. Now, if c is the center, then the elements x and $c-x$ commute. Therefore

$$\nu_{\mathfrak{A}}(c) \leqslant \nu_{\mathfrak{A}}(x)+\nu_{\mathfrak{A}}(c-x) \leqslant \|x\|_1+\|c-x\|_2.$$

It follows that $\nu_{\mathfrak{A}}(c) \leqslant \Delta(c)$.

COROLLARY (2.5.3). *If $\mathfrak{A}$ has an identity element, then $\mathfrak{S}$ must be a proper ideal.*

COROLLARY (2.5.4). *If $\mathfrak{A}$ is a simple algebra with an identity element, then any two norms under which $\mathfrak{A}$ is a Banach algebra are equivalent.*

LEMMA (2.5.5). *Let $\mathfrak{A}$ be a normed algebra under each of the norms $\|x\|_1$, $\|x\|_2$ and let e be an idempotent in $\mathfrak{A}$. If $\mathfrak{S}_e$ is the separating ideal for the two norms restricted to the sub-algebra $e\mathfrak{A}e$, then $\mathfrak{S}_e = e\mathfrak{S}e$.*

PROOF. It is obvious that $\mathfrak{S}_e \subseteq \mathfrak{S}$ and, since $e\mathfrak{S}_e e = \mathfrak{S}_e$, that $\mathfrak{S}_e \subseteq e\mathfrak{S}e$. Also, by property (4) above, we have

$$\Delta(ese) \leqslant \Delta(s)(\|e\|_1+\|e\|_2)^2.$$

Therefore $s \in \mathfrak{S}$ implies $ese \in \mathfrak{S}_e$. In other words, $\mathfrak{S}_e = e\mathfrak{S}e$.

THEOREM (2.5.6). *Let $\mathfrak{A}$ be a Banach algebra relative to each of the norms $\|x\|_1$, $\|x\|_2$. Then every element of the separating ideal $\mathfrak{S}$ is a 2-sided topological divisor of zero with respect to each norm.*

PROOF. Let $s \in \mathfrak{S}$. Then also $\lambda s \in \mathfrak{S}$ for every scalar λ. Hence there exists $\{x_n\} \subset \mathfrak{A}$ such that $\|x_n\|_1 \to 0$ and $\|\lambda s - x_n\|_2 \to 0$. Since $\|x_n\|_1 \to 0$, the elements x_n will be quasi-regular for large n. Thus λs, being a limit of quasi-regular elements with respect to the norm $\|x\|_2$, is either quasi-regular or $1-\lambda s$ is a 2-sided topological divisor of zero relative to this norm (by Lemma (1.5.9) (ii)). Consider first the case in which $1-\lambda s$ is a 2-sided topological divisor of zero for arbitrarily large λ. Then there exists a sequence $\{\lambda_n\}$ of scalars and a sequence $\{z_n\}$ of elements such that $\|z_n\|_2 = 1$, $\|\lambda_n s z_n - z_n\|_2 < 1$ for each n, and $|\lambda_n| \to \infty$. Since

$$\|sz_n\|_2 \leqslant \frac{1}{|\lambda_n|}(\|\lambda_n s z_n - z_n\|_2 + \|z_n\|_2) < \frac{2}{|\lambda_n|},$$

it follows that $\|sz_n\|_2 \to 0$, so that s is a left topological divisor of zero. A similar proof shows that s is also a right and hence a 2-sided topological divisor of zero with respect to $\|x\|_2$. Now consider the case in which λs is quasi-regular for arbitrarily large scalars λ. By Theorem (1.5.9) (iii), s is either a 2-sided topological divisor of zero with respect to $\|x\|_2$ or there exists a non-zero idempotent $e \in \mathfrak{A}$ such that $es = se = s$ and s is a regular element in the algebra $e\mathfrak{A}e$. Furthermore, it follows from Lemma (2.5.5) that s is a separating element for the two norms restricted to $e\mathfrak{A}e$. However, according to Corollary (2.5.3), the separating ideal in $e\mathfrak{A}e$ is proper and so cannot contain a regular element. Therefore s is in all cases a 2-sided topological divisor of zero with respect to $\|x\|_2$. By symmetry, a similar result holds for $\|x\|_1$, and so the proof is complete.

THEOREM (2.5.7). *Let $\mathfrak{A}$ be an algebra with socle $\mathfrak{F}$ and let $\mathfrak{A}$ be a normed algebra under $\|x\|_1$ and $\|x\|_2$. If $\mathfrak{S}$ is the separating ideal for these norms, then $\mathfrak{S}\mathfrak{F}$ and $\mathfrak{F}\mathfrak{S}$ are contained in the radical of $\mathfrak{A}$.*

PROOF. Recall that $\mathfrak{F}$ is a 2-sided ideal in $\mathfrak{A}$ equal to the sum of all minimal left (or right) ideals in $\mathfrak{A}$. Therefore it will be sufficient to prove that $\mathfrak{S}\mathfrak{L} \subseteq \mathfrak{R}$ for every minimal left ideal $\mathfrak{L}$. If $\mathfrak{L}^2 = (0)$, then already $\mathfrak{L} \subseteq \mathfrak{R}$, and so *a fortiori* $\mathfrak{S}\mathfrak{L} \subseteq \mathfrak{R}$. Hence we can assume $\mathfrak{L}^2 \neq (0)$. In this case there exists a non-zero minimal idempotent $e \in \mathfrak{A}$ such that $\mathfrak{L} = \mathfrak{A}e$. Furthermore, $e\mathfrak{A}e$ is a normed division algebra and so is either the reals, complexes or quaternions. Since $\mathfrak{S}$ is an ideal it will be sufficient in this case to prove that $\mathfrak{S}e = (0)$. Since $e\mathfrak{A}e$ is finite dimensional over the reals, all norms in $e\mathfrak{A}e$ are equivalent. Therefore the separating ideal $\mathfrak{S}_e$ for the two norms in $e\mathfrak{A}e$ must be zero. By Lemma (2.5.5) we have $\mathfrak{S}_e = e\,\mathfrak{S}e$, and so $e\mathfrak{S}e = (0)$. But this implies $\mathfrak{S}e = (0)$; for, if $\mathfrak{S}e \neq (0)$, then $\mathfrak{S}e = \mathfrak{A}e$ since $\mathfrak{A}e$ is minimal. Therefore $e\mathfrak{A}e = (0)$ and, in particular, $e = 0$ which is a contradiction. This completes the proof.

Corollary (2.5.8). *Let $\mathfrak{A}$ be a Banach algebra with socle $\mathfrak{F}$ such that $a\mathfrak{F} = (0)$ implies $a = 0$. Then $\mathfrak{A}$ has a unique norm topology.*

If $\mathfrak{A}$ is a primitive algebra with minimal ideals, then, by Corollary (2.4.15), the left regular representation of $\mathfrak{A}$ on its socle is faithful. Hence we have the following result.

Corollary (2.5.9). *Let $\mathfrak{A}$ be a primitive Banach algebra with minimal one-sided ideals. Then $\mathfrak{A}$ has a unique norm topology.*

Corollary (2.5.10). *Any strictly irreducible algebra of operators on a vector space, which contains operators of finite rank and which is a Banach algebra under some norm, has a unique norm topology. In particular, $\mathscr{B}(\mathfrak{X})$, for any Banach space, has a unique norm topology.*

Consider next an algebra $\mathfrak{A}$ which is a normed algebra under each of the norms $\|x\|_1$, $\|x\|_2$ and a 2-sided ideal $\mathfrak{I}$ in $\mathfrak{A}$ which is closed relative to each norm. Let $x \to \pi(x)$ be the natural homomorphism of $\mathfrak{A}$ onto $\mathfrak{A}/\mathfrak{I}$. Since $\mathfrak{I}$ is closed, the norms $\|x\|_1$, $\|x\|_2$ induce respectively norms $\|\pi(x)\|_1$ and $\|\pi(x)\|_2$ in $\mathfrak{A}/\mathfrak{I}$. Denote as usual by Δ and $\mathfrak{S}$ the separating function and ideal for the norms in $\mathfrak{A}$. Similarly, denote by Δ_π and $\mathfrak{S}_\pi$ the separating function and ideal for the induced norms in $\mathfrak{A}/\mathfrak{I}$. In this situation we have the following theorem.

Theorem (2.5.11). *It is always true that $\Delta_\pi(\pi(s)) \leqslant \Delta(s)$ and therefore $\pi(\mathfrak{S}) \subseteq \mathfrak{S}_\pi$. If $\mathfrak{I} \subseteq \mathfrak{S}$, then $\Delta_\pi(\pi(s)) = \Delta(s)$, so that $\pi(\mathfrak{S}) = \mathfrak{S}_\pi$ and $\pi^{-1}(\mathfrak{S}_\pi) = \mathfrak{S}$.*

Proof. The inequality $\Delta_\pi(\pi(s)) \leqslant \Delta(s)$ is an immediate consequence of the inequalities $\|\pi(x)\|_1 \leqslant \|x\|_1$ and $\|\pi(x)\|_2 \leqslant \|x\|_2$. Now, for arbitrary $\epsilon > 0$ and $s \in \mathfrak{A}$, choose $t \in \mathfrak{A}$ such that

$$\|\pi(t)\|_1 + \|\pi(s-t)\|_2 \leqslant \Delta_\pi(\pi(s)) + \epsilon.$$

Next choose $m_1, m_2 \in \mathfrak{I}$ such that

$$\|t+m_1\|_1 \leqslant \|\pi(t)\|_1 + \epsilon, \qquad \|s-t+m_2\|_2 \leqslant \|\pi(s-t)\|_2 + \epsilon.$$

Then $\|t+m_1\|_1 + \|s-t+m_2\|_2 \leqslant \Delta_\pi(\pi(s))+3\epsilon$. This implies $\Delta(s+m_1+m_2)$ $\leqslant \Delta_\pi(\pi(s))+3\epsilon$. The elements m_1 and m_2 depend on s and ϵ. However, if $\mathfrak{I} \subseteq \mathfrak{S}$, then $\Delta(m_1+m_2) = 0$ and we have $\Delta(s) = \Delta(s+m_1+m_2)$. Hence $\Delta(s) \leqslant \Delta_\pi(\pi(s))+3\epsilon$. Since ϵ is arbitrary, it follows that $\Delta(s) \leqslant \Delta_\pi(\pi(s))$ and therefore $\Delta(s) = \Delta_\pi(\pi(s))$.

COROLLARY (2.5.12). *Assume $\mathfrak{A}$ to be a Banach algebra under each of the norms $\|x\|_1, \|x\|_2$. Then in order for the induced norms in $\mathfrak{A}/\mathfrak{I}$ to be equivalent it is necessary that $\mathfrak{S} \subseteq \mathfrak{I}$ and sufficient that $\mathfrak{S} = \mathfrak{I}$.*

This corollary shows that, in order to settle the question of whether or not every semi-simple Banach algebra has a unique norm topology, it is sufficient to settle it for primitive Banach algebras.

THEOREM (2.5.13). *If $\mathfrak{A}$ is a Banach algebra under each of the norms $\|x\|_1, \|x\|_2$, then the separating ideal for these norms is contained in the strong radical. In particular, if $\mathfrak{A}$ is strongly semi-simple, then it has a unique norm topology.*

PROOF. Let $\|x\|_1, \|x\|_2$ be any two Banach algebra norms for $\mathfrak{A}$ with separating ideal $\mathfrak{S}$. If $\mathfrak{M}$ is a maximal modular 2-sided ideal in $\mathfrak{A}$, then $\mathfrak{A}/\mathfrak{M}$ is a simple algebra with an identity so has a unique norm topology. Therefore, by the above corollary, $\mathfrak{S} \subseteq \mathfrak{M}$.

THEOREM (2.5.14). *Let $x \to x^\tau$ be a homomorphism of a Banach algebra $\mathfrak{A}$ onto an arbitrary algebra $\mathfrak{B}$. Denote by $\mathfrak{K}$ the kernel of the homomorphism τ and $\bar{\mathfrak{K}}$ the closure of $\mathfrak{K}$ in $\mathfrak{A}$. Then τ maps $\bar{\mathfrak{K}}$ into the radical of $\mathfrak{B}$.*

PROOF. If $\mathfrak{B}$ is a radical algebra, then there is nothing to prove. Otherwise let $\mathfrak{L}'$ be any maximal modular left ideal in $\mathfrak{B}$. Then the counter image $\mathfrak{L}$ of $\mathfrak{L}'$ in $\mathfrak{A}$ is a maximal modular ideal in $\mathfrak{A}$. Now $\mathfrak{K} \subseteq \mathfrak{L}$ and $\mathfrak{L}$ is closed, since $\mathfrak{A}$ is a Banach algebra. Therefore $\bar{\mathfrak{K}} \subseteq \mathfrak{L}$ and hence τ maps $\bar{\mathfrak{K}}$ into $\mathfrak{L}'$. Since the radical of $\mathfrak{B}$ is equal to the intersection of all such $\mathfrak{L}'$, the desired result follows.

COROLLARY (2.5.15). *If $\mathfrak{B}$ is semi-simple, then the kernel of any homomorphism of a Banach algebra onto $\mathfrak{B}$ is automatically closed.*

THEOREM (2.5.16). *Let τ be any homomorphism of a Banach algebra $\mathfrak{A}$ onto a second Banach algebra $\mathfrak{B}$. If $\mathfrak{B}$ is semi-simple with a unique norm topology, then τ is automatically continuous.*

PROOF. By the above corollary, the kernel $\mathfrak{K}$ of the homomorphism

τ is a closed 2-sided ideal in $\mathfrak{A}$. Therefore $\mathfrak{B}$, which is isomorphic with $\mathfrak{A}/\mathfrak{R}$, is also a Banach algebra under the norm

$$\|b\|_1 = \inf_{a^\tau = b} \|a\|, \quad a \in \mathfrak{A}.$$

Since $\|a^\tau\|_1 \leqslant \|a\|$, the desired result follows from the equivalence of the norm $\|b\|_1$ with the given noım in $\mathfrak{B}$.

If $\mathfrak{B}$ is commutative, then the above theorem can be strengthened as follows:

THEOREM (2.5.17). *Let τ be any homomorphism of a Banach algebra $\mathfrak{A}$ into a semi-simple commutative Banach algebra $\mathfrak{C}$. Then τ is automatically continuous.*

PROOF. Note that τ is only assumed to be "into" rather than "onto". By Corollary (2.3.7) the image of $\mathfrak{A}$ in $\mathfrak{C}$ is semi-simple, so that the kernel of τ is a closed ideal in $\mathfrak{A}$. Therefore $\mathfrak{A}^\tau$ is a Banach algebra under the norm

$$\|a^\tau\|_1 = \inf_{a^\tau = x^\tau} \|x\|, \quad a, x \in \mathfrak{A}.$$

Since $Sp_{\mathfrak{C}}(b) \subseteq Sp_{\mathfrak{A}^\tau}(b)$, we have $\nu_{\mathfrak{C}}(b) \leqslant \|b\|_1$ as well as $\nu_{\mathfrak{C}}(b) \leqslant \|b\|$, for all $b \in \mathfrak{A}^\tau$. Hence

$$\nu_{\mathfrak{C}}(s) \leqslant \|b\| + \|s-b\|_1, \quad b \in \mathfrak{A}^\tau, \quad s \in \mathfrak{C}.$$

Now, if $\|s-b_n\|_1 \to 0$ while $\|b_n\| \to 0$, it follows that $\nu_{\mathfrak{C}}(s) = 0$ and this implies $s = 0$ since $\mathfrak{C}$ is semi-simple. Therefore, by the closed graph theorem, the embedding of $\mathfrak{A}^\tau$ in $\mathfrak{C}$ is continuous. In other words, there exists a constant β such that $\|a^\tau\| \leqslant \beta\|a^\tau\|_1 \leqslant \beta\|a\|$, for all $a \in \mathfrak{A}$. This completes the proof.

COROLLARY (2.5.18). *Any semi-simple commutative Banach algebra has a unique norm topology.*

We are now in a position to obtain the fundamental isomorphism theorem for primitive Banach algebras with minimal ideals. The purely algebraic portion of this theorem holds for general primitive rings with minimal ideals. (See Jacobson [4; 5, p. 79].) The results obtained above concerning uniqueness of the norm topology enable us to fill in the toplogical properties demanded in the case of Banach algebras. By Corollary (2.4.6), complex primitive Banach algebras are characterized by the property of being continuously isomorphic with strictly dense algebras of bounded operators on a complex Banach space. Also, by Lemma (2.4.10), a primitive Banach algebra will possess minimal one-sided ideals if and only if its associated algebra of operators contains operators of finite rank. The fundamental isomorphism theorem is concerned with the form of isomorphisms between such algebras of operators. We accordingly consider two complex Banach spaces $\mathfrak{X}_1$, $\mathfrak{X}_2$ and let $\mathfrak{B}_1$, $\mathfrak{B}_2$ be strictly dense sub-algebras of $\mathscr{B}(\mathfrak{X}_1)$, $\mathscr{B}(\mathfrak{X}_2)$ respectively. Assume also that each of the algebras contains operators of finite rank (that is, contains minimal one-sided ideals) and is a Banach algebra under some given norm which, by Theorem (2.4.14), automatically majorizes the operator bound. The fundamental isomorphism theorem can now be stated as follows:

THEOREM (2.5.19). *Let $T \to T^\tau$ be any algebra isomorphism of $\mathfrak{B}_1$ onto $\mathfrak{B}_2$. Then there exists a one-to-one bicontinuous linear transformation U of $\mathfrak{X}_1$ onto $\mathfrak{X}_2$ such that $T^\tau = UTU^{-1}$, for every $T \in \mathfrak{B}_1$.*

PROOF. By Corollary (2.5.10), τ maps a given minimal left ideal in $\mathfrak{B}_1$ homeomorphically onto a minimal left ideal in $\mathfrak{B}_2$. After this observation, the desired result is easily obtained from Corollary (2.4.15).

Most of the general results in this section are due to the author [3, 4]. Extensions of some of the results have been obtained by Yood [5, 10]. That $\mathscr{B}(\mathfrak{X})$ has a unique norm topology (given here by Corollary (2.5.10)) was proved by Eidelheit [2]. Uniqueness of the norm topology for semi-simple commutative Banach algebras was proved by Gelfand [4]. Theorem (2.5.17) was proved by Šilov [5]. For certain special cases, it is meaningful to consider the uniqueness of norm problem for norms which need not be complete. For example, in the case of the algebra $C(\Omega)$ of all continuous functions on a compact Hausdorff space Ω, it is a result of Kaplansky [5] that any norm under which $C(\Omega)$ is a normed algebra majorizes the natural norm. (See Corollary (3.7.7).) Whether or not $C(\Omega)$ admits such a norm not equivalent to its natural norm (i.e. not complete) is an open question. Bade and Curtis [1] have obtained some partial results on this question. Also, if $\mathfrak{X}$ is a Banach space, then Theorem (2.4.17) shows that any norm under which $\mathscr{B}(\mathfrak{X})$ is a normed algebra majorizes the operator bound. This may be regarded as an extension to $\mathscr{B}(\mathfrak{X})$ of the Kaplansky result for $C(\Omega)$.

§ **6. Structure of semi-simple Banach algebras. The structure spaces.** A result from general algebra theory is that any semi-simple algebra is isomorphic with a subdirect sum of primitive algebras (Jacobson [2]). Also, any strongly semi-simple algebra is isomorphic with a subdirect sum of simple algebras with identity elements. We examine briefly here these general structure theorems, along with some related questions, for the special case of Banach algebras. First, however, it is necessary to define a subdirect sum of Banach algebras which takes into account the norms.

Let $\{\mathfrak{A}_\lambda : \lambda \in \Lambda\}$ be a family of Banach algebras all of which are either real or complex. Denote by $\Sigma\, \mathfrak{A}_\lambda$ the class of all functions f defined on Λ with $f(\lambda) \in \mathfrak{A}_\lambda$, for each λ, and such that the quantity $|f|$ defined by

$$|f| = \sup_{\lambda \in \Lambda} \|f(\lambda)\|,$$

$\|f(\lambda)\|$ being the norm in $\mathfrak{A}_\lambda$, is finite. Algebra operations are defined in $\Sigma\, \mathfrak{A}_\lambda$ by the relations $(f+g)(\lambda) = f(\lambda)+g(\lambda)$, $(\alpha f)(\lambda) = \alpha(f(\lambda))$ and $(fg)(\lambda) = f(\lambda)g(\lambda)$. With these operations and $|f|$ as norm, $\Sigma\, \mathfrak{A}_\lambda$ is easily seen to be a Banach algebra. This algebra will be called the NORMED FULL DIRECT SUM of the algebras $\mathfrak{A}_\lambda$. Any subalgebra $\Sigma' \mathfrak{A}_\lambda$ of $\Sigma\, \mathfrak{A}_\lambda$, such that for each $\mu \in \Lambda$ the elements $f(\mu)$ exhaust $\mathfrak{A}_\mu$ as f ranges over $\Sigma' \mathfrak{A}_\lambda$, is called a NORMED SUBDIRECT SUM of the algebras $\mathfrak{A}_\lambda$. A normed subdirect sum is a normed algebra but not necessarily a Banach algebra with respect to the norm $|f|$.

Now consider any normed subdirect sum $\Sigma' \mathfrak{A}_\lambda$ and let $\mathfrak{I}_\mu$ be the set of all $f \in \Sigma' \mathfrak{A}_\lambda$ for which $f(\mu) = 0$. Then $\mathfrak{I}_\mu$ is a 2-sided ideal in $\Sigma' \mathfrak{A}_\lambda$ and $(\Sigma' \mathfrak{A}_\lambda)/\mathfrak{I}_\mu$ is isomorphic with $\mathfrak{A}_\mu$. If each $\mathfrak{A}_\lambda$ is primitive, then each $\mathfrak{I}_\lambda$ is a primitive ideal and, since $\bigcap \mathfrak{I}_\mu = (0)$, the algebra $\Sigma' \mathfrak{A}_\lambda$ is semi-simple. Similarly, if each $\mathfrak{A}_\lambda$ is a simple algebra with an identity element, then each $\mathfrak{I}_\mu$ is a maximal modular ideal and $\Sigma' \mathfrak{A}_\lambda$ is strongly semi-simple. The desired structure theorem can now be stated.

THEOREM (2.6.1).

(i) *Every semi-simple Banach algebra is continuously isomorphic with a normed subdirect sum of primitive Banach algebras.*

(ii) *Every strongly semi-simple Banach algebra is continuously isomorphic with a normed subdirect sum of simple Banach algebras with identity elements.*

PROOF. Let $\Pi_{\mathfrak{A}}$ denote the set of all primitive ideals and let $\Xi_{\mathfrak{A}}$ denote the set of all maximal modular 2-sided ideals in the Banach algebra $\mathfrak{A}$. When there is no chance of confusion the subscript $\mathfrak{A}$ on $\Pi_{\mathfrak{A}}$ and $\Xi_{\mathfrak{A}}$ will be omitted. For each $\mathfrak{P} \in \Pi$, let $\mathfrak{A}_{\mathfrak{P}} = \mathfrak{A}/\mathfrak{P}$. Then $\mathfrak{A}_{\mathfrak{P}}$ is a primitive Banach algebra. For $x \in \mathfrak{A}$ and $\mathfrak{P} \in \Pi$, define $\hat{x}(\mathfrak{P})$ as the image of x in $\mathfrak{A}_{\mathfrak{P}}$. If $\mathfrak{A}$ is semi-simple, then $\hat{x}(\mathfrak{P}) = 0$ for every $\mathfrak{P} \in \Pi$ is equivalent to $x = 0$. Also, since $\|\hat{x}(\mathfrak{P})\| \leqslant \|x\|$, it follows that $|\hat{x}| \leqslant \|x\|$, where $|\hat{x}|$ is the norm in the normed full direct sum $\Sigma\, \mathfrak{A}_{\mathfrak{P}}$. Therefore the mapping $x \to \hat{x}$ defines a continuous isomorphism of $\mathfrak{A}$ into $\Sigma\, \mathfrak{A}_{\mathfrak{P}}$. It is obvious that the image of $\mathfrak{A}$ in

$\Sigma\,\mathfrak{A}_{\mathfrak{P}}$ is a normed subdirect sum of the algebras $\mathfrak{A}_{\mathfrak{P}}$. This completes the proof of (i).

When $\mathfrak{A}$ is strongly semi-simple, let $\mathfrak{M} \in \Xi$ and define $\mathfrak{A}_{\mathfrak{M}} = \mathfrak{A}/\mathfrak{M}$. For $x \in \mathfrak{A}$, define $\hat{x}(\mathfrak{M})$ as the image of x in $\mathfrak{A}_{\mathfrak{M}}$. Then, just as in the above case, $x \to \hat{x}$ is a continuous isomorphism of $\mathfrak{A}$ with a normed subdirect sum of the algebras $\mathfrak{A}_{\mathfrak{M}}$. Since $\mathfrak{M}$ is a maximal modular ideal, $\mathfrak{A}_{\mathfrak{M}}$ is a simple Banach algebra with an identity element. Therefore statement (ii) is also proved.

Some of the properties of the set $\Pi_{\mathfrak{A}}$ of all primitive ideals and the set $\Xi_{\mathfrak{A}}$ of all maximal modular 2-sided ideals in $\mathfrak{A}$ will now be obtained. It is convenient to introduce the following notions of "hulls" and "kernels".

DEFINITION (2.6.2). *Let A be a subset of $\mathfrak{A}$ and F a subset of $\Pi_{\mathfrak{A}}$ (or of $\Xi_{\mathfrak{A}}$). Then the set $h(A)$ of all $\mathfrak{P} \in \Pi_{\mathfrak{A}}$ (or all $\mathfrak{M} \in \Xi_{\mathfrak{A}}$) which contain A is called the* HULL *of A in $\Pi_{\mathfrak{A}}$ (or in $\Xi_{\mathfrak{A}}$) and the intersection $k(F)$ of all the ideals in F is called the* KERNEL *of F in $\mathfrak{A}$. If $F = h(k(F))$, then F is called a* HULL *and, if $A = k(h(A))$, then A is called a* KERNEL.

In terms of hulls and kernels, closure operations can be introduced into Π and Ξ as follows. Let E be any subset of Π (or of Ξ). If E is empty, define $\bar{E} = E$. Otherwise define $\bar{E} = h(k(E))$. It is obvious that $E \subseteq \bar{E}$ and that $\bar{E} = \bar{\bar{E}}$. Furthermore, if E_1 and E_2 are any two subsets of Π (of Ξ), then it is immediate that $k(E_1 \cup E_2) = k(E_1) \cap k(E_2)$. Hence $\bar{E}_1 \cup \bar{E}_2 \subseteq \overline{E_1 \cup E_2}$. On the other hand, if $\mathfrak{P}$ is any primitive ideal (in particular, if $\mathfrak{P}$ is a maximal modular ideal) such that $k(E_1 \cup E_2) \subseteq \mathfrak{P}$ then

$$k(E_1)k(E_2) \subseteq k(E_1) \cap k(E_2) = k(E_1 \cup E_2) \subseteq \mathfrak{P}.$$

Therefore, by Theorem (2.2.9) (iv), either $k(E_1) \subseteq \mathfrak{P}$ or $k(E_2) \subseteq \mathfrak{P}$. In other words, either $\mathfrak{P} \in \bar{E}_1$ or $\mathfrak{P} \in \bar{E}_2$ and hence $\overline{E_1 \cup E_2} = \bar{E}_1 \cup \bar{E}_2$. Thus $E \to \bar{E}$ is indeed a closure operation. The topology determined in Π (and in Ξ) by this closure operation is called the HULL-KERNEL TOPOLOGY.

DEFINITION (2.6.3). *The spaces $\Pi_{\mathfrak{A}}$ and $\Xi_{\mathfrak{A}}$, under their hull-kernel topologies, are called respectively the* STRUCTURE SPACE *and the* STRONG STRUCTURE SPACE *of the algebra $\mathfrak{A}$.*

Since it is possible to have distinct primitive ideals $\mathfrak{P}_1$ and $\mathfrak{P}_2$ with $\mathfrak{P}_1 \subset \mathfrak{P}_2$, points of Π need not be closed in the hull-kernel topology.

Therefore Π is, in general, only a T_0-space. On the other hand, elements of Ξ are maximal ideals, so that Ξ is always a T_1-space. The injection mapping of Ξ into Π (recall that $\Xi \subseteq \Pi$) is obviously a homeomorphism.

THEOREM (2.6.4). *Let $\mathfrak{I}$ be a modular 2-sided ideal in $\mathfrak{A}$. Then the hull of $\mathfrak{I}$ in either $\Pi_{\mathfrak{A}}$ or $\Xi_{\mathfrak{A}}$ is compact.*

PROOF. Both cases can be disposed of simultaneously since $\Xi \subsetneq \Pi$. Let $\{F_\lambda\}$ be any family of closed subsets of $h(\mathfrak{I})$ with $\bigcap F_\lambda = 0$. Denote by $\mathfrak{K}$ the smallest 2-sided ideal of $\mathfrak{A}$ which contains each of the ideals $k(F_\lambda)$. Since $F_\lambda \subseteq h(\mathfrak{I})$, we have $\mathfrak{I} \subseteq k(h(\mathfrak{I})) \subseteq k(F_\lambda)$. Therefore $\mathfrak{I} \subseteq \mathfrak{K}$ and modularity of $\mathfrak{I}$ implies modularity of $\mathfrak{K}$. If $\mathfrak{K} \neq \mathfrak{A}$, then there exists $\mathfrak{M} \in \Xi$ such that $\mathfrak{K} \subseteq \mathfrak{M}$. But then $k(F_\lambda) \subseteq \mathfrak{M}$ and F_λ, being closed, must contain $\mathfrak{M}$ for every λ. Since this is contrary to the hypothesis, we conclude that $\mathfrak{K} = \mathfrak{A}$. In particular, if e is an identity modulo $\mathfrak{I}$, then there exist $m_i \in k(F_{\lambda_i})$ $(i = 1, \cdots, n)$ such that $e = m_1 + \cdots + m_n$. Since $\mathfrak{I} \subseteq k(F_\lambda)$ for all λ, it follows that $k(F_{\lambda_1}) + \cdots + k(F_{\lambda_n}) = \mathfrak{A}$. But this implies $F_{\lambda_1} \cap \cdots \cap F_{\lambda_n} = 0$, which proves that $h(\mathfrak{I})$ is compact.

COROLLARY (2.6.5). *If $\mathfrak{A}$ has an identity element, then both of its structure spaces are compact.*

It should be noted that neither the definition of the structure spaces of an algebra $\mathfrak{A}$ nor the above theorem depend in any way on $\mathfrak{A}$ being a Banach algebra or, for that matter, even an algebra. Since a number of the properties of the strong structure space Ξ are needed below, we consider it in some detail. Although analogous results hold for the space Π and are only slightly more difficult to obtain (See Jacobson [5, Chapter IX]), we restrict proofs to Ξ.

THEOREM (2.6.6). *Let $\mathfrak{I}$ be a 2-sided ideal in $\mathfrak{A}$ and set $\mathfrak{A}' = \mathfrak{A}/\mathfrak{I}$. Then the hull $h(\mathfrak{I})$ of the ideal $\mathfrak{I}$ in $\Xi_{\mathfrak{A}}$ is homeomorphic with $\Xi_{\mathfrak{A}'}$ under the mapping $\mathfrak{M} \to \mathfrak{M}/\mathfrak{I}$, and $\Xi_{\mathfrak{A}} - h(\mathfrak{I})$ is homeomorphic with $\Xi_{\mathfrak{I}}$ under the mapping $\mathfrak{M} \to \mathfrak{M} \cap \mathfrak{I}$.* Similar results hold for Π.

PROOF. It is straightforward to verify that $\mathfrak{M} \to \mathfrak{M}/\mathfrak{I}$ is a one-to-one mapping of $h(\mathfrak{I})$ onto $\Xi_{\mathfrak{A}'}$. Moreover, if F is any subset of $h(\mathfrak{I})$ and F' is its image in $\Xi_{\mathfrak{A}'}$, then $k(F') = k(F)/\mathfrak{I}$. Furthermore, for any $\mathfrak{M}$ in $h(\mathfrak{I})$, we have $k(F) \subseteq \mathfrak{M}$ if and only if $k(F') \subseteq \mathfrak{M}/\mathfrak{I}$. It follows that the mapping $\mathfrak{M} \to \mathfrak{M}/\mathfrak{I}$ is a homeomorphism of $h(\mathfrak{I})$ onto $\Xi_{\mathfrak{A}'}$, and so the first statement is proved.

Next let $\mathfrak{M} \in \Xi_{\mathfrak{A}} - h(\mathfrak{I})$ and let e be an identity for $\mathfrak{A}$ modulo $\mathfrak{M}$

Since $\mathfrak{M} \notin h(\mathfrak{J})$ and $\mathfrak{M}$ is maximal, $\mathfrak{M}+\mathfrak{J} = \mathfrak{A}$. Hence there exists $m \in \mathfrak{M}$ and $e' \in \mathfrak{J}$ such that $m+e' = e$. Thus e' is an identity in $\mathfrak{A}$ modulo $\mathfrak{M}$ and, if $\mathfrak{M}' = \mathfrak{M} \cap \mathfrak{J}$, then e' is an identity in $\mathfrak{J}$ modulo $\mathfrak{M}'$. If $\mathfrak{M}''$is any 2-sided ideal in $\mathfrak{J}$ which contains $\mathfrak{M}'$, then

$$\mathfrak{A}\mathfrak{M}'' \subseteq \mathfrak{M}\mathfrak{M}''+\mathfrak{J}\mathfrak{M}'' \subseteq \mathfrak{M}+\mathfrak{M}''.$$

Similarly, $\mathfrak{M}''\mathfrak{A} \subseteq \mathfrak{M}+\mathfrak{M}''$. It follows that $\mathfrak{M}+\mathfrak{M}''$ is a 2-sided ideal in $\mathfrak{A}$. Since $\mathfrak{M}$ is maximal, we have either $\mathfrak{M}+\mathfrak{M}'' = \mathfrak{M}$ or $\mathfrak{M}+\mathfrak{M}'' = \mathfrak{A}$. In the first case $\mathfrak{M}'' = \mathfrak{M}'$ and in the second $\mathfrak{M}'' = \mathfrak{J}$. Therefore $\mathfrak{M}' \in \Xi_{\mathfrak{J}}$. Suppose $\mathfrak{M}_1$ were another element of $\Xi_{\mathfrak{A}}$ such that $\mathfrak{M}_1 \cap \mathfrak{J} = \mathfrak{M}'$. Then $\mathfrak{M}+\mathfrak{M}_1 = \mathfrak{A}$. Hence $\mathfrak{J}\mathfrak{A} \subseteq \mathfrak{J}\mathfrak{M}+\mathfrak{J}\mathfrak{M}_1 \subseteq \mathfrak{M}'$. But also $\mathfrak{J}(1-e') \subseteq \mathfrak{M}'$. Therefore $\mathfrak{J} \subseteq \mathfrak{M}'$, a contradiction. This proves that $\mathfrak{M} \rightarrow \mathfrak{M} \cap \mathfrak{J}$ is a one-to-one mapping of $\Xi_{\mathfrak{A}}-h(\mathfrak{J})$ into $\Xi_{\mathfrak{J}}$. Next let $\mathfrak{M}'$ be any element of $\Xi_{\mathfrak{J}}$ with e' as an identity in $\mathfrak{J}$ modulo $\mathfrak{M}'$. Define $\mathfrak{M} = \mathfrak{M}'+\mathfrak{A}(1-e')$.
Then

$$\begin{aligned}(1-e')\mathfrak{A} &\subseteq (1-e')\mathfrak{A}(1-e')+(1-e')\mathfrak{A}e' \\ &\subseteq \mathfrak{A}(1-e')+e'\mathfrak{A}(1-e')+(1-e')\mathfrak{A}e' \\ &\subseteq \mathfrak{A}(1-e')+\mathfrak{J}(1-e')+(1-e')\mathfrak{J} \\ &\subseteq \mathfrak{A}(1-e')+\mathfrak{M}' = \mathfrak{M}.\end{aligned}$$

Also,

$$\begin{aligned}\mathfrak{A}\mathfrak{M}' &\subseteq (1-e')\mathfrak{A}\mathfrak{M}'+e'\mathfrak{A}\mathfrak{M}' \subseteq (1-e')\mathfrak{A}+\mathfrak{J}\mathfrak{M}' \\ &\subseteq \mathfrak{A}(1-e')+\mathfrak{M}' = \mathfrak{M}.\end{aligned}$$

Similarly, $\mathfrak{M}'\mathfrak{A} \subseteq \mathfrak{M}$. It follows that $\mathfrak{M}$ is a modular 2-sided ideal in $\mathfrak{A}$. Moreover, if $e' \in \mathfrak{M}$, then $e' = m'+a(1-e')$ where $m' \in \mathfrak{M}'$. Hence $a = e'-m'+ae' \in \mathfrak{J}$. But then $a(1-e') \in \mathfrak{M}'$ which implies $e' \in \mathfrak{M}'$, a contradiction. Therefore $e' \notin \mathfrak{M}$, so that $\mathfrak{M}$ is a proper ideal in $\mathfrak{A}$. Observe that $\mathfrak{M}+\mathfrak{J} = \mathfrak{A}$. Now let $\mathfrak{M}_1$ be any proper 2-sided ideal in $\mathfrak{A}$ which contains $\mathfrak{M}$. Then $\mathfrak{M}_1 \cap \mathfrak{J} = \mathfrak{M}'$ and

$$\mathfrak{M}_1\mathfrak{A} \subseteq \mathfrak{M}_1\mathfrak{M}+\mathfrak{M}_1\mathfrak{J} \subseteq \mathfrak{M}+\mathfrak{M}' \subseteq \mathfrak{M}.$$

Since also $\mathfrak{M}_1(1-e') \subseteq \mathfrak{M}$, it follows that $\mathfrak{M}_1 \subseteq \mathfrak{M}$. This shows that $\mathfrak{M}$ is an element of $\Xi_{\mathfrak{A}}-h(\mathfrak{J})$ and proves that the mapping $\mathfrak{M} \rightarrow \mathfrak{M} \cap \mathfrak{J}$ takes $\Xi_{\mathfrak{A}}-h(\mathfrak{J})$ onto $\Xi_{\mathfrak{J}}$. Finally, let F be a subset of $\Xi_{\mathfrak{A}}-h(\mathfrak{J})$ and denote its image in $\Xi_{\mathfrak{J}}$ by F'. Then $k(F') = k(F) \cap \mathfrak{J}$. Now, if $\mathfrak{M} \in \Xi_{\mathfrak{A}}-h(\mathfrak{J})$ and $\mathfrak{M}' = \mathfrak{M} \cap \mathfrak{J}$, then it is obvious that $\mathfrak{M} \supseteq k(F)$ implies $\mathfrak{M}' \supseteq k(F')$. Suppose, on the other hand, that $\mathfrak{M}' \supseteq k(F')$. If $\mathfrak{M} \not\supseteq k(F)$, then $\mathfrak{M}+k(F) = \mathfrak{A}$. Therefore $\mathfrak{J}\mathfrak{A} \subseteq \mathfrak{J}\mathfrak{M}+\mathfrak{J}k(F) \subseteq \mathfrak{M} \cap \mathfrak{J}+k(F) \cap \mathfrak{J} \subseteq \mathfrak{M}'$. Since $\mathfrak{M}'$ is modular in $\mathfrak{J}$, it follows that $\mathfrak{I} \subseteq \mathfrak{M}'$, a contradiction. In other words, $\mathfrak{M}' \supseteq k(F')$ implies $\mathfrak{M} \supseteq k(F)$. This proves that the mapping $\mathfrak{M} \rightarrow \mathfrak{M} \cap \mathfrak{I}$ is a homeomorphism and completes the proof of the theorem.

LEMMA (2.6.7). *Let $\mathfrak{I}_1$ and $\mathfrak{I}_2$ be any pair of 2-sided ideals in $\mathfrak{A}$. Then $h(\mathfrak{I}_1+\mathfrak{I}_2) = h(\mathfrak{I}_1) \cap h(\mathfrak{I}_2)$ and $h(\mathfrak{I}_1 \cap \mathfrak{I}_2) = h(\mathfrak{I}_1) \cup h(\mathfrak{I}_2)$ where the hulls are in $\Xi_{\mathfrak{A}}$.*

PROOF. Since $\mathfrak{I}_1+\mathfrak{I}_2$ contains both $\mathfrak{I}_1$ and $\mathfrak{I}_2$, the first equation is obvious. It is also obvious that $h(\mathfrak{I}_1) \cup h(\mathfrak{I}_2) \subseteq h(\mathfrak{I}_1 \cap \mathfrak{I}_2)$. Finally, let $\mathfrak{M} \in h(\mathfrak{I}_1 \cap \mathfrak{I}_2)$ and suppose that $\mathfrak{M} \notin h(\mathfrak{I}_1)$. Then, since $\mathfrak{M}$ is a maximal ideal in $\mathfrak{A}$, we have $\mathfrak{M}+\mathfrak{I}_1 = \mathfrak{A}$. As in the proof of Theorem (2.6.6), the ideal $\mathfrak{I}_1$ contains an identity e for $\mathfrak{A}$ modulo $\mathfrak{M}$. Thus $\mathfrak{I}_2 \subseteq \mathfrak{I}_2(1-e)+\mathfrak{I}_2 e \subseteq \mathfrak{M}+ \mathfrak{I}_1 \cap \mathfrak{I}_2 \subseteq \mathfrak{M}$. In other words, $\mathfrak{M} \in h(\mathfrak{I}_2)$ and the lemma is proved.

LEMMA (2.6.8). *Let $\mathfrak{I}_1$ and $\mathfrak{I}_2$ be any pair of 2-sided ideals in $\mathfrak{A}$. Then, in order for $\mathfrak{A} = \mathfrak{I}_1+\mathfrak{I}_2$, it is necessary and sufficient that $\mathfrak{I}_1+\mathfrak{I}_2$ be modular and that $h(\mathfrak{I}_1)$ and $h(\mathfrak{I}_2)$ be disjoint in $\Xi_{\mathfrak{A}}$.*

PROOF. By the preceding lemma, $h(\mathfrak{I}_1+\mathfrak{I}_2)$ is vacuous if and only if $h(\mathfrak{I}_1)$ and $h(\mathfrak{I}_2)$ are disjoint. Since $\mathfrak{A}$ is trivially modular, this proves the necessity. On the other hand, if $\mathfrak{I}_1+\mathfrak{I}_2$ is modular, then $h(\mathfrak{I}_1+\mathfrak{I}_2)$ can be vacuous only if $\mathfrak{I}_1+\mathfrak{I}_2 = \mathfrak{A}$. Hence the conditions are sufficient and the lemma is proved.

LEMMA (2.6.9). *Let $\mathfrak{I}$ be any ideal in $\mathfrak{A}$ and F a closed subset of $\Xi_{\mathfrak{A}}$ disjoint from $h(\mathfrak{I})$ such that $k(F)$ is modular. Then $\mathfrak{I}$ contains an identity for $\mathfrak{A}$ modulo $k(F)$.*

PROOF. By the preceding lemma, $k(F)+\mathfrak{I} = \mathfrak{A}$. Let u be any identity for $\mathfrak{A}$ modulo $k(F)$. Then there exist elements $d \in k(F)$ and $e \in \mathfrak{I}$ such that $d+e = u$. Since $e-u \in k(F)$, it follows that e is an identity for $\mathfrak{A}$ modulo $k(F)$, and so the lemma is proved.

The motivation for calling $\Pi_{\mathfrak{A}}$ and $\Xi_{\mathfrak{A}}$ structure spaces stems, of course, from their roles in the structure Theorem (2.6.1). (Segal [2] calls the strong structure space the *spectrum* of the algebra.) However, as far as general algebras are concerned, the fact that $\Pi_{\mathfrak{A}}$ and $\Xi_{\mathfrak{A}}$ are topological spaces does not appear to be especially significant for the structure theorems. On the other hand, the topology is of fundamental importance in the structure of certain special algebras. In this category fall the commutative Banach algebras which are taken up systematically in the next chapter. A major handicap, which makes it difficult to work with the structure spaces, lies in the fact that they are in general not Hausdorff. Therefore, as might be expected, the topology is a much more useful tool for those algebras which have Hausdorff structure spaces. In fact, for these algebras, topological properties become intimately bound up with structure properties. At this point it is worth noting that, if $\Pi_{\mathfrak{A}}$ is a Hausdorff space, then so is $\Xi_{\mathfrak{A}}$. Moreover, in case every primitive ideal in $\mathfrak{A}$ is contained in an element of $\Xi_{\mathfrak{A}}$ (in particular, if $\mathfrak{A}$ has an identity element), then the condition that $\Pi_{\mathfrak{A}}$ be a T_1-space already implies $\Pi_{\mathfrak{A}} = \Xi_{\mathfrak{A}}$. Therefore, in order to retain as much generality as possible, it is natural to consider algebras for which only the strong structure space is assumed Hausdorff. Banach algebras with this property are discussed in the next section.

A simple example of a Banach algebra whose structure spaces coincide but are still not Hausdorff is due to Mackey (see Kaplansky [5, p. 414]) and may be described as follows. Let $\mathscr{M}_2$ be the algebra of all 2×2 matrices over the complex numbers (with the operator bound as norm) and consider the algebra $\mathscr{S}_{\mathscr{M}_2}$ of all bounded sequences of elements of $\mathscr{M}_2$ discussed at the end of § 5, Chapter I. The desired algebra $\mathfrak{A}$ is the subalgebra of $\mathscr{S}_{\mathscr{M}_2}$ consisting of all sequences of elements of $\mathscr{M}_2$ which converge to a diagonal matrix. Observe that $\mathfrak{A}$ is even a B*-algebra with an identity element. Now, for any $\{M_k\} \in \mathfrak{A}$, set

$$\begin{pmatrix} \alpha & 0 \\ 0 & \beta \end{pmatrix} = \lim_{k \to \infty} M_k.$$

Then the set $\mathfrak{M}'_\infty$ of all $\{M_k\}$ such that $\alpha = 0$ is a maximal 2-sided ideal in $\mathfrak{A}$, since it is the kernel of the homomorphism $\{M_k\} \to \alpha$ of $\mathfrak{A}$ onto the complex field. Similarly, the set $\mathfrak{M}''_\infty$ of all $\{M_k\}$ such that $\beta = 0$ is also a maximal 2-sided ideal. Next define

$$\mathfrak{M}_n = \{\{M_k\} : M_n = 0\},$$

for $n = 1, 2, \cdots$. Then $\mathfrak{M}_n$ is the kernel of the homomorphism $\{M_k\} \to M_n$ of $\mathfrak{A}$ onto $\mathscr{M}_2$ and so is a maximal 2-sided ideal in $\mathfrak{A}$, since $\mathscr{M}_2$ is simple. It is not difficult to show that every primitive ideal in $\mathfrak{A}$ must coincide with one of the ideals $\mathfrak{M}'_\infty$, $\mathfrak{M}''_\infty$ or $\mathfrak{M}_n$ ($n = 1, 2, \cdots$). Hence $\Pi_{\mathfrak{A}} = \Xi_{\mathfrak{A}}$. Furthermore, it can also be shown that each $\mathfrak{M}_n$ is an isolated point of $\Xi_{\mathfrak{A}}$ while $\mathfrak{M}'_\infty$ and $\mathfrak{M}''_\infty$ are limit points which cannot be separated by open sets. Therefore $\Xi_{\mathfrak{A}}$ is not Hausdorff. We leave the details to the reader.

The hull–kernel method of topologizing the primitive ideals was discussed by Jacobson [3]. In a special case, these ideas were used earlier by Stone [1]. For commutative Banach algebras, Gelfand and Šilov [1] studied the hull-kernel topology for the space of maximal ideals.

§ **7. Completely regular algebras.** The class of algebras, which are considered in this section, reduces in the commutative case to the regular algebras of Šilov [5]. Most of the material presented here is due to Willcox [1] and generalizes results which were obtained by Šilov for the commutative case. The terminology "completely regular" is suggested by certain separation properties of the structure space, with respect to the algebra, which are analogous to properties of a completely regular topological space relative to the continuous functions. Our use of "completely regular" in place of Šilov's "regular" is an attempt to avoid confusion with an entirely different concept of regular algebra which was introduced by von Neumann [4].

The following is a precise definition of the class of algebras under consideration.

DEFINITION (2.7.1). *The algebra* $\mathfrak{A}$ *is said to be* COMPLETELY REGULAR *provided it satisfies both of the conditions*:

(i) *The strong structure space* $\Xi_{\mathfrak{A}}$ *of* $\mathfrak{A}$ *is Hausdorff.*

(ii) *Each point of* $\Xi_{\mathfrak{A}}$ *has a neighborhood* V *such that* $k(V)$ *is modular.*

Condition (ii) of this definition requires some motivation. In the first place, observe that (ii) is automatically satisfied if $\mathfrak{A}$ has an identity element (simply take $V = \Xi_{\mathfrak{A}}$!). In the second place, by Theorem (2.6.4), condition (ii) is a strong form of local compactness for $\Xi_{\mathfrak{A}}$. A consequence of this is that the one-point compactification of $\Xi_{\mathfrak{A}}$ (obtained by adjoining an infinite point whose neighborhoods are complements of compact sets) is Hausdorff. As will be seen below, the condition also ensures that, if $\mathfrak{A}$ is completely regular, then the algebra obtained from $\mathfrak{A}$ by adjunction of an identity element is also completely regular.

Some of the most important examples of completely regular algebras are commutative. These include, in addition to the algebra $C_0(\Omega)$ of all complex-valued functions which are continuous and vanish at infinity on a locally compact Hausdorff space Ω, the group algebra $L^1(\mathfrak{G})$ of a locally compact abelian group. (See Appendix, § 3 for a discussion of group algebras.) This is a fundamental property of group algebras. Other commutative examples will be found in the Appendix, § 2. Though commutative examples are perhaps first in importance, (at least from the point of view of applications) there are, nevertheless, some interesting cases of non-commutative completely regular Banach algebras. One such algebra is the group algebra of any compact topological group or, more generally, any algebra for which the right and left regular representations give rise to compact (that is, completely continuous) operators. (See Appendix, A.1.2.) A B*-algebra $\mathfrak{A}$ such that $\|\hat{x}(\mathfrak{P})\|$ is a continuous function of $\mathfrak{P} \in \Pi_{\mathfrak{A}}$, for each $x \in \mathfrak{A}$, is completely regular. (See Kaplansky [9] and Chapter IV, §10.) Also AW*-algebras, and hence W*-algebras (see Appendix, A.1.5), are completely regular. Further examples are given by Willcox [1].

THEOREM (2.7.2). *Let $\mathfrak{J}$ be a 2-sided ideal in $\mathfrak{A}$. If $\mathfrak{A}$ is completely regular, then so are the algebras $\mathfrak{A}/\mathfrak{J}$ and $\mathfrak{J}$.*

PROOF. In view of Theorem (2.6.6), we have only to prove that condition (ii) of Definition (2.7.1) is satisfied in both cases. To this end, let $\mathfrak{M}$ be any point of $h(\mathfrak{J})$ and V any neighborhood of $\mathfrak{M}$ in $\Xi_{\mathfrak{A}}$ such that $k(V)$ is modular. Since $k(V) \subseteq k(V \cap h(\mathfrak{J}))$, $k(V \cap h(\mathfrak{J}))$ is also modular. Denote by V' the image of $V \cap h(\mathfrak{J})$ in $\Xi_{\mathfrak{A}/\mathfrak{J}}$ given by Theorem (2.6.6). Since $k(V') = k(V \cap h(\mathfrak{J}))/\mathfrak{J}$, $k(V')$ is modular in $\mathfrak{A}/\mathfrak{J}$ and it follows that $\mathfrak{A}/\mathfrak{J}$ is completely regular.

Now let $\mathfrak{M}$ be any point of $\Xi_{\mathfrak{A}} - h(\mathfrak{J})$ and choose a neighborhood V of $\mathfrak{M}$ in $\Xi_{\mathfrak{A}}$ whose closure is disjoint from $h(\mathfrak{J})$ and such that $k(V)$ is modular. Let V' be the image of V in $\Xi_{\mathfrak{J}}$ given by Theorem (2.6.6). Then $k(V') = k(V) \cap \mathfrak{J}$. Since $h(k(V))$ is disjoint from $h(\mathfrak{J})$ and $k(V)$ is modular, it follows from Lemma (2.6.9) that $\mathfrak{J}$ contains an identity e for $\mathfrak{A}$ modulo $k(V)$. In particular, $\mathfrak{J}(1-e) \subseteq k(V) \cap \mathfrak{J}$ and $(1-e)\mathfrak{J} \subseteq k(V) \cap \mathfrak{J}$, which means that $k(V')$ is modular in $\mathfrak{J}$. This completes the proof.

THEOREM (2.7.3). *Let $\mathfrak{A}_1$ be the algebra obtained from $\mathfrak{A}$ by adjunction of an identity element. Then $\mathfrak{A}$ is completely regular if and only if $\mathfrak{A}_1$ is completely regular.*

PROOF. Since $\mathfrak{A}$ is a 2-sided ideal in $\mathfrak{A}_1$, the preceding theorem shows that complete regularity of $\mathfrak{A}_1$ implies complete regularity of $\mathfrak{A}$. On the other hand, assume $\mathfrak{A}$ to be completely regular. Since, by Theorem (2.6.6), the space $\Xi_{\mathfrak{A}}$ is homeomorphic with $\Xi_{\mathfrak{A}_1} - (\mathfrak{A})$, the complete regularity of $\mathfrak{A}_1$ will follow if we prove that $\Xi_{\mathfrak{A}_1}$ is Hausdorff at the point $\mathfrak{A}$. Therefore let $\mathfrak{M}'_0$ be any point of $\Xi_{\mathfrak{A}_1}$ distinct from $\mathfrak{A}$ and set $\mathfrak{M}_0 = \mathfrak{M}'_0 \cap \mathfrak{A}$. Then $\mathfrak{M}_0 \in \Xi_{\mathfrak{A}}$ and there exists a neighborhood V of $\mathfrak{M}_0$ in $\Xi_{\mathfrak{A}}$ such that $k(V)$ is a modular ideal in $\mathfrak{A}$. Let e be an identity for $\mathfrak{A}$ modulo $k(V)$ and denote by $\mathfrak{J}_1$ the 2-sided ideal $k(V) + \mathfrak{A}_1(1-e)$ in $\mathfrak{A}_1$. Obviously $\mathfrak{J}_1$ is not contained in $\mathfrak{A}$ so that $\mathfrak{A}$ is not in the hull $h'(\mathfrak{J}_1)$ in $\Xi_{\mathfrak{A}_1}$. Therefore the complement U' of $h'(\mathfrak{J}_1)$ is a neighborhood of $\mathfrak{A}$ in $\Xi_{\mathfrak{A}_1}$. Now let $\mathfrak{M} \in V$ and denote its image in $\Xi_{\mathfrak{A}_1}$ by $\mathfrak{M}'$. Then $\mathfrak{M} = \mathfrak{M}' \cap \mathfrak{A}$ and $\mathfrak{M}' = \mathfrak{M} + \mathfrak{A}_1(1-e)$.

Since $\mathfrak{M} \supseteq k(V)$, it follows that $\mathfrak{M}' \supseteq \mathfrak{I}_1$. In other words, the image V' of V in $\Xi_{\mathfrak{A}_1}$ is contained in $h'(\mathfrak{I}_1)$. Hence the two neighborhoods U' and V' are disjoint. Therefore $\Xi_{\mathfrak{A}_1}$ is Hausdorff at the point $\mathfrak{A}$ and the theorem is proved.

THEOREM (2.7.4). *Let $\mathfrak{R}_{\mathscr{S}}$ be the strong radical of $\mathfrak{A}$. Then $\Xi_{\mathfrak{A}} = \Xi_{\mathfrak{A}/\mathfrak{R}_{\mathscr{S}}}$ and $\mathfrak{A}$ is completely regular if and only if $\mathfrak{A}/\mathfrak{R}_{\mathscr{S}}$ is completely regular.*

PROOF. Since $h(\mathfrak{R}_{\mathscr{S}}) = \Xi_{\mathfrak{A}}$, we obtain $\Xi_{\mathfrak{A}} = \Xi_{\mathfrak{A}/\mathfrak{R}_{\mathscr{S}}}$ immediately from Theorem (2.6.6). Also, complete regularity of $\mathfrak{A}$ implies complete regularity of $\mathfrak{A}/\mathfrak{R}_{\mathscr{S}}$, by Theorem (2.7.2). Therefore assume $\mathfrak{A}/\mathfrak{R}_{\mathscr{S}}$ to be completely regular and let $\mathfrak{M}$ be any point of $\Xi_{\mathfrak{A}}$. In order to prove that $\mathfrak{A}$ is completely regular, we have only to produce a neighborhood V of $\mathfrak{M}$ such that $k(V)$ is modular. Let $\mathfrak{M}'$ be the element $\mathfrak{M}/\mathfrak{R}_{\mathscr{S}}$ of $\Xi_{\mathfrak{A}/\mathfrak{R}_{\mathscr{S}}}$ and choose a neighborhood V' of $\mathfrak{M}'$ in $\Xi_{\mathfrak{A}/\mathfrak{R}_{\mathscr{S}}}$ such that $k(V')$ is modular. If V is the corresponding neighborhood of $\mathfrak{M}$ in $\Xi_{\mathfrak{A}}$, then $k(V') = k(V)/\mathfrak{R}_{\mathscr{S}}$. Since $\mathfrak{R}_{\mathscr{S}} \subseteq k(V)$, modularity of $k(V')$ implies modularity of $k(V)$ and proves that $\mathfrak{A}$ is completely regular.

THEOREM (2.7.5). *Let $\mathfrak{A}$ be a Banach algebra with center $\mathfrak{C}$ and, for $\mathscr{E}$ any subset of $\mathfrak{A}$, define $\mathscr{E}^\sigma = \mathfrak{C} \cap \mathscr{E}$. If $\mathfrak{C}$ is completely regular, then $\mathfrak{P} \to \mathfrak{P}^\sigma$ is a continuous mapping of $\Pi_{\mathfrak{A}} - h(\mathfrak{C})$ onto a closed subset of $\Pi_{\mathfrak{C}}$. If also $\mathfrak{A}$ is semi-simple, then the mapping is onto $\Pi_{\mathfrak{C}}$. A similar result holds for $\Xi_{\mathfrak{A}}$ and $\Xi_{\mathfrak{C}}$.*

PROOF. Note that, since $\mathfrak{C}$ is commutative, $\Pi_{\mathfrak{C}} = \Xi_{\mathfrak{C}}$. Assume first that $\mathfrak{A}$ has an identity element, in which case $h(\mathfrak{C})$ is vacuous. For any $\mathfrak{P} \in \Pi_{\mathfrak{A}}$, observe that the mapping $c + \mathfrak{P}^\sigma \to c + \mathfrak{P}$ is an isomorphism of $\mathfrak{C}/\mathfrak{P}^\sigma$ into the center of $\mathfrak{A}/\mathfrak{P}$. Furthermore $\mathfrak{A}/\mathfrak{P}$, being primitive, has a center which is isomorphic to either the real or complex field. (See Corollary (2.4.5).) It follows that $\mathfrak{C}/\mathfrak{P}^\sigma$ is also isomorphic with either the real or complex field. Therefore $\mathfrak{P}^\sigma$ must be a maximal modular ideal in $\mathfrak{C}$, so that $\mathfrak{P} \to \mathfrak{P}^\sigma$ is indeed a mapping of $\Pi_{\mathfrak{A}}$ into $\Pi_{\mathfrak{C}}$. Let F be a closed set in $\Pi_{\mathfrak{C}}$ and denote by E the complete counter image of F in $\Pi_{\mathfrak{A}}$. If $\mathfrak{P}_0$ is a limit point of E in $\Pi_{\mathfrak{A}}$, then

$$\mathfrak{P}_0 \supseteq k(E) = \bigcap_{\mathfrak{P} \in E} \mathfrak{P}.$$

Also,

$$\mathfrak{P}_0^\sigma \supseteq \mathfrak{C} \cap k(E) = \bigcap_{\mathfrak{P} \in E} \mathfrak{P}^\sigma \supseteq k(F).$$

Therefore $\mathfrak{P}_0^\sigma \in F$, and hence $\mathfrak{P}_0 \in E$. Thus E is closed in $\Pi_{\mathfrak{A}}$, which proves that the mapping $\mathfrak{P} \to \mathfrak{P}^\sigma$ is continuous. Since $\Pi_{\mathfrak{C}}$ is Hausdorff, this continuity plus the compactness of $\Pi_{\mathfrak{A}}$ implies that the image of $\Pi_{\mathfrak{A}}$ in $\Pi_{\mathfrak{C}}$ is closed. If $\mathfrak{A}$ is semi-simple, then

$$\bigcap \mathfrak{P}^\sigma = \mathfrak{C} \cap (\bigcap \mathfrak{P}) = (0),$$

so that the image of $\Pi_{\mathfrak{A}}$ is dense in $\Pi_{\mathfrak{C}}$ and, being closed, must coincide with $\Pi_{\mathfrak{C}}$. This proves the theorem when $\mathfrak{A}$ has an identity element. If $\mathfrak{A}$ does not have an identity, adjoin one to obtain $\mathfrak{A}_1$. Denote the center of $\mathfrak{A}_1$ by $\mathfrak{C}_1$ and note that $\mathfrak{C}_1$ is obtained from $\mathfrak{C}$ by adjunction of the identity. By Theorem (2.6.6), $\Pi_{\mathfrak{A}_1}$ is homeomorphic with $\Pi_{\mathfrak{A}}$ plus a "point at infinity" (namely $\mathfrak{A}$), and a similar statement holds for $\Pi_{\mathfrak{C}_1}$ and $\Pi_{\mathfrak{C}}$. According to Theorem (2.7.3), $\mathfrak{C}_1$ is also completely regular. Now apply the result obtained above for the case of an identity and restrict the mapping $\mathfrak{P} \to \mathfrak{P}^\sigma$ to the space $\Pi_{\mathfrak{A}}$. Since $h(\mathfrak{C})$ is precisely the subset of $\Pi_{\mathfrak{A}}$ which maps onto the point at infinity of $\Pi_{\mathfrak{C}_1}$, the desired result follows. An identical proof yields the result for the strong structure spaces $\Xi_{\mathfrak{A}}$ and $\Xi_{\mathfrak{C}}$.

Definition (2.7.6). *An algebra $\mathfrak{A}$ with center $\mathfrak{C}$ is said to be* CENTRAL *provided $\mathfrak{P} \to \mathfrak{P}^\sigma$ is a one-to-one mapping of $\Pi_{\mathfrak{A}}$ into $\Pi_{\mathfrak{C}}$.* (Kaplansky [5].) *It is said to be* WEAKLY CENTRAL *provided $\mathfrak{M} \to \mathfrak{M}^\sigma$ is a one-to-one mapping of $\Xi_{\mathfrak{A}}$ into $\Xi_{\mathfrak{C}}$.* (Misonou [1].)

Lemma (2.7.7). *Let $\mathfrak{A}$ be a Banach algebra and $\mathfrak{P}$ any primitive ideal in $\mathfrak{A}$ which does not contain the center $\mathfrak{C}$ of $\mathfrak{A}$. Then $\mathfrak{P}$ is necessarily modular and $\mathfrak{C}$ contains an identity element for $\mathfrak{A}$ modulo $\mathfrak{P}$.*

Proof. Since the image of $\mathfrak{C}$ in $\mathfrak{A}/\mathfrak{P}$ is contained in the center of $\mathfrak{A}/\mathfrak{P}$, the latter is non-zero and so, by Corollary (2.4.5), is either the real or complex field. It also follows that $\mathfrak{C}$ contains an element e which maps onto the identity element of the center of $\mathfrak{A}/\mathfrak{P}$. Evidently $\mathfrak{A}e\mathfrak{A}(1-e) \subseteq \mathfrak{P}$. Therefore, according to Theorem (2.2.9) (iv), either $\mathfrak{A}e \subseteq \mathfrak{P}$ or $\mathfrak{A}(1-e) \subseteq \mathfrak{P}$. The first inclusion is obviously impossible, and so it follows that $\mathfrak{P}$ is modular with e an identity element for $\mathfrak{A}$ modulo $\mathfrak{P}$.

Theorem (2.7.8). *A central Banach algebra $\mathfrak{A}$ is automatically weakly central and $\Pi_{\mathfrak{A}} = \Xi_{\mathfrak{A}}$.*

Proof. By the above lemma, every primitive ideal $\mathfrak{P}$ is modular and is accordingly contained in a maximal modular 2-sided ideal $\mathfrak{M}$. But then $\mathfrak{P}^\sigma \subseteq \mathfrak{M}^\sigma$ and, since $\mathfrak{P}^\sigma$ is maximal, we have $\mathfrak{P}^\sigma = \mathfrak{M}^\sigma$.

The assumption that $\mathfrak{A}$ be central implies that $\mathfrak{P} = \mathfrak{M}$ and completes the proof.

THEOREM (2.7.9). *Let $\mathfrak{A}$ be a weakly central Banach algebra with a completely regular center $\mathfrak{C}$. Then $\mathfrak{A}$ is also completely regular and $\mathfrak{M} \to \mathfrak{M}^\sigma$ is a homeomorphism of $\Xi_\mathfrak{A}$ into $\Xi_\mathfrak{C}$.*

PROOF. We already know from Theorem (2.7.5) that the mapping $\mathfrak{M} \to \mathfrak{M}^\sigma$ is continuous. In the present case, it is also one-to-one and $\Xi_\mathfrak{C}$ is Hausdorff, so that we conclude immediately that $\Xi_\mathfrak{A}$ is Hausdorff. Next let $\mathfrak{M}_0$ be a fixed point of $\Xi_\mathfrak{A}$ and, by the complete regularity of $\mathfrak{C}$, choose a neighborhood V'_0 of $\mathfrak{M}_0{}^\sigma$ in $\Xi_\mathfrak{C}$ such that the ideal $k(V'_0)$ of $\mathfrak{C}$ is modular. Let e_0 be an element of $\mathfrak{C}$ which is an identity element for $\mathfrak{C}$ modulo $k(V'_0)$. Then e_0 is *a fortiori* an identity element for $\mathfrak{C}$ modulo each $\mathfrak{M}^\sigma \in V'_0$. Using Lemma (2.7.7) we obtain an element e of $\mathfrak{C}$ which is an identity for $\mathfrak{A}$ modulo $\mathfrak{M}$. The element e is also an identity for $\mathfrak{C}$ modulo $\mathfrak{M}^\sigma$. Therefore $e - e_0 \in \mathfrak{M}^\sigma$ and it follows that e_0 is an identity for $\mathfrak{A}$ modulo $\mathfrak{M}$. Since this holds for every $\mathfrak{M}$ such that $\mathfrak{M}^\sigma \in V'_0$, the counter image of V'_0 in $\Xi_\mathfrak{A}$ is a neighborhood V_0 of $\mathfrak{M}_0$ such that $k(V_0)$ is modular. This completes the proof that $\mathfrak{A}$ is completely regular. Finally, we observe that the restriction of the mapping $\mathfrak{M} \to \mathfrak{M}^\sigma$ to the closure of the neighborhood V_0 is a one-to-one continuous mapping of a compact (see Theorem (2.6.4)) Hausdorff space into a Hausdorff space and is therefore bicontinuous. It follows immediately that the mapping $\mathfrak{M} \to \mathfrak{M}^\sigma$ is a homeomorphism of $\Xi_\mathfrak{A}$ into $\Xi_\mathfrak{C}$. This completes the proof.

Throughout the remainder of this section the algebra $\mathfrak{A}$ will be assumed to be completely regular.

THEOREM (2.7.10). *Let F be any closed subset of $\Xi_\mathfrak{A}$. Then F is compact if and only if $k(F)$ is modular.*

PROOF. Since $F = h(k(F))$, modularity of $k(F)$ implies F compact, by Theorem (2.6.4). Therefore assume F compact. For each $\mathfrak{M} \in F$, there exists a neighborhood V such that $k(V)$ is modular. Since F is compact, it is covered by a finite number of such neighborhoods, say $V_1, \cdots, V_n$. Observe that $k(V_1) \cap \cdots \cap k(V_n) \subseteq k(F)$. Moreover, since each $k(V_i)$ is modular, the intersection of these ideals is modular, by Theorem (2.1.1). Therefore $k(F)$ is modular and the theorem is proved.

By Lemma (2.6.9), we have the following corollary to the above theorem.

COROLLARY (2.7.11). *Let $\mathfrak{I}$ be any 2-sided ideal in $\mathfrak{A}$ and let F be any compact subset of $\Xi_{\mathfrak{A}}$ disjoint from $h(\mathfrak{I})$. Then $\mathfrak{I}$ contains an identity for $\mathfrak{A}$ modulo $k(F)$.*

The next theorem gives a "partition of the identity" for completely regular algebras.

THEOREM (2.7.12). *Let F be a compact subset of $\Xi_{\mathfrak{A}}$ which is covered by a finite number of open sets $U_1, \cdots, U_n$. Then there exist elements $e_1, \cdots, e_n$ of $\mathfrak{A}$ such that the element $e_1 + \cdots + e_n$ is an identity modulo $k(F)$ and $e_i \in k(\Xi_{\mathfrak{A}} - U_i)$ for $i = 1, \cdots, n$.*

PROOF. Define $\mathfrak{I}_i = k(\Xi_{\mathfrak{A}} - U_i)$ and set $\mathfrak{I} = \mathfrak{I}_1 + \cdots + \mathfrak{I}_n$. Then, by Lemma (2.6.7),

$$h(\mathfrak{I}) = \bigcap_{i=1}^{n} h(\mathfrak{I}_i) = \bigcap_{i=1}^{n} (\Xi_{\mathfrak{A}} - U_i) = \Xi_{\mathfrak{A}} - \bigcup_{i=1}^{n} U_i.$$

Hence F and $h(\mathfrak{I})$ are disjoint. Since F is compact, $k(F)$ is modular. Therefore, by Lemma (2.6.9), $\mathfrak{I}$ contains an identity e for $\mathfrak{A}$ modulo $k(F)$. Now, since $e \in \mathfrak{I}$, there exist elements $e_i \in \mathfrak{I}_i$ such that $e = e_1 + \cdots + e_n$. This completes the proof.

As in the proof of Theorem (2.6.1), let $\mathfrak{A}_{\mathfrak{M}} = \mathfrak{A}/\mathfrak{M}$, for each $\mathfrak{M} \in \Xi_{\mathfrak{A}}$, and denote by $\Sigma\mathfrak{A}_{\mathfrak{M}}$ the full (normed) direct sum of the algebras $\mathfrak{A}_{\mathfrak{M}}$. If $\mathfrak{A}$ is strongly semi-simple, then the mapping $x \to \hat{x}$, where $\hat{x}(\mathfrak{M}) = x + \mathfrak{M}$, is a continuous isomorphism of $\mathfrak{A}$ with a (normed) subdirect sum $\Sigma'\mathfrak{A}_{\mathfrak{M}}$ of the algebras $\mathfrak{A}_{\mathfrak{M}}$. The subdirect sum $\Sigma'\mathfrak{A}_{\mathfrak{M}}$ is by definition a subalgebra of $\Sigma\,\mathfrak{A}_{\mathfrak{M}}$. When $\mathfrak{A}$ is completely regular, then one can obtain some information as to the "size" of $\Sigma'\mathfrak{A}_{\mathfrak{M}}$ in $\Sigma\,\mathfrak{A}_{\mathfrak{M}}$.

DEFINITION (2.7.13). *Let A be a subset of $\mathfrak{A}$ and f an element of $\Sigma\,\mathfrak{A}_{\mathfrak{M}}$. Then f is said to* BELONG TO A NEAR A POINT $\mathfrak{M} \in \Xi_{\mathfrak{A}}$ *(or* AT INFINITY*) provided there exists a neighborhood V of $\mathfrak{M}$ (or of infinity) and an element $x \in A$ such that $\hat{x}$ coincides with f in V. If f belongs to A near every point of $\Xi_{\mathfrak{A}}$ and at infinity, then f is said to* BELONG LOCALLY TO A.

THEOREM (2.7.14). *Let $\mathfrak{I}$ be a right (or left) ideal in $\mathfrak{A}$. Also let F be a closed subset of $\Xi_{\mathfrak{A}}$ which is covered by open sets $U_0, U_1, \cdots, U_n$ where the sets $U_1, \cdots, U_n$ have compact closure. If $a_0, a_1, \cdots, a_n$ are* *elements of* $\mathfrak{J}$ *such that* $\hat{a}_i(\mathfrak{M}) = \hat{a}_j(\mathfrak{M})$ *for* $\mathfrak{M} \in U_i \cap U_j$ $(i, j = 0, 1, \cdots, n)$, *then there exists an element* $a \in \mathfrak{J}$ *such that* $\hat{a}(\mathfrak{M}) = \hat{a}_i(\mathfrak{M})$ *for* $\mathfrak{M} \in F \cap U_i$ $(i = 0, 1, \cdots, n)$.

PROOF. By Theorem (2.7.12), there exist elements $e_1, \cdots, e_n \in \mathfrak{A}$ such that $e_i \in k(\Xi_{\mathfrak{A}} - U_i)$ for each i, and, if $e = e_1 + \cdots + e_n$, then e is an identity for $\mathfrak{A}$ modulo $k(F - U_0)$. Notice that, for any $\mathfrak{M} \in \Xi_{\mathfrak{A}}$,

$$\hat{e}(\mathfrak{M}) = \sum_{\mathfrak{M} \in U_j} \hat{e}_j(\mathfrak{M}).$$

Define

$$a = a_0(1-e) + a_1e_1 + \cdots + a_ne_n.$$

Then $a \in \mathfrak{J}$ and, for any $\mathfrak{M}$ in $F \cap U_i$ $(i = 0, 1, \cdots, n)$, we have

$$\hat{a}(\mathfrak{M}) = \begin{cases} \hat{a}_i(\mathfrak{M})[1 - \hat{e}(\mathfrak{M}) + \sum\limits_{\mathfrak{M} \in U_j} \hat{e}_j(\mathfrak{M})] = \hat{a}_i(\mathfrak{M}), & \text{if } \mathfrak{M} \in U_0 \\ \hat{a}_i(\mathfrak{M})\hat{e}(\mathfrak{M}) = \hat{a}_i(\mathfrak{M}), \text{ if } \mathfrak{M} \notin U_0, & \end{cases}$$

and the theorem is proved.

THEOREM (2.7.15). *Let* $\mathfrak{J}$ *be a right (or left) ideal in* $\mathfrak{A}$. *If an element* f *of* $\Sigma\, \mathfrak{A}_{\mathfrak{M}}$ *belongs to* $\mathfrak{J}$ *near each point of a compact set* F, *then there exists* $a \in \mathfrak{J}$ *such that* $\hat{a}(\mathfrak{M}) = f(\mathfrak{M})$ *for* $\mathfrak{M} \in F$.

PROOF. Since F is compact, there exists a finite covering of F by open neighborhoods $U_1, \cdots, U_n$ with compact closures and a corresponding finite set of elements $a_1, \cdots, a_n$ in $\mathfrak{J}$ such that $\hat{a}_i(\mathfrak{M}) = f(\mathfrak{M})$ for $\mathfrak{M} \in U_i$, $i = 1, \cdots, n$. Since $\hat{a}_i(\mathfrak{M}) = \hat{a}_j(\mathfrak{M})$ for $\mathfrak{M} \in U_i \cap U_j$ $(i, j = 1, \cdots, n)$, the desired result follows immediately from the preceding theorem.

THEOREM (2.7.16). *Let* $\mathfrak{J}$ *be a right (or left) ideal in* $\mathfrak{A}$. *If an element* f *of* $\Sigma\, \mathfrak{A}_{\mathfrak{M}}$ *belongs locally to* $\mathfrak{J}$, *then there exists* $a \in \mathfrak{J}$ *such that* $\hat{a} = f$.

PROOF. Since f belongs to $\mathfrak{J}$ at infinity, there exists an open set U_0 with compact complement in $\Xi_{\mathfrak{A}}$ and an element $a_0 \in \mathfrak{J}$ such that $\hat{a}_0(\mathfrak{M}) = f(\mathfrak{M})$ for $\mathfrak{M} \in U_0$. Since $\Xi_{\mathfrak{A}} - U_0$ is compact, there exists an open set U_1 with compact closure such that $\Xi_{\mathfrak{A}} - U_0 \subset U_1$. An application of the preceding theorem with $F = \overline{U_1}$ provides an element $a_1 \in \mathfrak{J}$ such that $\hat{a}_1(\mathfrak{M}) = f(\mathfrak{M})$ for $\mathfrak{M} \in \overline{U_1}$. Since U_0 and U_1 cover $\Xi_{\mathfrak{A}}$, the proof is completed by an application of Theorem (2.7.14) with $F = \Xi_{\mathfrak{A}}$.

COROLLARY (2.7.17). *If an element* f *of* $\Sigma\, \mathfrak{A}_{\mathfrak{M}}$ *belongs locally to* $\mathfrak{A}$, *then* $f \in \Sigma' \mathfrak{A}_{\mathfrak{M}}$.

THEOREM (2.7.18). *Let $\mathfrak{I}$ be a 2-sided ideal in $\mathfrak{A}$. Then, for every $a \in \mathfrak{A}$, the function $\hat{a}$ belongs to $\mathfrak{I}$ near every point interior to $h(a)$ or in the complement of $h(\mathfrak{I})$.*

PROOF. If $\mathfrak{M}_0$ is interior to $h(a)$, then $\hat{a}(\mathfrak{M}) = 0$ for every $\mathfrak{M}$ in a neighborhood of $\mathfrak{M}_0$. Since $0 \in \mathfrak{I}$, it follows that $\hat{a}$ belongs to $\mathfrak{I}$ near $\mathfrak{M}_0$. Now, if $\mathfrak{M}_0 \in \Xi_{\mathfrak{A}} - h(\mathfrak{I})$, choose a neighborhood V of $\mathfrak{M}_0$ with compact closure disjoint from $h(\mathfrak{I})$. By Corollary (2.7.11), there exists $u \in \mathfrak{I}$ such that u is an identity for $\mathfrak{A}$ modulo $k(V)$. This implies $\hat{u}(\mathfrak{M}) = 1$ for $\mathfrak{M} \in V$. Hence $\widehat{ua}(\mathfrak{M}) = \hat{a}(\mathfrak{M})$ for $\mathfrak{M} \in V$. Since $ua \in \mathfrak{I}$, this means that $\hat{a}$ belongs to $\mathfrak{I}$ near $\mathfrak{M}_0$ and completes the proof of the theorem.

COROLLARY (2.7.19). *If $\mathfrak{A}$ is strongly semi-simple, then an element $a \in \mathfrak{A}$ will belong to the ideal $\mathfrak{I}$ if and only if $\hat{a}$ belongs to $\mathfrak{I}$ near every point of $h(\mathfrak{I})$ and the point at infinity.*

COROLLARY (2.7.20). *If $\mathfrak{A}$ is strongly semi-simple and U is any open set which contains $h(\mathfrak{I})$ and has a compact complement, then $k(U) \subseteq \mathfrak{I}$.*

THEOREM (2.7.21). *Let $F_0, F_1, \cdots, F_n$ be disjoint closed subsets of of $\Xi_{\mathfrak{A}}$ with $F_1, \cdots, F_n$ compact. If $a_0, a_1, \cdots, a_n$ are arbitrary elements of $\mathfrak{A}$, then there exists a single element $a \in \mathfrak{A}$ such that $\hat{a}(\mathfrak{M}) = \hat{a}_i(\mathfrak{M})$, for $\mathfrak{M} \in F_i$, $i = 0, 1, \cdots, n$.*

PROOF. Let $F = F_0 \cup \cdots \cup F_n$ and define $\mathfrak{A}' = \mathfrak{A}/k(F)$. Then, by Theorem (2.6.6), $\Xi_{\mathfrak{A}'} = F$ and, by Theorem (2.7.2), $\mathfrak{A}'$ is also completely regular. Let $a'_i = a_i + k(F)$ and, regarding F_i as a subset of $\Xi_{\mathfrak{A}'}$, define $f(\mathfrak{M}) = \hat{a}'_i(\mathfrak{M})$ for $\mathfrak{M} \in F_i$ $(i = 0, 1, \cdots, n)$. Then f belongs locally to $\mathfrak{A}'$. Therefore, by Corollary (2.7.17), there exists $a' \in \mathfrak{A}'$ such that $\hat{a}'(\mathfrak{M}) = f(\mathfrak{M})$ for all $\mathfrak{M} \in \Xi_{\mathfrak{A}'}$. Now any element $a \in \mathfrak{A}$ such that $a' = a + k(F)$ has the property $\hat{a}(\mathfrak{M}) = \hat{a}_i(\mathfrak{M})$ for $\mathfrak{M} \in F_i$ $(i = 0, 1, \cdots, n)$. This proves the theorem.

Let F be an arbitrary hull in $\Xi_{\mathfrak{A}}$. There are, in general, many 2-sided ideals in $\mathfrak{A}$ with hull equal to F. One such ideal, which is maximal with respect to the property of having F as hull, is the kernel $k(F)$. In the next theorem we show that, if $\mathfrak{A}$ is strongly semi-simple as well as completely regular, then there also exists a 2-sided ideal which is minimal with respect to having F as hull. It is convenient first to make a definition.

DEFINITION (2.7.22). *Let F be any closed set in $\Xi_{\mathfrak{A}}$. Define $J(F)$ to be the set-theoretic union of all ideals $k(U)$, where U is any open set* *containing* F. *Define* $J(F, \infty)$ *to be the union of all ideals* $k(U)$, *where* U *is any open set containing* F *and having compact complement. If* F *is empty, we write* $J(F, \infty) = J(\infty)$ *and, if* F *consists of a single point* $\mathfrak{M}$, *we write* $J(F, \infty) = J(\mathfrak{M}, \infty)$.

Notice that, if U_1 and U_2 are open sets containing F, then $U_1 \cap U_2$ is also an open set containing F and will have a compact complement in case U_1 and U_2 do. Since $k(U_1)+k(U_2) \subseteq k(U_1 \cap U_2)$, it follows that $J(F)$, $J(F, \infty)$ and $J(\infty)$ are 2-sided ideals in $\mathfrak{A}$. Also $J(F, \infty) \subseteq J(\infty)$ for all F, and $J(F, \infty) = J(F) \cap J(\infty)$.

THEOREM (2.7.23). *If* $\mathfrak{A}$ *is strongly semi-simple, then* $J(F, \infty)$ *is minimal among those 2-sided ideals in* $\mathfrak{A}$ *with hull equal to* F.

PROOF. We prove first that $h(J(F, \infty)) = F$. It is obvious that $F \subseteq h(J(F, \infty))$. Therefore consider any point $\mathfrak{M}$ of $\Xi_{\mathfrak{A}}$ not in F and choose a neighborhood V of $\mathfrak{M}$ which has a compact closure disjoint from F. Let U be the complement of the closure of V. Then $k(U) \subseteq J(F, \infty)$, so that $h(J(F, \infty)) \subseteq h(k(U)) = \Xi_{\mathfrak{A}} - V$. Hence $\mathfrak{M} \notin h(J(F, \infty))$ and it follows that $h(J(F, \infty)) = F$. Next let $\mathfrak{J}$ be any ideal in $\mathfrak{A}$ with $h(\mathfrak{J}) = F$ and let U be any open set containing F and possessing a compact complement. By Corollary (2.7.20), we have $k(U) \subseteq \mathfrak{J}$. Therefore $J(F, \infty) \subseteq \mathfrak{J}$ and the theorem is proved.

COROLLARY (2.7.24). *If* $\mathfrak{A}$ *is a Banach algebra, then the closure of* $J(F, \infty)$ *is the smallest closed 2-sided ideal in* $\mathfrak{A}$ *with hull equal to* F.

THEOREM (2.7.25). *If* $\mathfrak{A}$ *is strongly semi-simple, then, in order for every proper 2-sided ideal in* $\mathfrak{A}$ *(modular or not) to be contained in some maximal modular 2-sided ideal, it is necessary and sufficient that* $J(\infty) = \mathfrak{A}$. *If* $\mathfrak{A}$ *is a Banach algebra, then the condition* $\overline{J(\infty)} = \mathfrak{A}$ *is necessary and sufficient for every proper closed 2-sided ideal to be contained in some maximal modular 2-sided ideal.*

PROOF. Observe that an ideal is contained in a maximal modular 2-sided ideal if and only if its hull is non-vacuous. Since the hull of the ideal $J(\infty)$ is vacuous, the necessity of the condition is immediate. On the other hand, if $\mathfrak{J}$ is any 2-sided ideal in $\mathfrak{A}$ with vacuous hull, then, by the preceding theorem, $J(\infty) \subseteq \mathfrak{J}$. Therefore, if $J(\infty) = \mathfrak{A}$, then $\mathfrak{J}$ is not proper. This proves that the condition $J(\infty) = \mathfrak{A}$ is sufficient. Finally, if $\mathfrak{A}$ is a Banach algebra, then $\overline{J(\infty)}$ is a closed 2-sided ideal with vacuous hull. Hence the condition $\overline{J(\infty)} = \mathfrak{A}$ is necessary for every proper closed 2-sided ideal to be contained in some maximal modular 2-sided ideal. Now, if $\mathfrak{J}$ is a 2-sided ideal with vacuous hull, then again $J(\infty) \subseteq \mathfrak{I}$ and, if $\mathfrak{I}$ is closed, then $\overline{J(\infty)} \subseteq \mathfrak{I}$. If $\overline{J(\infty)} = \mathfrak{A}$, then $\mathfrak{I}$ cannot be proper. This proves the sufficiency.

The L_1 group algebra of a locally compact abelian group satisfies the condition $\overline{J(\infty)} = \mathfrak{A}$. The proof of this fact, along with a proof of the fact that the L_1-algebra is completely regular, constitutes the major part of a proof of the Wiener Tauberian Theorem. (See Loomis [1, § 37A] and Appendix, A.3.2.) For this reason, it is appropriate to call a Banach algebra TAUBERIAN if it satisfies the condition $\overline{J(\infty)} = \mathfrak{A}$. (Willcox [1].)

DEFINITION (2.7.26). *An ideal* $\mathfrak{I}$ *is said to be* PRIMARY IN $\mathfrak{A}$ *if it is contained in exactly one maximal modular* 2*-sided ideal. The algebra* $\mathfrak{A}$ *is called a* PRIMARY ALGEBRA *if it contains exactly one maximal* 2*-sided ideal.*

That an ideal $\mathfrak{I}$ is primary in $\mathfrak{A}$ means that $h(\mathfrak{I})$ reduces to a single point of $\Xi_{\mathfrak{A}}$. That an algebra $\mathfrak{A}$ is a primary algebra means that $\Xi_{\mathfrak{A}}$ reduces to a single point. Note that $\mathfrak{A}$ will be a primary algebra if and only if (0) is a primary ideal in $\mathfrak{A}$. If $\mathfrak{I}$ is any ideal which is primary in $\mathfrak{A}$, then it is easy to verify that $\mathfrak{A}/\mathfrak{I}$ is a primary algebra. Every maximal modular 2-sided ideal is primary in $\mathfrak{A}$. If $\mathfrak{A}$ is strongly semi-simple and completely regular and if $\mathfrak{M}$ is any element of $\Xi_{\mathfrak{A}}$, then $J(\mathfrak{M}, \infty)$ is primary in $\mathfrak{A}$ and is minimal with this property.

A question which arises naturally in the structure theory of ideals is whether or not an ideal is equal to an intersection of maximal modular 2-sided ideals. This question is, of course, significant only for 2-sided ideals with non-vacuous hull and, in the case of a Banach algebra, only for closed ideals. Evidently an ideal $\mathfrak{I}$ has this property if and only if it is a kernel or, more precisely, if and only if $\mathfrak{I} = k(h(\mathfrak{I}))$. A Banach algebra, in which every closed 2-sided ideal with non-vacuous hull is a kernel, has been called an N-algebra. (Šilov [5], Willcox [1].) Note that, if $\mathfrak{A}$ is a strongly semi-simple completely regular Banach algebra, then, by Corollary (2.7.24), $\mathfrak{I} = k(h(\mathfrak{I}))$ if and only if $\overline{J(h(\mathfrak{I}), \infty)} = k(h(\mathfrak{I}))$. Another property of an algebra, which is relevant to the ideal structure, says that every closed ideal, primary in $\mathfrak{A}$, is maximal. In other words, every closed primary ideal is a kernel. Banach algebras with this property have been called N*-ALGEBRAS (Šilov [5], Willcox [1]). In a strongly semi-simple Banach algebra which is completely regular, this is equivalent to the condition

$\overline{J(\mathfrak{M}, \infty)} = \mathfrak{M}$ and is thus related to the condition $\overline{J(\infty)} = \mathfrak{A}$. It is obvious that an N-algebra is automatically an N*-algebra.

We now consider the above notions in some detail for a strongly semi-simple, completely regular Banach algebra $\mathfrak{A}$. In this case, $\mathfrak{A}$ is continuously isomorphic with a sub-direct sum $\Sigma'\mathfrak{A}_{\mathfrak{M}}$, $\mathfrak{M} \in \Xi_{\mathfrak{A}}$. Define $|x| = \text{lub}\ \|\hat{x}(\mathfrak{M})\|$, $\mathfrak{M} \in \Xi_{\mathfrak{A}}$. Then $\mathfrak{A}$ is a normed algebra under $|x|$ and $|x| \leqslant \|x\|$ for all x. In general, $\mathfrak{A}$ will not be complete with respect to $|x|$, but, if it is, then $|x|$ and $\|x\|$ are equivalent norms. We have another structure theorem for this case. First associate with each $\mathfrak{M}$ in $\Xi_{\mathfrak{A}}$ the minimal closed primary ideal $\overline{J(\mathfrak{M}, \infty)}$ and let $\mathfrak{B}_{\mathfrak{M}} = \mathfrak{A}/\overline{J(\mathfrak{M}, \infty)}$. Then $\mathfrak{B}_{\mathfrak{M}}$ is a primary algebra and the structure theorem can be stated as follows.

THEOREM (2.7.27). *The algebra $\mathfrak{A}$ is continuously isomorphic with a normed subdirect sum $\Sigma'\mathfrak{B}_{\mathfrak{M}}$ of the primary algebras $\mathfrak{B}_{\mathfrak{M}}$, $\mathfrak{M} \in \Xi_{\mathfrak{A}}$.*

PROOF. The isomorphism is given by $x \to \tilde{x}$, where $\tilde{x}(\overline{J(\mathfrak{M}, \infty)})$ is the image of x in $\mathfrak{A}/\overline{J(\mathfrak{M}, \infty)}$. Since $\|\tilde{x}(\overline{J(\mathfrak{M}, \infty)})\| \leqslant \|x\|$, it follows that the mapping $x \to \tilde{x}$ takes $\mathfrak{A}$ continuously onto a normed sub-direct sum of the algebras $\mathfrak{B}_{\mathfrak{M}}$. Moreover, since $\overline{J(\mathfrak{M}, \infty)} \subseteq \mathfrak{M}$ and $\mathfrak{A}$ is strongly semi-simple, the mapping $x \to \tilde{x}$ is an isomorphism. This completes the proof.

If we define $|x|' = \sup \|\tilde{x}(\overline{J(\mathfrak{M}, \infty)})\|$ for $\mathfrak{M} \in \Xi_{\mathfrak{A}}$, then $|x|' \leqslant \|x\|$ for all x in $\mathfrak{A}$. Again, $\mathfrak{A}$ is a, not necessarily complete, normed algebra under $|x|'$. If $\mathfrak{A}$ is complete under $|x|'$, then this norm is equivalent to $\|x\|$. In this case, the algebra $\mathfrak{A}$ has been defined to be of *type* C (Šilov [5], Willcox [1]). Since the norm $\|\tilde{x}(\overline{J(\mathfrak{M}, \infty)})\|$ is equal to the infimum of numbers $\|x+p\|$, where p ranges over $\overline{J(\mathfrak{M}, \infty)}$, and the norm $\|\hat{x}(\mathfrak{M})\|$ is equal to the infimum of numbers $\|x+m\|$, where m ranges over $\mathfrak{M}$, it follows from the inclusion $\overline{J(\mathfrak{M}, \infty)} \subseteq \mathfrak{M}$ that $\|\hat{x}(\mathfrak{M})\| \leqslant \|\tilde{x}(\overline{J(\mathfrak{M}, \infty)})\|$. Therefore $|x| \leqslant |x|'$ for all x in $\mathfrak{A}$. Thus the condition that $|x|$ and $\|x\|$ be equivalent implies equivalence of $|x|'$ and $\|x\|$. Hence equivalence of $|x|'$ and $\|x\|$ is, in general, a weaker restriction than equivalence of $|x|$ and $\|x\|$. If $\mathfrak{A}$ is an N*-algebra (that is, $\overline{J(\mathfrak{M}, \infty)} = \mathfrak{M}$), then, of course, $|x|' = |x|$.

For the next theorem, a definition is needed.

DEFINITION (2.7.28). *Let s be a scalar-valued function defined on $\Xi_{\mathfrak{A}}$. Then the sub-direct sum $\Sigma'\mathfrak{A}_{\mathfrak{M}}$ is said to be* CLOSED UNDER MULTIPLICATION BY s *provided, for every $f \in \Sigma'\mathfrak{A}_{\mathfrak{M}}$, there exists $g \in \Sigma'\mathfrak{A}_{\mathfrak{M}}$ such that $g(\mathfrak{M}) = s(\mathfrak{M})f(\mathfrak{M})$ for all $\mathfrak{M} \in \Xi_{\mathfrak{A}}$. We write $g = sf$.*

THEOREM (2.7.29). *Assume that the two norms* $|x|$, $\|x\|$ *are equivalent in* $\mathfrak{A}$ *and that the subdirect sum* $\Sigma'\mathfrak{A}_{\mathfrak{M}}$ *is closed under multiplication by bounded real-valued continuous functions on* $\Xi_{\mathfrak{A}}$. *Then the condition,* $\overline{J(\mathfrak{M}, \infty)} = \mathfrak{M}$ *for every point* $\mathfrak{M}$ *in* $\Xi_{\mathfrak{A}}$, *implies that* $\overline{J(F, \infty)} = k(F)$ *for every non-vacuous closed set* F *in* $\Xi_{\mathfrak{A}}$.

PROOF. Observe first that, since $J(\mathfrak{M}, \infty) \subseteq J(\infty)$ and $\overline{J(\mathfrak{M}, \infty)} = \mathfrak{M}$, it follows that $\overline{J(\infty)}$ contains every $\mathfrak{M}$ in $\Xi_{\mathfrak{A}}$. In particular, since F is non-vacuous, $k(F) \subseteq \overline{J(\infty)}$. Thus, if x is an arbitrary element of $k(F)$ and $\epsilon > 0$, then there exists an open set U_0 with compact complement and an element $u_0 \in k(U_0)$ such that $\|u_0 - x\| < \epsilon$. Let $F_0 = F - U_0$. Then F_0 is compact. Since $\overline{J(\mathfrak{M}, \infty)} = \mathfrak{M}$, there exists, for each $\mathfrak{M} \in F_0$, a neighborhood $U_{\mathfrak{M}}$ of $\mathfrak{M}$ and an element $u_{\mathfrak{M}} \in k(U_{\mathfrak{M}})$ such that $\|u_{\mathfrak{M}} - x\| < \epsilon$. We can also assume $U_{\mathfrak{M}}$ to have a compact closure. Since F_0 is compact, it is covered by a finite number of these neighborhoods $U_{\mathfrak{M}}$. Let $U_1, \cdots, U_n$ be such a finite set of neighborhoods and denote the associated elements of their kernels by $u_1, \cdots, u_n$. Since the union $U_0 \cup U_1 \cup \cdots \cup U_n$ contains F and has a compact complement, there exists an open set U_{n+1} containing this complement whose closure is compact and disjoint from F. We thus obtain a covering $U_0, U_1, \cdots, U_{n+1}$ of $\Xi_{\mathfrak{A}}$ where $U_1, \cdots, U_{n+1}$ have compact closures. By a well-known real-variable result, there is associated with this covering a partition of the identity into continuous functions. In other words, there exist real continuous functions $s_0, s_1, \cdots, s_{n+1}$ on $\Xi_{\mathfrak{A}}$ which satisfy the conditions: $s_i(\mathfrak{M}) = 0$, for $\mathfrak{M} \notin U_i$, $0 \leqslant s_i(\mathfrak{M}) \leqslant 1$ and $\Sigma\, s_i(\mathfrak{M}) = 1$, for all $\mathfrak{M}$. Define the element

$$u = s_0 u_0 + s_1 u_1 + \cdots + s_n u_n + s_{n+1} x,$$

and let $U = \Xi_{\mathfrak{A}} - \bar{U}_{n+1}$. Then clearly $u \in k(U)$. Furthermore, U is an open set which contains F and has a compact complement. Hence $u \in J(F, \infty)$. Moreover, for every $\mathfrak{M} \in \Xi_{\mathfrak{A}}$,

$$\begin{aligned}
\|\hat{u}(\mathfrak{M}) - \hat{x}(\mathfrak{M})\| &= \left\| \sum_{i=0}^{n} s_i(\mathfrak{M})\hat{u}_i(\mathfrak{M}) + s_{n+1}(\mathfrak{M})\hat{x}(\mathfrak{M}) - \sum_{i=0}^{n+1} s_i(\mathfrak{M})\hat{x}(\mathfrak{M}) \right\| \\
&= \left\| \sum_{i=0}^{n} s_i(\mathfrak{M})(\hat{u}_i(\mathfrak{M}) - \hat{x}(\mathfrak{M})) \right\| \\
&\leqslant \sum_{i=0}^{n} s_i(\mathfrak{M}) \|\hat{u}_i(\mathfrak{M}) - \hat{x}(\mathfrak{M})\| \\
&\leqslant \sum_{i=0}^{n} s_i(\mathfrak{M}) \|u_i - x\| < \epsilon.
\end{aligned}$$

Therefore, $|u-x| < \epsilon$. Since the two norms $|x|$ and $\|x\|$ are equivalent, it follows that $x \in \overline{J(F, \infty)}$ and hence that $k(F) \subseteq \overline{J(F, \infty)}$. On the other hand, we always have $\overline{J(F, \infty)} \subseteq k(F)$, so that the theorem is proved.

Corollary (2.7.30). *Under the hypotheses of the theorem, the condition that $\mathfrak{A}$ be an $N^\star$-algebra already implies that $\mathfrak{A}$ is an N-algebra.*

Another definition is needed for the next theorem.

Definition (2.7.31). *An element f of the normed full direct sum $\Sigma\, \mathfrak{A}_{\mathfrak{M}}$ is said to be* continuous at zero *if, for every $\mathfrak{M}_0 \in \Xi_{\mathfrak{A}}$ with $f(\mathfrak{M}_0) = 0$ and any $\epsilon > 0$, there exists a neighborhood V of $\mathfrak{M}_0$ in $\Xi_{\mathfrak{A}}$ such that $\|f(\mathfrak{M})\| < \epsilon$ for each $\mathfrak{M} \in V$. Also, f is said to* vanish at infinity *if, for any $\epsilon > 0$, there exists a compact set F in $\Xi_{\mathfrak{A}}$ such that $\|f(\mathfrak{M})\| < \epsilon$ for each $\mathfrak{M} \notin F$.*

Theorem (2.7.32). *Let $\mathfrak{A}$ be a strongly semi-simple completely regular Banach algebra such that*

(i) *the norms $|x|$ and $\|x\|$ are equivalent,*

(ii) *$\Sigma'\mathfrak{A}_{\mathfrak{M}}$ is closed under multiplication by bounded real-valued continuous functions on $\Xi_{\mathfrak{A}}$, and*

(iii) *the functions $\hat{x}$ in $\Sigma'\mathfrak{A}_{\mathfrak{M}}$ are continuous at zero and vanish at infinity.*

Then $\overline{J(F, \infty)} = k(F)$, for every closed set F in $\Xi_{\mathfrak{A}}$. In other words, $\mathfrak{A}$ is Tauberian ($\overline{J(\infty)} = \mathfrak{A}$) and is an N-algebra.

Proof. If we prove that $\overline{J(\infty)} = \mathfrak{A}$, and $\overline{J(\mathfrak{M}, \infty)} = \mathfrak{M}$, for every $\mathfrak{M} \in \Xi_{\mathfrak{A}}$, then the theorem will follow from the preceding theorem. Fix $\mathfrak{M}_0$ and let x be any element of $\mathfrak{M}_0$. Then, since $\hat{x}$ is continuous at zero and vanishes at infinity, there exists, for $\epsilon > 0$, an open set V with compact complement such that $\mathfrak{M}_0 \in V$ and $\|\hat{x}(\mathfrak{M})\| < \epsilon$ for every $\mathfrak{M} \in V$. Next choose an open set U, with compact complement, such that $\mathfrak{M}_0 \in U \subset \bar{U} \subset V$. Then there exists a bounded continuous real function s such that $0 \leqslant s(\mathfrak{M}) \leqslant 1$, for all $\mathfrak{M}$, $s(\mathfrak{M}) = 1$, for $\mathfrak{M} \notin V$, and $s(\mathfrak{M}) = 0$, for $\mathfrak{M} \in U$. Let $u = sx$. Then $u \in k(U)$ and

$$\|\hat{x}(\mathfrak{M}) - \hat{u}(\mathfrak{M})\| = \begin{cases} 0 & , \quad \mathfrak{M} \notin V. \\ |s(\mathfrak{M})|\|\hat{x}(\mathfrak{M})\| < \epsilon, & \mathfrak{M} \in V. \end{cases}$$

Therefore $|x-u| < \epsilon$ and equivalence of the norms $|x|$, $\|x\|$ implies $x \in \overline{J(\mathfrak{M}, \infty)}$. Finally, if x is any element of $\mathfrak{A}$, the above argument can be repeated, with U and V open sets just with compact complement, to obtain $\overline{J(\infty)} = \mathfrak{A}$. This completes the proof.

The problem of constructing completely regular Banach algebras out of either simple Banach algebras with an identity or primary Banach algebras is obviously suggested by Theorem (2.6.1) (ii) and Theorem (2.7.27). The idea is to consider a subdirect sum $\Sigma'\mathfrak{A}_\lambda$ of, say, simple Banach algebras $\mathfrak{A}_\lambda$ with identity and impose appropriate conditions so as to obtain a completely regular Banach algebra. Since only partial results are known in this direction for the general case, we omit further discussion on the problem. (See Silov [5] and Willcox [1].)

The von Neumann notion of "regularity" for a ring, referred to at the beginning of this section, is simply that every element x of the ring possess a RELATIVE INVERSE y such that $xyx = x$. Kaplansky [3] has proved that a Banach algebra which is regular in this sense must be finite dimensional. On the other hand, a large class of Banach algebras (including, for example, all W*-algebras) are "almost regular" in the sense that elements which possess relative inverses are dense in the algebra. (See Rickart [1].)

§ **8. Annihilator Algebras.** Let $\mathscr{E}$ be an arbitrary subset of an algebra $\mathfrak{A}$ and set

$$\mathscr{A}_l(\mathscr{E}) = \{x : x \in \mathfrak{A},\, x\mathscr{E} = (0)\}$$
$$\mathscr{A}_r(\mathscr{E}) = \{x : x \in \mathfrak{A},\, \mathscr{E}x = (0)\}.$$

Then $\mathscr{A}_l(\mathscr{E})$ is called the LEFT ANNIHILATOR and $\mathscr{A}_r(\mathscr{E})$ the RIGHT ANNIHILATOR of $\mathscr{E}$. It is obvious that $\mathscr{A}_l(\mathscr{E})$ is a left ideal and $\mathscr{A}_r(\mathscr{E})$ is a right ideal. If $\mathfrak{A}$ is a normed algebra, then these ideals are closed. Observe that $\mathscr{E} \subseteq \mathscr{A}_r(\mathscr{A}_l(\mathscr{E}))$, $\mathscr{E} \subseteq \mathscr{A}_l(\mathscr{A}_r(\mathscr{E}))$ and, if $\mathscr{E}_1 \subseteq \mathscr{E}_2$, then $\mathscr{A}_l(\mathscr{E}_2) \subseteq \mathscr{A}_l(\mathscr{E}_1)$, $\mathscr{A}_r(\mathscr{E}_2) \subseteq \mathscr{A}_r(\mathscr{E}_1)$. A left ideal $\mathfrak{L}$ is called a LEFT ANNIHILATOR IDEAL if it has the form $\mathfrak{L} = \mathscr{A}_l(\mathscr{E})$ for some set $\mathscr{E} \subseteq \mathfrak{A}$. Similarly, a right ideal of the form $\mathscr{A}_r(\mathscr{E})$ is called a RIGHT ANNIHILATOR IDEAL. It is easily verified that an ideal $\mathfrak{L}$ is a left annihilator ideal if and only if $\mathfrak{L} = \mathscr{A}_l(\mathscr{A}_r(\mathfrak{L}))$. Similarly, $\mathfrak{R}$ is a right annihilator ideal if and only if $\mathfrak{R} = \mathscr{A}_r(\mathscr{A}_l(\mathfrak{R}))$. Finally, we note that the left (right) annihilator of a left (right) ideal is a 2-sided ideal.

The class of algebras to be considered in this section can now be defined. They were introduced by Bonsall and Goldie [2], who obtained the main results concerning them.

DEFINITION (2.8.1). *A Banach algebra $\mathfrak{A}$ is called an* ANNIHILATOR ALGEBRA *if, for arbitrary closed left ideal $\mathfrak{L}$ and closed right ideal $\mathfrak{R}$ in $\mathfrak{A}$, both of the following conditions are satisfied:*

(i) $\mathscr{A}_r(\mathfrak{L}) = (0)$ *if and only if* $\mathfrak{L} = \mathfrak{A}$,
(ii) $\mathscr{A}_l(\mathfrak{R}) = (0)$ *if and only if* $\mathfrak{R} = \mathfrak{A}$.

If every closed (right or left) ideal in $\mathfrak{A}$ is an annihilator ideal, then $\mathfrak{A}$ is called a DUAL ALGEBRA.

The notion of a dual algebra was introduced by Kaplansky. It is obvious that a dual algebra is automatically an annihilator algebra. These concepts clearly apply to any topological algebra and, as such, include an even wider class of algebras (Kaplansky [4]). The objective here is to establish some structure theorems for annihilator Banach algebras. Although we assume throughout that $\mathfrak{A}$ is a semi-simple complex annihilator Banach algebra, many of the results can also be established for more general topological algebras. (See Wolfson [5].)

LEMMA (2.8.2). *Let u be any element of $\mathfrak{A}$. Then* $\mathscr{A}_l((u-1)\mathfrak{A}) = \{x : xu = x\}$, $\mathscr{A}_l(u\mathfrak{A}) = \{x : xu = 0\}$. *If* $u^2 = u$, *then* $\mathscr{A}_l((u-1)\mathfrak{A}) = \mathfrak{A}u$, $\mathscr{A}_l(u\mathfrak{A}) = \mathfrak{A}(u-1)$. *Similar statements hold for the right annihilators of* $\mathfrak{A}(u-1)$ *and* $\mathfrak{A}u$.

PROOF. The proof depends only on the property $\mathscr{A}_l(\mathfrak{A}) = \mathscr{A}_r(\mathfrak{A}) = (0)$. It is obvious that $\{x : xu = x\} \subseteq \mathscr{A}_l((u-1)\mathfrak{A})$. On the other hand, if $x \in \mathscr{A}_l((u-1)\mathfrak{A})$, then $(xu-x)\mathfrak{A} = x(u-1)\mathfrak{A} = (0)$. Hence $xu-x \in \mathscr{A}_l(\mathfrak{A})$ and this implies $xu = x$. If $u^2 = u$, then it is immediate that $\mathfrak{A}u = \{x : xu = x\}$. Similar proofs hold for $\mathscr{A}_l(u\mathfrak{A})$ and the right annihilators.

COROLLARY (2.8.3). *For any* $u \in \mathfrak{A}$, $u \in \mathscr{A}_r(\mathscr{A}_l(u\mathfrak{A}))$. *If $\mathfrak{A}$ is dual, then* $u \in \overline{u\mathfrak{A}} \cap \overline{\mathfrak{A}u}$.

LEMMA (2.8.4). *Let u be any right quasi-singular element of $\mathfrak{A}$. Then there exists a non-zero element $v \in \mathfrak{A}$ such that $vu = v$. An analogous result holds if u is left quasi-singular.*

PROOF. Since $\mathfrak{A}$ is a Banach algebra and u is right quasi-singular, the closure of $(u-1)\mathfrak{A}$ is a proper ideal in $\mathfrak{A}$. Since $\mathfrak{A}$ is an annihilator algebra, $\mathscr{A}_l((u-1)\mathfrak{A})$ contains a non-zero element v which, by the preceding lemma, has the property $vu = v$.

THEOREM (2.8.5). *If $\mathfrak{R}$ is a maximal-closed right ideal in $\mathfrak{A}$, then $\mathfrak{R}$ is a maximal modular right ideal, $\mathscr{A}_l(\mathfrak{R})$ is a minimal left ideal, and* $\mathfrak{R} = \mathscr{A}_r(\mathscr{A}_l(\mathfrak{R}))$. *Similarly, if $\mathfrak{L}$ is a minimal left ideal in $\mathfrak{A}$, then $\mathscr{A}_r(\mathfrak{L})$ is a maximal modular right ideal and* $\mathfrak{L} = \mathscr{A}_l(\mathscr{A}_r(\mathfrak{L}))$.

PROOF. Let u be any non-zero element of $\mathscr{A}_l(\mathfrak{R})$. Then $\mathfrak{R} \subseteq \mathscr{A}_r(\mathscr{A}_l(\mathfrak{R})) \subseteq \mathscr{A}_r(\mathfrak{A}u)$. Since $\mathfrak{A}u \neq (0)$, $\mathscr{A}_r(\mathfrak{A}u)$ is a proper closed right ideal so that $\mathfrak{R} = \mathscr{A}_r(\mathfrak{A}u)$, by the maximality of $\mathfrak{R}$. Because $\mathfrak{A}$ is semi-simple, the ideal $\mathfrak{A}u$ cannot be quasi-regular and must accordingly contain a quasi-singular element e. We prove that $e^2 = e$. Suppose that $e^2 \neq e$. Then the above argument gives $\mathfrak{R} = \mathscr{A}_r(\mathfrak{A}(e^2-e))$. By Lemma (2.8.4), there exists $v \in \mathfrak{A}$ such that $ev = v \neq 0$. Since

$(e^2-e)v = 0$, it follows that $v \in \mathfrak{R}$. But this implies $v = ev = 0$ and contradicts $v \neq 0$. Therefore $e^2 = e$. Again we have $\mathfrak{R} = \mathscr{A}_r(\mathfrak{A}e)$ and, by Lemma (2.8.2), $\mathfrak{R} = (e-1)\mathfrak{A}$ and $\mathscr{A}_l(\mathfrak{R}) = \mathfrak{A}e$. It follows that $\mathfrak{R}$ is modular and, being maximal-closed, is therefore maximal. Furthermore,

$$\mathscr{A}_l(\mathfrak{R}) = \mathfrak{A}e \subseteq \mathfrak{A}u \subseteq \mathscr{A}_l(\mathfrak{R})$$

and hence $\mathfrak{A}u = \mathscr{A}_l(\mathfrak{R})$, for every non-zero $u \in \mathscr{A}_l(\mathfrak{R})$. In other words, $\mathscr{A}_l(\mathfrak{R})$ is a minimal left ideal.

Now let $\mathfrak{L}$ be a minimal left ideal in $\mathfrak{A}$. Since $\mathfrak{A}$ is semi-simple, $\mathfrak{L} = \mathfrak{A}e$, where $e^2 = e$. Hence, by Lemma (2.8.2), $\mathscr{A}_r(\mathfrak{L}) = (e-1)\mathfrak{A}$ and $\mathscr{A}_l(\mathscr{A}_r(\mathfrak{L})) = \mathfrak{L}$. Let $\mathfrak{R}$ be any proper right ideal containing $(e-1)\mathfrak{A}$. Then $\mathfrak{R}$ is modular so that its closure is also proper. Therefore $\mathscr{A}_l(\mathfrak{R}) \neq 0$. Since $\mathscr{A}_l(\mathfrak{R}) \subseteq \mathscr{A}_l((e-1)\mathfrak{A}) = \mathfrak{A}e$, it follows that $\mathscr{A}_l(\mathfrak{R}) = \mathfrak{A}e$. Therefore

$$\mathfrak{R} \subseteq \mathscr{A}_r(\mathscr{A}_l(\mathfrak{R})) = \mathscr{A}_r(\mathfrak{A}e) = (e-1)\mathfrak{A}.$$

In other words, $(e-1)\mathfrak{A}$ is a maximal right ideal.

LEMMA (2.8.6). *Every non-zero left ideal in $\mathfrak{A}$ contains a minimal left ideal.*

PROOF. Let $\mathfrak{L}$ be a left ideal in $\mathfrak{A}$ which does not contain a minimal left ideal. We prove that $\mathfrak{L} = (0)$. Let $\mathfrak{R}$ be any maximal modular right ideal in $\mathfrak{A}$. By Theorem (2.8.5), $\mathfrak{R} = \mathscr{A}_r(\mathscr{A}_l(\mathfrak{R}))$ and $\mathscr{A}_l(\mathfrak{R}) = \mathfrak{A}e$, where $e^2 = e$ and $\mathfrak{A}e$ is a minimal left ideal. Since $\mathfrak{A}eu$ is either a minimal left ideal or zero for each $u \in \mathfrak{A}$ (see the proof of Lemma (2.1.11)), and since $\mathfrak{L}$ is assumed not to contain a minimal left ideal, it follows that $\mathfrak{A}e\mathfrak{L} = (0)$. Therefore $\mathfrak{L} \subseteq \mathscr{A}_r(\mathfrak{A}e) = \mathfrak{R}$. In other words, $\mathfrak{L}$ is contained in every maximal modular right ideal and so must reduce to zero by the semi-simplicity.

COROLLARY (2.8.7). *Every closed left ideal in $\mathfrak{A}$ is contained in a maximal modular left ideal.*

LEMMA (2.8.8). *Let $\mathfrak{L}$ be a minimal left ideal in $\mathfrak{A}$. Then the smallest closed 2-sided ideal $\mathfrak{J}$ which contains $\mathfrak{L}$ is minimal-closed.*

PROOF. Let $\mathfrak{J}'$ be a closed 2-sided ideal contained in $\mathfrak{J}$. Then $\mathfrak{J}' \cap \mathfrak{L}$ is a left ideal contained in $\mathfrak{L}$. Therefore, either $\mathfrak{J}' \cap \mathfrak{L} = (0)$ or $\mathfrak{J}' \cap \mathfrak{L} = \mathfrak{L}$. In the latter case, $\mathfrak{L} \subseteq \mathfrak{J}'$ and hence $\mathfrak{J}' = \mathfrak{J}$. Suppose $\mathfrak{J}' \cap \mathfrak{L} = (0)$. Then $\mathfrak{J}'\mathfrak{L} \subseteq \mathfrak{J}' \cap \mathfrak{L} = (0)$ and thus $\mathfrak{L} \subseteq \mathscr{A}_r(\mathfrak{J}')$. But $\mathscr{A}_r(\mathfrak{J}')$ is a closed 2-sided ideal in $\mathfrak{A}$ and hence contains $\mathfrak{J}$. Therefore $\mathfrak{J}' \subseteq \mathscr{A}_l(\mathscr{A}_r(\mathfrak{J}')) \subseteq \mathscr{A}_l(\mathfrak{J})$. In particular,

$(\mathfrak{I}')^2 = (0)$. Since $\mathfrak{A}$ is semi-simple, this implies $\mathfrak{I}' = (0)$ and completes the proof.

This lemma with the preceding one enables us to state the following corollary.

COROLLARY (2.8.9). *Every non-zero closed 2-sided ideal in $\mathfrak{A}$ contains a minimal-closed ideal.*

LEMMA (2.8.10). *Let $\mathfrak{I}$ be any 2-sided ideal in $\mathfrak{A}$. Then $\mathfrak{I} \cap \mathscr{A}_l(\mathfrak{I}) = (0)$, $\mathscr{A}_l(\mathfrak{I}) = \mathscr{A}_r(\mathfrak{I})$ and $\mathfrak{I}+\mathscr{A}_l(\mathfrak{I})$ is dense in $\mathfrak{A}$.*

PROOF. Note that $(\mathfrak{I} \cap \mathscr{A}_l(\mathfrak{I}))^2 = (0)$ and hence $\mathfrak{I} \cap \mathscr{A}_l(\mathfrak{I}) = (0)$, by the semi-simplicity of $\mathfrak{A}$. In particular, we have $\mathfrak{I}\mathscr{A}_l(\mathfrak{I}) = (0)$ which says that $\mathscr{A}_l(\mathfrak{I}) \subseteq \mathscr{A}_r(\mathfrak{I})$. By symmetry, also $\mathscr{A}_r(\mathfrak{I}) \subseteq \mathscr{A}_l(\mathfrak{I})$ and hence $\mathscr{A}_l(\mathfrak{I}) = \mathscr{A}_r(\mathfrak{I})$. Now let $\mathfrak{K} = \overline{\mathfrak{I}+\mathscr{A}_l(\mathfrak{I})}$. Since $\mathfrak{I} \subseteq \mathfrak{K}$, we have $\mathscr{A}_l(\mathfrak{K}) \subseteq \mathscr{A}_l(\mathfrak{I})$. Therefore $\mathscr{A}_l(\mathfrak{K}) \subseteq \mathfrak{K}$, so that $\mathscr{A}_l(\mathfrak{K})^2 = (0)$ and hence $\mathscr{A}_l(\mathfrak{K}) = (0)$. We thus obtain $\bar{\mathfrak{K}} = \mathfrak{A}$ completing the proof.

LEMMA (2.8.11). *Let $\mathfrak{I}$ be a closed 2-sided ideal in $\mathfrak{A}$. Then every closed left (right) ideal in the algebra $\mathfrak{I}$ is also a closed left (right) ideal in $\mathfrak{A}$.*

PROOF. By the preceding lemma, $\mathfrak{A} = \overline{\mathfrak{I}+\mathscr{A}_l(\mathfrak{I})}$. Let $\mathfrak{L}$ be any closed left ideal in the algebra $\mathfrak{I}$. Then $\mathscr{A}_l(\mathfrak{I})\mathfrak{L} = (0)$ and thus

$$\mathfrak{A}\mathfrak{L} = (\overline{\mathfrak{I}+\mathscr{A}(\mathfrak{I})})\mathfrak{L} \subseteq \overline{\mathfrak{I}\mathfrak{L}} \subseteq \mathfrak{L}.$$

Therefore $\mathfrak{L}$ is a left ideal in $\mathfrak{A}$.

THEOREM (2.8.12). *Let $\mathfrak{I}$ be a closed 2-sided ideal in $\mathfrak{A}$ such that $\overline{\mathfrak{A}\mathfrak{I}} = \overline{\mathfrak{I}\mathfrak{A}} = \mathfrak{I}$. Then $\mathfrak{I}$ is itself a semi-simple annihilator Banach algebra.*

PROOF. That $\mathfrak{I}$ is semi-simple is immediate from the above lemma. Denote by $\mathscr{A}'_r(\mathscr{E})$ the right annihilator in $\mathfrak{I}$ of a subset $\mathscr{E}$ of $\mathfrak{I}$. Then $\mathscr{A}'_r(\mathscr{E}) = \mathscr{A}_r(\mathscr{E}) \cap \mathfrak{I}$. Consider any closed left ideal $\mathfrak{L}$ in the algebra $\mathfrak{I}$. It will be sufficient to show that $\mathscr{A}'_r(\mathfrak{L}) = (0)$ if and only if $\mathfrak{L} = \mathfrak{I}$. Since $\mathscr{A}_r(\mathfrak{I}) \cap \mathfrak{I} = (0)$, it is immediate that $\mathscr{A}'_r(\mathfrak{I}) = (0)$. On the other hand, assume $\mathscr{A}'_r(\mathfrak{L}) = (0)$. Since $\mathfrak{L} \subseteq \mathfrak{I}$, we have $\mathscr{A}_r(\mathfrak{I}) \subseteq \mathscr{A}_r(\mathfrak{L})$. Also, since $\mathscr{A}_r(\mathfrak{L}) \cap \mathfrak{I} = (0)$, by assumption, we have $\mathscr{A}_r(\mathfrak{L})\mathfrak{I} = (0)$. Hence $\mathscr{A}_r(\mathfrak{L}) \subseteq \mathscr{A}_l(\mathfrak{I}) = \mathscr{A}_r(\mathfrak{I})$. Therefore $\mathscr{A}_r(\mathfrak{L}) = \mathscr{A}_r(\mathfrak{I})$. Next let $\mathfrak{K} = \mathfrak{L}+\mathscr{A}_r(\mathfrak{I})$. Then

$$\begin{aligned}\mathscr{A}_r(\mathfrak{K}) &= \mathscr{A}_r(\mathfrak{L}) \cap \mathscr{A}_r(\mathscr{A}_r(\mathfrak{I}))\\ &= \mathscr{A}_r(\mathfrak{I}) \cap \mathscr{A}_r(\mathscr{A}_r(\mathfrak{I})) = 0,\end{aligned}$$

the last equality being given by Lemma (2.8.10). Thus $\bar{\mathfrak{R}} = \mathfrak{A}$. Now, since $\mathfrak{L}$ is closed and $\mathfrak{I}\mathfrak{R} \subseteq \mathfrak{L}$, it follows that $\mathfrak{I}\mathfrak{A} \subseteq \mathfrak{L}$ and hence $\overline{\mathfrak{I}\mathfrak{A}} \subseteq \mathfrak{L}$. Therefore $\mathfrak{I} = \mathfrak{L}$ and the theorem is proved.

COROLLARY (2.8.13). *If $\mathfrak{I}$ is a minimal-closed 2-sided ideal in $\mathfrak{A}$, then $\mathfrak{I}$ is a semi-simple annihilator Banach algebra.*

THEOREM (2.8.14). *If $\mathfrak{A}$ is a dual algebra, then every closed 2-sided ideal in $\mathfrak{A}$ is also a dual algebra.*

PROOF. Let $\mathfrak{I}$ be a closed 2-sided ideal in $\mathfrak{A}$ and consider any closed left ideal $\mathfrak{L}$ in the algebra $\mathfrak{I}$. By Lemma (2.8.11), $\mathfrak{L}$ is also a closed left ideal in $\mathfrak{A}$ and thus $\mathfrak{L} = \mathscr{A}_l(\mathscr{A}_r(\mathfrak{L}))$. As in the proof of the preceding theorem, set $\mathscr{A}'_r(\mathfrak{L}) = \mathscr{A}_r(\mathfrak{L}) \cap \mathfrak{I}$. Then the problem is to show that $\mathscr{A}'_l(\mathscr{A}'_r(\mathfrak{L})) = \mathfrak{L}$. It is obvious that $\mathfrak{L} \subseteq \mathscr{A}'_l(\mathscr{A}'_r(\mathfrak{L}))$. On the other hand, since $\mathscr{A}_r(\mathfrak{L})\mathfrak{I} \subseteq \mathscr{A}'_r(\mathfrak{L})$, we have $\mathscr{A}_l(\mathscr{A}'_r(\mathfrak{L}))\mathscr{A}_r(\mathfrak{L})\mathfrak{I} = (0)$. Hence $\mathscr{A}'_l(\mathscr{A}'_r(\mathfrak{L}))\mathscr{A}_r(\mathfrak{L}) \subseteq \mathfrak{I} \cap \mathscr{A}_l(\mathfrak{I}) = (0)$ and this implies $\mathscr{A}'_l(\mathscr{A}'_r(\mathfrak{L})) \subseteq \mathscr{A}_l(\mathscr{A}_r(\mathfrak{L})) = \mathfrak{L}$. Therefore $\mathscr{A}'_l(\mathscr{A}'_r(\mathfrak{L})) = \mathfrak{L}$ and the proof is complete.

Definitions of the topological and direct topological sums in the next theorem will be found in § 1 of this chapter.

THEOREM (2.8.15). *The algebra $\mathfrak{A}$ is equal to the topological sum of its minimal left (right) ideals, and is equal to the direct topological sum of its minimal closed 2-sided ideals.*

PROOF. Let $\mathfrak{A}_0$ denote the topological sum of the minimal left or the minimal-closed 2-sided ideals in $\mathfrak{A}$. Since the 2-sided ideals in question are minimal, it is easily proved that the topological sum $\mathfrak{A}_0$ is a direct topological sum in this case. If $\mathfrak{A}e$ is a minimal left ideal and x is any element of $\mathfrak{A}$, then $\mathfrak{A}ex$ is either zero or is also a minimal left ideal. Therefore $\mathfrak{A}_0$ is a 2-sided ideal of $\mathfrak{A}$ in both cases. Hence $\mathscr{A}_l(\mathfrak{A}_0)$ is a closed 2-sided ideal in $\mathfrak{A}$. Now, if $\mathfrak{A}_0 \neq \mathfrak{A}$, then $\mathscr{A}_l(\mathfrak{A}_0) \neq (0)$. Therefore $\mathscr{A}_l(\mathfrak{A}_0)$ will contain a minimal left ideal and also a minimal-closed 2-sided ideal. Since $\mathfrak{A}_0 \cap \mathscr{A}_l(\mathfrak{A}_0) = (0)$, this is a contradiction and shows that $\mathfrak{A}_0 = \mathfrak{A}$, the desired result.

Recalling that the socle of $\mathfrak{A}$ is equal to the sum of all minimal left (or right) ideals in $\mathfrak{A}$, we can restate the first part of the above theorem as follows:

COROLLARY (2.8.16). *The socle $\mathfrak{F}$ of $\mathfrak{A}$ is dense in $\mathfrak{A}$.*

Since $\mathfrak{A}$ is semi-simple, an application of the above corollary along with Corollary (2.5.8) yields the following result.

COROLLARY (2.8.17). *$\mathfrak{A}$ has a unique norm topology.*

The next theorem shows that the structure space $\Pi_{\mathfrak{A}}$ of $\mathfrak{A}$ is almost discrete.

THEOREM (2.8.18). *The closure of each point of $\Pi_{\mathfrak{A}}$ is both open and closed.*

PROOF. Let $\mathfrak{P}$ be any point of $\Pi_{\mathfrak{A}}$. Then, by Lemma (2.8.10), $\mathfrak{P}\mathscr{A}_l(\mathfrak{P}) = (0)$. Therefore every primitive ideal in $\mathfrak{A}$ must contain either $\mathfrak{P}$ or $\mathscr{A}_l(\mathfrak{P})$. Moreover, if $\mathfrak{P}'$ is a primitive ideal for which both $\mathfrak{P} \subseteq \mathfrak{P}'$ and $\mathscr{A}_l(\mathfrak{P}) \subseteq \mathfrak{P}'$, then $\mathscr{A}_l(\mathfrak{P}') \subseteq \mathscr{A}_l(\mathfrak{P}) \subseteq \mathfrak{P}'$. This is impossible and proves that $\Pi_{\mathfrak{A}}$ is the union of the disjoint closed sets $\mathscr{h}(\mathfrak{P})$ and $\mathscr{h}(\mathscr{A}_l(\mathfrak{P}))$. In other words $\mathscr{h}(\mathfrak{P})$ is open and closed.

COROLLARY (2.8.19). *The strong structure space $\Xi_{\mathfrak{A}}$ is discrete, so that, in particular, $\mathfrak{A}$ is completely regular.*

Observe that a minimal-closed 2-sided ideal in $\mathfrak{A}$ is a TOPOLOGICALLY SIMPLE algebra in the sense that (0) is its only proper closed 2-sided ideal. Theorem (2.8.15), in a manner of speaking, thus reduces the study of semi-simple annihilator Banach algebras to the topologically simple case. We now obtain the structure of $\mathfrak{A}$ under the assumption that it be topologically simple.

Let $\mathfrak{A}e$ be any minimal left ideal in $\mathfrak{A}$ with e an idempotent. Since $\mathfrak{A}e$ is closed in $\mathfrak{A}$, it is a Banach space under the norm of $\mathfrak{A}$. We denote by $\mathfrak{X}_e$ the Banach space thus associated with $\mathfrak{A}e$. Consider the left regular representation $a \to A_a$ of $\mathfrak{A}$ on $\mathfrak{X}_e$. Then $a \to A_a$ is a continuous homomorphism of $\mathfrak{A}$ into $\mathscr{B}(\mathfrak{X}_e)$. Since $\mathscr{A}_l(\mathfrak{A}e) \neq \mathfrak{A}$, the kernel of the homomorphism $a \to A_a$ is a proper closed 2-sided ideal in $\mathfrak{A}$. Therefore, if $\mathfrak{A}$ is topologically simple, then $a \to A_a$ is an isomorphism of $\mathfrak{A}$ into $\mathscr{B}(\mathfrak{X}_e)$. Denote the image of $\mathfrak{A}$ in $\mathscr{B}(\mathfrak{X}_e)$ by $\mathfrak{B}_e$. Since $\mathfrak{A}e$ is minimal, $\mathfrak{B}_e$ is strictly irreducible and therefore, by Theorem (2.4.6), is strictly dense on $\mathfrak{X}_e$. When $\mathfrak{A}$ is topologically simple, the socle of $\mathfrak{A}$ is isomorphic under $a \to A_a$ with the socle of $\mathfrak{B}_e$ and the latter consists of all those operators in $\mathfrak{B}_e$ which have finite rank. (See § 4 above.)

LEMMA (2.8.20). *If $\mathfrak{A}$ is topologically simple, then $\mathfrak{B}_e$ contains all operators in $\mathscr{B}(\mathfrak{X}_e)$ with finite rank.*

PROOF. It is obviously sufficient to prove that $\mathfrak{B}_e$ contains every operator in $\mathscr{B}(\mathfrak{X}_e)$ of rank one. Hence let A be any such operator. Then A is of the form $A = v \otimes f$, where v is a fixed non-zero element of $\mathfrak{X}_e$ and f is a fixed non-zero bounded linear functional on $\mathfrak{X}_e$. Let $\mathfrak{N}$

be the zero space of f in $\mathfrak{X}_e$ and choose any u in $\mathfrak{X}_e$ such that $f(u) = 1$. Then $\mathfrak{N}$ is a closed subspace of $\mathfrak{X}_e$ and every element x in $\mathfrak{X}_e$ can be written in the form $x = f(x)u+n$, where $n \in \mathfrak{N}$. We observe next that $\mathscr{A}_l(\mathfrak{N}) \neq (0)$. In fact, let $[\mathfrak{N}\mathfrak{A}]$ be the right ideal generated in $\mathfrak{A}$ by the set $\mathfrak{N}\mathfrak{A}$. Then, since $\mathscr{A}_l(\mathfrak{N}) = \mathscr{A}_l(\mathfrak{N}\mathfrak{A}) = \mathscr{A}_l([\mathfrak{N}\mathfrak{A}])$, it follows that $\mathscr{A}_l(\mathfrak{N}) = (0)$ implies $\overline{[\mathfrak{N}\mathfrak{A}]} = \mathfrak{A}$. On the other hand, $\mathfrak{A}e$ is minimal, so that $e\mathfrak{A}e$ consists of scalar multiples of e and thus

$$\mathfrak{A}e = \overline{[\mathfrak{N}\mathfrak{A}]}e = \overline{[\mathfrak{N}e\,\mathfrak{A}]}e = \mathfrak{N}.$$

This contradicts the assumption $f \neq 0$ and shows that $\mathscr{A}_l(\mathfrak{N}) \neq (0)$. Choose any non-zero element b from $\mathscr{A}_l(\mathfrak{N})$. Then $A_b x = f(x)bu$, for each $x \in \mathfrak{X}_e$, and thus $A_b = (bu) \otimes f$. Since $b \neq 0$ implies $A_b \neq 0$, it follows that $bu \neq 0$. Hence, by the irreducibility of $\mathfrak{B}_e$, there exists a c in $\mathfrak{A}$ such that $cbu = v$. Thus we have

$$A_{cb} = (cbu) \otimes f = v \otimes f.$$

Therefore $v \otimes f$ belongs to $\mathfrak{B}_e$ and the lemma is proved.

Since the socle of $\mathfrak{A}$ is dense in $\mathfrak{A}$, it follows that the algebra $\mathfrak{B}_e$ is obtained by completion of the algebra of all operators in $\mathscr{B}(\mathfrak{X}_e)$ of finite rank with respect to the norm induced on these operators by $\mathfrak{A}$. This suggests consideration of the general case of such an algebra under the additional assumption that it be an annihilator algebra. We accordingly shift the remainder of the discussion to this general situation.

Let $\mathfrak{X}$ be an arbitrary complex Banach space. Denote the norm in $\mathfrak{X}$ by $|x|$ and the bound of a linear operator T on $\mathfrak{X}$ relative to this norm by $|T|$. Let $\mathfrak{F}$ be the subalgebra of $\mathscr{B}(\mathfrak{X})$ consisting of all the operators of finite rank. Consider a subalgebra $\mathfrak{B}$ of $\mathscr{B}(\mathfrak{X})$ which contains $\mathfrak{F}$. Assume that $\mathfrak{B}$ is a Banach algebra under some given norm $\|T\|$ and that $\mathfrak{F}$ is dense in $\mathfrak{B}$ relative to this norm. Note that, in view of Theorems (2.4.13) and (2.2.6), we can just as well assume that the norm $|x|$ in $\mathfrak{X}$ is given by

$$|x| = \inf \|T\|, \quad Tu = x, \quad T \in \mathfrak{B},$$

where u is a fixed vector in $\mathfrak{X}$, and hence that $|T| \leqslant \|T\|$. The algebra $\mathfrak{B}$ is obviously semi-simple and topologically simple and contains minimal one-sided ideals. Observe that $\mathfrak{B}$ can be regarded as obtained by completing $\mathfrak{F}$ with respect to a norm under which it is a normed algebra. We digress briefly at this point to prove the following result suggested by this observation.

THEOREM (2.8.21). *Let $\mathfrak{F}$ be a normed algebra with norm $\|T\|$ and let $\mathfrak{A}$ be the completion of $\mathfrak{F}$ with respect to this norm. Then there exists a representation $a \to T_a$ of $\mathfrak{A}$ on $\mathfrak{X}$ whose kernel is the radical of $\mathfrak{A}$ and such that each element of $\mathfrak{F}$ maps into itself. Thus $\mathfrak{A}$, modulo its radical, is an algebra $\mathfrak{B}$ of the kind described above.*

PROOF. By Theorem (2.4.17), the norm $\|T\|$ majorizes the operator bound. It follows easily from this fact that every element $a \in \mathfrak{A}$ has associated with it an operator $T_a \in \mathscr{B}(\mathfrak{X})$ such that, if $\{F_n\} \subset \mathfrak{F}$ and $\|F_n - a\| \to 0$, then $|F_n - T_a| \to 0$. The mapping $a \to T_a$ is clearly a homomorphism of $\mathfrak{A}$ into $\mathscr{B}(\mathfrak{X})$ such that each element of $\mathfrak{F}$ maps into itself. The image of $\mathfrak{A}$ in $\mathscr{B}(\mathfrak{X})$ is obviously semi-simple so that the kernel of the representation $a \to T_a$ contains the radical $\mathfrak{R}$ of $\mathfrak{A}$. On the other hand, suppose that $T_a = 0$ and choose $\{F_n\} \subset \mathfrak{F}$ such that $\|F_n - a\| \to 0$. Then $|F_n| \to 0$. Also,

$$\|(x \otimes f)F_n(y \otimes g)\| = |f(F_n y)|\|x \otimes g\|.$$

Therefore, letting $n \to \infty$, we obtain $(x \otimes f)a(y \otimes g) = 0$. Since $\mathfrak{F}$ is dense in $\mathfrak{A}$, it follows that $\mathfrak{A}a\mathfrak{A} = (0)$. This implies $a \in \mathfrak{R}$ and completes the proof.

We now return to the algebra $\mathfrak{B}$, assuming that $\mathfrak{F} \subseteq \mathfrak{B} \subseteq \mathscr{B}(\mathfrak{X})$, and that $\mathfrak{B}$ is a Banach algebra under a norm $\|T\|$ with respect to which $\mathfrak{F}$ is dense in $\mathfrak{B}$. Observe that the discussion preceding Lemma (2.4.11) applies to $\mathfrak{B}$, so that $\mathfrak{B}$ determines a space $\mathfrak{X}^{\mathfrak{B}}$ which is normed dual to $\mathfrak{X}$. Furthermore, since $\mathfrak{B}$ contains $\mathfrak{F}$, this space $\mathfrak{X}^{\mathfrak{B}}$ obviously coincides with the conjugate space $\mathfrak{X}'$ of $\mathfrak{X}$.

LEMMA (2.8.22). *The norm induced in $\mathfrak{X}'$ by $\mathfrak{B}$ is equivalent to the "natural" norm defined in $\mathfrak{X}'$ by the relation*

$$|f|' = \sup \frac{|(x, f)|}{|x|}, \quad x \in \mathfrak{X}.$$

PROOF. The norm induced in $\mathfrak{X}'$ by $\mathfrak{B}$ is given by

$$|f| = \inf_{T'h=f} \|T\|,$$

where h is a fixed non-zero element of $\mathfrak{X}'$. Also, since $\mathfrak{X}$ and $\mathfrak{X}'$ are normed dual relative to the norms $|x|$ and $|f|$, there exists a constant β such that

$$|(x, f)| \leqslant \beta|x||f|.$$

Therefore $|f|' \leqslant \beta |f|$. Now, since $\mathfrak{X}'$ is complete in both $|f|$ and $|f|'$, the equivalence of the two norms follows.

THEOREM (2.8.23). *In order for $\mathfrak{B}$ to be an annihilator Banach algebra, it is necessary and sufficient that the Banach space $\mathfrak{X}$ be reflexive.*

PROOF. Consider a closed right ideal $\mathfrak{K}$ in $\mathfrak{B}$ and let $\mathfrak{M}$ be the smallest closed linear subspace of $\mathfrak{X}$ which contains the range of every operator in $\mathfrak{K}$. Then, by Theorem (2.4.18), $\mathfrak{K}$ contains every element of $\mathfrak{F}$ with range in $\mathfrak{M}$. Since $\mathfrak{F}$ is dense in $\mathfrak{B}$, it follows that $\mathfrak{K}$ is proper if, and only if, $\mathfrak{M}$ is proper. Now, if $\mathfrak{M}$ is proper, then there exists a non-zero element $g \in \mathfrak{X}'$ such that $(\mathfrak{M}, g) = (0)$. It is obvious that $u \otimes g$ belongs to $\mathscr{A}_l(\mathfrak{K})$. Hence $\mathfrak{K} \neq \mathfrak{B}$ implies $\mathscr{A}_l(\mathfrak{K}) \neq (0)$. Also $\mathscr{A}_l(\mathfrak{B}) = (0)$, so that the half of the condition for an annihilator algebra which pertains to right ideals is automatically satisfied in $\mathfrak{B}$ without further assumptions. On the other hand, if $\mathfrak{L}$ is a closed left ideal in $\mathfrak{B}$, then $\mathfrak{L}'$ is a closed right ideal in $\mathfrak{B}'$ and the left annihilator of $\mathfrak{L}'$ in $\mathfrak{B}'$ is equal to $(\mathscr{A}_r(\mathfrak{L}))'$. Therefore, in case $\mathfrak{X}$ is reflexive, the above argument can be applied to $\mathfrak{B}'$ to obtain that $\mathscr{A}_r(\mathfrak{L}) = (0)$ if and only if $\mathfrak{L} = \mathfrak{B}$. This proves the sufficiency of reflexivity of $\mathfrak{X}$ for $\mathfrak{B}$ to be an annihilator algebra.

Now assume that $\mathfrak{B}$ is an annihilator algebra and let F be any non-zero bounded linear functional on the Banach space $\mathfrak{X}'$. Denote the zero space of F by $\mathfrak{X}'_0$ and let h be any element of $\mathfrak{X}'$ such that $F(h) = 1$. Then every element f in $\mathfrak{X}'$ can be written in the form $f = F(f)h + f'$, where $f' \in \mathfrak{X}'_0$. Next let $\mathfrak{L}$ be the set of all T in $\mathfrak{B}$ such that $T'\mathfrak{X}' \subseteq \mathfrak{X}'_0$. Then $\mathfrak{L}$ is a closed left ideal in $\mathfrak{B}$. Obviously, since $\mathfrak{X}'_0 \neq \mathfrak{X}'$, the ideal $\mathfrak{L}$ is proper. Therefore $\mathscr{A}_r(\mathfrak{L}) \neq (0)$. Let $v \otimes g$ be any element of rank one in $\mathscr{A}_r(\mathfrak{L})$. Then $(v \otimes g)'\mathfrak{L}' = (0)$ and, since $(v \otimes g)'f = (v, f)g$, it follows that $(v, f) = 0$ for every f in the range of any operator in $\mathfrak{L}'$. Since these f exhaust $\mathfrak{X}'_0$, it follows that $(v, \mathfrak{X}'_0) = (0)$. Therefore $(v, f) = F(f)(v, h)$, for every $f \in \mathfrak{X}'$. This implies reflexivity of $\mathfrak{X}$ and completes the proof.

We now obtain conditions under which $\mathfrak{B}$ is a dual Banach algebra.

LEMMA (2.8.24). *Let $\mathfrak{K}$ be a closed right ideal in $\mathfrak{B}$ and let $\mathfrak{M}$ denote the smallest closed linear subspace of $\mathfrak{X}$ which contains the range of each operator in $\mathfrak{K}$. Then*

$$\mathscr{A}_r(\mathscr{A}_l(\mathfrak{K})) = \{T : T \in \mathfrak{B}, \ T(\mathfrak{X}) \subseteq \mathfrak{M}\}.$$

PROOF. Set $\mathfrak{K}_0 = \{T : T \in \mathfrak{B}, \ T(\mathfrak{X}) \subseteq \mathfrak{M}\}$. Observe first that $\mathscr{A}_l(\mathfrak{K}) = \{T : T \in \mathfrak{B}, \ T(\mathfrak{M}) = (0)\}$. Therefore, if $T(\mathfrak{X}) \subseteq \mathfrak{M}$ and

$A \in \mathscr{A}_l(\mathfrak{K})$, then $AT = 0$. In other words, $\mathfrak{K}_0 \subseteq \mathscr{A}_r(\mathscr{A}_l(\mathfrak{K}))$. On the other hand, let $T \in \mathscr{A}_r(\mathscr{A}_l(\mathfrak{K}))$ and suppose that $T \notin \mathfrak{K}_0$. Then there exists $x_0 \in \mathfrak{X}$ such that $Tx_0 \notin \mathfrak{M}$. Since $\mathfrak{M}$ is closed, there exists $f \in \mathfrak{X}'$ such that $(\mathfrak{M}, f) = (0)$ and $(Tx_0, f) = 1$. Define $A = x_0 \otimes f$. Obviously $A(\mathfrak{M}) = (0)$, so that $A \in \mathscr{A}_l(\mathfrak{K})$. Therefore $AT = 0$. But then $0 = ATx_0 = (Tx_0, f)x_0 = x_0$. This contradicts the assumption $Tx_0 \notin \mathfrak{M}$ and proves that $\mathscr{A}_r(\mathscr{A}_l(\mathfrak{K})) \subseteq \mathfrak{K}_0$.

COROLLARY (2.8.25). *In order for a closed right ideal $\mathfrak{K}$ in $\mathfrak{B}$ to be an annihilator ideal it is necessary and sufficient that it be of the form*

$$\mathfrak{K} = \{T : T \in \mathfrak{B},\ T(\mathfrak{X}) \subseteq \mathfrak{M}\},$$

where $\mathfrak{M}$ is some closed linear subspace of $\mathfrak{X}$.

LEMMA (2.8.26). *If $\mathfrak{K}$ is any closed right ideal in $\mathfrak{B}$, then $\mathscr{A}_r(\mathscr{A}_l(\mathfrak{K}))\mathfrak{B} \subseteq \mathfrak{K}$.*

PROOF. As before, let $\mathfrak{M}$ be the closed linear subspace of $\mathfrak{X}$ spanned by the ranges of operators in $\mathfrak{K}$ and let T be any element of $\mathscr{A}_r(\mathscr{A}_l(\mathfrak{K}))$. By Lemma (2.8.24), $T(\mathfrak{X}) \subseteq \mathfrak{M}$. Also, by Theorem (2.4.17), $\mathfrak{K}$ contains every element of $\mathfrak{F}$ with range in $\mathfrak{M}$. Thus, since $T\mathfrak{F} \subseteq \mathfrak{F}$, it follows that $T\mathfrak{F} \subseteq \mathfrak{K}$. Therefore, by the fact that $\mathfrak{K}$ is closed and that $\mathfrak{F}$ is dense in $\mathfrak{B}$, we obtain $T\mathfrak{B} \subseteq \mathfrak{K}$. This completes the proof.

THEOREM (2.8.27). *In order for $\mathfrak{B}$ to be a dual Banach algebra, it is necessary and sufficient that $\mathfrak{X}$ be reflexive and that $T \in \overline{T\mathfrak{B}} \cap \overline{\mathfrak{B}T}$, for every $T \in \mathfrak{B}$.*

PROOF. The necessity is given directly by Theorem (2.8.23) and Corollary (2.8.3). For the proof of the sufficiency, the assumption that $\mathfrak{X}$ is reflexive reduces the problem to one of showing that $\mathscr{A}_r(\mathscr{A}_l(\mathfrak{K})) = \mathfrak{K}$ for a closed right ideal $\mathfrak{K}$. By the assumption $T \in \overline{T\mathfrak{B}}$ and Lemma (2.8.26), we obtain

$$\mathscr{A}_r(\mathscr{A}_l(\mathfrak{K})) \subseteq \overline{\mathscr{A}_r(\mathscr{A}_l(\mathfrak{K}))\mathfrak{B}} \subseteq \mathfrak{K}.$$

Therefore $\mathscr{A}_r(\mathscr{A}_l(\mathfrak{K})) = \mathfrak{K}$ and the theorem is proved.

THEOREM (2.8.28). *If the norm in $\mathfrak{B}$ is equivalent to the operator bound $|T|$, then a sufficient condition for $\mathfrak{B}$ to be dual is that $\mathfrak{X}$ be reflexive and there exist, for each $T \in \mathfrak{B}$, a projection in $\mathscr{B}(\mathfrak{X})$ with range equal to $\overline{T(\mathfrak{X})}$.*

PROOF. Again the reflexivity of $\mathfrak{X}$ enables us to restrict attention to closed right ideals $\mathfrak{K}$. Let $\mathfrak{M}$ be the closed subspace of $\mathfrak{X}$ spanned by the ranges of operators in $\mathfrak{K}$ and let T be any element of $\mathscr{A}_r(\mathscr{A}_l(\mathfrak{K}))$.

Since $\mathfrak{F}$ is dense in $\mathfrak{B}$, there exists $\{A_n\} \subset \mathfrak{F}$ such that $|T - A_n| \to 0$. Now let P be the bounded projection with range equal to $\overline{T(\mathfrak{X})}$. Then $PT = T$ and PA_n is an element of $\mathfrak{F}$ and so belongs to $\mathfrak{B}$. Moreover, we have $|T - PA_n| \to 0$. Since $\overline{T(\mathfrak{X})} \subseteq \mathfrak{M}$, it follows that $PA_n\mathfrak{X} \subseteq \mathfrak{M}$ and hence, by Theorem (2.4.17), that $PA_n \in \mathfrak{R}$. Thus T, being a limit of elements of $\mathfrak{R}$, belongs to $\mathfrak{R}$. In other words, $\mathscr{A}_r(\mathscr{A}_l(\mathfrak{R})) = \mathfrak{R}$ and the proof is complete.

We close this section with the following converse to Theorem (2.8.15).

THEOREM (2.8.29). *Let $\mathfrak{A}$ be a semi-simple Banach algebra which is equal to the topological sum of a given family $\{\mathfrak{J}_\lambda : \lambda \in \Lambda\}$ of its closed 2-sided ideals. If each $\mathfrak{J}_\lambda$ is an annihilator algebra, then $\mathfrak{A}$ is an annihilator algebra. If each $\mathfrak{J}_\lambda$ is dual and $a \in \overline{a\mathfrak{A}} \cap \overline{\mathfrak{A}a}$, for each $a \in \mathfrak{A}$, then $\mathfrak{A}$ is dual.*

PROOF. Let $\mathfrak{L}$ be any closed left ideal in $\mathfrak{A}$ and set $\mathfrak{L}_\lambda = \mathfrak{L} \cap \mathfrak{J}_\lambda$. Then $\mathfrak{L}_\lambda$ is a closed left ideal in $\mathfrak{J}_\lambda$. Denote by $\mathscr{A}_r^\lambda$ and $\mathscr{A}_l^\lambda$ the annihilator operations in $\mathfrak{J}_\lambda$. Since $\mathfrak{J}_\lambda\mathfrak{L} \subseteq \mathfrak{L}_\lambda$, we have $\mathfrak{J}_\lambda\mathfrak{L}\mathscr{A}_r^\lambda(\mathfrak{L}_\lambda) = (0)$. Therefore, if $\mathfrak{J}_\lambda$ is an annihilator algebra, then $\mathfrak{L}\mathscr{A}_r^\lambda(\mathfrak{L}_\lambda) = (0)$, so that $\mathscr{A}_r^\lambda(\mathfrak{L}_\lambda) \subseteq \mathscr{A}_r(\mathfrak{L})$. Now, if $\mathfrak{L} \neq \mathfrak{A}$, then, since $\mathfrak{A}$ is the topological sum of the ideals $\mathfrak{J}_\lambda$ and $\mathfrak{L}_\lambda \subseteq \mathfrak{L}$, there must exist $\mu \in \Lambda$ such that $\mathfrak{L}_\mu \neq \mathfrak{J}_\mu$. Hence $\mathscr{A}_r^\mu(\mathfrak{L}_\mu) \neq (0)$ and *a fortiori* $\mathscr{A}_r(\mathfrak{L}) \neq (0)$. If $\mathfrak{L} = \mathfrak{A}$, then $\mathscr{A}_r(\mathfrak{L}) = (0)$ by the semi-simplicity of $\mathfrak{A}$. In other words, $\mathscr{A}_r(\mathfrak{L}) = (0)$ if and only if $\mathfrak{L} = \mathfrak{A}$. A similar proof establishes the analogous result for right ideals and thus completes the proof that $\mathfrak{A}$ is an annihilator algebra.

Now assume that each $\mathfrak{J}_\lambda$ is dual and that $a \in \overline{a\mathfrak{A}} \cap \overline{\mathfrak{A}a}$ for each $a \in \mathfrak{A}$. If $\mathfrak{L}$ is a closed left ideal in $\mathfrak{A}$, then we obtain as before that $\mathscr{A}_r^\lambda(\mathfrak{L}_\lambda) \subseteq \mathscr{A}_r(\mathfrak{L})$. Let $a \in \mathscr{A}_l(\mathscr{A}_r(\mathfrak{L}))$. Then obviously $\mathfrak{J}_\lambda a\mathscr{A}_r^\lambda(\mathfrak{L}_\lambda) = (0)$. Thus $\mathfrak{J}_\lambda a \subseteq \mathscr{A}_l^\lambda(\mathscr{A}_r^\lambda(\mathfrak{L}_\lambda)) = \mathfrak{L}_\lambda \subseteq \mathfrak{L}$ for each λ. It follows that $\overline{\mathfrak{A}a} \subseteq \mathfrak{L}$ and therefore $a \in \mathfrak{L}$. This shows that $\mathscr{A}_l(\mathscr{A}_r(\mathfrak{L})) = \mathfrak{L}$. Similarly, if $\mathfrak{R}$ is a closed right ideal in $\mathfrak{A}$, then $\mathscr{A}_r(\mathscr{A}_l(\mathfrak{R})) = \mathfrak{R}$. In other words, $\mathfrak{A}$ is dual and the theorem is proved.

As an application of the above theorem, consider a family $\{\mathfrak{A}_\lambda : \lambda \in \Lambda\}$ of Banach algebras and their full direct sum $\Sigma\,\mathfrak{A}_\lambda$. Denote by $(\Sigma\,\mathfrak{A}_\lambda)_0$ the subset of $\Sigma\,\mathfrak{A}_\lambda$ consisting of all f such that, for arbitrary $\epsilon > 0$, the set $\{\lambda : \|f(\lambda)\| \geqslant \epsilon\}$ is finite. (See Kaplansky [5, p. 411].) It is straightforward to verify that $(\Sigma\,\mathfrak{A}_\lambda)_0$ is a subdirect sum of the algebras $\mathfrak{A}_\lambda$ and is a closed subalgebra of $\Sigma\,\mathfrak{A}_\lambda$. Observe that $(\Sigma\,\mathfrak{A}_\lambda)_0$ contains all f which are zero except at a finite number of the indices λ

and that these elements are dense in $(\Sigma\,\mathfrak{A}_\lambda)_0$. The set of those f which are zero except at the fixed index λ is a closed 2-sided ideal in $(\Sigma\,\mathfrak{A}_\lambda)_0$ which is isometrically isomorphic, as an algebra, with $\mathfrak{A}_\lambda$. Clearly, $(\Sigma\,\mathfrak{A}_\lambda)_0$ is a topological (direct) sum of these ideals. Now assume that each of the algebras $\mathfrak{A}_\lambda$ is a semi-simple annihilator algebra. It is easy to see that the semi-simplicity for each $\mathfrak{A}_\lambda$ implies semi-simplicity for $(\Sigma\,\mathfrak{A}_\lambda)_0$. Therefore Theorem (2.8.29) applies and we conclude that $(\Sigma\,\mathfrak{A}_\lambda)_0$ is an annihilator algebra. Furthermore, if each $\mathfrak{A}_\lambda$ is dual and has the property that $a \in \overline{a\mathfrak{A}_\lambda} \cap \overline{\mathfrak{A}_\lambda a}$ for each $a \in \mathfrak{A}$, then it is not difficult to show that Theorem (2.8.29) applies again enabling us to conclude that $(\Sigma\,\mathfrak{A}_\lambda)_0$ is dual.

If an algebra is subjected to only one of the conditions in Definition (2.8.1), it is called a RIGHT or LEFT ANNIHILATOR ALGEBRA according as condition (i) or condition (ii) is required. A number of the above results hold for these "one-sided" annihilator algebras. In particular, the analogue of Theorem (2.8.15) goes through, giving a decomposition of a semi-simple right or left annihilator Banach algebras into topologically simple algebras of the same kind. An example of a topologically simple left annihilator Banach algebra is the closure, $\overline{\mathfrak{F}}$, of the operators of finite rank in $\mathscr{B}(\mathfrak{X})$, where $\mathfrak{X}$ is any Banach space. Smiley [2], who introduced the one-sided annihilator algebras (actually, he considers certain topological rings) and proved the analogue of Theorem (2.8.15), also obtained an abstract characterization of the special simple algebras $\overline{\mathfrak{F}}$.

III. COMMUTATIVE BANACH ALGEBRAS

Introduction. It was with commutative algebras that Gelfand began the study of Banach algebras. He was in a large part motivated by the fact that many of the important examples of Banach algebras which arise in analysis are commutative. These examples naturally set the pattern for much of the discussion in the general case. In this chapter, we develop systematically a general theory of commutative Banach algebras. It is here that some of the most satisfying and complete results have been obtained.

As we saw in Corollary (2.2.10), primitive ideals in a commutative algebra are automatically maximal modular. Therefore the two structure spaces coincide and the radical is equal to the intersection of all maximal modular ideals. In a primitive commutative algebra, the zero ideal, being primitive, is maximal modular, and this implies that the algebra is a field. Thus, any primitive commutative normed algebra is isomorphic to either the real or complex numbers. It follows that every irreducible representation of a commutative Banach algebra is actually a homomorphism of the algebra into the complex numbers.

As might be expected from the above remarks, homomorphisms into the complex numbers constitute a useful tool for the study of commutative Banach algebras. Such homomorphisms, which never exist in sufficient numbers to be of much use in the non-commutative case, of course exist in abundance for semi-simple commutative Banach algebras. The entire theory of these algebras revolves about this important fact.

The class of all homomorphisms of a real or complex algebra into the complex numbers is, with an appropriate topology, called the "carrier space" of the algebra. This space is discussed in § 1 which also includes the Gelfand representation theorem. The Gelfand theorem provides a representation of a commutative Banach algebra as an algebra of continuous functions on the carrier space. In § 2 we investigate some general properties of algebras of functions. In § 3 the Šilov boundary is defined and some of its properties are obtained. Certain "concrete" representations of the carrier space are studied in § 4 and some of the methods used there are sharpened in § 5 and applied in § 6. Finally, § 7 contains a discussion of commutative completely regular algebras.

§ 1. The carrier space and the Gelfand representation theorem. Let $\mathfrak{A}$ be an arbitrary commutative real or complex algebra and denote by $\Phi_{\mathfrak{A}}$ the class of all non-zero homomorphisms of $\mathfrak{A}$ into the field of complex numbers. The image of $\mathfrak{A}$ under an element of $\Phi_{\mathfrak{A}}$ may be either the real or the complex numbers. Both possibilities can occur for real algebras while the second is the only one which can occur for complex algebras. It is convenient to denote by φ_∞ the homomorphism which maps $\mathfrak{A}$ into zero and by $\Phi_{\mathfrak{A}}{}^\infty$ the class $\Phi_{\mathfrak{A}}$ plus φ_∞. It has already been observed that, if $\mathfrak{A}$ is a Banach algebra, then irreducible representations of $\mathfrak{A}$ give rise to elements of $\Phi_{\mathfrak{A}}$, so that $\Phi_{\mathfrak{A}}$ is non-vacuous if $\mathfrak{A}$ is not a radical algebra. It is instructive to obtain this fundamental result as a consequence of the following slightly more inclusive theorem.

Theorem (3.1.1). *Let $\mathfrak{A}$ be a normed commutative algebra and let $\mathfrak{M}$ be a closed maximal ideal in $\mathfrak{A}$. Then the difference algebra $\mathfrak{A}/\mathfrak{M}$ either is a one-dimensional zero algebra (all products zero) or is isomorphic to the real or complex numbers.*

Proof. Since $\mathfrak{M}$ is maximal, the difference algebra $\mathfrak{A}' = \mathfrak{A}/\mathfrak{M}$ is simple (contains no non-trivial ideals). Thus, if $\mathfrak{J}$ is the set of all $x' \in \mathfrak{A}'$ such that $x'\mathfrak{A}' = (0)$, then $\mathfrak{J}$, being an ideal in $\mathfrak{A}'$, is equal to either $\mathfrak{A}'$ or (0). Let $x \to x'$ denote the natural homomorphism of $\mathfrak{A}$ onto $\mathfrak{A}'$. Since $\mathfrak{M}$ is maximal, if e is any element of $\mathfrak{A}$ not in $\mathfrak{M}$, then every element $x \in \mathfrak{A}$ can be written in the form $x = (\xi + a)e + m$, where $a \in \mathfrak{A}$, $m \in \mathfrak{M}$ and ξ is scalar. Therefore $x' = \xi e' + a'e'$. Now, if $\mathfrak{J} = \mathfrak{A}'$, then $\mathfrak{A}'$ is obviously a zero algebra. Moreover, $x' = \xi e'$ so that $\mathfrak{A}'$ is also one-dimensional. On the other hand, if $\mathfrak{J} = (0)$ and if x' is any non-zero element of $\mathfrak{A}'$, then the ideal $x'\mathfrak{A}'$ is non-zero and so must equal $\mathfrak{A}'$. This means first that $\mathfrak{A}'$ contains no zero divisors. In fact, $x' \neq 0$ and $y' \neq 0$ imply $x'y'\mathfrak{A}' = x'\mathfrak{A}' = \mathfrak{A}'$ and hence $x'y' \neq 0$. Next let a' be a fixed non-zero element of $\mathfrak{A}'$. Since $a'\mathfrak{A}' = \mathfrak{A}'$, there exists $e' \in \mathfrak{A}'$ such that $a'e' = a'$. Furthermore, since $a'(e'x' - x') = 0$, we have $e'x' = x'$ for every $x' \in \mathfrak{A}'$. Hence e' is an identity element for $\mathfrak{A}'$. Again, since $x'\mathfrak{A}' = \mathfrak{A}'$ for $x' \neq 0$, there exists $y' \in \mathfrak{A}'$ such that $x'y' = e'$. Therefore $\mathfrak{A}'$ is a field. Finally, since $\mathfrak{M}$ is closed, $\mathfrak{A}'$ is a normed field and is accordingly isomorphic to either the real or complex field, by Theorem (1.7.5).

COROLLARY (3.1.2). *$\mathfrak{A}/\mathfrak{M}$ is either the real or complex field if and only if $\mathfrak{M}$ is modular.*

If $\mathfrak{A}$ is not a radical algebra, then it necessarily contains maximal modular ideals. Furthermore, if $\mathfrak{A}$ is a Banach algebra, then a maximal modular ideal $\mathfrak{M}$ is automatically closed and so determines a non-zero homomorphism of $\mathfrak{A}$ into the complex field. In other words $\Phi_{\mathfrak{A}}$ is non-vacuous for such $\mathfrak{A}$.

Associated with each element x in $\mathfrak{A}$ is the function $\hat{x}$ defined on $\Phi_{\mathfrak{A}}$ with value at φ equal to the image $\hat{x}(\varphi)$ of x under the homomorphism φ. If $\varphi_1 \neq \varphi_2$, then there exists $\hat{x}$ such that $\hat{x}(\varphi_1) \neq \hat{x}(\varphi_2)$. Therefore these functions separate points of $\Phi_{\mathfrak{A}}$. We introduce into $\Phi_{\mathfrak{A}}{}^{\infty}$ the weakest topology (that is, with the smallest number of open sets) for which each of the functions $\hat{x}$ is continuous. It is easily verified that this topology is equivalent to the topology determined in $\Phi_{\mathfrak{A}}{}^{\infty}$ by the system of neighborhoods of points φ in $\Phi_{\mathfrak{A}}{}^{\infty}$ having the form,

$$V_{\varphi}(x_1, \cdots, x_n; \epsilon) = \{\varphi' : |\hat{x}_i(\varphi) - \hat{x}_i(\varphi')| < \epsilon, i = 1, \cdots, n\},$$

where $x_1, \cdots, x_n$ is any finite set of elements of $\mathfrak{A}$ and $\epsilon > 0$. It is convenient to refer to the topology defined here as the $\mathfrak{A}$-TOPOLOGY or the topology induced in $\Phi_{\mathfrak{A}}{}^{\infty}$ by the functions $\hat{x}$. Unless it is explicitly stated otherwise, the topology in $\Phi_{\mathfrak{A}}{}^{\infty}$ (and also in $\Phi_{\mathfrak{A}}$) will always be assumed to be the $\mathfrak{A}$-topology. Note that, since the functions $\hat{x}$ separate the points of $\Phi_{\mathfrak{A}}{}^{\infty}$, the $\mathfrak{A}$-topology is automatically Hausdorff.

DEFINITION (3.1.3). *The space $\Phi_{\mathfrak{A}}$, with the $\mathfrak{A}$-topology, is called the* CARRIER SPACE *of the algebra $\mathfrak{A}$.*

The carrier space is defined for any real or complex algebra which admits non-zero homomorphisms into the complex field. The carrier space is therefore defined for every commutative Banach algebra which is not a radical algebra, each maximal modular ideal in $\mathfrak{A}$ giving rise to an element of $\Phi_{\mathfrak{A}}$. Conversely, if φ is any element of $\Phi_{\mathfrak{A}}$ and $\mathfrak{M}$ is its kernel, then $\mathfrak{M}$ is a maximal modular ideal and $\hat{x}(\varphi) \leftrightarrow x + \mathfrak{M}$ is an isomorphism between the range of φ and $\mathfrak{A}/\mathfrak{M}$. This correspondence between elements of $\Phi_{\mathfrak{A}}$ and maximal modular ideals is obviously one-to-one if $\mathfrak{A}$ is complex. If $\mathfrak{A}$ is real, then the correspondence is also one-to-one for those maximal modular ideals $\mathfrak{M}$ such that $\mathfrak{A}/\mathfrak{M}$ is the real field. However, if $\mathfrak{A}$ is real and $\mathfrak{A}/\mathfrak{M}$ is the complex field, then there are two distinct elements of $\Phi_{\mathfrak{A}}$ associated with $\mathfrak{M}$. In fact, if φ is any homomorphism of the real algebra $\mathfrak{A}$ onto the complex field, then $\bar{\varphi}$, where $\hat{x}(\bar{\varphi})$ is the complex conjugate of $\hat{x}(\varphi)$, is a second homomorphism with the same kernel as φ. Evidently these are the only possibilities. This situation is clarified somewhat by passage to the complexification of the algebra.

THEOREM (3.1.4). *Let $\mathfrak{A}$ be a real commutative algebra and $\mathfrak{A}_C$ its complexification. Then there exists a unique homeomorphism $\varphi \leftrightarrow \varphi'$ between the carrier spaces $\Phi_{\mathfrak{A}}$ and $\Phi_{\mathfrak{A}_C}$ such that $\hat{x}(\varphi) = \hat{x}(\varphi')$ for every $x \in \mathfrak{A}$.*

PROOF. Since the restriction of any element of $\Phi_{\mathfrak{A}_C}$ to $\mathfrak{A}$ is obviously an element of $\Phi_{\mathfrak{A}}$, the substance of the theorem is that every element of $\Phi_{\mathfrak{A}}$ has a unique extension to all of $\mathfrak{A}_C$ as an element of $\Phi_{\mathfrak{A}_C}$. It is readily verified that, if $\varphi \in \Phi_{\mathfrak{A}}$ and $w = x+iy$ is an arbitrary element of $\mathfrak{A}_C$ with x and y in $\mathfrak{A}$, then the desired extension φ' is given by $\hat{w}(\varphi') = \hat{x}(\varphi)+i\hat{y}(\varphi)$. That the mapping $\varphi \rightarrow \varphi'$ is a homeomorphism is immediate from the definition of the topologies in $\Phi_{\mathfrak{A}}$ and $\Phi_{\mathfrak{A}_C}$.

COROLLARY (3.1.5). *If $\mathfrak{A}$ is a Banach algebra, then the mapping $\varphi \rightarrow \varphi'$ defines a one-to-one correspondence between elements of $\Phi_{\mathfrak{A}}$ and the maximal modular ideals of the complexification of $\mathfrak{A}$.*

The next theorem relates the carrier space to the spectra of elements in $\mathfrak{A}$.

THEOREM (3.1.6). *Let x be any element of the commutative Banach algebra $\mathfrak{A}$. Then*

$$Sp_{\mathfrak{A}}(x) - (0) \subseteq \{\hat{x}(\varphi) : \varphi \in \Phi_{\mathfrak{A}}\} \subseteq Sp_{\mathfrak{A}}(x).$$

If $\mathfrak{A}$ has an identity element, then the equality holds on the right.

PROOF. In view of the preceding theorem and the definition of spectrum for real algebras, it will be sufficient to restrict attention to complex $\mathfrak{A}$. First, let φ be any element of $\Phi_{\mathfrak{A}}$ and set $\alpha = \hat{x}(\varphi)$. If $\alpha = 0$, then x is in the kernel of φ, which is a proper ideal in $\mathfrak{A}$. Therefore x must be singular and so $\alpha \in Sp(x)$. If $\alpha \neq 0$, let $y = \alpha^{-1}x$ and note that $\hat{y}(\varphi) = 1$. But this implies y quasi-singular, since, if $y \circ z = 0$, then

$$0 = \hat{y}(\varphi)+\hat{z}(\varphi)-\hat{y}(\varphi)\,\hat{z}(\varphi) = 1+\hat{z}(\varphi)-\hat{z}(\varphi) = 1,$$

a contradiction. Therefore $\alpha \in Sp(x)$ and the right hand inclusion is proved. We note in passing that completeness of $\mathfrak{A}$ was not needed for this result. Now let α be any non-zero element of $Sp(x)$. Then $\alpha^{-1}x$ is quasi-singular, so that $(1-\alpha^{-1}x)\mathfrak{A}$ is a proper modular ideal in $\mathfrak{A}$ with $\alpha^{-1}x$ as an identity modulo the ideal. If $\mathfrak{M}$ is a maximal modular ideal containing $(1-\alpha^{-1}x)\mathfrak{A}$, let φ be the corresponding element of $\Phi_{\mathfrak{A}}$ with $\mathfrak{M}$ as kernel. Since $e = \alpha^{-1}x$ is also an identity modulo $\mathfrak{M}$, we have $\hat{e}(\varphi) = \alpha^{-1}\hat{x}(\varphi) = 1$ and hence $\hat{x}(\varphi) = \alpha$. This proves the left hand inclusion. If $\alpha = 0$ and $\mathfrak{A}$ has an identity element, then $x\mathfrak{A}$ is a proper ideal and so is contained in a maximal ideal. Hence again $\hat{x}(\varphi) = \alpha$ for some $\varphi \in \Phi_{\mathfrak{A}}$. Therefore the equality holds on the right when $\mathfrak{A}$ has an identity.

COROLLARY (3.1.7). $\nu_{\mathfrak{A}}(x) = \max|\hat{x}(\varphi)|$, $\varphi \in \Phi_{\mathfrak{A}}$. *In particular, each homomorphism φ is automatically continuous.*

COROLLARY (3.1.8). *An element x is in the radical of $\mathfrak{A}$ if and only if $\hat{x}(\varphi) = 0$ for every $\varphi \in \Phi_{\mathfrak{A}}$.*

COROLLARY (3.1.9). *An element x is quasi-regular in $\mathfrak{A}$ if and only if $\hat{x}(\varphi) \neq 1$ for every $\varphi \in \Phi_{\mathfrak{A}}$. If $\mathfrak{A}$ has an identity element, then x is regular in $\mathfrak{A}$ if and only if $\hat{x}(\varphi) \neq 0$ for every $\varphi \in \Phi_{\mathfrak{A}}$.*

We now obtain a useful concrete representation of the carrier space. However, it is necessary to discuss first the notion of a system of generators for an algebra.

Let $\mathfrak{A}$ be any normed algebra and A an arbitrary subset of $\mathfrak{A}$. Then the smallest closed subalgebra $\mathfrak{A}_0$ of $\mathfrak{A}$ which contains A is called the subalgebra of $\mathfrak{A}$ GENERATED BY A, and A is called a SYSTEM OF GENERATORS for $\mathfrak{A}_0$. It is evident that $\mathfrak{A}_0$ is equal to the closure, in the norm of $\mathfrak{A}$, of the set of all elements of $\mathfrak{A}$ which can be expressed as polynomials in elements of A with coefficients in the field of scalars of $\mathfrak{A}$. Observe that a trivial system of generators for an algebra $\mathfrak{A}$ is $\mathfrak{A}$ itself.

We remark in passing that, if $\mathfrak{A}$ has an identity element, then some writers would define the subalgebra of $\mathfrak{A}$ generated by a set A to be the smallest closed subalgebra which contains A *plus* the identity element. Although this definition has some advantages in certain special situations, the definition given above is more appropriate for our immediate purposes whether or not $\mathfrak{A}$ has an identity element.

Consider a commutative Banach algebra $\mathfrak{A}$ with a system of generators $\{z_\lambda : \lambda \in \Lambda\}$ indexed by an abstract set Λ. We prove first that the topology in the space $\Phi_{\mathfrak{A}}{}^\infty$ is determined by neighborhoods of the form,

$$V_\varphi(x_1, \cdots, x_n; \epsilon) = \{\varphi' : |\hat{x}_i(\varphi) - \hat{x}_i(\varphi')| < \epsilon, i = 1, \cdots, n\},$$

where the elements $x_1, \cdots, x_n$ are taken from the system of generators.

This is evidently equivalent to saying that the topology of $\Phi_{\mathfrak{A}}{}^{\infty}$ is the weakest topology in which all of the functions $\hat{z}_{\lambda}$ are continuous. For the proof, note that, if x is any element of $\mathfrak{A}$ and $\{p_k\}$ is a sequence of elements of $\mathfrak{A}$ which are polynomials in the generators such that $\|x-p_k\| \to 0$, then $\hat{p}_k(\varphi) \to \hat{x}(\varphi)$ uniformly for $\varphi \in \Phi_{\mathfrak{A}}{}^{\infty}$. If $p_k = P_k(\{z_{\lambda}\})$ where $P_k(\{\xi_{\lambda}\})$ denotes a polynomial in a finite number of the indeterminates $\{\xi_{\lambda}\,;\lambda \in \Lambda\}$, then $\hat{p}_k(\varphi) = P_k(\{\hat{z}_{\lambda}(\varphi)\})$, so that continuity of each $\hat{z}_{\lambda}$ implies continuity of $\hat{p}_k$ and hence continuity of $\hat{x}$. Therefore the desired conclusion follows. Now associate with each of the indices $\lambda \in \Lambda$ a complex plane K_{λ} and denote by K^{Λ} the cartesian product of the planes K_{λ} under the usual product space topology. Then $\varphi \to \{\hat{z}_{\lambda}(\varphi)\}$ defines a mapping of $\Phi_{\mathfrak{A}}{}^{\infty}$ into K^{Λ} which will be called the CANONICAL MAPPING of $\Phi_{\mathfrak{A}}{}^{\infty}$ into K^{Λ}. The image of $\Phi_{\mathfrak{A}}{}^{\infty}$ in K^{Λ} will be called the CANONICAL REPRESENTATION of $\Phi_{\mathfrak{A}}{}^{\infty}$ determined by the given system of generators.

THEOREM (3.1.10). *Let $\mathfrak{A}$ be a commutative Banach algebra and $\{z_{\lambda} : \lambda \in \Lambda\}$ any system of generators for $\mathfrak{A}$. Then the canonical mapping $\varphi \to \{\hat{z}_{\lambda}(\varphi)\}$ of $\Phi_{\mathfrak{A}}{}^{\infty}$ into K^{Λ} is a homeomorphism and the image of $\Phi_{\mathfrak{A}}{}^{\infty}$ in K^{Λ} is compact.*

PROOF. That the canonical mapping is a homeomorphism is immediate from the definition of the topology in K^{Λ} plus the fact that the topology in $\Phi_{\mathfrak{A}}{}^{\infty}$ is determined by the system of generators. Now let D_{λ} denote the closed disc $\{\zeta : |\zeta| \leqslant \nu_{\mathfrak{A}}(z_{\lambda})\}$ in the complex plane K_{λ}. Since each D_{λ} is compact, it follows by the Tychonoff theorem that the cartesian product Δ of all the D_{λ} is a compact subset of K^{Λ}. Furthermore, the image Ψ of $\Phi_{\mathfrak{A}}{}^{\infty}$ in K^{Λ} is contained in Δ. Therefore in order to prove compactness we have only to show that the image Ψ is closed. To this end let $\{\zeta_{\lambda}\}$ be a limit point of Ψ in K^{Λ}. The problem is to construct a $\psi \in \Phi_{\mathfrak{A}}{}^{\infty}$ such that $\zeta_{\lambda} = \hat{z}_{\lambda}(\psi)$ for each $\lambda \in \Lambda$. First let p be any element of $\mathfrak{A}$ which is equal to a polynomial $P(\{z_{\lambda}\})$ in the generators $z_{\lambda_1}, \cdots, z_{\lambda_n}$. For arbitrary $\delta > 0$, there exists $\varphi \in \Phi_{\mathfrak{A}}{}^{\infty}$ such that $|\hat{z}_{\lambda_i}(\varphi)-\zeta_{\lambda_i}| < \delta$ for $i = 1, \cdots, n$. By continuity of polynomials and the fact that $\hat{p}(\varphi) = P(\{\hat{z}_{\lambda}(\varphi)\})$, it follows that there exists, for $\epsilon > 0$, a $\varphi \in \Phi_{\mathfrak{A}}{}^{\infty}$ such that $|\hat{p}(\varphi)-P(\{\zeta_{\lambda}\})| < \epsilon$. Since $|\hat{p}(\varphi)| \leqslant \|p\|$, we conclude that $|P(\{\zeta_{\lambda}\})| \leqslant \|p\|$. Now let x be any element of $\mathfrak{A}$ and choose a sequence $\{p_k\}$ with $p_k = P_k(\{z_{\lambda}\})$, where P_k is a polynomial, such that $\|x-p_k\| \to 0$. If we define $\hat{p}_k(\psi) = P_k(\{\zeta_{\lambda}\})$, then it follows, from the inequality $|P(\{\zeta_{\lambda}\})| \leqslant \|p\|$ obtained above, that

$$\hat{x}(\psi) = \lim_{k\to\infty} \hat{p}_k(\psi)$$

exists. Furthermore $\hat{x}(\psi)$ is independent of the choice of $\{p_k\}$ since any other choice $\{q_k\}$ will have the property $\|p_k - q_k\| \to 0$. Finally, if x and y are any two elements of $\mathfrak{A}$ and $\{p_k\}$, $\{q_k\}$ are sequences of polynomials in the generators which converge to x, y respectively, then $\{p_k q_k\}$ converges to xy. Let $w = xy$ and $r_k = p_k q_k$. Then it is obvious that $\hat{r}_k(\psi) = \hat{p}_k(\psi)\hat{q}_k(\psi)$ and hence that $\hat{w}(\psi) = \hat{x}(\psi)\hat{y}(\psi)$. The other properties of a homomorphism are proved in a similar way and we therefore conclude that $\psi \in \Phi_{\mathfrak{A}}{}^{\infty}$. Since $\hat{z}_\lambda(\psi) = \zeta_\lambda$, for every $\lambda \in \Lambda$, the proof is complete.

Corollary (3.1.11). *$\Phi_{\mathfrak{A}}$ is a locally compact Hausdorff space with $\Phi_{\mathfrak{A}}{}^{\infty}$ as its one-point compactification. If $\mathfrak{A}$ also has an identity element, then φ_∞ is an isolated point of $\Phi_{\mathfrak{A}}{}^{\infty}$, so that $\Phi_{\mathfrak{A}}$ is compact.*

Corollary (3.1.12). *If $\{z_k\}$ is a countable system of generators for $\mathfrak{A}$, then the topology in $\Phi_{\mathfrak{A}}{}^{\infty}$ is equivalent to the topology defined by the metric*

$$d(\varphi_1, \varphi_2) = \sum_{k=1}^{\infty} \frac{|\hat{z}_k(\varphi_1) - \hat{z}_k(\varphi_2)|}{2^k}.$$

Suppose that the system of generators $\{z_\lambda : \lambda \in \Lambda\}$ in the above theorem contains an element z_{λ_0} such that $\hat{z}_{\lambda_0}$ is constant on $\Phi_{\mathfrak{A}}$. If Λ_0 is equal to the set Λ minus λ_0, then the λ_0-projection of K^Λ onto K^{Λ_0} evidently maps the image of $\Phi_{\mathfrak{A}}$ in K^Λ determined by $\{z_\lambda : \lambda \in \Lambda\}$ homeomorphically onto the image of $\Phi_{\mathfrak{A}}$ in K^{Λ_0} determined by $\{z_\lambda : \lambda \in \Lambda_0\}$. We can therefore state the following corollary.

Corollary (3.1.13). *Assume that $\mathfrak{A}$ has an identity element and that $\{z_\lambda : \lambda \in \Lambda\}$ plus the identity is a system of generators for $\mathfrak{A}$. Then the mapping $\varphi \to \{\hat{z}_\lambda(\varphi)\}$ of $\Phi_{\mathfrak{A}}$ into K^Λ is a homeomorphism.*

A natural question to raise at this point concerns the relationship between the carrier space $\Phi_{\mathfrak{A}}$ of a commutative Banach algebra $\mathfrak{A}$ discussed here and the structure spaces discussed in Chapter II, § 6. Since in a commutative algebra an ideal is primitive if and only if it is maximal modular, we see that the space $\Pi_{\mathfrak{A}}$ of primitive ideals reduces to the space $\Xi_{\mathfrak{A}}$ of maximal modular ideals. Now, if $\mathfrak{A}$ is also complex, then $\Xi_{\mathfrak{A}}$ is in one-to-one correspondence with $\Phi_{\mathfrak{A}}$ *via* the mapping which associates with each homomorphism in $\Phi_{\mathfrak{A}}$ its kernel ideal in $\Xi_{\mathfrak{A}}$. Therefore $\Phi_{\mathfrak{A}}$ inherits a hull–kernel topology from $\Xi_{\mathfrak{A}}$. The same is true for real $\mathfrak{A}$ provided we take instead of $\Xi_{\mathfrak{A}}$ the space $\Xi_{\mathfrak{A}_c}$ of maximal modular ideals in the complexification of $\mathfrak{A}$. It is convenient to formulate the notions of hull and kernel directly in $\Phi_{\mathfrak{A}}$.

DEFINITION (3.1.14). *Let A be a subset of $\mathfrak{A}$ and F a subset of $\Phi_{\mathfrak{A}}$. Then the set*

$$\mathscr{h}(A) = \{\varphi : \varphi \in \Phi_{\mathfrak{A}},\ \hat{a}(\varphi) = 0 \text{ for } a \in A\}$$

is the HULL *of A in $\Phi_{\mathfrak{A}}$ and the set*

$$\mathscr{k}(F) = \{a : a \in \mathfrak{A},\ \hat{a}(\varphi) = 0 \text{ for } \varphi \in F\}$$

is the KERNEL *of F in $\mathfrak{A}$. If $F = \mathscr{h}(\mathscr{k}(F))$, then F is called a* HULL *and, if $A = \mathscr{k}(\mathscr{h}(A))$, then A is called a* KERNEL.

The T_1-topology determined in $\Phi_{\mathfrak{A}}$ by the hulls as closed sets is called the HULL–KERNEL TOPOLOGY for $\Phi_{\mathfrak{A}}$. This topology is not in general equivalent to the $\mathfrak{A}$-topology. An example for which the two topologies are different is the algebra of all complex-valued functions continuous on the closed unit disc of the complex plane and holomorphic in the interior of the disc (See Appendix, A.2.6). On the other hand, the class of algebras for which these topologies are equivalent is an important one and will be discussed later in § 8. In order to avoid confusion, a closed set in the hull–kernel topology will always be referred to as a hull and all topological references will be to the $\mathfrak{A}$-topology unless explicitly stated otherwise.

In addition to the usual properties of hulls and kernels, which hold in any algebra, it is straightforward to verify the following properties: (1) $\mathscr{h}(A)$ is a closed subset of $\Phi_{\mathfrak{A}}$ and $\mathscr{k}(F)$ is a closed ideal in $\mathfrak{A}$. (2) If $\mathfrak{I}$ is the closed ideal generated in $\mathfrak{A}$ by A, then $\mathscr{h}(A) = \mathscr{h}(\mathfrak{I})$. If $\bar{F}$ is the closure of the set F in $\Phi_{\mathfrak{A}}$, then $\mathscr{k}(F) = \mathscr{k}(\bar{F})$. We also include here the following lemmas which will be needed later.

LEMMA (3.1.15). *Let F be an arbitrary subset of $\Phi_{\mathfrak{A}}$. Then the ideal $\mathscr{k}(F)$ is modular if and only if there exists $u \in \mathfrak{A}$ such that $\hat{u}(\varphi) = 1$ for $\varphi \in F$.*

PROOF. Assume first that u exists such that $\hat{u}(\varphi) = 1$ for $\varphi \in F$. For any $x \in \mathfrak{A}$, set $v = x - xu$. Then $\hat{v}(\varphi) = 0$, for every $\varphi \in F$. In other words $\mathfrak{A}(1-u) \subseteq \mathscr{k}(F)$ and $\mathscr{k}(F)$ is modular. Now assume $\mathscr{k}(F)$ modular and let $\mathfrak{A}(1-u) \subseteq \mathscr{k}(F)$. For arbitrary $\varphi \in F$, choose $x \in \mathfrak{A}$ such that $\hat{x}(\varphi) \neq 0$. Then $v = x - xu \in \mathscr{k}(F)$ and we have

$$\hat{x}(\varphi)(1 - \hat{u}(\varphi)) = \hat{v}(\varphi) = 0.$$

Since $\hat{x}(\varphi) \neq 0$ it follows that $\hat{u}(\varphi) = 1$, and the proof is complete.

LEMMA (3.1.16). *If u is any element of $\mathfrak{A}$ and α any scalar, then the set* $\{\varphi : \varphi \in \Phi_{\mathfrak{A}},\ \hat{u}(\varphi) = \alpha\}$ *is a hull.*

PROOF. Let $F_\alpha = \{\varphi : \varphi \in \Phi_{\mathfrak{A}},\ \hat{u}(\varphi) = \alpha\}$ and define $\mathfrak{J} = \mathfrak{A}u$, if $\alpha = 0$, and $\mathfrak{J} = \mathfrak{A}(1-\alpha^{-1}u)$, if $\alpha \neq 0$. It is obvious that $F_\alpha \subseteq h(\mathfrak{J})$ in either case. On the other hand, let $\varphi \in h(\mathfrak{J})$ and choose $a \in \mathfrak{A}$ such that $\hat{a}(\varphi) \neq 0$. If $\alpha = 0$ and $v = au$, then $\hat{a}(\varphi)\hat{u}(\varphi) = \hat{v}(\varphi) = 0$. If $\alpha \neq 0$ and $w = a(1-\alpha^{-1}u)$, then $\hat{a}(\varphi)(1-\alpha^{-1}\hat{u}(\varphi)) = \hat{w}(\varphi) = 0$. Hence $\hat{u}(\varphi) = \alpha$ in either case and we obtain $h(\mathfrak{J}) \subseteq F_\alpha$. Therefore $h(\mathfrak{J}) = F_\alpha$, and the lemma is proved.

Consider next a pair of algebras $\mathfrak{A}$ and $\mathfrak{B}$ along with a homomorphism τ of $\mathfrak{B}$ into $\mathfrak{A}$. If φ is any element of $\Phi_{\mathfrak{A}}{}^\infty$, then the mapping $b \to \hat{b}^\tau(\varphi)$ defines a homomorphism of $\mathfrak{B}$ into the complex field and so determines an element $\varphi^{\tau'}$ of $\Phi_{\mathfrak{B}}{}^\infty$. We thus obtain a mapping $\varphi \to \varphi^{\tau'}$ of $\Phi_{\mathfrak{A}}{}^\infty$ into $\Phi_{\mathfrak{B}}{}^\infty$ which will be called the DUAL of τ or the DUAL MAPPING ASSOCIATED WITH τ. If $V_{\varphi^{\tau'}}(b_1, \cdots, b_n;\epsilon)$ is any neighborhood of $\varphi^{\tau'}$ in $\Phi_{\mathfrak{B}}{}^\infty$, then the neighborhood $V_\varphi(b_1{}^\tau, \cdots, b_n{}^\tau;\epsilon)$ of φ in $\Phi_{\mathfrak{A}}{}^\infty$ is mapped by τ' into $V_{\varphi^{\tau'}}$. Therefore the dual mapping is always continuous. Observe that, if $\mathfrak{B}$ is a subalgebra of $\mathfrak{A}$ and τ is the injection mapping of $\mathfrak{B}$ into $\mathfrak{A}$, then the image of $\Phi_{\mathfrak{A}}{}^\infty$ in $\Phi_{\mathfrak{B}}{}^\infty$ under the associated dual mapping consists precisely of those homomorphisms of $\mathfrak{B}$ into the complex field which can be extended to all of $\mathfrak{A}$. If, in addition, $\mathfrak{A}$ is a Banach algebra and $\mathfrak{B}$ is a dense subalgebra of $\mathfrak{A}$, then the image of $\Phi_{\mathfrak{A}}{}^\infty$ in $\Phi_{\mathfrak{B}}{}^\infty$ consists of those homomorphisms of $\mathfrak{B}$ into the complex field which are continuous with respect to the $\mathfrak{A}$-norm in $\mathfrak{B}$. The image of $\Phi_{\mathfrak{A}}{}^\infty$ in $\Phi_{\mathfrak{B}}{}^\infty$, for this case, can also be described as the set of all $\psi \in \Phi_{\mathfrak{B}}{}^\infty$ such that $|\hat{x}(\psi)| \leqslant \|x\|$, for all $x \in \mathfrak{B}$, where $\|x\|$ is the norm in $\mathfrak{A}$. The embedding here is actually a homeomorphism (See Theorem (3.2.4)). It is obvious that, if τ is an isomorphism between $\mathfrak{B}$ and $\mathfrak{A}$, then the dual of τ is a homeomorphism between the two carrier spaces. We have, more generally, the following theorem.

THEOREM (3.1.17). *Let τ be a homomorphism of $\mathfrak{B}$ onto $\mathfrak{A}$ and let $\mathfrak{K}$ be the kernel of τ. Then the dual mapping of $\Phi_{\mathfrak{A}}{}^\infty$ into $\Phi_{\mathfrak{B}}{}^\infty$ takes $\Phi_{\mathfrak{A}}$ homeomorphically onto $h(\mathfrak{K})$, the hull in $\Phi_{\mathfrak{B}}$ of the ideal $\mathfrak{K}$.*

PROOF. Since $\hat{b}(\varphi^{\tau'}) = \hat{b}^\tau(\varphi)$, it is immediate that the image of $\Phi_{\mathfrak{A}}$ in $\Phi_{\mathfrak{B}}$ is contained in $h(\mathfrak{K})$. Furthermore, since $\mathfrak{B}$ is mapped *onto* $\mathfrak{A}$ by τ, it also follows that the dual mapping is one-to-one on $\Phi_{\mathfrak{A}}$. Next let ψ be any element of $h(\mathfrak{K})$. For arbitrary $a \in \mathfrak{A}$, choose $b \in \mathfrak{B}$ such that $b^\tau = a$ and define $\hat{a}(\varphi) = \hat{b}(\psi)$. If $b_1{}^\tau = b_2{}^\tau$, then $b_1 - b_2 \in \mathfrak{K}$ and hence $\hat{b}_1(\psi) = \hat{b}_2(\psi)$. Therefore the definition of $\hat{a}(\varphi)$ is independent of the choice of b. Evidently $\varphi \in \Phi_{\mathfrak{A}}$ and $\varphi^{\tau'} = \psi$. In other words, $\Phi_{\mathfrak{A}}$ is mapped onto $h(\mathfrak{R})$. Finally let $V_{\varphi_0}(a_1, \cdots, a_n ; \epsilon)$ be any neighborhood of the point φ_0 in $\Phi_{\mathfrak{A}}$. Choose $b_i \in \mathfrak{B}$ such that $b_i^{\tau} = a_i$. Then $\varphi \to \varphi^{\tau}$ takes the neighborhood V_{φ_0} *onto* the neighborhood $V_{\varphi_0^{\tau'}}(b_1, \cdots, b_n ; \epsilon)$ of $\varphi_0^{\tau'}$ in $h(\mathfrak{R})$. It follows that the dual of τ is a homeomorphism and so the theorem is proved.

The above theorem provides an identification of the carrier space of an algebra which is obtained from a given one by forming the difference algebra modulo an ideal. If $\mathfrak{A}$ were a complex Banach algebra and if $\Phi_{\mathfrak{A}}$ were topologized with the hull-kernel topology, then the above theorem would be a corollary of the first statement in Theorem (2.6.6). The next theorem provides the analogue of the result in the second statement of the same theorem.

THEOREM (3.1.18). *Let $\mathfrak{I}$ be any ideal in $\mathfrak{A}$. Then the dual mapping of $\Phi_{\mathfrak{A}}^{\infty}$ into $\Phi_{\mathfrak{I}}^{\infty}$, associated with the injection of $\mathfrak{I}$ into $\mathfrak{A}$, is a homeomorphism of $\Phi_{\mathfrak{A}} - h(\mathfrak{I})$ onto $\Phi_{\mathfrak{I}}$.*

PROOF. Let $\varphi \to \varphi'$ denote the dual mapping of $\Phi_{\mathfrak{A}}^{\infty}$ into $\Phi_{\mathfrak{I}}^{\infty}$. If $\varphi \in h(\mathfrak{I})$, then φ' is obviously the zero homomorphism of $\mathfrak{I}$. Furthermore, if φ_1 and φ_2 are any two points of $\Phi_{\mathfrak{A}}^{\infty}$, choose $u \in \mathfrak{A}$ such that $\hat{u}(\varphi_1) = 0$ while $\hat{u}(\varphi_2) = 1$. Now, if $\varphi'_1 = \varphi'_2$, then, for every $b \in \mathfrak{I}$, we have $v = bu \in \mathfrak{I}$ and hence $0 = \hat{v}(\varphi_1) = \hat{v}(\varphi_2) = \hat{b}(\varphi_2)$. In other words, $\varphi_2 \in h(\mathfrak{I})$. Similarly, $\varphi_1 \in h(\mathfrak{I})$. Therefore the mapping $\varphi \to \varphi'$ is one-to-one on $\Phi_{\mathfrak{A}} - h(\mathfrak{I})$. We now prove that $\Phi_{\mathfrak{A}} - h(\mathfrak{I})$ maps *onto* $\Phi_{\mathfrak{I}}$. To this end, let ψ be an arbitrary element of $\Phi_{\mathfrak{I}}$ and choose $u \in \mathfrak{I}$ such that $\hat{u}(\psi) = 1$. Now, for arbitrary $a \in \mathfrak{A}$, set $v = au$ and define $\hat{a}(\varphi) = \hat{v}(\psi)$. Then it is readily verified that $a \to \hat{a}(\varphi)$ is a homomorphism of $\mathfrak{A}$ into the complex field, so that $\varphi \in \Phi_{\mathfrak{A}}$. Furthermore, if $a \in \mathfrak{I}$, then $\hat{a}(\varphi) = \hat{a}(\psi)$. Therefore $\psi = \varphi'$ and it follows that $\Phi_{\mathfrak{A}} - h(\mathfrak{I})$ maps onto $\Phi_{\mathfrak{I}}$. Since the dual mapping is always continuous, it remains to prove that its inverse $\varphi' \to \varphi$ is also continuous. Let φ_0 be any element of $\Phi_{\mathfrak{A}} - h(\mathfrak{I})$ and let $V_{\varphi_0}(x_1, \cdots, x_n ; \epsilon)$ be a neighborhood of φ_0 in $\Phi_{\mathfrak{A}}$. Choose $u_0 \in \mathfrak{I}$ such that $\hat{u}_0(\varphi_0) \neq 0$ and define $u_i = u_0 x_i$ for $i = 1, \cdots, n$. Then $u_i \in \mathfrak{I}$ and, for arbitrary φ,

$$\begin{aligned} |\hat{u}_i(\varphi) - \hat{u}_i(\varphi_0)| &= |\hat{u}_0(\varphi)\hat{x}_i(\varphi) - \hat{u}_0(\varphi_0)\hat{x}_i(\varphi_0)| \\ &\geqslant |\hat{u}_0(\varphi)|\,|\hat{x}_i(\varphi) - \hat{x}_i(\varphi_0)| - |\hat{u}_0(\varphi) - \hat{u}_0(\varphi_0)|\,|\hat{x}_i(\varphi_0)|. \end{aligned}$$

Therefore, if $|\hat{u}_i(\varphi) - \hat{u}_i(\varphi_0)| < \delta$, for $i = 0, 1, \cdots, n$, where $0 < \delta < \frac{1}{2}|\hat{u}_0(\varphi_0)|$, then

$$|\hat{x}_i(\varphi) - \hat{x}_i(\varphi_0)| < 2\frac{1 + |\hat{x}_i(\varphi_0)|}{|\hat{u}_0(\varphi_0)|}\delta, \qquad i = 1, \cdots, n.$$

Hence, if we take

$$\delta < \frac{\epsilon|\hat{u}_0(\varphi_0)|}{2(1 + \max|\hat{x}_i(\varphi_0)|)},$$

then $|\hat{u}_i(\varphi) - \hat{u}_i(\varphi_0)| < \delta$ for $i = 0, 1, \cdots, n$ implies $|\hat{x}_i(\varphi) - \hat{x}_i(\varphi_0)| < \epsilon$ for $i = 1, \cdots, n$. In other words, the neighborhood $V_{\varphi_0}(u_0, u_1, \cdots, u_n; \delta)$ is mapped by the inverse of the dual mapping into the neighborhood $V_{\varphi_0}(x_1, \cdots, x_n; \epsilon)$. Therefore the inverse mapping is continuous and the theorem is proved.

COROLLARY (3.1.19). *Let e be an idempotent in $\mathfrak{A}$. Then the dual mapping associated with the injection of $e\mathfrak{A}$ into $\mathfrak{A}$ defines a homeomorphism of the subset $\{\varphi : \hat{e}(\varphi) = 1\}$ of $\Phi_{\mathfrak{A}}$ with the carrier space $\Phi_{e\mathfrak{A}}$ of the algebra $e\mathfrak{A}$.*

We turn now to the fundamental Gelfand [4] representation theorem for commutative Banach algebras. This theorem provides, in one sense, a complete solution of the structure problem for general semi-simple commutative Banach algebras. It shows that such an algebra is a "continuous sum" of its irreducible representations, the result being an algebra of continuous functions on a locally compact Hausdorff space. The theorem, at least in the complex case, can be regarded as a specialization of the structure Theorem (2.6.1) (ii) obtained in Chapter II. However, in the commutative case, the result is a far more concrete representation and consequently plays a much more important role in the theory. The substance of the proof has already been covered in the preceding pages, so that, aside from some notations, there is little more to do than to state the theorem.

Let Ω be any topological space. Then $C(\Omega)$ will denote the algebra of all bounded, complex-valued continuous functions on Ω with the usual algebra operations for functions. Thus, if Ω is a compact Hausdorff space, $C(\Omega)$ is the algebra of all continuous functions on Ω. If Ω is a locally compact Hausdorff space, then a function f, which is continuous on Ω, is said to VANISH AT INFINITY provided, for arbitrary $\epsilon > 0$, there exists a compact subset F of Ω such that $|f(\omega)| < \epsilon$ for $\omega \in \Omega - F$. The algebra of all complex-valued continuous functions on

Ω, which vanish at infinity, is denoted by $C_0(\Omega)$. If Ω is compact, then $C_0(\Omega) = C(\Omega)$. The corresponding algebras of real-valued functions will be denoted by $C^R(\Omega)$ and $C_0{}^R(\Omega)$ respectively. Notice that all of these algebras are Banach algebras under the norm $\|f\| = \sup|f(\omega)|$, $\omega \in \Omega$. The algebras $C(\Omega)$ and $C^R(\Omega)$ always possess an identity element, while $C_0(\Omega)$ and $C_0{}^R(\Omega)$ will possess an identity element if and only if Ω is compact.

THEOREM (3.1.20). *Let $\mathfrak{A}$ be any commutative Banach algebra with carrier space $\Phi_{\mathfrak{A}}$. Then there exists a continuous homomorphism of $\mathfrak{A}$ into the Banach algebra $C_0(\Phi_{\mathfrak{A}})$, the kernel of the homomorphism being equal to the radical of $\mathfrak{A}$.*

PROOF. As in the above discussion, we associate with each x in $\mathfrak{A}$ the function $\hat{x}$ defined on $\Phi_{\mathfrak{A}}$. By the definition of the topology in $\Phi_{\mathfrak{A}}$, $\hat{x}$ is continuous and vanishes at infinity on $\Phi_{\mathfrak{A}}$. It is obvious that $x \to \hat{x}$ is a homomorphism of $\mathfrak{A}$ into $C_0(\Phi_{\mathfrak{A}})$ and that the kernel of the homomorphism is equal to the radical. Furthermore since $\hat{x}(\varphi)$ belongs to $Sp(x)$, for every φ in $\Phi_{\mathfrak{A}}$, we have

$$\|\hat{x}\| = \max_{\varphi \in \Phi_{\mathfrak{A}}} |\hat{x}(\varphi)| \leqslant \|x\|$$

for every $x \in \mathfrak{A}$. In other words, the homomorphism $x \to \hat{x}$ of $\mathfrak{A}$ into $C_0(\Phi_{\mathfrak{A}})$ is continuous and the proof is complete.

It has already been noted that, if $\mathfrak{A}$ is a real algebra, then it can happen that, for some $\varphi \in \Phi_{\mathfrak{A}}$, the image of $\mathfrak{A}$ under φ is the complex field. It is natural to ask when only the real numbers arise, thus ensuring that all of the functions in the Gelfand representation are real.

THEOREM (3.1.21). *Let $\mathfrak{A}$ be a commutative Banach algebra. Then, in order for $\hat{x}(\varphi)$ to be real for every $x \in \mathfrak{A}$ and $\varphi \in \Phi_{\mathfrak{A}}$, it is necessary and sufficient that $-x^2$ be quasi-regular for every $x \in \mathfrak{A}$.*

PROOF. Observe first that, if $\hat{x}(\varphi)$ is always real, then $\mathfrak{A}$ must be a real algebra. Furthermore, if $-x^2$ is not quasi-regular, then $-1 \in Sp(x^2)$, and so there exists by Theorem (3.1.6) a $\varphi \in \Phi_{\mathfrak{A}}$ such that $\hat{x}(\varphi)^2 = -1$. In other words $\hat{x}(\varphi) = \pm i$, contrary to hypothesis. This proves the necessity. Now suppose $\hat{x}(\varphi) = \alpha + \beta i$ where α, β are real and $\beta \neq 0$. Choose $e \in \mathfrak{A}$ such that $\hat{e}(\varphi) = 1$ and set $y = \beta^{-1}(x - \alpha e)$. Then $\hat{y}(\varphi) = i$ and this implies that $-y^2$ is quasi-singular, by Corollary (3.1.9). This proves the sufficiency.

An interesting fact here is that, in any Banach algebra, quasi-regularity of $-x^2$, for every x, already implies commutativity modulo the radical, that is, $xy - yx$ belongs to the radical for all x and y (Kaplansky [5]).

In the case of a complex Banach algebra, we have observed that the carrier space can be identified with the class of maximal modular ideals of the algebra. This is the form in which the space was first introduced by Gelfand [4]. It is important to remark, however, that the topology of the carrier space so represented is, in general, different from the hull–kernel topology. In order to emphasize this distinction, we have restricted the use of the terminology "structure space" to apply only to the space of maximal modular ideals under the hull–kernel topology. This is in contrast to a common practice of referring to the carrier space as the "maximal ideal space" or "structure space" of the algebra. The terminology "carrier space" has also been used recently by Gelfand [8] essentially as we have used it here. (See remarks at the end of § 6, Chapter II.)

§ 2. **Algebras of functions.** The Gelfand representation theorem shows that the study of semi-simple commutative Banach algebras reduces to a study of certain algebras of continuous functions on a locally compact Hausdorff space. With this motivition, we examine in this section a few general properties of algebras of complex-valued functions. As the starting point, consider any topological space Ω and let $\mathfrak{C}$ be a real or complex algebra of complex-valued continuous functions on Ω, the algebra operations in $\mathfrak{C}$ being the usual ones for functions. It will be assumed throughout that $\mathfrak{C}$ SEPARATES THE POINTS of Ω in the sense that there exists for any pair of points ω_1, ω_2 in Ω an element f of $\mathfrak{C}$ such that $f(\omega_1) \neq f(\omega_2)$. Since the functions in $\mathfrak{C}$ are continuous, this separation condition forces Ω to be Hausdorff. If $\mathfrak{C}$ separates points of Ω and if in addition there exists for each $\omega \in \Omega$ an $f \in \mathfrak{C}$ such that $f(\omega) \neq 0$, then $\mathfrak{C}$ is said to SEPARATE STRONGLY the points of Ω. The weakest topology in Ω for which each $f \in \mathfrak{C}$ is continuous will be called the $\mathfrak{C}$-topology in accordance with the terminology used in the preceding section. It is determined by neighborhoods of the form

$$V_\omega(f_1, \cdots, f_n; \epsilon) = \{\omega' : |f_i(\omega) - f_i(\omega')| < \epsilon, i = 1, \cdots, n\},$$

where $f_1, \cdots, f_n$ is any finite set of elements from $\mathfrak{C}$ and $\epsilon > 0$.

Let ω be a fixed point of Ω and consider the mapping $f \to f(\omega)$ of $\mathfrak{C}$ into the complex numbers. This mapping is obviously a homomorphism and so defines an element φ_ω of the carrier space $\Phi_{\mathfrak{C}}^\infty$ of $\mathfrak{C}$ such that $\hat{f}(\varphi_\omega) = f(\omega)$. Since $f(\omega) = 0$ for every $\omega \in \Omega$ means, by definition, that $f = 0$, it follows that $\mathfrak{C}$ is automatically semi-simple. The mapping $\omega \to \varphi_\omega$ defined here will be called the NATURAL EMBEDDING of Ω in $\Phi_{\mathfrak{C}}^\infty$. Notice that if $\mathfrak{C}$ separates strongly the points of Ω, then the image of Ω under the natural embedding lies in $\Phi_{\mathfrak{C}}$.

The question of the relationship between Ω and $\Phi_{\mathfrak{C}}$ appears, in one form or another, as a basic problem in the study of any algebra of functions.

THEOREM (3.2.1). *The natural embedding of Ω in $\Phi_{\mathfrak{C}}{}^{\infty}$ is one-to-one and continuous. It is a homeomorphism if and only if the given topology in Ω is equivalent to the $\mathfrak{C}$-topology.*

PROOF. It is obvious that the mapping $\omega \rightarrow \varphi_{\omega}$ is one-to-one since $\mathfrak{C}$ separates the points of Ω. It follows immediately from the definition of the $\mathfrak{C}$-topologies in Ω and in $\Phi_{\mathfrak{C}}{}^{\infty}$ that the natural embedding is a homeomorphism with respect to these topologies. Furthermore, since the $\mathfrak{C}$-topology is, by definition, equivalent to or weaker than the given topology in Ω, the mapping is always continuous, and the theorem follows.

COROLLARY (3.2.2). *If $\mathfrak{C}$ is a Banach algebra under any norm whatsoever, then the functions in $\mathfrak{C}$ are bounded and $|f(\omega)| \leqslant \nu(f) \leqslant \|f\|$ for all $\omega \in \Omega$ and $f \in \mathfrak{C}$.*

COROLLARY (3.2.3). *Assume that, for every closed set F in Ω and every point ω_0 of Ω not in F, there exists a function u in $\mathfrak{C}$ which is constant on F with value different from $u(\omega_0)$. Then the topology in Ω is equivalent to the $\mathfrak{C}$-topology, so that the natural embedding of Ω in $\Phi_{\mathfrak{C}}{}^{\infty}$ is a homeomorphism.*

THEOREM (3.2.4). *Let Ω be locally compact and let $\mathfrak{C}$ be a (real or complex) subalgebra of $C_0(\Omega)$. Then, if $\mathfrak{C}$ separates strongly the points of Ω, the natural embedding of Ω into $\Phi_{\mathfrak{C}}$ is a homeomorphism which takes Ω onto a closed subset of $\Phi_{\mathfrak{C}}$.*

PROOF. By the preceding theorem the natural embedding is one-to-one and continuous. Therefore the theorem will follow if we prove that every closed set F in Ω maps onto a closed set F' in $\Phi_{\mathfrak{C}}$. Let φ_0 be any point of $\Phi_{\mathfrak{C}}$ not in F' and choose any $f_0 \in \mathfrak{C}$ such that $|f_0(\varphi_0)| = 2\delta_0 > 0$. Since f_0 vanishes at infinity on Ω, the set F_0 of points in F such that $|f_0(\omega)| \geqslant \delta_0$ is compact in Ω. Now, since $\varphi_0 \notin F'$, there exists for each $\omega \in F_0$ an $f_{\omega} \in \mathfrak{C}$ such that $|f_{\omega}(\omega) - f_{\omega}(\varphi_0)| = 2\delta_{\omega} > 0$. Define

$$G_{\omega} = \{\omega' : \omega' \in \Omega, |f_{\omega}(\omega') - f_{\omega}(\varphi_0)| > \delta_{\omega}\}.$$

Then G_{ω} is an open set which contains ω. Since these sets cover F_0 and F_0 is compact, a finite number will cover F_0. Let $H_1, \cdots, H_n$ denote this finite collection of sets G_{ω}. Let f_i be the function f_{ω} associated with H_i and let δ_i be the corresponding δ_{ω}. Finally, define

ϵ to be the least of the positive numbers $\delta_0, \delta_1, \cdots, \delta_n$. Then the neighborhood $V_{\varphi_0}(f_0, f_1, \cdots, f_n; \epsilon)$ of φ_0 in $\Phi_{\mathfrak{C}}$ does not intersect F'. In other words, F' is closed and the theorem is proved.

COROLLARY (3.2.5). *If Ω is locally compact and if $\mathfrak{C}$ is a subalgebra of $C_0(\Omega)$ which separates strongly the points of Ω, then the given topology in Ω is equivalent to the $\mathfrak{C}$-topology.*

DEFINITION (3.2.6). *The algebra $\mathfrak{C}$ is said to be* SELF-ADJOINT ON A SUBSET *S of Ω provided $\mathfrak{C}$ contains with every f a function g such that $g(\omega) = \overline{f(\omega)}$, the complex conjugate of $f(\omega)$, for every $\omega \in S$. A general commutative (real or complex) algebra $\mathfrak{A}$ is said to be* SELF-ADJOINT *provided the associated algebra of functions is self-adjoint on the carrier space $\Phi_{\mathfrak{A}}$ of $\mathfrak{A}$.*

THEOREM (3.2.7). *Let $\mathfrak{C}$ be a complex algebra which is self-adjoint on Ω. Also assume that any element f of $\mathfrak{C}$, such that $\inf_\omega |1-f(\omega)| > 0$, is quasi-regular in $\mathfrak{C}$. Then the image of Ω in $\Phi_{\mathfrak{C}}$ under the natural embedding is dense in $\Phi_{\mathfrak{C}}$.*

PROOF. If the image Ω' of Ω in $\Phi_{\mathfrak{C}}$ is not dense, then there exists $\varphi_0 \in \Phi_{\mathfrak{C}}$ and a neighborhood $V_{\varphi_0}(f_1, \cdots, f_n; \epsilon)$ of φ_0 disjoint from Ω'. Since $\varphi_0 \neq \varphi_\infty$ there is no loss in assuming $\hat{f}_j(\varphi_0) \neq 0$ for at least one j. Choose, for each j, an element $g_j \in \mathfrak{C}$ such that $g_j(\omega) = \overline{f_j(\omega)}$, $\omega \in \Omega$. Define $\lambda_j = \hat{f}_j(\varphi_0)$, $\beta = \Sigma|\lambda_j|^2$, $u_j = \beta^{-1}(\lambda_j g_j + \bar{\lambda}_j f_j - f_j g_j)$ and $u = \Sigma u_j$. Then

$$\hat{u}(\varphi_0) = \beta^{-1} \sum (\lambda_j \bar{\lambda}_j + \bar{\lambda}_j \lambda_j - \lambda_j \bar{\lambda}_j) = 1,$$

and, for $\omega \in \Omega$,

$$\begin{aligned} u(\omega) &= \beta^{-1} \sum (\lambda_j \overline{f_j(\omega)} + \bar{\lambda}_j f_j(\omega) - |f_j(\omega)|^2) \\ &= \beta^{-1} \sum (-(f_j(\omega) - \lambda_j)\overline{(f_j(\omega) - \lambda_j)} + |\lambda_j|^2) \\ &= -\beta^{-1} \sum |f_j(\omega) - \lambda_j|^2 + 1 \\ &\leqslant 1 - \epsilon^2 \beta^{-1}. \end{aligned}$$

It follows that $\epsilon^2\beta^{-1} \leqslant 1 - u(\omega)$ for every $\omega \in \Omega$. Therefore u must be quasi-regular in $\mathfrak{C}$. Since this contradicts $\hat{u}(\varphi_0) = 1$, the image of Ω must be dense in $\Phi_{\mathfrak{C}}$, and the theorem is proved.

Observe that, if $\mathfrak{C}$ is a Banach algebra under any norm whatsoever, then the condition that the image of Ω be dense in $\Phi_{\mathfrak{C}}$ implies that $Sp_{\mathfrak{C}}(f)$ is equal to the closure of the range of f on Ω. Therefore, if $\inf_\omega |1-f(\omega)| > 0$, then $1 \notin Sp_{\mathfrak{C}}(f)$, so that f is quasi-regular in $\mathfrak{C}$.

Using Theorem (3.2.4), we obtain the following corollaries to the above theorem.

COROLLARY (3.2.8). *Let Ω be locally compact and let $\mathfrak{C}$ be a subalgebra of $C_0(\Omega)$ which separates strongly the points of Ω and is self-adjoint on Ω. If also* $\inf_\omega |1-f(\omega)| > 0$ *for* $f \in \mathfrak{C}$ *implies f quasi-regular in $\mathfrak{C}$, then Ω is homeomorphic with $\Phi_{\mathfrak{C}}$ under the natural embedding.*

COROLLARY (3.2.9). *Let Ω be locally compact. Then the carrier spaces of both $C_0(\Omega)$ and $C_0^R(\Omega)$ are homeomorphic with Ω under the natural embeddings.*

THEOREM (3.2.10). *Let Ω be a completely regular topological space. Then the natural embedding of Ω in $\Phi_{C(\Omega)}$ is a homeomorphism onto a dense subset of $\Phi_{C(\Omega)}$.*

PROOF. It is essentially the definition of complete regularity that the given topology in Ω is equivalent to the $C(\Omega)$-topology. Therefore the natural mapping is a homeomorphism by Theorem (3.2.1). If f is a bounded continuous function on Ω such that $\inf_\omega |1-f(\omega)| > 0$, then the function g defined by

$$g(\omega) = \frac{f(\omega)}{f(\omega)-1}, \qquad \omega \in \Omega,$$

is bounded and continuous on Ω and hence belongs to $C(\Omega)$. Obviously $f \circ g = 0$, so that f is quasi-regular in $C(\Omega)$. Since $C(\Omega)$ is self-adjoint on Ω, the preceding theorem applies to complete the proof.

Stone [1] and Čech [1] proved that every completely regular space Ω is homeomorphic with a dense subspace of a compact Hausdorff space Γ in such a way that every bounded continuous function on Ω can be extended to a continuous function on Γ. The space Γ, which is uniquely determined up to a homeomorphism by these properties, is called the STONE–ČECH COMPACTIFICATION of Ω.

THEOREM (3.2.11). *If Ω is completely regular, then $\Phi_{C(\Omega)}$ is equal to the Stone–Čech compactification of Ω.*

PROOF. Since $C(\Omega)$ has an identity element, $\Phi_{C(\Omega)}$ is compact. Therefore, by the preceding theorem, we have only to prove the uniqueness. Let Γ be any compact Hausdorff space which contains Ω homeomorphically as a dense subspace and which has the property that every bounded continuous function on Ω can be extended as a continuous function to Γ. Then $C(\Omega) = C(\Gamma)$. Since Γ is compact, it follows by

Corollary (3.2.9) that Γ is homeomorphic with $\Phi_{C(\Omega)}$. This completes the proof.

We include at this point Stone's [1;4] generalization of the Weierstrass polynomial approximation theorem.

STONE–WEIERSTRASS THEOREM (3.2.12). *Let Ω be a locally compact Hausdorff space and let $\mathfrak{C}$ be a subalgebra of $C_0^R(\Omega)$ which separates strongly the points of Ω. Then $\mathfrak{C}$ is dense in $C_0^R(\Omega)$. The same result holds for $C_0(\Omega)$ if $\mathfrak{C}$ is self-adjoint on Ω.*

PROOF. We prove first that the absolute value of every element of $\mathfrak{C}$ belongs to the closure $\bar{\mathfrak{C}}$ of $\mathfrak{C}$. In other words, if $f \in \mathfrak{C}$ and f_a is the function defined by the relation $f_a(\omega) = |f(\omega)|$, $\omega \in \Omega$, then $f_a \in \bar{\mathfrak{C}}$. By the classical Weierstrass approximation theorem, there exists, for arbitrary $\epsilon > 0$, a polynomial P with real coefficients such that $|P(\xi) - |\xi|\,| < \epsilon$ for $-\|f\| \leqslant \xi \leqslant \|f\|$. Furthermore, it is easy to see that P can be chosen so that $P(0) = 0$. It follows that $P(f)$ is an element of $\mathfrak{C}$ and that $\|P(f) - f_a\| < \epsilon$. Therefore $f_a \in \bar{\mathfrak{C}}$.

Next let f, g be arbitrary elements of $\mathfrak{C}$ and define the functions $f \wedge g$, $f \vee g$ by the relations

$$(f \wedge g)(\omega) = \min\,[f(\omega), g(\omega)], \qquad (f \vee g)(\omega) = \max\,[f(\omega), g(\omega)],$$

for $\omega \in \Omega$. Then $f \wedge g$ and $f \vee g$ belong to $C_0^R(\Omega)$. Moreover,

$$f \wedge g = \tfrac{1}{2}[f+g-(f-g)_a], \qquad f \vee g = \tfrac{1}{2}[f+g+(f-g)_a],$$

so that $f \wedge g$ and $f \vee g$ actually belong to $\bar{\mathfrak{C}}$.

Now consider an arbitrary function F in $C_0^R(\Omega)$ and let μ, ν be any pair of (not necessarily distinct) points of Ω. Since $\mathfrak{C}$ separates strongly the points of Ω, it is not difficult to show that there exists $f_{\mu,\nu}$ in $\mathfrak{C}$ which coincides with F at each of the points μ and ν. For arbitrary $\epsilon > 0$ and fixed ν, let

$$G_\mu = \{\omega : F(\omega) - \epsilon < f_{\mu,\nu}(\omega)\}.$$

Then G_μ is an open set in Ω which contains the point μ. Furthermore, since F and $f_{\mu,\nu}$ belong to $C_0^R(\Omega)$, the complement of G_μ is compact. It follows that a finite number of these sets, say $G_{\mu_1}, \cdots, G_{\mu_m}$, cover Ω. Define

$$f_\nu = f_{\mu_1,\nu} \vee f_{\mu_2,\nu} \vee \cdots \vee f_{\mu_m,\nu}.$$

Then $f_\nu \in \bar{\mathfrak{C}}$, $f_\nu(\nu) = F(\nu)$, and $F(\omega) - \epsilon < f_\nu(\omega)$, for all $\omega \in \Omega$. Next let

$$H_\nu = \{\omega : f_\nu(\omega) < F(\omega) + \epsilon\}.$$

Then H_ν is open, contains the point ν, and has a compact complement. Therefore, a finite number of these sets, say $H_{\nu_1}, \cdots, H_{\nu_n}$, covers Ω. Define

$$f = f_{\nu_1} \wedge f_{\nu_2} \wedge \cdots \wedge f_{\nu_n}.$$

Then $f \in \bar{\mathfrak{C}}$ and $F(\omega) - \epsilon < f(\omega) < F(\omega) + \epsilon$ for all $\omega \in \Omega$. In other words, $\|F - f\| < \epsilon$ and hence $F \in \bar{\mathfrak{C}}$. This completes the proof for $C_0^R(\Omega)$.

Finally, consider the algebra $C_0(\Omega)$ and let $\mathfrak{C}$ be a subalgebra of $C_0(\Omega)$ which separates strongly the points of Ω. If $\mathfrak{C}$ is self-adjoint on Ω, then the real-valued functions in $\mathfrak{C}$ constitute a subalgebra of $C_0^R(\Omega)$ which also separates strongly the points of Ω and is therefore dense in $C_0^R(\Omega)$. This implies that $\bar{\mathfrak{C}}$ contains $C_0^R(\Omega)$. It follows immediately that $\bar{\mathfrak{C}}$ exhausts $C_0(\Omega)$ and so the theorem is proved.

It is not difficult to obtain the following corollary to the above theorem.

Corollary (3.2.13). *Let Ω be compact and let $\mathfrak{C}$ be a subalgebra of $C^R(\Omega)$ which separates the points of Ω. Then either $\bar{\mathfrak{C}}$ coincides with $C^R(\Omega)$ or is equal to a maximal ideal of $C^R(\Omega)$. In particular, if $\mathfrak{C}$ contains the constant functions, then $\bar{\mathfrak{C}} = C^R(\Omega)$. The same results hold for $C(\Omega)$ if $\mathfrak{C}$ is self-adjoint on Ω.*

Now consider a compact Hausdorff space Ω and a decomposition $\{\Omega_\lambda : \lambda \in \Lambda\}$ of Ω into pairwise disjoint closed sets Ω_λ. The index set Λ inherits from Ω a natural topology which can be described as follows: *A subset Γ of Λ is defined to be closed provided the union of the sets Ω_λ, for $\lambda \in \Gamma$, is a closed set in Ω.* This is the strongest topology in Λ which ensures that the mapping of Ω onto Λ, defined by the condition $\omega \to \lambda$ for $\omega \in \Omega_\lambda$, is continuous. The resulting topological space Λ is obviously a T_1-space and, being the continuous image of a compact space, is also compact. However, Λ need not be Hausdorff. In fact, since Ω is compact, it is not difficult to prove that a necessary and sufficient condition for Λ to be Hausdorff is that the decomposition $\{\Omega_\lambda : \lambda \in \Lambda\}$ be upper semi-continuous. In other words, if F is any closed set in Ω, then the set F', consisting of the union of all of the sets Ω_λ which have a non-vacuous intersection with F, is also closed in Ω. This is equivalent to the condition that the union of all of the sets Ω_λ which are contained in an open set of Ω is also open in Ω.

Definition (3.2.14). *Let $\mathfrak{C}$ be any family of functions on Ω. If ω is* *any point of* Ω, *then the set* $\tilde{\omega}$, *consisting of all* ω' *in* Ω *such that* $f(\omega') = f(\omega)$, *for every* f *in* $\mathfrak{C}$, *is called a* SET OF CONSTANCY *for* $\mathfrak{C}$.

LEMMA (3.2.15). *Let* $\mathfrak{C}$ *be any family of (real or complex) continuous functions defined on the compact Hausdorff space* Ω. *Then the sets of constancy for* $\mathfrak{C}$ *constitute an upper semi-continuous decomposition of* Ω.

PROOF. It is obvious that the sets of constancy are pairwise disjoint. They are also closed sets, since the functions in $\mathfrak{C}$ are continuous. Let F be any closed set in Ω. Denote by F' the union of all those sets of constancy which intersect F non-vacuously and let ω_0 be any limit point of F' in Ω. For any finite set $\pi = (f_1, \cdots, f_n)$ of elements of $\mathfrak{C}$ and arbitrary $\epsilon > 0$, define

$$F_\epsilon(\pi) = \{\omega : |f_i(\omega) - f_i(\omega_0)| \leqslant \epsilon, i = 1, \cdots, n\}.$$

Then $F_\epsilon(\pi)$ is a closed set in Ω. Moreover, since ω_0 is a limit point of F', there will exist a point ω_1 of F' in $F_\epsilon(\pi)$. But $\tilde{\omega}_1$ intersects F, and hence $F \cap F_\epsilon(\pi)$ is non-vacuous. Since any finite intersection of the sets $F_\epsilon(\pi)$ obviously contains a set of the same form, it follows from the compactness of F that there exists a point ω'_0 of F which is contained in every set $F_\epsilon(\pi)$. It follows that ω'_0 belongs to $\tilde{\omega}_0$ and this implies that $\omega_0 \in F'$. In other words, F' is closed in Ω, so that the decomposition is upper semi-continuous and the lemma is proved.

By the above lemma, the family $\tilde{\Omega}$ of the sets of constancy for $\mathfrak{C}$ can be topologized as a compact Hausdorff space so that the mapping $\omega \rightarrow \tilde{\omega}$ of Ω onto $\tilde{\Omega}$ is continuous. Since the elements of $\mathfrak{C}$ are constant on each of the sets $\tilde{\omega}$, the relation $\tilde{f}(\tilde{\omega}) = f(\omega)$ defines unambiguously a function $\tilde{f}$ which is continuous on $\tilde{\Omega}$. With these notations, we state the next theorem due essentially to Stone [1, Theorem 87]. (See Rickart [1, § 1]).

THEOREM (3.2.16). *If* $\mathfrak{C}$ *is a closed subalgebra of* $C^R(\Omega)$, *which contains the identity element, then* $f \rightarrow \tilde{f}$ *is an isometric, isomorphic mapping of* $\mathfrak{C}$ *onto* $C^R(\tilde{\Omega})$. *If* $\mathfrak{C}$ *is a closed subalgebra of* $C(\Omega)$ *which contains the identity element and is self-adjoint on* Ω, *then* $f \rightarrow \tilde{f}$ *is an isometric, isomorphic mapping of* $\mathfrak{C}$ *onto* $C(\tilde{\Omega})$ *which preserves conjugates.*

PROOF. It is immediate from definitions that $f \rightarrow \tilde{f}$ is an isometric isomorphism of $\mathfrak{C}$ into the corresponding algebra of continuous functions on $\tilde{\Omega}$. Since the image of $\mathfrak{C}$ separates the points of $\tilde{\Omega}$ (and is self-adjoint on $\tilde{\Omega}$ in the complex case), the Stone–Weierstrass theorem completes the proof.

COROLLARY (3.2.17). *Let Ω be a locally compact Hausdorff space. Then every closed subalgebra of the algebra $C_0{}^R(\Omega)$ is an algebra of the same type. The same statement holds in the case of $C_0(\Omega)$ for subalgebras which are self-adjoint on Ω.*

COROLLARY (3.2.18). *Let Ω be a compact Hausdorff space and let $\mathfrak{C}_0$ and $\mathfrak{C}_1$ be closed subalgebras of $C^R(\Omega)$ both of which possess the identity element. If $\mathfrak{C}_1$ separates every pair of points of Ω which are separated by $\mathfrak{C}_0$, then $\mathfrak{C}_0 \subseteq \mathfrak{C}_1$.*

DEFINITION (3.2.19). *Let $\mathfrak{C}$ be any family of functions on Ω and Γ a subset of Ω. Then a given function f defined on Ω is said to* BELONG TO $\mathfrak{C}$ ON THE SET Γ *provided there exists g in $\mathfrak{C}$ such that $g(\omega) = f(\omega)$ for $\omega \in \Gamma$.*

The following theorem, which generalizes the Stone–Weierstrass theorem, is due to Šilov [13].

THEOREM (3.2.20). *Let Ω be a compact Hausdorff space. Assume given a subalgebra $\mathfrak{C}_0$ of $C(\Omega)$, which contains the identity element and is self-adjoint on Ω, and let $\mathfrak{C}$ be any closed subalgebra of $C(\Omega)$ which contains $\mathfrak{C}_0$. Then, in order for an element f of $C(\Omega)$ to belong to $\mathfrak{C}$, it is necessary and sufficient that it belong to $\mathfrak{C}$ on every set of constancy for $\mathfrak{C}_0$.*

PROOF. The necessity of the condition is obvious. We prove the sufficiency. Since $\mathfrak{C}$ is a closed subalgebra of $C(\Omega)$, it may as well be assumed that $\mathfrak{C}_0$ is also closed. By Lemma (3.2.15), the sets of constancy $\tilde{\Omega}$ for $\mathfrak{C}_0$ constitute an upper semi-continuous decomposition of Ω. Also, by Theorem (3.2.16), $\mathfrak{C}_0$ is isomorphic with $C(\tilde{\Omega})$ and hence contains every continuous function which is constant on each of the sets of constancy. Now let f be any element of $C(\Omega)$ which belongs to $\mathfrak{C}$ on every set of constancy for $\mathfrak{C}_0$. For $\tilde{\omega}_0$ a fixed element of $\tilde{\Omega}$, denote by g_0 an element of $\mathfrak{C}$ such that $g_0(\omega) = f(\omega)$ for $\omega \in \tilde{\omega}_0$. For arbitrary $\epsilon > 0$, define

$$V = \{\omega : |f(\omega) - g_0(\omega)| < \epsilon\}.$$

Then V is an open set in Ω which contains the set $\tilde{\omega}_0$. Since $\tilde{\Omega}$ is an upper semi-continuous decomposition of Ω, the union U of all sets $\tilde{\omega}$

which are contained in V is also an open set in Ω. By the compactness of Ω, a finite number of the sets U, say $U_1, \cdots, U_n$, will cover Ω. Denote by g_i the element of $\mathfrak{C}$ associated with U_i. Then

$$|f(\omega)-g_i(\omega)| < \epsilon, \quad \omega \in U_i.$$

Now the images $\tilde{U}_1, \cdots, \tilde{U}_n$ of these sets in $\tilde{\Omega}$ constitute an open covering of $\tilde{\Omega}$. Therefore there exist real continuous functions $e_1, \cdots, e_n$ on $\tilde{\Omega}$ such that $0 \leqslant e_i(\tilde{\omega}) \leqslant 1$ for all $\tilde{\omega} \in \tilde{\Omega}$, $e_i(\tilde{\omega}) = 0$ for $\tilde{\omega} \notin \tilde{U}_i$, and $e_1 + \cdots + e_n = 1$. Denote by $u_1, \cdots, u_n$ the corresponding elements of $\mathfrak{C}_0$. Then $0 \leqslant u_i(\omega) \leqslant 1$ for all $\omega \in \Omega$, $u_i(\omega) = 0$ for $\omega \notin U_i$, and $u_1 + \cdots + u_n = 1$. Therefore, if

$$g = u_1 g_1 + \cdots + u_n g_n,$$

then $g \in \mathfrak{C}$ and

$$|f(\omega)-g(\omega)| \leqslant \sum_{i=1}^{n} |u_i(\omega)||f(\omega)-g_i(\omega)| < \epsilon$$

for all $\omega \in \Omega$. In other words, $\|f-g\| < \epsilon$. Since $\mathfrak{C}$ is closed, it follows that $f \in \mathfrak{C}$ and the theorem is proved.

If $\mathfrak{C}$ is self-adjoint on Ω (in particular, if $\mathfrak{C}$ consists of real functions), then the above theorem is contained in Theorem (3.2.16). Therefore the force of the result lies in the fact that $\mathfrak{C}$ need not be self-adjoint on Ω. Observe that this theorem reduces to the Stone–Weierstrass theorem if $\mathfrak{C} = \mathfrak{C}_0$ and $\mathfrak{C}_0$ separates the points of Ω.

We now prove a theorem which gives the carrier spaces of certain subdirect sums of commutative Banach algebras. Let $\{\mathfrak{A}_\lambda : \lambda \in \Lambda\}$ be a family of (real or complex) commutative Banach algebras each of which is assumed to possess an identity element. Denote the carrier space of $\mathfrak{A}_\lambda$ by Φ_λ and let Ψ be the set-theoretic union of the spaces Φ_λ regarded as distinct abstract sets. Consider a normed subdirect sum $\mathfrak{A} = \Sigma' \mathfrak{A}_\lambda$ which is a closed subalgebra of the normed full direct sum $\Sigma\, \mathfrak{A}_\lambda$. Under certain conditions, the carrier space of $\mathfrak{A}$ can be identified with the set Ψ. The next theorem gives such a result. For notational convenience, we write f_λ instead of $f(\lambda)$ for the value in $\mathfrak{A}_\lambda$ of an element f of $\Sigma\, \mathfrak{A}_\lambda$.

THEOREM (3.2.21). *Assume Λ to be a compact Hausdorff space and let the subdirect sum algebra $\mathfrak{A}$ satisfy the following conditions:*

(i) *$\mathfrak{A}$ contains the function e such that e_λ is equal to the identity element of $\mathfrak{A}_\lambda$ for each λ. Thus e is an identity element for $\mathfrak{A}$.*

(ii) $\mathfrak{A}$ *is closed under multiplication by elements of* $C^R(\Lambda)$. (*See Definition* (2.7.28).)

(iii) *For each* f *in* $\mathfrak{A}$, *the real function* $\|f_\lambda\|$, $\lambda \in \Lambda$, *is upper semi-continuous. (In other words, the set* $\{\lambda : \|f_\lambda\| < \epsilon\}$ *is open in* Λ *for each* $\epsilon > 0$.)

Then there exists a one-to-one mapping, $\psi \to \psi^\sigma$, *of* Ψ *onto* $\Phi_{\mathfrak{A}}$ *such that, for each* f *in* $\mathfrak{A}$,

$$\hat{f}(\psi^\sigma) = \hat{f}_\lambda(\psi), \quad \psi \in \Phi_\lambda.$$

PROOF. Fix λ and let ψ be any element of Φ_λ. Then the mapping $f \to \hat{f}_\lambda(\psi)$ obviously defines a homomorphism of $\mathfrak{A}$ into the complex field and hence determines an element ψ^σ of $\Phi_{\mathfrak{A}}$ with $\hat{f}(\psi^\sigma) = \hat{f}_\lambda(\psi)$ for $f \in \mathfrak{A}$. Since $\mathfrak{A}$ is a subdirect sum and is closed under multiplication by elements of $C^R(\Lambda)$, it is easily verified that the mapping $\psi \to \psi^\sigma$ of Ψ into $\Phi_{\mathfrak{A}}$ is one-to-one. It only remains to prove that $\Phi_{\mathfrak{A}}$ is covered by this mapping. To this end, let φ be an arbitrary element of $\Phi_{\mathfrak{A}}$. By conditions (i) and (ii), $C^R(\Lambda)$ can be regarded as a (real) subalgebra of $\mathfrak{A}$. Therefore φ induces a homomorphism of $C^R(\Lambda)$ into the complex field and accordingly determines a point λ_0 of Λ such that $\hat{s}(\varphi) = s_{\lambda_0}$ for all $s \in C^R(\Lambda)$. We shall now show that $\varphi = \psi^\sigma$, for some ψ in Φ_{λ_0}. Consider first any two elements f and g of $\mathfrak{A}$ with $f_{\lambda_0} = g_{\lambda_0}$. For arbitrary $\epsilon > 0$, define the set

$$U = \{\lambda : \|f_\lambda - g_\lambda\| < \epsilon\}.$$

Condition (iii) implies that U is open in Λ. Note that $\lambda_0 \in U$. Next choose s in $C^R(\Lambda)$ such that $s_{\lambda_0} = 1$, $|s_\lambda| \leqslant 1$ for all λ, and $s_\lambda = 0$ for $\lambda \notin U$. Since $\hat{s}(\varphi) = s_{\lambda_0} = 1$, we have

$$\widehat{(sf - sg)}(\varphi) = \hat{f}(\varphi) - \hat{g}(\varphi).$$

Moreover, for arbitrary $\lambda \in \Lambda$, $(sf - sg)_\lambda = s_\lambda(f_\lambda - g_\lambda)$ and therefore $\|(sf - sg)_\lambda\| = |s_\lambda| \, \|f_\lambda - g_\lambda\|$. Since $s_\lambda = 0$ for $\lambda \notin U$, it follows that

$$\|sf - sg\| = \sup_\lambda \|(sf - sg)_\lambda\| \leqslant \epsilon.$$

In particular,

$$|\hat{f}(\varphi) - \hat{g}(\varphi)| = |\widehat{(sf - sg)}(\varphi)| \leqslant \|sf - sg\| \leqslant \epsilon.$$

Since ϵ is an arbitrary positive number, we conclude that $f_{\lambda_0} = g_{\lambda_0}$ implies $\hat{f}(\varphi) = \hat{g}(\varphi)$. In other words, $\hat{f}(\varphi)$ depends only on the component

f_{λ_0}. Now, for any x in $\mathfrak{A}_{\lambda_0}$, choose an f in $\mathfrak{A}$ such that $f_{\lambda_0} = x$. Such f exist, since $\mathfrak{A}$ is a subdirect sum. Since $\hat{f}(\varphi)$ depends only on f_{λ_0}, the mapping $x \to \hat{f}(\varphi)$ defines a homomorphism of $\mathfrak{A}_{\lambda_0}$ into the complex field and so determines an element ψ in Φ_{λ_0}. Evidently, for every f in $\mathfrak{A}$, $\hat{f}(\varphi) = \hat{f}_{\lambda_0}(\psi)$. Therefore $\varphi = \psi^\sigma$ and the theorem is proved.

As an application of the above theorem, consider a compact Hausdorff space Ω and an upper semi-continuous decomposition $\{F_\lambda : \lambda \in \Lambda\}$ of Ω into closed sets. Then, as has already been observed, Ω induces a compact Hausdorff topology on Λ such that the mapping $\omega \to \lambda$, for $\omega \in F_\lambda$, is continuous. Now assume given, for each $\lambda \in \Lambda$, a closed subalgebra $\mathfrak{A}_\lambda$ of $C(F_\lambda)$ which has F_λ as its carrier space. Let $\mathfrak{A}$ be the subalgebra of $C(\Omega)$ consisting of all elements of $C(\Omega)$ whose restrictions to each F_λ give elements of $\mathfrak{A}_\lambda$. Evidently $\mathfrak{A}$ is a closed subalgebra of $C(\Omega)$. If, in addition, $\mathfrak{A}$ is a subdirect sum of the algebras $\mathfrak{A}_\lambda$, then all of the conditions of Theorem (3.2.21) are satisfied. Therefore the carrier space of $\mathfrak{A}$ is equal to Ω. This result is due to Holladay [1]. It is perhaps worth noting here that, if $\mathfrak{A}_0$ is any closed subalgebra in $C(\Omega)$ which is a subdirect sum of the algebras $\mathfrak{A}_\lambda$ and which contains all elements of $C(\Omega)$ which are constant on each of the sets F_λ, then, by Theorem (3.2.20), $\mathfrak{A}_0$ must already coincide with $\mathfrak{A}$.

An interesting special decomposition of the above type is one in which all but a finite number of the sets F_λ reduce to single points. In this case the decomposition is automatically upper semi-continuous and $\mathfrak{A}$ is a subdirect sum.

Another special case of interest is obtained when Ω is the cartesian product of two compact Hausdorff spaces Φ and Λ. If $F_\lambda = \Phi \times (\lambda)$, then $\{F_\lambda : \lambda \in \Lambda\}$ is an upper semi-continuous decomposition of Ω. Now let $\mathfrak{A}_0$ be a closed subalgebra of $C(\Phi)$ whose carrier space is Φ. Then, if $\mathfrak{A}$ is the subalgebra of $C(\Phi \times \Lambda)$ consisting of all those functions $f(\varphi, \lambda)$ which belong to $\mathfrak{A}_0$ for each fixed λ in Λ, then Theorem (3.2.21) applies to give $\Phi \times \Lambda$ as the carrier space of $\mathfrak{A}$. Again, by Theorem (3.2.20), if $\mathfrak{A}'_0$ is any closed subalgebra in $C(\Phi \times \Lambda)$ whose elements reduce to elements of $\mathfrak{A}_0$ for fixed λ and which contains all elements $f(\varphi, \lambda)$ of $C(\Phi \times \Lambda)$ which are constant with respect to φ, then $\mathfrak{A}'_0$ must coincide with the algebra $\mathfrak{A}$.

Consider next the cartesian product $\Delta \times \Lambda$, where Δ is the closed unit disc $\{\zeta : |\zeta| \leqslant 1\}$ in the complex plane and Λ is the unit interval $[0,1]$. Let $\mathfrak{A}$ denote the subalgebra of $C(\Delta \times \Lambda)$ consisting of all those f such that $f(\zeta, \lambda)$ is a holomorphic function of ζ in the interior of Δ for each fixed λ with $0 < \lambda \leqslant 1$. We thus have the case in which $F_\lambda = \Delta$ for each $\lambda \in \Lambda$, $\mathfrak{A}_0 = C(\Delta)$ and $\mathfrak{A}_\lambda = \mathscr{A}(\Delta)$ for $0 < \lambda \leqslant 1$, where $\mathscr{A}(\Delta)$ is the algebra of all complex functions continuous on Δ and holomorphic in the interior of Δ. (See Appendix, A.2.6) Since elements f of $C(\Delta \times \Lambda)$ are uniformly continuous, it follows that

$$\lim_{\lambda \to 0} f(\zeta, \lambda) = f(\zeta, 0)$$

uniformly for $\zeta \in \Delta$. Therefore $f(\zeta, 0)$, being a uniform limit of holomorphic functions, must belong to $\mathscr{A}(\Delta)$. Since $\mathscr{A}(\Delta)$ is a proper subalgebra of $C(\Delta)$, this shows that $\mathfrak{A}$ is not a subdirect sum of the algebras $\mathfrak{A}_\lambda$, $\lambda \in \Lambda$, as defined above. This example was called to our attention by F. Quigley.

We conclude this section with another application of the above remarks plus results from the preceding section. Let Ω_1 and Ω_2 be two compact Hausdorff spaces and let Ω denote the space which is equal to the disjoint union of Ω_1, Ω_2 such that the sets Ω_1, Ω_2 are closed and the topology in each set is the given one. Fix points $\omega_1{}^0 \in \Omega_1$ and $\omega_2{}^0 \in \Omega_2$ and denote by Ω_0 the space obtained from Ω by identification of the two points $\omega_1{}^0$ and $\omega_2{}^0$. Now let $\mathfrak{A}_1$ and $\mathfrak{A}_2$ be subalgebras of $C(\Omega_1)$ and $C(\Omega_2)$ respectively such that $\Phi_{\mathfrak{A}_1} = \Omega_1$ and $\Phi_{\mathfrak{A}_2} = \Omega_2$. Denote by $\mathfrak{A}_0$ the subalgebra of $C(\Omega_0)$ consisting of every f whose restriction to Ω_1 belongs to $\mathfrak{A}_1$ and restriction to Ω_2 belongs to $\mathfrak{A}_2$. We prove that $\Phi_{\mathfrak{A}_0} = \Omega_0$. First let $\mathfrak{A}$ denote the subalgebra of $C(\Omega)$ consisting of every f whose restrictions to Ω_1 and Ω_2 belong to $\mathfrak{A}_1$ and $\mathfrak{A}_2$ respectively. Then we know that $\Phi_{\mathfrak{A}} = \Omega$. Observe that $\mathfrak{A}_0$ is isomorphic with the subalgebra of $\mathfrak{A}$ consisting of those f for which $f(\omega_1{}^0) = f(\omega_2{}^0)$. Moreover, if $\mathfrak{I}$ is the ideal in $\mathfrak{A}$ consisting of those f such that $f(\omega_1{}^0) = f(\omega_2{}^0) = 0$, then $\mathfrak{A}_0$ is isomorphic with the algebra obtained by adjunction of an identity element to $\mathfrak{I}$. By Theorem (3.1.18), $\Phi_{\mathfrak{I}} = \Omega - \mathscr{h}(\mathfrak{I})$. But any finite set of points is already a hull (points are closed in the hull–kernel topology), so that we obtain $\mathscr{h}(\mathfrak{I}) = (\omega_1{}^0, \omega_2{}^0)$. It follows that $\Phi_{\mathfrak{I}^\infty} = \Omega_0$ and hence that $\Phi_{\mathfrak{A}_0} = \Omega_0$. An iteration of this method can be used to deal with the case in which any finite number of pairs of points are identified. The situation becomes more complicated with an infinite number of identifications and will not be discussed here. Holladay [1] has some results for the infinite case.

A variety of examples of algebras of functions will be found in § 2 of the Appendix. The algebra $C_0(\Omega)$ is discussed systematically in § 2 of Chapter IV. Much of the material in the first part of this section was obtained by Gelfand and Šilov [1]. Holladay [1] determines the carrier spaces of a number of special algebras of functions including those discussed here. If Ω is a circle or a closed interval and $\mathfrak{C}$ is a subalgebra of $C(\Omega)$ which separates points and contains constant functions, then Helson and Quigley [2] give a sufficient condition on $\mathfrak{C}$ that the natural embedding map Ω into a proper subset of $\Phi_{\mathfrak{C}}$.

§ **3. The Šilov boundary.** We consider in this section some results for general algebras of functions which are suggestive of certain properties of holomorphic functions. The motivating example for much of the discussion is the algebra of all complex-valued functions which are continuous on the closure of and holomorphic in the interior of the unit disc of the complex plane. The key to the situation lies in the fact that an analogue of the maximum modulus principle can be formulated for the general case.

Our starting point is a locally compact Hausdorff space Ω and a family $\mathscr{C}$ of (real or complex) functions which are continuous and vanish at infinity on Ω. It follows that, if F is any closed subset of Ω and f any element of $\mathscr{C}$, then there exists $\omega_0 \in F$ such that $|f(\omega)| \leqslant |f(\omega_0)|$ for every $\omega \in F$. A closed subset Γ in Ω with the property that

$$\max_{\omega \in \Gamma} |f(\omega)| = \max_{\omega \in \Omega} |f(\omega)|$$

for every $f \in \mathscr{C}$ is called a MAXIMIZING SET FOR $\mathscr{C}$ or, more briefly, a $\mathscr{C}$-SET. A $\mathscr{C}$-set which does not properly contain any other $\mathscr{C}$-set is called MINIMAL. If a $\mathscr{C}$-set has the much stronger minimal property of being contained in *every* $\mathscr{C}$-set, then it is called the $\mathscr{C}$-BOUNDARY of Ω and is denoted by $\partial_{\mathscr{C}}\Omega$. The $\mathscr{C}$-boundary, which is obviously uniquely determined when it exists and whose existence for an algebra of functions is given by the next theorem, is also called the ŠILOV BOUNDARY since it was Šilov (See Gelfand, Raikov and Šilov [1, § 24].) who first proved its existence for the algebra of functions associated with a commutative Banach algebra in the Gelfand representation theorem.

Before stating the next theorem, we observe that minimal $\mathscr{C}$-sets exist without further conditions on $\mathscr{C}$. To show this, denote by $\mathscr{E}$ the collection of all $\mathscr{C}$-sets in Ω. Since Ω is itself a $\mathscr{C}$-set, $\mathscr{E}$ is not vacuous. By Zorn's lemma, there exists a decreasing chain $\mathscr{E}_0$ of $\mathscr{C}$-sets (ordered by inclusion) which is maximal in the sense that no $\mathscr{C}$-set is properly contained in every element of $\mathscr{E}_0$. Denote by Γ_0 the intersection of all the sets in $\mathscr{E}_0$. We prove that Γ_0 is a $\mathscr{C}$-set, which will show incidentally that Γ_0 is non-vacuous. Let f be any element of $\mathscr{C}$ and define

$$F_f = \{\omega' : |f(\omega')| = \max_{\omega \in \Omega} |f(\omega)|\}.$$

If $f = 0$, then $F_f = \Omega$ and automatically $\Gamma_0 \subseteq F_f$. If $f \neq 0$, then F_f is compact since f vanishes at infinity. We have

$$F_f \cap \Gamma_0 = \bigcap_{\Gamma \in \mathscr{E}_0} (F_f \cap \Gamma).$$

Now $\mathscr{E}_0$ is decreasing and each of the sets $F_f \cap \Gamma$ is non-vacuous and compact; therefore $F_f \cap \Gamma_0$ is non-vacuous. This conclusion holds for every $f \in \mathscr{C}$ and proves that Γ_0 is a $\mathscr{C}$-set. From the maximality of $\mathscr{E}_0$, it follows that Γ_0 is minimal.

THEOREM (3.3.1). *If $\mathfrak{C}$ is a complex subalgebra of $C_0(\Omega)$ which separates the points of Ω, then $\partial_{\mathfrak{C}}\Omega$ exists.*

PROOF. Observe first that we can assume without loss of generality that $\mathfrak{C}$ separates strongly the points of Ω. In fact, if every $f \in \mathfrak{C}$ vanishes at some point $\omega_0 \in \Omega$, replace Ω by $\Omega_0 = \Omega - (\omega_0)$ and note that $\mathfrak{C}$ separates strongly the points of Ω_0. If $\partial_{\mathfrak{C}}\Omega_0$ exists, then obviously $\partial_{\mathfrak{C}}\Omega$ exists and is equal to the closure of $\partial_{\mathfrak{C}}\Omega_0$ in Ω. By Corollary (3.2.5), we can accordingly assume that the given topology in Ω is equivalent to the $\mathfrak{C}$-topology.

We already know that a minimal $\mathfrak{C}$-set Γ_0 exists. The problem here is to show that Γ_0 is contained in every $\mathfrak{C}$-set and hence that $\Gamma_0 = \partial_{\mathfrak{C}}\Omega$. To this end, let F be any closed subset of Ω which does not contain Γ_0 and choose $\omega_0 \in \Gamma_0 - F$. Since F is closed in the $\mathfrak{C}$-topology, there exists a finite number of elements of $\mathfrak{C}$, say $f_1, \cdots, f_k$, and $\epsilon > 0$ such that the open set

$$G = \{\omega : |f_i(\omega) - f_i(\omega_0)| < \epsilon; \quad i = 1, \cdots, k\}$$

does not intersect F. Since $\omega_0 \in G$, $\Gamma_0 - G$ is a proper subset of Γ_0 and so is not a $\mathfrak{C}$-set. Therefore there exists $g \in \mathfrak{C}$ such that

$$\max_{\omega \in \Gamma_0 - G} |g(\omega)| < \max_{\omega \in \Omega} |g(\omega)|.$$

Let ω_1 be any point of Ω and ω_2 any point of $\Gamma_0 - G$ such that

$$|g(\omega_1)| = \max_{\omega \in \Omega} |g(\omega)|, \qquad |g(\omega_2)| = \max_{\omega \in \Gamma_0 - G} |g(\omega)|.$$

Since $|g(\omega_2)||g(\omega_1)|^{-1} < 1$, we have for large n

$$\left(\frac{|g(\omega_2)|}{|g(\omega_1)|}\right)^n < \left(1 + \sum_{i=1}^{k} \max_{\omega \in \Omega} |f_i(\omega) - f_i(\omega_0)|\right)^{-1} \epsilon = \delta.$$

Let $h = g^n$. Then

$$|g(\omega_1)|^n = \max_{\omega \in \Omega} |h(\omega)|, \qquad |g(\omega_2)|^n = \max_{\omega \in \Gamma_0 - G} |h(\omega)|,$$

and hence

$$\max_{\omega \in \Gamma_0 - G} |h(\omega)| < \delta \max_{\omega \in \Omega} |h(\omega)|.$$

Now, if $\omega \in G$, then $|f_i(\omega) - f_i(\omega_0)| < \epsilon$, so that

$$|(f_i h - f_i(\omega_0)h)(\omega)| < \epsilon \max_{\omega \in \Omega} |h(\omega)|.$$

On the other hand, if $\omega \in \Gamma_0 - G$, then

$$|h(\omega)| < \delta \max_{\omega \in \Omega} |h(\omega)|,$$

so that again

$$|(f_i h - f_i(\omega_0)h)(\omega)| < \epsilon \max_{\omega \in \Omega} |h(\omega)|.$$

Since Γ_0 is a $\mathfrak{C}$-set and $f_i h - f_i(\omega_0)h \in \mathfrak{C}$, it follows that

$$\max_{\omega \in \Omega} |(f_i h - f_i(\omega_0)h)(\omega)| < \epsilon \max_{\omega \in \Omega} |h(\omega)|.$$

Let ω'_0 be any point of Ω with

$$|h(\omega'_0)| = \max_{\omega \in \Omega} |h(\omega)|.$$

Then

$$|h(\omega'_0)| |f_i(\omega'_0) - f_i(\omega_0)| = |(f_i h - f_i(\omega_0)h)(\omega'_0)| < \epsilon |h(\omega'_0)|.$$

Therefore $|f_i(\omega'_0) - f_i(\omega_0)| < \epsilon$. Since this holds for each i, it follows that $\omega'_0 \in G$. In other words, h is an element of $\mathfrak{C}$ which does not assume its maximum outside G. In particular, F is not a $\mathfrak{C}$-set. In other words, every $\mathfrak{C}$-set must contain Γ_0 and the theorem is proved.

In the above argument, the assumption that $\mathfrak{C}$ be a complex algebra was used only to ensure that $\mathfrak{C}$ contain the functions $f_i h - f_i(\omega_0)h$. In particular, the complex scalars are needed only because $f_i(\omega_0)$ may be complex. It follows that the theorem is true for real algebras provided $\mathfrak{C}$ contains enough real-valued functions to determine the topology in Ω. On the other hand, an example shows (See Appendix, A.2.9) that the theorem is not true for arbitrary real algebras of complex functions. If the functions in $\mathfrak{C}$ determine the topology of Ω in the stronger sense that each point ω_0 has a basis of neighborhoods of the form

$\{\omega : |f_i(\omega)| < \epsilon; i = 1, \cdots, k\}$, then obviously the only algebra condition needed on $\mathfrak{C}$ is that it be closed under multiplication. (See Arens and Singer [1]).

THEOREM (3.3.2). *If the complex algebra $\mathfrak{C}$ is dense in $C_0(\Omega)$, in particular if $\mathfrak{C}$ is self-adjoint on Ω, then $\partial_{\mathfrak{C}}\Omega = \Omega$.*

PROOF. Notice that a point ω_0 is an element of $\partial_{\mathfrak{C}}\Omega$ if and only if for every neighborhood V of ω_0 there exists $f \in \mathfrak{C}$ such that

$$\max_{\omega \notin V} |f(\omega)| < \max_{\omega \in \Omega} |f(\omega)|.$$

Now, if V is a compact neighborhood of ω_0, then there exists $u \in C_0(\Omega)$ such that $u(\omega_0) = 1$ and $u(\omega) = 0$ for $\omega \notin V$. If $\mathfrak{C}$ is dense in $C_0(\Omega)$, then there exists $f \in \mathfrak{C}$ such that $|f(\omega) - u(\omega)| < \frac{1}{2}$ for all $\omega \in \Omega$. Since $|f(\omega)| < \frac{1}{2}$ for $\omega \notin V$ and $|f(\omega_0)| > \frac{1}{2}$, it follows that $\omega_0 \in \partial_{\mathfrak{C}}\Omega$.

THEOREM (3.3.3). *If $\mathfrak{C}$ is a complex subalgebra of $C_0(\Omega)$ which separates strongly the points of Ω and if $\partial_{\mathfrak{C}}\Omega \neq \Omega$, then $\partial_{\mathfrak{C}}\Omega$ contains an infinite number of points.*

PROOF. Let ω_0 and ω'_0 be any pair of distinct points of Ω. We prove first that there exists $u \in \mathfrak{C}$ such that $u(\omega_0) \neq 0$ while $u(\omega'_0) = 0$. This is, of course, trivial if $\mathfrak{C}$ contains an identity element, but requires some argument in the general case. Let f be any element of $\mathfrak{C}$ with $f(\omega_0) \neq f(\omega'_0)$. If $f(\omega'_0) = 0$, then we can take $u = f$. If $f(\omega'_0) \neq 0$, there is no loss in assuming $f(\omega'_0) = 1$, so that we have $f(\omega_0) \neq 1$. If also $f(\omega_0) \neq 0$, take $u = f - f^2$. Then $u(\omega'_0) = 0$ while $u(\omega_0) = f(\omega_0)(1 - f(\omega_0)) \neq 0$. This leaves the case $f(\omega_0) = 0$ and $f(\omega'_0) = 1$. Choose any $g \in \mathfrak{C}$ with $g(\omega_0) \neq 0$. If $g(\omega'_0) = 0$, take $u = g$. If $g(\omega'_0) \neq 0$, take $u = f - g(\omega'_0)^{-1}g$. Then $u(\omega'_0) = 0$ while $u(\omega_0) = -g(\omega'_0)^{-1}g(\omega_0) \neq 0$. Therefore u exists in all cases. Now let $\omega_1, \cdots, \omega_n$ be any finite set of elements of $\partial_{\mathfrak{C}}\Omega$ and choose any $\omega_0 \notin \partial_{\mathfrak{C}}\Omega$. For each i choose $u_i \in \mathfrak{C}$ such that $u_i(\omega_0) \neq 0$ while $u_i(\omega_i) = 0$. If $v = u_1 u_2 \cdots u_n$, then $v(\omega_0) \neq 0$ while $v(\omega_i) = 0$ for each $i = 1, \cdots, n$. This shows that the points $\omega_1, \cdots, \omega_n$ cannot exhaust $\partial_{\mathfrak{C}}\Omega$ and completes the proof.

Let $\mathfrak{C}$ be any complex subalgebra of $C_0(\Omega)$ which separates the points of Ω and let $\mathfrak{C}_1$ be the algebra obtained from $\mathfrak{C}$ by adjunction of an identity element. The algebra $\mathfrak{C}_1$ can be regarded as a subalgebra of $C(\Omega^\infty)$, where Ω^∞ is the one-point compactification of Ω obtained by adjunction of a point at infinity ω_∞. Moreover, $\mathfrak{C}$ is equal to the maximal ideal in $\mathfrak{C}_1$ consisting of all of those functions in $\mathfrak{C}_1$ which vanish on the point ω_∞. The next theorem shows the effect of this construction on the Šilov boundary.

THEOREM (3.3.4). *Assume Ω compact and let $\mathfrak{C}$ be any complex subalgebra of $C(\Omega)$ which contains the identity of $C(\Omega)$ and separates the points of Ω. Let ω_0 be a fixed point of Ω and denote by $\mathfrak{M}_0$ the maximal ideal in $\mathfrak{C}$ consisting of all f which vanish at ω_0. Then*

$$\partial_{\mathfrak{M}_0}\Omega \subseteq \partial_{\mathfrak{C}}\Omega \subseteq \partial_{\mathfrak{M}_0}\Omega \cup (\omega_0).$$

PROOF. It is immediate that $\mathfrak{M}_0$ still separates points of Ω, so that $\partial_{\mathfrak{M}_0}\Omega$ exists. Furthermore, since $\mathfrak{M}_0 \subseteq \mathfrak{C}$, it is also immediate that $\partial_{\mathfrak{M}_0}\Omega \subseteq \partial_{\mathfrak{C}}\Omega$. If $\partial_{\mathfrak{M}_0}\Omega \cup (\omega_0)$ does not contain $\partial_{\mathfrak{C}}\Omega$, then there must exist $f \in \mathfrak{C}$ such that

$$\max_{\omega \in \partial_{\mathfrak{M}_0}\Omega \cup (\omega_0)} |f(\omega)| < \mu < \max_{\omega \in \Omega} |f(\omega)|.$$

For g equal to a sufficiently high power of $\mu^{-1}f$, we obtain

$$\max_{\omega \in \partial_{\mathfrak{M}_0}\Omega \cup (\omega_0)} |g(\omega)| < 1 < 3 < \max_{\omega \in \Omega} |g(\omega)|.$$

In particular, $|g(\omega_0)| < 1$. Therefore, since $g - g(\omega_0) \in \mathfrak{M}_0$,

$$\begin{aligned} \max_{\omega \in \Omega} |g(\omega) - g(\omega_0)| &= \max_{\omega \in \partial_{\mathfrak{M}_0}\Omega} |g(\omega) - g(\omega_0)| \\ &\leqslant \max_{\omega \in \partial_{\mathfrak{M}_0}\Omega} |g(\omega)| + 1 \leqslant 2. \end{aligned}$$

On the other hand, since $|g(\omega)| \leqslant |g(\omega) - g(\omega_0)| + 1$, we have

$$3 < \max_{\omega \in \Omega} |g(\omega)| \leqslant \max_{\omega \in \Omega} |g(\omega) - g(\omega_0)| + 1,$$

and hence

$$2 < \max_{\omega \in \Omega} |g(\omega) - g(\omega_0)|.$$

This is a contradiction and shows that $\partial_{\mathfrak{C}}\Omega \subseteq \partial_{\mathfrak{M}_0}\Omega \cup (\omega_0)$.

COROLLARY (3.3.5). *Either $\partial_{\mathfrak{M}_0}\Omega = \partial_{\mathfrak{C}}\Omega$ or ω_0 is an isolated point of $\partial_{\mathfrak{C}}\Omega$.*

THEOREM (3.3.6). *Let Ω be locally compact and let $\mathfrak{C}$ be a subalgebra of $C_0(\Omega)$. Then, for every $f \in \mathfrak{C}$,*

$$\min_{\omega \in \partial_{\mathfrak{C}}\Omega} |f(\omega)| = \inf_{g \in \mathfrak{C}} \frac{\|fg\|}{\|g\|}.$$

PROOF. Denote the quantity on the right hand side of this equation by μ and consider any non-zero $g \in \mathfrak{C}$. Choose $\omega_0 \in \partial_{\mathfrak{C}}\Omega$ such that $|g(\omega_0)| = \|g\|$. Then

$$\frac{\|fg\|}{\|g\|} \geqslant \frac{|f(\omega_0)|\,|g(\omega_0)|}{|g(\omega_0)|} = |f(\omega_0)| \geqslant \min_{\omega \in \partial_{\mathfrak{C}}\Omega} |f(\omega)|.$$

If $\mu = 0$, the proof is complete. If $\mu > 0$, define

$$F = \{\omega : |f(\omega)| \geqslant \mu\}.$$

Since $\mu > 0$, the set F is compact. The theorem will follow if we show that F is a $\mathfrak{C}$-set and consequently contains $\partial_{\mathfrak{C}}\Omega$. If F is not a $\mathfrak{C}$-set, then there exists $g \in \mathfrak{C}$ such that $\max_{\omega \in F} |g(\omega)| < \|g\|$. Since $\max_{\omega\in F}|g(\omega)|^n = \max_{\omega\in F}|g^n(\omega)|$ and $\|g^n\| = \|g\|^n$, it follows that

$$\lim_{n\to\infty} \frac{\max_{\omega\in F} |g^n(\omega)|}{\|g^n\|} = 0.$$

Now, for each n, choose $\omega_n \in \Omega$ such that

$$|f(\omega_n)g^n(\omega_n)| = \|fg^n\|.$$

Since

$$\mu \leqslant \frac{\|fg^n\|}{\|g^n\|} \leqslant \frac{|f(\omega_n)g^n(\omega_n)|}{|g^n(\omega_n)|} = |f(\omega_n)|,$$

it follows that $\omega_n \in F$. Therefore

$$\mu \leqslant \frac{\|fg^n\|}{\|g^n\|} = \frac{|f(\omega_n)||g^n(\omega_n)|}{\|g^n\|} \leqslant \|f\| \frac{\max_{\omega\in F} |g^n(\omega)|}{\|g^n\|}.$$

Since the right hand side of this inequality converges to zero as $n \to \infty$, we obtain $\mu = 0$, contrary to hypothesis. In other words, F is a $\mathfrak{C}$-set and the proof is complete.

COROLLARY (3.3.7). *The function f is a topological divisor of zero in $\mathfrak{C}$ if and only if it vanishes at some point of $\partial_{\mathfrak{C}}\Omega$.*

COROLLARY (3.3.8). *Let $f \in \mathfrak{C}$ and denote by $\tilde{f}$ the function obtained by restricting f to the set $\partial_{\mathfrak{C}}\Omega$. Then $f \to \tilde{f}$ is an isometric embedding of $\mathfrak{C}$ in $C(\partial_{\mathfrak{C}}\Omega)$ and the element $\tilde{f}$ is regular in $C(\partial_{\mathfrak{C}}\Omega)$ if and only if f is not a topological divisor of zero in $\mathfrak{C}$.*

As was observed in the proof of Theorem (3.3.2), the Šilov boundary $\partial_{\mathfrak{C}}\Omega$ consists of all points ω with the property that, for every neighborhood V of ω, there exists $f \in \mathfrak{C}$ such that the maximum absolute value of f is assumed only inside V. Notice that this maximum value need not be assumed at ω itself. This suggests the following definition.

DEFINITION (3.3.9). *A point $\omega \in \Omega$ is called a* STRONG BOUNDARY POINT *of Ω (relative to $\mathfrak{C}$) provided there exists, for each neighborhood V of ω, a function $f \in \mathfrak{C}$ whose maximum absolute value is assumed at ω but at no point outside of V.*

It is obvious that every strong boundary point belongs to $\partial_{\mathfrak{C}}\Omega$. It will be proved below that, if Ω is compact and $\mathfrak{C}$ is a closed subalgebra of $C(\Omega)$ which separates the points of Ω and contains the identity of $C(\Omega)$, then each function in $\mathfrak{C}$ assumes its maximum absolute value on the strong boundary points which, therefore, are dense in $\partial_{\mathfrak{C}}\Omega$. For this we need some preliminary results. The space Ω is assumed compact throughout the remainder of the discussion.

A subset of Ω, which consists of all those points at which the maximum absolute value of a given $f \in \mathfrak{C}$ is assumed, will be called a MAXIMUM SET (associated with f). If, in addition, the function f is constantly equal to 1 on this set, then the set is called a SPECIAL MAXIMUM SET. Notice that maximum sets are compact and, if S_f and S_g are (special) maximum sets associated with f and g respectively, then $S_f \cap S_g$ is either void or is a (special) maximum set associated with fg. Therefore the intersection of any finite collection of (special) maximum sets is either void or is a (special) maximum set. The result in the following lemma was proved by Holladay [1].

LEMMA (3.3.10). *Consider a non-zero function f in $C(\Omega)$ and let ω_0 be a point of Ω such that $|f(\omega_0)| = \|f\|$. Set $\mu = f(\omega_0)$ and define $g = \frac{1}{2}(\mu^{-1}f+1)$. Then*

$$\{\omega : f(\omega) = f(\omega_0)\} = \{\omega : g(\omega) = 1\},$$

and the set on the right is the maximum set for g.

PROOF. It is obvious that $\|g\| = 1$. Furthermore, if $|g(\omega_1)| = 1$, then, since $|f(\omega_1)| \leqslant |\mu|$,

$$1 = \tfrac{1}{2}|\mu^{-1}f(\omega_1)+1| \leqslant \tfrac{1}{2}(|\mu|^{-1}|f(\omega_1)|+1) \leqslant 1.$$

Therefore the equality must hold throughout, and hence

$$|\mu^{-1}f(\omega_1)+1| = 2, \quad |\mu|^{-1}|f(\omega_1)| = 1.$$

These equations imply that $f(\omega_1) = \mu$. On the other hand, if $f(\omega) = \mu$, then $g(\omega) = 1$ and the lemma follows.

COROLLARY (3.3.11). *If $\mathfrak{C}$ is a subalgebra of $C(\Omega)$ which contains the identity element of $C(\Omega)$, then every maximum set associated with an element of $\mathfrak{C}$ contains a special maximum set.*

Now let us call the intersection of an arbitrary collection of special maximum sets associated with elements of $\mathfrak{C}$ simply a SPECIAL SET associated with $\mathfrak{C}$. It is obvious that special sets are compact and that the intersection of any family of special sets is again a special set. Observe that a set consisting of a single strong boundary point is a special set and, conversely, if a special set contains only one point, then that point is a strong boundary point. A special set F is called MINIMAL if it is non-vacuous and does not properly contain any non-vacuous special sets. This amounts to demanding that every special maximum set either contain F or be disjoint from it. If $\mathfrak{C}$ contains the identity element of $C(\Omega)$, then, by a simple application of the above corollary and Zorn's Lemma, it follows that every maximum set contains a minimal special set. Our next objective is to prove that, if $\mathfrak{C}$ is also a closed subalgebra of $C(\Omega)$ which separates the points of Ω, then every minimal special set reduces to a single point. This will follow from the next lemma.

LEMMA (3.3.12). *Let $\mathfrak{C}$ be a closed subalgebra of $C(\Omega)$ which contains the identity element of $C(\Omega)$ and let F be any special set associated with $\mathfrak{C}$. Also let F_0 be a subset of F which is a special set associated with the subalgebra of $C(F)$ obtained by restriction of functions in $\mathfrak{C}$ to the set F. Then F_0 is also a special set associated with $\mathfrak{C}$.*

PROOF. It is evidently sufficient to make the proof for the case in which F_0 is a special maximum set associated with the restriction of some function in $\mathfrak{C}$ to the set F. For this it is sufficient to prove the existence of a special maximum set, associated with an element of $\mathfrak{C}$, whose intersection with F is equal to F_0. We accordingly assume given a function $f \in \mathfrak{C}$ such that $|f(\omega)| < 1$, for $\omega \in F - F_0 = \{\omega : \omega \in F, f(\omega) = 1\}$. For each positive integer n, let

$$G_n = \left\{\omega : \omega \in \Omega, \quad |f(\omega)| < 1+\frac{1}{2^n}\right\}.$$

Then G_n is an open set in Ω which contains the set F. Since F is special and Ω is compact, there exists a special maximum set F_n, associated with some $f_n \in \mathfrak{C}$, such that $F \subseteq F_n \subset G_n$. Now, since $\max|f_n(\omega)| < 1$, for $\omega \notin G_n$, there exists an integer k_n such that

$$|f_n(\omega)|^{k_n}|f(\omega)| < \frac{1}{2^n}$$

for $\omega \notin G_n$. Define

$$g = \sum_{n=1}^{\infty} \frac{1}{2^n} f_n{}^{k_n} f.$$

Then $g \in \mathfrak{C}$ since $\mathfrak{C}$ is closed in $C(\Omega)$. Let ω be an arbitrary point of Ω. If $\omega \in G_n$, for all n, then $|f(\omega)| \leqslant 1$ and therefore

$$|g(\omega)| \leqslant \sum_{n=1}^{\infty} \frac{1}{2^n} = 1.$$

If $\omega \notin G_n$, for some n, then there exists m such that $\omega \in G_{m-1}$ while $\omega \notin G_n$, for all $n \geqslant m$. Thus

$$|(f_n{}^{k_n} f)(\omega)| < 1 + \frac{1}{2^{m-1}} \quad \text{for } n = 1, \cdots, m-1,$$

and

$$|(f_n{}^{k_n} f)(\omega)| < \frac{1}{2^n} < \frac{1}{2^{m-1}} \quad \text{for } n \geqslant m.$$

Therefore

$$\begin{aligned} |g(\omega)| &\leqslant \left(1 + \frac{1}{2^{m-1}}\right) \sum_{n=1}^{m-1} \frac{1}{2^n} + \frac{1}{2^{m-1}} \sum_{n=m}^{\infty} \frac{1}{2^n} \\ &\leqslant \left(1 + \frac{1}{2^{m-1}}\right)\left(1 - \frac{1}{2^{m-1}}\right) + \frac{1}{2^{m-1}} \frac{1}{2^{m-1}} = 1. \end{aligned}$$

Hence $\|g\| = 1$. Also, since f_n is equal to 1 on F, it follows that $g(\omega) = f(\omega)$, for $\omega \in F$. Therefore $F_0 = F \cap \{\omega : \omega \in \Omega, g(\omega) = 1\}$ and the proof is complete.

COROLLARY (3.3.13). *Let F be a special maximum set associated with some element of $\mathfrak{C}$. Then any subset of F, which is a special maximum set associated with the restriction of some element of $\mathfrak{C}$ to the set F, is also a special maximum set associated with an element of $\mathfrak{C}$.*

COROLLARY (3.3.14). *If $\mathfrak{C}$ separates the points of Ω, then every* *minimal special set associated with $\mathfrak{C}$ reduces to a single strong boundary point.*

We can now complete the proof of the result promised above.

THEOREM (3.3.15). *Let $\mathfrak{C}$ be a closed subalgebra of $C(\Omega)$ which separates the points of Ω and contains the identity element of $C(\Omega)$. Then each function in $\mathfrak{C}$ assumes its maximum absolute value in the set of strong boundary points of Ω relative to $\mathfrak{C}$.*

PROOF. It is immediate from Corollaries (3.3.11) and (3.3.14) that every maximum set associated with an element of $\mathfrak{C}$ contains a strong boundary point. Therefore the theorem follows.

We call the set of strong boundary points of Ω the STRONG BOUNDARY of Ω relative to $\mathfrak{C}$.

By definition, a strong boundary point ω_0 is contained in arbitrarily small maximum sets. The question arises as to whether or not ω_0 itself constitutes a maximum set. In other words, is ω_0 a UNIQUE MAXIMUM POINT in the sense that there exists a function in $\mathfrak{C}$ whose maximum absolute value is attained at ω_0 and at no other point? An answer to this question is provided in the next theorem.

THEOREM (3.3.16). *Let $\mathfrak{C}$ be a closed subalgebra of $C(\Omega)$ which contains the identity element of $C(\Omega)$, and let ω_0 be a strong boundary point of Ω relative to $\mathfrak{C}$. Then, in order for ω_0 to be a unique maximum point, it is necessary and sufficient that ω_0 be a G_δ-set.*

PROOF. By definition, the condition means that ω_0 is an intersection of a countable sequence of open sets. Assume first that ω_0 is a unique maximum point for a function $f \in \mathfrak{C}$ with $f(\omega_0) = 1$. Then the sets

$$G_n = \{\omega : 1 - \frac{1}{n} < |f(\omega)|\}, \quad n = 1, 2, \cdots,$$

are open and intersect in the point ω_0. This proves the necessity. Now assume a given sequence $\{G_n\}$ of open sets which intersect in ω_0. Since ω_0 is a strong boundary point, there exists, for each n, a special maximum set F_n which contains ω_0 and is contained in G_n. Let f_n be a function in $\mathfrak{C}$ with F_n as its maximum set and equal to 1 on F_n. Define

$$f = \sum_{n=1}^{\infty} \frac{1}{2^n} f_n.$$

Then it is straightforward to verify that $\|f\| = 1$, $f(\omega_0) = 1$, and

$|f(\omega)| < 1$ for $\omega \neq \omega_0$. In other words, ω_0 is a unique maximum point for f. This proves the sufficiency.

The result in the following corollary is due to E. A. Bishop [4] who, in this case, calls the set of unique maximum points the MINIMAL BOUNDARY of Ω.

COROLLARY (3.3.17). *If Ω is a compact metric space and $\mathfrak{C}$ is a closed subalgebra of $C(\Omega)$ which separates the points of Ω and contains the identity element of $C(\Omega)$, then each function in $\mathfrak{C}$ assumes its maximum absolute value in the set of unique maximum points.*

In the remainder of this section, we specialize to the case of a complex commutative Banach algebra $\mathfrak{A}$. The algebra $\hat{\mathfrak{A}}$ of functions on the carrier space $\Phi_{\mathfrak{A}}$, associated with $\mathfrak{A}$ by the Gelfand representation theorem, obviously satisfies the conditions of Theorem (3.3.1). Therefore, the Šilov boundary exists. In this situation, we denote the boundary by $\partial_{\mathfrak{A}}\Phi_{\mathfrak{A}}$ and call it the $\mathfrak{A}$-BOUNDARY of $\Phi_{\mathfrak{A}}$. Similarly, if F is a subset of $\Phi_{\mathfrak{A}}$, then $\partial_{\mathfrak{A}}F$ is the $\mathfrak{A}$-boundary of the functions in $\hat{\mathfrak{A}}$ restricted to F. When there is no chance for confusion, we write $\partial\Phi_{\mathfrak{A}}$ in place of $\partial_{\mathfrak{A}}\Phi_{\mathfrak{A}}$.

THEOREM (3.3.18). *For every $x \in \mathfrak{A}$*, bdry $Sp_{\mathfrak{A}}(x) \subseteq \hat{x}(\partial\Phi_{\mathfrak{A}}) \cup (0)$.

PROOF. Let λ_0 be any boundary point of $Sp(x)$ and suppose that $\lambda_0 \notin \hat{x}(\partial\Phi_{\mathfrak{A}}) \cup (0)$. It is easily verified that $\hat{x}(\partial\Phi_{\mathfrak{A}}) \cup (0)$ is a closed set in the complex plane. Hence there exists $\delta > 0$ such that $|\hat{x}(\varphi)-\lambda_0| > \delta\nu(x)$ for every $\varphi \in \partial\Phi_{\mathfrak{A}}$. Let λ_1 be any non-zero complex number such that $\lambda_1 \notin Sp(x)$ and $|\lambda_0-\lambda_1| < (\delta/2)|\lambda_0|$. Then $\lambda_1^{-1}x$ is quasi-regular. Moreover, if $u = (\lambda_1^{-1}x)^\circ$, then

$$\hat{u}(\varphi) = \frac{\hat{x}(\varphi)}{\hat{x}(\varphi)-\lambda_1}, \quad \varphi \in \Phi_{\mathfrak{A}}.$$

Also,

$$\tfrac{1}{2}\delta\nu(x) = \delta\nu(x) - \tfrac{1}{2}\delta\nu(x) < |\hat{x}(\varphi)-\lambda_0| - |\lambda_0-\lambda_1| \leqslant |\hat{x}(\varphi)-\lambda_1|.$$

Therefore

$$\max_{\varphi\in\partial\Phi_{\mathfrak{A}}} |\hat{u}(\varphi)| \leqslant \max_{\varphi\in\partial\Phi_{\mathfrak{A}}} \frac{2|\hat{x}(\varphi)|}{\delta\nu(x)} \leqslant 2\delta^{-1}.$$

On the other hand,

$$\max_{\varphi\in\Phi_{\mathfrak{A}}} |\hat{u}(\varphi)| = \max_{\varphi\in\Phi_{\mathfrak{A}}} \frac{|\hat{x}(\varphi)|}{|\hat{x}(\varphi)-\lambda_1|} \geqslant \frac{|\lambda_0|}{|\lambda_0-\lambda_1|} > 2\delta^{-1}.$$

This contradicts the preceding inequality showing that $\hat{x}(\partial\Phi_{\mathfrak{A}}) \cup (0)$ must contain the boundary of $Sp(x)$.

THEOREM (3.3.19). *If* $\mathfrak{A}$ *has an identity element, then*

$$\text{bdry}Sp(x) \subseteq \hat{x}(\partial\Phi_{\mathfrak{A}}).$$

PROOF. By the preceding theorem, we have only to show that if $0 \in \text{bdry}Sp(x)$, then $0 \in \hat{x}(\partial\Phi_{\mathfrak{A}})$. Since $\mathfrak{A}$ has an identity element, $\Phi_{\mathfrak{A}}$ and hence $\partial\Phi_{\mathfrak{A}}$ are compact. Therefore $\hat{x}(\partial\Phi_{\mathfrak{A}})$ is a closed set in the complex plane. Suppose $0 \in \text{bdry}Sp(x)$ but $0 \notin \hat{x}(\partial\Phi_{\mathfrak{A}})$, and let $\delta = \min|\lambda|$ for $\lambda \in \hat{x}(\partial\Phi_{\mathfrak{A}})$. Choose any $\lambda_1 \notin Sp(x)$ such that $|\lambda_1| < \delta/2$. Then $x-\lambda_1$ is regular in $\mathfrak{A}$. Let $u = (x-\lambda_1)^{-1}$. Then we have

$$\nu(u) = \max_{\varphi\in\partial\Phi_{\mathfrak{A}}} |\hat{u}(\varphi)| = (\min_{\varphi\in\partial\Phi_{\mathfrak{A}}} |\hat{x}(\varphi)-\lambda_1|)^{-1} \leqslant 2\delta^{-1}.$$

On the other hand, since $0 \in Sp(x)$, there exists $\varphi_0 \in \Phi_{\mathfrak{A}}$ such that $\hat{x}(\varphi_0) = 0$. Therefore

$$\nu(u) \geqslant |\hat{u}(\varphi_0)| = |\lambda_1|^{-1} > 2\delta^{-1}.$$

This contradicts the preceding inequality and shows that $0 \in \hat{x}(\partial\Phi_{\mathfrak{A}})$.

THEOREM (3.3.20). *Let u be an element of $\mathfrak{A}$ and φ_0 any point of $\Phi_{\mathfrak{A}}$ such that $|\hat{u}(\varphi_0)| = \nu(u)$. Let U be the set of all those points of $\Phi_{\mathfrak{A}}$ at which $\hat{u}$ takes the value $\hat{u}(\varphi_0)$. Then $\partial_{\mathfrak{A}}U$ exists and is contained in $U\cap\partial\Phi_{\mathfrak{A}}$. In particular, $h(k(U\cap\partial\Phi_{\mathfrak{A}})) = U$.*

PROOF. Let $\mathfrak{A}_1$ be the algebra obtained by adjunction of an identity element to $\mathfrak{A}$ and note that $\Phi_{\mathfrak{A}_1} = \Phi_{\mathfrak{A}}{}^{\infty}$. By Lemma (3.3.10), we can choose $u_1 \in \mathfrak{A}_1$ such that $\hat{u}_1(\varphi) = 1$ for $\varphi \in U$, and U is the maximum set associated with u_1. Now, if $U\cap\partial\Phi_{\mathfrak{A}}$ does not contain $\partial_{\mathfrak{A}}U$, then there exists $v \in \mathfrak{A}$ such that, if $\alpha = \max|\hat{v}(\varphi)|$ for $\varphi \in U$, then $\alpha \neq 0$ and

$$U\cap\partial\Phi_{\mathfrak{A}} \subset \{\varphi : \varphi \in \Phi_{\mathfrak{A}},\ \ |\hat{v}(\varphi)| < \alpha\}.$$

Denote the open set on the right by G. Since

$$U\cap\partial\Phi_{\mathfrak{A}} = \{\varphi : \varphi \in \partial\Phi_{\mathfrak{A}},\ \ |\hat{u}_1(\varphi)| = 1\},$$

it follows that

$$\max_{\varphi\in\partial\Phi_{\mathfrak{A}}-G} |\hat{u}_1(\varphi)| < 1,$$

and hence, for large k,

$$\max_{\varphi\in\partial\Phi_{\mathfrak{A}}-G} |\hat{u}_1(\varphi)|^k < \alpha\nu(v)^{-1}.$$

Set $w = vu_1^k$. Then $w \in \mathfrak{A}$ and

$$\max_{\varphi \in U} |\hat{w}(\varphi)| = \alpha \leqslant \nu(w).$$

For any $\varphi \in G$, we have $|\hat{v}(\varphi)| < \alpha$ and thus $|\hat{w}(\varphi)| < \alpha$. Also, for any $\varphi \in \partial \Phi_{\mathfrak{A}} - G$, we have

$$|\hat{v}(\varphi)||\hat{u}_1(\varphi)|^k < |\hat{v}(\varphi)|\alpha \nu(v)^{-1} \leqslant \alpha,$$

and so again $|\hat{w}(\varphi)| < \alpha$. Since $\alpha \leqslant \nu(w)$, this contradicts the fact that $\partial \Phi_{\mathfrak{A}}$ is an $\mathfrak{A}$-set and proves that $\partial_{\mathfrak{A}} U \subseteq U \cap \partial \Phi_{\mathfrak{A}}$. In particular, $\hat{x}(U \cap \partial \Phi_{\mathfrak{A}}) = (0)$ implies $\hat{x}(U) = (0)$, so that $h(k(U \cap \partial \Phi_{\mathfrak{A}})) \supseteq U$. On the other hand, by Lemma (3.1.16), the set U is a hull and therefore

$$U = h(k(U)) \supseteq h(k(U \cap \partial \Phi_{\mathfrak{A}})) \supseteq U.$$

In other words, $U = h(k(U \cap \partial \Phi_{\mathfrak{A}}))$, and the theorem is proved.

Since any finite set of points is already a hull, it follows immediately from the above theorem that the set $U \cap \partial \Phi_{\mathfrak{A}}$ is necessarily infinite if U contains points not in $\partial \Phi_{\mathfrak{A}}$. This result, which was observed by Holladay [1], is strengthened in the next theorem. The stronger result was called to our attention by K. Hoffman whose proof however was quite different being based on a use of measure. (See remarks at the end of this section).

THEOREM (3.3.21). *If* $|\hat{u}(\varphi_0)| = \nu(u) \neq 0$, *where* $\varphi_0 \notin \partial \Phi_{\mathfrak{A}}$, *then the function* $\hat{u}$ *assumes the value* $\hat{u}(\varphi_0)$ *on a subset of* $\partial \Phi_{\mathfrak{A}}$ *which contains a perfect set.*

PROOF. Let U be the set of all those points of $\Phi_{\mathfrak{A}}$ at which $\hat{u}$ takes the value $\hat{u}(\varphi_0)$. Then U is compact and, by the preceding theorem, $\partial_{\mathfrak{A}} U$ exists and is contained in $U \cap \partial \Phi_{\mathfrak{A}}$. In particular, $\partial_{\mathfrak{A}} U$ is a closed subset of $U \cap \partial \Phi_{\mathfrak{A}}$ such that

$$|\hat{x}(\varphi_0)| \leqslant \max_{\varphi \in \partial_{\mathfrak{A}} U} |\hat{x}(\varphi)|$$

for every $x \in \mathfrak{A}$. By the compactness of U and a straightforward application of Zorn's lemma (for example, as in the argument preceding Theorem (3.3.1)), we can obtain a set $\Gamma \subseteq \partial_{\mathfrak{A}} U$ which is closed and is minimal with respect to the property,

$$|\hat{x}(\varphi_0)| \leqslant \max_{\varphi \in \Gamma} |\hat{x}(\varphi)|$$

for every $x \in \mathfrak{A}$. We prove that Γ is a perfect set. Suppose, on the contrary, that φ_1 were an isolated point of Γ. Let $\Gamma_1 = \Gamma-(\varphi_1)$. By the assumed minimal character of Γ, there obviously must exist $v \in \mathfrak{A}$ such that

$$\rho = \max_{\varphi\in\Gamma_1} |\hat{v}(\varphi)| < \hat{v}(\varphi_0) = 1.$$

Choose $w \in \mathfrak{A}$ such that $\hat{w}(\varphi_0) = 1$ and $\hat{w}(\varphi_1) = 0$. Let k be a positive integer such that $\rho^k\nu(w) < 1$, and define $z = v^k w$. Then

$$\max_{\varphi\in\Gamma_1} |\hat{z}(\varphi)| \leqslant \rho^k\nu(w) < 1.$$

Moreover, $\hat{z}(\varphi_0) = 1$ and $\hat{z}(\varphi_1) = 0$, so that

$$\max_{\varphi\in\Gamma} |\hat{z}(\varphi)| < 1 = |\hat{z}(\varphi_0)|.$$

This contradicts the defining property of Γ and shows that Γ is perfect. Since $\Gamma \subseteq U\cap\partial\Phi_{\mathfrak{A}}$, the theorem is therefore proved.

The next theorem is a mild generalization of Rouche's Theorem for holomorphic functions in the plane to the algebra $\hat{\mathfrak{A}}$. It is due to Holladay [1].

THEOREM (3.3.22). *Assume $\mathfrak{A}$ to possess an identity element and let u, v be two elements of $\mathfrak{A}$ such that $|\hat{u}(\varphi)-\hat{v}(\varphi)| < |\hat{u}(\varphi)|$ for every $\varphi \in \partial\Phi_{\mathfrak{A}}$. Then $\hat{u}$ will have a zero in $\Phi_{\mathfrak{A}}$ if and only if $\hat{v}$ does.*

PROOF. Since $\partial\Phi_{\mathfrak{A}}$ is compact, there exists a positive integer n such that

$$n \min_{\varphi\in\partial\Phi_{\mathfrak{A}}} [|\hat{u}(\varphi)|-|\hat{u}(\varphi)-\hat{v}(\varphi)|] > \nu(u-v).$$

Consider the following elements of $\mathfrak{A}$:

$$nu, \quad (n-1)u+v, \quad (n-2)u+2v, \quad \cdots, \quad u+(n-1)v, \quad nv.$$

Assuming the theorem false, one obtains k with $0 \leqslant k \leqslant n$ such that $(n-k)\hat{u}+k\hat{v}$ is never zero on $\Phi_{\mathfrak{A}}$, while one of the two elements $(n-k\mp 1)\hat{u}+(k\pm 1)\hat{v}$ does have a zero at some point φ_0 of $\Phi_{\mathfrak{A}}$. Since $(n-k)\hat{u}+k\hat{v}$ is never zero on $\Phi_{\mathfrak{A}}$, the element $(n-k)u+kv$ has an inverse w in $\mathfrak{A}$. Moreover, $\hat{w}(\varphi) = [(n-k)\hat{u}(\varphi)+k\hat{v}(\varphi)]^{-1}$ and hence

$$\max_{\varphi\in\partial\Phi_{\mathfrak{A}}} |(n-k)\hat{u}(\varphi)+k\hat{v}(\varphi)|^{-1} = \max_{\varphi\in\Phi_{\mathfrak{A}}} |(n-k)\hat{u}(\varphi)+k\hat{v}(\varphi)|^{-1}.$$

Therefore

$$\min_{\varphi\in\partial\Phi_{\mathfrak{A}}} |(n-k)\hat{u}(\varphi)+k\hat{v}(\varphi)| = \min_{\varphi\in\Phi_{\mathfrak{A}}} |(n-k)\hat{u}(\varphi)+k\hat{v}(\varphi)|.$$

Now we have

$$\begin{aligned}\nu(u-v) &< n \min_{\varphi\in\partial\Phi_{\mathfrak{A}}} (|\hat{u}(\varphi)| - |\hat{u}(\varphi)-\hat{v}(\varphi)|)\\ &\leqslant \min_{\varphi\in\partial\Phi_{\mathfrak{A}}} (n|\hat{u}(\varphi)| - k|\hat{u}(\varphi)-\hat{v}(\varphi)|)\\ &\leqslant \min_{\varphi\in\partial\Phi_{\mathfrak{A}}} |(n-k)\hat{u}(\varphi)+k\hat{v}(\varphi)| = \min_{\varphi\in\Phi_{\mathfrak{A}}} |(n-k)\hat{u}(\varphi)+k\hat{v}(\varphi)|\\ &\leqslant |(n-k)\hat{u}(\varphi_0)+k\hat{v}(\varphi_0)-[(n-k\mp 1)\hat{u}(\varphi_0)+(k\pm 1)\hat{v}(\varphi_0)]|\\ &= |\hat{u}(\varphi_0)-\hat{v}(\varphi_0)| \leqslant \nu(u-v).\end{aligned}$$

This is a contradiction and the theorem follows.

THEOREM (3.3.23). *Assume $\mathfrak{A}$ to possess an identity element. Let x be an element of $\mathfrak{A}$ and ξ_0 be any complex number in the range of the function $\hat{x}$ which is not assumed by $\hat{x}$ on the Šilov boundary $\partial\Phi_{\mathfrak{A}}$. Then the range of $\hat{x}$ contains every complex number ξ such that*

$$|\xi-\xi_0| < \min_{\varphi\in\partial\Phi_{\mathfrak{A}}} |\hat{x}(\varphi)-\xi_0|.$$

PROOF. Apply the preceding theorem to the pair of elements $u = x-\xi_0$ and $v = x-\xi$.

THEOREM (3.3.24). *Let $\mathfrak{A}$ possess an identity element and let there exist in $\mathfrak{A}$ an element u such that the function $\hat{u}$ assumes a value in $\Phi_{\mathfrak{A}}-\partial\Phi_{\mathfrak{A}}$ not assumed in $\partial\Phi_{\mathfrak{A}}$. Then both of the sets $\partial\Phi_{\mathfrak{A}}$ and $\Phi_{\mathfrak{A}}-\partial\Phi_{\mathfrak{A}}$ must be non-denumerable.*

PROOF. Let α be the exceptional value assumed by $\hat{u}$ in $\Phi_{\mathfrak{A}}-\partial\Phi_{\mathfrak{A}}$ and define $v = u-\alpha$. Then $\hat{v}$ takes the value zero in $\Phi_{\mathfrak{A}}-\partial\Phi_{\mathfrak{A}}$ but not in $\partial\Phi_{\mathfrak{A}}$. By the preceding theorem, if $|\beta| < \min_{\varphi\in\partial\Phi_{\mathfrak{A}}} |\hat{v}(\varphi)|$, then there exists $\varphi\in\Phi_{\mathfrak{A}}-\partial\Phi_{\mathfrak{A}}$ such that $\hat{v}(\varphi) = \beta$. It follows immediately that $\Phi_{\mathfrak{A}}-\partial\Phi_{\mathfrak{A}}$ is non-denumerable. Now the set $Sp(v)$ is a bounded non-denumerable subset of the complex plane, and so bdry$Sp(v)$ is also non-denumerable. On the other hand, bdry$Sp(v) \subseteq \hat{v}(\partial\Phi_{\mathfrak{A}})$ by Theorem (3.3.19), and it follows that $\partial\Phi_{\mathfrak{A}}$ must also be non-denumerable.

In the next theorem, the Šilov boundary associated with a given algebra is related to the Šilov boundaries associated with subalgebras of the given algebra. Actually it is desirable to consider the more general situation provided by a pair of complex commutative Banach algebras $\mathfrak{A}$ and $\mathfrak{B}$ along with a homomorphism τ of $\mathfrak{B}$ into $\mathfrak{A}$. No topological assumptions are imposed on τ. As in § 1, we denote by $\varphi \to \varphi^{\tau'}$ the dual mapping of $\Phi_{\mathfrak{A}}{}^{\infty}$ into $\Phi_{\mathfrak{B}}{}^{\infty}$ induced by τ. Recall that the dual mapping is continuous and so, by the compactness of $\Phi_{\mathfrak{A}}{}^{\infty}$, maps closed sets of $\Phi_{\mathfrak{A}}{}^{\infty}$ onto closed sets in $\Phi_{\mathfrak{B}}{}^{\infty}$.

For the case in which $\mathfrak{B}$ is a closed subalgebra of $\mathfrak{A}$, the first part of the next theorem and its corollary were proved by Šilov. (See Gelfand, Raikov and Šilov [1, § 27] and Šilov [3].)

THEOREM (3.3.25). *If $\nu_{\mathfrak{B}}(x) = \nu_{\mathfrak{A}}(x^{\tau})$ for every $x \in \mathfrak{B}$, then the image of $\partial\Phi_{\mathfrak{A}}{}^{\infty}$ under the dual mapping $\varphi \to \varphi^{\tau'}$ of $\Phi_{\mathfrak{A}}{}^{\infty}$ into $\Phi_{\mathfrak{B}}{}^{\infty}$ contains $\partial\Phi_{\mathfrak{B}}{}^{\infty}$. Furthermore, $\partial\Phi_{\mathfrak{B}}{}^{\infty}$ is the largest closed subset of $\Phi_{\mathfrak{B}}{}^{\infty}$ that has this property for every such $\mathfrak{A}$.*

PROOF. For arbitrary $x \in \mathfrak{B}$, we have

$$\max_{\psi \in (\partial\Phi_{\mathfrak{A}}{}^{\infty})^{\tau'}} |\hat{x}(\psi)| = \max_{\varphi \in \partial\Phi_{\mathfrak{A}}{}^{\infty}} |\hat{x}^{\tau}(\varphi)| = \nu_{\mathfrak{A}}(x^{\tau}).$$

Since $\nu_{\mathfrak{A}}(x^{\tau}) = \nu_{\mathfrak{B}}(x)$, it follows that $(\partial\Phi_{\mathfrak{A}}{}^{\infty})^{\tau'}$ is a $\mathfrak{B}$-set in $\Phi_{\mathfrak{B}}{}^{\infty}$ and, being closed, must contain the Šilov boundary $\partial\Phi_{\mathfrak{B}}{}^{\infty}$. In order to show that $\partial\Phi_{\mathfrak{B}}{}^{\infty}$ is characterized by this property, we have only to take $\mathfrak{A}$ as the algebra $C(\partial\Phi_{\mathfrak{B}}{}^{\infty})$ of all complex-valued continuous functions on $\partial\Phi_{\mathfrak{B}}{}^{\infty}$. Then the mapping $x \to \hat{x}$, where the function $\hat{x}$ is restricted to $\partial\Phi_{\mathfrak{B}}{}^{\infty}$, is a homomorphism of $\mathfrak{B}$ into $\mathfrak{A} = C(\partial\Phi_{\mathfrak{B}}{}^{\infty})$ such that $\nu_{\mathfrak{B}}(x) = \nu_{\mathfrak{A}}(\hat{x})$ for each $x \in \mathfrak{B}$. In this case, $\Phi_{\mathfrak{A}}{}^{\infty} = \partial\Phi_{\mathfrak{B}}{}^{\infty}$ and $\partial\Phi_{\mathfrak{A}}{}^{\infty} = \partial\Phi_{\mathfrak{B}}{}^{\infty}$. Furthermore, the associated dual mapping of $\Phi_{\mathfrak{A}}{}^{\infty}$ into $\Phi_{\mathfrak{B}}{}^{\infty}$ is just the injection mapping of $\partial\Phi_{\mathfrak{B}}{}^{\infty}$ into $\Phi_{\mathfrak{B}}{}^{\infty}$. In other words, the image of $\partial\Phi_{\mathfrak{A}}{}^{\infty}$ in $\Phi_{\mathfrak{B}}{}^{\infty}$ is exactly $\partial\Phi_{\mathfrak{B}}{}^{\infty}$.

COROLLARY (3.3.26). *Let $\mathfrak{B}$ denote a self-adjoint complex commutative Banach algebra and let $\mathfrak{A}$ be any complex commutative Banach algebra which contains $\mathfrak{B}$ as a subalgebra. If $\nu_{\mathfrak{A}}(x) = \nu_{\mathfrak{B}}(x)$ for every $x \in \mathfrak{B}$, then every homomorphism of $\mathfrak{B}$ into the complex field can be extended to all of $\mathfrak{A}$.*

In the next theorem we have an improvement of a previous result obtained in Theorem (1.6.12).

THEOREM (3.3.27). *Let $\mathfrak{A}$ and $\mathfrak{B}$ denote two complex Banach algebras such that $\mathfrak{B}$ is a subalgebra of $\mathfrak{A}$ with the property that $\nu_{\mathfrak{A}}(b) = \nu_{\mathfrak{B}}(b)$ for every $b \in \mathfrak{B}$. Then, for each $b \in \mathfrak{B}$, we have $Sp_{\mathfrak{A}}(b) \subseteq Sp_{\mathfrak{B}}(b) \cup (0)$ while* bdry $Sp_{\mathfrak{B}}(b) \subseteq$ bdry $Sp_{\mathfrak{A}}(b)$.

PROOF. Let b denote any fixed element of $\mathfrak{B}$. Then there exists a maximal commutative subalgebra $\mathfrak{C}_1$ of $\mathfrak{B}$ such that $b \in \mathfrak{C}_1$ and a maximal commutative subalgebra $\mathfrak{C}_2$ of $\mathfrak{A}$ such that $\mathfrak{C}_1 \subseteq \mathfrak{C}_2$. Since $Sp_{\mathfrak{B}}(b) = Sp_{\mathfrak{C}_1}(b)$ and $Sp_{\mathfrak{C}_2}(b) = Sp_{\mathfrak{A}}(b)$, we can accordingly limit attention to the case in which $\mathfrak{A}$ and $\mathfrak{B}$ are both commutative. The inclusion $Sp_{\mathfrak{A}}(b) \subseteq Sp_{\mathfrak{B}}(b) \cup (0)$ is an immediate consequence of the fact that $\mathfrak{B}$ is a subalgebra of $\mathfrak{A}$ and is independent of the condition $\nu_{\mathfrak{A}}(b) = \nu_{\mathfrak{B}}(b)$. If $\varphi \to \varphi^\tau$ is the dual mapping of $\Phi_{\mathfrak{A}}{}^\infty$ into $\Phi_{\mathfrak{B}}{}^\infty$ associated with the injection mapping of $\mathfrak{B}$ into $\mathfrak{A}$, then, by the preceding theorem, $(\partial\Phi_{\mathfrak{A}}{}^\infty)^\tau \supseteq \partial\Phi_{\mathfrak{B}}{}^\infty$. Moreover, by Theorem (3.3.18), bdry $Sp_{\mathfrak{B}}(b) \subseteq \hat{b}(\partial\Phi_{\mathfrak{B}}{}^\infty) \cup (0)$. Let $\lambda \in$ bdry $Sp_{\mathfrak{B}}(b)$ and choose $\psi \in \partial\Phi_{\mathfrak{B}}{}^\infty$ such that $\lambda = \hat{b}(\psi)$. Choose $\varphi \in \partial\Phi_{\mathfrak{A}}{}^\infty$ such that $\varphi^\tau = \psi$. Then $\hat{b}(\varphi^\tau) = \hat{b}(\psi) = \lambda$. Thus $\lambda \in Sp_{\mathfrak{A}}(b)$ and we obtain that bdry $Sp_{\mathfrak{B}}(b) \subseteq Sp_{\mathfrak{A}}(b)$. This inclusion, along with $Sp_{\mathfrak{A}}(b) \subseteq Sp_{\mathfrak{B}}(b) \cup (0)$, implies bdry $Sp_{\mathfrak{B}}(b) \subseteq$ bdry $Sp_{\mathfrak{A}}(b)$ and completes the proof.

Holladay [1] has obtained a variety of special maximizing properties of subsets of a compact Hausdorff space Ω with respect to subalgebras of $C(\Omega)$. Arens and Singer [2] obtain more direct generalization of properties of holomorphic functions (on the disc) by considering certain special subalgebras of the group algebra $L^1(\mathfrak{G})$ of a locally compact abelian group $\mathfrak{G}$. (See Appendix, A.3.2.) More precisely, they assume given a closed semi-group $\mathfrak{G}_+$ in $\mathfrak{G}$, which generates $\mathfrak{G}$ and which is equal to the closure of its interior, and then take $\mathfrak{A}$ as the collection of all $f \in L^1(\mathfrak{G})$ which vanish outside of $\mathfrak{G}_+$. Note that $\mathfrak{A}$ is a closed subalgebra of $L^1(\mathfrak{G})$. The classical case is obtained if $\mathfrak{G}$ is the additive group of the integers and $\mathfrak{G}_+$ is the semi-group of all non-negative integers. In this case, $\Phi_{\mathfrak{A}}$ is the closed unit disc on the complex plane and an element $f \in \mathfrak{A}$ is mapped, *via* the Gelfand representation, into a function $\hat{f}$ which is continuous on the disc and holomorphic on the interior of the disc. The Šilov boundary of $\Phi_{\mathfrak{A}}$ is equal to the topological boundary and can be identified with the character group of $\mathfrak{G}$. In the general case, the functions $\hat{f}$ are called GENERALIZED ANALYTIC FUNCTIONS. The study of these functions has been continued by Arens [9; 11] and Hoffman [1]. H. Rossi [1] has recently proved a local maximum principle for elements of a function algebra.

A device which is useful in some of these considerations can be described as follows. Let $\mathfrak{C}$ be a subalgebra of $C(\Omega)$ and recall that $\mathfrak{C}$ can also be regarded, *via* restriction to $\partial_{\mathfrak{C}}\Omega$, as a subalgebra of $C(\partial_{\mathfrak{C}}\Omega)$. Consider a fixed point $\omega_0 \in \Omega$ and, for $f \in \mathfrak{C}$, define $F(f) = f(\omega_0)$. Then F is a linear functional on $\mathfrak{C}$. Since

$$|F(f)| \leqslant \max_{\omega \in \partial_{\mathfrak{C}}\Omega} |f(\omega)|,$$

F can be extended to a linear functional on $C(\partial_{\mathfrak{C}}\Omega)$ with bound equal to 1. Therefore, by the Riesz–Kakutani representation theorem, there exists a regular measure μ defined on the Borel subsets of $\partial_{\mathfrak{C}}\Omega$ such that

$$f(\omega_0) = \int_{\partial_{\mathfrak{C}}\Omega} f(\omega)\mu(\partial\omega), \quad f \in \mathfrak{C},$$

where $\mu(\partial_{\mathfrak{C}}\Omega) = 1$. If $\omega_0 \in \partial_{\mathfrak{C}}\Omega$, then μ is a point measure concentrated at ω_0. On the other hand, if $\omega_0 \notin \partial_{\mathfrak{C}}\Omega$, then μ cannot be a point measure. In this case, the above formula can be regarded as a crude version of the Cauchy integral formula. Its usefulness depends in any given case on how much information can be obtained concerning the dependence of μ on the point ω_0.

§ 4. Representations of the carrier space. The canonical representation of the carrier space of a commutative normed algebra, associated with a given system of generators for the algebra, was introduced in § 1 primarily to obtain the compactness properties of the carrier space of a commutative Banach algebra. We return now for a closer and more systematic examination of this important notion. It is convenient to make a few preliminary observations. Throughout the discussion we have in mind a given real or complex commutative Banach algebra $\mathfrak{A}$.

Consider a system of indeterminates $\{\xi_\lambda : \lambda \in \Lambda\}$, where Λ is a completely arbitrary index set. By a polynomial in this system of indeterminates, we will mean a polynomial, with coefficients in the scalar field of $\mathfrak{A}$, which involves any finite subset of the indeterminates ξ_λ. The collection $\mathscr{P}(\Lambda)$ of all such polynomials is an algebra over the scalar field of $\mathfrak{A}$ with respect to the usual algebra operations for polynomials. If $P(\xi_{\lambda_1}, \cdots, \xi_{\lambda_n})$ is any element of $\mathscr{P}(\Lambda)$ which involves the indeterminates $\xi_{\lambda_1}, \cdots, \xi_{\lambda_n}$, then we write, for brevity, $P(\{\xi_\lambda\})$ in place of the usual $P(\xi_{\lambda_1}, \cdots, \xi_{\lambda_n})$. It is obvious that $\mathscr{P}(\Lambda)$ can be regarded as an algebra of complex-valued continuous functions on the product space K^Λ of "Λ" complex planes K. We denote by $\mathscr{P}_0(\Lambda)$ the subalgebra of $\mathscr{P}(\Lambda)$ consisting of all those polynomials with constant term equal to zero. These are the polynomials which vanish at the origin of K^Λ. When there is no chance of confusion, we shall write $\mathscr{P}$ in place of $\mathscr{P}(\Lambda)$ and $\mathscr{P}_0$ in place of $\mathscr{P}_0(\Lambda)$. Observe that the elements of $\mathscr{P}_0$ separate the points of K^Λ. Furthermore, it is an almost immediate consequence of definitions that the usual product space topology in K^Λ is equivalent to the $\mathscr{P}_0$-topology. Therefore, by Theorem (3.2.1), the natural embedding of K^Λ in the carrier space $\Phi_{\mathscr{P}_0}{}^\infty$ is a homeomorphism. Moreover, if φ is any element of $\Phi_{\mathscr{P}_0}{}^\infty$ and P_λ is the polymonial ξ_λ, define $\mu_\lambda = \hat{P}_\lambda(\varphi)$. Then $\{\mu_\lambda\}$ is an element of K^Λ and, if P is any element of $\mathscr{P}_0$, then $P(\{\mu_\lambda\}) = \hat{P}(\varphi)$. This shows that the natural embedding of K^Λ covers $\Phi_{\mathscr{P}_0}{}^\infty$, so that K^Λ and $\Phi_{\mathscr{P}_0}{}^\infty$ are homeomorphic. We take the usual liberties with notations and write $\Phi_{\mathscr{P}_0}{}^\infty = K^\Lambda$.

Now let $\{z_\lambda : \lambda \in \Lambda\}$ be an arbitrary subset of the Banach algebra $\mathfrak{A}$ indexed by the same set Λ involved in the definition of the polynomial algebra $\mathscr{P}_0$ discussed above. If $P(\xi_{\lambda_1}, \cdots, \xi_{\lambda_n})$ is any element of $\mathscr{P}_0$ and if we write $P(\{z_\lambda\}) = P(z_{\lambda_1}, \cdots, z_{\lambda_n})$, then $P(\{z_\lambda\})$ is an element of $\mathfrak{A}$ and the mapping $P \rightarrow P(\{z_\lambda\})$ is a homomorphism of $\mathscr{P}_0$ into $\mathfrak{A}$. We note in passing that every homomorphism of $\mathscr{P}_0$ into $\mathfrak{A}$ is obviously obtained in this way. The dual mapping of $\Phi_{\mathfrak{A}}{}^{\infty}$ into K^{Λ} associated with this homomorphism is given explicitly by $\varphi \to \{\hat{z}_{\lambda}(\varphi)\}$. By analogy with the case of a single element, the image in K^{Λ} of $\Phi_{\mathfrak{A}}$ or of $\Phi_{\mathfrak{A}}{}^{\infty}$ (according as $\mathfrak{A}$ does or does not possess an identity element) will be called the JOINT SPECTRUM of the elements z_{λ} and denoted by $Sp_{\mathfrak{A}}(\{z_{\lambda}\})$. (See Arens and Calderon [2].) Since the dual mapping is continuous (See § 1), it follows that $Sp_{\mathfrak{A}}(\{z_{\lambda}\})$ is a compact subset of K^{Λ}. Note that $Sp_{\mathfrak{A}}(\{z_{\lambda}\})$ is contained in the compact set Δ in K^{Λ} which is equal to the product of all the discs $D_{\lambda} = \{\zeta : |\zeta| \leqslant \nu(z_{\lambda})\}$. The kernel $\mathfrak{K}_0$ of the homomorphism of $\mathscr{P}_0$ into $\mathfrak{A}$, associated with the set $\{z_{\lambda} : \lambda \in \Lambda\}$, consists of all polynomial relations satisfied in $\mathfrak{A}$ by the elements z_{λ}. If Γ_P denotes the set of all zeros in K^{Λ} of the polynomial P, then the hull in $\Phi_{\mathscr{P}_0}{}^{\infty} = K^{\Lambda}$ of the ideal $\mathfrak{K}_0$ of $\mathscr{P}_0$ is equal to the intersection Γ of all Γ_P for $P \in \mathfrak{K}_0$. We thus conclude that $Sp_{\mathfrak{A}}(\{z_{\lambda}\}) \subseteq \Gamma \cap \Delta$. Notice that, if $\mathfrak{A}$ is a real algebra, then, as in the case of a single element, the joint spectrum $Sp_{\mathfrak{A}}(\{z_{\lambda}\})$ is self-conjugate. In other words, if $\{\mu_{\lambda}\} \in Sp_{\mathfrak{A}}(\{z_{\lambda}\})$, then also $\{\bar{\mu}_{\lambda}\} \in Sp_{\mathfrak{A}}(\{z_{\lambda}\})$, where $\bar{\mu}_{\lambda}$ is the complex conjugate of μ_{λ}.

In the next theorem, we specialize to the case in which $\{z_{\lambda} : \lambda \in \Lambda\}$ is a system of generators for $\mathfrak{A}$. Then the dual mapping reduces to the canonical mapping which, by Theorem (3.1.10), is a homeomorphism between $\Phi_{\mathfrak{A}}{}^{\infty}$ and the joint spectrum $Sp_{\mathfrak{A}}(\{z_{\lambda}\})$. We take the liberty again in this situation of writing $\Phi_{\mathfrak{A}}{}^{\infty} = Sp_{\mathfrak{A}}(\{z_{\lambda}\})$.

THEOREM (3.4.1.). *If the system of generators $\{z_{\lambda} : \lambda \in \Lambda\}$ exhausts $\mathfrak{A}$, then $\Phi_{\mathfrak{A}}{}^{\infty} = \Gamma$. If the generators constitute a subalgebra of $\mathfrak{A}$, then $\Phi_{\mathfrak{A}}{}^{\infty} = \Gamma \cap \Delta$.*

PROOF. If the generators exhaust $\mathfrak{A}$, then $P \to P(\{z_{\lambda}\})$ is a homomorphism of $\mathscr{P}_0$ onto $\mathfrak{A}$. Since Γ is the hull of the kernel of this homomorphism, it follows immediately from Theorem (3.1.17) that $\Phi_{\mathfrak{A}}{}^{\infty} = \Gamma$. Now assume only that the generators constitute a subalgebra $\mathfrak{A}_0$ of $\mathfrak{A}$. By the definition of a system of generators, $\mathfrak{A}_0$ is dense in $\mathfrak{A}$. Let $\{\mu_{\lambda}\}$ be any point of $\Gamma \cap \Delta$. Then, since $\{\mu_{\lambda}\} \in \Gamma$, the mapping $z_{\lambda} \to \mu_{\lambda}$ is a homomorphism of $\mathfrak{A}_0$ into the complex field (i.e. $\{\mu_{\lambda}\} \in \Phi_{\mathfrak{A}_0}{}^{\infty}$). Furthermore, since $\{\mu_{\lambda}\} \in \Delta$, we have $|\mu_{\lambda}| \leqslant \|z_{\lambda}\|$ for every $z_{\lambda} \in \mathfrak{A}_0$. In other words, the homomorphism is continuous on $\mathfrak{A}_0$ and, since $\mathfrak{A}_0$ is dense in $\mathfrak{A}$, can therefore be extended to all of $\mathfrak{A}$. Hence $\{\mu_{\lambda}\} \in \Phi_{\mathfrak{A}}{}^{\infty}$. This shows that $\Gamma \cap \Delta \subseteq \Phi_{\mathfrak{A}}{}^{\infty}$ and, along with the opposite inclusion obtained previously, proves that $\Phi_{\mathfrak{A}}{}^{\infty} = \Gamma \cap \Delta$ and establishes the theorem.

The above theorem shows that the carrier space of $\mathfrak{A}$ can be represented as an "algebraic variety" in a certain (infinite) cartesian product of complex planes. This, however, requires an extensive system of generators. If no conditions are imposed on the system of generators, then it is still possible to obtain a weaker "algebraic" representation of the carrier space as an "algebraic polyhedron". In the following discussion we denote by $\|P\|$ the norm of the element $P(\{z_\lambda\})$ in $\mathfrak{A}$ and by $|P|$ the maximum value of $|P(\{\mu_\lambda\})|$ for $\{\mu_\lambda\} \in Sp_{\mathfrak{A}}(\{z_\lambda\})$. Note that $|P| = \nu_{\mathfrak{A}}(P(\{z_\lambda\})) \leqslant \|P\|$.

THEOREM (3.4.2). *For any system* $\{z_\lambda : \lambda \in \Lambda\}$ *of generators for* $\mathfrak{A}$, *it is true that*

$$\Phi_{\mathfrak{A}}{}^{\infty} = \bigcap_{P \in \mathscr{P}_0} \{\{\mu_\lambda\} : |P(\{\mu_\lambda\})| \leqslant \|P\|\}.$$

PROOF. Define $\Psi_P = \{\{\mu_\lambda\} : |P(\{\mu_\lambda\})| \leqslant \|P\|\}$ and set $\Psi = \bigcap \Psi_P, P \in \mathscr{P}_0$. The problem is to show that $\Psi = \Phi_{\mathfrak{A}}{}^{\infty}$. This reduces to proving that $\Psi \subseteq \Phi_{\mathfrak{A}}{}^{\infty}$, the opposite inclusion being obvious. Since $\|P\| = 0$ for every $P \in \mathfrak{K}_0$, it is immediate that $\Psi \subseteq \Gamma$. Next let $\{\mu_\lambda\}$ be any point of Γ not in $\Phi_{\mathfrak{A}}{}^{\infty}$. If $\mathfrak{A}_0$ is the homomorphic image of $\mathscr{P}_0$ in $\mathfrak{A}$, then $\{\mu_\lambda\} \in \Phi_{\mathfrak{A}_0}{}^{\infty}$. Since $\mathfrak{A}_0$ is dense in $\mathfrak{A}$, the homomorphism $P(\{z_\lambda\}) \to P(\{\mu_\lambda\})$ of $\mathfrak{A}_0$ into the field of complex numbers cannot be continuous with respect to the norm in $\mathfrak{A}$. Otherwise the homomorphism could be extended to all of $\mathfrak{A}$, so that $\{\mu_\lambda\} \in \Phi_{\mathfrak{A}}{}^{\infty}$ contrary to hypothesis. Therefore there exists $P \in \mathscr{P}_0$ such that $|P(\{\mu_\lambda\})| > \|P\|$. This completes the proof.

COROLLARY (3.4.3).

$$\Phi_{\mathfrak{A}}{}^{\infty} = \bigcap_{P \in \mathscr{P}_0} \{\{\mu_\lambda\} : |P(\{\mu_\lambda\})| \leqslant |P|\}.$$

The next theorem gives a characterization of those subsets of a product space K^Λ which can serve as the carrier space of a commutative Banach algebra. (See Gelfand [8].)

THEOREM (3.4.4.) *Let* Λ *be an arbitrary abstract point set and let* Φ *be any subset of* K^Λ. *Then, in order for there to exist a commutative Banach algebra* $\mathfrak{A}$ *with a system* $\{z_\lambda : \lambda \in \Lambda\}$ *of generators such that* Φ *is the canonical image of* $\Phi_{\mathfrak{A}}{}^{\infty}$ *determined by this system of generators, it is necessary and sufficient that* Φ *be compact and contain the origin of* K^Λ *and that*

$$\Phi = \bigcap_{P \in \mathscr{P}_0} \{\{\mu_\lambda\} : |P(\{\mu_\lambda\})| \leqslant |P|_\Phi\},$$

where $|P|_\Phi$ *denotes the maximum value of* $|P(\{\mu_\lambda\})|$ *for* $\{\mu_\lambda\} \in \Phi$.

Proof. The necessity is given by the corollary to the preceding theorem. In order to prove the sufficiency, we have only to take as $\mathfrak{A}$ the algebra of all continuous functions on Φ which are obtained as uniform limits on Φ of polynomials from $\mathscr{P}_0$. Then $\mathfrak{A}$ is obviously generated by the polynomials z_α defined by $z_\alpha(\{\xi_\lambda\}) = \xi_\alpha$. Therefore $\Phi_{\mathfrak{A}}{}^\infty = \Phi$, by the preceding theorem, and the proof is complete.

The characterization in the above theorem involves both topological and algebraic conditions. However, for algebras with one generator, in which case the carrier spaces are subsets of the complex plane, Šilov [4] has given a purely topological characterization.

Theorem (3.4.5). *A subset Φ of the complex plane is the carrier space $\Phi_{\mathfrak{A}}{}^\infty$ of a commutative Banach algebra $\mathfrak{A}$ with one generator if and only if it is compact, contains the origin and does not separate the plane.*

Proof. If $\mathfrak{A}$ is an algebra with one generator, then $\Phi_{\mathfrak{A}}{}^\infty$ is obviously a compact set in the plane which contains the origin. Furthermore, by Corollary (3.4.3) and the maximum modulus principle for polynomials, it follows that $\Phi_{\mathfrak{A}}{}^\infty$ cannot separate the plane. Conversely, let Φ be any compact subset of the complex plane which contains the origin and does not separate the plane. Take as $\mathfrak{A}$ the algebra of all complex-valued functions on Φ which are uniform limits on Φ of polynomials with constant term zero. Then $\mathfrak{A}$ is a closed subalgebra of the algebra $C(\Phi)_0$ of all complex-valued functions which are continuous on Φ and vanish at the origin. Note that $\mathfrak{A}$ is an algebra with the single generator z where $z(\zeta) = \zeta$, $\zeta \in \Phi$. It remains to prove that $\Phi_{\mathfrak{A}}{}^\infty = \Phi$; that is, $\Phi = \{\hat{z}(\varphi) : \varphi \in \Phi_{\mathfrak{A}}{}^\infty\}$. Since $\Phi = \Phi_{C(\Phi)_0}{}^\infty$, we have, by Theorem (3.1.6), $Sp_{C(\Phi)_0}(z) = \Phi$ and $Sp_{\mathfrak{A}}(z) = \Phi_{\mathfrak{A}}{}^\infty$. In particular, $Sp_{C(\Phi)_0}(z)$ does not separate the plane. Since $\mathfrak{A}$ is a closed subalgebra of $C(\Phi)_0$, it follows by Theorem (1.6.13) that $Sp_{\mathfrak{A}}(z) = Sp_{C(\Phi)_0}(z)$. In other words, $\Phi_{\mathfrak{A}}{}^\infty = \Phi$ and the proof is complete.

Since the maximum modulus principle holds for polynomials in several complex variables, it follows, as in the above proof, that the carrier space $\Phi_{\mathfrak{A}}{}^\infty$ of an algebra with n generators is a compact set in K^n which contains the origin of K^n and does not separate K^n. On the other hand, there are examples, already for $n = 2$, which show that these topological conditions are no longer sufficient for a subset of K^n to be the carrier space of an algebra with n generators. (See Appendix, A.2.7.)

Suppose that $\mathfrak{A}$ has an identity element. Then, as has already been observed (Corollary (3.1.13)), if the set $\{z_\lambda : \lambda \in \Lambda\}$ plus the identity is a system of generators for $\mathfrak{A}$, then the mapping $\varphi \to \{z_\lambda(\varphi)\}$ of $\Phi_\mathfrak{A}$ into K^Λ is a homeomorphism. Using this result and Theorem (3.4.4), one can easily show that a subset Φ of K^Λ represents in this way a carrier space $\Phi_\mathfrak{A}$ if and only if it is compact and of the form

$$\Phi = \bigcap_{P \in \mathscr{P}} \{\{\mu_\lambda\} : |P(\{\mu_\lambda\})| \leqslant |P|_\Phi\}.$$

Similarly, we can use Theorem (3.4.5) to show that a subset Φ of the complex plane is homeomorphic *via* a mapping $\varphi \to \hat{z}(\varphi)$ with the carrier space $\Phi_\mathfrak{A}$ of a commutative Banach algebra $\mathfrak{A}$ generated by z plus an identity element, if and only if Φ is compact and does not separate the plane. This is the form in which Šilov obtained the result.

In the remainder of this section we consider some results which give, in a sense, approximations to the carrier space of a Banach algebra $\mathfrak{A}$ by the carrier spaces of certain finitely generated closed subalgebras of $\mathfrak{A}$. It will be assumed throughout that $\{z_\lambda : \lambda \in \Lambda\}$ is a system of generators for $\mathfrak{A}$. Again, a few notational preliminaries are needed.

If Ψ is any subset of the product space K^Λ and if Λ_0 is a subset of Λ, then the PROJECTION OF Ψ INTO K^{Λ_0} consists of all $\{\mu_\lambda\} \in K^{\Lambda_0}$ such that there exists $\{\mu'_\lambda\} \in K^\Lambda$ with $\mu'_\lambda = \mu_\lambda$ for $\lambda \in \Lambda_0$. This projection of Ψ will be denoted by $\Psi(\Lambda_0)$. Also, for any subset Λ_0 of Λ, the closed subalgebra of $\mathfrak{A}$ generated by the set $\{z_\lambda : \lambda \in \Lambda_0\}$ will be denoted by $\mathfrak{A}_{\Lambda_0}$. The set Δ, as before, is equal to the product of all the discs $D_\lambda = \{\zeta : |\zeta| \leqslant \nu(z_\lambda)\}$.

THEOREM (3.4.6). *Let Θ be any open set in K^Λ which contains $\Phi_\mathfrak{A}^\infty$. Then there exists a finite subset π_0 of the index set Λ such that, if π is any subset of Λ containing π_0, then*

$$\Phi_\mathfrak{A}^\infty(\pi) \subseteq \Phi_{\mathfrak{A}_\pi}^\infty \subseteq \Theta(\pi).$$

PROOF. Since $\mathfrak{A}_\pi$ is a subalgebra of $\mathfrak{A}$, the first inclusion is given immediately by the dual mapping of $\Phi_\mathfrak{A}^\infty$ into $\Phi_{\mathfrak{A}_\pi}^\infty$. Since the set Δ is compact and $\Phi_{\mathfrak{A}_\pi}^\infty \subseteq \Delta \cap \Theta$, Theorem (3.4.2) implies the existence of a finite number of polynomials $P_1, \cdots, P_n$ in $\mathscr{P}_0$ such that

$$\Delta \cap \Psi_{P_1} \cap \ldots \cap \Psi_{P_n} \subseteq \Theta,$$

where, as before,

$$\Psi_P = \{\{\mu_\lambda\} : |P(\{\mu_\lambda\})| \leqslant \|P\|\}.$$

Let π_0 be the finite subset of Λ consisting of all indices involved in the polynomials $P_1, \cdots, P_n$. Now if π is any set of indices containing π_0, then it is evident that $\Psi_{P_i}(\pi)$, the projection of Ψ_{P_i} into K^π, is given by

$$\Psi_{P_i}(\pi) = \{\{\mu'_\lambda\} : \{\mu'_\lambda\} \in K^\pi, \ |P_i(\{\mu'_\lambda\})| \leqslant \|P_i\|\}.$$

Furthermore,

$$\Phi_{\mathfrak{A}_\pi}{}^\infty \subseteq \Delta(\pi) \cap \Psi_{P_1}(\pi) \cap \cdots \cap \Psi_{P_n}(\pi).$$

Now, if $\{\mu'_\lambda\}$ is any element of K^π which belongs to $\Delta(\pi) \cap \Psi_{P_i}(\pi)$ and if $\{\mu_\lambda\}$ is any element of Δ which projects onto $\{\mu'_\lambda\}$, then $\{\mu_\lambda\}$ automatically belongs to Ψ_{P_i}. This implies that

$$\Delta(\pi) \cap \Psi_{P_1}(\pi) \cap \cdots \cap \Psi_{P_n}(\pi) \subseteq \Theta(\pi)$$

and completes the proof.

THEOREM (3.4.7). *Let Θ be any open set in K^Λ which contains $\Phi_{\mathfrak{A}}{}^\infty$. Then there exists a finite subset π_0 of the index set Λ such that, for every finite subset π of Λ containing π_0, there exists a bounded closed algebraic polyhedron Ω_π in K^π which is contained in $\Theta(\pi)$ and which contains $\Phi_{\mathfrak{A}_\pi}{}^\infty$ in its interior.*

PROOF. Observe that, in the proof of the preceding theorem, the set $\Delta(\pi) \cap \Psi_{P_1}(\pi) \cap \cdots \cap \Psi_{P_n}(\pi)$ is actually a closed algebraic polyhedron in K^π which is contained in $\Theta(\pi)$ and which contains $\Phi_{\mathfrak{A}_\pi}{}^\infty$. It is necessary to modify this polyhedron slightly to get $\Phi_{\mathfrak{A}_\pi}{}^\infty$ into the interior. First let $\Delta^{(1)}$ denote the set of those points $\{\zeta_\lambda\}$ in K^π with $|\zeta_\lambda| \leqslant \nu_{\mathfrak{A}}(z_\lambda)+1, \lambda \in \pi$. Then $\Delta^{(1)}$ is a compact set in K^π which contains $\Delta(\pi)$ in its interior. Next, for k an integer, define $\Psi_{P_i}{}^{(k)}$ to be the set of those points $\{\zeta_\lambda\}$ in K^π such that $|P_i(\{\zeta_\lambda\})| \leqslant \|P_i\|+1/k$. Then $\Psi_{P_i}{}^{(k)}$, for each k, contains $\Psi_{P_i}(\pi)$ in its interior. Finally define

$$\Gamma_k = (\Delta^{(1)} - \Theta(\pi)) \bigcap_{i=1}^{n} \Psi_{P_i}{}^{(k)}.$$

Then, since

$$\bigcap_{k=1}^{\infty} \Psi_{P_i}{}^{(k)} = \Psi_{P_i}(\pi) \qquad \text{and} \qquad (\Delta^{(1)} - \Theta(\pi)) \bigcap_{i=1}^{n} \Psi_{P_i}(\pi) = 0,$$

it follows that

$$\bigcap_{k=1}^{\infty} \Gamma_k = 0.$$

By the compactness and the fact that $\Gamma_{k+1} \subseteq \Gamma_k$, there exists k_0 such that $\Gamma_{k_0} = 0$. We can therefore take

$$\Omega_\pi = \Delta^{(1)} \cap \Psi_{P_i}^{(k_0)} \cap \cdots \cap \Psi_{P_n}^{(k_0)}$$

and the theorem is proved.

The above theorem shows that the "approximation" of $\Phi_{\mathfrak{A}_\pi}{}^\infty$ to $\Phi_{\mathfrak{A}}{}^\infty$ is within an algebraic polyhedron. If the system of generators $\{z_\lambda : \lambda \in \Lambda\}$ is a subalgebra of $\mathfrak{A}$, then Theorem (3.4.1) can be used in place of Theorem (3.4.2) in the above argument to obtain an approximation in terms of an algebraic variety. More precisely, if Θ is any open set in K^Λ containing $\Phi_{\mathfrak{A}}{}^\infty$, then there exists a finite set of indices π_0 such that, for any subset π of Λ containing π_0, there exists an algebraic variety Ω_π in K^π such that

$$\Phi_{\mathfrak{A}_\pi}{}^\infty \subseteq \Delta(\pi) \subseteq \Omega_\pi \subseteq \Theta(\pi).$$

In fact, the polynomials which define Ω_π involve only the indices in π_0.

THEOREM (3.4.8). *Let $\Phi_{\mathfrak{A}}{}^\infty$ be equal to a union of a finite number of disjoint open and closed sets $\Phi_1, \cdots, \Phi_n$. Then there exists in $\mathfrak{A}$ a closed finitely generated subalgebra $\mathfrak{A}'$ whose carrier space $\Phi_{\mathfrak{A}'}{}^\infty$, is equal to a union of a finite number of disjoint open and closed sets $\Phi'_1, \cdots, \Phi'_n$ such that the dual mapping of $\Phi_{\mathfrak{A}}{}^\infty$ into $\Phi_{\mathfrak{A}'}{}^\infty$ takes Φ_k into Φ'_k ($k = 1, \cdots, n$).*

PROOF. Let $\{z_\lambda : \lambda \in \Lambda\}$ be any system of generators for $\mathfrak{A}$ and identify $\Phi_{\mathfrak{A}}{}^\infty$ with its canonical representation in K^Λ. Then $\Phi_{\mathfrak{A}}{}^\infty$ is the union in K^Λ of the finite collection of pairwise disjoint compact sets $\Phi_1, \cdots, \Phi_n$. Hence there exist pairwise disjoint open sets $\Theta_1, \cdots, \Theta_n$ in K^Λ such that $\Phi_k \subseteq \Theta_k$ for $k = 1, \cdots, n$. Let Θ be the union of the sets $\Theta_1, \cdots, \Theta_n$ and apply Theorem (3.4.6). Observe that, since Φ_k is compact, each of the sets Θ_k can be assumed to be determined by a finite number of the indices in Λ. Therefore the total number of indices involved in the specification of the sets $\Theta_1, \cdots, \Theta_n$ is finite. Let π be any finite set of indices which contains those indices which determine the sets $\Theta_1, \cdots, \Theta_n$ and also contains the set π_0 given by Theorem (3.4.6). Then we have

$$\Phi_{\mathfrak{A}}{}^\infty(\pi) \subseteq \Phi_{\mathfrak{A}_\pi}{}^\infty \subseteq \Theta(\pi).$$

Define $\Phi'_k = \Phi_{\mathfrak{A}_\pi}{}^\infty \cap \Theta_k(\pi)$. Since π contains all of the indices involved in the sets $\Theta_1, \cdots, \Theta_n$, it is immediate that

$$\Theta(\pi) = \Theta_1(\pi) \cup \cdots \cup \Theta_n(\pi)$$

and the $\Theta_k(\pi)$ are disjoint open sets in K^π. Therefore the Φ'_k are disjoint closed sets in K^π. Furthermore, since $\Phi_k \subseteq \Theta_k$, we have $\Phi_k(\pi) \subseteq \Theta_k(\pi)$. Hence $\Phi_k(\pi) \subseteq \Phi'_k$ and the theorem follows.

§ 5. Homomorphisms of certain function algebras into a Banach algebra. The method of studying the structure of a commutative Banach algebra in terms of homomorphisms of polynomial algebras into it was used effectively in the preceding section. It is desirable to sharpen this method by extending it to algebras more inclusive than polynomial algebras. The existence of non-trivial homomorphisms, which was no problem in the case of polynomials, becomes a major difficulty in more general cases. In order to avoid uninteresting complications, we limit attention throughout to a complex algebra $\mathfrak{A}$.

The first extension to be considered is close to the polynomial case. Let Λ be an arbitrary index set and denote by $\mathscr{P}$, as in the preceding section, the algebra of all polynomials in the system of indeterminates $\{\xi_\lambda : \lambda \in \Lambda\}$. Next let Ω be any compact subset of K^Λ and denote by $\mathscr{P}_\Omega$ the set of all those polynomials in $\mathscr{P}$ which are never zero in Ω. Then the set of all rational functions P/Q with $P \in \mathscr{P}$ and $Q \in \mathscr{P}_\Omega$ constitutes an algebra $\mathscr{R}(\Omega)$ which will be called the algebra of rational functions on Ω. The carrier space of $\mathscr{R}(\Omega)$ will not be needed below, hence we only remark without proof that it can be identified with the set of all those points $\{\mu_\lambda\} \in K^\Lambda$ with the property that, if $Q \in \mathscr{P}$ and $Q(\{\omega_\lambda\}) \neq 0$ for every $\{\omega_\lambda\} \in \Omega$, then $Q(\{\mu_\lambda\}) \neq 0$.

Now assume $\mathfrak{A}$ to possess an identity element and let $\{z_\lambda : \lambda \in \Lambda\}$ be any collection of elements of $\mathfrak{A}$ such that $Sp_{\mathfrak{A}}(\{z_\lambda\}) \subseteq \Omega$. If P is any polynomial in $\mathscr{P}$ with constant term α, then $P = \alpha + P_0$, where $P_0 \in \mathscr{P}_0$. Denote by $P(\{z_\lambda\})$ the element $\alpha + P_0(\{z_\lambda\})$ of $\mathfrak{A}$. Then $P \to P(\{z_\lambda\})$ is a homomorphism of $\mathscr{P}$ into $\mathfrak{A}$. If $Q \in \mathscr{P}_\Omega$, then $Q(\{\hat{z}_\lambda(\varphi)\}) \neq 0$ for each $\varphi \in \Phi_{\mathfrak{A}}$. Therefore $Q(\{z_\lambda\})^{-1}$ exists in $\mathfrak{A}$, and the mapping $P/Q \to P(\{z_\lambda\})Q(\{z_\lambda\})^{-1}$ is a homomorphism τ of $\mathscr{R}(\Omega)$ into $\mathfrak{A}$ such that, for every $f \in \mathscr{R}(\Omega)$,

$$(\star) \qquad \widehat{f^\tau}(\varphi) = f(\{\hat{z}_\lambda(\varphi)\}), \quad \varphi \in \Phi_{\mathfrak{A}}.$$

Observe that $\mathscr{P}$ is a subalgebra of $\mathscr{R}(\Omega)$ and that τ is an extension of the homomorphism defined previously for $\mathscr{P}$. When $\mathfrak{A}$ does not possess an identity element, assume that Ω contains the origin $\{0\}$ of K^Λ and consider, in place of $\mathscr{R}(\Omega)$, the subalgebra $\mathscr{R}_0(\Omega)$ consisting of all f in $\mathscr{R}(\Omega)$ with $f(\{0\}) = 0$. Then we can still define $f(\{z_\lambda\})$ and so obtain a homomorphism of $\mathscr{R}_0(\Omega)$ into $\mathfrak{A}$. This homomorphism can also be realized as the restriction to $\mathscr{R}_0(\Omega)$ of the previous homomorphism τ of $\mathscr{R}(\Omega)$ into $\mathfrak{A}_1$, where $\mathfrak{A}_1$ is the algebra obtained from $\mathfrak{A}$ by adjunction of an identity element. Our objective is to extend τ to a much wider class of functions associated with Ω so as to preserve condition (*). In order to do this, we need to specialize to the case of a finite index set $\Lambda = (1, 2, \cdots n)$. In this case, we write $K^n = K^\Lambda$. The algebra of functions to be used will now be constructed.

A complex-valued function f is said to be HOLOMORPHIC ON Ω provided there exists an open set Θ, containing Ω, *on each component of which* f is a holomorphic function of n complex variables. It is important to notice that f is not required to be holomorphic in the usual sense and might more accurately be called only "piecewise" or "locally" holomorphic. In particular, if Θ is the union of two disjoint sets Θ_1 and Θ_2, then the function f which is equal to zero on Θ_1 and to one on Θ_2 is holomorphic on Ω. Two functions holomorphic on Ω are defined to be EQUIVALENT provided they coincide in some open set containing Ω. Under this equivalence relation, the class of all functions holomorphic on Ω decomposes into mutually disjoint equivalence classes. The equivalence class which contains a given function f is called the GERM OF f ON Ω. The class of all germs of holomorphic functions on Ω is denoted by $\mathscr{H}(\Omega)$. In the obvious way, algebra operations can be introduced into $\mathscr{H}(\Omega)$, *via* these operations for functions, so that $\mathscr{H}(\Omega)$ becomes a complex commutative algebra with an identity element. If one associates with a rational function on Ω its germ on Ω, the result is clearly an isomorphism of $\mathscr{R}(\Omega)$ with a subalgebra of $\mathscr{H}(\Omega)$. It is convenient to treat $\mathscr{H}(\Omega)$ as the class of all functions holomorphic on Ω in which two functions are defined as equal if they are equivalent. Thus, with the usual ambiguity of notation, f will denote either a function holomorphic on Ω or its germ. Each f in $\mathscr{H}(\Omega)$ determines a function f_Ω defined on Ω, obtained by restriction of elements of f to Ω. The mapping $f \to f_\Omega$ is a homomorphism of $\mathscr{H}(\Omega)$ into $C(\Omega)$. It will be an isomorphism if Ω is equal to the closure of its interior.

We now come to the problem of constructing homomorphisms of $\mathscr{H}(\Omega)$ into $\mathfrak{A}$. For reasons of simplicity, the case $n = 1$ will be dealt with first, although the resulting theorem is essentially contained in the theorem for arbitrary n.

THEOREM (3.5.1). *Assume $\mathfrak{A}$ to possess an identity element and let Ω be a compact subset of the complex plane. If z is any element of $\mathfrak{A}$ with*

$Sp_{\mathfrak{A}}(z) \subseteq \Omega$, then there exists a homomorphism $f \to f^{\tau}$ of $\mathscr{H}(\Omega)$ into $\mathfrak{A}$ such that

$$\widehat{f^{\tau}}(\varphi) = f(\hat{z}(\varphi)), \quad \varphi \in \Phi_{\mathfrak{A}}.$$

Proof. Let f be any element of $\mathscr{H}(\Omega)$. Since the domain of definition of f is an open set which contains Ω, there obviously exists an open set Θ, which contains Ω and whose closure is contained in the domain of f, such that the boundary of Θ consists of a finite number of rectifiable simple closed curves. These boundary curves are assumed to be positively oriented in the usual manner as contours of integration about the set Ω. Denote this oriented boundary by B. Now, since $Sp(z) \subseteq \Omega$ and B is bounded, it follows that $f(\zeta)(\zeta - z)^{-1}$ is a uniformly continuous function of $\zeta \in B$ with values in $\mathfrak{A}$. It is straightforward to define and prove the existence in $\mathfrak{A}$ of the vector-valued contour integral

$$f(z) = \frac{1}{2\pi i} \int_B f(\zeta)(\zeta - z)^{-1} \, d\zeta.$$

Furthermore, if we define $f^{\tau} = f(z)$, then $f \to f^{\tau}$ is a homomorphism of the algebra $\mathscr{H}(\Omega)$ into $\mathfrak{A}$. The details here, which are not substantially different from those for the case of complex-valued functions, may be found in Hille [2, Sec. 5.17] or Dunford and Schwartz [1, VII. 3.10]. It suffices for us to recall that the above integral is obtained as a limit of finite sums of the form

$$\frac{1}{2\pi i} \sum_{k=1}^{m} f(\zeta'_k)(\zeta'_k - z)^{-1}(\zeta_k - \zeta_{k-1})$$

with respect to the norm in $\mathfrak{A}$. Since homomorphisms of $\mathfrak{A}$ into the complex field are continuous, we obtain that

$$\widehat{f(z)}(\varphi) = \frac{1}{2\pi i} \int_B f(\zeta)(\zeta - \hat{z}(\varphi))^{-1} \, d\zeta = f(\hat{z}(\varphi)),$$

for every $\varphi \in \Phi_{\mathfrak{A}}$. Thus $f \to f^{\tau}$ is the desired homomorphism and the theorem is proved.

Notice that, if $\mathfrak{A}$ is semi-simple, then the fact that $f \to f^{\tau}$ is a homomorphism of $\mathscr{H}(\Omega)$ into $\mathfrak{A}$ follows easily from the relation $\widehat{f^{\tau}}(\varphi) = f(\hat{z}(\varphi))$, $\varphi \in \Phi_{\mathfrak{A}}$. Notice also that the homomorphism $f \to f^{\tau}$ is an extension of the homomorphism defined previously for $\mathscr{R}(\Omega)$. In particular, it maps the identity element of $\mathscr{H}(\Omega)$ onto the identity of $\mathfrak{A}$ and the function f, defined by $f(\zeta) = \zeta$, onto the element z.

We turn now to the case $n > 1$ for which the situation is much less elementary. As might be guessed from the case $n = 1$, the key to the problem lies in a general Cauchy integral formula for holomorphic functions of several variables. Such a formula has been obtained by A. Weil [1]. The Weil formula, which applies to functions holomorphic on an *analytic* polyhedron, is an exceedingly sharp result since it recovers the given function from its values on the distinguished boundary of the polyhedron. This is a set with real dimension equal to n as opposed to a real dimension of $2n$ for the space K^n. The proof of the formula involves a number of very difficult points, one of which is an appeal to a deep result due to van der Waerdon concerning triangulation of analytic loci. Arens [10] has obtained a restricted version of the formula, the proof of which avoids most of the difficulties encountered in the general formula. Actually, for our purposes the full precision of the Weil formula is not needed. In fact, all that we require is a certain strong kind of approximation of the given function by rational functions which is implied by the formula. This can as well be obtained from a much less demanding, and accordingly more easily proved, generalized Cauchy integral formula which has been discussed by Michel Hervé [1]. We now describe a special case of this formula which is adequate for the problem at hand. The set Ω is again an arbitrary compact subset of the space K^n.

Let Ψ denote a bounded (open) algebraic polyhderon in K^n which contains the set Ω. By definition, there exists a finite set of polynomials $P_1, \cdots, P_m$ $(m \geqslant n)$ in n complex variables such that

$$\Psi = \bigcap_{j=1}^{m} \{\tilde{\zeta} : |P_j(\tilde{\zeta})| < 1\},$$

where $\tilde{\zeta}$ denotes the point $(\zeta_1, \cdots, \zeta_n)$ in K^n. It is not difficult to show that there also exist polynomials $P_{jk}(\tilde{\zeta}, \tilde{\omega})$, in the $2n$ variables $\zeta_1, \cdots, \zeta_n, \omega_1, \cdots, \omega_n$, such that

$$P_j(\tilde{\zeta}) - P_j(\tilde{\omega}) = \sum_{k=1}^{n} (\zeta_k - \omega_k) P_{jk}(\tilde{\zeta}, \tilde{\omega}),$$

where $j = 1, 2, \cdots, m$.

Now let Θ be an open set in K^n which contains the closure of the polyhedron Ψ. Then there exists a constant δ with $1 < \delta$ such that the (closed) polyhedron

$$\Psi_\delta = \bigcap_{j=1}^{m} \{\tilde{\zeta} : |P_j(\tilde{\zeta})| \leqslant \delta\}$$

is contained in Θ. Observing that Ψ_δ contains the closure of Ψ in its interior, we denote by Δ the "annular" region $\Psi_\delta - \Psi$. Let u be a real-valued function defined in the plane K with the following properties: u is infinitely differentiable at each point of the plane; $u(\xi) = 1$ for $|\xi| \leqslant 1$; and $u(\xi) = 0$ for $|\xi| \geqslant \delta$. Set

$$v_j(\tilde{\zeta}) = u(P_j(\tilde{\zeta})), \quad \tilde{\zeta} \in K^n.$$

Then v_j is an infinitely differentiable function (of $2n$ real variables) defined throughout K^n. Each v_j is identically equal to 1 on Ψ and, if $v = v_1 v_2 \cdots v_m$, then the support of v is contained in Ψ_δ. Our next step is to define a differential form D which will appear as the kernel of the desired integral formula.

First let

$$A_j = [P_j(\tilde{\zeta}) - P_j(\tilde{\omega})]^{-1} \sum_{k=1}^{n} P_{jk}(\tilde{\zeta}, \tilde{\omega}) d\zeta_k$$

and

$$B_j = A_j \wedge dv_j, \quad j = 1, \cdots, m,$$

where the symbol "$\wedge$" denotes the exterior product of the forms involved. Then define

$$D(\tilde{\zeta}, \tilde{\omega}) = \sum_{j_1 < \cdots < j_n} \frac{v}{v_{j_1} \cdots v_{j_n}} B_{j_1} \wedge \cdots \wedge B_{j_n}.$$

For fixed $\tilde{\omega} \in \Omega$, D is a differential $2n$-form which is defined for all $\tilde{\zeta} \in K^n$ and vanishes outside of Δ.

Finally, let f be any function which is holomorphic in each component of Θ. Then, for $\tilde{\omega} \in \Omega$, it is true that

$$f(\tilde{\omega}) = \frac{1}{(2\pi i)^n} \int_\Delta f(\tilde{\zeta}) D(\tilde{\zeta}, \tilde{\omega}).$$

This is the desired special case of the Hervé generalization of the Cauchy formula mentioned above. The proof, which is tedious and will not be attempted here, depends on elementary theory of integration of differential forms including Stokes's theorem. For our purposes, it is sufficient to note that the integral appears as a limit of finite sums of rational functions of $\omega_1, \cdots, \omega_n$ and that the limit still exists in the norm of $\mathfrak{A}$ when $\omega_1, \cdots, \omega_n$ are replaced respectively by elements $z_1, \cdots, z_n$ of $\mathfrak{A}$ with $Sp_{\mathfrak{A}}(z_1, \cdots, z_n) \subseteq \Omega$. In fact, if $Sp(z_1, \cdots, z_n) \subseteq \Omega$ and if we write $\tilde{z} = (z_1, \cdots, z_n)$, then $[P_j(\tilde{\zeta}) - P_j(\tilde{z})]^{-1}$ exists for $\tilde{\zeta} \notin \Omega$ and $f(\tilde{\zeta})D(\tilde{\zeta}, \tilde{z})$ is a vector-valued differential $2n$-form which is uniformly continuous on Δ. The existence of the vector-valued integral follows from this observation. We now define

$$f(z_1, \cdots, z_n) = \frac{1}{(2\pi i)^n} \int_{\Delta} f(\tilde{\zeta}) D(\tilde{\zeta}, \tilde{z}).$$

Since the integral exists as a limit in the norm of $\mathfrak{A}$, we have

$$\widehat{f(z_1, \cdots, z_n)}(\varphi) = f(\hat{z}_1(\varphi), \cdots, \hat{z}_n(\varphi)), \quad \varphi \in \Phi_{\mathfrak{A}}.$$

This result, which was obtained by Šilov [15] using the general Weil formula, will now be used to complete the proof of the following theorem. (See Arens and Calderón [2].)

THEOREM (3.5.2). *Assume $\mathfrak{A}$ to be semi-simple with an identity element and let $z_1, \cdots, z_n$ be any set of n elements of $\mathfrak{A}$ such that $Sp_{\mathfrak{A}}(z_1, \cdots, z_n) \subseteq \Omega$. Then there exists a homomorphism τ of $\mathscr{H}(\Omega)$ into $\mathfrak{A}$ such that*

$$\widehat{f^{\tau}}(\varphi) = f(\hat{z}_1(\varphi), \cdots, \hat{z}_n(\varphi)), \quad \varphi \in \Phi_{\mathfrak{A}}.$$

PROOF. Consider any element f in $\mathscr{H}(\Omega)$. Since there may not exist an algebraic polyhedron which contains Ω in its interior and whose closure is contained in the domain of definition of f, the Šilov result cannot be applied directly to f. However, it turns out that this difficulty can be overcome by increasing sufficiently the dimension n. More precisely, choose any system $\{z_\lambda : \lambda \in \Lambda\}$ of generators for $\mathfrak{A}$ which contains the set $z_1, \cdots, z_n$. Let $\pi_n = (1, 2, \cdots, n)$ and denote by Θ the open set in K^Λ consisting of all points whose projections into K^n belong to the domain of f. Then the projection $\Theta(\pi_n)$ of Θ into K^n is equal to the domain of f in K^n. Since $Sp(z_1, \cdots, z_n) \subseteq \Omega$, the set Θ contains the canonical representation of $\Phi_{\mathfrak{A}}$ in K^Λ determined by the generators $\{z_\lambda : \lambda \in \Lambda\}$. Now, by Theorem (3.4.7), there exists a finite subset π of Λ and a bounded closed algebraic polyhedron Ψ_π in K^π, such that π contains π_n, Ψ_π is contained in $\Theta(\pi)$ and contains $\Phi_{\mathfrak{A}_\pi}$ (and hence $\Phi_{\mathfrak{A}}(\pi)$) in its interior. Let $\pi = (1, 2, \cdots, n, n+1, \cdots, p)$. Then $\Phi_{\mathfrak{A}}(\pi) = Sp_{\mathfrak{A}}(z_1, \cdots, z_p)$. Since the projection of $\Theta(\pi)$ from K^p into K^n is equal to the domain of f in K^n, it follows that f can be regarded as a function of p-variables which is holomorphic in each component of $\Theta(\pi)$. The Šilov result applies to this extension of f and we obtain an element $f(z_1, \cdots, z_n)$ in $\mathfrak{A}$ such that, if $w = f(z_1, \cdots, z_n)$, then

$$\hat{w}(\varphi) = f(\hat{z}_1(\varphi), \cdots, \hat{z}_n(\varphi)), \quad \varphi \in \Phi_{\mathfrak{A}}.$$

It appears that the element $f(z_1, \cdots, z_n)$ depends on the choice of π, since its definition involves all of the elements $z_1, \cdots, z_p$. However, $\hat{w}(\varphi)$ depends only on the values of f for points of Ω, so that semi-simplicity of $\mathfrak{A}$ implies that $f(z_1, \cdots, z_n)$ is not only independent of the choice of π but depends only on the germ of f on Ω. Semi-simplicity also shows that $f \to f(z_1, \cdots, z_n)$ is a homomorphism of $\mathscr{H}(\Omega)$ into $\mathfrak{A}$ which maps the identity element of $\mathscr{H}(\Omega)$ onto the identity of $\mathfrak{A}$ and the function f_k, defined for each k by the relation $f_k(\zeta_1, \cdots, \zeta_n) = \zeta_k$, onto the element z_k. It is obvious that this homomorphism is an extension of the one previously defined for $\mathscr{R}(\Omega)$.

Observe that the result for the case $n = 1$ does not require semi-simplicity. On the other hand, semi-simplicity seems to enter in an essential way in the proof for $n > 1$. Whether or not this assumption can be removed in general we do not know.

In the above theorem, $\mathfrak{A}$ was assumed to possess an identity element. If such is not the case, then the joint spectrum $Sp(z_1, \cdots, z_n)$ always contains the point $(0, \cdots, 0)$ and it is accordingly necessary to assume that Ω contains this point. In this case, define $\mathscr{H}_0(\Omega)$ to be the subalgebra of $\mathscr{H}(\Omega)$ consisting of all those f for which $f(0, \cdots, 0) = 0$.

THEOREM (3.5.3). *Let $\mathfrak{A}$ be semi-simple (with or without identity element) and let $z_1, \cdots, z_n$ be any set of n elements of $\mathfrak{A}$ with $Sp(z_1, \cdots, z_n) \subseteq \Omega$, where Ω is assumed to contain $(0, \cdots, 0)$. Then there exists a homomorphism $f \to f^\tau$ of $\mathscr{H}_0(\Omega)$ into $\mathfrak{A}$ such that*

$$\widehat{f^\tau}(\varphi) = f(\hat{z}_1(\varphi), \cdots, \hat{z}_n(\varphi))$$

for every $\varphi \in \Phi_{\mathfrak{A}}{}^\infty$.

PROOF. If $\mathfrak{A}$ has an identity element, the desired homomorphism is obtained by restriction of the homomorphism of $\mathscr{H}(\Omega)$ given by the preceding theorem. If $\mathfrak{A}$ does not have an identity, let $\mathfrak{A}_1$ be the algebra obtained by adjunction of an identity element to $\mathfrak{A}$. Then $Sp_{\mathfrak{A}}(z_1, \cdots, z_n) = Sp_{\mathfrak{A}_1}(z_1, \cdots, z_n)$. Therefore the preceding theorem applies again to give a homomorphism τ of $\mathscr{H}(\Omega)$ into $\mathfrak{A}_1$. For $f \in \mathscr{H}(\Omega)$, let $f^\tau = \alpha + a$, with $a \in \mathfrak{A}$ and α a scalar. Since $\hat{a}(\varphi_\infty) = 0$ and $\alpha + \hat{a}(\varphi) = f(\hat{z}_1(\varphi), \cdots, \hat{z}_n(\varphi))$, $\varphi \in \Phi_{\mathfrak{A}_1} = \Phi_{\mathfrak{A}}{}^\infty$, it follows that $f(0, \cdots, 0) = \alpha$. Therefore f^τ lies in $\mathfrak{A}$ if and only if $f \in \mathscr{H}_0(\Omega)$. Thus the restriction of τ to $\mathscr{H}_0(\Omega)$ is the desired homomorphism and the theorem is proved.

Consider a bounded open set Θ in K^n and denote by $\mathscr{A}(\Theta)$ the family of all complex functions which are continuous on the closure of Θ and holomorphic in each component of Θ. Then $\mathscr{A}(\Theta)$ is a closed subalgebra of all complex-valued continuous functions on the closure of Θ. Thus, in particular, $\mathscr{A}(\Theta)$ is a Banach algebra. If Θ contains the point $(0, \cdots, 0)$, then the closed subalgebra of $\mathscr{A}(\Theta)$, consisting of all those functions which vanish at this point, will be denoted by $\mathscr{A}_0(\Theta)$.

THEOREM (3.5.4). *Let $\mathfrak{A}$ be semi-simple and let $z_1, \cdots, z_n$ be any set of n elements of $\mathfrak{A}$ such that $Sp_{\mathfrak{A}}(z_1, \cdots, z_n)$ is contained in Θ. If $\mathfrak{A}$ has an identity element, then there exists a continuous homomorphism τ of the Banach algebra $\mathscr{A}(\Theta)$ into $\mathfrak{A}$ such that*

$$\widehat{f^{\tau}}(\varphi) = f(\hat{z}_1(\varphi), \cdots, \hat{z}_n(\varphi)),$$

for each $\varphi \in \Phi_{\mathfrak{A}}$. If $\mathfrak{A}$ does not have an identity element, then the above statement is true with $\mathscr{A}(\Theta)$ replaced by $\mathscr{A}_0(\Theta)$.

PROOF. Let $\Omega = Sp(z_1, \cdots, z_n)$ and observe that each function in $\mathscr{A}(\Theta)$ is holomorphic on Ω. Moreover, since Θ is an open set, the mapping $f \to f$ of $\mathscr{A}(\Theta)$ into $\mathscr{H}(\Omega)$ is an isomorphism, Therefore the existence of τ is provided by Theorem (3.5.2) or Theorem (3.5.3) and the continuity of τ is given by Theorem (2.15.7).

The homomorphisms obtained in Theorems (3.5.2) and (3.5.3) represent very substantial extensions of the homomorphism of $\mathscr{R}(\Omega)$ into $\mathfrak{A}$ defined previously, In this connection, it is interesting to note that there actually exists, in a certain sense, a maximal extension which includes those of the above theorems. Before describing precisely the sense in which this statement is true, we prove a theorem on which it is based.

THEOREM (3.5.5.) *Let Λ be an arbitrary index set and Ω a compact subset of K^{Λ}. If $\mathfrak{A}$ is semi-simple and $\{z_\lambda : \lambda \in \Lambda\}$ is a subset of $\mathfrak{A}$ such that $Sp_{\mathfrak{A}}(\{z_\lambda\}) \subseteq \Omega$, then there exists a subalgebra $C_{\mathfrak{A}}(\Omega)$ of $C(\Omega)$ and a homomorphism $f \to f^{\tau}$ of $C_{\mathfrak{A}}(\Omega)$ into $\mathfrak{A}$ such that*

$$\widehat{f^{\tau}}(\varphi) = f(\{\hat{z}_\lambda(\varphi)\}), \quad \varphi \in \Phi_{\mathfrak{A}}.$$

Furthermore, if $\mathfrak{C}$ is any subalgebra of $C(\Omega)$ with these properties, then $\mathfrak{C}$ is contained in $C_{\mathfrak{A}}(\Omega)$ and τ is an extension of the given homomorphism of $\mathfrak{C}$ into $\mathfrak{A}$.

PROOF. Let $C_{\mathfrak{A}}(\Omega)$ be the family of all f in $C(\Omega)$ for which there exists a_f in $\mathfrak{A}$ with $\hat{a}_f(\varphi) = f(\{\hat{z}_\lambda(\varphi)\})$ for every $\varphi \in \Phi_{\mathfrak{A}}$. It is obvious that

$C_{\mathfrak{A}}(\Omega)$ is a subalgebra of $C(\Omega)$. If we define $f^\tau = a_f$, then it is immediate from the semi-simplicity of $\mathfrak{A}$ and the definition of a_f that $f \to f^\tau$ is a homomorphism of $C_{\mathfrak{A}}(\Omega)$ into $\mathfrak{A}$ such that $\widehat{f^\tau}(\varphi) = f(\{\hat{z}_\lambda(\varphi)\})$ for every $\varphi \in \Phi_{\mathfrak{A}}$. Furthermore, if $\mathfrak{C}$ is any subalgebra of $C(\Omega)$ and σ is a homomorphism of $\mathfrak{C}$ into $\mathfrak{A}$ such that $\widehat{f^\sigma}(\varphi) = f\{z_\lambda(\varphi)\}$) for $\varphi \in \Phi_{\mathfrak{A}}$, then, by the definition of $C_{\mathfrak{A}}(\Omega)$, the algebra $\mathfrak{C}$ is contained in $C_{\mathfrak{A}}(\Omega)$. Also, by definition of τ, $f^\tau = f^\sigma$ for $f \in \mathfrak{C}$. This completes the proof.

Now let $f \in \mathscr{R}(\Omega)$ and denote by f_Ω the function obtained by restriction of f to Ω. Then $f \to f_\Omega$ is a homomorphism of $\mathscr{R}(\Omega)$ into $C(\Omega)$. Denote the image of $\mathscr{R}(\Omega)$ in $C(\Omega)$ by $\mathscr{R}'(\Omega)$. The homomorphism τ of $\mathscr{R}(\Omega)$ into $\mathfrak{A}$ evidently maps the kernel of the homomorphism $f \to f_\Omega$ into the radical of $\mathfrak{A}$. Therefore, if $\mathfrak{A}$ is semi-simple, then τ defines a homomorphism of $\mathscr{R}'(\Omega)$ into $\mathfrak{A}$. Similarly, if Λ is finite, the homomorphism $f \to f_\Omega$ maps $\mathscr{H}(\Omega)$ onto a subalgebra $\mathscr{H}'(\Omega)$ of $C(\Omega)$ and the homomorphism τ given in Theorem (3.5.2) defines a homomorphism of $\mathscr{H}'(\Omega)$ into $\mathfrak{A}$. These remarks, in the presence of Theorem (3.5.5), give the sense in which the maximal extension referred to above exists. If it happens that Ω is such that $f \to f_\Omega$ is an isomorphism, then $\mathscr{R}(\Omega)$ (or $\mathscr{H}(\Omega)$) can be identified with a subalgebra of $C(\Omega)$ and the homomorphism of $C_{\mathfrak{A}}(\Omega)$ obtained in theorem (3.5.5) is truly a maximal extension within $C(\Omega)$. The usefulness of the result in Theorem (3.5.5) is limited by the difficulty of determining when an element of $C(\Omega)$ belongs to $C_{\mathfrak{A}}(\Omega)$. Actually, the force of Theorems (3.5.2) and (3.5.3) stems from the fact that they specify a large class of functions which do belong to $C_{\mathfrak{A}}(\Omega)$.

We have already considered the notion of a subalgebra generated by a subset $\{z_\lambda : \lambda \in \Lambda\}$ of $\mathfrak{A}$. It can be regarded as the closure of the image of $\mathscr{P}_0$ in $\mathfrak{A}$ under the homomorphism of $\mathscr{P}_0$ into $\mathfrak{A}$ determined by the set $\{z_\lambda : \lambda \in \Lambda\}$. It would perhaps be more appropriate to call this the subalgebra which is POLYNOMIALLY GENERATED by the set $\{z_\lambda : \lambda \in \Lambda\}$. Similarly, the closure of the image of $\mathscr{R}_0(Sp_{\mathfrak{A}}(\{z_\lambda\}))$ in $\mathfrak{A}$ is the subalgebra which is RATIONALLY GENERATED by the set $\{z_\lambda : \lambda \in \Lambda\}$. When Λ is finite, the closure of the image of $\mathscr{H}_0(Sp_{\mathfrak{A}}(\{z_\lambda\}))$ in $\mathfrak{A}$ is called the subalgebra which is HOLOMORPHICALLY GENERATED by the set $\{z_\lambda : \lambda \in \Lambda\}$. Also, when Λ is finite, let Θ be a fixed open set which contains $Sp_{\mathfrak{A}}(\{z_\lambda\})$, and consider the algebra $\mathscr{A}_0(\Theta)$ of all functions which are holomorphic in each component of Θ and which vanish at the origin. This algebra can obviously be regarded as a subalgebra of

$\mathscr{H}_0(Sp_{\mathfrak{A}}(\{z_\lambda\}))$. The closure of its image in $\mathfrak{A}$ is called the subalgebra of $\mathfrak{A}$ which is Θ-HOLOMORPHICALLY GENERATED by the set $\{z_\lambda : \lambda \in \Lambda\}$. This subalgebra is obviously contained in the preceding one. We can now state the next theorem.

THEOREM (3.5.6). *Let $z_1, \cdots, z_n$ be any finite set of elements in the semi-simple commutative Banach algebra $\mathfrak{A}$, and let Θ be an arbitrary open set in K^n which contains $Sp_{\mathfrak{A}}(z_1, \cdots, z_n)$. Then there exist elements $z_{n+1}, \cdots, z_p$ in $\mathfrak{A}$ such that the subalgebra of $\mathfrak{A}$ which is rationally generated by $z_1, \cdots, z_p$ contains the subalgebra which is Θ-holomorphically generated by $z_1, \cdots, z_n$.*

PROOF. This theorem follows directly from the definition of $f(z_1, \cdots, z_n)$ given in the proof of Theorem (3.5.2) for a function f holomorphic in each component of Θ. Observe firstly that the choice of π in the definition of $f(z_1, \cdots, z_n)$ depends only on Θ, so that the elements $z_1, \cdots, z_p$ are independent of f, and secondly that the integrals involved in the general Cauchy formula are limits of finite sums of rational functions of $z_1, \cdots, z_p$.

The ideas involved in Theorem (3.5.5) suggest yet another notion of a subalgebra which is generated by the set $\{z_\lambda : \lambda \in \Lambda\}$. Denote by $\mathfrak{A}_0$ the set of all elements x in $\mathfrak{A}$ such that there exists a function f in $C(Sp(\{z_\lambda\}))$ with $f(\{\hat{z}_\lambda(\varphi)\}) = \hat{x}(\varphi)$ for every $\varphi \in \Phi_{\mathfrak{A}}$. It is easily verified that $\mathfrak{A}_0$ is a closed subalgebra of $\mathfrak{A}$, which automatically contains the elements z_λ and the identity element, if there is one. We call $\mathfrak{A}_0$ the subalgebra which is CONTINUOUSLY GENERATED by the set $\{z_\lambda : \lambda \in \Lambda\}$. If $\mathfrak{A}_0 = \mathfrak{A}$, then $\mathfrak{A}$ is said to be CONTINUOUSLY GENERATED by $\{z_\lambda : \lambda \in \Lambda\}$. (See Mirkil [1].)

THEOREM (3.5.7). *In order for $\mathfrak{A}$ to be continuously generated by the set $\{z_\lambda : \lambda \in \Lambda\}$, it is necessary that the functions $\{\hat{z}_\lambda : \lambda \in \Lambda\}$ separate the points of $\Phi_{\mathfrak{A}}$ and sufficient that they separate strongly the points of $\Phi_{\mathfrak{A}}$.*

PROOF. Let φ_1 and φ_2 be distinct points of $\Phi_{\mathfrak{A}}$ and choose $x \in \mathfrak{A}$ such that $\hat{x}(\varphi_1) \neq \hat{x}(\varphi_2)$. If $\mathfrak{A}$ is continuously generated by $\{z_\lambda : \lambda \in \Lambda\}$, then there exists f in $C(Sp(\{z_\lambda\}))$ such that $f(\{\hat{z}_\lambda(\varphi)\}) = \hat{x}(\varphi)$ for every $\varphi \in \Phi_{\mathfrak{A}}$. Since $\hat{x}(\varphi_1) \neq \hat{x}(\varphi_2)$, also $\{\hat{z}_\lambda(\varphi_1)\} \neq \{\hat{z}_\lambda(\varphi_2)\}$. In other words, the functions $\{\hat{z}_\lambda : \lambda \in \Lambda)$ separate the points of $\Phi_{\mathfrak{A}}$. Now assume that these functions separate strongly the points of $\Phi_{\mathfrak{A}}$. Then they separate the points of $\Phi_{\mathfrak{A}}^\infty$. Hence the mapping $\varphi \to \{\hat{z}_\lambda(\varphi)\}$ of $\Phi_{\mathfrak{A}}^\infty$ into K^Λ is one-to-one. Since $\Phi_{\mathfrak{A}}^\infty$ is compact and this mapping is always continuous, it follows that $\varphi \to \{\hat{z}_\lambda(\varphi)\}$ is a homeomorphism. Therefore, if

x is any element of $\mathfrak{A}$ and f_x is defined on $Sp(\{z_\lambda\})$ by the relation $f_x(\{\hat{z}_\lambda(\varphi)\} = \hat{x}(\varphi)$, then $f_x \in C(Sp(\{z_\lambda\}))$. Thus, $\mathfrak{A}$ is continuously generated by $\{z_\lambda : \lambda \in \Lambda\}$.

Notice that, in general, the necessary condition is not sufficient and the sufficient condition is not necessary. Consider, for example, an algebra $\mathfrak{A}$ with an identity element, and let $\{z_\lambda : \lambda \in \Lambda\}$ be the set of all elements in a maximal ideal of $\mathfrak{A}$. Then the subalgebra, continuously generated by $\{z_\lambda : \lambda \in \Lambda\}$, contains the maximal ideal and the identity element so must coincide with $\mathfrak{A}$. However, the functions $\{\hat{z}_\lambda : \lambda \in \Lambda\}$ do not separate strongly the points of $\Phi_\mathfrak{A}$. This shows that the sufficient condition is not necessary. Now consider an algebra $\mathfrak{A}$ which does not have an identity element and let the set $\{z_\lambda : \lambda \in \Lambda\}$ coincide with a maximal modular ideal in $\mathfrak{A}$. Then the functions $\{\hat{z}_\lambda : \lambda \in \Lambda\}$ separate the points of $\Phi_\mathfrak{A}$. Let φ_0 be the element of $\Phi_\mathfrak{A}$ corresponding to the ideal $\{z_\lambda : \lambda \in \Lambda\}$ and let e be any element of $\mathfrak{A}$ with $\hat{e}(\varphi_0) = 1$. Suppose that e were in the subalgebra continuously generated by $\{z_\lambda : \lambda \in \Lambda\}$ and let f be a continuous function on $Sp(\{z_\lambda\})$ with $f(\{\hat{z}_\lambda(\varphi)\}) = \hat{e}(\varphi)$ for all $\varphi \in \Phi_\mathfrak{A}$. Since $\hat{z}_\lambda(\varphi_0) = 0$ for each λ and $\hat{e}(\varphi_0) = 1$, we have $f(\{0\}) = 1$. Hence there exists a neighborhood V of $\{0\}$ in K^Λ such that $\{\hat{z}_\lambda(\varphi)\} \in V$ implies $|f(\{\hat{z}_\lambda(\varphi)\})| \geqslant \frac{1}{2}$. On the other hand, the mapping $\varphi \to \{\hat{z}_\lambda(\varphi)\}$ of $\Phi_\mathfrak{A}{}^\infty$ onto $Sp(\{z_\lambda\})$ is continuous. There accordingly exists a neighborhood W of φ_∞ which maps into V. But W contains points φ with $|\hat{e}(\varphi)| < \frac{1}{2}$. Therefore it follows that $\mathfrak{A}$ is not continuously generated by the set $\{z_\lambda : \lambda \in \Lambda\}$. This example shows that the necessary condition is not sufficient.

When $\mathfrak{A}$ has an identity element, then $\Phi_\mathfrak{A}$ is compact and the sufficiency argument in the proof of the above theorem requires only that the functions $\{\hat{z}_\lambda : \lambda \in \Lambda\}$ separate the points of $\Phi_\mathfrak{A}$. Therefore in this case the necessary condition is sufficient and we have the following corollaries.

Corollary (3.5.8). *If $\mathfrak{A}$ has an identity element, then a necessary and sufficient condition for $\mathfrak{A}$ to be continuously generated by $\{z_\lambda : \lambda \in \Lambda\}$ is that the set of functions $\{\hat{z}_\lambda : \lambda \in \Lambda\}$ separate the points of $\Phi_\mathfrak{A}$.*

Corollary (3.5.9). *If $\mathfrak{A}$ has an identity element, then a necessary and sufficient condition for $\mathfrak{A}$ to be continuously generated by $\{z_\lambda : \lambda \in \Lambda\}$, is that the mapping $\varphi \to \{\hat{z}_\lambda(\varphi)\}$ be a homeomorphism of $\Phi_\mathfrak{A}$ onto $Sp(\{z_\lambda\})$.*

THEOREM (3.5.10). *Let* $\mathfrak{A}_0$ *be the subalgebra of* $\mathfrak{A}$ *which is continuously generated by the set* $\{z_\lambda : \lambda \in \Lambda\}$. *Then, for every* $x \in \mathfrak{A}_0$, *we have* $Sp_{\mathfrak{A}_0}(x) = Sp_{\mathfrak{A}}(x)$.

PROOF. Since $\mathfrak{A}_0$ contains the identity element, if there is one, it will be sufficient to prove that an element of $\mathfrak{A}_0$ which is quasi-regular in $\mathfrak{A}$ is also quasi-regular in $\mathfrak{A}_0$. Let x be such an element with $\hat{x}(\varphi) = f(\{\hat{z}_\lambda(\varphi)\})$, for $\varphi \in \Phi_{\mathfrak{A}}$, where f is continuous on $Sp_{\mathfrak{A}}(\{z_\lambda\})$. Since x is quasi-regular, $\hat{x}(\varphi) \neq 1$ for every φ. Therefore the function $g = f/(f-1)$ is continuous on $\mathrm{Sp}_{\mathfrak{A}}(\{z_\lambda\})$. Since

$$g(\{\hat{z}_\lambda(\varphi)\}) = \frac{f(\{\hat{z}_\lambda(\varphi)\})}{f(\{z_\lambda(\varphi)\})-1}$$

$$= \frac{\hat{x}(\varphi)}{\hat{x}(\varphi)-1} = \hat{x^\circ}(\varphi), \quad \varphi \in \Phi_{\mathfrak{A}},$$

the theorem is proved.

In this section, our use of material from complex function theory has gone far beyond a mere appeal to elementary or well-known results. This is especially so in the case of functions of several variables. On the other hand, a fruitful application of the theory of commutative Banach algebras to certain kinds of problems in the theory of functions of several variables appears promising. This is an area that is currently receiving considerable attention and will undoubtedly receive a great deal more attention in the future. However, since the study of functions of several variables involves one immediately in the very special problems of analysis and topology which surround this subject, we shall not pursue these matters further here. Finally, it should be pointed out that the proof of Theorem (3.5.1) involves only a small fragment of a well-developed theory of holomorphic functions in Banach algebras. The interested reader can obtain a more complete picture of this subject in Hille [2, Ch. 5] or Hille–Phillips [1, Ch. 5].

The problem of describing more precisely those functions which belong to $C_{\mathfrak{A}}(\Omega)$ is a difficult one. For the case of an algebra with an identity element and one generator, some results in this direction are obtained by Šilov [4]. A related problem concerns the question of whether or not a given function f, which is defined on a subset Δ of the complex plane, OPERATES ON $\mathfrak{A}$ in the sense that, if $x \in \mathfrak{A}$ with $Sp(x) \subseteq \Delta$, then there exists $y \in \mathfrak{A}$ such that $\hat{y}(\varphi) = f(\hat{x}(\varphi))$ for all $\varphi \in \Phi_{\mathfrak{A}}$. This question, in the case of some special algebras, has been studied in detail by Helson, Kahane, Katznelson and Rudin [1]. If every continuous function operates on $\mathfrak{A}$, then Katznelson [2] has shown that $\mathfrak{A} = C(\Phi_{\mathfrak{A}})$.

§ 6. Direct-sum decompositions and related results.

Let $\mathfrak{A}$ be a complex commutative Banach algebra. Our starting point in this section is the problem of representing $\mathfrak{A}$ as a direct sum of non-zero ideals. When this is possible the algebra is said to be DECOMPOSABLE. The simplest possible decomposition of $\mathfrak{A}$ is one induced by a non-trivial idempotent e; that is, $\mathfrak{A} = \mathfrak{A}(1-e)+\mathfrak{A}e$. As might be expected, decompositions of $\mathfrak{A}$ are closely related to decompositions of the carrier space $\Phi_{\mathfrak{A}}$. By lemma (2.6.8), if $\mathfrak{J}_1$ and $\mathfrak{J}_2$ are any two ideals in $\mathfrak{A}$, then

$\mathfrak{A} = \mathfrak{I}_1 + \mathfrak{I}_2$ if and only if the ideal $\overline{\mathfrak{I}_1 + \mathfrak{I}_2}$ is modular and $h(\mathfrak{I}_1)$ and $h(\mathfrak{I}_2)$ are disjoint. Also, if $\mathfrak{A} = \overline{\mathfrak{I}_1 + \mathfrak{I}_2}$, then $h(\mathfrak{I}_1)$ and $h(\mathfrak{I}_2)$ are disjoint. It follows from Lemma (2.6.7) that $\Phi_{\mathfrak{A}} = h(\mathfrak{I}_1) \cup h(\mathfrak{I}_2)$ if and only if $\mathfrak{I}_1 \cap \mathfrak{I}_2$ is contained in the radical.

THEOREM (3.6.1). *Let $\mathfrak{A} = \mathfrak{I}_1 \oplus \mathfrak{I}_2$, where $\mathfrak{I}_1$ and $\mathfrak{I}_2$ are non-zero ideals in $\mathfrak{A}$, If $\mathfrak{I}_1$ is modular, then there exists an idempotent e in $\mathfrak{A}$ such that $\mathfrak{I}_1 = \mathfrak{A}(1-e)$ and $\mathfrak{I}_2 = \mathfrak{A}e$. Also, the hull $h(\mathfrak{I}_1)$ is a compact open and closed subset of $\Phi_{\mathfrak{A}}$.*

PROOF. Observe that $\mathfrak{I}_2$ is isomorphic with $\mathfrak{A}/\mathfrak{I}_1$ and, since $\mathfrak{A}/\mathfrak{I}_1$ has an identity element, there exists an idempotent e in $\mathfrak{I}_2$ such that $ae = a$ for every $a \in \mathfrak{I}_2$. It follows that $\mathfrak{I}_2 = \mathfrak{A}e$ and hence $\mathfrak{I}_1 = \mathfrak{A}(1-e)$. Evidently $h(\mathfrak{I}_1) = \{\varphi : \hat{e}(\varphi) = 1\}$ and $h(\mathfrak{I}_2) = \{\varphi : \hat{e}(\varphi) = 0\}$. Since $e^2 = e$, we have $\hat{e}(\varphi) = 0$ or 1 for every $\varphi \in \Phi_{\mathfrak{A}}$. Therefore continuity of $\hat{e}$ implies that $h(\mathfrak{I}_1)$ is a compact open subset of $\Phi_{\mathfrak{A}}$.

COROLLARY (3.6.2). *If $\mathfrak{A} = \mathfrak{I}_1 \oplus \mathfrak{I}_2$ and either of the ideals is modular, then $\mathfrak{I}_1$ and $\mathfrak{I}_2$ are automatically closed.*

The next theorem, which provides a converse to the preceding theorem, is due to Šilov [15]. Its proof involves almost the full force of the machinery in the preceding section.

THEOREM (3.6.3). *Let Ψ be a non-vacuous compact open and closed subset of $\Phi_{\mathfrak{A}}$. Then there exists a non-zero idempotent e in $\mathfrak{A}$ such that $\Psi = \{\varphi : \hat{e}(\varphi) = 1\}$.*

PROOF. Assume first that $\mathfrak{A}$ is semi-simple and set $\Psi_0 = \Phi_{\mathfrak{A}}^\infty - \Psi$. Then $\Phi_{\mathfrak{A}}^\infty = \Psi_0 \cup \Psi$ is a decomposition of $\Phi_{\mathfrak{A}}^\infty$ into disjoint closed sets with $\varphi_\infty \in \Psi_0$. By Theorem (3.4.8), there exists a finite set $z_1, \cdots, z_n$ of elements of $\mathfrak{A}$ such that, if $\mathfrak{B}$ is the subalgebra of $\mathfrak{A}$ generated by these elements, then $\Phi_{\mathfrak{B}}^\infty = \Psi'_0 \cup \Psi'$ where Ψ'_0 and Ψ' are disjoint closed sets in $\Phi_{\mathfrak{B}}^\infty$ and the dual mapping of $\Phi_{\mathfrak{A}}^\infty$ into $\Phi_{\mathfrak{B}}^\infty$ takes Ψ_0 into Ψ'_0 and Ψ into Ψ'. Let Ω denote the canonical representation of $\Phi_{\mathfrak{B}}^\infty$ in K^n determined by $z_1, \cdots, z_n$ and consider the homomorphism $f \to f(z_1, \cdots, z_n)$ of $\mathscr{H}_0(\Omega)$ into $\mathfrak{B}$ given in Theorem (3.5.3). Since Ω is the union of the disjoint closed sets Ψ'_0 and Ψ', there exists $h \in \mathscr{H}_0(\Omega)$ which is equal to zero in a neighborhood of Ψ'_0 and equal to one in a neighborhood of Ψ'. The element h is obviously an idempotent in $\mathscr{H}_0(\Omega)$, so that its image $e = h(z_1, \cdots, z_n)$ is also idempotent in $\mathfrak{B}$. Furthermore, $\hat{e}(\varphi) = 0$ for $\varphi \in \Psi'_0$ and $\hat{e}(\varphi) = 1$ for $\varphi \in \Psi'$. Hence the theorem is proved in the semi-simple case.

If $\mathfrak{A}$ is not semi-simple, let $\mathfrak{A}' = \mathfrak{A}/\mathfrak{R}$, where $\mathfrak{R}$ is the radical of $\mathfrak{A}$. Then $\mathfrak{A}'$ is semi-simple and $\Phi_{\mathfrak{A}'}{}^{\infty} = \Phi_{\mathfrak{A}}{}^{\infty}$. The above argument thus gives an idempotent e' in $\mathfrak{A}'$ with the desired properties. Now, by Theorem (2.3.9), there exists an idempotent e in $\mathfrak{A}$ such that $e' = e+\mathfrak{R}$. Since $\hat{e}(\varphi) = \hat{e}'(\varphi)$ for $\varphi \in \Phi_{\mathfrak{A}}{}^{\infty}$, this completes the proof.

The next corollary is obtained with the help of Lemma (3.1.16) and Theorem (3.1.17).

COROLLARY (3.6.4). *If F_0, F_1 are disjoint closed sets with F_1 compact and if $F_0 \cup F_1$ is a hull, then F_0 and F_1 are also hulls.*

THEOREM (3.6.5). *Let $\Phi_{\mathfrak{A}}$ be equal to the union of a finite number of disjoint closed sets $\Phi_0, \Phi_1, \cdots, \Phi_n$ where $\Phi_1, \cdots, \Phi_n$ are compact. Then there exist closed ideals $\mathfrak{J}_0, \mathfrak{J}_1, \cdots, \mathfrak{J}_n$ in $\mathfrak{A}$ such that $\mathfrak{A} = \mathfrak{J}_0 \oplus \mathfrak{J}_1 \oplus \cdots \oplus \mathfrak{J}_n$ and $\Phi_{\mathfrak{J}_k} = \Phi_k$ for $k = 0, 1, \cdots, n$.*

PROOF. By the preceding theorem, there exists for each $k = 1, \cdots, n$ an indempotent e_k in $\mathfrak{A}$ such that $e_k(\varphi) = 0$ for $\varphi \notin \Phi_k$ and $\hat{e}_k(\varphi) = 1$ for $\varphi \in \Phi_k$. Define $e = e_1 + \cdots + e_n$, $\mathfrak{J}_0 = \mathfrak{A}(1-e)$ and $\mathfrak{J}_k = \mathfrak{A}e_k$ for $k = 1, \cdots, n$. Then each of the ideals $\mathfrak{J}_k$ is closed and $\mathfrak{A} = \mathfrak{J}_0 \oplus \mathfrak{J}_1 \oplus \cdots \oplus \mathfrak{J}_n$. Finally, it is obvious that $h(\mathfrak{J}_k) = \Phi_{\mathfrak{A}} - \Phi_k$ and therefore $\Phi_{\mathfrak{J}_k} = \Phi_{\mathfrak{A}} - h(\mathfrak{J}_k) = \Phi_k$ for each k.

THEOREM (3.6.6). *If $\mathfrak{A}$ is semi-simple, then it has an identity element if and only if $\Phi_{\mathfrak{A}}$ is compact.*

PROOF. If $\mathfrak{A}$ has an identity element, then compactness of $\Phi_{\mathfrak{A}}$ has already been observed (Corollary (3.1.12)) even without semi-simplicity. If, on the other hand, $\Phi_{\mathfrak{A}}$ is compact, then, by Theorem (3.6.3), there exists in $\mathfrak{A}$ an idempotent e such that $\hat{e}(\varphi) = 1$ for every $\varphi \in \Phi_{\mathfrak{A}}$. It follows that $(a-ae)(\varphi) = 0$ for every $\varphi \in \Phi_{\mathfrak{A}}$. Since $\mathfrak{A}$ is semi-simple, this implies $a = ae$ for every $a \in \mathfrak{A}$ and completes the proof.

In the above proof, we have assumed that $\mathfrak{A}$ is complex. However, in view of Theorem (3.1.5) and the fact that a real algebra has an identity element if and only if its complexification does, the theorem is also true for real algebras.

Let $\mathfrak{A}'$ be a semi-simple algebra with an identity element and $\mathfrak{R}$ a radical algebra. Define $\mathfrak{A} = \mathfrak{A}' \oplus \mathfrak{R}$, where the algebra operations are given by the relations $(a \oplus r)+(b \oplus s) = (a+b) \oplus (r+s)$, $\alpha(a \oplus r) = (\alpha a) \oplus (\alpha r)$, and $(a \oplus r)(b \oplus s) = (ab) \oplus (rs)$, where $a, b \in \mathfrak{A}'$, $r, s \in \mathfrak{R}$, and α is a scalar. Also, define the norm in $\mathfrak{A}$ by the relation $\|a \oplus r\| = \|a\| + \|r\|$. If $\mathfrak{A}'$ and $\mathfrak{R}$ are Banach algebras, then so is $\mathfrak{A}$. The radical of $\mathfrak{A}$ is equal to $\mathfrak{R}$. Evidently $\Phi_{\mathfrak{A}} = \Phi_{\mathfrak{A}'}$, so that $\Phi_{\mathfrak{A}}$ is compact. However, $\mathfrak{A}$ does not possess an identity element. This shows that the semi-simplicity is needed in the above theorem.

THEOREM (3.6.7). *A hull Φ in $\Phi_{\mathfrak{A}}$ is compact if and only if $k(\Phi)$ is a modular ideal.*

PROOF. Let $\mathfrak{A}' = \mathfrak{A}/k(\Phi)$. Then $\Phi_{\mathfrak{A}'} = h(k(\Phi)) = \Phi$. Note also that $\mathfrak{A}'$ is semi-simple. By the preceding theorem, Φ is compact if and only if $\mathfrak{A}'$ has an identity element. Since $\mathfrak{A}'$ has an identity if and only if $k(\Phi)$ is modular, the theorem follows.

COROLLARY (3.6.8). *If Φ is any closed subset of $\Phi_{\mathfrak{A}}$ such that $k(\Phi)$ is modular, then Φ is compact.*

THEOREM (3.6.9). *Let $\mathfrak{J}$ be any ideal in $\mathfrak{A}$ and let Φ be a compact hull disjoint from $h(\mathfrak{J})$. Then there exists $u \in \mathfrak{J}$ such that $\hat{u}(\varphi) = 1$ for $\varphi \in \Phi$.*

PROOF. Observe that $k(\Phi)$ is a modular ideal by the preceding theorem. Also $h(k(\Phi)) = \Phi$. Since $k(\Phi)$ is modular, so is the ideal $\mathfrak{J}+k(\Phi)$. Hence, by Lemma (2.6.8), we have $\mathfrak{A} = \mathfrak{J}+k(\Phi)$. Let w be any element of $\mathfrak{A}$ such that $\hat{w}(\varphi) = 1$ for $\varphi \in \Phi$. Then $w = u+v$ with $u \in \mathfrak{J}$ and $v \in k(\Phi)$. Since $\hat{v}(\varphi) = 0$ for $\varphi \in \Phi$, it follows that $\hat{u}(\varphi) = 1$ for $\varphi \in \Phi$ and the theorem is proved.

COROLLARY (3.6.10). *Let Φ_0, Φ_1 be disjoint hulls in $\Phi_{\mathfrak{A}}$ with Φ_1 compact. Then there exists $u \in \mathfrak{A}$ such that $\hat{u}(\varphi) = 0$ for $\varphi \in \Phi_0$ and $\hat{u}(\varphi) = 1$ for $\varphi \in \Phi_1$.*

The following definition provides a condition under which some of the above results can be extended to sets Φ which are not hulls.

DEFINITION (3.6.11). *The algebra $\mathfrak{A}$ is said to* CONTAIN LOCAL IDENTITIES *provided, for every $\varphi_0 \in \Phi_{\mathfrak{A}}$ there exists an element $u \in \mathfrak{A}$ such that $\hat{u}(\varphi) = 1$ in some neighborhood of φ_0.*

Notice that, if $\mathfrak{A}$ possesses an identity element modulo its radical, then it automatically contains local identities.

LEMMA (3.6.12). *In order for $\mathfrak{A}$ to contain local identities it is necessary and sufficient that there exist for each $\varphi \in \Phi_{\mathfrak{A}}$ a neighborhood V of φ such that $k(V)$ is modular.*

PROOF. If $k(V)$ is modular, then $\mathfrak{A}/k(V)$ has an identity element. Since $\Phi_{\mathfrak{A}/k(V)} = h(k(V)) \supseteq V$, it follows that there exists $u \in \mathfrak{A}$ such that $\hat{u}(\varphi) = 1$ for $\varphi \in V$. Therefore the condition is sufficient. On the other hand, assume given a $u \in \mathfrak{A}$ such that $\hat{u}(\varphi) = 1$ for $\varphi \in V$ and define $\mathfrak{J} = \mathfrak{A}(1-u)$. Then $\mathfrak{J}$ is a modular ideal and, since $\mathfrak{J} \subseteq k(V)$, the ideal $k(V)$ is also modular. This completes the proof.

The next theorem extends Theorem (3.6.7).

THEOREM (3.6.13). *Let $\mathfrak{A}$ contain local identities. Then an arbitrary closed set Φ in $\Phi_{\mathfrak{A}}$ is compact if and only if $k(\Phi)$ is modular.*

PROOF. If $k(\Phi)$ is modular, then $\mathfrak{A}/k(\Phi)$ has an identity element so that $h(k(\Phi))$, and hence Φ, is compact. Now assume Φ compact. Since each point of Φ has a neighborhood V such that $k(V)$ is modular, it follows from compactness that Φ is covered by a finite number of such neighborhoods, say $V_1, \cdots, V_n$. Since $\Phi \subseteq V_1 \cup \cdots \cup V_n$, we have $k(\Phi) \supseteq k(V_1) \cap \cdots \cap k(V_n)$. But any finite intersection of modular ideals is modular (Theorem (2.1.1)). Therefore $k(\Phi)$ is also modular and the theorem is proved.

COROLLARY (3.6.14). *If $\mathfrak{A}$ contains local identities and Φ is a compact set in $\Phi_{\mathfrak{A}}$, then the hull $h(k(\Phi))$ is also compact.*

All of the results from (3.6.4) to (3.6.10) depend on Theorem (3.6.3) whose proof is decidedly non-elementary in character since it appeals to the results in the preceding section. When $\mathfrak{A}$ contains local identities, Theorem (3.6.13) can be used to free the results (3.6.6) to (3.6.10), from dependence on § 5. It is conceivable that the proof of Theorem (3.6.3) will eventually be reduced by elementary arguments at least to the point where only the Cauchy formula for one variable is needed. In any case, the proof does simplify a great deal in certain special situations. For example, whenever the separation of $\Phi_{\mathfrak{A}}^{\infty}$, determined in the proof of Theorem (3.6.3) by the elements $z_1, \cdots, z_n$, can be effected by a single element z, then homomorphisms of holomorphic functions of only one variable into $\mathfrak{A}$ (Theorem (3.5.1)) suffice to give the idempotent e. In this case the spectrum $Sp_{\mathfrak{A}}(z)$ is a union of two disjoint closed sets S_0 and S such that $\Psi_0 = \{\varphi : \hat{z}(\varphi) \in S_0\}$ and $\Psi = \{\varphi : \hat{z}(\varphi) \in S\}$. If, in addition, the sets S_0 and S can be separated by a circle with center at the origin, then the homomorphisms of § 5 can be avoided completely, so that not even the Cauchy formula for one variable is needed. The argument goes as follows. Choose $\delta > 0$ so that S_0 lies interior to and S exterior to the circle $|\zeta| = \delta$. Next let ω_j be the nth roots of unity and set $\delta_j = \delta\omega_j$ $(j = 1, \cdots, n)$. As in the proof of Theorem (1.6.3), we have

$$(\delta^{-n}z^n)^{\circ} = \frac{1}{n}\sum_{j=1}^{n}(\delta_j^{-1}z)^{\circ}.$$

Since $(\zeta^{-1}z)^\circ$ is uniformly continuous on the circle $|\zeta| = \delta$, it follows easily, by a standard Riemann integral type of argument, that

$$\lim_{n\to\infty} (\delta^{-n}z^n)^\circ = e$$

exists in $\mathfrak{A}$. Moreover, if $u_n = (\delta^{-n}z^n)^\circ$, then

$$\hat{u}_n(\varphi) = \frac{\delta^{-n}\hat{z}(\varphi)^n}{\delta^{-n}\hat{z}(\varphi)^n - 1}, \quad \varphi \in \Phi_{\mathfrak{A}},$$

and we have

$$\hat{e}(\varphi) = \lim_{n\to\infty} \hat{u}_n(\varphi) = \begin{cases} 0 \text{ if } |\hat{z}(\varphi)| < \delta \\ 1 \text{ if } |\hat{z}(\varphi)| > \delta. \end{cases}$$

Therefore $\hat{e}(\varphi) = 0$ for $\varphi \in \Psi_0$ and $\hat{e}(\varphi) = 1$ for $\varphi \in \Psi$. Since e is an idempotent modulo the radical, an application of Theorem (2.3.9) provides an idempotent in $\mathfrak{A}$ with the desired properties. (See Reisz and Sz.-Nagy [1, § 149] and Lorch [1, p. 243].)

The above argument applies to Theorem (3.6.6), if an element z is given such that $\hat{z}(\varphi) \neq 0$ for every $\varphi \in \Phi_{\mathfrak{A}}$. A similar remark holds, of course, for those results which depend on Theorem (3.6.6). A special case which is covered here is the following.

THEOREM (3.6.15). *Let Φ be a hull in $\Phi_{\mathfrak{A}}$ and let u be an element of $\mathfrak{A}$ such that $|\hat{u}(\varphi)| \geqslant \delta > 0$ for $\varphi \in \Phi$. Then $k(\Phi)$ is modular and there exists $v \in \mathfrak{A}$ such that $\widehat{(uv)}(\varphi) = 1$ for $\varphi \in \Phi$.*

PROOF. Let $\mathfrak{A}' = \mathfrak{A}/k(\Phi)$ and $u' = u + k(\Phi)$, the element of $\mathfrak{A}'$ corresponding to u. Since $|\hat{u}'(\varphi)| \geqslant \delta > 0$ for $\varphi \in \Phi_{\mathfrak{A}'}$, the elementary argument given above applies to give an identity element in $\mathfrak{A}'$. In other words $k(\Phi)$ is modular. Since $\hat{u}'(\varphi) \neq 0$ for every $\varphi \in \Phi_{\mathfrak{A}'}$ and $\mathfrak{A}'$ has an identity element, it follows that u' has an inverse v' in $\mathfrak{A}'$. Therefore there exists $v \in \mathfrak{A}$ such that $\widehat{(uv)}(\varphi) = 1$ for $\varphi \in \Phi$. This completes the proof.

We note finally that the above elementary situation applies when $\mathfrak{A}$ is self-adjoint on $\Phi_{\mathfrak{A}}$, since, in this case, the algebra of functions $\hat{\mathfrak{A}}$ is dense in $C_0(\Phi_{\mathfrak{A}})$ by the Stone–Weierstrass theorem. Thus, if $\Phi_{\mathfrak{A}}{}^\infty = \Psi_0 \cup \Psi$, as before, then the function f which is equal to zero on Ψ_0 and equal to one on Ψ belongs to $C_0(\Phi_{\mathfrak{A}})$. Hence there exists $z \in \mathfrak{A}$ such that $|\hat{z}(\varphi) - f(\varphi)| < 1/3$ for all $\varphi \in \Phi_{\mathfrak{A}}$. Therefore $|\hat{z}(\varphi)| < 1/3$ for $\varphi \in \Psi_0$ and $|\hat{z}(\varphi)| > 2/3$ for $\varphi \in \Psi$. By a similar argument, if Φ is any compact subset of $\Phi_{\mathfrak{A}}$, then there exists $u \in \mathfrak{A}$ such that $|\hat{u}(\varphi)| \geqslant \delta > 0$ for $\varphi \in \Phi$. This result requires only that $\mathfrak{A}$ be self-adjoint on Φ.

§ **7. Completely regular commutative Banach algebras.** General completely regular algebras were discussed in § 7 of Chapter II. In this section we examine some of the special properties of these algebras in the commutative case. We restrict attention throughout to a complex commutative Banach algebra $\mathfrak{A}$. By Definition (2.7.1), the algebra $\mathfrak{A}$ is completely regular provided it satisfies the two conditions: (i) $\Phi_{\mathfrak{A}}$ is Hausdorff in the hull–kernel topology and (ii) each point of $\Phi_{\mathfrak{A}}$ has a hull–kernel neighborhood V with $k(V)$ modular. The study of these algebras was initiated by Šilov [5] who assumed an identity element. Šilov called his algebras REGULAR.

A good example of a completely regular commutative Banach algebra is the algebra of all functions which are continuous and vanish at infinity on a locally compact Hausdorff space. However, the most important example is undoubtedly the group algebra of a locally compact abelian group (Appendix, A.3.2). Many of the results for this special case have been extended in one form or another to more general commutative Banach algebras which are completely regular. These results, some of which are direct specializations of the results obtained in § 7 of Chapter II, properly come under the heading of abstract harmonic analysis. Since this field is adequately covered by Loomis [1] in his book on the subject, we restrict attention here to other matters. Some examples of commutative completely regular algebras are discussed in the Appendix (A.2.1, A.2.3, A.2.4, A.2.5).

The following theorem gives a necessary and sufficient condition that $\mathfrak{A}$ be completely regular in terms of the usual topology of the carrier space $\Phi_{\mathfrak{A}}$. This condition is essentially Šilov's definition of regular algebra. The form used by Šilov as a definition is given below in Corollary (3.7.2).

THEOREM (3.7.1). *In order for $\mathfrak{A}$ to be completely regular, it is necessary and sufficient that the hull–kernel topology in $\Phi_{\mathfrak{A}}$ be equivalent to the $\mathfrak{A}$-topology.*

PROOF. Since hulls are automatically closed in the $\mathfrak{A}$-topology, the hull–kernel topology is always either equivalent to or weaker (fewer open sets) than the $\mathfrak{A}$-topology. Hence the problem is to show that complete regularity is equivalent to the condition that every closed set in $\Phi_{\mathfrak{A}}$ be a hull. Observe that, in order for a closed set F to be a hull, it is necessary and sufficient that there exist for each $\varphi \notin F$, an element $u \in \mathfrak{A}$ such that $\hat{u}(\varphi) \neq 0$ while $\hat{u}(F) = (0)$.

Assume first that $\mathfrak{A}$ is completely regular. Let F be any closed set in $\Phi_{\mathfrak{A}}$ and let φ_0 be any point of $\Phi_{\mathfrak{A}}$ not in F. By definition of complete regularity, there exists a hull–kernel neighborhood V of φ_0 such that $\mathfrak{k}(V)$ is modular. Set $F_0 = F \cap \mathfrak{h}(\mathfrak{k}(V))$. By Theorem (3.6.7), the hull $\mathfrak{h}(\mathfrak{k}(V))$, and hence the set F_0, is compact. Since the hull–kernel topology is Hausdorff and $\varphi_0 \notin F_0$, there exists an open set U about each φ in F_0 such that $\varphi_0 \notin \mathfrak{h}(\mathfrak{k}(U))$. The set F_0, being compact, is covered by a finite number of these sets, say $U_1, \cdots, U_n$. Since $\varphi_0 \notin \mathfrak{h}(\mathfrak{k}(U_i))$, there exists for each i an element $v_i \in \mathfrak{A}$ such that $\hat{v}_i(\varphi_0) \neq 0$ while $\hat{v}_i(U_i) = (0)$. Also, $\varphi_0 \notin \Phi_{\mathfrak{A}} - V$ and $\Phi_{\mathfrak{A}} - V$ is a hull, so that there exists $v_0 \in \mathfrak{A}$ such that $\hat{v}_0(\varphi_0) \neq 0$ while $\hat{v}_0(\Phi_{\mathfrak{A}} - V) = (0)$. Define $v = v_0 v_1 \cdots v_n$. Then $\hat{v}(\varphi_0) \neq 0$ and $\hat{v}(\varphi) = 0$ for every φ in the set $(U_1 \cup \cdots \cup U_n) \cup (\Phi_{\mathfrak{A}} - V)$. Since $V \subseteq \mathfrak{h}(\mathfrak{k}(V))$, the above set contains F. Therefore $\hat{v}(F) = (0)$. It follows that F is a hull and that the two topologies are equivalent.

Now assume that the two topologies are equivalent. Since the $\mathfrak{A}$-topology is always Hausdorff, it follows that the hull–kernel topology is Hausdorff, so that the first condition for complete regularity is satisfied. Moreover, if φ_0 is any point of $\Phi_{\mathfrak{A}}$, then there exists u in $\mathfrak{A}$ such that $\hat{u}(\varphi_0) \neq 0$. Define $V = \{\varphi : |\hat{u}(\varphi)| > \frac{1}{2}|\hat{u}(\varphi_0)|\}$. Then V is an open set with closure $\bar{V}$ equal to the set $\{\varphi : |\hat{u}(\varphi)| \geqslant \frac{1}{2}|\hat{u}(\varphi_0)|\}$, which is compact. Since the topologies are equivalent, $\bar{V}$ is a hull. Therefore, by Theorem (3.6.15), $\mathfrak{k}(\bar{V})$ is modular. But $\mathfrak{k}(V) = \mathfrak{k}(\bar{V})$; hence condition (ii) for complete regularity is satisfied. This completes the proof of the theorem.

COROLLARY (3.7.2). *In order for $\mathfrak{A}$ to be completely regular, it is necessary and sufficient that there exist, for each closed set F in $\Phi_{\mathfrak{A}}$ and each point $\varphi_0 \notin F$, an element $u \in \mathfrak{A}$ such that $\hat{u}(\varphi_0) \neq 0$ while $\hat{u}(F) = (0)$.*

COROLLARY (3.7.3). *If $\mathfrak{A}$ is completely regular, then it contains local identities.*

THEOREM (3.7.4). *Let $\mathscr{E}$ denote the subset of $\mathfrak{A}$ consisting of those elements z such that the subalgebra of $\mathfrak{A}$ which is continuously generated by z (See § 5) is completely regular. Then, if the functions $\{\hat{z} : z \in \mathscr{E}\}$ separate strongly the points of $\Phi_{\mathfrak{A}}$, the algebra $\mathfrak{A}$ is completely regular.*

PROOF. Let F be an arbitrary closed set in $\Phi_{\mathfrak{A}}$ and φ_0 a point of $\Phi_{\mathfrak{A}} - F$. By Corollary (3.2.5), the topology in $\Phi_{\mathfrak{A}}$ is equivalent to the

$\mathscr{E}$-topology. Therefore there exists a neighborhood $V_{\varphi_0}(z_1, \cdots, z_n;\epsilon)$ of φ_0, disjoint from F, with $z_1, \cdots, z_n \in \mathscr{E}$. Let $\mathfrak{A}_i$ denote the subalgebra of $\mathfrak{A}$ which is continuously generated by z_i. Let $\varphi \to \varphi'$ denote the mapping of $\Phi_{\mathfrak{A}}$ into $\Phi_{\mathfrak{A}_i}$ which is dual to the injection of $\mathfrak{A}_i$ into $\mathfrak{A}$. Define

$$F_i = \{\psi : \psi \in \Phi_{\mathfrak{A}_i},\quad |\hat{z}_i(\psi) - \hat{z}_i(\varphi_0)| \geqslant \epsilon\}.$$

Then F_i is a closed subset of $\Phi_{\mathfrak{A}_i}$ and $\varphi'_0 \notin F_i$. Since $\mathfrak{A}_i$ is completely regular, there exists $u_i \in \mathfrak{A}_i$ such that $\hat{u}_i(\varphi_0) \neq 0$ and $\hat{u}_i(F_i) = (0)$. Let $u = u_1 u_2 \cdots u_n$. Then $\hat{u}(\varphi_0) \neq 0$. Furthermore, if $\varphi \in F$, then there exists z_i such that $|\hat{z}_i(\varphi) - \hat{z}_i(\varphi_0)| \geqslant \epsilon$. Hence $\varphi' \in F_i$, so that $\hat{u}_i(\varphi) = \hat{u}_i(\varphi') = 0$. Therefore $\hat{u}(\varphi) = 0$, for $\varphi \in F$, and the theorem is proved. (See Mirkil [1].)

It follows immediately from Corollary (3.7.2) that, for a completely regular commutative Banach algebra $\mathfrak{A}$, the Šilov boundary $\partial\Phi_{\mathfrak{A}}$ must exhaust the carrier space $\Phi_{\mathfrak{A}}$. Therefore, if $\mathfrak{A}$ is a closed subalgebra of any other commutative Banach algebra $\mathfrak{B}$, then, by Theorem (3.3.25), the associated dual mapping of $\Phi_{\mathfrak{B}}$ into $\Phi_{\mathfrak{A}}$ must cover $\Phi_{\mathfrak{A}}$. When $\mathfrak{A}$ is semi-simple, we actually have a much stronger result in which no topological conditions are imposed on the embedding of $\mathfrak{A}$ in $\mathfrak{B}$. (See Rickart [5].)

THEOREM (3.7.5). *Let $\mathfrak{A}$ be a semi-simple completely regular commutative Banach algebra and let τ be any isomorphism of $\mathfrak{A}$ into an arbitrary commutative Banach algebra $\mathfrak{B}$. Then the associated dual mapping maps $\Phi_{\mathfrak{B}}{}^{\infty}$ onto $\Phi_{\mathfrak{A}}{}^{\infty}$.*

PROOF. Let Φ denote the image of $\Phi_{\mathfrak{B}}{}^{\infty}$ in $\Phi_{\mathfrak{A}}{}^{\infty}$ under the dual mapping. We have to prove that $\Phi = \Phi_{\mathfrak{A}}{}^{\infty}$. Suppose there exists $\varphi_0 \in \Phi_{\mathfrak{A}}{}^{\infty} - \Phi$. Then, for every $\psi \in \Phi_{\mathfrak{B}}$, there exists $a_\psi \in \mathfrak{A}$ such that $\hat{a}_\psi(\varphi_0) \neq \hat{a}_\psi{}^{\tau}(\psi)$. Set $\epsilon_\psi = \frac{1}{2}|\hat{a}_\psi{}^{\tau}(\psi) - \hat{a}_\psi(\varphi_0)|$ and define the set

$$G_\psi = \{\psi' : |\hat{a}_\psi{}^{\tau}(\psi') - \hat{a}_\psi(\varphi_0)| > \epsilon_\psi,\quad \psi' \in \Phi_{\mathfrak{B}}{}^{\infty}\}.$$

Then G_ψ is an open set in $\Phi_{\mathfrak{B}}{}^{\infty}$ and contains ψ. Since $\Phi_{\mathfrak{B}}{}^{\infty}$ is compact, there exists a finite number of sets $G_{\psi_1}, \cdots, G_{\psi_n}$ which cover $\Phi_{\mathfrak{B}}{}^{\infty}$. Set $a_i = a_{\psi_i}$, $\epsilon = \min_i \epsilon_{\psi_i}$, and consider the neighborhood

$$V = V_{\varphi_0}(a_1, \cdots, a_n;\epsilon)$$

in $\Phi_{\mathfrak{A}}{}^{\infty}$. Then V is disjoint from Φ. Now choose in $\Phi_{\mathfrak{A}}{}^{\infty}$ an open set U which contains φ_0 and whose closure is compact and contained in V. By Corollary (3.6.10), there exist elements u and v in $\mathfrak{A}$ such that $\hat{u}(\varphi_0) = 1$, $\hat{u}(\varphi) = 0$ for $\varphi \notin U$, $\hat{v}(\varphi) = 1$ for $\varphi \in U$, and $\hat{v}(\varphi) = 0$ for

$\varphi \notin V$. Then $\widehat{(uv)}(\varphi) = \hat{u}(\varphi)$ for every $\varphi \in \Phi_{\mathfrak{A}}$, and therefore $uv = u$ by the semi-simplicity of $\mathfrak{A}$. Since $\hat{v}^{\tau}(\psi) = 0$ for every $\psi \in \Phi_{\mathfrak{B}}{}^{\infty}$, the element v^{τ} is quasi-regular in $\mathfrak{B}$. In other words, there exists w in $\mathfrak{B}$ such that $v^{\tau} \circ w = 0$. Therefore, since $u \circ v = v$, we have $0 = v^{\tau} \circ w = u^{\tau} \circ v^{\tau} \circ w = u^{\tau}$. Since $u \neq 0$ and τ is an isomorphism, this is a contradiction and completes the proof.

COROLLARY (3.7.6). *Let $\mathfrak{A}$ be a semi-simple, commutative, completely regular Banach algebra which is algebraically embedded in an arbitrary Banach algebra $\mathfrak{B}$. Then $Sp_{\mathfrak{A}}(x) \cup (0) = Sp_{\mathfrak{B}}(x) \cup (0)$ for every $x \in \mathfrak{A}$.*

Observe that, if $\mathfrak{A}$ is a normed algebra under a second norm $\|x\|'$, then the completion of $\mathfrak{A}$ with respect to this norm is a Banach algebra $\mathfrak{B}$ in which $\mathfrak{A}$ is algebraically embedded. Since $\nu_{\mathfrak{B}}(x) \leqslant \|x\|'$, an application of the above corollary gives the following result, which is especially interesting when $\nu_{\mathfrak{A}}(x) = \|x\|$.

COROLLARY (3.7.7). *Let $\mathfrak{A}$ be a semi-simple, completely regular Banach algebra and let $\|x\|'$ be any norm (complete or not) under which $\mathfrak{A}$ is a normed algebra. Then $\nu_{\mathfrak{A}}(x) \leqslant \|x\|'$ for every $x \in \mathfrak{A}$.*

When $\mathfrak{A} = C_0(\Omega)$, where Ω is a locally compact Hausdorff space, the above corollary reduces to a result of Kaplansky's [5], which asserts that the natural norm in $C_0(\Omega)$ is minimal among *all* norms in $C_0(\Omega)$ which possess the multiplicative property.

Some of the results obtained for general completely regular algebras in § 7 of Chapter II are of special interest in the commutative case since the subdirect sum representation reduces to the algebra $\hat{\mathfrak{A}}$ of continuous functions on the carrier space $\Phi_{\mathfrak{A}}$, Therefore the various results obtained in the general case concerning the relationship of the subdirect sum $\Sigma'\mathfrak{A}_{\mathfrak{M}}$ to the full direct sum $\Sigma\mathfrak{A}_{\mathfrak{M}}$ become in the commutative case results concerning the relationship of the algebra of functions $\hat{\mathfrak{A}}$ to the full algebra of continuous functions $C_0(\Phi_{\mathfrak{A}})$. We leave it to the reader to specialize these general results to the commutative case. The remainder of this section is devoted to a brief description of the representation of a completely regular Banach algebra as a subdirect sum of primary algebras (See Theorem (2.7.27)). We also limit attention to algebras with an identity element. Our first step is to restrict further the subdirect sums which are to be used.

Let Ω be a compact Hausdorff space and assume given for each $\omega \in \Omega$ a complex commutative primary Banach algebra $\mathfrak{A}_{\omega}$ with an identity element. Since $\mathfrak{A}_{\omega}$ is primary, its carrier space $\Phi_{\mathfrak{A}_{\omega}}$ reduces to a single point φ_ω. A normed subdirect sum $\Sigma'\mathfrak{A}_\omega$ will be called a CONTINUOUS SUBDIRECT SUM of the algebras $\mathfrak{A}_\omega$, $\omega \in \Omega$, provided, for each $f \in \Sigma'\mathfrak{A}_\omega$, the complex function F defined by the relation

$$F(\omega) = \widehat{f(\omega)}(\varphi_\omega), \quad \omega \in \Omega,$$

belongs to $C(\Omega)$.

If $\mathfrak{A}$ is a completely regular, semi-simple, commutative Banach algebra with an identity element, then associated with each $\varphi \in \Phi_{\mathfrak{A}}$ is the minimal closed primary ideal $\overline{J(\varphi)}$, where $J(\varphi)$ consists of all $x \in \mathfrak{A}$ such that $\hat{x}$ vanishes in some neighborhood of φ. (See Definition (2.7.22).) Denote the primary algebra $\mathfrak{A}/\overline{J(\varphi)}$ by $\mathfrak{A}_\varphi$. With each $x \in \mathfrak{A}$, associate the function $\tilde{x}$ defined on $\Phi_{\mathfrak{A}}$ with value at φ given by

$$\tilde{x}(\varphi) = x + \overline{J(\varphi)} \in \mathfrak{A}_\varphi.$$

Denote the single element of the carrier space of $\mathfrak{A}_\varphi$ by ψ_φ. Then ψ_φ maps $x + \overline{J(\varphi)}$ into $\hat{x}(\varphi)$, so that

$$\widehat{\tilde{x}(\varphi)}(\psi_\varphi) = \hat{x}(\varphi), \quad \varphi \in \Phi_{\mathfrak{A}}.$$

Therefore it follows that $x \to \tilde{x}$ is an isomorphism of $\mathfrak{A}$ with a continuous subdirect sum of the primary algebras $\mathfrak{A}_\varphi$. It is always true that $x \to \tilde{x}$ is a continuous mapping of $\mathfrak{A}$ into the normed direct sum $\Sigma\mathfrak{A}_\varphi$. In case this mapping is a homeomorphism, the algebra $\mathfrak{A}$ is said to be of TYPE C (Šilov [7]). This amounts to the condition that the norm

$$\|x\|' = \sup_{\varphi \in \Phi_{\mathfrak{A}}} \left(\inf_{m \in J(\varphi)} \|x + m\| \right)$$

be equivalent to the given norm $\|x\|$ in $\mathfrak{A}$. Examples of these algebras are discussed in the Appendix, § 2.

IV. ALGEBRAS WITH AN INVOLUTION

Introduction. Let $\mathfrak{A}$ be any real algebra. A mapping $x \to x^\star$ of $\mathfrak{A}$ onto itself is called an INVOLUTION provided the following conditions are satisfied:

(i) $(x^\star)^\star = x$

(ii) $(x+y)^\star = x^\star + y^\star$

(iii) $(xy)^\star = y^\star x^\star$

(iv) $(\alpha x)^\star = \alpha x^\star$, α real.

If $\mathfrak{A}$ is a complex algebra, it is customary to impose the following strengthened form of condition (iv) in the definition of the involution:

(iv)′ $(\alpha x)^\star = \bar{\alpha} x^\star$, α complex.

Therefore, unless otherwise stated, an involution in a complex algebra will be assumed to satisfy condition (iv)′. An algebra with an involution is called a $\star$-ALGEBRA. A subalgebra $\mathfrak{B}$ of a $\star$-algebra $\mathfrak{A}$ is called a $\star$-SUBALGEBRA of $\mathfrak{A}$ provided $\mathfrak{B}^\star = \mathfrak{B}$.

In view of conditions (iii) and (iv)′, the identity mapping $x \to x$ will be an involution if and only if the algebra is real and commutative. Most of our discussion will be concerned with complex $\star$-algebras and it is only in this and the next section that real $\star$-algebras are considered at all.

Many important Banach algebras naturally carry an involution. One of the most important of these is a self-adjoint algebra of bounded operators on a Hilbert space $\mathfrak{H}$, that is, a subalgebra of $\mathscr{B}(\mathfrak{H})$ which contains with T the adjoint operator $T^\star$. This example motivates most of the terminology for $\star$-algebras. Thus, an element h such that $h^\star = h$ is called HERMITIAN, and an idempotent p such that $p^\star = p$ is called a PROJECTION. Elements of the form $x + x^\star$, $xx^\star$, the zero element and the identity element, if it exists, are all hermitian. An element x such that $xx^\star = x^\star x$ is called NORMAL. Obviously, every hermitian element is normal. A subset $\mathscr{E}$ of $\mathfrak{A}$ is called NORMAL provided the set $\mathscr{E} \cup \mathscr{E}^\star$ is commutative (that is, every pair of elements commute). If $\mathfrak{A}$ is a complex $\star$-algebra, then every element has a unique representation in the form $x = h+ik$ where h and k are hermitian. In fact,

$$h = \frac{1}{2}(x+x^\star) \quad \text{and} \quad k = \frac{1}{2i}(x-x^\star).$$

The elements h and k are called the HERMITIAN COMPONENTS of x. Note that the set $\mathscr{H}_{\mathfrak{A}}$ of all hermitian elements of $\mathfrak{A}$ is a real linear subspace of $\mathfrak{A}$.

If $\mathfrak{A}$ is a complex $\star$-algebra which does not possess an identity element, adjoin an identity to obtain $\mathfrak{A}_1$. If $\alpha+x$ is any element of $\mathfrak{A}_1$, define $(\alpha+x)^\star = \bar{\alpha}+x^\star$. Then $\alpha+x \to (\alpha+x)^\star$ is an involution in $\mathfrak{A}_1$. Moreover, if $\mathfrak{A}$ is normed and the involution in $\mathfrak{A}$ is continuous, then so is its extension to $\mathfrak{A}_1$. A similar extension can, of course, be made in the real case. Now let $\mathfrak{A}$ be a real $\star$-algebra and $\mathfrak{A}_C$ its complexification. For $x+iy$ in $\mathfrak{A}_C$, define $(x+iy)^\star = x^\star - iy^\star$. Then $x+iy \to (x+iy)^\star$ is readily verified to be an involution in $\mathfrak{A}_C$ as a complex algebra. Again, if the involution in $\mathfrak{A}$ is continuous, then its extension to $\mathfrak{A}_C$ is also continuous. In each of the above instances, $\mathfrak{A}$ is a $\star$-subalgebra of the larger algebra.

The importance of the involution in any $\star$-algebra $\mathfrak{A}$ stems from the symmetry which it imposes on the algebra. For example, the mapping $x \to x^\star$ transforms in a one-to-one manner every left (right) ideal of $\mathfrak{A}$ into a right (left) ideal, preserving properties such as modularity and maximality. Thus, a 2-sided ideal is transformed into a 2-sided ideal. If any ideal has the property that $\mathfrak{I}^\star = \mathfrak{I}$, then it is automatically 2-sided and is called a $\star$-IDEAL. It follows from these remarks that the radical of any algebra with involution is a $\star$-ideal.

It is easily verified that the transformation $\mathfrak{M} \to \mathfrak{M}^\star$ is a homeomorphic mapping of the strong structure space $\Xi_{\mathfrak{A}}$ onto itself. On the other hand, let $\mathfrak{P}$ be any primitive ideal in $\mathfrak{A}$, then $\mathfrak{P} = \mathfrak{L} : \mathfrak{A}$ where $\mathfrak{L}$ is a maximal modular left ideal in $\mathfrak{A}$. Hence $\mathfrak{P}$ should be called LEFT PRIMITIVE. Similarly, the quotient of a maximal modular right ideal might be called RIGHT PRIMITIVE. Whether or not every right primitive ideal is also left primitive is still an open question in ring theory and it is even conjectured that the answer is in the negative (Jacobson [5, p. 4].) Therefore a result for the structure space $\Pi_{\mathfrak{A}}$, similar to that observed above for $\Xi_{\mathfrak{A}}$, may not be available without further restrictions.

Let $\mathfrak{A}$ and $\mathfrak{B}$ denote two $\star$-algebras. Then a homomorphism $a \to a^\tau$ of $\mathfrak{A}$ into $\mathfrak{B}$ is called a $\star$-HOMOMORPHISM if $(a^\star)^\tau = (a^\tau)^\star$ for every $a \in \mathfrak{A}$. Similarly, an isomorphism with this property is called a $\star$-ISOMORPHISM. The image of $\mathfrak{A}$ in $\mathfrak{B}$ under a $\star$-homomorphism is obviously a $\star$-subalgebra of $\mathfrak{B}$ and the kernel of the homomorphism is a $\star$-ideal. Conversely, let $\mathfrak{I}$ be any $\star$-ideal in $\mathfrak{A}$ and consider the algebra $\mathfrak{A}/\mathfrak{I}$. If $x^\tau = x + \mathfrak{I}$, then $x \to x^\tau$ is a homomorphism of $\mathfrak{A}$ onto $\mathfrak{A}/\mathfrak{I}$. Define $(x^\tau)^\star = (x^\star)^\tau$ for $x^\tau \in \mathfrak{A}/\mathfrak{I}$; then the fact that $\mathfrak{I}$ is a $\star$-ideal implies that $(x^\tau)^\star$ depends only on the equivalence class x^τ and not on x. It follows that $x^\tau \to (x^\tau)^\star$ is an involution in $\mathfrak{A}/\mathfrak{I}$ and hence $\mathfrak{A}/\mathfrak{I}$ is a $\star$-algebra. Furthermore, the homomorphism $x \to x^\tau$ of $\mathfrak{A}$ onto $\mathfrak{A}/\mathfrak{I}$ is a $\star$-homomorphism. Therefore the $\star$-homomorphisms of $\mathfrak{A}$ onto $\star$-algebras are in one-to-one correspondence with the $\star$-ideals in $\mathfrak{A}$.

An involution in a normed $\star$-algebra may or may not be continuous. The simplest condition for continuity is that the involution be an isometry; that is, $\|x^\star\| = \|x\|$. This is, in a sense, the general case; because, whenever the involution is continuous, an equivalent norm $\|x\|'$ (for example, take $\|x\|' = \max(\|x\|, \|x^\star\|)$) can be introduced into $\mathfrak{A}$ so that the isometry condition is satisfied. It is convenient to refer to a normed $\star$-algebra, in which $\|x^\star\| = \|x\|$, as a $\star$-NORMED algebra. If $\mathfrak{A}$ is a complex normed $\star$-algebra with a continuous involution, then a sequence $\{x_n\}$ of elements of $\mathfrak{A}$ will converge to an element x if and only if the hermitian components of x_n converge respectively to the corresponding hermitian components of x. In particular, the real space $\mathscr{H}_{\mathfrak{A}}$ of hermitian elements will be a Banach space if and only if $\mathfrak{A}$ is a Banach algebra. Furthermore, if $\mathfrak{A}$ is any complex Banach $\star$-algebra, then the closed graph theorem can be used to show that continuity of the involution is equivalent to the space $\mathscr{H}_{\mathfrak{A}}$ being closed in $\mathfrak{A}$. In many of the situations in which continuity of the involution is used, it suffices to impose the weaker condition that the involution be continuous in every maximal commutative $\star$-subalgebra of $\mathfrak{A}$. In this case we say that the involution is LOCALLY CONTINUOUS.

A much stronger linking of the involution with the norm, than that involved in continuity, is given by the condition $\|x^\star x\| = \|x\|^2$. Any Banach $\star$-algebra which satisfies it is called a B*-ALGEBRA. Since the inequality $\|x^\star x\| \leqslant \|x^\star\|\,\|x\|$ always holds in a normed $\star$-algebra, the B*-condition clearly implies that $\|x^\star\| = \|x\|$. Also, if $h^\star = h$, then

$\|h^{2^n}\| = \|h\|^{2^n}$ for all n, which implies that $\|h\| = \nu(h)$. In particular, $\|h^n\| = \|h\|^n$ for all n. As an example, consider a bounded operator T on a Hilbert space $\mathfrak{H}$. Let $|T|$ be the bound of T and let $|f|$ be the norm of $f \in \mathfrak{H}$. Then

$$|Tf|^2 = (Tf, Tf) = (T^\star Tf, f) \leqslant |T^\star T||f|^2$$

for all $f \in \mathfrak{H}$, so that $|T|^2 \leqslant |T^\star T| \leqslant |T^\star||T|$. In particular, $|T| \leqslant |T^\star|$ and hence, by symmetry, $|T^\star| = |T|$. Therefore $|T^\star T| = |T|^2$ and we see that any closed self-adjoint subalgebra of $\mathscr{B}(\mathfrak{H})$ is a B★-algebra. These algebras are called C★-ALGEBRAS and are understood to carry with them the particular Hilbert space on which they operate. We regard B★-algebras as abstract C★-algebras. As will be seen later (§ 9), every complex B★-algebra is isometrically ★-isomorphic to a C★-algebra. Whether or not the same is true for real B★-algebras is an open question. In many situations involving B★-algebras, the condition $\|x^\star x\| = \|x\|^2$ can be weakened to $\|x\|^2 \leqslant \beta\|x^\star x\|$, β constant.

A Banach ★-algebra in which there is defined a second norm $|x|$ which satisfies, in addition to the multiplicative condition $|xy| \leqslant |x||y|$, the B★-condition $|x|^2 = |x^\star x|$, is called an A★-ALGEBRA. This second norm will be called an AUXILIARY NORM. Note that completeness of the algebra in the auxiliary norm is not required and no *a priori* conditions relating the given norm and the involution are imposed. It will be shown in a later section (§ 9) that the defining properties of the A★-algebra characterize those self-adjoint subalgebras of $\mathfrak{B}(\mathfrak{H})$ which are Banach algebras under some norm. The A★-algebras obviously include the B★-algebras. An important example of an A★-algebra, which is not in general a B★-algebra, is the L_1 algebra of a locally compact topological group (see Appendix, A.3.1). Another example of an A★-algebra is a semi-simple real commutative Banach algebra. Here the involution is the identity mapping and the auxiliary norm is the spectral radius, the required properties being given by Theorem (1.4.1).

The next section (§ 1) contains a brief discussion of some of the properties of A★-algebras along with a variety of miscellaneous results for ★-algebras including properties of the groups of regular elements and some resulting spectral properties. A systematic discussion of general B★-algebras is postponed to later sections. In § 2 commutative ★-algebras are considered and, among other things, the Gelfand–Naǐmark abstract characterization of the algebras $C_0(\Omega)$ is obtained. In § 3, ★-representations on self-dual vector spaces are introduced and it is proved that every complex ★-normed algebra admits a faithful

$\star$-representation of this kind. In §§ 5, 6 and 7, we study $\star$-representations on Hilbert space and, in § 8, show the existence of many such representations for a special class of $\star$-algebras. In §§ 9, 10 we specialize to B$\star$-algebras and obtain many of their fundamental properties, including some structure theorems. The last section (§ 11) is devoted to a study of certain $\star$- algebras with minimal ideals.

§ 1. **Miscellaneous properties of $\star$-algebras.** If $\mathfrak{A}$ is a $\star$-algebra with an identity element, then an element r in $\mathfrak{A}$ is (left, right) regular if and only if $r^\star$ is (right, left) regular. Hence the involution is an anti-automorphism of the group G of regular elements. Thus $G^\star = G$ and, if $r \in G$, then $(r^\star)^{-1} = (r^{-1})^\star$. A hermitian element h will be regular if it is either left or right regular. Any element x in $\mathfrak{A}$ will be left (right) regular if the element $x^\star x$ (the element $xx^\star$) is regular. Hence an element x is in G if and only if both $x^\star x$ and $xx^\star$ are in G. Similar remarks hold for quasi-regularity and involve the elements $x^\star \circ x$ and $x \circ x^\star$ instead of $x^\star x$ and $xx^\star$. In particular, $(G^q)^\star = G^q$ and, if $r \in G^q$, then $(r^\star)^\circ = (r^\circ)^\star$.

LEMMA (4.1.1). *Let $\mathfrak{A}$ be any $\star$-algebra. Then, for every $x \in \mathfrak{A}$, $Sp_{\mathfrak{A}}(x^\star)$ is equal to the complex conjugate of $Sp_{\mathfrak{A}}(x)$. If $\mathfrak{A}$ is a real $\star$-algebra, then $Sp_{\mathfrak{A}}(x^\star) = Sp_{\mathfrak{A}}(x)$.*

PROOF. This lemma follows directly from the above comments plus the fact that every element in a real algebra has a self-conjugate spectrum (Corollary (1.6.7)).

COROLLARY (4.1.2). *If $\mathfrak{A}$ is a Banach $\star$-algebra, then $\nu_{\mathfrak{A}}(x^\star) = \nu_{\mathfrak{A}}(x)$, for every $x \in \mathfrak{A}$.*

Let $\mathscr{E}$ be a normal subset of the $\star$-algebra $\mathfrak{A}$. Then, by definition, $\mathscr{E} \cup \mathscr{E}^\star$ is commutative. By Zorn's Lemma, there will exist a maximal normal subset of $\mathfrak{A}$ which contains $\mathscr{E}$. Just as in the case of maximal commutative subsets of an algebra, the maximal normal subsets automatically possess certain algebraic and topological properties. (See Civin and Yood [3].)

THEOREM (4.1.3). *Every maximal normal subset $\mathfrak{C}$ of a normed $\star$-algebra $\mathfrak{A}$ is a closed maximal commutative $\star$-subalgebra of $\mathfrak{A}$ such that $Sp_{\mathfrak{C}}(c) = Sp_{\mathfrak{A}}(c)$ for every $c \in \mathfrak{C}$.*

PROOF. If $\mathscr{E}$ is any normal subset of $\mathfrak{A}$, then it is obvious from the definition that $\mathscr{E} \cup \mathscr{E}^\star$ is also a normal subset. Therefore, since $\mathfrak{C}$ is maximal, $\mathfrak{C}^\star = \mathfrak{C}$. It follows from this observation that, in order to prove a given element x belongs to $\mathfrak{C}$, we have only to show (1) that x is normal and (2) that x commutes with every element of $\mathfrak{C}$. For, in this case, $\mathfrak{C}$ plus x is clearly normal, so that $x \in \mathfrak{C}$ by the maximality of $\mathfrak{C}$. Now the proof that $\mathfrak{C}$ is a subalgebra, and hence is a maximal commutative ⋆-subalgebra, is easy and will be omitted. That $\mathfrak{C}$ contains the identity element of $\mathfrak{A}$, if it exists, is also trivial. Next let $\{c_n\}$ be a sequence of elements of $\mathfrak{C}$ which converges to an element $x \in \mathfrak{A}$. Since each c_n commutes with every element of $\mathfrak{C}$, so does the element x. Furthermore, since $\mathfrak{C}$ is a ⋆-subalgebra, $x^\star$ will also commute with every element of $\mathfrak{C}$. In particular, $c_n x^\star = x^\star c_n$ for each n. Passing to the limit, we obtain $xx^\star = x^\star x$. In other words, x is normal, so that $x \in \mathfrak{C}$ and hence $\mathfrak{C}$ is closed. Finally, let c be any element of $\mathfrak{C}$ which is quasi-regular in $\mathfrak{A}$. Then, since c is normal, so is its quasi-inverse c°. Also, c° commutes with every element which commutes with c. Therefore $c^\circ \in \mathfrak{C}$ and it follows that $Sp_{\mathfrak{A}}(c) = Sp_{\mathfrak{C}}(c)$.

The next lemma is used at a number of points in the remainder of this chapter. In order to cover these applications, the lemma is formulated more generally than would be required by its use in this section.

LEMMA (4.1.4). *Let $\mathfrak{A}$ be a Banach algebra and h an element of $\mathfrak{A}$ with $\nu(h) < 1$. Then there exists an element $k \in \mathfrak{A}$ such that $k \circ k = h$. If $\mathfrak{A}$ is a Banach ⋆-algebra with a locally continuous involution and h is hermitian, then k is also hermitian.*

PROOF. Consider the function f defined in terms of the binomial series as follows:

$$f(\zeta) = -\sum_{n=1}^{\infty} \binom{1/2}{n} (-\zeta)^n.$$

Note that f is defined and $2f(\zeta) - f(\zeta)^2 = \zeta$ for all $|\zeta| \leqslant 1$. Since the binomial series converges absolutely for $|\zeta| < 1$ and since $\nu(h) < 1$, it follows that the vector-valued series

$$-\sum_{n=1}^{\infty} \binom{1/2}{n} (-h)^n$$

converges absolutely to an element $k \in \mathfrak{A}$ such that $k \circ k = 2k - k^2 = h$. In the ⋆-algebra case with h hermitian, let $\mathfrak{C}$ be a maximal commutative ⋆-subalgebra of $\mathfrak{A}$ which contains h. Then $\mathfrak{C}$ is closed and therefore contains k. Moreover, by definition of local continuity, the involution is continuous in $\mathfrak{C}$, so that k is also hermitian and the lemma is proved.

In a $\star$-algebra with an identity element, an element u is said to be UNITARY if $u^\star u = uu^\star = 1$. The above lemma enables us to show that under quite general conditions a $\star$-algebra is spanned by its unitary elements. (See Dixmier [15, p.4].)

THEOREM (4.1.5). *Let $\mathfrak{A}$ be a complex Banach $\star$-algebra with an identity element and a locally continuous involution. Then every element of $\mathfrak{A}$ is a linear combination of unitary elements.*

PROOF. It is obviously sufficient to make the proof for a hermitian element h with $\nu(h) < 1$. Since $\nu(h^2) = \nu(h)^2 < 1$, an application of the above lemma to h^2 yields a hermitian element k such that $k \circ k = h^2$. This implies $(1-k)^2 = 1-h^2$. Now define $u = h+i(1-k)$. Then $u^\star = h-i(1-k)$ and $u^\star u = uu^\star = 1$. Moreover, $h = \frac{1}{2}(u+u^\star)$, so that the theorem follows.

DEFINITION (4.1.6). *An involution in a Banach $\star$-algebra is said to be* HERMITIAN *if every hermitian element has a real spectrum.*

LEMMA (4.1.7). *In order for the involution in a Banach $\star$-algebra $\mathfrak{A}$ to be hermitian, it is necessary and sufficient that every element of the form $-h^2$, where $h^\star = h$, be quasi-regular.*

PROOF. If the involution is hermitian, then the spectrum of h is real and, since $Sp(h^2) = (Sp(h))^2$, it follows that $Sp(h^2)$ is non-negative. In particular, $-1 \notin Sp(h^2)$, so that $-h^2$ is quasi-regular. This proves the necessity. Now suppose that h is a hermitian element whose spectrum contains a complex number $\alpha+\beta i$ with $\beta \neq 0$. Define the element

$$k = \beta^{-1}(\alpha^2+\beta^2)^{-1}(\alpha h^2+(\beta^2-\alpha^2)h).$$

Then k is hermitian and, by Theorem (1.6.10), its spectrum will contain i. Hence the spectrum of k^2 must contain -1, so that $-k^2$ is quasi-singular by Definition (1.6.1) or Corollary (1.6.7). This proves the sufficiency and establishes the lemma.

THEOREM (4.1.8). *Let $\mathfrak{A}$ be a Banach $\star$-algebra with a hermitian involution. Then $S^q = Z^q \cup (Z^q)^\star$. If $\mathfrak{A}$ has an identity element, then $S = Z \cup Z^\star$.*

PROOF. It will be sufficient to make the proof for the real case without assumption of an identity element. Consider first any hermitian element h in S^q. Then also $h \circ h \in S^q$. Since the involution is hermitian, each of the elements $|\alpha_n|^{-2}(2h-h^2)$, where $\alpha_n = 1+n^{-1}i$ and

$n = 1, 2, \cdots$, is quasi-regular (Theorem (1.6.6)). Moreover,

$$|\alpha_n|^{-2}(2h - h^2) = \frac{n^2}{n^2+1}(h \circ h)$$

and hence

$$\lim_{n\to\infty} |\alpha_n|^{-2}(2h - h^2) = h \circ h.$$

It follows from Theorem (1.5.9) (ii) that $1-(h \circ h)$ is a topological divisor of zero. In other words, $h \circ h \in Z^q$ and, by Theorem (1.5.9) (i), this implies $h \in Z^q$. Now let s be an arbitrary element of S^q. Then either $s \circ s^\star$ or $s^\star \circ s$ is in S^q. Since these elements are hermitian, it follows that either $s \circ s^\star$ or $s^\star \circ s$ belongs to Z^q. In either case, another application of Theorem (1.5.9) (i) shows that either s or $s^\star$ belongs to Z^q and so completes the proof.

THEOREM (4.1.9). *Let $\mathfrak{A}$ be a Banach ⋆-algebra with hermitian involution and let $\mathfrak{B}$ denote any closed ⋆-subalgebra of $\mathfrak{A}$. Then $\mathfrak{B}$ contains quasi-inverses in the sense that, if $b \in \mathfrak{B}$ and b° exists in $\mathfrak{A}$, then $b^\circ \in \mathfrak{B}$.*

PROOF. By Theorem (1.6.13), the involution is also hermitian in $\mathfrak{B}$. Hence, if s is a quasi-singular element of $\mathfrak{B}$, then either $1-s$ or $1-s^\star$ is a topological divisor of zero in $\mathfrak{B}$ and hence in $\mathfrak{A}$. Therefore s must be quasi-singular in $\mathfrak{A}$.

COROLLARY (4.1.10). *For every $b \in \mathfrak{B}$, $Sp_{\mathfrak{A}}(b) \cup (0) = Sp_{\mathfrak{B}}(b) \cup (0)$. If $\mathfrak{B}$ contains an identity element for $\mathfrak{A}$, then $Sp_{\mathfrak{A}}(b) = Sp_{\mathfrak{B}}(b)$.*

THEOREM (4.1.11). *Let $\mathfrak{A}$ be a Banach ⋆-algebra whose involution is both hermitian and continuous. Then $S^q = Z^q$ and, if $\mathfrak{A}$ has an identity element, then $S = Z$.*

PROOF. Since the involution is continuous, there exists a constant $\beta > 0$ such that $\|x^\star\| \leqslant \beta\|x\|$ for all $x \in \mathfrak{A}$. Hence

$$\frac{\|x - z^\star x\|}{\|x\|} \leqslant \beta^2 \frac{\|x^\star - x^\star z\|}{\|x^\star\|}.$$

It follows that $\lambda^q(z^\star) \leqslant \beta^2 \rho^q(z)$ and this implies $(Z^{rq})^\star \subseteq Z^{lq}$. Similarly, $(Z^{lq})^\star \subseteq Z^{rq}$, so that $Z^{lq} \subseteq (Z^{rq})^\star$. Therefore $(Z^{rq})^\star = Z^{lq}$, $(Z^{lq})^\star = Z^{rq}$ and $(Z^q)^\star = Z^q$. If $\mathfrak{A}$ has an identity element, then a similar argument gives $(Z^r)^\star = Z^l$, $(Z^l)^\star = Z^r$ and $Z^\star = Z$. The theorem now follows immediately from the preceding theorem.

The first part of the above proof used only the continuity of the involution. Therefore we can state the following corollary.

COROLLARY (4.1.12). *Let* $\mathfrak{A}$ *be any Banach* $\star$*-algebra with a continuous involution. Then* $(Z^{rq})^\star = Z^{lq}$, $(Z^{lq})^\star = Z^{rq}$ *and* $(Z^q)^\star = Z^q$. *If* $\mathfrak{A}$ *has an identity element, then* $(Z^r)^\star = Z^l$, $(Z^l)^\star = Z^r$ *and* $Z^\star = Z$.

The remainder of this section is devoted to a discussion of A*-algebras. Some of the properties of these algebras are needed below for the study of $\star$-representations of Hilbert space. Recall that a Banach $\star$-algebra is an A*-algebra if it possesses, in addition to its given complete norm $\|x\|$, a second (not necessarily complete) AUXILIARY NORM $|x|$ which satisfies the B*-condition, $|x^\star x| = |x|^2$. For the moment, the algebra can be either real or complex and need not possess an identity element. On the other hand, the following lemma shows that an identity element can always be adjoined so as to preserve the A*-character of the algebras. (See Yood [9, Lemma 4.39].)

LEMMA (4.1.13). *Let* $\mathfrak{A}$ *be a normed* $\star$*-algebra whose norm* $|x|$ *satisfies the* B**-condition* $|x^\star x| = |x|^2$. *Then there exists a second normed* $\star$*-algebra* $\mathfrak{B}$ *and an isometric* $\star$*-isomorphism of* $\mathfrak{A}$ *into* $\mathfrak{B}$ *with the following properties: (i)* $\mathfrak{B}$ *has an identity element and its norm satisfies the* B**-condition. (ii) If* $\mathfrak{A}'$ *is the image of* $\mathfrak{A}$ *in* $\mathfrak{B}$, *then* $\mathfrak{B}$ *is either equal to* $\mathfrak{A}'$ *or generated by* $\mathfrak{A}'$ *plus the identity element, according as* $\mathfrak{A}$ *does or does not possess an identity.*

PROOF. Consider the left regular representation $a \to A_a$ of $\mathfrak{A}$ on itself. If $|A_a|$ is the bound of A_a as an element of $\mathscr{B}(\mathfrak{A})$, then it is always true that $|A_a| \leqslant |a|$. On the other hand, using the B*-condition, we obtain

$$|a|^2 = |aa^\star| = |A_a a^\star| \leqslant |A_a||a^\star| = |A_a||a|.$$

Therefore $|a| \leqslant |A_a|$ and hence $|A_a| = |a|$. This proves that $a \to A_a$ is an isometric isomorphism of $\mathfrak{A}$ into $\mathscr{B}(\mathfrak{A})$. Now take $\mathfrak{B}$ as the subalgebra of $\mathscr{B}(\mathfrak{A})$ generated by the identity operator and the image of $\mathfrak{A}$ in $\mathscr{B}(\mathfrak{A})$. Note that $\mathfrak{B}$ consists of all operators of the form $A_a + \alpha I$, α a scalar and $a \in \mathfrak{A}$. Define

$$(A_a + \alpha I)^\star = A_{a^\star} + \bar{\alpha} I.$$

Then $A_a + \alpha I \to (A_a + \alpha I)^\star$ is an involution in $\mathfrak{B}$ and $a \to A_a$ becomes a $\star$-isomorphism of $\mathfrak{A}$ into $\mathfrak{B}$. Property (ii) is obviously satisfied, so that it only remains to prove that the operator norm in $\mathfrak{B}$ has the B*-property relative to the involution just defined. Let $B = A_a + \alpha I$. Then

$$|Bx|^2 = |ax + \alpha x|^2 = |(ax + \alpha x)^\star(ax + \alpha x)|$$
$$= |x^\star(B^\star Bx)| \leqslant |B^\star B||x|^2.$$

Therefore $|B|^2 \leqslant |B^\star B| \leqslant |B^\star||B|$, which implies $|B|^2 = |B^\star B|$ and completes the proof.

It is immediate from the above lemma that one can always adjoin an identity element to a B⋆-algebra and obtain a B⋆-algebra. For an A⋆-algebra, observe that the above lemma takes care of the auxiliary norm in $\mathfrak{A}$. If $\mathfrak{A}$ does not already have an identity element, define $\|A_a + \alpha I\| = \|a\| + |\alpha|$. Then $\mathfrak{B}$ is a Banach algebra under this norm and so is an A⋆-algebra. Note that the ⋆-isomorphism $a \to A_a$ here preserves both the auxiliary norm and the complete norm.

LEMMA (4.1.14). *Let $\mathfrak{A}$ be an $A^\star$-algebra with norm $\|x\|$ and auxiliary norm $|x|$. Then $|h| \leqslant \nu_{\mathfrak{A}}(h)$ for hermitian h, and $|x|^2 \leqslant \nu_{\mathfrak{A}}(x^\star x)$ for all x.*

PROOF. Let h be any hermitian element. Then $|h^{2^{m-1}}|^2 = |h^{2^m}|$ and, by iteration, $|h|^{2^m} = |h^{2^m}|$. If $\nu_0(x) = \lim|x^n|^{1/n}$, then it follows that $|h| = \nu_0(h)$. By Theorems (1.6.3) and (1.6.4), we have $\nu_0(h) \leqslant \nu_{\mathfrak{A}}(h)$. Therefore $|h| \leqslant \nu_{\mathfrak{A}}(h)$. If $h = xx^\star$, then $|x|^2 = |x^\star x| \leqslant \nu_{\mathfrak{A}}(x^\star x)$, and the lemma is proved.

THEOREM (4.1.15). *The involution in an $A^\star$-algebra is necessarily continuous with respect to both norms.*

PROOF. As has already been observed, the B⋆-condition implies that the involution is an isometry with respect to the auxiliary norm. Since $x \to x^\star$ is a linear mapping of a real Banach space onto itself, the continuity of the involution will follow from the closed graph theorem if we prove that $x_n \to a$ and $x_n^\star \to b$ implies $b = a^\star$. Observe first that $|b - a^\star| \leqslant |b - x_n^\star| + |x_n^\star - a^\star|$. By the above lemma, $|x|^2 \leqslant \nu_{\mathfrak{A}}(x^\star x) \leqslant \|x^\star\|\,\|x\|$, so that

$$|b - x_n^\star|^2 \leqslant \|b - x_n^\star\|\,\|b^\star - x_n\|$$

and

$$|x_n^\star - a^\star|^2 \leqslant \|x_n^\star - a^\star\|\,\|x_n - a\|.$$

In the right-hand side of each of these inequalities, one factor is bounded while the other converges to zero as $n \to \infty$. Therefore both $|b - x_n^\star| \to 0$ and $|x_n^\star - a^\star| \to 0$. This implies $|b - a^\star| = 0$, and hence $b = a^\star$, which is the desired result.

COROLLARY (4.1.16). *There exists a constant β such that $|x| \leqslant \beta\|x\|$ for all x.*

THEOREM (4.1.17). *Let $\mathfrak{A}$ be an $A^\star$-algebra with norm $\|x\|$ and auxiliary norm $|x|$ and let $\mathfrak{B}$ denote a ⋆-subalgebra of $\mathfrak{A}$ which is itself* *a Banach algebra under another norm* $\|x\|'$. *Then there exists a constant* γ *such that* $\|x\| \leqslant \gamma\|x\|'$ *for every* $x \in \mathfrak{B}$; *that is, the injection mapping of* $\mathfrak{B}$ *into* $\mathfrak{A}$ *is continuous.*

PROOF. By the corollary to the preceding theorem we know that $|x| \leqslant \beta\|x\|$ for all $x \in \mathfrak{A}$. Moreover, observe that $\mathfrak{B}$ is an A*-algebra in its own right, so that there exists a constant β' such that $|x| \leqslant \beta'\|x\|'$ for $x \in \mathfrak{B}$. Now consider the injection mapping of $\mathfrak{B}$ as a Banach space into $\mathfrak{A}$ as a Banach space. The theorem will be proved if we show that this mapping is continuous and hence bounded. Again, the closed graph theorem is used to obtain the desired result. Let $\{x_n\}$ be a sequence of elements of $\mathfrak{B}$ which converges to an element $b \in \mathfrak{B}$ in the norm of $\mathfrak{B}$ and to an element $a \in \mathfrak{A}$ in the norm of $\mathfrak{A}$. But

$$|a-b| \leqslant |a-x_n|+|x_n-b| \leqslant \beta\|a-x_n\|+\beta'\|x_n-b\|'.$$

Since $\|a-x_n\| \to 0$ and $\|x_n-b\|' \to 0$, it follows that $a = b$ and the proof is complete.

COROLLARY (4.1.18). *If a* **-algebra* $\mathfrak{A}$ *has an auxiliary norm, then all norms which make* $\mathfrak{A}$ *into a Banach algebra are equivalent*; *that is, if* $\mathfrak{A}$ *has a complete norm topology, then that topology is uniquely determined.*

It follows from the next theorem that all A*-algebras are semi-simple.

THEOREM (4.1.19). *Any *-subalgebra of an A*-algebra* $\mathfrak{A}$ *is semi-simple.*

PROOF. By Lemma (4.1.14), for every x in $\mathfrak{A}$, $|x|^2 \leqslant \nu_{\mathfrak{A}}(x^\star x)$. Let $\mathfrak{B}$ be a *-subalgebra of $\mathfrak{A}$ with radical $\mathfrak{R}_0$. If $q \in \mathfrak{R}_0$, then also $q^\star q \in \mathfrak{R}_0$. Since $\mathfrak{B}$ is a normed algebra, $q^\star q$ is topologically nilpotent. Therefore $\nu_{\mathfrak{A}}(q^\star q) = 0$, which implies $|q| = 0$ and hence $q = 0$. Thus $\mathfrak{R}_0 = (0)$ and $\mathfrak{B}$ is semi-simple.

This theorem, along with results in § 5 of Chapter II, enables us to strengthen Theorem (4.1.17).

THEOREM (4.1.20). *Let* $x \to x^\tau$ *be a homomorphism of an arbitrary Banach algebra* $\mathfrak{B}$ *into an A*-algebra* $\mathfrak{A}$. *If the image of* $\mathfrak{B}$ *in* $\mathfrak{A}$ *is a *-subalgebra of* $\mathfrak{A}$, *then the homomorphism is automatically continuous.*

PROOF. Since $\mathfrak{B}^\tau$ is a *-subalgebra of $\mathfrak{A}$, it is semi-simple by the preceding theorem. Therefore, by Corollary (2.5.15), the kernel of the homomorphism is a closed ideal $\mathfrak{K}$. It follows that $\mathfrak{B}^\tau$, which is isomorphic with $\mathfrak{B}/\mathfrak{K}$, is a Banach algebra under the norm $\|x^\tau\|_1 = \inf\|y\|$

for $y^\tau = x^\tau$. Since $\|x^\tau\|_1 \leqslant \|x\|$, the desired result follows immediately from Theorem (4.1.17).

The main results obtained in this section are due to the author [1, 2, 3]. Civin and Yood [3] make a systematic study of properties of involutions on a Banach algebra.

§ **2. Commutative ⋆-algebras.** Let $\mathfrak{A}$ be a complex commutative Banach algebra and let $x \to x^\star$ be any involution in $\mathfrak{A}$. For each φ in the carrier space $\Phi_{\mathfrak{A}}$, define $\varphi^\star$ by the relation

$$\hat{x}(\varphi^\star) = \overline{\hat{x}^\star(\varphi)}, \quad x \in \mathfrak{A}.$$

Then it is readily verified that $\varphi^\star$ is an element of $\Phi_{\mathfrak{A}}$ and that the mapping $\varphi \to \varphi^\star$ is a homeomorphism of $\Phi_{\mathfrak{A}}$ onto $\Phi_{\mathfrak{A}}$ with period two. We note in passing that this homeomorphism maps the Šilov boundary $\partial\Phi_{\mathfrak{A}}$ onto itself. In fact,

$$\max_{\varphi \in \partial\Phi_{\mathfrak{A}}} |\hat{x}(\varphi^\star)| = \max_{\varphi \in \partial\Phi_{\mathfrak{A}}} |\hat{x}^\star(\varphi)| = \nu_{\mathfrak{A}}(x^\star) = \nu_{\mathfrak{A}}(x)$$

for every $x \in \mathfrak{A}$. It follows that $(\partial\Phi_{\mathfrak{A}})^\star$ is a maximizing set for $\mathfrak{A}$ and accordingly $\partial\Phi_{\mathfrak{A}} \subseteq (\partial\Phi_{\mathfrak{A}})^\star$. Therefore $(\partial\Phi_{\mathfrak{A}})^\star \subseteq (\partial\Phi_{\mathfrak{A}})^{\star\star} = \partial\Phi_{\mathfrak{A}}$, so that $(\partial\Phi_{\mathfrak{A}})^\star = \partial\Phi_{\mathfrak{A}}$.

Now denote by $\Phi_{\mathfrak{A}}^{(\star)}$ the subset of $\Phi_{\mathfrak{A}}$ consisting of the fixed points of the homeomorphism $\varphi \to \varphi^\star$. Then $\Phi_{\mathfrak{A}}^{(\star)}$ is a closed subset of $\Phi_{\mathfrak{A}}$. It is obvious that $\Phi_{\mathfrak{A}}^{(\star)}$ consists precisely of those elements φ in $\Phi_{\mathfrak{A}}$ such that $\hat{x}^\star(\varphi) = \overline{\hat{x}(\varphi)}$, for every $x \in \mathfrak{A}$. Furthermore, since every element of $\mathfrak{A}$ can be written in the form $h+ik$ with h and k hermitian, it follows that φ belongs to $\Phi_{\mathfrak{A}}^{(\star)}$ if and only if $\hat{h}(\varphi)$ is real for every hermitian element h in $\mathfrak{A}$. Thus, in order for an involution to be hermitian, it is necessary and sufficient that $\Phi_{\mathfrak{A}}^{(\star)} = \Phi_{\mathfrak{A}}$. By Lemma (4.1.7), we also know that the involution will be hermitian if and only if the function $\hat{h}^2$ never assumes the value -1 on $\Phi_{\mathfrak{A}}$. A more subtle characterization of a hermitian involution in a commutative Banach ⋆-algebra is given in the following lemma.

Lemma (4.2.1). *In order for an involution $x \to x^\star$ in $\mathfrak{A}$ to be hermitian, it is necessary and sufficient that $\nu(x^\star x) = \nu(x)^2$ for every $x \in \mathfrak{A}$.*

Proof. If the involution is hermitian, then $\hat{x}^\star(\varphi) = \overline{\hat{x}(\varphi)}$ and we have

$$\widehat{(x^\star x)}(\varphi) = |\hat{x}(\varphi)|^2, \quad \varphi \in \Phi_{\mathfrak{A}}.$$

Therefore $\nu(x^\star x) = \nu(x)^2$, so that the condition is necessary.

Now assume that the condition is satisfied but that the involution is not hermitian. Then there exists a hermitian element h and a φ_0 in $\Phi_{\mathfrak{A}}$ such that $\hat{h}(\varphi_0) = \alpha+\beta i$, where α and β are real and $\beta \neq 0$. Set $\mu = \beta^{-1}\alpha$ and define $u = \beta^{-1}h$. Then u is hermitian and $\hat{u}(\varphi_0) = \mu+i$. Also choose e in $\mathfrak{A}$ such that $\hat{e}(\varphi_0) = 1$, and define

$$v = (u-\mu+ni)^m e,$$

where m and n are positive integers. Then

$$v^\star = (u-\mu-ni)^m e^\star, \qquad v^\star v = [(u-\mu)^2+n^2]^m e^\star e,$$

and

$$\hat{v}(\varphi_0) = i^m(1+n)^m, \qquad \hat{v}^\star(\varphi_0{}^\star) = (-i)^m(1+n)^m.$$

It follows that

$$(1+n)^m \leqslant \nu(v), \qquad (1+n)^m \leqslant \nu(v^\star).$$

Therefore

$$\begin{aligned}(1+n)^{2m} &\leqslant \nu(v^\star)\nu(v) = \nu(v^\star v) = \nu([(u-\mu)^2+n^2]^m e^\star e)\\ &\leqslant ([\nu(u)+|\mu|]^2+n^2)^m \nu(e^\star e).\end{aligned}$$

Hence

$$(1+n)^2 \leqslant ([\nu(u)+|\mu|]^2+n^2)(\nu(e^\star e))^{1/m}.$$

Letting $m \to \infty$, we obtain

$$(1+n)^2 \leqslant [\nu(u)+|\mu|^2]+n^2$$

or

$$1+2n \leqslant [\nu(u)+|\mu|]^2.$$

Since this inequality cannot hold for all n, we have a contradiction and so conclude that the involution is hermitian. This completes the proof.

The next theorem, which is due essentially to Gelfand and Naïmark [1], provides an abstract characterization of the algebra $C_0(\Omega)$, where Ω is a locally compact Hausdorff space. Note that $C_0(\Omega)$ is a $B^\star$-algebra with involution $f \to f^\star$ defined by the equation $f^\star(\omega) = \overline{f(\omega)}$, $\omega \in \Omega$.

THEOREM (4.2.2.). *Let $\mathfrak{A}$ be a complex commutative Banach $\star$-algebra which satisfies the weakened $B^\star$-condition $\|x^\star\|\,\|x\| \leqslant \beta\|x^\star x\|$. Then the mapping $x \to \hat{x}$ is a homeomorphic $\star$-isomorphism of $\mathfrak{A}$ onto $C_0(\Phi_{\mathfrak{A}})$. If $\beta = 1$, then $\mathfrak{A}$ is a $B^\star$-algebra and the isomorphism is an isometry.*

PROOF. For arbitrary positive integer n, we have

$$\|x^{\star n}\|\,\|x^n\| \leqslant \beta\|x^{\star n}x^n\| = \beta\|(x^\star x)^n\|.$$

Taking the nth root of this inequality and letting $n \to \infty$, we obtain $\nu(x^\star)\nu(x) \leqslant \nu(x^\star x)$. Since always $\nu(x^\star x) \leqslant \nu(x^\star)\nu(x)$ and $\nu(x^\star) = \nu(x)$, it follows that $\nu(x)^2 = \nu(x^\star x)$. Therefore, by Lemma (4.2.1), $\hat{x}^\star(\varphi) = \overline{\hat{x}(\varphi)}$ for $\varphi \in \Phi_{\mathfrak{A}}$ and $x \in \mathfrak{A}$. Hence the mapping $x \to \hat{x}$ is at least a $\star$-homomorphism of $\mathfrak{A}$ into $C_0(\Phi_{\mathfrak{A}})$. Moreover, the functions $\hat{x}$ separate strongly the points of $\Phi_{\mathfrak{A}}$ and so, by the Stone–Weierstrass Theorem (3.2.12), the image of $\mathfrak{A}$ is dense in $C_0(\Phi_{\mathfrak{A}})$.

If h is any hermitian element of $\mathfrak{A}$, then repeated application of the B*-condition leads to the inequality

$$\|h\| \leqslant \beta^{(2^n-1)/2^n}\|h^{2^n}\|^{1/2^n}, \quad n = 1, 2, \cdots.$$

Letting $n \to \infty$, we obtain $\|h\| \leqslant \beta\nu(h)$. Therefore

$$\|x^\star\|\,\|x\| \leqslant \beta\|x^\star x\| \leqslant \beta^2\nu(x^\star x) = \beta^2\nu(x)^2 \leqslant \beta^2\|x\|^2$$

and hence, in particular, $\|x^\star\| \leqslant \beta^2\|x\|$. Replacing x by $x^\star$, we obtain $\|x\| \leqslant \beta^2\|x^\star\|$, so that $\|x^2\| \leqslant \beta^2\|x^\star\|\,\|x\|$. It follows that $\|x\| \leqslant \beta^2\nu(x) \leqslant \beta^2\|x\|$, which means that $\nu(x)$ is a norm in $\mathfrak{A}$ and is equivalent to the given norm $\|x\|$. Thus, $x \to \hat{x}$ is a homeomorphism of $\mathfrak{A}$ into $C_0(\Phi_{\mathfrak{A}})$. Since $\mathfrak{A}$ is complete and the image of $\mathfrak{A}$ is dense in $C_0(\Phi_{\mathfrak{A}})$, it follows that $x \to \hat{x}$ maps $\mathfrak{A}$ onto $C_0(\Phi_{\mathfrak{A}})$. This proves the first statement of the theorem. Finally, if $\beta = 1$, then $\|x\| = \nu(x)$, so that $\mathfrak{A}$ is a B*-algebra, $x \to \hat{x}$ is an isometry, and the theorem is proved.

We obtain next a result of the above type for real algebras. It is due to Arens and Kaplansky [1]. Let Ω be a locally compact Hausdorff space and let $\omega \to \omega^\tau$ be a homeomorphism of Ω onto itself. Denote by $C_0(\Omega, \tau)$ the collection of all f in $C_0(\Omega)$ such that $f(\omega^\tau) = \overline{f(\omega)}$, for all $\omega \in \Omega$. Then $C_0(\Omega, \tau)$ is a closed real $\star$-subalgebra of $C_0(\Omega)$.

THEOREM (4.2.3). *Let $\mathfrak{A}$ be a real Banach $\star$-algebra such that $\|x\|^2 \leqslant \beta\|x^\star x + y^\star y\|$ for all x and y in $\mathfrak{A}$, where β is a constant. Then there exists an involutoric homeomorphism τ of $\Phi_{\mathfrak{A}}$ onto itself such that $x \to \hat{x}$ is a homeomorphic $\star$-isomorphism of $\mathfrak{A}$ onto $C_0(\Phi_{\mathfrak{A}}, \tau)$. If $\beta = 1$, then the isomorphism is an isometry.*

PROOF. Let $\mathfrak{A}_C$ be the complexification of $\mathfrak{A}$ and let $x+iy$ be an arbitrary element of $\mathfrak{A}_C$ with $x, y \in \mathfrak{A}$. Then $\mathfrak{A}_C$ is a $\star$-algebra under the involution $(x+iy)^\star = x^\star - iy^\star$. Since $\|x\|^2 \leqslant \beta\|x^\star x + y^\star y\|$ and also $\|y\|^2 \leqslant \beta\|x^\star x+y^\star y\|$, we have

$$\|x+iy\| \leqslant \|x\|+\|y\| \leqslant 2\beta^{1/2}\|x^\star x+y^\star y\|^{1/2}$$

and hence

$$\|x+iy\|^2 \leqslant 4\beta\|x^\star x+y^\star y\|.$$

Observe that

$$(x+iy)^\star(x+iy) = x^\star x+y^\star y+i(x^\star y-y^\star x).$$

Thus, by the proof of Theorem (1.3.2)

$$\|x^\star x+y^\star y\| \leqslant \sqrt{2}\|(x+iy)^\star(x+iy)\|$$

and therefore

$$\|x+iy\|^2 \leqslant 4\beta\sqrt{2}\|(x+iy)^\star(x+iy)\|.$$

In other words, $\mathfrak{A}_C$ satisfies the hypotheses of Theorem (4.2.2) and is homeomorphically $\star$-isomorphic with $C_0(\Phi_{\mathfrak{A}_C})$. By Theorem (3.1.4), $\Phi_{\mathfrak{A}}$ is homeomorphic with $\Phi_{\mathfrak{A}_C}$ under a mapping $\varphi \to \varphi'$ such that $\hat{x}(\varphi) = \hat{x}(\varphi')$ for every $x \in \mathfrak{A}$. Hence $C_0(\Phi_{\mathfrak{A}_C}) = C_0(\Phi_{\mathfrak{A}})$, and it only remains to identify the image of $\mathfrak{A}$ in $C_0(\Phi_{\mathfrak{A}})$. We have

$$\widehat{(x+iy)}^\star(\varphi') = \overline{\widehat{(x+iy)}(\varphi')} = \overline{\hat{x}(\varphi)}-i\overline{\hat{y}(\varphi)}.$$

Also, since $(x+iy)^\star = x^\star - iy^\star$, we have

$$\overline{\hat{x}(\varphi)}-i\overline{\hat{y}(\varphi)} = \widehat{x^\star}(\varphi)-i\widehat{y^\star}(\varphi).$$

This holds for all $x, y \in \mathfrak{A}$. Taking $y = 0$, we obtain $\widehat{x^\star}(\varphi) = \overline{\hat{x}(\varphi)}$. Therefore $x \to \hat{x}$ is a $\star$-isomorphism of $\mathfrak{A}$ into $C_0(\Phi_{\mathfrak{A}})$. Now define φ^τ by the relation $\hat{x}(\varphi^\tau) = \overline{\hat{x}(\varphi)}$. Then φ^τ is clearly an element of $\Phi_{\mathfrak{A}}$ and the mapping $\varphi \to \varphi^\tau$ is an involutoric homeomorphism of $\Phi_{\mathfrak{A}}$ onto itself. We have already shown that the image of $\mathfrak{A}$ in $C_0(\Phi_{\mathfrak{A}})$ is contained in $C_0(\Phi_{\mathfrak{A}}, \tau)$. On the other hand, let f be an arbitrary element of $C_0(\Phi_{\mathfrak{A}}, \tau)$. Since $f \in C_0(\Phi_{\mathfrak{A}})$, there exist u, v in $\mathfrak{A}$ such that

$$f(\varphi) = \hat{u}(\varphi)+i\hat{v}(\varphi), \quad \varphi \in \Phi_{\mathfrak{A}}.$$

Since $f(\varphi^\tau) = \overline{f(\varphi)}$, we have

$$\hat{u}(\varphi^\tau)+i\hat{v}(\varphi^\tau) = \overline{\hat{u}(\varphi)}-i\overline{\hat{v}(\varphi)}.$$

But also, $\hat{u}(\varphi^\tau) = \overline{\hat{u}(\varphi)}$ and $\hat{v}(\varphi^\tau) = \overline{\hat{v}(\varphi)}$. Hence

$$\overline{\hat{u}(\varphi)}+i\overline{\hat{v}(\varphi)} = \overline{\hat{u}(\varphi)}-i\overline{\hat{v}(\varphi)}.$$

This implies $\hat{v}(\varphi) = 0$. In other words, $f(\varphi) = \hat{u}(\varphi)$ for all $\varphi \in \Phi_{\mathfrak{A}}$.

Therefore the image of $\mathfrak{A}$ exhausts $C_0(\Phi_{\mathfrak{A}}, \tau)$. If $\beta = 1$, then $\|x\| = \nu_{\mathfrak{A}_C}(x) = \nu_{\mathfrak{A}}(x)$ for $x \in \mathfrak{A}$, so that $x \to \hat{x}$ is an isometry and the theorem is proved.

THEOREM (4.2.4). *Let $\mathfrak{A}$ be a complex commutative $B^\star$-algebra and let $\mathfrak{I}$ be a closed ideal in $\mathfrak{A}$. Then $\mathfrak{I} = k(h(\mathfrak{I}))$, $\mathfrak{I}$ is a $\star$-ideal, and $\mathfrak{A}/\mathfrak{I}$ is isometrically $\star$-isomorphic with $C_0(h(\mathfrak{I}))$.*

PROOF. The fact that $\mathfrak{A}$ can be identified with $C_0(\Phi_{\mathfrak{A}})$ implies that $\mathfrak{A}$ is completely regular in the sense of Chapter II, § 7 (see also Chapter III, § 7). Therefore, by Corollary (2.7.20), if U is any open set in $\Phi_{\mathfrak{A}}$ which contains $h(\mathfrak{I})$ and has compact complement, then $k(U) \subseteq \mathfrak{I}$. Therefore, if we denote by $\mathfrak{I}_0$ the sum of all these ideals $k(U)$, then $\mathfrak{I}_0 \subseteq \mathfrak{I}$. Since $\mathfrak{I} \subseteq k(h(\mathfrak{I}))$, the conclusion $\mathfrak{I} = k(h(\mathfrak{I}))$ will follow if we prove that the closure of $\mathfrak{I}_0$ exhausts $k(h(\mathfrak{I}))$. Let $c \in k(h(\mathfrak{I}))$ and, for $\epsilon > 0$, define $U = \{\varphi : |\hat{c}(\varphi)| < \epsilon\}$. Then U is open, contains $h(\mathfrak{I})$, and has a compact complement. For any $\varphi \in \Phi_{\mathfrak{A}}$, write $\hat{c}(\varphi) = \rho e^{i\theta}$, where $\rho \geqslant 0$, and define

$$g(\varphi) = \begin{cases} 0 & \varphi \in U \\ (\rho - \epsilon)e^{i\theta}, & \varphi \notin U. \end{cases}$$

Then g is continuous on $\Phi_{\mathfrak{A}}$. Hence there exists $u \in \mathfrak{A}$ such that $\hat{u}(\varphi) = g(\varphi)$, $\varphi \in \Phi_{\mathfrak{A}}$. Obviously, $u \in k(h(\mathfrak{I}))$ and $\|u - c\| \leqslant \epsilon$. Therefor the closure of $\mathfrak{I}_0$ is equal to $k(h(\mathfrak{I}))$ and hence $\mathfrak{I} = k(h(\mathfrak{I}))$.

Consider next the $\star$-homomorphism $c \to \hat{c}'$ of $\mathfrak{A}$ *onto* $C_0(h(\mathfrak{I}))$ obtained by associating with c the restriction $\hat{c}'$ of the function $\hat{c}$ to the set $h(\mathfrak{I})$. It is obvious that the kernel of this homomorphism is equal to $k(h(\mathfrak{I})) = \mathfrak{I}$. Therefore, if c' denotes the image $c + \mathfrak{I}$ of c in $\mathfrak{A}/\mathfrak{I}$, then $c' \to \hat{c}'$ is a $\star$-isomorphism of $\mathfrak{A}/\mathfrak{I}$ with $C_0(h(\mathfrak{I}))$. It only remains to show that

$$\|c'\| = \inf_{m \in \mathfrak{I}} \|c + m\| = \max_{\varphi \in h(\mathfrak{I})} |\hat{c}(\varphi)| = \|\hat{c}'\|.$$

Since $c' \to \hat{c}'$ is actually the Gelfand representation of $\mathfrak{A}/\mathfrak{I}$, it is immediate that $\|\hat{c}'\| \leqslant \|c'\|$. On the other hand, for arbitrary $\epsilon > 0$, define $G = \{\varphi : |\hat{c}(\varphi)| < \|\hat{c}'\| + \epsilon\}$. Then G is open and contains $h(\mathfrak{I})$. Next choose $u \in \mathfrak{A}$ such that $0 \leqslant \hat{u}(\varphi) \leqslant 1$ for all φ, $\hat{u}(\varphi) = 1$ for $\varphi \in h(\mathfrak{I})$, and $\hat{u}(\varphi) = 0$ for $\varphi \notin G$. Then $c - cu \in \mathfrak{I}$ and we have

$$\|c'\| = \|c'u'\| \leqslant \|cu\| = \max_{\varphi \in \Phi_{\mathfrak{A}}} |\hat{c}(\varphi)\hat{u}(\varphi)|$$

$$\leqslant \sup_{\varphi \in G} |\hat{c}(\varphi)| \leqslant \|\hat{c}'\| + \epsilon.$$

It follows that $\|c'\| \leqslant \|\hat{c}'\|$, which completes the proof.

In the notation of Definition (2.7.17), the ideal $\mathfrak{J}_0$ in the above proof is equal to $J(\hbar(\mathfrak{J}), \infty)$. Since every closed set in $\Phi_{\mathfrak{A}}$ is a hull, we have the following result.

COROLLARY (4.2.5). *For every closed set F in $\Phi_{\mathfrak{A}}$, $\overline{J(F, \infty)} = \mathfrak{k}(F)$.*

The ideal $J(F, \infty)$ consists of all $x \in \mathfrak{A}$ such that $\hat{x}$ vanishes in some neighborhood of F and outside some compact set. If F is vacuous, then $J(F, \infty)$ is the ideal $J(\infty)$ of all $x \in \mathfrak{A}$ such that $\hat{x}$ vanishes outside some compact set. Since $J(\infty)$ is obviously a proper ideal if φ_∞ is not an isolated point of $\Phi_{\mathfrak{A}}^\infty$ (that is, if $\mathfrak{A}$ does not possess an identity element), we obtain the following result.

COROLLARY (4.2.6). *If $\mathfrak{A}$ does not possess an identity element, then $J(\infty)$ is a proper ideal in $\mathfrak{A}$ which is not contained in any maximal ideal.*

Lemma (4.2.1) is due essentially to Gelfand and Naĭmark [1]. The proof given here reduces to a proof of Arens [1; 4] when $\mathfrak{A}$ has an identity element. Theorem (4.2.4) is due essentially to Stone [1, Theorem 85], Arens [5] has extended the result in Theorem [4.2.3] to certain non-commutative real Banach $\star$-algebras. The algebras considered are called $BQ^\star$-ALGEBRAS and the resulting representation is an algebra of continuous quaternion-valued functions on a compact Hausdorff space. Further generalizations have been made by Arens and Kaplansky [1].

§ **3. Self-dual vector spaces and $\star$-representations.** In the case of $\star$-algebras, it is desirable to consider representations on certain special vector spaces in order to exploit fully the properties of the involution. These vector spaces are described in the following definition.

DEFINITION (4.3.1). *A complex vector space $\mathfrak{X}$ is said to be* SELF-DUAL *provided there exists a function defined on $\mathfrak{X} \times \mathfrak{X}$ to the complexes, whose value on the pair x, y will be denoted by (x, y) and which satisfies the following conditions:*

(*i*) $(x, y) = 0$, *for every y, implies $x = 0$.*

(*ii*) (x, y) *is linear in x for each fixed y.*

(*iii*) $(x, y) = \overline{(y, x)}$, *for all x and y.*

If the space $\mathfrak{X}$ is also normed, then it is called a NORMED SELF-DUAL *space provided (x, y) satisfies the additional condition,*

(*iv*) *there exists a constant β, called a* BOUND *for (x, y), independent of x and y such that $|(x, y)| \leqslant \beta\|x\|\,\|y\|$, for all x and y.*

The function (x, y) is called a SCALAR PRODUCT in $\mathfrak{X}$. Condition (iv) means that (x, y) is a continuous function on $\mathfrak{X} \times \mathfrak{X}$. Observe that, if $\mathfrak{X}$ is a Banach space, then by the Uniform Boundedness theorem a sufficient condition for (iv) to hold is that (x, y) be continuous in x and y separately. By virtue of condition (i), the scalar product is called NON-DEGENERATE. Condition (iii) implies that the number (x, x) is necessarily real although it can be negative or zero. In case the scalar product is positive (that is, $(x, x) \geqslant 0$ for all x), then a standard proof yields a Cauchy–Schwartz inequality: $|(x, y)|^2 \leqslant (x, x)(y, y)$. From the non-degeneracy, it follows that positivity already implies positive definiteness (that is, $(x, x) > 0$ for $x \neq 0$). Thus, if the scalar product is positive, then it is an inner product and $\mathfrak{X}$ is a pre-Hilbert space. We note in passing that if $(x, x) = 0$ implies $x = 0$, then the scalar product is automatically definite (that is, either $(x, x) > 0$ for all x or $(x, x) < 0$ for all x). Conditions (ii) and (iii) imply that (x, y) is conjugate linear in y for each fixed x; in other words, (x, y) is additive in y but $(x, \alpha y) = \bar{\alpha}(x, y)$. The relation $f_y(x) = (x, y)$ defines a linear functional f_y on the linear vector space $\mathfrak{X}$. These functionals will be bounded if $\mathfrak{X}$ is normed self-dual. The mapping $y \rightarrow f_y$ of $\mathfrak{X}$ into the vector space of linear functionals on $\mathfrak{X}$ is conjugate linear, since (x, y) is conjugate linear in y, and is one-to-one, since the scalar product is non-degenerate. Two normed self-dual spaces are called EQUIVALENT if there exists a linear isomorphism between them which takes scalar product into scalar product and is a homeomorphism with respect to the norms.

Assume, for the moment, that the scalar product (x, y) is degenerate (that is, condition (i) is not satisfied) and set

$$\mathfrak{N} = \{x : (x, y) = 0 \quad \text{for every} \quad y \in \mathfrak{X}\}.$$

Then $\mathfrak{N}$ is obviously a linear subspace of $\mathfrak{X}$ and, in the normed case, is also closed. Now form the difference space $\mathfrak{X}' = \mathfrak{X} - \mathfrak{N}$ and denote by x' the element $x + \mathfrak{N}$ of $\mathfrak{X}'$. For arbitrary x' and y' in $\mathfrak{X}'$, define

$$(x', y') = (x, y).$$

If $x'_1 = x'$, then $x_1 = x + n$, where $n \in \mathfrak{N}$, and we have

$$(x'_1, y') = (x+n, y) = (x, y) + (n, y) = (x, y).$$

Therefore the definition of (x', y') depends only on the equivalence class x' and not on x. Similarly, (x', y') depends on y' but not on y.

If x' is an element of $\mathfrak{X}'$ such that $(x', y') = 0$ for every y' in $\mathfrak{X}'$, then it follows that $(x, y) = 0$ for every y in $\mathfrak{X}$. Therefore $x \in \mathfrak{N}$, so that $x' = 0$. In other words (x', y') is non-degenerate in $\mathfrak{X}'$. Since (x', y') clearly satisfies conditions (ii) and (iii) it is a non-degenerate scalar product in $\mathfrak{X}'$. Moreover, in the normed case, since $\mathfrak{N}$ is closed, the space $\mathfrak{X}'$ is normed with $\|x'\| = \inf\|x+n\|$, $n \in \mathfrak{N}$. Hence

$$|(x', y')| = |(x+n_1, y+n_2)| \leqslant \beta\|x+n_1\| \|y+n_2\|$$

for an arbitrary n_1 and n_2 in $\mathfrak{N}$. Taking the infimum over n_1 and n_2 on the right, we obtain $|(x', y')| \leqslant \beta\|x'\| \|y'\|$. Therefore the scalar product is bounded and $\mathfrak{X}'$ is a normed self-dual space.

DEFINITION (4.3.2). *Let T be a (bounded) linear operator on the (normed) self-dual space $\mathfrak{X}$. Then a (bounded) linear operator $T^\star$ on $\mathfrak{X}$ such that*

$$(Tx, y) = (x, T^\star y),$$

for all x and y in $\mathfrak{X}$, is called the ADJOINT *of T with respect to the scalar product (x, y).*

Note that the non-degeneracy of the scalar product ensures the uniqueness of $T^\star$ if it exists. Furthermore, if $T^\star$ exists, then $(T^\star)^\star$ exists and is equal to T. The collection of all T such that $T^\star$ exists is clearly an algebra of linear operators on $\mathfrak{X}$ and has $T \to T^\star$ as an involution. Recall that, if $\mathfrak{X}$ is a Hilbert space with inner product (x, y), then $T^\star$ exists for every T in $\mathscr{B}(\mathfrak{X})$. In fact, for this case, existence of the adjoint is equivalent to boundedness for any linear operator on $\mathfrak{X}$. If $\mathfrak{X}$ is a Banach space, then existence of the adjoint still implies boundedness. In fact, let T be any linear operator on $\mathfrak{X}$ such that $T^\star$ exists. If $\{x_n\}$ is a sequence of elements of $\mathfrak{X}$ such that $x_n \to 0$ while $Tx_n \to y$ relative to the norm in $\mathfrak{X}$, then, since the scalar product is continuous,

$$0 = \lim_{n\to\infty} (x_n, T^\star x) = \lim_{n\to\infty} (Tx_n, x) = (y, x)$$

for all $x \in \mathfrak{X}$. Therefore $y = 0$ and continuity of T follows from the closed graph theorem.

DEFINITION (4.3.3). *Let $\mathfrak{A}$ be a (normed) $\star$-algebra and $\mathfrak{X}$ a (normed) self-dual space. Then a (normed) representation $a \to T_a$ of $\mathfrak{A}$ on $\mathfrak{X}$ is called a* $\star$-REPRESENTATION *provided $T_a{}^\star$ exists and is equal to $T_{a^\star}$ for every $a \in \mathfrak{A}$.*

We need to construct a direct sum of $\star$-representations. In order to do this, it is necessary first to construct a direct sum of self-dual spaces. We restrict attention to the normed case. Let $\{\mathfrak{X}_\lambda : \lambda \in \Lambda\}$ be a family of normed self-dual spaces whose scalar products are uniformly bounded in the sense that there exists a constant β independent of λ such that

$$|(x_\lambda, y_\lambda)| \leqslant \beta \|x_\lambda\| \, \|y_\lambda\|$$

for all vectors x_λ and y_λ in $\mathfrak{X}_\lambda$. Denote by $\Sigma^{(2)}\mathfrak{X}_\lambda$ the collection of all functions f defined on Λ such that $f(\lambda)$ is in $\mathfrak{X}_\lambda$ for each λ and

$$\|f\| = \Big(\sum_{\lambda \in \Lambda} \|f(\lambda)\|^2\Big)^{1/2} < \infty.$$

For $f, g \in \Sigma^{(2)}\mathfrak{X}_\lambda$ and α a scalar, define

$$(\alpha f)(\lambda) = \alpha f(\lambda), \qquad (f+g)(\lambda) = f(\lambda)+g(\lambda).$$

Then it is not difficult to show that

$$\|\alpha f\| = |\alpha| \, \|f\|, \qquad \|f+g\| \leqslant \|f\|+\|g\|,$$

so that $\Sigma^{(2)}\mathfrak{X}_\lambda$ is a normed linear space. Furthermore, if each $\mathfrak{X}_\lambda$ is a Banach space, then $\Sigma^{(2)}\mathfrak{X}_\lambda$ is also a Banach space. Finally, if

$$(f, g) = \sum (f(\lambda), g(\lambda)),$$

where $(f(\lambda), g(\lambda))$ is the given scalar product in $\mathfrak{X}_\lambda$, then

$$|(f, g)| \leqslant \beta \|f\| \, \|g\|,$$

and it follows that $\Sigma^{(2)}\mathfrak{X}_\lambda$ is normed self-dual with (f, g) as its scalar product. Observe that, if the scalar product in each of the spaces $\mathfrak{X}_\lambda$ is positive definite, then (f, g) is also positive definite.

Now, for each λ in Λ, let $a \to T_a^{(\lambda)}$ be a $\star$-representation of the $\star$-algebra $\mathfrak{A}$ on the self-dual space $\mathfrak{X}_\lambda$. For any f in $\Sigma^{(2)}\mathfrak{X}_\lambda$, define

$$(T_a f)(\lambda) = T_a^{(\lambda)} f(\lambda), \quad \lambda \in \Lambda.$$

If it happens that $T_a f$ belongs to $\Sigma^{(2)}\mathfrak{X}_\lambda$, for every $a \in \mathfrak{A}$ and $f \in \Sigma^{(2)}\mathfrak{X}_\lambda$, then $a \to T_a$ is clearly a representation of $\mathfrak{A}$ on $\Sigma^{(2)}\mathfrak{X}_\lambda$. Moreover,

$$\begin{aligned}(T_a f, g) &= \sum (T_a^{(\lambda)} f(\lambda), g(\lambda)) \\ &= \sum (f(\lambda), T_{a^\star}^{(\lambda)} g(\lambda)) = (f, T_{a^\star} g)\end{aligned}$$

for all f and g in $\Sigma^{(2)}\mathfrak{X}_\lambda$. In other words, $a \to T_a$ is a $\star$-representation.

If $\mathfrak{A}$ is normed and the representations $a \to T_a^{(\lambda)}$ are continuous uniformly in λ, in the sense there exists for each $a \in \mathfrak{A}$ a constant γ_a independent of λ such that

$$\|T_a^{(\lambda)}\| \leqslant \gamma_a, \quad \lambda \in \Lambda,$$

then the above situation prevails. In fact,

$$\sum \|(T_a f)(\lambda)\|^2 = \sum \|T_a^{(\lambda)} f(\lambda)\|^2 \leqslant \gamma_a^2 \sum \|f(\lambda)\|^2,$$

so that $T_a f \in \Sigma^{(2)}\mathfrak{X}_\lambda$ for all $a \in \mathfrak{A}$ and $f \in \Sigma^{(2)}\mathfrak{X}_\lambda$. Therefore the representation $a \to T_a$ is defined and furthermore $\|T_a\| \leqslant \gamma_a$, $a \in \mathfrak{A}$. An important special case is obtained when there exists a constant γ, independent of $a \in \mathfrak{A}$ and $\lambda \in \Lambda$, such that $\|T_a^{(\lambda)}\| \leqslant \gamma \|a\|$.

DEFINITION (4.3.4). *The representation $a \to T_a$ on $\Sigma^{(2)}\mathfrak{X}_\lambda$, when it is defined, is called the* DIRECT SUM *of the representations $a \to T_a^{(\lambda)}$, $\lambda \in \Lambda$.*

The next problem is the construction of $\star$-representations for a given $\star$-algebra $\mathfrak{A}$. This is done by means of certain linear functionals on $\mathfrak{A}$. Consider first any $\star$-representation of $\mathfrak{A}$ on a self-dual space $\mathfrak{X}$. Let f_0 be a fixed vector in $\mathfrak{X}$ and define

$$F(a) = (T_a f_0, f_0), \quad a \in \mathfrak{A}.$$

Then F is obviously a linear functional on $\mathfrak{A}$. Moreover, since

$$(T_{a^\star} f_0, f_0) = (f_0, T_a f_0) = \overline{(T_a f_0, f_0)},$$

it follows that F has the property

$$F(a^\star) = \overline{F(a)}, \quad a \in \mathfrak{A}.$$

Any linear functional on $\mathfrak{A}$ with this property will be called HERMITIAN. If $\mathfrak{A}$ and $\mathfrak{X}$ are normed and the representation is strongly continuous, with $\|T_a f\| \leqslant \gamma(f)\|a\|$, then

$$|F(a)| = |(T_a f_0, f_0)| \leqslant \beta\gamma(f_0)\|f_0\|\,\|a\|,$$

for all $a \in \mathfrak{A}$. Thus F is also a bounded functional. As will be seen below, this situation is typical in that essentially every hermitian functional can be obtained in this way. The algebra $\mathfrak{A}$ is assumed throughout the remainder of this section to be a complex $\star$-algebra.

Now let F_0 be any linear functional on the real vector space $\mathscr{H}_{\mathfrak{A}}$ of the hermitian elements of $\mathfrak{A}$; that is, $h \to F_0(h)$ is a linear mapping of

$\mathscr{H}_{\mathfrak{A}}$ into the real numbers. If x is any element of $\mathfrak{A}$ with hermitian components h and k, define

$$F(x) = F_0(h) + iF_0(k).$$

Then it is readily verified that F is a hermitian linear functional on $\mathfrak{A}$; that is, $x \to F(x)$ is a linear mapping of $\mathfrak{A}$ as a complex vector space into the complex numbers, such that $F(x^\star) = \overline{F(x)}$. Moreover, if $\mathfrak{A}$ is $\star$-normed and F_0 is bounded, with bound $\|F_0\|$, then the extension F of F_0 to $\mathfrak{A}$ is also bounded. In fact,

$$\begin{aligned} |F(x)| &= \left| F_0\left(\frac{x+x^\star}{2}\right) + iF_0\left(\frac{x-x^\star}{2i}\right) \right| \\ &\leqslant \|F_0\|\left(\left\|\frac{x+x^\star}{2}\right\| + \left\|\frac{x-x^\star}{2i}\right\|\right) \\ &\leqslant \frac{\|F_0\|}{2}(2\|x\| + 2\|x^\star\|) = 2\|F_0\|\,\|x\|. \end{aligned}$$

Therefore, if $\|F\|$ is the bound of F on $\mathfrak{A}$, then $\|F\| \leqslant 2\|F_0\| \leqslant 2\|F\|$. Note that F_0 is obtained from F by restriction to $\mathscr{H}_{\mathfrak{A}}$.

Now let F' be any complex linear functional on $\mathfrak{A}$ and denote by F'_0 its restriction to $\mathscr{H}_{\mathfrak{A}}$. In general, F' will assume complex values on $\mathscr{H}_{\mathfrak{A}}$, so that F'_0 will not be a linear functional on $\mathscr{H}_{\mathfrak{A}}$ as a real vector space. On the other hand, if F' does assume only real values on $\mathscr{H}_{\mathfrak{A}}$, then F'_0 is a linear functional on the real space $\mathscr{H}_{\mathfrak{A}}$ and, if $\mathfrak{A}$ is $\star$-normed, is bounded on $\mathscr{H}_{\mathfrak{A}}$ if and only if F' is bounded on $\mathfrak{A}$.

Lemma (4.3.5). *In order for a linear functional F on $\mathfrak{A}$ to assume only real values on $\mathscr{H}_{\mathfrak{A}}$ it is necessary and sufficient that it be hermitian. Conversely, if $F(u)$ is real for every (bounded) hermitian functional F, then the element u is hermitian.*

Proof. If $h^\star = h$, then the hermitian condition implies $F(h) = \overline{F(h)}$, so that $F(h)$ is real and the sufficiency is proved. On the other hand, let x be any element of $\mathfrak{A}$ with hermitian components h and k. Then $x = h + ik$ and $x^\star = h - ik$. If F assumes real values on $\mathscr{H}_{\mathfrak{A}}$, then

$$F(x^\star) = F(h) - iF(k) = \overline{F(h) + iF(k)} = \overline{F(x)}.$$

Therefore F is hermitian and the first statement is proved. Now, if $F(u)$ is real for every (bounded) hermitian functional F and $u = h + ik$, where h and k are hermitian, then $F(k) = 0$ for every such F. Therefore $F_0(k) = 0$ for every (bounded) linear functional on $\mathscr{H}_{\mathfrak{A}}$. This clearly implies $k = 0$ and completes the proof.

It is obvious that the hermitian functionals on $\mathfrak{A}$ constitute a real linear subspace of the complex space of all linear functionals on $\mathfrak{A}$. If F is any hermitian functional on $\mathfrak{A}$, denote by F_0 the restriction of F to $\mathscr{H}_{\mathfrak{A}}$. Then the mapping $F \to F_0$ is a linear isomorphism of the space of all hermitian functionals on $\mathfrak{A}$ with the space of all linear functionals on the real space $\mathscr{H}_{\mathfrak{A}}$. For bounded functionals on a $\star$-normed algebra, this isomorphism is a homeomorphism with $\|F\| \leqslant 2\|F_0\| \leqslant 2\|F\|$. Note that in this case the bounded hermitian functionals constitute a closed subspace of the space of all bounded linear functionals on $\mathfrak{A}$.

LEMMA (4.3.6). *Every linear functional F on $\mathfrak{A}$ can be written uniquely in the form $F = F_1 + iF_2$, where F_1 and F_2 are hermitian. In fact, F_1 and F_2 are given by*

$$F_1(x) = \tfrac{1}{2}[F(x) + \overline{F(x^\star)}], \quad F_2(x) = [F(x) - \overline{F(x^\star)}]/2i.$$

PROOF. It is straightforward to verify that F_1 and F_2 as defined are hermitian and that $F = F_1 + iF_2$. On the other hand, let $F = F'_1 + iF'_2$ be any decomposition of F with F'_1 and F'_2 hermitian. Then

$$F(x^\star) = F'_1(x^\star) + iF'_2(x^\star) = \overline{F'_1(x)} + i\overline{F'_2(x)}.$$

Therefore $\overline{F(x^\star)} = F'_1(x) - iF'_2(x)$ and we obtain

$$F(x) + \overline{F(x^\star)} = 2F'_1(x), \quad F(x) - \overline{F(x^\star)} = 2iF'_2(x).$$

This gives $F'_1 = F_1$ and $F'_2 = F_2$ and completes the proof.

Consider any hermitian functional F on $\mathfrak{A}$. For any pair of elements x and y in $\mathfrak{A}$, define

$$(x, y) = F(y^\star x).$$

Then (x, y) is clearly a scalar product on $\mathfrak{A}$. However, this scalar product is in general degenerate, so that a reduction is necessary to obtain non-degeneracy. To this end, define

$$\mathfrak{L}_F = \{x : F(y^\star x) = 0 \quad \text{for every} \quad y \in \mathfrak{A}\}.$$

Then $\mathfrak{L}_F$ is obviously a left ideal in $\mathfrak{A}$. Let $\mathfrak{X}_F = \mathfrak{A} - \mathfrak{L}_F$ and set

$x' = x+\mathfrak{L}_F$. Then $\mathfrak{X}_F$ is a self-dual vector space under the scalar product

$$(x', y') = F(y^\star x).$$

When $\mathfrak{A}$ is normed and F is bounded, the ideal $\mathfrak{L}_F$ is closed and $\inf \|x+m\|$, for $m \in \mathfrak{L}_F$, defines a norm $\|x'\|$ for $\mathfrak{X}_F$. Furthermore, since

$$|(x', y')| \leqslant \|F\| \|x+m\| \|(y+n)^\star\|, \quad |(x', y')| \leqslant \|F\| \|(x+m)^\star\| \|y+n\|,$$

for all m, $n \in \mathfrak{L}_F$, it follows that the scalar product is continuous in x' and y' separately. Therefore, if $\mathfrak{A}$ is a Banach algebra, then $\mathfrak{X}_F$ is normed self-dual. If the involution is continuous, then it follows immediately from the above inequalities that $\mathfrak{X}_F$ is normed self-dual even without completeness.

THEOREM (4.3.7). *Let F be any hermitian functional on the algebra $\mathfrak{A}$. Then there exists a self-dual vector space $\mathfrak{X}$ and a $\star$-representation $a \to T_a$ of $\mathfrak{A}$ on $\mathfrak{X}$ such that*

$$F(a) = (T_a f_0, f_0), \quad a \in \mathfrak{A},$$

where f_0 is a fixed vector in $\mathfrak{X}$. If $\mathfrak{A}$ is $\star$-normed and F is bounded, then $\mathfrak{X}$ is normed self-dual, $a \to T_a$ is a normed representation and $\|T_a\| \leqslant \|a\|$ for all $a \in \mathfrak{A}$.

PROOF. Assume first that $\mathfrak{A}$ has an identity element and take $\mathfrak{X}$ as the self-dual space $\mathfrak{X}_F$ constructed above. Also, let $a \to T_a$ be the representation of $\mathfrak{A}$ induced on $\mathfrak{X}_F$ by the left regular representation of $\mathfrak{A}$. Thus, $T_a x' = (ax)'$. When $\mathfrak{A}$ is $\star$-normed and F is bounded, $\mathfrak{X}_F$ is a normed self-dual space and $\|T_a\| \leqslant \|a\|$ for all $a \in \mathfrak{A}$. Furthermore

$$(T_a x', y') = F(y^\star ax) = F((a^\star y)^\star x) = (x', T_{a^\star} y'),$$

so that $a \to T_a$ is a $\star$-representation. Taking $f_0 = 1'$, we have

$$(T_a f_0, f_0) = (a', 1') = F(a)$$

and the theorem is proved when $\mathfrak{A}$ has an identity element. If $\mathfrak{A}$ does not have an identity element, adjoin one to obtain $\mathfrak{A}_1$, and extend the involution to $\mathfrak{A}_1$ by the definition $(\alpha+x)^\star = \bar{\alpha}+x^\star$. Note that, if $\mathfrak{A}$ is $\star$-normed, then so is $\mathfrak{A}_1$. The definition $F(\alpha+x) = \alpha+F(x)$ also extends the functional F to $\mathfrak{A}_1$. Since

$$F(\bar{\alpha}+x^\star) = \bar{\alpha}+F(x^\star) = \bar{\alpha}+\overline{F(x)} = \overline{F(\alpha+x)},$$

the extension of F is hermitian on $\mathfrak{A}_1$, and is bounded if F is bounded.

This reduces the problem to the case in which there is an identity element and completes the proof of the theorem.

From the way in which f_0 was chosen, we have immediately the following corollary.

COROLLARY (4.3.8). *If $\mathfrak{A}$ has an identity element, then the vector f_0 in the above theorem is strictly cyclic for the representation $a \to T_a$. If $\mathfrak{A}$ does not have an identity element, then the set $\{T_a f_0 : a \in \mathfrak{A}\}$ is a maximal linear subspace of $\mathfrak{X}$ which omits the vector f_0.*

We arrive now at the main result of this section. It is due essentially to Schatz [1].

THEOREM (4.3.9). *Let $\mathfrak{A}$ be any complex $\star$-normed algebra. Then there exists a normed self-dual space $\mathfrak{X}$ and a $\star$-representation $a \to T_a$ of $\mathfrak{A}$ on $\mathfrak{X}$ which is a homeomorphism of $\mathfrak{A}$ into $\mathscr{B}(\mathfrak{X})$ such that $\|a\| \leqslant 2\|T_a\| \leqslant 2\|a\|$ for all $a \in \mathfrak{A}$, and $\|T_h\| = \|h\|$ for $h \in \mathscr{H}_{\mathfrak{A}}$.*

PROOF. Since the specified properties of the representation are preserved in passing to a $\star$-subalgebra, it will be sufficient to make the proof for the case in which $\mathfrak{A}$ has an identity element.

Denote by $\{F_\lambda : \lambda \in \Lambda\}$ the set of all hermitian functionals on $\mathfrak{A}$ with norm equal to one. Let $\mathfrak{X}_\lambda$ be the normed self-dual space $\mathfrak{X}_{F_\lambda}$ associated with the hermitian functional F_λ. If x_λ and y_λ are elements of $\mathfrak{X}_\lambda$, then

$$|(x_\lambda, y_\lambda)| = |F_\lambda(y^\star x)| \leqslant \|x\|\,\|y\|,$$

where x and y are any elements of $\mathfrak{A}$ in the equivalence classes x_λ and y_λ respectively. Taking the infimum over all such x and y, we obtain

$$|(x_\lambda, y_\lambda)| \leqslant \|x_\lambda\|\,\|y_\lambda\|.$$

In other words, the scalar products in the spaces $\mathfrak{X}_\lambda$ are uniformly bounded with 1 as a common bound. Therefore the direct sum $\mathfrak{X} = \Sigma^{(2)}\mathfrak{X}_\lambda$ is defined and $|(f, g)| \leqslant \|f\|\,\|g\|$ for all f and g in $\mathfrak{X}$. Now let $a \to T_a{}^{(\lambda)}$ be the $\star$-representation of $\mathfrak{A}$ on $\mathfrak{X}_\lambda$ obtained in Theorem (4.3.7). Since $\|T_a{}^{(\lambda)}\| \leqslant \|a\|$ for all $a \in \mathfrak{A}$ and $\lambda \in \Lambda$, it follows that the direct sum of these representations is a $\star$-representation $a \to T_a$ of $\mathfrak{A}$ on $\mathfrak{X}$ also with the property $\|T_a\| \leqslant \|a\|$. It remains to show that this representation has the properties specified in the theorem.

For any element h in $\mathscr{H}_{\mathfrak{A}}$, the Hahn–Banach extension theorem provides the existence of a linear functional F on $\mathfrak{A}$ such that $\|F\| = 1$

and $F(h) = \|h\|$. Consider the hermitian functional F_1 defined by the relation

$$F_1(x) = \frac{F(x)+F(x^\star)}{2}, \quad x \in \mathfrak{A}.$$

It is obvious that $F_1(h) = \|h\|$ and hence that $\|F_1\| \geqslant 1$. Moreover, since $\|F\| = 1$,

$$|F_1(x)| \leqslant \tfrac{1}{2}(|F(x)|+|F(x^\star)|) \leqslant \tfrac{1}{2}(\|x\|+\|x^\star\|) = \|x\|.$$

Therefore $\|F_1\| = 1$. Notice also that, since $\mathfrak{A}$ is assumed to possess an identity element, the functional F_1 must vanish on its associated ideal $\mathfrak{L}_{F_1}$. In fact, if $n \in \mathfrak{L}_{F_1}$, then $F_1(n) = F_1(1n) = 0$. Therefore

$$\|h\| = F_1(h) = F_1(h+n) \leqslant \|h+n\|,$$

for all $n \in \mathfrak{L}_{F_1}$. Taking the infimum over all $n \in \mathfrak{L}_{F_1}$, we obtain that $\|h\| = \|h'\|$, where h' is the image of h in $\mathfrak{X}_{F_1}$. This proves that, for every h in $\mathscr{H}_{\mathfrak{A}}$, there exists μ in Λ such that

$$\|h\| = \|h_\mu\|, \qquad F_\mu(h) = \|h\|.$$

For a fixed $\mu \in \Lambda$, define, for each $\lambda \in \Lambda$,

$$f_\mu(\lambda) = \begin{cases} 1_\mu, & \lambda = \mu \\ 0\,, & \lambda \neq \mu. \end{cases}$$

Then $f_\mu \in \mathfrak{X}$, $\|f_\mu\| = 1$ and

$$(T_a f_\mu, f_\mu)| = F_\mu(a), \quad a \in \mathfrak{A}.$$

Since

$$|(T_a f_\mu, f_\mu)| \leqslant \|T_a f_\mu\|\,\|f_\mu\| \leqslant \|T_a\|,$$

we have

$$|F_\mu(a)| \leqslant \|T_a\|$$

for all $a \in \mathfrak{A}$ and $\mu \in \Lambda$. Now let $a = h+ik$, where h and k are the hermitian components of a. Choose μ in Λ such that $F_\mu(h) = \|h\|$. Since

$$F_\mu(a) = F_\mu(h)+iF_\mu(k),$$

where $F_\mu(h)$ and $F_\mu(k)$ are real numbers, it follows that

$$\|h\| = F_\mu(h) \leqslant |F_\mu(a)| \leqslant \|T_a\|.$$

Similarly, if F_μ is chosen so that $F_\mu(k) = \|k\|$, then $\|k\| \leqslant \|T_a\|$. Therefore

$$\max(\|h\|, \|k\|) \leqslant \|T_a\| \leqslant \|a\|.$$

In particular, if $k = 0$, then $\|T_h\| = \|h\|$. Also, since

$$\|a\| \leqslant \|h\|+\|k\| \leqslant 2\max(\|h\|, \|k\|),$$

we have

$$\|a\| \leqslant 2\|T_a\| \leqslant 2\|a\|$$

for all $a \in \mathfrak{A}$. This completes the proof of the theorem.

If the norm in $\mathfrak{A}$ satisfies the B*-condition $\|a^\star a\| = \|a\|^2$, then we have

$$\|a\|^2 = \|a^\star a\| = \|T_{a^\star a}\| \leqslant \|T_{a^\star}\|\,\|T_a\| \leqslant \|a^\star\|\,\|a\| = \|a\|^2.$$

Hence $\|a\|^2 = \|T_a\|\,\|T_{a^\star}\|$. Since always $\|T_a\| \leqslant \|a\|$ and $\|T_{a^\star}\| \leqslant \|a\|$, this implies the following corollary.

COROLLARY (4.3.10). *If the norm in $\mathfrak{A}$ satisfies the condition $\|a^\star a\| = \|a\|^2$, then the $\star$-representation $a \to T_a$ of $\mathfrak{A}$ on $\mathfrak{X}$ is an isometry; that is, $\|T_a\| = \|a\|$ for every $a \in \mathfrak{A}$.*

We conclude this section with the remark that in case $\mathfrak{A}$ is a $\star$-algebra without an identity element, then certain non-hermitian linear functionals also give rise to $\star$-representations on a self-dual space. In fact, if F is any linear functional on $\mathfrak{A}$ which has the weakened hermitian property $F(y^\star x) = \overline{F(x^\star y)}$, then the above construction of a $\star$-representation for a hermitian functional goes through without change. However, if $F = F_1+iF_2$, where F_1 and F_2 are hermitian, then

$$\begin{aligned} F_1(y^\star x)+iF_2(y^\star x) &= \overline{F(x^\star y)} \\ &= \overline{F_1(x^\star y)}-i\overline{F_2(x^\star y)} = F_1(y^\star x)-iF_2(y^\star x). \end{aligned}$$

Therefore $F_2(y^\star x) = 0$ and hence $F(y^\star x) = F_1(y^\star x)$, for all x and y. In other words, the $\star$-representation associated with F is identical with the $\star$-representation associated with the hermitian functional F_1. Of course, if $\mathfrak{A}$ has an identity element, the condition $F(y^\star x) = \overline{F(x^\star y)}$ already implies that F is hermitian. On the other hand, if $\mathfrak{A}^2$ spans a proper linear subspace of $\mathfrak{A}$, then there exists a non-zero linear functional F on $\mathfrak{A}$ which vanishes on $\mathfrak{A}^2$. Thus, in particular, $F(y^\star x) = 0$

for all $x, y \in \mathfrak{A}$. Either F itself or iF will be an example of a non-hermitian functional which satisfies the condition $F(y^\star x) = \overline{F(x^\star y)}$.

§ **4. Representations on Hilbert space.** There is obviously an enormous advantage in dealing with $\star$-representations which act on a Hilbert space. We accordingly examine such representations in some detail. Since on a Hilbert space $\mathfrak{H}$ a linear operator is bounded if and only if it possesses an adjoint relative to the inner product in $\mathfrak{H}$, a $\star$-representation on $\mathfrak{H}$ as a self-dual space is automatically normed. Another automatic topological result for this case is that any $\star$-representation of a Banach $\star$-algebra on a Hilbert space is necessarily continuous. This is a consequence of Theorem (4.1.20). All algebras considered here are assumed to be complex.

The inner product norm $(x, x)^{1/2}$ in a Hilbert space $\mathfrak{H}$ will be denoted by $|x|$. Similarly, if T is a bounded linear operator on $\mathfrak{H}$, then $|T|$ will denote the bound of T. Recall that the operator bound $|T|$ satisfies the B*-condition $|T^\star T| = |T|^2$ and therefore, if T is hermitian, then $|T^n| = |T|^n$ for all n.

Let $a \to T'_a$ and $a \to T''_a$ be two $\star$-representations of a $\star$-algebra $\mathfrak{A}$ on Hilbert spaces $\mathfrak{H}'$ and $\mathfrak{H}''$ respectively. Then the two representations are said to be UNITARILY EQUIVALENT provided there exists a unitary transformation U of $\mathfrak{H}''$ onto $\mathfrak{H}'$ such that $T''_a = U^{-1}T'_aU$ for every $a \in \mathfrak{A}$. Recall that U is unitary provided $(Uf'', Ug'') = (f'', g'')$, for all $f'', g'' \in \mathfrak{H}''$, and this is equivalent to the condition $|Uf''| = |f''|$, for every $f'' \in \mathfrak{H}''$. Throughout the following discussion, the terms "cyclic" and "irreducible" will mean "topologically cyclic" and "topologically irreducible" unless explicitly stated otherwise.

Now, let $a \to T_a$ be a $\star$-representation of a $\star$-algebra $\mathfrak{A}$ on a Hilbert space $\mathfrak{H}$ and let $\mathfrak{M}$ be a closed linear subspace of $\mathfrak{H}$ which is invariant with respect to the representation. Then the orthogonal complement $\mathfrak{M}^\perp$ of $\mathfrak{M}$ in $\mathfrak{H}$ is also an invariant subspace. In fact, if $f \in \mathfrak{M}$ and $g \in \mathfrak{M}^\perp$, then

$$(f, T_a g) = (T_{a^\star} f, g) = 0, \quad a \in \mathfrak{A},$$

since $T_{a^\star} f \in \mathfrak{M}$. Therefore $T_a g \in \mathfrak{M}^\perp$, so that $\mathfrak{M}^\perp$ is invariant. The subset $\mathfrak{N}$ of $\mathfrak{H}$, consisting of all f such that $T_a f = 0$ for every $a \in \mathfrak{A}$, is obviously a closed invariant subspace of $\mathfrak{H}$. In case $\mathfrak{N} = (0)$, we say that the representation is ESSENTIAL. Observe that the restriction of the given representation to the invariant subspace $\mathfrak{N}^\perp$ is an essential representation. If $\mathfrak{A}$ has an identity element and $T_1 = I$, the identity operator on $\mathfrak{H}$, then the representation $a \to T_a$ is obviously essential.

If the restriction of the representation $a \to T_a$ to an invariant subspace $\mathfrak{M}$ is (topologically) cyclic, then $\mathfrak{M}$ is called a CYCLIC SUBSPACE of $\mathfrak{H}$ with respect to the representation. Consider a fixed vector $f \in \mathfrak{H}$ and set

$$\mathfrak{H}_f = \overline{\{T_a f : a \in \mathfrak{A}\}}.$$

Then $\mathfrak{H}_f$ is obviously invariant.

LEMMA (4.4.1). *If the representation $a \to T_a$ is essential, then each of the subspaces $\mathfrak{H}_f$ is cyclic with f as a cyclic vector.*

PROOF. We have only to prove that $f \in \mathfrak{H}_f$. Decompose the vector f in the form $f = f' + f''$, where $f' \in \mathfrak{H}_f$ and $f'' \in \mathfrak{H}_f^{\perp}$. Then $f'' = f - f'$ and, since $\mathfrak{H}_f$ is invariant,

$$T_a f'' = T_a f - T_a f' \in \mathfrak{H}_f.$$

On the other hand, $\mathfrak{H}_f^{\perp}$ is invariant, so that $T_a f'' \in \mathfrak{H}_f^{\perp}$. Therefore we have $T_a f'' = 0$ for every $a \in \mathfrak{A}$. Since the representation is essential, this implies $f'' = 0$ and hence that $f \in \mathfrak{H}_f$.

COROLLARY (4.4.2). *Every non-zero closed invariant subspace of $\mathfrak{H}$ contains a non-zero cyclic subspace.*

The next theorem provides a criterion for unitary equivalence of cyclic representations.

THEOREM (4.4.3). *Let $a \to T'_a$ and $a \to T''_a$ be two cyclic $\star$-representations of a $\star$-algebra $\mathfrak{A}$ on the Hilbert spaces $\mathfrak{H}'$ and $\mathfrak{H}''$ respectively. Then a necessary and sufficient condition for these representations to be unitarily equivalent is that there exist cyclic vectors $f'_0 \in \mathfrak{H}'$ and $f''_0 \in \mathfrak{H}''$ such that*

$$(T'_x f'_0, f'_0) = (T''_x f''_0, f''_0)$$

for all x in $\mathfrak{A}$.

PROOF. Assume first that the representations are equivalent under a unitary transformation U of $\mathfrak{H}''$ onto $\mathfrak{H}'$. Let f''_0 be any cyclic vector in $\mathfrak{H}''$ and define $f'_0 = U f''_0$. Then

$$T'_x f'_0 = T'_x U f''_0 = U T''_x f''_0.$$

Since elements of the form $T''_x f''_0$ are dense in $\mathfrak{H}''$ and U is a unitary transformation of $\mathfrak{H}''$ onto $\mathfrak{H}'$, elements of the form $T'_x f'_0$ are dense in $\mathfrak{H}'$. In other words, f'_0 is a cyclic vector in $\mathfrak{H}'$. Also,

$$\begin{aligned}(T'_x f'_0, f'_0) &= (T'_x U f''_0, U f''_0)\\ &= (U T''_x f''_0, U f''_0)\\ &= (T''_x f''_0, f''_0)\end{aligned}$$

for all x in $\mathfrak{A}$. This proves the necessity.

Now assume the condition satisfied. For each element in $\mathfrak{H}''$ of the form $T''_x f''_0$, define $UT''_x f''_0 = T'_x f'_0$. Then

$$|UT''_x f''_0|^2 = (T'_x f'_0, T'_x f'_0) = (T''_x f''_0, T''_x f''_0) = |T''_x f''_0|^2.$$

Therefore $|UT''_x f''_0| = |T''_x f''_0|$, and thus U maps a dense subset of $\mathfrak{H}''$ isometrically onto a dense subset of $\mathfrak{H}'$. Furthermore, U is obviously linear and can therefore be extended to a unitary transformation of $\mathfrak{H}''$ onto $\mathfrak{H}'$. By the definition of U, we have

$$UT''_a T''_x f''_0 = T'_a U T''_x f''_0,$$

for all a, x in $\mathfrak{A}$. Again, since the elements $T''_x f''_0$ are dense in $\mathfrak{H}''$, it follows that $UT''_a = T'_a U$, $a \in \mathfrak{A}$. In other words, the representations are unitarily equivalent and the theorem is proved.

The proof of the necessity above enables us to state the following corollary.

Corollary (4.4.4). *If two $\star$-representations of $\mathfrak{A}$ on Hilbert space are unitarily equivalent and if one of the representations is cyclic (or irreducible), then so is the other.*

Observe that in the proof of the sufficiency above, we needed only the hypothesis that

$$(T'_x f'_0, T'_y f'_0) = (T''_x f''_0, T''_y f''_0)$$

for all $x, y \in \mathfrak{A}$. Furthermore, since

$$\begin{aligned}(Uf''_0, T'_x f'_0) &= (T'_{x^\star} U f''_0, f'_0) = (UT''_{x^\star} f''_0, f'_0)\\ &= (T'_{x^\star} f'_0, f'_0) = (f'_0, T'_x f'_0)\end{aligned}$$

for all $x \in \mathfrak{A}$, it follows that $Uf''_0 = f'_0$. Therefore

$$\begin{aligned}(T'_a f'_0, f'_0) &= (T'_a U f''_0, U f''_0)\\ &= (UT''_a f''_0, U f''_0) = (T''_a f''_0, f''_0),\end{aligned}$$

and we obtain the following corollary.

COROLLARY (4.4.5). *Let $a \to T'_a$ and $a \to T''_a$ be $\star$-representations of $\mathfrak{A}$ on Hilbert space for which there exist cyclic vectors f'_0 and f''_0 such that*

$$(T'_x f'_0, T'_y f'_0) = (T''_x f''_0, T''_y f''_0)$$

for all $x, y \in \mathfrak{A}$. Then also

$$(T'_a f'_0, f'_0) = (T''_a f''_0, f'')$$

for all $a \in \mathfrak{A}$.

The following lemma makes it possible to construct the direct sum of an arbitrary family of $\star$-representations of a Banach $\star$-algebra on Hilbert space.

LEMMA (4.4.6). *Let $a \to T_a$ be a continuous $\star$-representation of a normed $\star$-algebra $\mathfrak{A}$ on a Hilbert space $\mathfrak{H}$. Then, for every hermitian element h in $\mathfrak{A}$, $|T_h| \leqslant \nu(h)$.*

PROOF. Since the representation is continuous, there exists a constant β such that $|T_a| \leqslant \beta\|a\|$ for all $a \in \mathfrak{A}$. In particular, if h is hermitian and n is a positive integer, then

$$|T_h|^n = |T_{h^n}| \leqslant \beta\|h^n\|,$$

and hence

$$|T_h| \leqslant \beta^{1/n}\|h^n\|^{1/n}.$$

Letting $n \to \infty$, we obtain the desired result.

THEOREM (4.4.7). *Let $\mathfrak{A}$ be a Banach $\star$-algebra and $\{\mathfrak{H}_\lambda : \lambda \in \Lambda\}$ a family of Hilbert spaces. For each $\lambda \in \Lambda$, let $a \to T_a^{(\lambda)}$ be a $\star$-representation of $\mathfrak{A}$ on $\mathfrak{H}_\lambda$. Then the direct sum of the representations $a \to T_a^{(\lambda)}$ is defined.*

PROOF. Since $|(f, g)| \leqslant |f||g|$ in a Hilbert space, the direct sum $\Sigma^{(2)}\mathfrak{H}_\lambda$ of the spaces $\mathfrak{H}_\lambda$ is defined in the sense of § 3. Recall that $\Sigma^{(2)}\mathfrak{H}_\lambda$ consists of all functions f defined on Λ with $f(\lambda) \in \mathfrak{H}_\lambda$ such that $\Sigma|f(\lambda)|^2 < \infty$. The inner product in $\Sigma^{(2)}\mathfrak{H}_\lambda$ is given by $(f, g) = \Sigma(f(\lambda), g(\lambda))$. Now, for $f \in \Sigma^{(2)}\mathfrak{H}_\lambda$, define

$$(T_a f)(\lambda) = T_a^{(\lambda)} f(\lambda),\ \lambda \in \Lambda, \qquad a \in \mathfrak{A}.$$

We have only to show that $T_a f$ belongs to $\Sigma^{(2)}\mathfrak{H}_\lambda$ for every $a \in \mathfrak{A}$ and $f \in \Sigma^{(2)}\mathfrak{H}_\lambda$. (See the discussion preceding Definition (4.3.4).) Since $\mathfrak{A}$ is a Banach algebra, each of the representations $a \to T_a^{(\lambda)}$ is continuous.

Therefore, by the above lemma, $|T_{a^\star a}{}^{(\lambda)}| \leqslant \nu(a^\star a)$, for all $a \in \mathfrak{A}$ and $\lambda \in \Lambda$. Thus for any $a \in \mathfrak{A}$ and $f \in \Sigma^{(2)}\mathfrak{H}_\lambda$, we have

$$\begin{aligned} |(T_a f)(\lambda)|^2 &= |T_a{}^{(\lambda)} f(\lambda)|^2 = (T_a{}^{(\lambda)} f(\lambda),\, T_a{}^{(\lambda)} f(\lambda)) \\ &= (T_{a^\star a}{}^{(\lambda)} f(\lambda), f(\lambda)) \\ &\leqslant |T_{a^\star a}{}^{(\lambda)}|\,|f(\lambda)|^2 \leqslant \nu(a^\star a)|f(\lambda)|^2. \end{aligned}$$

It follows that $T_a f \in \Sigma^{(2)}\mathfrak{H}_\lambda$, and so the theorem is proved. Note that T_a is automatically bounded.

The proof of the above theorem also holds for any normed $\star$-algebra provided each of the representations $a \to T_a{}^{(\lambda)}$ is assumed to be continuous. If the involution is continuous, then one can also conclude in this case that the direct sum of the representations is continuous. In fact, if γ is a constant such that $\|a^\star\| \leqslant \gamma^2\|a\|$, for all $a \in \mathfrak{A}$, then

$$|T_a|^2 = |T_{a^\star a}| \leqslant \nu(a^\star a) \leqslant \|a^\star\|\;\|a\| \leqslant \gamma^2\|a\|^2.$$

Therefore $|T_a| \leqslant \gamma\|a\|$, and so $a \to T_a$ is continuous. Continuity is, of course, automatic in the Banach algebra case.

THEOREM (4.4.8). *Every essential $\star$-representation of a $\star$-algebra $\mathfrak{A}$ on Hilbert space is unitarily equivalent to a direct sum of cyclic representations.*

PROOF. Let $a \to T_a$ be a $\star$-representation of $\mathfrak{A}$ on Hilbert space $\mathfrak{H}$. Since the representation is assumed to be essential, there exist non-zero cyclic subspaces of $\mathfrak{H}$. Let $\{\mathfrak{H}_\lambda : \lambda \in \Lambda\}$ be a maximal family of non-zero cyclic subspaces such that $\mathfrak{H}_{\lambda_1}$ and $\mathfrak{H}_{\lambda_2}$ are orthogonal for $\lambda_1 \neq \lambda_2$. The existence of such a maximal family is established by a simple application of Zorn's lemma. Since the subspaces $\mathfrak{H}_\lambda$ are pairwise orthogonal in $\mathfrak{H}$, the series $\Sigma f(\lambda)$ converges to an element of $\mathfrak{H}$ for each f in $\Sigma^{(2)}\mathfrak{H}_\lambda$. Therefore, $f \to \Sigma f(\lambda)$ defines a unitary transformation U of $\Sigma^{(2)}\mathfrak{H}_\lambda$ onto a closed subspace $\mathfrak{H}_0$ of $\mathfrak{H}$. Note that $\mathfrak{H}_0$ is equal to the smallest closed linear subspace of $\mathfrak{H}$ which contains all of the subspaces $\mathfrak{H}_\lambda$, $\lambda \in \Lambda$. Note also that $\mathfrak{H}_0$ is an invariant subspace of $\mathfrak{H}$. Since the representation is essential, $\mathfrak{H}_0{}^\perp$ must reduce to zero; otherwise, by Corollary (4.4.2), there would exist a non-zero cyclic subspace contained in $\mathfrak{H}_0{}^\perp$ thus contradicting the maximality of the family $\{\mathfrak{H}_\lambda : \lambda \in \Lambda\}$. Therefore $\mathfrak{H}_0 = \mathfrak{H}$. Denote by $a \to T_a{}^{(\lambda)}$ the restriction of the representation $a \to T_a$ to the subspace $\mathfrak{H}_\lambda$. Then each of the representations $a \to T_a{}^{(\lambda)}$ is topologically cyclic. Since $|T_a{}^{(\lambda)}| \leqslant |T_a|$, for all $\lambda \in \Lambda$, the direct sum of the representations

$a \to T_a^{(\lambda)}$ is defined and is a representation $a \to T'_a$ on $\Sigma^{(2)} \mathfrak{H}_\lambda$. Furthermore, for $f \in \Sigma^{(2)}\mathfrak{H}_\lambda$,

$$\sum (T'_a f)(\lambda) = \sum T_a^{(\lambda)} f(\lambda)$$
$$= \sum T_a f(\lambda) = T_a \sum f(\lambda).$$

Therefore $UT'_a = T_a U$ for all $a \in \mathfrak{A}$, which says that the direct sum representation is unitarily equivalent to the given representation.

We introduce next the notion of a $\star$-radical for any $\star$-algebra $\mathfrak{A}$.

DEFINITION (4.4.9). *The intersection of the kernels of all topologically irreducible $\star$-representations of $\mathfrak{A}$ on Hilbert space is called the* $\star$-RADICAL *of $\mathfrak{A}$ and is denoted by $\mathfrak{R}^{(\star)}$. If $\mathfrak{R}^{(\star)} = (0)$, then $\mathfrak{A}$ is said to be* $\star$-SEMI-SIMPLE.

THEOREM (4.4.10). *The $\star$-radical $\mathfrak{R}^{(\star)}$ of a Banach $\star$-algebra $\mathfrak{A}$ has the following properties:*

(*i*) *$\mathfrak{R}^{(\star)}$ is a closed $\star$-ideal.*

(*ii*) *$\mathfrak{R}^{(\star)}$ contains the Jacobson radical $\mathfrak{R}$.*

(*iii*) *$\mathfrak{A}/\mathfrak{R}^{(\star)}$ is $\star$-semi-simple.*

PROOF. Since $\star$-representations of $\mathfrak{A}$ on Hilbert space are automatically continuous, the kernels of such representations are closed $\star$-ideals. Therefore statement (i) follows.

Next let q be any element of the Jacobson radical $\mathfrak{R}$. Then also $q^\star q \in \mathfrak{R}$ and, by Theorem (2.3.5), $\nu(q^\star q) = 0$. Therefore, by Lemma (4.4.6), $q^\star q$ belongs to the kernel of every $\star$-representation $a \to T_a$ of $\mathfrak{A}$ on Hilbert space. But, if $T_{q^\star q} = 0$, then $T_q^\star T_q = 0$, which implies $T_q = 0$. Therefore q belongs to the kernel of $a \to T_a$. It follows that $\mathfrak{R} \subseteq \mathfrak{R}^{(\star)}$ and (ii) is proved.

Since $\mathfrak{R}^{(\star)}$ is a closed $\star$-ideal, $\mathfrak{A}/\mathfrak{R}^{(\star)}$ is a Banach $\star$-algebra. Let $a \to a^\tau$ be the natural homomorphism of $\mathfrak{A}$ onto $\mathfrak{A}/\mathfrak{R}^{(\star)}$. Then $(a^\tau)^\star = (a^\star)^\tau$ and $\|a^\tau\| = \inf \|b\|$, for $b^\tau = a^\tau$. Consider any irreducible $\star$-representation $a \to T_a$ of $\mathfrak{A}$ on Hilbert space and denote its kernel by $\mathfrak{K}$. Then $\mathfrak{R}^{(\star)} \subseteq \mathfrak{K}$. For each $a^\tau \in \mathfrak{A}/\mathfrak{R}^{(\star)}$, define $T_{a^\tau} = T_a$. Since $a^\tau = b^\tau$ implies $b - a \in \mathfrak{R}^{(\star)}$, it follows that $T_a = T_b$, so that T_{a^τ} is well-defined. It is obvious that $a^\tau \to T_{a^\tau}$ is an irreducible $\star$-representation of $\mathfrak{A}/\mathfrak{R}^{(\star)}$ on Hilbert space. Since $a \notin \mathfrak{K}$ implies $T_{a^\tau} \neq 0$ and $\mathfrak{R}^{(\star)}$ is equal to the intersection of all such $\mathfrak{K}$, it follows that $\mathfrak{A}/\mathfrak{R}^{(\star)}$ is $\star$-semi-simple and statement (iii) is proved.

The proof of statement (ii) in the above theorem shows that the radical $\mathfrak{R}$ is actually contained in the intersection of the kernels of *all*

$\star$-representations of $\mathfrak{A}$ on Hilbert space. A stronger result, which will be proved later (Theorem (4.6.7)), is that $\mathfrak{R}^{(\star)}$ itself is equal to the intersection of the kernels of all $\star$-representations of $\mathfrak{A}$ on Hilbert space. If $\mathfrak{A}$ is a $\star$-semi-simple Banach algebra, then an application of Theorem (4.4.7) to the irreducible $\star$-representations of $\mathfrak{A}$ shows that $\mathfrak{A}$ is continuously $\star$-isomorphic to a $\star$-subalgebra of $\mathscr{B}(\mathfrak{H})$ for some Hilbert space $\mathfrak{H}$. In particular, $\star$-semi-simplicity is sufficient for $\mathfrak{A}$ to be an A*-algebra. It will be proved later (Corollary (4.8.12)) that every A*-algebra is $\star$-semi-simple. Thus, $\star$-semi-simplicity distinguishes within the class of all Banach $\star$-algebras precisely the subclass of all A*-algebras. The following theorem generalizes the uniqueness of norm property of an A*-algebra.

THEOREM (4.4.11). *Let $\mathfrak{A}$ be a $\star$-algebra which is a Banach algebra under two different norms $\|x\|_1$ and $\|x\|_2$. Then $\mathfrak{R}^{(\star)}$ contains the separating ideal $\mathfrak{S}$ for the two norms.*

PROOF. Note that $\mathfrak{R}^{(\star)}$ is closed relative to both norms. Therefore $\mathfrak{A}/\mathfrak{R}^{(\star)}$ is a Banach $\star$-algebra under each of the norms induced in it by $\|x\|_1$ and $\|x\|_2$. Since $\mathfrak{A}/\mathfrak{R}^{(\star)}$ is $\star$-semi-simple, it is an A*-algebra and hence, by Corollary (4.1.16), has a unique norm topology. Therefore, by Corollary (2.5.12), $\mathfrak{S} \subseteq \mathfrak{R}^{(\star)}$.

We close this section with a generalization of Schur's lemma to the case of (topologically) irreducible $\star$-representations of a $\star$-algebra on Hilbert space. More precisely, the result concerns an irreducible $\star$-subalgebra of $\mathscr{B}(\mathfrak{H})$, where $\mathfrak{H}$ is a Hilbert space.

THEOREM (4.4.12). *Let $\mathfrak{H}$ be a Hilbert space and $\mathfrak{B}$ any $\star$-subalgebra of $\mathscr{B}(\mathfrak{H})$. Then, in order for $\mathfrak{B}$ to be irreducible on $\mathfrak{H}$, it is necessary and sufficient that the centralizer $\mathfrak{B}'$ of $\mathfrak{B}$ in $\mathscr{B}(\mathfrak{H})$ reduce to scalar multiples of the identity operator.*

PROOF. By definition, $\mathfrak{B}'$ consists of all elements of $\mathscr{B}(\mathfrak{H})$ which commute with each element of $\mathfrak{B}$. Since $\mathfrak{B}$ is a $\star$-subalgebra of $\mathscr{B}(\mathfrak{H})$, it is readily verified that $\mathfrak{B}'$ is a closed $\star$-subalgebra of $\mathscr{B}(\mathfrak{H})$ containing the identity operator and is thus a C*-algebra with an identity element. If $\mathfrak{B}$ is not irreducible, then there exists a closed subspace $\mathfrak{X}$ of $\mathfrak{H}$ different from (0) and $\mathfrak{H}$ such that $T\mathfrak{X} \subseteq \mathfrak{X}$ for every $T \in \mathfrak{B}$. Denote by P the projection of $\mathfrak{H}$ onto $\mathfrak{X}$. Then P is obviously not a scalar multiple of the identity operator. However, since $T\mathfrak{X} \subseteq \mathfrak{X}$, we have $PTP = TP$ for every $T \in \mathfrak{B}$. Therefore

$$PT = (T^\star P)^\star = (PT^\star P)^\star = PTP = TP$$

for every $T \in \mathfrak{B}$. This means that $P \in \mathfrak{B}'$ and proves the sufficiency.

Now assume $\mathfrak{B}$ to be irreducible. Let f be any non-zero vector in $\mathfrak{H}$. Then $\{Tf : T \in \mathfrak{B}\}$ is dense in $\mathfrak{H}$. If $S \in \mathfrak{B}'$, then $STf = TSf$ and hence $Sf = 0$ implies $S = 0$. It follows, in particular, that $\mathfrak{B}'$ contains no zero divisors. In fact, if R is any non-zero element of $\mathscr{B}(\mathfrak{H})$, then $Rf \neq 0$ for some $f \in \mathfrak{H}$. Hence, if $S \in \mathfrak{B}'$, then $SR = 0$ implies $SRf = 0$ and hence $S = 0$. A similar argument applied to $S^\star$ and $R^\star$ shows also that $RS = 0$ implies $S = 0$. Next let H be any hermitian element of $\mathfrak{B}'$ and denote by $\mathfrak{C}$ a maximal commutative $\star$-subalgebra of $\mathfrak{B}'$ which contains H. Then $\mathfrak{C}$ is a B*-algebra, and so is isomorphic with $C(\Phi_{\mathfrak{C}})$, by Theorem (4.2.2). But the algebra $C(\Phi_{\mathfrak{C}})$ obviously contains zero divisors unless $\Phi_{\mathfrak{C}}$ reduces to a single point, which accordingly must be the case here. In particular, $Sp_{\mathfrak{C}}(H)$ contains a single real number α, and $\alpha - H$ is a hermitian element whose spectrum in $\mathfrak{C}$ reduces to zero. Therefore $|\alpha - H| = \nu_{\mathfrak{C}}(H) = 0$. In other words, H is a scalar multiple of the identity operator. Since every element of $\mathfrak{B}'$ is a linear combination of hermitian elements in $\mathfrak{B}'$, it follows that every element of $\mathfrak{B}'$ is a scalar multiple of the identity operator. This proves the necessity and establishes the theorem.

A result more general than that in the above theorem is valid. The operators in $\mathfrak{B}$ can be from one Hilbert space to another and the "centralizer" need not be restricted to bounded operators. (See Naĭmark [1, § 7].) Also, Naĭmark [6; 7, § 26] has obtained a "continuous analogue of Schur's lemma".

§ 5. Positive functionals and ★-representations on Hilbert space. Let $\mathfrak{A}$ be a complex $\star$-algebra. We are interested in using linear functionals to construct $\star$-representations of $\mathfrak{A}$ on Hilbert space. Consider a hermitian functional F on $\mathfrak{A}$ and let $\mathfrak{X}_F$ be the self-dual space associated with F. Then $\mathfrak{X}_F = \mathfrak{A} - \mathfrak{L}_F$, where

$$\mathfrak{L}_F = \{x : F(y^\star x) = 0, \text{ for every } y \in \mathfrak{A}\},$$

and the scalar product is given by the relation $(x', y') = F(y^\star x)$, where $x' = x + \mathfrak{L}_F$ and $y' = y + \mathfrak{L}_F$. (See § 3 above.) This scalar product will be positive definite, so that $\mathfrak{L}_F$ will be a pre-Hilbert space, in case $F(x^\star x) \geqslant 0$ for every $x \in \mathfrak{A}$. With this motivation, we define a linear functional F to be POSITIVE if $F(x^\star x) \geqslant 0$ for all x.

Consider any positive linear functional F on $\mathfrak{A}$. Let ξ and η be arbitrary complex numbers and set $u = \xi x + \eta y$ where $x, y \in \mathfrak{A}$. Then

$$F(u^\star u) = |\xi|^2 F(x^\star x) + \bar{\xi}\eta F(x^\star y) + \xi\bar{\eta} F(y^\star x) + |\eta|^2 F(y^\star y).$$

Since $F(z^\star z)$ is always real, it follows that the quantity

$$\xi\bar{\eta}F(x^\star y) + \bar{\xi}\eta F(y^\star x)$$

is real for all ξ, η. The choice $\xi = \eta = 1$ shows that $F(x^\star y)+F(y^\star x)$ is real and the choice $\xi = 1$, $\eta = i$ shows that $iF(x^\star y)-iF(y^\star x)$ is real. Therefore F has the hermitian property:

$$F(y^\star x) = \overline{F(x^\star y)}. \tag{1}$$

Now let ξ be any real number and set $\eta = F(y^\star x)$. Then, since $F(u^\star u) \geqslant 0$, we have

$$\xi^2 F(x^\star x) + 2\xi|F(y^\star x)|^2 + |F(y^\star x)|^2 F(y^\star y) \geqslant 0.$$

Since this holds for all real ξ, the discriminant of the quadratic is negative or zero. Therefore F satisfies the following Cauchy–Schwartz inequality:

$$|F(y^\star x)|^2 \leqslant F(y^\star y)F(x^\star x). \tag{2}$$

If $\mathfrak{A}$ has an identity element, then property (1) shows that every positive functional F on $\mathfrak{A}$ is hermitian and property (2) shows that $|F(x)|^2 \leqslant F(1)F(x^\star x)$. On the other hand, if $\mathfrak{A}$ does not have an identity, then a positive functional need not be hermitian. However, if F is positive then there always exists a positive hermitian functional F_1 such that $F(y^\star x) = F_1(y^\star x)$ for all x, y. (See the remark at the end of § 3.) Notice that, if F is positive, then, by property (2), the ideal $\mathfrak{L}_F$ consists of all elements x such that $F(x^\star x)=0$.

We have seen that positivity of a hermitian functional F is precisely the condition needed for $\mathfrak{X}_F$ to be a pre-Hilbert space. However, in order to extend the associated $\star$-representation $a \to T_a$ of $\mathfrak{A}$ on $\mathfrak{X}_F$ to the Hilbert space completion of $\mathfrak{X}_F$, we need the additional condition that each of the operators T_a be bounded relative to the inner product norm in $\mathfrak{X}_F$. This condition, formulated in terms of F itself, is simply that

$$\sup_{x\in\mathfrak{A}} \frac{F(x^\star a^\star a x)}{F(x^\star x)} < \infty$$

for each $a \in \mathfrak{A}$. Positive functionals which satisfy this condition will be called ADMISSIBLE. In the case of a normed $\star$-algebra, all bounded positive functionals are admissible and, in the case of a Banach $\star$-algebra with a locally continuous involution, *all* positive functionals are admissible. Before proving these assertions we establish a lemma.

LEMMA (4.5.1). *Let $\mathfrak{A}$ be a normed $\star$-algebra and F a bounded linear functional on $\mathfrak{A}$ such that*

$$|F(h)|^2 \leqslant \beta F(h^2), \quad h \in \mathscr{H}_{\mathfrak{A}},$$

where β is a positive real constant independent of h. Then

$$|F(h)| \leqslant \beta\nu(h), \quad h \in \mathscr{H}_{\mathfrak{A}}.$$

PROOF. Successive application of the assumed inequality to the elements $h, h^2, h^4, \cdots, h^{2^k}$ leads to the inequality

$$|F(h)|^{2^k} \leqslant \beta^{2^k-1}F(h^{2^k}) \leqslant \beta^{2^k-1}\|F\| \, \|h^{2^k}\|.$$

By taking the 2^kth root of this inequality and then letting $k \to \infty$, we obtain the desired result.

Let F be a linear functional on the $\star$-algebra $\mathfrak{A}$ and, for a fixed element $u \in \mathfrak{A}$, define

$$F_u(x) = F(u^\star xu), \quad x \in \mathfrak{A}.$$

Then F_u is a linear functional which is positive and hermitian if F is positive. When $\mathfrak{A}$ is normed, the functional F is said to be RELATIVELY BOUNDED in case F_u is bounded for each $u \in \mathfrak{A}$. It is obvious that boundedness implies relative boundedness and that the two notions coincide if $\mathfrak{A}$ has an identity element.

THEOREM (4.5.2). *Let $\mathfrak{A}$ be a normed $\star$-algebra and F any positive functional on $\mathfrak{A}$. If either F is relatively bounded or $\mathfrak{A}$ is a Banach $\star$-algebra with a locally continuous involution, then*

$$|F(u^\star hu)| \leqslant \nu(h)F(u^\star u), \quad u \in \mathfrak{A}, \quad h \in \mathscr{H}_{\mathfrak{A}},$$

so that F is admissible.

PROOF. By the Cauchy–Schwartz inequality,

$$|F(u^\star hu)|^2 \leqslant F(u^\star u)F(u^\star h^2 u).$$

In other words, $|F_u(h)|^2 \leqslant F(u^\star u)F_u(h^2)$ for $h \in \mathscr{H}_{\mathfrak{A}}$. Therefore, if F is relatively bounded, the desired result follows from the preceding lemma.

Now assume that $\mathfrak{A}$ is a Banach $\star$-algebra with a locally continuous involution and let h be an element of $\mathscr{H}_{\mathfrak{A}}$ with $\nu(h) < 1$. By Lemma (4.1.4), there exist elements $r,s \in \mathscr{H}_{\mathfrak{A}}$ such that $r \circ r = h$ and $s \circ s = -h$. For any $u \in \mathfrak{A}$, set $v = (1-r)u$ and $w = (1-s)u$. Then

$$v^\star v = u^\star(1-r)^2u = u^\star(1-h)u$$

and

$$w^\star w = u^\star(1-s)^2u = u^\star(1+h)u.$$

Therefore

$$F(u^\star(1-h)u) \geqslant 0, \qquad F(u^\star(1+h)u) \geqslant 0.$$

These inequalities imply that $|F_u(h)| \leqslant F(u^\star u)$ if $\nu(h) < 1$. Next, for arbitrary $h \in \mathscr{H}_{\mathfrak{A}}$ and $\epsilon > 0$, set $h_\epsilon = (\nu(h)+\epsilon)^{-1}h$. Then $\nu(h_\epsilon) < 1$, so that we have $|F_u(h_\epsilon)| \leqslant F(u^\star u)$. Hence,

$$|F(u^\star hu)| \leqslant (\nu(h)+\epsilon)F(u^\star u)$$

for all $\epsilon > 0$, and therefore

$$|F(u^\star hu)| \leqslant \nu(h)F(u^\star u).$$

Since this property obviously implies admissibility, the proof is complete.

Corollary (4.5.3). *If $\mathfrak{A}$ is a Banach $\star$-algebra with a locally continuous involution, then every positive functional is relatively bounded. If $\mathfrak{A}$ also has an identity element, then every positive functional F is bounded and $\|F\| = F(1)$.*

It is convenient at this point to assemble, in the form of an existence theorem, the various facts concerning the $\star$-representations associated with positive functionals.

Theorem (4.5.4). *Let F be an admissible positive hermitian functional on the $\star$-algebra $\mathfrak{A}$. Then there exists a $\star$-representation $a \to T_a$ of $\mathfrak{A}$ on a Hilbert space $\mathfrak{H}$ with the following properties:*

(*i*) *The kernel of the representation is $\mathfrak{L}_F : \mathfrak{A}$.*

(*ii*) *There exists a linear mapping $u \to f_u$ of $\mathfrak{A}$ onto a dense subspace of $\mathfrak{H}$ such that*

$$F(u^\star au) = (T_a f_u, f_u), \quad a \in \mathfrak{A}.$$

(*iii*) *If $\mathfrak{A}$ has an identity element, then the representation is topologically cyclic with a cyclic vector $f_1 \in \mathfrak{H}$ such that*

$$F(a) = (T_a f_1, f_1), \quad a \in \mathfrak{A}.$$

(*iv*) *If $\mathfrak{A}$ is normed and F is relatively bounded, then $|T_h| \leqslant \|h\|$ for $h \in \mathscr{H}_{\mathfrak{A}}$. If also $\mathfrak{A}$ is $\star$-normed, then $|T_a| \leqslant \|a\|$, for all $a \in \mathfrak{A}$.*

Proof. The desired representation is, of course, the representation $a \to T_a$ on $\mathfrak{H}_F$ constructed previously. Note that $\mathfrak{L}_F : \mathfrak{A}$ is the kernel of the left regular representation of $\mathfrak{A}$ on the difference space $\mathfrak{X}_F = \mathfrak{A} - \mathfrak{L}_F$ and that $a \to T_a$ coincides on $\mathfrak{X}_F$ with the left regular representation. Since $\mathfrak{X}_F$ is dense in $\mathfrak{H}_F$, an operator T_a will vanish on $\mathfrak{X}_F$ if and only if it vanishes on $\mathfrak{H}_F$. Therefore $\mathfrak{L}_F : \mathfrak{A}$ is the kernel of $a \to T_a$ and (i) is proved. If f_u denotes the image of u in $\mathfrak{H}_F$ *via* $\mathfrak{X}_F$ (that is, $f_u = u' = u + \mathfrak{L}_F$), then

$$F(u^\star au) = ((au)', u') = (T_a f_u, f_u), \quad a \in \mathfrak{A},$$

giving (ii). If $\mathfrak{A}$ has an identity element, then $T_a f_1 = a'$, so that elements of the form $T_a f_1$ exhaust $\mathfrak{X}_F$ and are therefore dense in $\mathfrak{H}_F$. This proves (iii). Finally, in the case of (iv), we have, by Theorem (4.5.2), that

$$|T_h|^2 = \sup \frac{F(u^\star h^2 u)}{F(u^\star u)} \leqslant \nu(h^2) = \nu(h)^2$$

for $h \in \mathscr{H}_{\mathfrak{A}}$. Hence $|T_h| \leqslant \nu(h) \leqslant \|h\|$. If $\mathfrak{A}$ is $\star$-normed, then $\|x^\star\| = \|x\|$, so that $|T_a|^2 = |T_{a^\star a}| \leqslant \|a^\star a\| \leqslant \|a\|^2$. Therefore $|T_a| \leqslant \|a\|$ and the theorem is proved.

Consider any $\star$-representation $a \to T_a$ of a $\star$-algebra $\mathfrak{A}$ on a Hilbert space $\mathfrak{H}$. Let f_0 be a fixed vector in $\mathfrak{H}$ and define $F(a) = (T_a f_0, f_0)$ for $a \in \mathfrak{A}$. Then F is a positive functional on $\mathfrak{A}$ and, since

$$F(x^\star a^\star ax) = |T_{ax} f_0|^2 \leqslant |T_a|^2 |T_x f_0|^2 = |T_a|^2 F(x^\star x),$$

F is also admissible. Part (iii) of the above theorem shows that, if $\mathfrak{A}$ has an identity element, then every admissible positive functional is of this form where the representation is (topologically) cyclic and f_0 is a cyclic vector. In the general case, those functionals which can be so obtained are of such importance that we distinguish them by a definition.

Definition (4.5.5). *Let F be a functional on the $\star$-algebra $\mathfrak{A}$ and let $a \to T_a$ be a $\star$-representation of $\mathfrak{A}$ on a Hilbert space $\mathfrak{H}$. Then F is said to be* REPRESENTABLE *by $a \to T_a$ provided there exists a (topologically) cyclic vector f_0 in $\mathfrak{H}$ such that $F(a) = (T_a f_0, f_0)$, $a \in \mathfrak{A}$.*

The following lemmas bring out more precisely the relationship between a representable positive functional and the representation which represents it.

Lemma (4.5.6). *Let $a \to T_a$ be any $\star$-representation of a $\star$-algebra $\mathfrak{A}$ on a Hilbert space $\mathfrak{H}$. Let f_0 be a non-zero vector in $\mathfrak{H}$ and define $F(a) = (T_a f_0, f_0)$, $a \in \mathfrak{A}$. Then there exists a closed invariant subspace $\mathfrak{H}_0$ in $\mathfrak{H}$ such that F is representable by the restriction of $a \to T_a$ to $\mathfrak{H}_0$. If $a \to T_a$ is essential, then also $f_0 \in \mathfrak{H}_0$.*

PROOF. Let $\mathfrak{N}$ be the zero space of the given representation consisting of all $f \in \mathfrak{H}$ such that $T_a f = 0$ for every $a \in \mathfrak{A}$. Then the restriction of $a \to T_a$ to the space $\mathfrak{N}^\perp$ is essential. Now let f'_0 denote the projection of f_0 on the space $\mathfrak{N}^\perp$. It is readily verified that $F(a) = (T_a f'_0, f'_0)$, $a \in \mathfrak{A}$. Let

$$\mathfrak{H}_0 = \overline{\{T_a f'_0 : a \in \mathfrak{A}\}}.$$

Then, by Lemma (4.4.1), $\mathfrak{H}_0$ is cyclic with f'_0 as a cyclic vector, and so the lemma is proved.

By Theorem (4.5.4) (ii) and the above lemma, we can state the following corollary.

COROLLARY (4.5.7). *If F is an admissible positive hermitian functional and u is any element of $\mathfrak{A}$, then F_u is representable by a restriction of the $\star$-representation of $\mathfrak{A}$ associated with F.*

LEMMA (4.5.8). *If a positive functional F on a $\star$-algebra $\mathfrak{A}$ is representable by a $\star$-representation $a \to T_a$ of $\mathfrak{A}$, then the $\star$-representation of $\mathfrak{A}$ associated with F is unitarily equivalent to $a \to T_a$.*

PROOF. By definition, there exists a cyclic vector f_0 in the Hilbert space $\mathfrak{H}$ of the representation $a \to T_a$ such that $F(a) = (T_a f_0, f_0)$ for $a \in \mathfrak{A}$. Let $a \to T'_a$ be the $\star$-representation on $\mathfrak{H}_F$ associated with F. For each x' in $\mathfrak{X}_F$, define $Ux' = T_x f_0$. Then

$$|Ux'|^2 = (T_x f_0, T_x f_0) = (T_{x^\star x} f_0, f_0) = F(x^\star x) = |x'|^2.$$

Therefore $|Ux'| = |x'|$ and U can be extended as a unitary transformation of $\mathfrak{H}_F$ onto $\mathfrak{H}$. Furthermore, for $x' \in \mathfrak{X}_F$,

$$UT'_a x' = U(ax)' = T_{ax} f_0 = T_a T_x f_0 = T_a U x'.$$

Since $\mathfrak{X}_F$ is dense in $\mathfrak{H}_F$, it follows that $UT'_a = T_a U$ for all $a \in \mathfrak{A}$. In other words, the representations $a \to T'_a$ and $a \to T_a$ are unitarily equivalent.

COROLLARY (4.5.9). *If a positive functional F on a $\star$-algebra $\mathfrak{A}$ is representable, then it is representable by its associated $\star$-representation of $\mathfrak{A}$.*

LEMMA (4.5.10). *If F_1 and F_2 are representable positive functionals such that $F_1(y^\star x) = F_2(y^\star x)$ for all $x, y \in \mathfrak{A}$, then $F_1 = F_2$.*

PROOF. This result follows immediately from Corollary (4.4.5).

The next theorem provides necessary and sufficient conditions for a positive functional on a Banach $\star$-algebra to be representable.

THEOREM (4.5.11). *Let F be a hermitian functional on the Banach $\star$-algebra $\mathfrak{A}$. Then, in order for F to be representable, it is necessary and sufficient that*

(*i*) *F is bounded, and*

(*ii*) $|F(x)|^2 \leqslant \mu F(x^\star x)$, $x \in \mathfrak{A}$,

where μ is a positive real constant independent of x.

PROOF. Assume first that F is representable by a representation $a \to T_a$ with $F(a) = (T_a f_0, f_0)$, $a \in \mathfrak{A}$. Since $\mathfrak{A}$ is a Banach algebra, $a \to T_a$ is automatically continuous, so that there exists a constant β such that $|T_a| \leqslant \beta\|a\|$, $a \in \mathfrak{A}$. Therefore $|F(x)| \leqslant \beta|f_0|^2\|x\|$, and hence F is bounded. Also,

$$|F(x)|^2 \leqslant |T_x f_0|^2 |f_0|^2 = (T_x f_0, T_x f_0)|f_0|^2 = F(x^\star x)|f_0|^2,$$

which gives condition (ii) with $\mu = |f_0|^2$. This proves the necessity.

Now assume that F satisfies the two conditions and denote by $\mathfrak{A}_1$ the Banach $\star$-algebra obtained by adjunction of an identity element to $\mathfrak{A}$. Extend the functional F to $\mathfrak{A}_1$ by the definition, $F(a+\alpha) = F(a)+\alpha\mu$ for $a \in \mathfrak{A}$ and α a scalar. It is obvious that this extension of F is a bounded linear functional on $\mathfrak{A}_1$. The sufficiency will follow from Theorems (4.5.2), (4.5.4) (iii) and Lemma (4.5.6) if we show that the extension of F is a positive functional on $\mathfrak{A}_1$. Since

$$\begin{aligned} F((a+\alpha)^\star(a+\alpha)) &= F(a^\star a)+\bar{\alpha}F(a)+\alpha F(a^\star)+\mu|\alpha|^2 \\ &\geqslant F(a^\star a)-2|\alpha||F(a)|+\mu|\alpha|^2 \\ &\geqslant F(a^\star a)-2|\alpha|\mu^{1/2}F(a^\star a)^{1/2}+\mu|\alpha|^2 \\ &= (F(a^\star a)^{1/2}-|\alpha|\mu^{1/2})^2, \end{aligned}$$

F is indeed a positive functional on $\mathfrak{A}_1$ and the theorem is proved.

Notice that, if $\mathfrak{A}$ is any $\star$-algebra, then the above proof shows that condition (ii) is necessary and sufficient that F be extendible to the algebra $\mathfrak{A}_1$ as a positive functional. (See Loomis [1, 26H].)

For the sufficiency half of the above theorem, boundedness of F was used only to ensure that the extension of F to $\mathfrak{A}_1$ be admissible, so that Theorem (4.5.4) could be applied. Since admissibility is automatic if the involution is locally continuous (see Theorem (4.5.2)), we have the following corollary to the theorem.

COROLLARY (4.5.12). *If the involution in $\mathfrak{A}$ is locally continuous, then condition* (*ii*) *is necessary and sufficient for F to be representable.*

If $\mathfrak{A}$ has an identity element, then, by the Cauchy–Schwartz inequality, we have $|F(x)|^2 \leqslant F(1)F(x^\star x)$ for any positive functional F. Thus, condition (ii) is automatically satisfied and we can state the next corollary.

COROLLARY (4.5.13). *If $\mathfrak{A}$ has an identity element, then every bounded positive functional is representable. If in addition the involution is locally continuous, then every positive functional is representable.*

THEOREM (4.5.14). *Let $\mathfrak{A}$ be a Banach $\star$-algebra with a continuous involution and an approximate identity $\{e_\lambda\}$. Then every bounded positive functional F on $\mathfrak{A}$ is representable.*

PROOF. Since the involution is continuous,

$$\lim xe_\lambda = \lim e_\lambda{}^\star x = x, \quad x \in \mathfrak{A}.$$

We prove first that F is hermitian. Since

$$F((x+e_\lambda)^\star(x+e_\lambda)) = F(x^\star x)+F(x^\star e_\lambda)+F(e_\lambda{}^\star x)+F(e_\lambda{}^\star e_\lambda),$$

the positivity of F implies that $F(x^\star e_\lambda)+F(e_\lambda{}^\star x)$ is real for every λ. Using the boundedness of F, we obtain

$$\lim (F(x^\star e_\lambda)+F(e_\lambda{}^\star x)) = F(x^\star)+F(x).$$

Therefore $F(x^\star)+F(x)$ is real and this implies that F is hermitian. From the continuity of the involution plus the fact that $\|e_\lambda\| \leqslant 1$ for all λ, it follows that there exists a constant β such that $\|e_\lambda{}^\star\| \leqslant \beta$ for all λ. By the Cauchy–Schwartz inequality,

$$|F(e_\lambda x)|^2 \leqslant F(e_\lambda e_\lambda{}^\star)F(x^\star x) \leqslant \beta\|F\|F(x^\star x).$$

Hence, after taking the limit with respect to λ, we obtain

$$|F(x)|^2 \leqslant \beta\|F\|F(x^\star x), \quad x \in \mathfrak{A}.$$

Therefore, by Theorem (4.5.11), F is representable, and the theorem is proved.

Observe that, if the approximate identity consists of hermitian elements, then the continuity of the involution is not required in the above proof.

Let F be a representable positive functional on a $\star$-algebra $\mathfrak{A}$ and let

$$F(a) = (T_a f_0, f_0), \quad a \in \mathfrak{A},$$

where $a \to T_a$ is the $\star$-representation associated with F and f_0 is a cyclic vector in the Hilbert space $\mathfrak{H}_F$ of the representation. Consider a bounded operator B on $\mathfrak{H}_F$ and define

$$F'(a) = (T_a B f_0, f_0), \quad a \in \mathfrak{A}.$$

If B commutes with each of the operators T_a and if $(Bf, f) \geqslant 0$ for every $f \in \mathfrak{H}_F$, then F' is readily seen also to be a positive functional on $\mathfrak{A}$. A positive functional F' which is obtained from F in this way is said to be INCLUDED IN F and we write $F' \prec F$. We wish to characterize those positive functionals which are included in F. (See Naĭmark [1, § 9].)

THEOREM (4.5.15). *A necessary and sufficient condition for a representable positive functional F' to be included in F is that there exist a constant λ such that $\lambda F - F'$ is a positive functional.*

PROOF. The condition is clearly necessary since

$$\begin{aligned} F'(a^\star a) &= |(BT_a f_0, T_a f_0)| \\ &\leqslant |B||T_a f_0|^2 = |B| F(a^\star a), \end{aligned}$$

so that $\lambda F - F'$ is positive if $\lambda \geqslant |B|$. On the other hand, assume that $\lambda F - F'$ is a positive functional. Then it is obvious that $\lambda \geqslant 0$. Define

$$\langle T_x f_0, T_y f_0 \rangle = F'(y^\star x).$$

Then

$$\begin{aligned} |\langle T_x f_0, T_y f_0 \rangle|^2 &\leqslant F'(x^\star x) F'(y^\star y) \\ &\leqslant \lambda^2 F(x^\star x) F(y^\star y) = \lambda^2 |T_x f_0|^2 |T_y f_0|^2. \end{aligned}$$

In other words, $\langle T_x f_0, T_y f_0 \rangle$ is a bilinear functional which is defined and bounded on a dense subspace of $\mathfrak{H}_F$. It can therefore be extended uniquely to a bilinear functional $\langle f, g \rangle$ defined on all of $\mathfrak{H}_F$ with the property $|\langle f, g \rangle| \leqslant \lambda |f||g|$. By a standard result from Hilbert space theory (Riesz and Sz-Nagy [1, p. 202]), there exists a bounded operator B on $\mathfrak{H}_F$ such that

$$\langle f, g \rangle = (Bf, g), \quad f, g \in \mathfrak{H}_F.$$

Since F' is a positive hermitian functional, it follows that B is a hermitian operator and $(Bf, f) \geqslant 0$ for all $f \in \mathfrak{H}_F$. Also,

$$(T_a B T_x f_0, T_y f_0) = F'(y^\star a x) = (B T_a T_x f_0, T_y f_0)$$

and, since elements of the form $T_x f_0$ are dense in $\mathfrak{H}_F$, it follows that $T_a B = B T_a$ for all $a \in \mathfrak{A}$. If $\mathfrak{A}$ has an identity element then immediately $F'(a) = (T_a B f_0, f_0)$ and the theorem is proved. If there is no identity element, then an additional argument is needed to establish this result.

Let $\mathfrak{N} = \{f : Bf = 0\}$ and denote the orthogonal complement of $\mathfrak{N}$ in $\mathfrak{H}_F$ by $\mathfrak{H}'_0$. Then $\langle f, g\rangle$ is an inner product in $\mathfrak{H}'_0$ and

$$\langle T_a f_0, f_0\rangle = \langle T_a f'_0, f'_0\rangle, \quad a \in \mathfrak{A},$$

where f'_0 is the projection of f_0 on the space $\mathfrak{H}'_0$. Set $|f|_0^2 = \langle f, f\rangle$ for $f \in \mathfrak{H}'_0$. Since F' is representable, it is admissible, so that there exists a constant β_a such that

$$F'(x^\star a^\star a x) \leqslant \beta_a F'(x^\star x), \quad x \in \mathfrak{A}.$$

Hence

$$|T_a T_x f'_0|_0^2 = F'(x^\star a^\star a x) \leqslant \beta_a F'(x^\star x) = \beta_a |T_x f'_0|_0^2.$$

In other words, T_a is bounded on the space $\{T_x f'_0 : x \in \mathfrak{A}\}$ and therefore has a unique extension to the completion, $\mathfrak{H}_0$, of this space with respect to the norm $|f|_0$. Thus, $a \to T_a$ becomes a $\star$-representation of $\mathfrak{A}$ on $\mathfrak{H}_0$. Finally, if we define

$$F''(a) = \langle T_a f'_0, f'_0\rangle, \quad a \in \mathfrak{A},$$

then F'' is a representable positive functional and $F''(y^\star x) = F'(y^\star x)$ for all $x, y \in \mathfrak{A}$. Therefore $F'' = F'$, by Lemma (4.5.10), and we have

$$F'(a) = \langle T_a f'_0, f'_0\rangle = (T_a B f_0, f_0), \quad a \in \mathfrak{A}.$$

In other words, $F' \prec F$ and the theorem is proved.

Except for some of the side effects resulting from not assuming an identity element, our discussion of positive functionals and their relation to $\star$-representations on Hilbert space follows the standard approach used by Gelfand and Naĭmark [1; 4], Naĭmark [1], Raikov [2], Kelley and Vaught [1], Segal [3], and many others.

§ 6. Positive functionals and irreducible $\star$-representations. Let $\mathfrak{A}$ be a Banach $\star$-algebra and consider an irreducible $\star$-representation $a \to T_a$ of $\mathfrak{A}$ on a Hilbert space $\mathfrak{H}$. If f_0 is any non-zero vector in $\mathfrak{H}$ and F is the positive functional defined by the relation $F(a) = (T_a f_0, f_0)$, then it follows from Lemma (4.5.8) that the $\star$-representation associated with F is unitarily equivalent to the representation $a \to T_a$ and so is irreducible. In other words, those positive functionals which are representable by an irreducible representation have irreducible associated $\star$-representations. Note also that, up to unitary equivalence, all irreducible $\star$-representations of $\mathfrak{A}$ on Hilbert space are obtained as $\star$-representations associated with representable positive functionals. The first problem considered in this section is to obtain conditions on a representable positive functional in order that its associated $\star$-representation be irreducible. This will provide a method for construction of irreducible representations and lead to a characterization of the $\star$-radical in terms of positive functionals.

Let F be a positive hermitian functional on $\mathfrak{A}$ and define

$$\mu_F = \sup_x \frac{|F(x)|^2}{F(x^\star x)}, \quad x \in \mathfrak{A}.$$

Since $\mathfrak{A}$ is a Banach $\star$-algebra, it follows by Theorem (4.5.11) that F is representable if and only if it is bounded and $\mu_F < \infty$. Furthermore, since multiplication of F by a positive constant does not alter essentially its associated representation, we can limit attention here to the subclass of the positive functionals specified in the following definition:

Definition (4.6.1). *For $\mathfrak{A}$ any Banach $\star$-algebra, denote by $\mathscr{P}_{\mathfrak{A}}$ the class of all those bounded positive hermitian functionals F on $\mathfrak{A}$ such that $\mu_F \leqslant 1$.*

Observe that, if $\mathfrak{A}$ has an identity element, then $\mathscr{P}_{\mathfrak{A}}$ consists of all those bounded positive functionals such that $F(1) \leqslant 1$.

After restriction of the functionals in $\mathscr{P}_{\mathfrak{A}}$ to the subspace $\mathscr{H}_{\mathfrak{A}}$ of hermitian elements of $\mathfrak{A}$, we can regard $\mathscr{P}_{\mathfrak{A}}$ as a subset of the dual space $\mathscr{H}'_{\mathfrak{A}}$ consisting of all bounded linear functionals on $\mathscr{H}_{\mathfrak{A}}$. Although $\mathscr{H}_{\mathfrak{A}}$ is not complete unless the involution is continuous, its dual space $\mathscr{H}'_{\mathfrak{A}}$ is always complete and is accordingly a real Banach space. In addition to its norm topology, the space $\mathscr{H}'_{\mathfrak{A}}$ carries the $\mathscr{H}_{\mathfrak{A}}$-topology which is, by definition, the weakest topology (smallest number of open sets) in which every element of $\mathscr{H}_{\mathfrak{A}}$ is continuous when considered as a function on $\mathscr{H}'_{\mathfrak{A}}$. This topology is Hausdorff and is determined by the system of neighborhoods,

$$V_{F_0}(h_1, \cdots, h_n ; \epsilon) = \{F : |F(h_i) - F_0(h_i)| < \epsilon; i = 1, \cdots, n\},$$

where F_0 is any element of $\mathscr{H}'_{\mathfrak{A}}$, $\epsilon > 0$ and $\{h_1, \cdots, h_n\}$ is an arbitrary finite subset of $\mathscr{H}_{\mathfrak{A}}$. An application of the Tychonoff theorem similar to that in the proof of Theorem (3.1.10) leads to the result that the unit ball of $\mathscr{H}'_{\mathfrak{A}}$ (that is, all F with $\|F\| \leqslant 1$) is compact in the $\mathscr{H}_{\mathfrak{A}}$-topology.

Lemma (4.6.2). *As a subset of $\mathscr{H}'_{\mathfrak{A}}$, $\mathscr{P}_{\mathfrak{A}}$ is a bounded convex set which is compact in the $\mathscr{H}_{\mathfrak{A}}$-topology of $\mathscr{H}'_{\mathfrak{A}}$.*

PROOF. Observe first that, by Lemma (4.5.1), we have $|F(h)| \leqslant \nu(h) \leqslant \|h\|$ for every $F \in \mathscr{P}_{\mathfrak{A}}$ and $h \in \mathscr{H}_{\mathfrak{A}}$. In other words, $\mathscr{P}_{\mathfrak{A}}$ is contained in the unit sphere of $\mathscr{H}'_{\mathfrak{A}}$ and so is bounded. Next let F_1, F_2 be any two elements of $\mathscr{P}_{\mathfrak{A}}$ and let α_1, α_2 be non-negative real numbers such that $\alpha_1+\alpha_2 = 1$. Then, by the Cauchy inequality,

$$\begin{aligned}|\alpha_1F_1(a)+\alpha_2F_2(a)| &\leqslant \alpha_1{}^{1/2}|\alpha_1{}^{1/2}F_1(a)|+\alpha_2{}^{1/2}|\alpha_2{}^{1/2}F_2(a)| \\ &\leqslant (\alpha_1+\alpha_2)^{1/2}(\alpha_1|F_1(a)|^2+\alpha_2|F_2(a)|^2)^{1/2} \\ &\leqslant (\alpha_1F_1(a^\star a)+\alpha_2F_2(a^\star a))^{1/2}.\end{aligned}$$

Therefore

$$|(\alpha_1F_1+\alpha_2F_2)(a)|^2 \leqslant (\alpha_1F_1+\alpha_2F_2)(a^\star a),$$

which proves that $\mathscr{P}_{\mathfrak{A}}$ is convex.

Since $\mathscr{P}_{\mathfrak{A}}$ is contained in the unit ball of $\mathscr{H}'_{\mathfrak{A}}$, which is compact in the $\mathscr{H}_{\mathfrak{A}}$-topology, it only remains to prove that $\mathscr{P}_{\mathfrak{A}}$ is closed in this topology. Let F_0 be a limit point of $\mathscr{P}_{\mathfrak{A}}$. Then, since the unit ball is closed, $\|F_0\| \leqslant 1$. For arbitrary $x \in \mathfrak{A}$, let $x = h+ik$ with $h, k \in \mathscr{H}_{\mathfrak{A}}$. Then, for $\epsilon > 0$, there exists $F \in \mathscr{P}_{\mathfrak{A}}$ such that

$$|F(h)-F_0(h)| < \epsilon, \quad |F(k)-F_0(k)| < \epsilon, \quad |F(x^\star x)-F_0(x^\star x)| < \epsilon.$$

Hence, in particular, $0 \leqslant F(x^\star x) \leqslant F_0(x^\star x)+\epsilon$ and

$$|F(x)-F_0(x)| \leqslant |F(h)-F_0(h)|+|F(k)-F_0(k)| < 2\epsilon.$$

Therefore F_0 is positive and

$$\begin{aligned}|F_0(x)|^2 &\leqslant |F(x)|^2+|F_0(x)^2-F(x)^2| \leqslant |F(x)|^2+2|F_0(x)-F(x)|\|x\| \\ &\leqslant F(x^\star x)+4\|x\|\epsilon \leqslant F_0(x^\star x)+(4\|x\|+1)\epsilon.\end{aligned}$$

Since this holds for all $\epsilon > 0$ independently of x, it follows that $|F_0(x)|^2 \leqslant F_0(x^\star x)$. In other words, $F_0 \in \mathscr{P}_{\mathfrak{A}}$ and so $\mathscr{P}_{\mathfrak{A}}$ is compact.

LEMMA (4.6.3). *If F is an extreme point of $\mathscr{P}_{\mathfrak{A}}$, then $\mu_F = 1$.*

PROOF. An extreme point of $\mathscr{P}_{\mathfrak{A}}$ is, by definition, a non-zero element $F \in \mathscr{P}_{\mathfrak{A}}$ such that a relation of the form $F = \alpha_1F_1+\alpha_2F_2$, with $\alpha_1 > 0$, $\alpha_2 > 0$, $\alpha_1+\alpha_2 = 1$ and $F_1, F_2 \in \mathscr{P}_{\mathfrak{A}}$, implies $F_1 = F_2 = F$. If $F \neq 0$, then $0 < \mu_F \leqslant 1$ and $\mu_F{}^{-1}F \in \mathscr{P}_{\mathfrak{A}}$. Also, $0 \in \mathscr{P}_{\mathfrak{A}}$ and

$$F = (1-\mu_F)0+\mu_F(\mu_F{}^{-1}F).$$

Thus, if F is an extreme point, then $\mu_F = 1$.

THEOREM (4.6.4). *In order for the $\star$-representation of $\mathfrak{A}$ associated with a functional F in $\mathscr{P}_{\mathfrak{A}}$ to be irreducible, it is necessary and sufficient that F be an extreme point of the convex set $\mathscr{P}_{\mathfrak{A}}$.*

PROOF. Let $a \to T_a$ be the $\star$-representation on the Hilbert space $\mathfrak{H}_F$ associated with F and let f_0 be a vector in $\mathfrak{H}_F$ such that $F(a) = (T_af_0, f_0)$, $a \in \mathfrak{A}$. Assume first that F is an extreme point of $\mathscr{P}_{\mathfrak{A}}$. Since f_0 is a cyclic vector, elements of the form T_af_0 are dense in $\mathfrak{H}_F$, and we have

$$\sup_{a \in \mathfrak{A}} \frac{|F(a)|^2}{F(a^\star a)} = \sup_{a \in \mathfrak{A}} \frac{|(T_af_0, f_0)|^2}{|T_af_0|^2} = |f_0|^2.$$

Therefore $|f_0| = 1$. Now suppose that $a \to T_a$ is not irreducible. Then there exists a projection P different from 0 and I such that $PT_a = T_aP$ for every $a \in \mathfrak{A}$. Note that, since elements of the form T_af_0 are dense in $\mathfrak{H}_F$, we have $Pf_0 \neq 0$ and $(I-P)f_0 \neq 0$. Define

$$\alpha_1 = |Pf_0|^2, \quad f_1 = \alpha_1^{-1/2}Pf_0, \quad F_1(a) = (T_af_1, f_1),$$

$$\alpha_2 = |(I-P)f_0|^2, \quad f_2 = \alpha_2^{-1/2}(I-P)f_0, \quad F_2(a) = (T_af_2, f_2).$$

Then $F = \alpha_1F_1 + \alpha_2F_2$ and

$$\alpha_1 + \alpha_2 = |Pf_0|^2 + |(I-P)f_0|^2 = |f_0|^2 = 1.$$

Since F is an extreme point, we must have $F_1 = F_2 = F$. However, if $F_1 = F$, then

$$(T_af_0, f_0) = (T_af_1, f_1) = \alpha_1^{-1}(T_aPf_0, Pf_0) = \alpha_1^{-1}(T_af_0, Pf_0)$$

for all $a \in \mathfrak{A}$. Again, since f_0 is a cyclic vector, it follows that $Pf_0 = \alpha_1 f_0$. Thus, $\alpha_1 = |Pf_0|^2 = \alpha_1^2|f_0|^2 = \alpha_1^2$. Therefore $\alpha_1 = 1$ and we obtain $Pf_0 = f_0$. But then $(I-P)f_0 = 0$, which is a contradiction. In other words, the representation $a \to T_a$ must be irreducible. This proves the sufficiency.

Now assume that $a \to T_a$ is irreducible and that F can be written in the form $F = \alpha_1F_1 + \alpha_2F_2$, where $\alpha_1 > 0$, $\alpha_2 > 0$, $\alpha_1 + \alpha_2 = 1$ and F_1, F_2 belong to $\mathscr{P}_{\mathfrak{A}}$. The problem is to show that $F_1 = F_2 = F$. Since $\alpha_1^{-1}F - F_1 = \alpha_1^{-1}\alpha_2F_2$, it follows, by Theorem (4.5.15), that $F_1 \prec F$. In other words, there exists an operator B in $\mathscr{B}(\mathfrak{H}_F)$, which commutes with each T_a, such that

$$F_1(a) = (T_aBf_0, f_0), \quad a \in \mathfrak{A}.$$

Since $a \to T_a$ is irreducible and B commutes with each T_a, it follows by Schur's Lemma (Theorem (4.4.12)) that B is equal to a scalar multiple, say λ_1, of the identity operator. Thus $F_1 = \lambda_1 F$ and, since F_1 is positive, $\lambda_1 \geqslant 0$. Furthermore, since $F_1(x^\star x) \leqslant \alpha_1^{-1}F(x^\star x)$, it follows that $\lambda_1 \leqslant \alpha_1^{-1}$ and hence that $\alpha_1\lambda_1 \leqslant 1$. Similarly, there exists

$\lambda_2 \geqslant 0$ such that $F_2 = \lambda_2 F$ and $\alpha_2\lambda_2 \leqslant 1$. Since $F = \alpha_1 F_1 + \alpha_2 F_2$ we obtain $\alpha_1\lambda_1 + \alpha_2\lambda_2 = 1$. This result, along with $\alpha_1 + \alpha_2 = 1$ and the inequalities $\alpha_1\lambda_1 \leqslant 1$ and $\alpha_2\lambda_2 \leqslant 1$, implies $\lambda_1 = \lambda_2 = 1$. Therefore $F_1 = F_2 = F$ and the theorem is proved.

COROLLARY (4.6.5). *In order for a non-zero element $F \in \mathscr{P}_{\mathfrak{A}}$ to be an extreme point, it is necessary and sufficient that the conditions $F' \in \mathscr{P}_{\mathfrak{A}}$ and $F' \prec F$ shall imply $F' = \lambda F$, for some scalar λ. If $\mu_{F'} = 1$, then $\lambda = 1$.*

LEMMA (4.6.6). *Let h be any element of $\mathscr{H}_{\mathfrak{A}}$ with the property that $F_0(h) \neq 0$ for some $F_0 \in \mathscr{P}_{\mathfrak{A}}$. Then there exists an extreme point F in $\mathscr{P}_{\mathfrak{A}}$ such that $F(h) \neq 0$.*

PROOF. Since $\mathscr{P}_{\mathfrak{A}}$ is a convex set which is compact in the $\mathscr{H}_{\mathfrak{A}}$-topology, the Krein–Mil'man Theorem (see Dunford and Schwartz [1, p. 440]) applies, so that we can conclude that the smallest convex subset of $\mathscr{P}_{\mathfrak{A}}$ which contains the extreme points and is closed in the $\mathscr{H}_{\mathfrak{A}}$-topology is the set $\mathscr{P}_{\mathfrak{A}}$ itself. Hence, for arbitrary $\epsilon > 0$, there exists a finite number of extreme points $F_1, \cdots, F_n$ and positive real numbers $\alpha_1, \cdots, \alpha_n$ such that $\alpha_1 + \cdots + \alpha_n = 1$ and

$$|F_0(h) - \sum_{j=1}^{n} \alpha_j F_j(h)| < \epsilon.$$

If $\epsilon < \frac{1}{2}|F_0(h)|$, then necessarily $F_j(h) \neq 0$ for at least one value of $j = 1, \cdots, n$. This proves the lemma.

THEOREM (4.6.7). *The $\star$-radical of a Banach $\star$-algebra $\mathfrak{A}$ is equal to the intersection of the kernels of all $\star$-representations of $\mathfrak{A}$ on Hilbert space.*

PROOF. Let $a \to T_a$ be any $\star$-representation of $\mathfrak{A}$ on a Hilbert space $\mathfrak{H}$. We have only to prove that the $\star$-radical $\mathfrak{R}^{(\star)}$ is contained in the kernel of $a \to T_a$. This is equivalent to showing that $T_u \neq 0$ implies $u \notin \mathfrak{R}^{(\star)}$. Now, if $T_u \neq 0$, then also $T_{u^\star} \neq 0$ and there exists a vector $f_0 \in \mathfrak{H}$ with $|f_0| = 1$ such that $T_{u^\star} f_0 \neq 0$. Define

$$F_0(a) = (T_a f_0, f_0), \quad a \in \mathfrak{A}.$$

Then $F_0 \in \mathscr{P}_{\mathfrak{A}}$ and $F_0(uu^\star) \neq 0$. By the above lemma, there exists an extreme point $F \in \mathscr{P}_{\mathfrak{A}}$ such that $F(uu^\star) \neq 0$. Let $a \to T'_a$ be the $\star$-representation associated with F. By Theorem (4.6.4), $a \to T'_a$ is irreducible. Furthermore, since $F \in \mathscr{P}_{\mathfrak{A}}$, we have $F(uu^\star)^2 \leqslant F(uu^\star uu^\star)$, so that $uu^\star \notin \mathfrak{L}_F$. This means that $u \notin \mathfrak{L}_F : \mathfrak{A}$. Since $\mathfrak{L}_F : \mathfrak{A}$ is the kernel of the irreducible representation $a \to T'_a$, it contains $\mathfrak{R}^{(\star)}$. Therefore $u \notin \mathfrak{R}^{(\star)}$ and the theorem is proved.

COROLLARY (4.6.8). *The $\star$-radical of $\mathfrak{A}$ is given by* $\mathfrak{R}^{(\star)} = \bigcap (\mathfrak{L}_F : \mathfrak{A}) = \bigcap \mathfrak{L}_F$, $F \in \mathscr{P}_{\mathfrak{A}}$.

THEOREM (4.6.9). *In any Banach $\star$-algebra $\mathfrak{A}$, there exists a pseudo-norm $|x|$ which satisfies the $B^\star$-condition $|x^\star x| = |x|^2$ and for which*

$$|F(x)| \leqslant \mu_F |x|, \quad x \in \mathfrak{A},$$

where F is any representable positive functional on $\mathfrak{A}$.

PROOF. Let $a \to T_a$ denote the $\star$-representation of $\mathfrak{A}$ obtained by forming the direct sum of all $\star$-representations associated with elements of $\mathscr{P}_{\mathfrak{A}}$. Define $|x|$ to be equal to the bound $|T_x|$ of the operator T_x. Then $|x|$ is clearly a pseudo-norm such that $|x^\star x| = |x|^2$. If F is any representable positive functional on $\mathfrak{A}$, then $\mu_F^{-1}F \in \mathscr{P}_{\mathfrak{A}}$ and there exists a vector f_0 in the Hilbert space of the representation $a \to T_a$ such that $|f_0| = 1$ and

$$\mu_F^{-1}F(x) = (T_x f_0, f_0), \quad x \in \mathfrak{A}.$$

It follows that $|F(x)| \leqslant \mu_F |x|$ and the theorem is proved.

COROLLARY (4.6.10). *The pseudo-norm $|x|$ can also be defined by the equation*

$$|x|^2 = \sup F(x^\star x), \quad F \in \mathscr{P}_{\mathfrak{A}}.$$

The $\star$-radical of $\mathfrak{A}$ consists of all x such that $|x| = 0$. In particular, if $\mathfrak{A}$ is $\star$-semi-simple, then it is an $A^\star$-algebra with $|x|$ as an auxiliary norm.

If the Banach algebra $\mathfrak{A}$ has an identity element and an involution which is locally continuous (that is, continuous in every maximal commutative $\star$-subalgebra), then the $\star$-radical has another interesting characterization which is due to Kelley and Vaught [1], except that they restricted attention to the $\star$-normed case (that is, $\|x^\star\| = \|x\|$). Before obtaining this, we note that local continuity of the involution is automatically satisfied in case all maximal commutative $\star$-subalgebras of $\mathfrak{A}$ are semi-simple. This follows from the fact that these subalgebras are always closed (Theorem (4.1.3)) plus uniqueness of the norm topology for semi-simple commutative Banach algebras (Corollary (2.5.18)). Another condition on the involution which yields local continuity is that $\nu(h) = 0$, for a hermitian element h, shall imply $h = 0$. In this case it is not difficult to show that *every* $\star$-subalgebra of $\mathfrak{A}$ is semi-simple. (See proof of Theorem (4.1.20).) We are indebted to Yood for these remarks as well as for the observation that the Kelley–Vaught characterization of the $\star$-radical could be extended to the more general situation.

Now assume that $\mathfrak{A}$ is a complex Banach $\star$-algebra with an identity element and a locally continuous involution. Denote by $\mathscr{K}_0$ the subset of $\mathscr{H}_{\mathfrak{A}}$ consisting of all finite sums of elements of the form $x^\star x$. It is readily verified that $\mathscr{K}_0$ is a convex set in $\mathscr{H}_{\mathfrak{A}}$ and is a CONE in the sense that $k_1+k_2 \in \mathscr{K}_0$ and $\alpha k \in \mathscr{K}_0$ for any k_1, k_2, $k \in \mathscr{K}_0$ and non-negative real scalar α. However, there may exist non-zero elements k such that both k and $-k$ belong to $\mathscr{K}_0$. The elements 0 and 1 obviously belong to $\mathscr{K}_0$ and the latter is even an interior point of $\mathscr{K}_0$. In fact, if $h \in \mathscr{H}_{\mathfrak{A}}$ and $\|1-h\| < 1$, then, by Lemma (4.1.4), there exists $k \in \mathscr{H}_{\mathfrak{A}}$ such that $k \circ k = 1-h$ and hence $(1-k)^2 = h$. It follows that $h \in \mathscr{K}_0$, which proves that 1 is an interior point of $\mathscr{K}_0$.

Next denote the closure of $\mathscr{K}_0$ in $\mathscr{H}_{\mathfrak{A}}$ by $\mathscr{K}$. Then $\mathscr{K}$ is also a cone. An element h of $\mathscr{H}_{\mathfrak{A}}$ will belong to $\mathscr{K}$ if and only if $\alpha+(1-\alpha)h \in \mathscr{K}_0$ for all α such that $0 < \alpha \leqslant 1$. It is obvious that this condition implies $h \in \mathscr{K}$ since $\lim(\alpha+(1-\alpha)h) = h$ as $\alpha \to 0$. On the other hand, if $h \in \mathscr{K}$, then, for arbitrary real scalar β, there exists $k \in \mathscr{K}_0$ such that $\|\beta(h-k)\| < 1$. Since $\|1-(1+\beta(h-k))\| < 1$, it follows that $1+\beta(h-k) \in \mathscr{K}_0$. If $\beta \geqslant 0$, then $\beta k \in \mathscr{K}_0$ and hence $1+\beta h \in \mathscr{K}_0$. Now, for arbitrary α with $0 < \alpha \leqslant 1$, set $\beta = \alpha^{-1}(1-\alpha)$. Then $\beta \geqslant 0$ and $\alpha+(1-\alpha)h = \alpha(1+\beta h) \in \mathscr{K}_0$.

Observe that a bounded linear functional F on $\mathfrak{A}$ is positive if and only if $F(k) \geqslant 0$ for every $k \in \mathscr{K}$. The way is thus opened for construction of positive functionals on $\mathfrak{A}$ with the help of the following extension theorem of M. G. Krein [7].

Let $\mathfrak{M}$ be a linear subspace of the real vector space $\mathscr{H}_{\mathfrak{A}}$ and let F_0 be a linear functional on $\mathfrak{M}$ such that $F_0(k) \geqslant 0$ for $k \in \mathfrak{M} \cap \mathscr{K}$. Then there exists a linear functional F defined on all of $\mathscr{H}_{\mathfrak{A}}$ such that $F(k) \geqslant 0$ for $k \in \mathscr{K}$ and $F(h) = F_0(h)$ for $h \in \mathfrak{M}$.

Aside from an application of Zorn's Lemma, the proof of this extension theorem reduces to showing that the extension can be made to the linear space spanned by $\mathfrak{M}$ and a single element h not in $\mathfrak{M}$. Let $\lambda = \sup F_0(m)$ for $h-m \in \mathscr{K}$, and $\mu = \inf F_0(m)$ for $m-h \in \mathscr{K}$. Then it is straightforward to prove that $\lambda \leqslant \mu$ and that any choice of $F(h)$ with $\lambda \leqslant F(h) \leqslant \mu$ leads to the required extension.

We are now ready to give the promised characterization of the $\star$-radical.

THEOREM (4.6.11). *Let $\mathfrak{A}$ be a complex Banach $\star$-algebra with an identity element and a locally continuous involution. Then the $\star$-radical of $\mathfrak{A}$ consists of all $r \in \mathfrak{A}$ such that $-r^\star r \in \mathscr{K}$. The set $\mathscr{K} \cap (-\mathscr{K})$ coincides with the set of all hermitian elements of $\mathfrak{R}^{(\star)}$.*

PROOF. If $-r^\star r \in \mathscr{K}$, then it is immediate that $F(r^\star r) = 0$ for every $F \in \mathscr{P}_{\mathfrak{A}}$. Therefore $r \in \mathfrak{R}^{(\star)}$ by Corollary (4.6.8). On the other hand, suppose that $-r^\star r \notin \mathscr{K}$ and let $\mathfrak{M}_0$ be the linear subspace of $\mathscr{H}_{\mathfrak{A}}$ spanned by the elements 1 and $r^\star r$. Let ρ denote the infimum of all real λ such that $\lambda - r^\star r \in \mathscr{K}$. Since $\mathscr{K}$ is closed, we have $\rho - r^\star r \in \mathscr{K}$. If $\rho \leqslant 0$, then $-r^\star r = |\rho| + \rho - r^\star r \in \mathscr{K}$ contrary to hypothesis. Therefore $\rho > 0$. Now define $F_0(\alpha + \beta r^\star r) = \alpha + \beta\rho$, where $\alpha + \beta r^\star r$ is an arbitrary element of $\mathfrak{M}_0$. Then F_0 is a linear functional on $\mathfrak{M}_0$. Let $\alpha + \beta r^\star r \in \mathscr{K}$. If $\beta \geqslant 0$, then $\beta(\rho - r^\star r) \in \mathscr{K}$ and hence

$$\alpha + \beta\rho = (\alpha + \beta r^\star r) + \beta(\rho - r^\star r) \in \mathscr{K}.$$

Since $-1 \notin \mathscr{K}$ (otherwise $-\rho \in \mathscr{K}$ so $-r^\star r = -\rho + (\rho - r^\star r) \in \mathscr{K}$), it follows that $\alpha + \beta\rho \geqslant 0$. Also, if $\beta < 0$, then $-\alpha\beta^{-1} - r^\star r \in \mathscr{K}$ and thus $\rho \leqslant -\alpha\beta^{-1}$, by the definition of ρ, so that again $\alpha + \beta\rho \geqslant 0$. In other words, $F_0(k) \geqslant 0$ for $k \in \mathscr{K} \cap \mathfrak{M}_0$. Since $F_0(1) = 1$, the extension theorem yields an element $F \in \mathscr{P}_{\mathfrak{A}}$ such that $F(x) = F_0(x)$ for $x \in \mathfrak{M}_0$. Finally, since $F_0(r^\star r) = \rho \neq 0$, it follows that $r \notin \mathfrak{R}^{(\star)}$ and the first assertion of the theorem is proved.

Now let $h \in \mathscr{K} \cap (-\mathscr{K})$. Since $x^\star \mathscr{K} x \subseteq \mathscr{K}$ for any $x \in \mathfrak{A}$, it follows that each of the elements $-h$, $-h^3$ and $(1-h)h(1-h)$ belongs to $\mathscr{K}$. Observe that $-h^2 = (1-h)h(1-h) - h - h^3$. Therefore $-h^2 \in \mathscr{K}$, so that $h \in \mathfrak{R}^{(\star)}$ by the first part of the theorem. On the other hand, let h be an arbitrary hermitian element of $\mathfrak{R}^{(\star)}$. Then $\nu(\alpha^{-1}h) = 0$ for any non-zero scalar α. When α is real this implies, as was observed earlier, that $1 \pm \alpha^{-1}h \in \mathscr{K}_0$. It follows that $\alpha \pm h \in \mathscr{K}_0$ for $\alpha > 0$. Letting $\alpha \to 0$, we obtain $\pm h \in \mathscr{K}$. In other words, $h \in \mathscr{K} \cap (-\mathscr{K})$ and the theorem is proved.

We conclude this section with some remarks on the case of a commutative Banach $\star$-algebra $\mathfrak{C}$. For any $\varphi \in \Phi_{\mathfrak{C}}$, define $F_\varphi(x) = \hat{x}(\varphi)$, $x \in \mathfrak{C}$. Then F_φ is a bounded linear functional on $\mathfrak{C}$. Observe that F_φ will be hermitian if and only if

$$\widehat{x^\star}(\varphi) = \overline{\hat{x}(\varphi)}, \quad x \in \mathfrak{C}.$$

In other words, the hermitian functionals of the form F_φ are precisely those functionals corresponding to elements of $\Phi_{\mathfrak{C}}{}^{(\star)}$. This is the set of fixed points under the homeomorphism $\varphi \to \varphi^\star$ of $\Phi_{\mathfrak{C}}$ onto itself, where $\hat{x}(\varphi^\star) = \overline{\widehat{x^\star}(\varphi)}$ for $x \in \mathfrak{C}$. Actually, we have a much stronger result given in the next theorem.

THEOREM (4.6.12). *For any commutative Banach $\star$-algebra $\mathfrak{C}$, $\{F_\varphi : \varphi \in \Phi_{\mathfrak{C}}^{(\star)}\}$ coincides with the set of all extreme points of the convex set $\mathscr{P}_{\mathfrak{C}}$.*

PROOF. If $\hat{x}^\star(\varphi) = \overline{\hat{x}(\varphi)}$, then $F_\varphi(x^\star x) = |F_\varphi(x)|^2$, so that $\{F_\varphi : \varphi \in \Phi_{\mathfrak{C}}^{(\star)}\} \subseteq \mathscr{P}_{\mathfrak{C}}$. Let F be an extreme point of $\mathscr{P}_{\mathfrak{C}}$ and let $c \to T_c$ be the associated $\star$-representation with $F(x) = (T_x f_0, f_0)$, $x \in \mathfrak{C}$. Since the representation is irreducible, it follows immediately from Schur's Lemma (Theorem (4.4.12)) that each T_x is a scalar multiple of the identity operator. Therefore there exists $\varphi \in \Phi_{\mathfrak{C}}$ such that $F(x) = \hat{x}(\varphi)|f_0|^2$. Since F is an extreme point, also $|f_0| = 1$. Hence $F = F_\varphi$. On the other hand, the $\star$-representation associated with each F_φ, for $\varphi \in \Phi_{\mathfrak{C}}^{(\star)}$, is obviously one-dimensional and so is irreducible. Therefore F_φ is an extreme point of $\mathscr{P}_{\mathfrak{C}}$ and the theorem is proved.

COROLLARY (4.6.13). *The $\star$-radical of $\mathfrak{C}$ coincides with the set of all $x \in \mathfrak{C}$ such that $\hat{x}$ vanishes on $\Phi_{\mathfrak{C}}^{(\star)}$.*

LEMMA (4.6.14). *The pseudo-norm $|x|$ in $\mathfrak{C}$, given by Theorem (4.6.9), is equal to $\max|\hat{x}(\varphi)|$ for $\varphi \in \Phi_{\mathfrak{C}}^{(\star)}$.*

PROOF. Set $|\hat{x}| = \max|\hat{x}(\varphi)|$ for $\varphi \in \Phi_{\mathfrak{C}}^{(\star)}$. By Corollary (4.6.10), we know that

$$|x|^2 = \sup F(x^\star x), \quad F \in \mathscr{P}_{\mathfrak{C}}.$$

Therefore it follows immediately that $|\hat{x}| \leqslant |x|$. On the other hand, for any $F \in \mathscr{P}_{\mathfrak{A}}$, $x \in \mathfrak{C}$, and $\epsilon > 0$, there exist, by the above theorem and the Krein–Mil'man theorem, positive scalars $\alpha_1, \cdots, \alpha_n$ and elements $\varphi_1, \cdots, \varphi_n$ of $\Phi_{\mathfrak{C}}^{(\star)}$ such that $\alpha_1 + \cdots + \alpha_n = 1$ and

$$\left|F(x^\star x) - \sum \alpha_i |\hat{x}(\varphi_i)|^2\right| < \epsilon.$$

Hence

$$\begin{aligned} F(x^\star x) &\leqslant \sum \alpha_i |x(\varphi_i)|^2 + \epsilon \\ &\leqslant |\hat{x}|^2 + \epsilon. \end{aligned}$$

This implies $|x|^2 \leqslant |\hat{x}|^2 + \epsilon$. Since $\epsilon > 0$ is arbitrary, it follows that $|x| \leqslant |\hat{x}|$ and the proof is complete.

We close with an integral representation for positive functionals. (Gelfand, Raikov, and Šilov [1, Theorem 19].)

THEOREM (4.6.15). *Every representable positive functional F on $\mathfrak{C}$ has the form*

$$F(x) = \int_{\Phi_{\mathfrak{C}}^{(\star)}} \hat{x}(\varphi) m(d\varphi), \quad x \in \mathfrak{C},$$

where m is a regular non-negative, real measure defined on the Borel subsets of $\Phi_{\mathfrak{C}}^{(\star)}$.

PROOF. Consider the $\star$-subalgebra $\mathfrak{C}_0$ of $C_0(\Phi_{\mathfrak{C}}^{(\star)})$ obtained by restricting the functions $\hat{x}$ to the set $\Phi_{\mathfrak{C}}^{(\star)}$ and observe that $\mathfrak{C}_0$ is dense in $C_0(\Phi_{\mathfrak{C}}^{(\star)})$ by the Stone–Weierstrass theorem. Now, by Theorem (4.6.9) and the above lemma, we have

$$|F(x)| \leqslant \mu_F \max |\hat{x}(\varphi)|, \quad \varphi \in \Phi_{\mathfrak{C}}^{(\star)}.$$

Therefore F may be regarded as a bounded linear functional on $\mathfrak{C}_0$ and can accordingly be extended to all of $C_0(\Phi_{\mathfrak{C}}^{(\star)})$. The desired result now follows from the Riesz–Kakutani representation theorem for bounded linear functionals on a Banach space of the type $C_0(\Phi_{\mathfrak{A}}^{(\star)})$.

Kelley and Vaught [1] define the $\star$-radical to be equal to the intersection of the kernels of all $\star$-representations on Hilbert space. (See Theorem (4.6.7).) The intersection of all ideals $\mathfrak{L}_F$, for $F \in \mathscr{P}_{\mathfrak{A}}$, which, by Corollary (4.6.8), is also the $\star$-radical, has been called the REDUCING IDEAL by Naĭmark [1]. When the reducing ideal is equal to (0), he calls the algebra REDUCED. The method of constructing irreducible $\star$-representations out of extreme points of $\mathscr{P}_{\mathfrak{A}}$ was used by Segal [3] to prove that a locally compact topological group admits a complete set of irreducible unitary representations. (See the Appendix, A.3.1.)

§ **7. Symmetric $\star$-algebras.** In this section we consider certain algebraic and topological conditions on a Banach $\star$-algebra which ensure the existence of many positive functionals and hence, by the preceding section, many $\star$-representations on Hilbert space. Our first step is to introduce another weaker notion of positivity for hermitian functionals.

DEFINITION (4.7.1). *Let $\mathfrak{A}$ be any $\star$-algebra and F a hermitian functional on $\mathfrak{A}$. Then F is said to be* WEAKLY POSITIVE *in case $F(h^2) \geqslant 0$ for every $h \in \mathscr{H}_{\mathfrak{A}}$.*

It is obvious that every positive functional is weakly positive. Since the concept of weak positivity is less restrictive than positivity, it is easier to construct weakly positive functionals than positive ones. This observation, plus the fact that the two notions coincide for an important class of Banach ⋆-algebras, motivates most of the discussion which follows.

As in the case of positive functionals, it is not difficult to establish for weakly positive functionals the following weak version of the Cauchy–Schwartz inequality:

$$|F(hk+kh)|^2 \leqslant 4F(h^2)F(k^2), \quad h, k \in \mathscr{H}_{\mathfrak{A}}.$$

Thus, if h and k commute, then $|F(hk)|^2 \leqslant F(h^2)F(k^2)$ and, if $\mathfrak{A}$ has an identity element, then $|F(h)|^2 \leqslant F(1)F(h^2)$.

Observe that, if h has a real spectrum, then h^2 has a non-negative spectrum. The following lemma provides a partial converse to this statement.

Lemma (4.7.2). *Let $\mathfrak{A}$ be a Banach algebra with an identity element. If u is any element of $\mathfrak{A}$ with a positive real spectrum, then there exists an element v in $\mathfrak{A}$ with real spectrum such that $v^2 = u$. If $\mathfrak{A}$ has a locally continuous involution and $u \in \mathscr{H}_{\mathfrak{A}}$, then also $v \in \mathscr{H}_{\mathfrak{A}}$.*

Proof. It will be sufficient to make the proof for an element u such that $0 < Sp(u) < 1$. In this case, we also have that $0 < Sp(1-u) < 1$. Therefore, in particular, $\nu(1-u) < 1$. It follows, by Lemma (4.1.4), that there exists $k \in \mathfrak{A}$ such that $k \circ k = 1-u$. Set $v = 1-k$. Then $v^2 = u$. In the case of an involution, $h \in \mathscr{H}_{\mathfrak{A}}$ implies $k \in \mathscr{H}_{\mathfrak{A}}$ and hence $v \in \mathscr{H}_{\mathfrak{A}}$. Since v is a limit of real polynomials in u, it therefore has a real spectrum, by Theorems (1.6.10) and (1.6.16). This completes the proof.

If h is a hermitian element in a Banach ⋆-algebra $\mathfrak{A}$, then it is convenient for the discussion which follows to write $h \geqslant 0$ in case $Sp(h) \geqslant 0$. Similarly, we write $h \leqslant k$ provided $k-h \geqslant 0$.

Theorem (4.7.3). *Let $\mathfrak{A}$ be a Banach ⋆-algebra with an identity element and a locally continuous hermitian involution. Then the following conditions on a hermitian functional F are equivalent.*

(*i*) *F is weakly positive.*

(*ii*) *$F(h) \geqslant 0$, for $h \geqslant 0$.*

(*iii*) *$|F(h)| \leqslant F(1)\nu(h)$, for every $h \in \mathscr{H}_{\mathfrak{A}}$.*

Proof. Assume first that (i) is true and consider any $h \geqslant 0$. For arbitrary $\delta > 0$, we have $0 < Sp(h+\delta)$. Thus, by Lemma (4.7.2), there exists $k \in \mathscr{H}_{\mathfrak{A}}$ such that $k^2 = h+\delta$. It follows that $0 \leqslant F(h+\delta)$ and hence that $-\delta F(1) \leqslant F(h)$ for all $\delta > 0$. Therefore $0 \leqslant F(h)$ and we have that (i) implies (ii).

Next assume (ii) true and let h be any element of $\mathscr{H}_{\mathfrak{A}}$. Since $Sp(\nu(h)-h) \geqslant 0$, it follows that $F(\nu(h)-h) \geqslant 0$. Hence $F(h) \leqslant F(1)\nu(h)$. Similarly,

$$-F(h) = F(-h) \leqslant F(1)\nu(-h) = F(1)\nu(h),$$

and so we obtain $|F(h)| \leqslant F(1)\nu(h)$. Therefore (ii) implies (iii).

Finally, we show that (iii) implies (i). In order to prove that $F(h^2) \geqslant 0$ for $h \in \mathscr{H}_{\mathfrak{A}}$, it is clearly sufficient to consider only h such that $\nu(h) \leqslant 1$. Then also $\nu(h^2) \leqslant 1$ and we have $0 \leqslant Sp(h^2) \leqslant 1$. It follows that $0 \leqslant Sp(1-h^2) \leqslant 1$ and hence that $\nu(1-h^2) \leqslant 1$. Now

$$F(1) = F(h^2)+F(1-h^2) \leqslant F(h^2)+F(1)\nu(1-h^2) \leqslant F(h^2)+F(1).$$

Therefore $0 \leqslant F(h^2)$ and the proof is complete.

LEMMA (4.7.4). *Let $\mathfrak{A}$ be a Banach ⋆-algebra with an identity element and a locally continuous hermitian involution. Then the following two conditions are equivalent.*

(*i*) $\nu(h+k) \leqslant \nu(h)+\nu(k)$, *for all h, k in $\mathscr{H}_{\mathfrak{A}}$.*

(*ii*) *If $h \geqslant 0$ and $k \geqslant 0$, then $h+k \geqslant 0$.*

PROOF. Consider any h, k such that $h \geqslant 0$ and $k \geqslant 0$. For arbitrary $\epsilon > 0$, choose $\lambda > 0$ so that, if $h' = \lambda^{-1}(h+\epsilon)$ and $k' = \lambda^{-1}(k+\epsilon)$, then $\nu(h') < 1$ and $\nu(k') < 1$. Clearly, $0 < Sp(h') < 1$ and $0 < Sp(k') < 1$. Therefore we also have $\nu(1-h') < 1$ and $\nu(1-k') < 1$. Now, assuming (i), we have

$$\nu\left(1-\frac{h'+k'}{2}\right) \leqslant \tfrac{1}{2}[\nu(1-h')+\nu(1-k')] < 1.$$

Since

$$\nu\left(1-\frac{h'+k'}{2}\right) = \max|1-\alpha|, \quad \alpha \in Sp\left(\frac{h'+k'}{2}\right),$$

it follows that

$$0 < Sp\left(\frac{h'+k'}{2}\right)$$

This implies $-2\epsilon < Sp(h+k)$. Since $\epsilon > 0$ is arbitrary, we obtain $Sp(h+k) \geqslant 0$, so that (i) implies (ii).

Next assume (ii) and let $\alpha > \nu(h)$ and $\beta > \nu(k)$. Since $Sp(\alpha \pm h) \geqslant 0$ and $Sp(\beta \pm k) \geqslant 0$, we have $Sp((\alpha \pm h)+(\beta \pm k)) \geqslant 0$. Moreover,

$$Sp((\alpha \pm h)+(\beta \pm k)) = \alpha+\beta \pm Sp(h+k).$$

Therefore,

$$-(\alpha+\beta) \leqslant Sp(h+k) \leqslant \alpha+\beta,$$

which implies $\nu(h+k) \leqslant \alpha+\beta$. Since α and β are arbitrary positive numbers greater than $\nu(h)$ and $\nu(k)$ respectively, it follows that $\nu(h+k) \leqslant \nu(h)+\nu(k)$, completing the proof of the lemma.

We turn now to a class of ⋆-algebras for which the notions of positivity and weak positivity coincide.

DEFINITION (4.7.5). *A Banach ⋆-algebra $\mathfrak{A}$ is called* SYMMETRIC *provided every element of the form $-x^\star x$ is quasi-regular in $\mathfrak{A}$.*

THEOREM (4.7.6). *Let $\mathfrak{A}$ be a symmetric Banach ⋆-algebra. Then (i) the involution in $\mathfrak{A}$ is hermitian and (ii) $x^\star x \geqslant 0$ for every $x \in \mathfrak{A}$.*

PROOF. Since elements of the form $-h^2$, where $h \in \mathscr{H}_{\mathfrak{A}}$, are quasi-regular, the first statement is given immediately by Lemma (4.1.7). Furthermore, let λ be any negative real number and set $z = |\lambda|^{-1/2}x$. Then $\lambda^{-1}x^\star x = -z^\star z$, so that $\lambda^{-1}x^\star x$ is quasi-regular. Therefore $Sp(x^\star x) \geqslant 0$ and the proof is complete.

Statement (i), along with Theorem (4.1.9), gives the following corollary.

COROLLARY (4.7.7). *If $\mathfrak{B}$ is a closed ⋆-subalgebra of $\mathfrak{A}$, then $\mathfrak{B}$ is also symmetric.*

By Theorem (4.7.3), we can state the next corollary.

COROLLARY (4.7.8). *If $\mathfrak{A}$ has an identity element and a locally continuous involution, then a hermitian functional F on $\mathfrak{A}$ is positive if and only if it is weakly positive.*

Notice that a commutative Banach ⋆-algebra $\mathfrak{C}$ is symmetric if and only if its involution is hermitian; that is $\widehat{x^\star}(\varphi) = \overline{\hat{x}(\varphi)}$ for every $x \in \mathfrak{C}$ and $\varphi \in \Phi_{\mathfrak{C}}$. In other words, $\varphi^\star = \varphi$ for every $\varphi \in \Phi_{\mathfrak{C}}$, so that $\Phi_{\mathfrak{C}}{}^{(\star)} = \Phi_{\mathfrak{C}}$.

The next theorem is due to Yood [12].

THEOREM (4.7.9). *Let $\mathfrak{A}$ be a symmetric Banach ⋆-algebra without an identity element and let $\mathfrak{A}_1$ be the Banach ⋆-algebra obtained by adjunction of an identity element to $\mathfrak{A}$. Then $\mathfrak{A}_1$ is also symmetric.*

PROOF. Let $\xi+x$ be an arbitrary element of $\mathfrak{A}_1$ and set

$$h = \bar{\xi}x+\xi x^\star+x^\star x.$$

Then $h \in \mathscr{H}_{\mathfrak{A}}$ and $(\xi+x)^\star(\xi+x) = |\xi|^2+h$. Now let $\mathfrak{C}$ be a maximal commutative $\star$-subalgebra of $\mathfrak{A}$ which contains h. Then, by Theorem (4.1.3), $\mathfrak{C}$ is a closed $\star$-subalgebra of $\mathfrak{A}$ and is accordingly a symmetric Banach $\star$-algebra in its own right. Let φ be an arbitrary element of $\Phi_{\mathfrak{C}}$ and choose any $u \in \mathfrak{C}$ with $\hat{u}(\varphi) = 1$. Then also $\widehat{u^\star}(\varphi) = 1$. Set $y = (\xi + x)u$. Then $y^\star y = u^\star(|\xi|^2 + h)u$ and, since $\mathfrak{A}$ is symmetric, $0 \leqslant Sp_{\mathfrak{A}}(y^\star y) = Sp_{\mathfrak{C}}(y^\star y)$. Therefore, in particular,

$$|\xi|^2 + \hat{h}(\varphi) = \widehat{u^\star}(\varphi)(|\xi|^2 + \hat{h}(\varphi))\hat{u}(\varphi) = (\widehat{y^\star y})(\varphi) \geqslant 0.$$

It follows that $0 \leqslant |\xi|^2 + Sp_{\mathfrak{C}}(h)$. Since

$$Sp_{\mathfrak{A}_1}(|\xi|^2 + h) = |\xi|^2 + Sp_{\mathfrak{A}}(h) = |\xi|^2 + Sp_{\mathfrak{C}}(h),$$

we conclude that $(\xi + x)^\star(\xi + x) \geqslant 0$ and hence that $\mathfrak{A}_1$ is symmetric, thus completing the proof.

In the remainder of our discussion of symmetric Banach $\star$-algebras, we shall assume the existence of an identity element. This is mainly for convenience, since most of the discussion could be pushed through in one form or another for the general case with the help of the above theorem.

Lemma (4.7.10). *Let $\mathfrak{A}$ be a symmetric Banach $\star$-algebra with an identity element and a locally continuous involution. Then $h \geqslant 0$ and $k \geqslant 0$ imply $h + k \geqslant 0$. Also, for arbitrary h and k in $\mathscr{H}_{\mathfrak{A}}$,*

$$\nu(h + k) \leqslant \nu(h) + \nu(k).$$

Proof. Let $\lambda > 0$ and set $h' = h + \lambda$ and $k' = k + \lambda$. Then $0 < Sp(h')$ and $0 < Sp(k')$. By Lemma (4.7.2), there exist hermitian elements u and v such that $u^2 = h'$ and $v^2 = k'$. Also, since h' and k' are regular, so are the elements u and v regular. Hence

$$\begin{aligned} h + k + 2\lambda &= u^2 + v^2 = u(1 + u^{-1}v^2u^{-1})u \\ &= u(1 + (vu^{-1})^\star(vu^{-1}))u. \end{aligned}$$

Therefore $h + k + 2\lambda$ is regular. Since this holds for all $\lambda > 0$, it follows that $Sp(h + k) \geqslant 0$. The last statement of the Lemma follows by Lemma (4.7.4).

Consider next a symmetric Banach $\star$-algebra $\mathfrak{A}$ with an identity element and a locally continuous involution, and let $\mathfrak{B}$ denote a closed $\star$-subalgebra of $\mathfrak{A}$ which contains the identity element of $\mathfrak{A}$. Then, by Corollary (4.7.7), $\mathfrak{B}$ is also symmetric. For F any positive functional on $\mathfrak{A}$, denote by F' the restriction of F to the subalgebra $\mathfrak{B}$.

THEOREM (4.7.11). *The mapping $F \to F'$ takes the class of all positive functionals on $\mathfrak{A}$ onto the class of all positive functionals on $\mathfrak{B}$ in such a way that $\mathscr{P}_{\mathfrak{A}}$ is mapped onto $\mathscr{P}_{\mathfrak{B}}$ and the extreme points of $\mathscr{P}_{\mathfrak{B}}$ are images of extreme points of $\mathscr{P}_{\mathfrak{A}}$.*

PROOF. It is obvious that F' is a positive functional on $\mathfrak{B}$. We prove that all positive functionals on $\mathfrak{B}$ are obtained in this way. Observe first that $\mathscr{H}_{\mathfrak{B}}$ is a linear subspace of $\mathscr{H}_{\mathfrak{A}}$. If F_0 is any positive functional on $\mathfrak{B}$, then, by Theorem (4.7.3) (iii), $|F_0(h)| \leqslant F_0(1)\nu(h)$, $h \in \mathscr{H}_{\mathfrak{B}}$. Therefore, since $\nu(h)$ is subadditive in $\mathscr{H}_{\mathfrak{B}}$ (Lemma (4.7.10)), the Hahn–Banach extension theorem applies, so that we can extend F_0 as a linear functional to $\mathscr{H}_{\mathfrak{A}}$ preserving the property $|F_0(h)| \leqslant F_0(1)\nu(h)$, $h \in \mathscr{H}_{\mathfrak{A}}$. Let F be the hermitian functional obtained by extending F_0 to all of $\mathfrak{A}$. Then, by Theorem (4.7.3) and Corollary (4.7.8), F is a positive functional on $\mathfrak{A}$. Clearly $F' = F_0$ on $\mathfrak{B}$, so that the mapping $F \to F'$ covers the positive functionals on $\mathfrak{B}$. Since $F \in \mathscr{P}_{\mathfrak{A}}$ if and only if $F(1) \leqslant 1$, the fact that $\mathscr{P}_{\mathfrak{A}}$ maps onto $\mathscr{P}_{\mathfrak{B}}$ is immediate.

Finally, let E'_0 be an extreme point of $\mathscr{P}_{\mathfrak{B}}$ and denote by $\mathscr{E}$ the set of all $F \in \mathscr{P}_{\mathfrak{A}}$ such that $F' = E'_0$. It is straightforward to verify that $\mathscr{E}$ is a convex subset of $\mathscr{P}_{\mathfrak{A}}$ which is closed in the $\mathscr{H}_{\mathfrak{A}}$-topology. Hence $\mathscr{E}$ contains an extreme point, say F_0. We have only to prove that F_0 is actually an extreme point of $\mathscr{P}_{\mathfrak{A}}$. Therefore, suppose that $F_0 = \alpha_1 F_1 + \alpha_2 F_2$, where $\alpha_1 > 0$, $\alpha_2 > 0$, $\alpha_1 + \alpha_2 = 1$, and $F_1, F_2 \in \mathscr{P}_{\mathfrak{A}}$. Then $E'_0 = \alpha_1 F'_1 + \alpha_2 F'_2$. Since E'_0 is an extreme point of $\mathscr{P}_{\mathfrak{B}}$ it follows that $F'_1 = F'_2 = E'_0$. In other words $F_1, F_2 \in \mathscr{E}$. Since F_0 is an extreme point of $\mathscr{E}$, it follows that $F_1 = F_2 = F_0$. Therefore F_0 is indeed an extreme point of $\mathscr{P}_{\mathfrak{A}}$ and the proof is complete.

THEOREM (4.7.12). *Let $\mathfrak{A}$ be a symmetric Banach ⋆-algebra with an identity element and a locally continuous involution. If c is a normal element of $\mathfrak{A}$, then*

$$Sp_{\mathfrak{A}}(c) \subseteq \{F(c) : F \text{ an extreme point of } \mathscr{P}_{\mathfrak{A}}\}.$$

PROOF. Consider a maximal commutative ⋆-subalgebra $\mathfrak{C}$ of $\mathfrak{A}$ which contains c. For any $\varphi_0 \in \Phi_{\mathfrak{C}}$, define $F_0(x) = \hat{x}(\varphi_0)$, $x \in \mathfrak{C}$. Then, by Theorem (4.6.12), F_0 is an extreme point of $\mathscr{P}_{\mathfrak{C}}$. Therefore, by the above theorem, there exists an extreme point F of $\mathscr{P}_{\mathfrak{A}}$ such that $F(x) = F_0(x)$ for $x \in \mathfrak{C}$. Since

$$Sp_{\mathfrak{A}}(c) = Sp_{\mathfrak{C}}(c) = \{\hat{c}(\varphi) : \varphi \in \Phi_{\mathfrak{C}}\}$$

the theorem follows.

COROLLARY (4.7.13). *A hermitian element* h *in* $\mathfrak{A}$ *has a non-negative spectrum if and only if* $F(h) \geqslant 0$ *for every* F *in* $\mathscr{P}_{\mathfrak{A}}$.

THEOREM (4.7.14). *Let* $\mathfrak{A}$ *be a symmetric Banach* $\star$*-algebra with an identity element and a locally continuous involution, and let* $\mathfrak{L}$ *be a maximal left ideal in* $\mathfrak{A}$. *Then there exists an extreme point* F *of* $\mathscr{P}_{\mathfrak{A}}$ *such that* $\mathfrak{L}_F = \mathfrak{L}$.

PROOF. Set $\mathscr{H}_{\mathfrak{L}} = \mathscr{H}_{\mathfrak{A}} \cap \mathfrak{L}$ and define

$$\mathscr{H}'_{\mathfrak{L}} = \{k+\lambda : k \in \mathscr{H}_{\mathfrak{L}},\ \lambda \text{ real}\}.$$

Then $\mathscr{H}'_{\mathfrak{L}}$ is a real linear subspace of $\mathscr{H}_{\mathfrak{A}}$. Now define

$$F_0(k+\lambda) = \lambda, \quad k+\lambda \in \mathscr{H}'_{\mathfrak{L}}.$$

Then F_0 is a real linear functional on $\mathscr{H}'_{\mathfrak{L}}$ with $F_0(1) = 1$. Since $k+\lambda \in \mathscr{H}'_{\mathfrak{L}}$ implies $\lambda-(k+\lambda) \in \mathfrak{L}$, it follows that $\lambda \in Sp(k+\lambda)$. Therefore $|\lambda| \leqslant \nu(k+\lambda)$ and we have

$$|F_0(k+\lambda)| \leqslant \nu(k+\lambda), \quad k+\lambda \in \mathscr{H}'_{\mathfrak{L}}.$$

Again, by the Hahn–Banach extension theorem, F_0 can be extended as a linear functional to $\mathscr{H}_{\mathfrak{A}}$ preserving the property $|F_0(h)| \leqslant \nu(h)$. Let F be the hermitian functional determined on $\mathfrak{A}$ by this extension. Note that F is automatically positive, by Theorem (4.7.3) and Corollary (4.7.8). If $x \in \mathfrak{L}$, then also $x^\star x \in \mathfrak{L}$, so that $F(x^\star x) = 0$. This means that $\mathfrak{L} \subseteq \mathfrak{L}_F$. On the other hand, since $\mathfrak{L}$ is maximal $\mathfrak{L} = \mathfrak{L}_F$. Note that $F \in \mathscr{P}_{\mathfrak{A}}$. Now consider the class $\mathscr{E}$ of all $F \in \mathscr{P}_{\mathfrak{A}}$ with $\mathfrak{L} = \mathfrak{L}_F$. Then it is readily verified that $\mathscr{E}$ is a convex subset of $\mathscr{P}_{\mathfrak{A}}$ which is closed in the $\mathscr{H}_{\mathfrak{A}}$-topology. Furthermore, if $F \in \mathscr{E}$ and $F = \alpha_1 F_1 + \alpha_2 F_2$, where $\alpha_1 > 0$, $\alpha_2 > 0$, $\alpha_1+\alpha_2 = 1$, and $F_1, F_2 \in \mathscr{P}_{\mathfrak{A}}$, then $F(x^\star x) = 0$ implies $F_1(x^\star x) = F_2(x^\star x) = 0$, so that $\mathfrak{L} = \mathfrak{L}_{F_1} = \mathfrak{L}_{F_2}$. In other words, $F_1, F_2 \in \mathscr{E}$. Therefore an extreme point of $\mathscr{E}$ is also an extreme point of $\mathscr{P}_{\mathfrak{A}}$. This proves the theorem.

THEOREM (4.7.15). *If* $\mathfrak{A}$ *is a symmetric Banach* $\star$*-algebra with an identity element and a locally continuous involution, then the radical of* $\mathfrak{A}$ *coincides with the* $\star$*-radical and the latter consists of all elements* r *such that* $Sp(r^\star r) = (0)$.

PROOF. Since the $\star$-radical $\mathfrak{R}^{(\star)}$ of a Banach $\star$-algebra always contains the radical $\mathfrak{R}$ (Theorem (4.4.10)), we have first to verify the opposite inclusion. Let $\mathfrak{L}$ be a maximal ideal in $\mathfrak{A}$ and, by Theorem (4.7.14), choose a positive functional $F \in \mathscr{P}_{\mathfrak{A}}$ such that $\mathfrak{L}_F = \mathfrak{L}$. The desired inclusion now follows from the facts that $\mathfrak{R}$ is equal to the intersection of all maximal left ideals $\mathfrak{L}$ (Theorem (2.3.2)) and that $\mathfrak{R}^{(\star)}$ is equal to the intersection of all ideals $\mathfrak{L}_F$ with $F \in \mathscr{P}_{\mathfrak{A}}$ (Corollary (4.6.8)). Now consider the set $\mathscr{H}_{\mathfrak{A}}^+$ of all $h \in \mathscr{H}_{\mathfrak{A}}$ such that $h \geqslant 0$. Then, by Corollary (4.7.13), $\mathscr{H}_{\mathfrak{A}}^+$ is closed. Recall the cone $\mathscr{K}$ introduced in the preceding section and observe that in the present case $\mathscr{K} \subseteq \mathscr{H}_{\mathfrak{A}}^+$. Furthermore, if $h \in \mathscr{H}_{\mathfrak{A}}^+$ and δ is a positive scalar, then $Sp(h+\delta) > 0$, so that there exists $k \in \mathscr{H}_{\mathfrak{A}}$ such that $k^2 = h+\delta$ (Lemma (4.7.2)). Since $h+\delta \rightarrow h$ as $\delta \rightarrow 0$, it follows that $h \in \mathscr{K}$. In other words, $\mathscr{K} = \mathscr{H}_{\mathfrak{A}}^+$. Now, by Theorem (4.6.11), $r \in \mathfrak{R}^{(\star)}$ if and only if $-r^\star r \in \mathscr{H}_{\mathfrak{A}}^+$. Since $r^\star r \in \mathscr{H}_{\mathfrak{A}}^+$, the condition $-r^\star r \in \mathscr{H}_{\mathfrak{A}}^+$ is obviously equivalent to the condition $Sp(r^\star r) = (0)$, and so the proof is complete.

Corollary (4.7.16). *If $\mathfrak{A}$ is semi-simple, then it has a faithful ⋆-representation on Hilbert space and is thus an $A^\star$-algebra.*

Theorem (4.7.17). *Let $\mathfrak{A}$ be a symmetric Banach ⋆-algebra with an identity element and a locally continuous involution, and let $\mathfrak{B}$ denote a closed ⋆-subalgebra of $\mathfrak{A}$ which contains the identity element of $\mathfrak{A}$. Then every maximal left (right) ideal $\mathfrak{L}'$ in $\mathfrak{B}$ is of the form $\mathfrak{L}' = \mathfrak{L} \cap \mathfrak{B}$, where $\mathfrak{L}$ is a maximal left (right) ideal in $\mathfrak{A}$.*

Proof. By Theorem (4.7.14), there exists a positive functional F' on $\mathfrak{B}$ such that $\mathfrak{L}_{F'} = \mathfrak{L}'$. Let F be any positive functional on $\mathfrak{A}$ whose restriction to $\mathfrak{B}$ is equal to F'. Then $\mathfrak{L}' = \mathfrak{L}_F \cap \mathfrak{B}$. If $\mathfrak{L}$ is any maximal left ideal in $\mathfrak{A}$ which contains $\mathfrak{L}_F$, then it is obvious that $\mathfrak{L}' = \mathfrak{L} \cap \mathfrak{B}$.

Corollary (4.7.18). *Any element b of $\mathfrak{B}$ which is left (right) regular in $\mathfrak{A}$ is also left (right) regular in $\mathfrak{B}$.*

By the above theorem, the radical of $\mathfrak{B}$ is contained in $\mathfrak{R} \cap \mathfrak{B}$, where $\mathfrak{R}$ is the radical of $\mathfrak{A}$. On the other hand, if u is an element of $\mathfrak{B}$ not in $\mathfrak{R}$, then, by Corollary (4.6.8), there exists $F \in \mathscr{P}_{\mathfrak{A}}$ such that $F(u^\star u) \neq 0$. Let F' be the restriction of F to $\mathfrak{B}$. Then $F'(u^\star u) \neq 0$ and, again by Corollary (4.6.8), u is not in the radical of $\mathfrak{B}$. We therefore obtain the next corollary.

Corollary (4.7.19). *The radical of $\mathfrak{B}$ is equal to $\mathfrak{R} \cap \mathfrak{B}$.*

In the following theorem on extension of ⋆-representations, the algebras $\mathfrak{A}$ and $\mathfrak{B}$ are as in the above theorem.

Theorem (4.7.20). *Let $b \rightarrow T'_b$ be any ⋆-representation of $\mathfrak{B}$ on a*

Hilbert space $\mathfrak{H}'$. *Then there exists a* $\star$*-representation* $a \to T_a$ *of* $\mathfrak{A}$ *on a Hilbert space* $\mathfrak{H}$ *with the following properties:*

(*i*) $\mathfrak{H}'$ *is a closed subspace of* $\mathfrak{H}$,

(*ii*) $T'_b f' = T_b f'$ *for all* $b \in \mathfrak{B}$ *and* $f' \in \mathfrak{H}'$,

(*iii*) *if* $b \to T'_b$ *is irreducible, then* $a \to T_a$ *is irreducible.*

PROOF. We can obviously assume the representation $b \to T'_b$ to be essential. Then it can be written as a direct sum of cyclic representations (Theorem (4.4.8)). It is not difficult to verify that we have only to extend each of the cyclic components of the given representation and then to form the direct sum of the resulting representations in order to complete the proof. Hence assume that $b \to T'_b$ is cyclic on $\mathfrak{H}'$ with f'_0 as a cyclic vector with norm $|f'_0| = 1$. Define

$$F'_0(b) = (T'_b f'_0, f'_0), \quad b \in \mathfrak{B}.$$

Then F'_0 is a positive functional on $\mathfrak{B}$ which belongs to $\mathscr{P}_{\mathfrak{B}}$. Let F_0 denote any element of $\mathscr{P}_{\mathfrak{A}}$ whose restriction to $\mathfrak{B}$ is equal to F'_0 and denote by $a \to T_a$ the $\star$-representation of $\mathfrak{A}$ on a Hilbert space $\mathfrak{H}$ associated with F_0. Then $F_0(a) = (T_a f_0, f_0)$, where f_0 is a cyclic vector in $\mathfrak{H}$. Since F_0 is an extension of F'_0, we have

$$(T_b f_0, f_0) = (T'_b f'_0, f'_0), \quad b \in \mathfrak{B}.$$

If $\mathfrak{H}_0$ denotes the closed subspace of $\mathfrak{H}$ spanned by the set of elements $\{T_b f_0 : b \in \mathfrak{B}\}$, then the restriction of the representation $b \to T_b$ to $\mathfrak{H}_0$ is a cyclic representation of $\mathfrak{B}$ which, by Theorem (4.4.3), is unitarily equivalent to $b \to T'_b$. Under the unitary mapping which implements this equivalence, the space $\mathfrak{H}'$ can be identified with $\mathfrak{H}_0$. Therefore, properties (i) and (ii) follow. Finally, if $b \to T'_b$ is irreducible, then F'_0 is an extreme point of $\mathscr{P}_{\mathfrak{B}}$ and, by Theorem (4.7.11), F_0 may be taken as an extreme point of $\mathscr{P}_{\mathfrak{A}}$. Then $a \to T_a$ is also irreducible and the theorem is proved.

We close this section with a criterion for symmetry of a Banach $\star$-algebra which is due to Raikov [2].

THEOREM (4.7.21). *Let* $\mathfrak{A}$ *be a Banach* $\star$*-algebra with an identity element and a locally continuous involution. Then, in order for* $\mathfrak{A}$ *to be symmetric, it is necessary and sufficient that, for each* x *in* $\mathfrak{A}$, $\nu(x^\star x) = \sup F(x^\star x)$, F *an extreme point of* $\mathscr{P}_{\mathfrak{A}}$.

PROOF. Assume first that $\mathfrak{A}$ is symmetric and, for a given $x \in \mathfrak{A}$, let $\mathfrak{C}$ denote a maximal commutative $\star$-subalgebra of $\mathfrak{A}$ which contains

$x^\star x$. Then $\mathfrak{C}$ is also symmetric and hence $\widehat{c^\star}(\varphi) = \overline{\hat{c}(\varphi)}$ for every $c \in \mathfrak{C}$ and $\varphi \in \Phi_{\mathfrak{C}}$. Therefore the relation $F'_\varphi(c) = \hat{c}(\varphi)$ defines a positive functional on $\mathfrak{C}$ for each $\varphi \in \Phi_{\mathfrak{C}}$. Furthermore F'_φ is an extreme point of $\mathscr{P}_{\mathfrak{C}}$. Denote by F_φ an extension of F'_φ to a positive functional on $\mathfrak{A}$. Then, since $F_\varphi(1) = 1$, $F_\varphi \in \mathscr{P}_{\mathfrak{A}}$ and, by Theorem (4.7.11), F_φ can be assumed to be an extreme point of $\mathscr{P}_{\mathfrak{A}}$. Also we have

$$\nu(x^\star x) = \max_{\varphi} F_\varphi(x^\star x) \leqslant \max_{F \in \mathscr{P}_{\mathfrak{A}}} F(x^\star x).$$

Since the inequality $F(x^\star x) \leqslant \nu(x^\star x)$ holds for every $F \in \mathscr{P}_{\mathfrak{A}}$, the necessity of the condition follows.

Now assume the condition satisfied. Again let x be any element of $\mathfrak{A}$ and define $u = \nu(x^\star x) - x^\star x$. Then

$$u^\star u = u^2 = \nu(x^\star x)^2 - 2\nu(x^\star x)x^\star x + x^\star x x^\star x,$$

and hence

$$F(u)^2 \leqslant \nu(x^\star x)^2 - 2\nu(x^\star x)F(x^\star x) + F(x^\star x x^\star x)$$

for each $F \in \mathscr{P}_{\mathfrak{A}}$. By Theorems (4.5.3) and (1.4.1) (iv),

$$F(x^\star x x^\star x) \leqslant F(x^\star x)\nu(x x^\star) = F(x^\star x)\nu(x^\star x).$$

Therefore

$$F(u^2) \leqslant \nu(x^\star x)^2 - \nu(x^\star x)F(x^\star x) \leqslant \nu(x^\star x)^2.$$

Since, by hypothesis, $\nu(u)^2 = \nu(u^2) = \sup F(u^2)$, F an extreme point of $\mathscr{P}_{\mathfrak{A}}$, it follows that $\nu(u) \leqslant \nu(x^\star x)$. On the other hand,

$$\nu(u) = \max_{\lambda \in Sp(x^\star x)} |\nu(x^\star x) - \lambda|.$$

This, together with the inequality $\nu(u) \leqslant \nu(x^\star x)$, implies that the set $Sp(x^\star x)$ lies within a circle with center at $\nu(x^\star x)$ and radius equal to $\nu(x^\star x)$. In particular, $-1 \notin Sp(x^\star x)$ and therefore $1 + x^\star x$ is regular. This establishes the sufficiency and completes proof of the theorem.

In our definition of a symmetric Banach $\star$-algebra, we have followed Raikov [2] who introduced the notion in generalizing results obtained by Gelfand and Naĭmark [1] in their abstract characterization of C*-algebras. More recently, Naĭmark [7, § 23], in his book on normed rings, calls these algebras "totally symmetric" and uses the term "symmetric" with reference to *any* $\star$-algebra.

§ 8. General properties of B*-algebras. Recall that a B*-algebra is a Banach $\star$-algebra whose norm satisfies the condition $\|x^\star x\| = \|x\|^2$. In particular, $\|x^\star\| = \|x\|$, so that these algebras are $\star$-normed. Being A*-algebras, they are also semi-simple, by Theorem (4.1.19). In this section, we present a systematic account of some general properties of

B*-algebras. The most useful tool in the study of these algebras is given by Theorem (4.2.2), which asserts that the Gelfand representation of any complex commutative B*-algebra $\mathfrak{C}$ is an isometric $\star$-isomorphism of $\mathfrak{C}$ with $C_0(\Phi_{\mathfrak{C}})$. Throughout this section, $\mathfrak{A}$ will be a complex B*-algebra.

LEMMA (4.8.1). *The B*-algebra $\mathfrak{A}$ has the following properties:*

(*i*) *The involution in $\mathfrak{A}$ is hermitian.*

(*ii*) *For arbitrary x in $\mathfrak{A}$, $\|x\|^2 = \nu(x^\star x)$ and, if x is normal, $\|x\| = \nu(x)$.*

(*iii*) *If $h \geqslant 0$ and $k \geqslant 0$, then $h+k \geqslant 0$.*

PROOF. Let c be any normal element of $\mathfrak{A}$ and let $\mathfrak{C}$ be a maximal commutative $\star$-subalgebra of $\mathfrak{A}$ which contains c. Then, since $\mathfrak{C}$ is a commutative B*-algebra, it can be identified with $C_0(\Phi_{\mathfrak{C}})$. Since $Sp_{\mathfrak{A}}(c) = Sp_{\mathfrak{C}}(c)$, it follows that $Sp_{\mathfrak{A}}(h)$ is real for every hermitian element h. It also follows that $\|c\| = \nu(c)$ for any normal element c, and hence $\|x\|^2 = \|x^\star x\| = \nu(x^\star x)$ for arbitrary x. This establishes (i) and (ii).

For the proof of (iii), observe first that there is no loss in assuming $\mathfrak{A}$ to have an identity element. Also, by property (ii), the spectral radius coincides with the norm for hermitian elements. Therefore (iii) follows from Lemma (4.7.4).

Since the involution is hermitian, an application of Corollary (4.1.8) yields the following result.

COROLLARY (4.8.2). *If $\mathfrak{A}_0$ is any closed $\star$-subalgebra of $\mathfrak{A}$, then $Sp_{\mathfrak{A}}(x) \cup (0) = Sp_{\mathfrak{A}_0}(x) \cup (0)$ for every $x \in \mathfrak{A}_0$.*

THEOREM (4.8.3). *Let $\mathfrak{B}$ denote any Banach algebra which contains $\mathfrak{A}$ as a (not necessarily closed) subalgebra. Denote the norms in $\mathfrak{A}$ and $\mathfrak{B}$ by $\|x\|$ and $\|x\|_1$ respectively. Then*

(*i*) *$Sp_{\mathfrak{A}}(c) \cup (0) = Sp_{\mathfrak{B}}(c) \cup (0)$ for every normal element $c \in \mathfrak{A}$.*

(*ii*) *$\|x\|^2 \leqslant \|x^\star\|_1 \|x\|_1$ for every $x \in \mathfrak{A}$.*

(*iii*) *$\nu_{\mathfrak{A}}(x) = \nu_{\mathfrak{B}}(x)$ for every $x \in \mathfrak{A}$.*

PROOF. Let c be a normal element of $\mathfrak{A}$ and let $\mathfrak{C}$ be a maximal commutative $\star$-subalgebra of $\mathfrak{A}$ which contains c. Note that $Sp_{\mathfrak{A}}(c) = Sp_{\bar{\mathfrak{C}}}(c)$. Furthermore, by Corollary (3.7.6), $Sp_{\mathfrak{C}}(c) \cup (0) = Sp_{\mathfrak{B}}(c) \cup (0)$. Hence, $Sp_{\mathfrak{A}}(c) \cup (0) = Sp_{\mathfrak{B}}(c) \cup (0)$ and (i) is proved. In particular, $\nu_{\mathfrak{A}}(c) = \nu_{\mathfrak{B}}(c)$ for normal $c \in \mathfrak{A}$.

Now, for arbitrary $x \in \mathfrak{A}$, we have

$$\|x\|^2 = \|x^\star x\| = \nu_{\mathfrak{A}}(x^\star x) = \nu_{\mathfrak{B}}(x^\star x) \leqslant \|x^\star\|_1 \|x\|_1,$$

which proves (ii). It follows from (ii) that

$$\|x^n\|^2 \leqslant \|(x^\star)^n\|_1 \|x^n\|_1$$

for all n. Taking the nth root and letting $n \to \infty$, we obtain $\nu_{\mathfrak{A}}(x)^2 \leqslant \nu_{\mathfrak{B}}(x^\star)\nu_{\mathfrak{B}}(x)$. On the other hand, since $\mathfrak{A}$ is a subalgebra of $\mathfrak{B}$, we always have $\nu_{\mathfrak{B}}(x) \leqslant \nu_{\mathfrak{A}}(x)$ for $x \in \mathfrak{A}$. Hence,

$$\nu_{\mathfrak{B}}(x^\star)\nu_{\mathfrak{B}}(x) \leqslant \nu_{\mathfrak{A}}(x^\star)\nu_{\mathfrak{A}}(x) = \nu_{\mathfrak{A}}(x)^2.$$

Therefore $\nu_{\mathfrak{A}}(x)^2 = \nu_{\mathfrak{B}}(x^\star)\nu_{\mathfrak{B}}(x)$. This, together with the inequalities $\nu_{\mathfrak{B}}(x) \leqslant \nu_{\mathfrak{A}}(x)$ and $\nu_{\mathfrak{B}}(x^\star) \leqslant \nu_{\mathfrak{A}}(x^\star) = \nu_{\mathfrak{A}}(x)$, implies $\nu_{\mathfrak{A}}(x) = \nu_{\mathfrak{B}}(x)$ and completes the proof.

COROLLARY (4.8.4). *Let* $\|x\|$ *be the given norm and let* $\|x\|_0$ *be a second norm in* $\mathfrak{A}$ *under which* $\mathfrak{A}$ *is just a normed algebra. Then* $\|x\|^2 \leqslant \|x^\star\|_0 \|x\|_0$ *and, if also* $\|x^\star\|_0 = \|x\|_0$, *then* $\|x\| \leqslant \|x\|_0$ *for all* x.

THEOREM (4.8.5). *If* $\mathfrak{B}$ *is a Banach* $\star$*-algebra which contains* $\mathfrak{A}$ *as a* $\star$*-subalgebra, then* $Sp_{\mathfrak{A}}(x) \cup (0) = Sp_{\mathfrak{B}}(x) \cup (0)$, *for every* $x \in \mathfrak{A}$. *If* $\mathfrak{B}$ *is also a B***-algebra, then the embedding of* $\mathfrak{A}$ *in* $\mathfrak{B}$ *is an isometry, so that* $\mathfrak{A}$ *is a closed subalgebra of* $\mathfrak{B}$.

PROOF. The first statement follows from part (i) of the preceding theorem plus the fact that an element x in any $\star$-algebra is quasi-regular if and only if both $x^\star \circ x$ and $x \circ x^\star$ are quasi-regular. The second statement of the theorem follows from part (iii) of the preceding theorem plus the fact that $\|x\|^2 = \nu(x^\star x)$ in a B*-algebra.

COROLLARY (4.8.6). *Let* $\|x\|_0$ *be any norm in* $\mathfrak{A}$ *with the B***-property. Then* $\|x\|_0 = \|x\|$ *for all* $x \in \mathfrak{A}$.

The next theorem provides an elementary operational calculus for normal elements of the B*-algebra $\mathfrak{A}$. If Ω is a subset of the complex plane which contains zero, then $C(\Omega)_0$ denotes the algebra of all $f \in C(\Omega)$ such that $f(0) = 0$.

THEOREM (4.8.7). *For every normal element* $c \in \mathfrak{A}$, *there exists an isometric* $\star$*-isomorphism,* $f \to f(c)$, *of* $C(Sp_{\mathfrak{A}}(c))$ *or of* $C(Sp_{\mathfrak{A}}(c))_0$, *according as* $\mathfrak{A}$ *does or does not have an identity element, into* $\mathfrak{A}$ *with the following properties.*

(*i*) *If* $f(\zeta) = \zeta$ *for all* $\zeta \in Sp_{\mathfrak{A}}(c)$, *then* $f(c) = c$.

(*ii*) $Sp_{\mathfrak{A}}(f(c)) = f(Sp_{\mathfrak{A}}(c))$.

(*iii*) $f(c)$ *is contained in every* ★*-subalgebra of* $\mathfrak{A}$ *which contains c along with the identity element if one exists.*

PROOF. We make the proof only for the case in which $\mathfrak{A}$ has an identity element and leave the case of no identity to the reader. Let $\mathfrak{C}$ be any closed commutative ★-subalgebra which contains c along with the identity element of $\mathfrak{A}$. Then $\mathfrak{C}$ is isometrically ★-isomorphic with $C(\Phi_{\mathfrak{C}})$ under the Gelfand mapping $x \to \hat{x}$. From Theorem (4.8.3) (i), we have $Sp_{\mathfrak{A}}(c) = Sp_{\mathfrak{C}}(c)$ and hence, by Theorem (3.1.6), $Sp_{\mathfrak{A}}(c) = \{\hat{c}(\varphi) : \varphi \in \Phi_{\mathfrak{C}}\}$. Now let $f \in C(Sp_{\mathfrak{A}}(c))$ and, for $\varphi \in \Phi_{\mathfrak{C}}$, define $g(\varphi) = f(\hat{c}(\varphi))$. Then $g \in C(\Phi_{\mathfrak{C}})$, so that there exists an element $f_{\mathfrak{C}}(c) \in \mathfrak{C}$ with

$$\widehat{f_{\mathfrak{C}}(c)}(\varphi) = g(\varphi), \quad \varphi \in \Phi_{\mathfrak{C}}.$$

It is obvious that the mapping $f \to f_{\mathfrak{C}}(c)$ is a ★-homomorphism of $C(Sp_{\mathfrak{A}}(c))$ into $\mathfrak{C}$ which has properties (i) and (ii). Moreover, since

$$\|f_{\mathfrak{C}}(c)\| = \max_{\varphi \in \Phi_{\mathfrak{C}}} |f(\hat{c}(\varphi))| = \max_{\zeta \in Sp_{\mathfrak{A}}(c)} |f(\zeta)| = \|f\|,$$

the mapping is an isometry. In order to complete the proof, it will be sufficient to show that $f_{\mathfrak{C}}(c)$ is actually independent of $\mathfrak{C}$ and so is contained in every closed commutative ★-subalgebra which contains c and the identity element. The problem is to show that $f_{\mathfrak{C}_1}(c) = f_{\mathfrak{C}_2}(c)$ for every pair $\mathfrak{C}_1$ and $\mathfrak{C}_2$ of such subalgebras. Since $\mathfrak{C}_1 \cap \mathfrak{C}_2$ is another such algebra, it is clearly sufficient to make the proof for the case $\mathfrak{C}_2 \subseteq \mathfrak{C}_1$. Let $\varphi \to \varphi'$ denote the natural mapping of $\Phi_{\mathfrak{C}_1}$ onto $\Phi_{\mathfrak{C}_2}$ obtained by restriction of the homomorphism φ to the subalgebra $\mathfrak{C}_2$. Then, for every $\varphi \in \Phi_{\mathfrak{C}_1}$,

$$\widehat{f_{\mathfrak{C}_2}(c)}(\varphi) = \widehat{f_{\mathfrak{C}_2}(c)}(\varphi') = f(\hat{c}(\varphi'))$$

$$= f(\hat{c}(\varphi)) = \widehat{f_{\mathfrak{C}_1}(c)}(\varphi).$$

Therefore $f_{\mathfrak{C}_2}(c) = f_{\mathfrak{C}_1}(c)$, and the theorem is proved.

Consider the real functions f_+ and f_- defined for all real λ by the relations

$$f_+(\lambda) = \begin{cases} 0, & \lambda \leqslant 0 \\ \lambda, & \lambda > 0 \end{cases}, \qquad f_-(\lambda) = \begin{cases} -\lambda, & \lambda \leqslant 0 \\ 0, & \lambda > 0. \end{cases}$$

If h is any hermitian element of the B★-algebra $\mathfrak{A}$ and $\Omega = Sp_{\mathfrak{A}}(h) - (0)$, then both f_+ and f_- belong to $C_0(\Omega)$. Therefore, by the above theorem we can define

$$h_+ = f_+(h), \qquad h_- = f_-(h).$$

Since the functions f_+ and f_- are real and non-negative, the elements h_+ and h_- are hermitian and have non-negative spectra; that is, $h_+ \geqslant 0$ and $h_- \geqslant 0$. Moreover, $f_+(\lambda)-f_-(\lambda) = \lambda$, for all λ, and $f_+f_- = f_-f_+ = 0$. Therefore we have

$$h = h_+ - h_-, \qquad h_+h_- = h_-h_+ = 0.$$

Also, let h_a denote the element of $\mathfrak{A}$ which corresponds to the function $|\lambda|$ in $C_0(\Omega)$. Then h_a is called the ABSOLUTE VALUE of h and, since $|\lambda| = f_+(\lambda)+f_-(\lambda)$, we have $h_a = h_+ + h_-$. Evidently, $h \geqslant 0$ if and only if $h_- = 0$, so that $h = h_+ = h_a$. The elements h_- and h_+ are uniquely determined by the properties $h = h_+ - h_-$, $h_a = h_+ + h_-$.

Consider next the real function f defined by the relation

$$f(\lambda) = \lambda^{1/2}, \quad \lambda \geqslant 0.$$

If h is any hermitian element with $Sp_{\mathfrak{A}}(h) \geqslant 0$, then $f(h)$ is a hermitian element of $\mathfrak{A}$ with non-negative spectrum and is such that $(f(h))^2 = h$. We define, in this case, $h^{1/2} = f(h)$. If k is any hermitian element of $\mathfrak{A}$ such that $k^2 = h$ and $Sp_{\mathfrak{A}}(k) \geqslant 0$, then $k = h^{1/2}$. In fact, if $\mathfrak{C}$ is any closed commutative *-subalgebra which contains k, then $\mathfrak{C}$ contains h and therefore contains $h^{1/2}$. That $h^{1/2} = k$ now follows from the representation of $\mathfrak{C}$ as $C_0(\Phi_{\mathfrak{C}})$. (Compare with Lemma (4.7.2).)

We prove next that B*-algebras are symmetric. The first step is a lemma due to Kaplansky.

LEMMA (4.8.8). *$x^*x \leqslant 0$ implies $x = 0$.*

PROOF. By Lemma (1.4.17) (iii), the non-zero portions of the spectra $Sp_{\mathfrak{A}}(x^*x)$ and $Sp_{\mathfrak{A}}(xx^*)$ are equal. Hence $x^*x \leqslant 0$ implies $xx^* \leqslant 0$. Now, if $x = h+ik$, with h and k hermitian, then $x^*x = 2h^2+2k^2-xx^*$. Since $2h^2 \geqslant 0$, $2k^2 \geqslant 0$, and $-xx^* \geqslant 0$, it follows that $x^*x \geqslant 0$, by Lemma (4.8.1) (iii). This, together with $x^*x \leqslant 0$, implies $x^*x = 0$ and therefore $x = 0$.

THEOREM (4.8.9). *Every complex B*-algebra is symmetric.*

PROOF. Since x^*x is hermitian, we can write $x^*x = h-k$, where $h \geqslant 0$, $k \geqslant 0$, and $hk = kh = 0$. Set $z = xk$. Then $z^*z = kx^*xk = -k^3$. Since $k \geqslant 0$, this implies $z^*z \leqslant 0$ and hence $z = 0$, by the above lemma. This obviously implies $k = 0$, so that $x^\star x = h$. Therefore $x^\star x \geqslant 0$ and, in particular, $-x^\star x$ is quasi-regular. In other words, the algebra is symmetric.

Since $\|x\|^2 = \nu(x^\star x)$ in a B*-algebra, we can now apply Theorem (4.7.21) to obtain the following result.

COROLLARY (4.8.10). *The norm in a B*-algebra $\mathfrak{A}$ is given by the equation* $\|x\|^2 = \sup F(x^\star x)$ *for F an extreme point of* $\mathscr{P}_{\mathfrak{A}}$.

THEOREM (4.8.11). *Every complex B*-algebra is isometrically $\star$-isomorphic to a C*-algebra.*

PROOF. If the B*-algebra $\mathfrak{A}$ does not possess an identity element, then, by Lemma (4.1.11), we can adjoin one at the same time preserving the B*-property. If the resulting B*-algebra with an identity element is a C*-algebra, then it is obvious that $\mathfrak{A}$ is a C*-algebra. Therefore we can assume that $\mathfrak{A}$ has an identity element. Since $\mathfrak{A}$ is semi-simple and symmetric, Corollary (4.7.16) applies to give a faithful $\star$-representation of $\mathfrak{A}$ on a Hilbert space. By Theorem (4.8.5), this representation is an isometry, so that the theorem is proved.

Since the B*-property is obviously preserved under completion, we obtain the following corollary.

COROLLARY (4.8.12). *Any complex normed $\star$-algebra, whose norm satisfies the B*-condition, is $\star$-semi-simple and admits a faithful norm-preserving $\star$-representation on Hilbert space. In particular, any complex A*-algebra admits a faithful $\star$-representation on Hilbert space which is an isometry with respect to the auxiliary norm.*

LEMMA (4.8.13). *Let $h \geqslant 0$ and define*

$$u = h(1+h)^{-1}, \qquad v = h(1+h)^{-2}.$$

Then

$$\|u\| = \frac{\|h\|}{1+\|h\|}, \qquad \|v\| \leqslant \tfrac{1}{4}.$$

PROOF. We can obviously assume $h \neq 0$. Let $\mathfrak{C}$ be a closed commutative $\star$-subalgebra of $\mathfrak{A}$ which contains h. Then also $u, v \in \mathfrak{C}$ and

$$|\hat{u}(\varphi)| = \frac{\hat{h}(\varphi)}{1+\hat{h}(\varphi)} = \frac{1}{\hat{h}(\varphi)^{-1}+1}, \quad \varphi \in \Phi_{\mathfrak{C}}, \quad \hat{h}(\varphi) \neq 0.$$

Therefore $|\hat{u}(\varphi)|$ and $\hat{h}(\varphi)$ assume their maximum values at the same point. It follows that

$$\|u\| = \frac{\|h\|}{1+\|h\|}.$$

Similarly,

$$|\hat{v}(\varphi)| = \frac{\hat{h}(\varphi)}{(1+\hat{h}(\varphi))^2}, \quad \varphi \in \Phi_{\mathfrak{C}}.$$

It is elementary to verify that the function $t(1+t)^{-2}$ has a maximum value at $t = 1$. Therefore $\|v\| \leqslant \frac{1}{4}$ and the lemma is proved.

We can prove next that $\mathfrak{A}$ has an approximate identity (see § 1, Chapter I). This is due to Segal [3].

THEOREM (4.8.14). *A $B^\star$-algebra has an approximate identity consisting of hermitian elements.*

PROOF. Let Λ be the collection of all finite subsets of $\mathfrak{A}$ ordered by inclusion. Let $\lambda = (x_1, \cdots, x_n)$ be an arbitrary element of Λ and set $h = x_1^\star x_1 + \cdots + x_n^\star x_n$. Since $h \geqslant 0$, the element $-nh$ is quasi-regular. Define

$$d_\lambda = nh(1+nh)^{-1}.$$

Then $d_\lambda^\star = d_\lambda$. Also, by Lemma (4.8.13),

$$\|d_\lambda\| = \frac{n\|h\|}{1+n\|h\|} \leqslant 1,$$

and

$$\|(1-d_\lambda)h(1-d_\lambda)\| \leqslant \frac{1}{4n}.$$

Furthermore, since

$$\sum [x_i(1-d_\lambda)]^\star[x_i(1-d_\lambda)] = (1-d_\lambda)h(1-d_\lambda),$$

we have

$$[x_i(1-d_\lambda)]^\star[x_i(1-d_\lambda)] \leqslant (1-d_\lambda)h(1-d_\lambda),$$

for $i = 1, \cdots, n$. Therefore

$$\|[x_i(1-d_\lambda)]^\star[x_i(1-d_\lambda)]\| \leqslant \frac{1}{4n},$$

and this implies

$$\|x_i(1-d_\lambda)\| \leqslant \frac{1}{2n^{1/2}}.$$

Now, for arbitrary $x \in \mathfrak{A}$ and $\epsilon > 0$, choose λ_ϵ to be any finite set of n elements of $\mathfrak{A}$ such that $x \in \lambda_\epsilon$ and $n > \epsilon^{-2}$. Then, for any $\lambda \geqslant \lambda_\epsilon$,

$$\|x - xd_\lambda\| < \epsilon.$$

In other words,

$$\lim_\lambda xd_\lambda = x$$

for every $x \in \mathfrak{A}$. Also, $\lim x^\star d_\lambda = x^\star$ and, by continuity of the involution, we obtain

$$\lim_\lambda d_\lambda x = x.$$

Observe finally that

$$\lim_\lambda \|d_\lambda\| = 1.$$

Therefore, if $e_\lambda = \|d_\lambda\|^{-1} d_\lambda$, then $\|e_\lambda\| = 1$ and $\{e_\lambda\}$ is an approximate identity for $\mathfrak{A}$.

We obtain some properties of positive functionals on the B*-algebra $\mathfrak{A}$. The first theorem shows that all positive functionals on a B*-algebra are representable in the sense of Definition (4.5.5). (See Theorem (4.5.11).)

THEOREM (4.8.15). *Let F be a positive functional on $\mathfrak{A}$. Then F is bounded and*

$$|F(x)|^2 \leqslant \|F\| F(x^\star x), \quad x \in \mathfrak{A}.$$

PROOF. We prove that F is bounded. For this it is sufficient to prove boundedness on $\mathscr{H}_\mathfrak{A}$. Note that, if $h \in \mathscr{H}_\mathfrak{A}$ and h_a is the absolute value of h, then $\|h\| = \|h_a\|$, $\pm h \leqslant h_a$ and, since F is positive, $|F(h)| \leqslant F(h_a)$. Therefore, if F is not bounded on $\mathscr{H}_\mathfrak{A}$, then there exists a sequence $\{h_n\}$ of elements of $\mathscr{H}_\mathfrak{A}$ such that $h_n \geqslant 0$, $\|h_n\| = 1$, and $F(h_n) \geqslant 2^n$ for each n. Define $h = \Sigma 2^{-n} h_n$. Then $h \in \mathscr{H}_\mathfrak{A}$ and

$$h - \sum_{k=1}^{n} 2^{-k} h_k = \sum_{k=n+1}^{\infty} 2^{-k} h_k = u_n.$$

By Lemma (4.7.10) and Corollary (4.7.13), $u_n \geqslant 0$. Therefore

$$F(h) \geqslant \sum_{k=1}^{n} 2^{-k} F(h_k) \geqslant n$$

for all n. This is impossible and shows that F must be bounded. Now let $\{e_\lambda\}$ be an approximate identity in $\mathfrak{A}$. Then

$$|F(e_\lambda x)|^2 \leqslant F(e_\lambda{}^2) F(x^\star x) \leqslant \|F\| F(x^\star x).$$

Since F is bounded,

$$\lim_{\lambda} F(e_\lambda x) = F(x)$$

and the desired result follows.

THEOREM (4.8.16). *If $\mathfrak{A}$ has an identity element, then a linear functional F on $\mathfrak{A}$ is positive if and only if $\|F\| = F(1)$.*

PROOF. That every positive linear functional satisfies this condition has already been proved in Corollary (4.5.3). We therefore assume the condition satisfied and write $F = F_1 + iF_2$, where F_1 and F_2 are hermitian functionals. (See Lemma (4.3.6).) We can assume without loss of generality that $F(1) = 1$. Since $F(1)$, $F_1(1)$ and $F_2(1)$ are real, it follows that $F_2(1) = 0$. We prove first that $F_2 = 0$. Let h be an arbitrary hermitian element of $\mathfrak{A}$ and set $u = \lambda - ih$, where λ is an arbitrary real number. Then

$$\|u\|^2 = \|\lambda^2 + h^2\| \leqslant \lambda^2 + \|h\|^2.$$

Also,

$$\begin{aligned} |F(u)|^2 &= |\lambda - iF_1(h) + F_2(h)|^2 \\ &= \lambda^2 + 2\lambda F_2(h) + F_2(h)^2 + F_1(h)^2. \end{aligned}$$

Hence

$$\begin{aligned} \|u\|^2 &\leqslant |F(u)|^2 - 2\lambda F_2(h) + \|h\|^2 \\ &\leqslant \|u\|^2 - 2\lambda F_2(h) + \|h\|^2. \end{aligned}$$

Therefore

$$\lambda F_2(h) \leqslant \|h\|^2.$$

Since this inequality holds for all hermitian h and real λ, it follows immediately that $F_2 = 0$. In other words, F is already a hermitian functional. Now suppose there exists a hermitian element h such that $h \geqslant 0$ while $F(h) < 0$. We can assume $0 \leqslant h \leqslant 1$, so that also $0 \leqslant 1 - h \leqslant 1$ and hence $\|1 - h\| \leqslant 1$. Then

$$1 = F(1) = F(1-h) + F(h) < F(1-h) \leqslant \|1-h\| \leqslant 1.$$

This is a contradiction and shows that F is a positive functional.

COROLLARY (4.8.17). *Any linear isometry between two $B^\star$-algebras which takes identity element into identity element also preserves positivity of hermitian elements.*

THEOREM (4.8.18). *The involution in a $B^\star$-algebra is uniquely determined.*

PROOF. There is evidently no loss in assuming that the algebra has an identity element. Let $x \to x^\star$ be the given involution and suppose that $x \to x'$ were a second involution with the B*-property $\|x'x\| = \|x\|^2$. By the preceding theorem, the positive functionals on $\mathfrak{A}$ are the same for both involutions. Now let h be any element of $\mathfrak{A}$ such that $h' = h$. Then, for any positive functional F, $F(h)$ is real. Also, $F(h^\star) = \overline{F(h)} = F(h)$, so that $F(h^\star - h) = 0$. By Theorem (4.7.12), $i(h^\star - h)$ is an element of $\mathscr{H}_{\mathfrak{A}}$ with zero spectrum. Therefore $h^\star = h$. In other words, $h' = h$ implies $h^\star = h$. By symmetry, $h^\star = h$ implies $h' = h$. It follows that the two involutions are identical.

COROLLARY (4.8.19). *Any isometric isomorphism between two B*-algebras is automatically a $\star$-isomorphism.*

The fact that a B*-algebra can be represented as a C*-algebra was first proved by Gelfand and Naïmark [1] under the additional assumption of symmetry. At the same time, however, they conjectured that the symmetry assumption was not needed. The key step in the proof of symmetry of a B*-algebra is that $h \geqslant 0$ and $k \geqslant 0$ imply $h+k \geqslant 0$. This was established independently by Fukamiya [3] and Kelley and Vaught [1]. The proof of symmetry was completed by Kaplansky. (See Schatz's review of Fukamiya's paper in *Math. Reviews*, vol. 14, p. 887.) Actually, Gelfand and Naïmark made the stronger conjecture that the condition $\|x^\star x\| = \|x^\star\|\,\|x\|$ is sufficient for the existence of a representation as a C*-algebra. That this is indeed the case has only recently been proved by Ono [1]. Yood [13] has shown that any Banach $\star$-algebra $\mathfrak{A}$ with an identity element and a hermitian involution such that $\nu(h) = \|h\|$ for $h \in \mathscr{H}_{\mathfrak{A}}$ admits a bicontinuous $\star$-representation on Hilbert space. The characterization of positive functionals given in Theorem (4.8.16) was observed by Bohnenblust and Karlin [1]. They also obtained the results in Theorem (4.8.18) and Corollary (4.8.19). Kadison [3] obtains the general form of a linear isometry between B*-algebras which generalizes the Banach–Stone theorem for $C(\Omega)$. (See Stone [1, Theorem 83].) At this point, it is worth noting that many of the properties which hold for arbitrary B*-algebras are natural generalizations of well-known properties of $C(\Omega)$.

§ 9. Structure of ideals and representations of B*-algebras.

We assume throughout this section that $\mathfrak{A}$ is a complex B*-algebra.

LEMMA (4.9.1). *Let $\mathfrak{J}$ be a closed (right or left) ideal and h a hermitian element of $\mathfrak{A}$. Also let f be any complex-valued continuous function defined on $Sp_{\mathfrak{A}}(h)$ such that $f(0) = 0$. If $h \in \mathfrak{J}$, then also $f(h) \in \mathfrak{J}$. In particular, the elements h_-, h_+, h_a and $h_a^{1/2}$ belong to $\mathfrak{J}$.*

PROOF. Let $\mathfrak{C}$ be any closed commutative $\star$-subalgebra which contains h and set $\mathfrak{K} = \mathfrak{J} \cap \mathfrak{C}$. Then $\mathfrak{K}$ is a closed ideal in $\mathfrak{C}$ and $\mathfrak{K} = k(h(\mathfrak{K}))$ by Theorem (4.2.4). Note that $f(h) \in \mathfrak{C}$. Now, if $h \in \mathfrak{J}$, then $\hat{h}(\varphi) = 0$ for all $\varphi \in h(\mathfrak{K})$. Therefore $\widehat{f(h)}(\varphi) = f(\hat{h}(\varphi)) = 0$ for all $\varphi \in h(\mathfrak{K})$, so that $f(h) \in k(h(\mathfrak{K}))$. This implies $f(h) \in \mathfrak{K}$ and proves the lemma.

The next theorem extends Theorem (4.2.4) to the non-commutative case. (See Segal [5] and Kaplansky [5].)

THEOREM (4.9.2). *Let $\mathfrak{I}$ be a closed 2-sided ideal in $\mathfrak{A}$. Then $\mathfrak{I}^\star = \mathfrak{I}$ and $\mathfrak{A}/\mathfrak{I}$ is also a $B^\star$-algebra.*

PROOF. Let x be any element of $\mathfrak{A}$ and set $h = x^\star x$. Since $h \geqslant 0$, the element $-\alpha h$ is quasi-regular for every $\alpha > 0$. Set $k = (-\alpha h)^\circ$ and define $w = x(1-k)$. Then $k = \alpha h(1+\alpha h)^{-1}$ and

$$w^\star w = (1-k)x^\star x(1-k) = h(1-k)^2 = h(1+\alpha h)^{-2}.$$

By Lemma (4.8.13), we have

$$\|w\|^2 = \|w^\star w\| \leqslant \frac{1}{4\alpha}.$$

Therefore $w \to 0$ and hence $xk \to x$ as $\alpha \to \infty$. Now, if $x^\star \in \mathfrak{I}$, then $h \in \mathfrak{I}$. Since $k - \alpha h + \alpha kh = 0$, also $k \in \mathfrak{I}$ and therefore $xk \in \mathfrak{I}$. Since $\mathfrak{I}$ is closed, it follows that $x \in \mathfrak{I}$. This proves that $\mathfrak{I}^\star \subseteq \mathfrak{I}$. An application of the involution to this inclusion gives $\mathfrak{I} = (\mathfrak{I}^\star)^\star \subseteq \mathfrak{I}^\star$, and so we conclude that $\mathfrak{I}^\star = \mathfrak{I}$.

Since $\mathfrak{I}$ is a $\star$-ideal, the difference algebra $\mathfrak{A}/\mathfrak{I}$ is a $\star$-algebra under the involution $x' \to (x')^\star = (x^\star)'$, where $x' = x+\mathfrak{I}$. It remains to show that the usual infimum norm in $\mathfrak{A}/\mathfrak{I}$ has the B*-property relative to this involution. With x, h, k, and w as in the first part of the proof, choose a closed commutative $\star$-subalgebra $\mathfrak{C}$ which contains h. Then also $k \in \mathfrak{C}$. Set $\mathfrak{K} = \mathfrak{I} \cap \mathfrak{C}$. Then $\mathfrak{K}$ is a closed ideal in $\mathfrak{C}$. Denote the algebra $\mathfrak{C}/\mathfrak{K}$ by $\mathfrak{C}''$ and set $c'' = c+\mathfrak{K}$ for $c \in \mathfrak{C}$. Also, denote the image of $\mathfrak{C}$ in $\mathfrak{A}/\mathfrak{I}$ by $\mathfrak{C}'$. The mapping $c' \to c''$ is obviously a $\star$-isomorphism of $\mathfrak{C}'$ onto $\mathfrak{C}''$. Since $\mathfrak{C}'' = C_0(\Phi_{\mathfrak{C}/\mathfrak{K}})$, it follows from Corollary (3.7.7) that $\|c''\| \leqslant \|c'\|$. On the other hand, since $\mathfrak{K} \subseteq \mathfrak{I}$, it is immediate, from the infimum definition of these norms, that $\|c'\| \leqslant \|c''\|$. Therefore $\|c'\| = \|c''\|$ for all $c \in \mathfrak{C}'$. In other words, the norm in $\mathfrak{A}/\mathfrak{I}$ has the B*-property on $\mathfrak{C}'$. We now have

$$\begin{aligned} \|x'\| &\leqslant \|x'-x'k'\|+\|x'k'\| \\ &\leqslant \|w\|+\|x'\|\,\|k'\| \\ &\leqslant \frac{1}{2\sqrt{\alpha}}+\|x'\|\frac{\alpha\|h'\|}{1+\alpha\|h'\|}, \end{aligned}$$

where the last inequality is given by the inequality for $\|w\|^2$ obtained above plus another application of Lemma (4.8.13) to the element

$k' = \alpha h'(1+\alpha h')^{-1}$. This result holds for all $\alpha > 0$. Let $\alpha = \|h'\|^{-1}$; then

$$\|x'\| \leqslant \tfrac{1}{2}\|h'\|^{1/2}+\tfrac{1}{2}\|x'\|.$$

Hence

$$\|x'\|^2 \leqslant \|h'\| = \|x'^\star x'\| \leqslant \|x'^\star\|\,\|x'\|.$$

In particular, $\|x'\| \leqslant \|x'^\star\|$, which implies $\|x'^\star\| = \|x'\|$. Therefore $\|x'\|^2 = \|x'^\star x'\|$ and the theorem is proved.

The above proof also yields the following corollary. (See Fukamiya [3].)

Corollary (4.9.3). *If $\mathfrak{L}$ is a closed left ideal in $\mathfrak{A}$ and $x^\star x \in \mathfrak{L}$, then $x \in \mathfrak{L}$.*

Let $\mathfrak{L}$ be a closed left ideal in the B*-algebra $\mathfrak{A}$ and let $a \to T_a$ be the associated left regular representation of $\mathfrak{A}$ on $\mathfrak{A}-\mathfrak{L}$. Denote the bound of T_a as an operator on $\mathfrak{A}-\mathfrak{L}$ by $\|T_a\|_0$ and let

$$\|T_a\| = \inf \|a+m\|, \quad m \in \mathfrak{L} : \mathfrak{A}.$$

Then, since $\mathfrak{A}/(\mathfrak{L} : \mathfrak{A})$ is a B*-algebra, Corollary (4.8.4) plus the fact that always $\|T_a\|_0 \leqslant \|T_a\|$ establishes the following result.

Corollary (4.9.4). $\|T_a\|_0 = \|T_a\|$, *for all* $a \in \mathfrak{A}$.

The following lemma shows that the operational calculus for normal elements obtained in Theorem (4.8.7) is preserved in passing from $\mathfrak{A}$ to $\mathfrak{A}/\mathfrak{J}$, where $\mathfrak{J}$ is a closed 2-sided ideal in $\mathfrak{A}$. We denote the natural homomorphism of $\mathfrak{A}$ onto $\mathfrak{A}/\mathfrak{J}$ by $x \to x'$ and set $\mathfrak{A}' = \mathfrak{A}/\mathfrak{J}$.

Lemma (4.9.5). *Let c be a normal element of $\mathfrak{A}$ and let f be a complex-valued continuous function defined on the set $Sp_{\mathfrak{A}}(c)$ (with $f(0) = 0$, if $\mathfrak{A}$ does not have an identity element). Then the elements $f(c)$ and $f(c')$ are both defined and $f(c') = f(c)'$.*

Proof. It is immediate from definitions that $Sp_{\mathfrak{A}'}(c') \subseteq Sp_{\mathfrak{A}}(c)$. Therefore f is continuous on $Sp_{\mathfrak{A}'}(c')$, so that both $f(c)$ and $f(c')$ are defined. Let $\mathfrak{C}$ be a closed commutative $\star$-subalgebra of $\mathfrak{A}$ which contains c and denote its image in $\mathfrak{A}'$ by $\mathfrak{C}'$. Then $\mathfrak{C}'$ is a closed commutative $\star$-subalgebra of $\mathfrak{A}'$. In fact, as in the proof of the preceding theorem, $\mathfrak{C}'$ can be identified with $\mathfrak{C}/(\mathfrak{C} \cap \mathfrak{J})$. It is understood, of course, that $\mathfrak{C}$ contains the identity element of $\mathfrak{A}$ if one exists. Let φ' be any element of $\Phi_{\mathfrak{C}'}$ and denote by φ the element of $\Phi_{\mathfrak{C}}$ defined by the homomorphism $x \to \hat{x}'(\varphi')$, $x \in \mathfrak{C}$ (that is, $\varphi' \to \varphi$ is the dual mapping of $\Phi_{\mathfrak{C}'}$ into $\Phi_{\mathfrak{C}}$ associated with the homomorphism $x \to x'$). We then have

$$\widehat{f(c')}(\varphi') = f(\hat{c'}(\varphi')) = f(\hat{c}(\varphi)) = \widehat{f(c)}(\varphi) = \widehat{f(c)'}(\varphi').$$

Therefore $f(c') = f(c)'$ and the lemma is proved.

THEOREM (4.9.6). *Every proper closed 2-sided ideal in $\mathfrak{A}$ is an intersection of primitive ideals.*

PROOF. If $\mathfrak{J}$ is a closed 2-sided ideal in $\mathfrak{A}$, let $\mathfrak{A}' = \mathfrak{A}/\mathfrak{J}$. Then, by the preceding theorem, $\mathfrak{A}'$ is also a B*-algebra. In particular, $\mathfrak{A}'$ is semi-simple. Therefore the intersection of all primitive ideals in $\mathfrak{A}'$ reduces to zero. Now, if $\mathfrak{P}'$ is any primitive ideal in $\mathfrak{A}'$, let $\mathfrak{P}$ denote the complete counter image of $\mathfrak{P}'$ in $\mathfrak{A}$. Then $\mathfrak{P}$ is a closed 2-sided ideal in $\mathfrak{A}$ which contains $\mathfrak{J}$, and $\mathfrak{A}'/\mathfrak{P}'$ is isomorphic with $\mathfrak{A}/\mathfrak{P}$. It follows that $\mathfrak{P}$ is a primitive ideal in $\mathfrak{A}$. Since the primitive ideals $\mathfrak{P}'$ intersect in zero, the ideal $\mathfrak{J}$ is equal to the intersection of those primitive ideals which contain it.

COROLLARY (4.9.7). *A 2-sided ideal $\mathfrak{J}$ in $\mathfrak{A}$ will be dense in $\mathfrak{A}$ if and only if its hull $h(\mathfrak{J})$ in $\Pi_{\mathfrak{A}}$ is vacuous.*

Next is an intersection theorem for one-sided ideals.

THEOREM (4.9.8). *Let $\mathfrak{L}$ be a closed left ideal in $\mathfrak{A}$. Then $\mathfrak{L}$ is equal to the intersection of all ideals $\mathfrak{L}_F$, where F is an extreme point of $\mathscr{P}_{\mathfrak{A}}$ and $\mathfrak{L} \subseteq \mathfrak{L}_F$.*

PROOF. Since $\mathfrak{L}$ is also a closed left ideal in the B*-algebra obtained by adjunction of an identity element, it is obvious that there is no loss of generality in assuming an identity element. First set $\mathfrak{K} = \bigcap \mathfrak{L}_F$ for $\mathfrak{L}_F \supseteq \mathfrak{L}$, and let u be an arbitrary element of $\mathfrak{K}$. Set

$$Q_n = \{F : F(u^\star u) \geqslant n^{-2},\ F \in \mathscr{P}_{\mathfrak{A}}\}.$$

Note that Q_n is a closed and hence compact subset of $\mathscr{P}_{\mathfrak{A}}$ relative to the $\mathscr{H}_{\mathfrak{A}}$-topology. Also, for each $F \in Q_n$, there exists $m \in \mathfrak{L}$ such that $F(m^\star m) \neq 0$. Otherwise $\mathfrak{L} \subseteq \mathfrak{L}_F$ and hence $\mathfrak{K} \subseteq \mathfrak{L}_F$. But, since $u \in \mathfrak{K}$, this implies $F(u^\star u) = 0$, a contradiction. Now, since Q_n is compact, there exist elements $m_1, \cdots, m_k \in \mathfrak{L}$ such that, for each $F \in Q_n$, $F(m_i^\star m_i) \neq 0$ for some i. Choose $h \geqslant 0$ such that

$$h^2 = m_1^\star m_1 + \cdots + m_n^\star m_n.$$

Then $h \in \mathfrak{L}$ and $F(h^2) > 0$ for every $F \in Q_n$. Since Q_n is compact, there exists $\delta > 0$ such that $F(h^2) \geqslant \delta$ for all $F \in Q_n$. Hence there exists $\beta > 0$ such that $F(\beta h^2) \geqslant F(u^\star u)$ for all $F \in Q_n$. Let $k^2 = \beta h^2$, $k \geqslant 0$. Then $F(k^2)+n^{-2} \geqslant F(u^\star u)$ for all $F \in \mathscr{P}_{\mathfrak{A}}$. It follows that $F(u^\star u) \leqslant F(k^2+n^{-2})$, for *every* positive functional F. Now, let F be any positive functional on $\mathfrak{A}$ and define

$$G(x) = F\left(\left(k-\frac{i}{n}\right)^{-1} x\left(k+\frac{i}{n}\right)^{-1}\right).$$

Then G is a positive functional and accordingly

$$G(u^\star u) \leqslant G(k^2+n^{-2}) = F(1).$$

Therefore

$$F\left(\left(k-\frac{i}{n}\right)^{-1} u^\star u\left(k+\frac{i}{n}\right)^{-1}\right) \leqslant F(1)$$

for every positive functional F on $\mathfrak{A}$. By Corollary (4.8.10), this implies

$$\left\|\left(k-\frac{i}{n}\right)^{-1} u^\star u\left(k+\frac{i}{n}\right)^{-1}\right\| \leqslant 1.$$

Furthermore, observe that

$$u-u\left(k+\frac{i}{n}\right)^{-1} k = \frac{i}{n}u\left(k+\frac{i}{n}\right)^{-1},$$

and hence

$$\left\|u-u\left(k+\frac{i}{n}\right)^{-1} k\right\|^2 = \frac{1}{n^2}\left\|\left(k-\frac{i}{n}\right)^{-1} u^\star u\left(k+\frac{i}{n}\right)^{-1}\right\|.$$

Therefore

$$\left\|u-u\left(k+\frac{i}{n}\right)^{-1} k\right\| \leqslant \frac{1}{n}.$$

Since $k \in \mathfrak{L}$ and $\mathfrak{L}$ is closed, it follows that $u \in \mathfrak{L}$, so that $\mathfrak{R} = \mathfrak{L}$. It remains to prove that $\mathfrak{L}$ is equal to the intersection of all $\mathfrak{L}_F$ where F is an extreme point of $\mathscr{P}_{\mathfrak{A}}$ such that $\mathfrak{L} \subseteq \mathfrak{L}_F$. Note first that the set $\mathscr{E}$ of all $F \in \mathscr{P}_{\mathfrak{A}}$, such that $\mathfrak{L} \subseteq \mathfrak{L}_F$, is a convex subset of $\mathscr{P}_{\mathfrak{A}}$ and is closed in the $\mathscr{H}_{\mathfrak{A}}$-topology. If $u \notin \mathfrak{L}$, then, since $\mathfrak{R} = \mathfrak{L}$, there will exist $F \in \mathscr{E}$ such that $F(u^\star u) \neq 0$. By the Krein–Mil'man theorem, there also exists an extreme point F_0 of $\mathscr{E}$ such that $F_0(u^\star u) \neq 0$. Furthermore, if $F_0 = \alpha_1 F_1+\alpha_2 F_2$, where $\alpha_1 > 0$, $\alpha_2 > 0$, $\alpha_1+\alpha_2 = 1$, and F_1, $F_2 \in \mathscr{P}_{\mathfrak{A}}$, then $F_0(x^\star x) = 0$ obviously implies

$$F_1(x^\star x) = F_2(x^\star x) = 0.$$

It follows that $F_1, F_2 \in \mathscr{E}$ and hence that $F_1 = F_2 = F_0$. This proves that F_0 is also an extreme point of $\mathscr{P}_{\mathfrak{A}}$ and establishes the theorem.

THEOREM (4.9.9). *If $\mathfrak{I}$ is a closed 2-sided ideal in $\mathfrak{A}$, then*

$$\mathfrak{I} = \bigcap (\mathfrak{L}_F \cap \mathfrak{L}_F^\star), \quad \mathfrak{I} \subseteq \mathfrak{L}_F.$$

PROOF. By the above theorem, $\mathfrak{I} = \bigcap \mathfrak{L}_F$ for all F such that $\mathfrak{I} \subseteq \mathfrak{L}_F$. Since $\mathfrak{I}$ is a 2-sided ideal, $\mathfrak{I} \subseteq \mathfrak{L}_F$ implies $mm^\star \in \mathfrak{L}_F$ for every $m \in \mathfrak{I}$. Thus $F((mm^\star)^2) = 0$ and, since

$$|F(mm^\star)|^2 \leqslant \|F\| F((mm^\star)^2) = 0,$$

it follows that $\mathfrak{I}^\star \subseteq \mathfrak{L}_F$. Therefore, $\mathfrak{I} \subseteq \mathfrak{L}_F \bigcap \mathfrak{L}_F^\star$, which obviously implies the desired result. (See Kadison [14].)

Observe that this theorem provides another proof of the fact that closed 2-sided ideals in $\mathfrak{A}$ are $\star$-ideals.

We now obtain a remarkable result which was established by Kadison [14].

THEOREM (4.9.10). *In the case of $\star$-representations of a B*-algebra on Hilbert space, topological irreducibility and strict irreducibility are equivalent.*

PROOF. Let $a \to T_a$ be any $\star$-representation of a B*-algebra $\mathfrak{A}$ on Hilbert space $\mathfrak{H}$ and denote by $\mathfrak{B}$ the image of $\mathfrak{A}$ in $\mathscr{B}(\mathfrak{H})$. Since $a \to T_a$ is automatically continuous, its kernel $\mathfrak{K}$ is a closed 2-sided ideal in $\mathfrak{A}$. Therefore, by Theorem (4.9.2), $\mathfrak{A}/\mathfrak{K}$ is also a B*-algebra. Since $\mathfrak{A}/\mathfrak{K}$ is $\star$-isomorphic with $\mathfrak{B}$, we conclude from Theorem (4.8.5), that $\mathfrak{B}$ is a closed subalgebra of $\mathscr{B}(\mathfrak{H})$. Therefore the problem reduces to showing that any C*-algebra $\mathfrak{B}$ which is topologically irreducible on its Hilbert space $\mathfrak{H}$ is necessarily strictly irreducible.

If $\mathfrak{B}$ is topologically irreducible on $\mathfrak{H}$, then, by Schur's lemma (Theorem (4.4.12)), the centralizer $\mathfrak{B}'$ of $\mathfrak{B}$ in $\mathscr{B}(\mathfrak{H})$ reduces to scalar multiples of the identity operator. Therefore the double centralizer $\mathfrak{B}''$ coincides with $\mathscr{B}(\mathfrak{H})$. It follows (see Dixmier [15, p. 43]) that $\mathfrak{B}$ is dense in $\mathscr{B}(\mathfrak{H})$ relative to the strong neighborhood topology for operators. Therefore, by a theorem of Kaplansky (see Dixmier [15, p. 46]), the unit ball of $\mathfrak{B}$ is dense in the unit ball of $\mathscr{B}(\mathfrak{H})$ with respect to the strong neighborhood topology.

Now let f_0, f_1 be arbitrary elements of $\mathfrak{H}$ with $f_0 \neq 0$. It is required to show the existence of $B \in \mathfrak{B}$ such that $Bf_0 = f_1$. For this we can assume $|f_0| = 1$. Let T be any operator in $\mathscr{B}(\mathfrak{H})$ such that $Tf_0 = f_1$

and $|T| = |f_1|$. Then, by the Kaplansky theorem, there exists $B_1 \in \mathfrak{B}$ such that $|B_1| \leqslant |f_1|$ and $|Tf_0 - B_1 f_0| \leqslant 2^{-1}|f_1|$. Hence, $|B_1| \leqslant |f_1|$ and $|f_1 - B_1 f_0| \leqslant 2^{-1}|f_1|$. Similarly, there exists $B_2 \in \mathfrak{B}$ such that $|B_2| \leqslant |f_1 - B_1 f_0|$ and

$$|f_1 - B_1 f_0 - B_2 f_0| \leqslant 2^{-1}|f_1 - B_1 f_0|.$$

Thus, $|B_2| \leqslant 2^{-1}|f_1|$ and

$$|f_1 - B_1 f_0 - B_2 f_0| \leqslant 4^{-1}|f_1|.$$

Repeating this process, we obtain a sequence $\{B_n\} \subseteq \mathfrak{B}$ such that

$$|B_n| \leqslant 2^{1-n}|f_1|, \qquad |f_1 - \sum_{k=1}^{n} B_k f_0| \leqslant 2^{-n}|f_1|$$

for each n. Define

$$B = \sum_{k=1}^{\infty} B_k.$$

Then the series converges in norm to an element B of $\mathfrak{B}$. It is obvious that $Bf_0 = f_1$ and so the theorem is proved.

We obtain now some consequences of the above theorem. For any positive functional F on $\mathfrak{A}$, let $\mathfrak{X}_F = \mathfrak{A} - \mathfrak{L}_F$ and, for $x' = x + \mathfrak{L}_F$, denote by $|x'|$ the inner product norm $F(x^{\star}x)^{1/2}$ determined in $\mathfrak{X}_F$ by the functional F. Let $\mathfrak{H}_F$ be the completion of $\mathfrak{X}_F$ with respect to $|x'|$. The usual infimum norm in $\mathfrak{X}_F$ is given by

$$\|x'\| = \inf_{m \in \mathfrak{L}_F} \|x+m\|.$$

LEMMA (4.9.11). *If F is an extreme point of $\mathscr{P}_{\mathfrak{A}}$, then $\mathfrak{H}_F = \mathfrak{X}_F$, so that the norms $|x'|$ and $\|x'\|$ are equivalent.*

PROOF. By Theorem (4.6.4), the $\star$-representation on $\mathfrak{H}_F$ associated with F is topologically irreducible and hence, by the preceding theorem, is strictly irreducible. Since $\mathfrak{X}_F$ is an invariant subspace of $\mathfrak{H}_F$, it follows that $\mathfrak{X}_F = \mathfrak{H}_F$. Now, since $|x'| \leqslant \|x'\|$ and $\mathfrak{X}_F$ is complete under both norms, equivalence of the two norms follows by the closed graph theorem.

THEOREM (4.9.12). *In order for a positive functional F to be an extreme point of $\mathscr{P}_{\mathfrak{A}}$, it is necessary and sufficient that $\mathfrak{L}_F$ be a maximal left ideal in $\mathfrak{A}$ and*

$$\mu_F = \sup \frac{|F(x)|^2}{F(x^{\star}x)} = 1, \quad x \in \mathfrak{A}.$$

PROOF. Assume first that F is an extreme point of $\mathscr{P}_{\mathfrak{A}}$. Then, by Lemma (4.6.3), $\mu_F = 1$. Also, by the above lemma, the $\star$-representation of $\mathfrak{A}$ on $\mathfrak{X}_F$ is strictly irreducible. Since this representation is just the left regular representation of $\mathfrak{A}$ on $\mathfrak{X}_F$, it follows, by Theorem (2.2.1), that $\mathfrak{L}_F$ is maximal. This proves the necessity. Now assume that $\mu_F = 1$ and that $\mathfrak{L}_F$ is maximal. By Theorem (4.7.14), there exists an extreme point F_0 of $\mathscr{P}_{\mathfrak{A}}$ such that $\mathfrak{L}_F = \mathfrak{L}_{F_0}$. For $x' = x+\mathfrak{L}_F$, define $|x'|_0 = F_0(x^\star x)^{1/2}$. By Lemma (4.9.11), the two norms $|x'|_0$ and $\|x'\|$ are equivalent in $\mathfrak{X}_F$. In other words, there exists a constant α such that $\|x'\| \leqslant \alpha|x'|_0$ for all $x' \in \mathfrak{X}_F$. Let $a \to T_a$ be the left regular representation on $\mathfrak{X}_F$. Since $\mathfrak{L}_F$ is maximal, $a \to T_a$ is strictly irreducible. This representation also coincides on $\mathfrak{X}_F$ with the $\star$-representation associated with F. Denote by $\mathfrak{B}$ the image of $\mathfrak{A}$ in $\mathscr{B}(\mathfrak{X}_F)$ and let $\|T_a\|_0$ be the bound of T_a relative to $\|x'\|$. By Corollary (4.9.4), $\mathfrak{B}$ is a B*-algebra with respect to $\|T_a\|_0$. If $|T_a|$ is the bound of T_a relative to $|x'|$, then the norm $|T_a|$ has the B*-property and so, by Corollary (4.8.6), must coincide with $\|T_a\|_0$. Now choose a fixed non-zero element u' in $\mathfrak{X}_F$ and define

$$\|x'\|_0 = \inf \|T_a\|_0, \quad T_a u' = x', \quad a \in \mathfrak{A}.$$

Then, by Theorem (2.2.6), $\mathfrak{X}_F$ is complete with respect to $\|x'\|_0$. Now, for any $a \in \mathfrak{A}$ such that $T_a u' = x'$, we have

$$|x'| = |T_a u'| \leqslant |T_a||u'| = \|T_a\|_0|u'|.$$

Therefore it follows that $|x'| \leqslant |u'|\|x'\|_0$. Similarly, $|x'|_0 \leqslant |u'|_0\|x'\|_0$. Since $\mathfrak{X}_F$ is complete under both $|x'|_0$ and $\|x'\|_0$, it follows, by the closed graph theorem, that there exists a constant β such that $\|x'\|_0 \leqslant \beta|x'|_0$. Therefore $|x'| \leqslant \beta|u'||x'|_0$. Hence,

$$F(x^\star x) \leqslant \beta^2|u'|^2F_0(x^\star x)$$

for all $x \in \mathfrak{A}$. Since $\mu_F = 1$ and F_0 is an extreme point of $\mathscr{P}_{\mathfrak{A}}$, it follows by Corollary (4.6.5), that $F = F_0$. This proves the theorem.

THEOREM (4.9.13). *Every closed left ideal in $\mathfrak{A}$ is an intersection of maximal left ideals.*

PROOF. By Theorem (4.9.8), a closed left ideal $\mathfrak{L}$ is equal to $\bigcap \mathfrak{L}_F$ where F ranges over the extreme points of $\mathscr{P}_{\mathfrak{A}}$ such that $\mathfrak{L} \subseteq \mathfrak{L}_F$. By the above theorem, these $\mathfrak{L}_F$ are maximal left ideals, and so the theorem follows.

We conclude this section with a few results, due mainly to Kaplansky [5, 9], concerning the structure space $\Pi_{\mathfrak{A}}$ of a B*-algebra $\mathfrak{A}$ and the representation of $\mathfrak{A}$ as a subdirect sum of the primitive algebras $\mathfrak{A}_{\mathfrak{P}} = \mathfrak{A}/\mathfrak{P}$, $\mathfrak{P} \in \Pi_{\mathfrak{A}}$. Note that each of the algebras $\mathfrak{A}_{\mathfrak{P}}$ is a B*-algebra. It is readily verified that the normed full direct sum of the algebras $\mathfrak{A}_{\mathfrak{P}}$ is also a B*-algebra under its natural norm

$$\|f\| = \sup \|f(\mathfrak{P})\|, \quad \mathfrak{P} \in \Pi_{\mathfrak{A}}.$$

Therefore, by Theorem (4.8.5), the isomorphism $a \to \hat{a}$ of $\mathfrak{A}$ into this full direct sum is an isometry; that is,

$$\|a\| = \sup \|\hat{a}(\mathfrak{P})\|, \quad \mathfrak{P} \in \Pi_{\mathfrak{A}},$$

where $\hat{a}(\mathfrak{P})$ denotes the image of a in the algebra $\mathfrak{A}_{\mathfrak{P}}$. It turns out that the supremum $\|a\|$ is actually attained by $\|\hat{a}(\mathfrak{P})\|$ for some $\mathfrak{P} \in \Pi_{\mathfrak{A}}$. In fact, we have the following even stronger result.

THEOREM (4.9.14). *Let Δ be an arbitrary closed subset of $\Pi_{\mathfrak{A}}$. Then, for every $a \in \mathfrak{A}$, there exists $\mathfrak{P}_a \in \Delta$ such that*

$$\|\hat{a}(\mathfrak{P}_a)\| = \sup \|\hat{a}(\mathfrak{P})\|, \quad \mathfrak{P} \in \Delta.$$

PROOF. Set $\mathfrak{J} = k(\Delta)$. Then $\mathfrak{J}$ is a closed 2-sided ideal in $\mathfrak{A}$ and, since Δ is closed, $\Delta = h(\mathfrak{J})$. By Theorem (4.9.2), $\mathfrak{A}/\mathfrak{J}$ is also a B*-algebra. Furthermore, the mapping $\mathfrak{P} \to \mathfrak{P}' = \mathfrak{P}/\mathfrak{J}$ is a homeomorphism of the set Δ with the structure space $\Pi_{\mathfrak{A}'}$. This is established by a proof identical with the first part of the proof of Theorem (2.6.6) in which a similar result is obtained for $\Xi_{\mathfrak{A}}$. Thus, if $a' = a+\mathfrak{J}$ then $\|\hat{a}'(\mathfrak{P}')\| = \|\hat{a}(\mathfrak{P})\|$ for $\mathfrak{P} \in \Delta$, and hence

$$\|a'\| = \sup_{\mathfrak{P}'} \|\widehat{a'}(\mathfrak{P}')\| = \sup_{\mathfrak{P}} \|\hat{a}(\mathfrak{P})\|,$$

where $\mathfrak{P}' \in \Pi_{\mathfrak{A}'}$ and $\mathfrak{P} \in \Delta$. This reduces the problem to the case in which $\Delta = \Pi_{\mathfrak{A}}$.

Now suppose that $\|\hat{a}(\mathfrak{P})\| < \|a\|$ and set $h = a^\star a$. Then also $\|\hat{h}(\mathfrak{P})\| < \|h\|$. If $|\lambda| = \|h\|$, then it follows that $\lambda^{-1}\hat{h}(\mathfrak{P})$ is quasi-regular in $\mathfrak{A}_{\mathfrak{P}}$. Thus, if $\|\hat{a}(\mathfrak{P})\| < \|a\|$ for every $\mathfrak{P} \in \Pi_{\mathfrak{A}}$, then $\lambda^{-1}h$ is quasi-regular modulo every primitive ideal in $\mathfrak{A}$. By Theorem (2.2.9) (v), it follows that $\lambda^{-1}h$ is quasi-regular in $\mathfrak{A}$ for every λ such that $|\lambda| = \|h\|$. On the other hand, this is impossible, since $\nu_{\mathfrak{A}}(h) = \|h\|$. Therefore $\|\hat{a}(\mathfrak{P})\| = \|a\|$ for some $\mathfrak{P} \in \Pi_{\mathfrak{A}}$. This completes the proof.

We now obtain some continuity properties of $\|\hat{a}(\mathfrak{P})\|$ regarded as function on $\Pi_{\mathfrak{A}}$ for fixed $a \in \mathfrak{A}$.

LEMMA (4.9.15). *Let* Δ_1 *and* Δ_2 *be subsets of* $\Pi_{\mathfrak{A}}$ *such that*

$$\alpha = \sup_{\mathfrak{P} \in \Delta_1} \|\hat{a}(\mathfrak{P})\| < \inf_{\mathfrak{P} \in \Delta_2} \|\hat{a}(\mathfrak{P})\| = \beta$$

for some $a \in \mathfrak{A}$. *Then there exists* $u \in \mathfrak{A}$ *such that* $\hat{u}(\mathfrak{P}) = 0$ *for* $\mathfrak{P} \in \Delta_1$, *and* $\|\hat{u}(\mathfrak{P})\| = 1$ *for* $\mathfrak{P} \in \Delta_2$.

PROOF. Set $h = (a^\star a)^{1/2}$. Then $\|\hat{h}(\mathfrak{P})\| = \|\hat{a}(\mathfrak{P})\|$ for all $\mathfrak{P}$, so that we can use the positive element h instead of a. Now define the real function

$$f(\lambda) = \begin{cases} 0 & , \lambda \leqslant \alpha \\ \dfrac{\lambda - \alpha}{\beta - \alpha}, & \alpha < \lambda < \beta \\ 1 & , \beta \leqslant \lambda. \end{cases}$$

Then f is defined and continuous for all real λ. Therefore $f(h)$ and $f(\hat{h}(\mathfrak{P}))$ are defined. Let $u = f(h)$. Then, by Lemma (4.9.5), we have

$$\hat{u}(\mathfrak{P}) = f(\hat{h}(\mathfrak{P})), \quad \mathfrak{P} \in \Pi_{\mathfrak{A}}.$$

Since $\|\hat{h}(\mathfrak{P})\| \leqslant \alpha$, the spectrum of $\hat{h}(\mathfrak{P})$ lies in the interval $[0, \alpha]$ for $\mathfrak{P} \in \Delta_1$. Therefore, $\hat{u}(\mathfrak{P}) = 0$ for $\mathfrak{P} \in \Delta_1$. On the other hand, since $\|\hat{h}(\mathfrak{P})\| \geqslant \beta$, there must be points of the spectrum of $\hat{h}(\mathfrak{P})$ in the interval $[\beta, \|h\|]$ for every $\mathfrak{P} \in \Delta_2$. It follows that $\|\hat{u}(\mathfrak{P})\| = 1$ for $\mathfrak{P} \in \Delta_2$, and the lemma is proved.

The above proof holds for the case $\alpha = 0$ and Δ_1 equal to the empty set. Therefore we can state the following corollary.

COROLLARY (4.9.16). *Let* Δ *be a subset of* $\Pi_{\mathfrak{A}}$ *such that, for some* $a \in \mathfrak{A}$, $\inf \|\hat{a}(\mathfrak{P})\| > 0$, $\mathfrak{P} \in \Delta$. *Then there exists* $u \in \mathfrak{A}$ *such that* $\|\hat{u}(\mathfrak{P})\| = 1$ *for* $\mathfrak{P} \in \Delta$.

THEOREM (4.9.17). *For arbitrary real number* ρ *and element* $a \in \mathfrak{A}$, *the set* Γ'_ρ *of all* $\mathfrak{P} \in \Pi_{\mathfrak{A}}$ *such that* $\|\hat{a}(\mathfrak{P})\| \leqslant \rho$ *is closed in* $\Pi_{\mathfrak{A}}$. *In other words, the function* $\|\hat{a}(\mathfrak{P})\|$ *is upper semi-continuous.*

PROOF. Let $\mathfrak{P}_0$ be any point of $\Pi_{\mathfrak{A}}$ such that $\rho < \|\hat{a}(\mathfrak{P}_0)\|$. Then, by an application of the preceding lemma, there exists $u \in \mathfrak{A}$ such that $\hat{u}(\mathfrak{P}_0) \neq 0$ and $\hat{u}(\mathfrak{P}) = 0$ for all $\mathfrak{P} \in \Gamma'_\rho$. Thus, $u \in k(\Gamma'_\rho)$ and $u \notin \mathfrak{P}_0$. It follows that $\mathfrak{P}_0$ is not in the closure of Γ'_ρ and hence that Γ'_ρ is already a closed set.

The next theorem shows that the functions $\hat{a}$ vanish at infinity on the structure space $\Pi_{\mathfrak{A}}$.

THEOREM (4.9.18). *For arbitrary $\rho > 0$ and element $a \in \mathfrak{A}$, the set Γ''_ρ of all $\mathfrak{P} \in \Pi_\mathfrak{A}$ such that $\|\hat{a}(\mathfrak{P})\| \geqslant \rho$ is a compact subspace of $\Pi_\mathfrak{A}$.*

PROOF. Let $\{\Delta_\mu\}$ be a family of closed subsets of $\Pi_\mathfrak{A}$ such that the sets $\Delta''_\rho \cap \Delta_\mu$ have a vacuous intersection. The problem is to prove that a finite number of these sets have a vacuous intersection. Set $\mathfrak{J}_\mu = k(\Delta_\mu)$ and denote by $\mathfrak{J}$ the smallest 2-sided ideal in $\mathfrak{A}$ which contains each of the ideals $\mathfrak{J}_\mu$. Observe that the hull $h(\mathfrak{J})$ does not intersect Γ''_ρ since $\mathfrak{P} \supseteq \mathfrak{J}$ implies $\mathfrak{P} \supseteq \mathfrak{J}_\mu$, so that $\mathfrak{P} \in \Delta_\mu$ for each μ. It follows that $\|\hat{a}(\mathfrak{P})\| < \rho$ for every $\mathfrak{P} \in h(\mathfrak{J})$. Since $h(\mathfrak{J})$ is closed, we conclude from Theorem (4.9.14) that $\sup \|\hat{a}(\mathfrak{P})\| < \rho$ for $\mathfrak{P} \in h(\mathfrak{J})$. Now Lemma (4.9.15) can be applied to give an element $u \in \mathfrak{A}$ such that $\hat{u}(\mathfrak{P}) = 0$ for $\mathfrak{P} \in h(\mathfrak{J})$, and $\|\hat{u}(\mathfrak{P})\| = 1$ for $\mathfrak{P} \in \Gamma''_\rho$. In particular, we have $u \in k(h(\mathfrak{J}))$. Let $\bar{\mathfrak{J}}$ denote the closure of the ideal $\mathfrak{J}$ in $\mathfrak{A}$. Then, by Theorem (4.9.6), the ideal $\bar{\mathfrak{J}}$ is a kernel, so that $k(h(\mathfrak{J})) = k(h(\bar{\mathfrak{J}})) = \bar{\mathfrak{J}}$. Therefore $u \in \bar{\mathfrak{J}}$ and there exists $v \in \mathfrak{J}$ such that $\|u - v\| < 1$. Observe that v is contained in the sum of a finite number of the ideals $\mathfrak{J}_\mu$, say $\mathfrak{J}_{\mu_1}, \cdots, \mathfrak{J}_{\mu_n}$. In conclusion, suppose that $\mathfrak{P}_0$ were a point in the intersection of the sets $\Delta_{\mu_1}, \cdots, \Delta_{\mu_n}$. Then $\hat{v}(\mathfrak{P}_0) = 0$ and hence $\|\hat{u}(\mathfrak{P}_0)\| < 1$. On the other hand, $\|\hat{u}(\mathfrak{P})\| = 1$ for all $\mathfrak{P} \in \Gamma''_\rho$. Therefore $\mathfrak{P}_0$ cannot belong to Γ''_ρ and we conclude that the sets $\Gamma''_\rho \cap \Delta_{\mu_i}$ have a vacuous intersection.

It is important to emphasize here that, although the set Γ''_ρ in the above theorem is a compact subspace of $\Pi_\mathfrak{A}$, it need not be closed in $\Pi_\mathfrak{A}$. This pathology can occur, of course, only when $\Pi_\mathfrak{A}$ is not Hausdorff. Furthermore, that $\Pi_\mathfrak{A}$ need not be Hausdorff is shown by the example discussed at the end of § 6, Chapter II.

THEOREM (4.9.19). *In order for $\|\hat{a}(\mathfrak{P})\|$ to be a continuous function on $\Pi_\mathfrak{A}$ for each $a \in \mathfrak{A}$, it is necessary and sufficient that the structure space $\Pi_\mathfrak{A}$ be Hausdorff.*

PROOF. Since the functions $\|\hat{a}(\mathfrak{P})\|$ separate the points of $\Pi_\mathfrak{A}$, the necessity of the condition is immediate. Now assume $\Pi_\mathfrak{A}$ to be Hausdorff and consider an element $a \in \mathfrak{A}$ and any real number ρ. Then it follows, by Theorem (4.9.18), that the set $\{\mathfrak{P} : \|\hat{a}(\mathfrak{P})\| \geqslant p\}$ is closed. In other words, $\|\hat{a}(\mathfrak{P})\|$ is lower semi-continuous. On the other hand, by Theorem (4.9.17), these functions are always upper semi-continuous and so must be continuous. This proves the sufficiency.

COROLLARY (4.9.20). *If $\Pi_\mathfrak{A}$ is Hausdorff, then it is locally compact.*

LEMMA (4.9.21). *Let $\mathfrak{J}$ and $\mathfrak{K}$ be closed 2-sided ideals in $\mathfrak{A}$ such that*

$\mathfrak{I} \cap \mathfrak{K} = (0)$ *and* $\mathfrak{I}+\mathfrak{K}$ *is dense in* $\mathfrak{A}$. *Then* $\mathfrak{I}+\mathfrak{K} = \mathfrak{A}$ *and* $\|m+n\| = \max(\|m\|, \|n\|)$, *for* $m \in \mathfrak{I}$ *and* $n \in \mathfrak{K}$.

Proof. Denote by $\mathfrak{A}_0$ the direct sum $\mathfrak{I} \oplus \mathfrak{K}$ of the two B*-algebras $\mathfrak{I}$ and $\mathfrak{K}$. Then $\mathfrak{A}_0$ is a B*-algebra under the norm $\|m \oplus n\| = \max(\|m\|, \|n\|)$. Observe that $m \oplus n \to m+n$ defines a $\star$-isomorphism of $\mathfrak{A}_0$ onto a dense subset of $\mathfrak{A}$. By Theorem (4.8.5), $\mathfrak{A}_0$ must map onto $\mathfrak{A}$ isometrically, and thus the lemma is proved.

Corollary (4.9.22). *If* $\mathfrak{I}$ *and* $\mathfrak{K}$ *are closed 2-sided ideals such that* $\mathfrak{I} \cap \mathfrak{K} = (0)$, *then* $\mathfrak{I}+\mathfrak{K}$ *is also a closed 2-sided ideal in* $\mathfrak{A}$.

Theorem (4.9.23). *A B***-algebra* $\mathfrak{A}$ *is a direct sum of non-zero 2-sided ideals if and only if its structure space* $\Pi_{\mathfrak{A}}$ *is disconnected.*

Proof. If $\mathfrak{A} = \mathfrak{I}+\mathfrak{K}$, where $\mathfrak{I}$ and $\mathfrak{K}$ are disjoint non-zero two-sided ideals, then the hulls $h(\mathfrak{I})$ and $h(\mathfrak{K})$ in $\Pi_{\mathfrak{A}}$ are obviously disjoint sets. Moreover, if $\mathfrak{P}$ is any primitive ideal in $\mathfrak{A}$, then $\mathfrak{I}\mathfrak{K} = (0) \subseteq \mathfrak{P}$, so that either $\mathfrak{I} \subseteq \mathfrak{P}$ or $\mathfrak{K} \subseteq \mathfrak{P}$, by Theorem (2.2.8)(iv). Therefore $\Pi_{\mathfrak{A}} = h(\mathfrak{I}) \cup h(\mathfrak{K})$ and $\Pi_{\mathfrak{A}}$ is disconnected. On the other hand, let $\Pi_{\mathfrak{A}} = \Gamma_1 \cup \Gamma_2$, where Γ_1 and Γ_2 are disjoint closed sets. Define $\mathfrak{I} = k(\Gamma_1)$ and $\mathfrak{K} = k(\Gamma_2)$. Then $\mathfrak{I}+\mathfrak{K}$ is not contained in any primitive ideal and so, by Corollary (4.9.7), must be dense in $\mathfrak{A}$. Since $\mathfrak{I} \cap \mathfrak{K}$ is contained in every $\mathfrak{P} \in \Gamma_1 \cup \Gamma_2$, semi-simplicity implies $\mathfrak{I} \cap \mathfrak{K} = (0)$. Therefore, an application of the above lemma gives $\mathfrak{A} = \mathfrak{I}+\mathfrak{K}$ and completes the proof.

For the next theorem, we need the special subdirect sum $(\Sigma\mathfrak{A}_\lambda)_0$ of a family $\{\mathfrak{A}_\lambda : \lambda \in \Lambda\}$ of normed algebras which was discussed at the end of § 8 in Chapter II. It consists of all $f \in \Sigma\mathfrak{A}_\lambda$ such that $\{\lambda : \|f(\lambda)\| \geqslant \epsilon\}$ is a finite subset of Λ for each $\epsilon > 0$. If Λ is given the discrete topology, then $(\Sigma\mathfrak{A}_\lambda)_0$ consists of those $f \in \Sigma\mathfrak{A}_\lambda$ such that $\|f(\lambda)\|$ vanishes at infinity on Λ. If each $\mathfrak{A}_\lambda$ is a B*-algebra, then $(\Sigma\mathfrak{A}_\lambda)_0$ is obviously a $\star$-subalgebra of $\Sigma\mathfrak{A}_\lambda$ and so is also a B*-algebra.

Theorem (4.9.24). *A B***-algebra* $\mathfrak{A}$ *has a discrete structure space* $\Pi_{\mathfrak{A}}$ *if and only if it is of the form* $(\Sigma\mathfrak{A}_\lambda)_0$, *where each* $\mathfrak{A}_\lambda$ *is a topologically simple B***-algebra.*

Proof. Assume first that $\Pi_{\mathfrak{A}}$ is discrete. Then, in particular, $\Pi_{\mathfrak{A}}$ is Hausdorff and this implies that each primitive ideal $\mathfrak{P}$ is maximal-closed. Thus $\mathfrak{A}_{\mathfrak{P}}$ is topologically simple. Now, for each $\mathfrak{P} \in \Pi_{\mathfrak{A}}$, define $\mathfrak{I}_{\mathfrak{P}} = k(\Pi_{\mathfrak{A}} - (\mathfrak{P}))$. Then $\mathfrak{I}_{\mathfrak{P}} \cap \mathfrak{P} = (0)$. Since $\Pi_{\mathfrak{A}}$ is discrete, $\Pi_{\mathfrak{A}} - (\mathfrak{P})$ is closed and hence $h(\mathfrak{I}_{\mathfrak{P}}) = \Pi_{\mathfrak{A}} - (\mathfrak{P})$. Therefore $h(\mathfrak{I}_{\mathfrak{P}} + \mathfrak{P})$ is vacuous and $\mathfrak{I}_{\mathfrak{P}} + \mathfrak{P}$ is dense in $\mathfrak{A}$, by Corollary (4.9.7). Applying

Lemma (4.9.21), we obtain $\mathfrak{A} = \mathfrak{I}_\mathfrak{P} + \mathfrak{P}$. This means that the difference algebra $\mathfrak{A}_\mathfrak{P}$ can be identified with the ideal $\mathfrak{I}_\mathfrak{P}$. Furthermore, if $\mathfrak{P}_1, \cdots, \mathfrak{P}_n$ is any finite set of primitive ideals with $\mathfrak{K}$ as their kernel, then it is readily verified that

$$\mathfrak{A} = \mathfrak{K} \oplus \mathfrak{I}_{\mathfrak{P}_1} \oplus \cdots \oplus \mathfrak{I}_{\mathfrak{P}_n}$$

and moreover, by repeated application of Lemma (4.9.21), we obtain that

$$\|m_0 + m_1 + \cdots + m_n\| = \max (\|m_0\|, \cdots, \|m_n\|),$$

where $m_0 \in \mathfrak{K}$ and $m_i \in \mathfrak{I}_{\mathfrak{P}_i}$ for $i = 1, \cdots, n$. Now let $\mathfrak{I}$ denote the join of all of the ideals $\mathfrak{I}_\mathfrak{P}$. If $\mathfrak{P} \supseteq \mathfrak{I}$, then a fortiori $\mathfrak{P} \supseteq \mathfrak{I}_\mathfrak{P}$, which is impossible since $h(\mathfrak{I}_\mathfrak{P}) = \Pi_\mathfrak{A} - (\mathfrak{P})$. Therefore $h(\mathfrak{I})$ is vacuous and $\mathfrak{I}$ is dense in $\mathfrak{A}$. For arbitrary $a \in \mathfrak{I}$, there exist $\mathfrak{P}_1, \cdots, \mathfrak{P}_n$ such that $a \in \mathfrak{I}_{\mathfrak{P}_1} + \cdots + \mathfrak{I}_{\mathfrak{P}_n}$. Thus, $\hat{a}(\mathfrak{P}) = 0$ for $\mathfrak{P}$ different from $\mathfrak{P}_1, \cdots, \mathfrak{P}_n$. It follows that $a \to \hat{a}$ maps $\mathfrak{I}$ isometrically onto the subalgebra of $\Sigma\mathfrak{A}_\mathfrak{P}$ consisting of those functions which vanish except on a finite subset of $\Pi_\mathfrak{A}$. This subalgebra is clearly dense in $(\Sigma\mathfrak{A}_\mathfrak{P})_0$. Therefore $a \to \hat{a}$ maps $\mathfrak{A}$ onto $(\Sigma\mathfrak{A}_\mathfrak{P})_0$. This proves the first half of the theorem.

Now assume that $\mathfrak{A}$ is of the form $(\Sigma\mathfrak{A}_\lambda)_0$, where each $\mathfrak{A}_\lambda$ is a topologically simple B*-algebra. If $\mathfrak{I}$ is a closed 2-sided ideal in $\mathfrak{A}$, then the simplicity of the algebra $\mathfrak{A}_\lambda$ implies that $\mathfrak{I}$ consists of all functions in $(\Sigma\mathfrak{A}_\lambda)_0$ which vanish on a certain subset Λ_0 of Λ. Suppose that Λ_0 contains more than one point. Then it is equal to a union of two disjoint sets Λ_1 and Λ_2. Let $\mathfrak{I}_1$ and $\mathfrak{I}_2$ be the ideals consisting of all f in $\mathfrak{A}$ which vanish on Λ_1 and Λ_2 respectively. Then $\mathfrak{I}_1\mathfrak{I}_2 \subseteq \mathfrak{I}$. Since neither $\mathfrak{I}_1$ nor $\mathfrak{I}_2$ is contained in $\mathfrak{I}$, it follows by Theorem (2.2.8)(iv) that $\mathfrak{I}$ is not primitive. In other words, a primitive ideal in $\mathfrak{A}$ consists of all functions which vanish at a single point of Λ. That $\Pi_\mathfrak{A}$ is discrete follows immediately from this result.

Kadison [11; 15] has given a system of unitary invariants for *-representations of C*-algebras on Hilbert space. He [10] has also obtained criteria under which a general representation (not necessarily *-representation !) of a B*-algebra on Hilbert space is similar to a *-representation. In the commutative case, this problem was treated by Mackey [5, p. 146]. Some more results of this kind were obtained by R. B. Smith [1].

§ 10. Banach *-algebras with minimal ideals.

Before discussing the special algebras, which are the main concern of this section, we consider briefly some properties of minimal ideals in a *-algebra. The following lemma is an adaptation of Lemma (2.1.5) to the present situation. (See Rickart [4].)

LEMMA (4.10.1). *Let* $\mathfrak{A}$ *be an arbitrary* $\star$*-algebra in which* $x^\star x = 0$ *implies* $x = 0$. *Then every minimal left ideal* $\mathfrak{L}$ *in* $\mathfrak{A}$ *is of the form* $\mathfrak{L} = \mathfrak{A}p$, *where* p *is a unique hermitian idempotent. A similar result holds for right ideals.*

PROOF. Let x be any non-zero element of $\mathfrak{L}$ and set $h = x^\star x$. Then h is a non-zero hermitian element of $\mathfrak{L}$. Also, since $\mathfrak{L}$ is minimal and $h^2 \neq 0$, we have $\mathfrak{L}h = \mathfrak{L}$. Now let z be any element of $\mathfrak{L}$ such that $zh = 0$. If $z \neq 0$, then $\mathfrak{L} = \mathfrak{A}z$. But $\mathfrak{L} = \mathfrak{L}h = \mathfrak{A}zh = (0)$, a contradiction. In other words, the left annihilator of h in $\mathfrak{L}$ is zero. Now, since $\mathfrak{L} = \mathfrak{L}h$, there exists $e \in \mathfrak{L}$ such that $eh = h$. Moreover, $(e^2 - e)h = 0$ and hence $e^2 = e$. Since $h \in \mathfrak{L}$ and $\mathfrak{L} = \mathfrak{L}e$, it follows that $h = he$. Applying the involution to this equation, we obtain $h = e^\star h$. Define $p = e^\star e$. Then $p \in \mathfrak{L}$, $ph = h$ and thus $(p^2 - p)h = 0$ which implies $p^2 = p$. Furthermore, p is a non-zero element of $\mathfrak{L}$, so that $\mathfrak{L} = \mathfrak{A}p$. Finally, if p' were another hermitian idempotent such that $\mathfrak{L} = \mathfrak{L}p'$, then $p'p = p'$ and $pp' = p$. Therefore, $p' = (p')^\star = (p'p)^\star = pp' = p$, and the lemma is proved.

LEMMA (4.10.2). *Let* $\mathfrak{A}$ *be an arbitrary* $\star$*-algebra in which* $x^\star x = 0$ *implies* $x = 0$. *If* $\mathfrak{A}$ *contains minimal one-sided ideals, then its socle* $\mathfrak{F}$ *is defined and is a* $\star$*-ideal.*

PROOF. Note that any ideal $\mathfrak{J}$ different from zero will contain a non-zero hermitian element h. Since $h^2 \neq 0$, it follows that $\mathfrak{J}^2 \neq (0)$. Therefore (0) is the only ideal with square equal to zero. It follows, by Lemma (2.1.12), that the socle $\mathfrak{F}$ is defined. Moreover, if $\mathfrak{L}$ is any minimal left ideal, then $\mathfrak{L}^\star$ is a minimal right ideal. That $\mathfrak{F}$ is a $\star$-ideal now follows from the fact that it is the join of all minimal left ideals or all minimal right ideals.

THEOREM (4.10.3). *Let* $\mathfrak{A}$ *be a complex Banach* $\star$*-algebra in which* $x^\star x = 0$ *implies* $x = 0$ *and let* $\mathfrak{L}$ *be a minimal left ideal in* $\mathfrak{A}$. *Then an inner product* (x, y) *can be introduced into* $\mathfrak{L}$ *such that the left regular representation,* $a \to T_a$, *of* $\mathfrak{A}$ *on* $\mathfrak{L}$ *is a* $\star$*-representation relative to* (x, y) *and every* T_a *is bounded relative to the inner product norm* $|x|_0 = (x, x)^{1/2}$.

PROOF. By Lemma (4.10.1), there exists a hermitian idempotent p such that $\mathfrak{L} = \mathfrak{A}p$. Also, by Corollary (2.1.6), $p\mathfrak{A}p$ consists of scalar multiples of p. Now, if x and y are any two elements of $\mathfrak{L}$, then $y^\star x \in p\mathfrak{A}p$ and hence there exists a scalar (x, y) such that $y^\star x = (x, y)p$. We prove that (x, y) is the desired inner product. It is obvious that (x, y) is linear in x for fixed y. Also,

$$(y, x)p = x^\star y = (y^\star x)^\star = ((x, y)p)^\star = \overline{(x, y)}p.$$

Hence $(y, x) = \overline{(x, y)}$. Moreover, since $(x, x)p = x^\star x$, $(x, x) = 0$ implies $x = 0$. Therefore (x, y) is positive definite and so is indeed an inner product. Next we have

$$(T_a x, y)p = y^\star a x = (a^\star y)^\star x = (x, T_{a^\star} y)p$$

and thus obtain $T_{a^\star} = T_a{}^\star$, which shows that $a \to T_a$ is a $\star$-representation on $\mathfrak{L}$. Finally, define

$$F(a) = (T_a p, p), \quad a \in \mathfrak{A}.$$

Then F is clearly a positive functional on $\mathfrak{A}$. Moreover,

$$|F(a)| \|p\| = \|pap\| \leqslant \|p\|^2 \|a\|,$$

so that F is bounded. It follows, by Theorem (4.5.2), that

$$|F(x^\star a^\star a x)| \leqslant F(x^\star x) \nu(a^\star a).$$

This can be written as

$$|T_a x|_0{}^2 \leqslant |x|_0{}^2 \nu(a^\star a),$$

and shows that T_a is bounded relative to the inner product norm. This completes the proof.

Since the operators T_a are bounded relative to the inner product norm, they can be extended to the completion of $\mathfrak{L}$ by this norm, so that $a \to T_a$ becomes a $\star$-representation on Hilbert space. Also, since $|T_a|^2 \leqslant \nu(a^\star a)$, the direct sum of all such $\star$-representations exists. Therefore we obtain the following corollary.

COROLLARY (4.10.4). *Let $\mathfrak{A}$ be a complex Banach $\star$-algebra in which $x^\star x = 0$ implies $x = 0$. Let $\mathfrak{F}$ be the socle of $\mathfrak{A}$ and assume that $a\mathfrak{F} = (0)$ implies $a = 0$. Then $\mathfrak{A}$ admits a faithful $\star$-representation on Hilbert space and so is an $A^\star$-algebra.*

We specialize now to a primitive complex Banach $\star$-algebra $\mathfrak{A}$ with minimal one-sided ideals. Observe that Theorem (2.4.12) applies to this case giving a representation of $\mathfrak{A}$ in terms of a pair of normed-dual Banach spaces. The next theorem records the effect of an involution on this representation. If $\mathfrak{H}$ is a Hilbert space and g, h are vectors in $\mathfrak{H}$, then we denote by $g \otimes h$ the linear operator on $\mathfrak{H}$ defined by the relation $(g \otimes h)f = (f, h)g$, $f \in \mathfrak{H}$. Observe that $(g \otimes h)^\star = h \otimes g$.

THEOREM (4.10.5). *Let $\mathfrak{A}$ be a primitive complex Banach $\star$-algebra which has minimal one-sided ideals and in which $x^\star x = 0$ implies $x = 0$. Then there exists a faithful $\star$-representation of $\mathfrak{A}$ on a Hilbert space $\mathfrak{H}$*

such that the image of $\mathfrak{A}$ in $\mathscr{B}(\mathfrak{H})$ contains every operator on $\mathfrak{H}$ of the form $g \otimes h$, where g and h range over a certain dense subspace $\mathfrak{H}_0$ in $\mathfrak{H}$.

PROOF. Let $\mathfrak{L} = \mathfrak{A}p$ be a minimal left ideal in $\mathfrak{A}$, with $p^2 = p$ and $p^\star = p$, and let $a \to T_a$ be the left regular representation of $\mathfrak{A}$ on $\mathfrak{L}$. Since $\mathfrak{A}$ is primitive, the representation $a \to T_a$ is already faithful. Let (x, y) be the inner product introduced into $\mathfrak{L}$ in Theorem (4.10.3) and denote by $\mathfrak{H}$ the completion of $\mathfrak{L}$ under the inner product norm, $|x|_0 = (x, x)^{1/2}$. Then $a \to T_a$ is a $\star$-representation of $\mathfrak{A}$ in $\mathscr{B}(\mathfrak{H})$. Note that $\mathfrak{L}$ is isomorphic with a dense subspace of $\mathfrak{H}$ which we denote by $\mathfrak{H}_0$. Now let f, g and h be arbitrary elements of $\mathfrak{H}_0$ and denote by the same symbols the corresponding elements of $\mathfrak{L}$. We then have (in $\mathfrak{L}$)

$$\begin{aligned}(g \oplus h)f &= (f, h)g = (f, h)gp \\ &= g(f, h)p = gh^\star f = T_{gh^\star}f.\end{aligned}$$

It follows that $T_{gh^\star} = g \otimes h$, and the theorem is proved.

We remark in passing that, by the fundamental isomorphism theorem for primitive Banach algebras with minimal ideals (Theorem (2.5.19)), the representation $a \to T_a$ of $\mathfrak{A}$ on dual Banach spaces $\mathfrak{X}$ and $\mathfrak{Y}$, obtained in Theorem (2.4.12), is topologically equivalent to the left regular representation, $a \to A_a$, of $\mathfrak{A}$ on $\mathfrak{L}$ (regarded as a Banach space under the norm of $\mathfrak{A}$). In this case, there exists a bicontinuous linear transformation U of $\mathfrak{L}$ onto $\mathfrak{X}$ and a bicontinuous *conjugate* linear transformation V of $\mathfrak{L}$ onto $\mathfrak{Y}$ such that

$$(Ux, Vy) = (x, y), \quad x, y \in \mathfrak{L},$$

and

$$UA_a x = T_a Ux, \quad VA_{a^\star}y = T'_a Vy, \quad a \in \mathfrak{A}.$$

A situation of special importance in the above theorem occurs when $\mathfrak{H}_0 = \mathfrak{H}$. In this case, $\mathfrak{L}$ is already complete in the inner product norm and the image of $\mathfrak{A}$ in $\mathscr{B}(\mathfrak{H})$ contains all bounded operators of finite rank. In the following theorem, we have a necessary and sufficient condition for this situation to hold.

THEOREM (4.10.6). *In order for $\mathfrak{L}$ to be complete in the inner product norm $|x|_0$, it is necessary and sufficient that there exist a constant β such that $\|x\|^2 \leqslant \beta\|x^\star x\|$ for every $x \in \mathfrak{L}$.*

PROOF. Since the involution in $\mathfrak{A}$ is continuous, there exists a constant α such that $\|a^\star\| \leqslant \alpha\|a\|$ for all $a \in \mathfrak{A}$. Hence

$$|x|_0^2\|p\| = \|x^\star x\| \leqslant \alpha\|x\|^2, \quad x \in \mathfrak{L},$$

and it follows that always $|x|_0 \leqslant \mu\|x\|$, where $\mu^2 = \alpha\|p\|^{-1}$. Since $\mathfrak{L}$ is complete relative to $||x||$, this shows that $\mathfrak{L}$ will be complete relative to $|x|_0$ if and only if the two norms $|x|_0$ and $||x||$ are equivalent. Assume first that β exists such that $||x||^2 \leqslant \beta||x^\star x||$, $x \in \mathfrak{L}$. Then

$$||x||^2 \leqslant \beta||x^\star x|| = \beta|x_0|^2||p||, \quad x \in \mathfrak{L}.$$

Therefore $||x|| \leqslant \gamma|x|_0$, where $\gamma^2 = \beta^{-1}||p||$. Hence, $|x|_0$ and $||x||$ are equivalent and the sufficiency is proved. On the other hand, if the norms are equivalent, let γ be a constant such that $||x|| \leqslant \gamma|x|_0$. Then

$$||x||^2 \leqslant \gamma^2|x|_0{}^2 = \gamma^2||p||^{-1}||x^\star x||, \quad x \in \mathfrak{L}.$$

Therefore $||x||^2 \leqslant \beta||x^\star x||$, with $\beta = \gamma^2||p||^{-1}$, and the necessity is proved.

It is instructive to approach the question considered in Theorem (4.10.3) from a slightly different point of view, obtained by starting with a given representation of the algebra as an irreducible algebra of bounded operators on a general Banach space. Thus, let $\mathfrak{X}$ be a complex Banach space with norm $|x|$ and denote the bound of an operator $T \in \mathscr{B}(\mathfrak{X})$ by $|T|$. Let $\mathfrak{B}$ denote a strictly irreducible subalgebra of $\mathscr{B}(\mathfrak{X})$ which contains minimal one-sided ideals and which is a Banach algebra under a norm $||T||$. The problem can now be regarded as one of describing the influence of an involution in $\mathfrak{B}$ on the space $\mathfrak{X}$. Before continuing, we introduce a more restricted kind of irreducibility for normed subalgebras of $\mathscr{B}(\mathfrak{X})$.

A normed subalgebra of $\mathscr{B}(\mathfrak{X})$ is called STRONGLY IRREDUCIBLE provided there exists, for each $y \in \mathfrak{X}$, a constant α_y with the following property: If $x \in \mathfrak{X}$ and $|x| = 1$, then there exists a T in the subalgebra such that $Tx = y$ and $||T|| \leqslant \alpha_y$. If the subalgebra is strictly irreducible, then the above condition imposed for a single fixed non-zero y already implies strong irreducibility. Note that $\mathscr{B}(\mathfrak{X})$ itself is strongly irreducible with respect to the norm $|T|$. (See Rickart [7].)

THEOREM (4.10.7). *Let $T \to T^\star$ be any involution in $\mathfrak{B}$ such that $T^\star T = 0$ implies $T = 0$. Then an inner product (x, y) can be introduced into $\mathfrak{X}$ with the following properties:*

(*i*) *Each $T \in \mathfrak{B}$ is bounded relative to the inner product norm $|x|_0 = (x, x)^{1/2}$ and, if $|T|_0$ is the bound of T for $|x|_0$, then there exists a constant γ such that $|T|_0 \leqslant \gamma||T||$ for all $T \in \mathfrak{B}$.*

(*ii*) *$(Tx, y) = (x, T^\star y)$ for all $x, y \in \mathfrak{X}$ and $T \in \mathfrak{B}$.*

(*iii*) *There exists a constant β such that $|x|_0 \leqslant \beta|x|$ for all $x \in \mathfrak{X}$.*

(*iv*) *If $\mathfrak{B}$ is strongly irreducible, then the two norms $|x|$ and $|x|_0$ are equivalent.*

PROOF. By Lemma (2.4.13), the space $\mathfrak{X}$ is equivalent to a minimal left ideal in $\mathfrak{B}$ under a correspondence $x \leftrightarrow x \otimes g$, where g is a fixed bounded linear functional on $\mathfrak{X}$. Since $Tx \leftrightarrow (Tx) \otimes g = T(x \otimes g)$, Theorem (4.10.3) provides an inner product in $\mathfrak{X}$ with property (ii). The relationship between the norms in (i) is given by Corollary (4.1.16) and in (iii) is given by Theorem (2.2.7). For the proof of (iv) let u be a fixed non-zero vector in $\mathfrak{X}$. Then, by strong irreducibility, there exists for each non-zero $x \in \mathfrak{X}$ an operator $T \in \mathfrak{B}$ such that $\|T\| \leqslant \alpha$ and $Tx = |x|u$, where α is a constant. Therefore

$$|x||u|_0 = |Tx|_0 \leqslant |T|_0|x|_0 \leqslant \gamma\alpha|x|_0 \leqslant \beta\gamma\alpha|x|,$$

so that the norms $|x|$, $|x|_0$ are equivalent and the theorem is proved.

Since $\mathscr{B}(\mathfrak{X})$ is strongly irreducible, we obtain as a corollary to the above theorem a result due to Kakutani and Mackey [2].

COROLLARY (4.10.8). *If $\mathscr{B}(\mathfrak{X})$ admits an involution $T \to T^\star$ such that $T^\star T = 0$ implies $T = 0$, then an inner product can be introduced into $\mathfrak{X}$ so that it becomes a Hilbert space with norm equivalent to the given norm in $\mathfrak{X}$ and so that $T^\star$ is the adjoint of T relative to the inner product.*

We obtain next a sharpened form of the fundamental isomorphism theorem (Theorem (2.5.19)) for ⋆-algebras. Let $\mathfrak{H}_1$ and $\mathfrak{H}_2$ be two Hilbert spaces and let $\mathfrak{B}_1$ and $\mathfrak{B}_2$ denote (strictly) irreducible ⋆-subalgebras of $\mathscr{B}(\mathfrak{H}_1)$ and $\mathscr{B}(\mathfrak{H}_2)$ respectively. These algebras are assumed to contain minimal one-sided ideals and to be Banach algebras under norms which may differ from the operator bounds. Notice that these norms automatically majorize the operator bounds, by Theorem (4.1.17).

THEOREM (4.10.9). *Let $T \to T^\tau$ be any ⋆-isomorphism of $\mathfrak{B}_1$ onto $\mathfrak{B}_2$. Then there exists a unitary transformation U of $\mathfrak{H}_1$ onto $\mathfrak{H}_2$ such that $T^\tau = UTU^\star$ for every $T \in \mathfrak{B}_1$.*

PROOF. By the isomorphism theorem, there exists a one-to-one bicontinuous linear transformation V of $\mathfrak{H}_1$ onto $\mathfrak{H}_2$ such that $T^\tau = VTV^{-1}$ for $T \in \mathfrak{B}_1$. Since τ is a ⋆-isomorphism, it follows that also $T^\tau = (V^\star)^{-1}TV^\star$, where $V^\star$ is the adjoint of V and maps $\mathfrak{H}_2$ onto $\mathfrak{H}_1$. Therefore we have $V^\star VT = TV^\star V$ for all $T \in \mathfrak{B}_1$. Since $\mathfrak{B}_1$ is irreducible, it follows by Schur's lemma (Theorem (4.4.12)) that $V^\star V$ reduces to a scalar multiple of the identity operator on $\mathfrak{H}_1$, say $V^\star V = \lambda I$. Evidently, $\lambda > 0$, so that $\lambda = \beta^2$, $\beta > 0$. The desired unitary operator U is equal to $\beta^{-1}V$.

In view of Theorem (4.9.10), we can state the following result.

COROLLARY (4.10.10). *If the algebras $\mathfrak{B}_1$, $\mathfrak{B}_2$ are complete with respect to the operator bounds, then strict irreducibility can be replaced by topological irreducibility in the above theorem.*

The remainder of this section will be devoted to the study of a semi-simple annihilator Banach $\star$-algebra $\mathfrak{A}$ in which $x^\star x = 0$ implies $x = 0$. Since these algebras have a unique norm topology (see Corollary (2.8.17)), the involution in $\mathfrak{A}$ is automatically continuous. The following result is due to Civin and Yood [3].

THEOREM (4.10.11). *A semi-simple annihilator Banach $\star$-algebra $\mathfrak{A}$ in which $x^\star x = 0$ implies $x = 0$ is necessarily symmetric.*

PROOF. Suppose u were an element of $\mathfrak{A}$ such that $-u^\star u$ is quasi-singular. Then $(1+u^\star u)\mathfrak{A}$ is a proper modular right ideal and so is contained in a maximal modular right ideal $\mathfrak{K}$. By Theorem (2.8.5)(ii), $\mathscr{A}_l(\mathfrak{K})$ is a minimal left ideal. Therefore, Lemma (4.10.1) provides a minimal hermitian idempotent p such that $\mathscr{A}_l(\mathfrak{K}) = \mathfrak{A}p$. In particular, $p(1+u^\star u)\mathfrak{A} = (0)$ and hence $pu^\star u = -p$. Since p is minimal, there exists a scalar $\zeta = \alpha + \beta i$ (α, β real) such that $pup = \zeta p$. Now, if ξ is any real number, then

$$(up-\xi p)^\star(up-\xi p) = (\xi^2 - 2\alpha\xi - 1)p.$$

The quadratic $\xi^2 - 2\alpha\xi - 1$ has real roots, so that there exists a real number ξ such that $up = \xi p$. But then, $\xi^2 p = pu^\star up = -p$, which implies $\xi^2 = -1$. This contradicts the fact that ξ is real and shows that $\mathfrak{A}$ must be symmetric.

Our next lemma strengthens slightly the result that $\mathfrak{A}$ is equal to the topological sum of its minimal left (or right) ideals. (See Theorem (2.8.15).)

LEMMA (4.10.12). *Let $\{p_\lambda : \lambda \in \Lambda\}$ be a maximal family of pairwise orthogonal, minimal, hermitian idempotents in $\mathfrak{A}$. Then $\mathfrak{A}$ is equal to the topological sum of the minimal left ideals $\mathfrak{A}p_\lambda$ and also of the minimal right ideals $p_\lambda\mathfrak{A}$.*

PROOF. Let $\mathfrak{A}_0$ denote the topological sum of the left ideals $\mathfrak{A}p_\lambda$. Then $\mathfrak{A}_0$ is a closed left ideal in $\mathfrak{A}$. If $\mathfrak{A}_0 \neq \mathfrak{A}$, then $\mathscr{A}_r(\mathfrak{A}_0) \neq (0)$. By Lemmas (2.8.6) and (4.10.1), the ideal $\mathscr{A}_r(\mathfrak{A}_0)$ must contain a minimal hermitian idempotent p. Note that $p_\lambda p = 0$ and, since these elements are hermitian, also $pp_\lambda = 0$ for all λ. This contradicts the maximality of the family $\{p_\lambda : \lambda \in \Lambda\}$ and proves that $\mathfrak{A}_0 = \mathfrak{A}$. The result for right ideals follows by a similar argument.

LEMMA (4.10.13). *Let $\mathfrak{J}$ be a minimal-closed 2-sided ideal in $\mathfrak{A}$. Then $\mathfrak{J}^\star = \mathfrak{J}$.*

PROOF. By Lemmas (2.8.6) and (4.10.1), $\mathfrak{J}$ contains a minimal hermitian idempotent p. In particular, $p \in \mathfrak{J} \cap \mathfrak{J}^\star$. But $\mathfrak{J}^\star$ is also a minimal-closed 2-sided ideal in $\mathfrak{A}$ and must therefore be equal to $\mathfrak{J}$ since $\mathfrak{J} \cap \mathfrak{J}^\star \neq (0)$.

This lemma, along with the fact that $\mathfrak{A}$ is equal to the direct topological sum of its minimal-closed 2-sided ideals (Theorem (2.8.15)), in effect, reduces the study of these algebras to the simple case. However, before specializing to the simple case we obtain a sharpened form of this structure theorem in the case of a B*-algebra. For a definition of the subdirect sum in the next theorem, see the discussion preceding Theorem (4.9.24).

THEOREM (4.10.14). *Let $\mathfrak{A}$ be an annihilator $B^\star$-algebra with $\{\mathfrak{J}_\lambda : \lambda \in \Lambda\}$ as its family of minimal-closed 2-sided ideals. Then $\mathfrak{A} = (\Sigma\mathfrak{J}_\lambda)_0$.*

PROOF. Let $\mathfrak{J}$ be the sum of all of the ideals $\mathfrak{J}_\lambda$. Then, by Theorem (2.8.15), $\mathfrak{J}$ is dense in $\mathfrak{A}$. For arbitrary $a \in \mathfrak{J}$, there exist indices $\lambda_1, \cdots, \lambda_n$ and elements $u_i \in \mathfrak{J}_{\lambda_i}$ such that $a = u_1 + \cdots + u_n$. Repeated application of Lemma (4.9.21) yields the result

$$\|a\| = \max(\|u_1\|, \cdots, \|u_n\|).$$

Therefore, if we define $f_a(\lambda) = u_i$ for $\lambda = \lambda_i$ and $f_a(\lambda) = 0$ otherwise, then $f_a \in (\Sigma\mathfrak{J}_\lambda)_0$ and $a \to f_a$ is an isometric $\star$-isomorphism of $\mathfrak{J}$ onto a dense subalgebra of $(\Sigma\mathfrak{J}_\lambda)_0$. The desired result now follows from the density of $\mathfrak{J}$ in $\mathfrak{A}$.

The following corollary is obtained from the above theorem plus Theorem (4.9.24).

COROLLARY (4.10.15). *The structure space $\Pi_{\mathfrak{A}}$ of $\mathfrak{A}$ is discrete.*

We now return to general annihilator Banach $\star$-algebras which are semi-simple and also topologically simple.

THEOREM (4.10.16). *Let $\mathfrak{A}$ be a topologically simple, semi-simple annihilator Banach $\star$-algebra in which $x^\star x = 0$ implies $x = 0$. Then there exists a faithful $\star$-representation of $\mathfrak{A}$ on a Hilbert space $\mathfrak{H}$ such that the socle of $\mathfrak{A}$ maps onto the socle of $\mathscr{B}(\mathfrak{H})$.*

PROOF. Let $\mathfrak{L}$ be a minimal left ideal in $\mathfrak{A}$ and write $\mathfrak{L} = \mathfrak{A}p$, $p^2 = p$, $p^\star = p$. Then $y^\star x = (x, y)p$, where (x, y) is an inner product on $\mathfrak{L}$. In view of Theorem (4.10.5) (note that $\mathfrak{H}_0 = \mathfrak{L}$), we have only to prove that $\mathfrak{L}$ is complete with respect to the inner product norm $|x|_0$. Now regard $\mathfrak{L}$ as a Banach space under the norm $\|x\|$ of $\mathfrak{A}$. Then we know from Lemma (2.8.20) that the image of $\mathfrak{A}$ in $\mathscr{B}(\mathfrak{L})$ under the left regular representation $a \to A_a$ on $\mathfrak{L}$ contains *every* operator of the form $p \otimes F$, where F is a bounded linear functional on $\mathfrak{L}$ and $(p \otimes F)x = F(x)p$. Denote the bound of F by $\|F\|$ and set $\|F\|' = \|a\|$, where $A_a = p \otimes F$. By Lemmas (2.8.22) and (2.4.13), the two norms $\|F\|$ and $\|F\|'$ are equivalent. Hence there exists a constant α such that $\|F\|' \leqslant \alpha\|F\|$. Now, for a given $x \in \mathfrak{L}$, choose F such that $F(x) = \|x\|$ and $\|F\| = 1$. Then $(p \otimes F)x = \|x\|p$ and $\|F\|' \leqslant \alpha$. Since $|p|_0 = 1$, we have

$$\|x\| = |(p \otimes F)x|_0 \leqslant \|F\|'|x|_0 \leqslant \alpha|x|_0.$$

On the other hand, by Theorem (4.10.7) (iii), there exists a constant β such that $|x|_0 \leqslant \beta\|x\|$. Therefore the norms $\|x\|$, $|x|_0$ are equivalent and the proof is complete.

The above theorem has a number of interesting consequences which we record as a series of corollaries. The converse statement in the first one is easily established with help of Theorem (2.8.23).

COROLLARY (4.10.17). *The image of $\mathfrak{A}$ in $\mathscr{B}(\mathfrak{H})$ is a $\star$-algebra of compact operators and is obtained by completion of the operators of finite rank relative to a norm which majorizes the operator bound. Conversely, every $\star$-subalgebra of the compact operators on $\mathfrak{H}$ obtained in this way is a topologically simple annihilator Banach $\star$-algebra.*

Since a projection is compact if and only if its range is finite dimensional and the image of $\mathfrak{A}$ in $\mathscr{B}(\mathfrak{H})$ contains all operators of finite rank, we obtain the next result.

COROLLARY (4.10.18). *If e is any hermitian idempotent in $\mathfrak{A}$, then the algebra $e\mathfrak{A}e$ is finite dimensional and isomorphic to a full matrix algebra over the complex numbers. In particular, $\mathfrak{A}$ is finite dimensional (and hence isomorphic to a full matrix algebra) if and only if it possesses an identity element.*

It is easy to prove that any simple ring, whose annihilator is equal to zero and which contains a non-zero central element, must possess an identity element. Therefore we can state the next corollary.

COROLLARY (4.10.19). *The algebra $\mathfrak{A}$ is infinite dimensional if and only if its center reduces to the zero element.*

If $\mathfrak{A}$ is a B⋆-algebra, then the ⋆-representation in $\mathscr{B}(\mathfrak{H})$ is an isometry. Note also that a B⋆-algebra is automatically semi-simple and $x^\star x = 0$ implies $x = 0$. Therefore, since every closed subspace of $\mathfrak{H}$ is the range of a bounded projection, Theorem (2.8.28) and Corollary (4.10.17) apply to give the following result.

COROLLARY (4.10.20). *Every topologically simple annihilator B⋆-algebra is dual and is equal to the algebra of all compact operators on a Hilbert space.*

In the following three theorems, $\mathfrak{A}$ is assumed to be a topologically simple, semi-simple, Banach ⋆-algebra in which $x^\star x = 0$ implies $x = 0$. The first of the theorems gives an important structure property of these algebras.

THEOREM (4.10.21). *There exists a family $\{e_{\lambda\mu} : \lambda, \mu \in \Lambda\}$ of elements in $\mathfrak{A}$ with the following properties:*

(*i*) $e_{\lambda\mu}{}^\star = e_{\mu\lambda}$, $e_{\lambda\mu}e_{\rho\sigma} = \delta_{\mu\rho}e_{\lambda\sigma}$.
(*ii*) $\{e_{\lambda\lambda} : \lambda \in \Lambda\}$ *is a maximal family of pairwise orthogonal, minimal, hermitian idempotents.*
(*iii*) *Finite linear combinations of the elements $e_{\lambda\mu}$ are dense in $\mathfrak{A}$.*

PROOF. Let $a \to T_a$ be the representation of $\mathfrak{A}$ on Hilbert space $\mathfrak{H}$ given by Theorem (4.10.16) and denote by $\{f_\lambda : \lambda \in \Lambda)$ a complete orthonormal system of vectors in $\mathfrak{H}$. Define $E_{\lambda\mu} = f_\lambda \otimes f_\mu$ and let $e_{\lambda\mu}$ be the corresponding element of $\mathfrak{A}$. It is obvious that the operators $E_{\lambda\mu}$, and hence the elements $e_{\lambda\mu}$, satisfy the properties in (i). Note also that each $e_{\lambda\lambda}$ is a minimal hermitian idempotent and that these idempotents are pairwise orthogonal. Let e be any hermitian idempotent which is orthogonal to each $e_{\lambda\mu}$ and denote its image in $\mathscr{B}(\mathfrak{H})$ by E. Then $EE_{\lambda\lambda} = (Ef_\lambda) \otimes f_\lambda = 0$, and hence, $Ef_\lambda = 0$ for all λ. Therefore $E = 0$ and property (ii) is proved. Next we observe that

$$E_{\lambda\lambda}TE_{\mu\mu} = (f_\lambda, Tf_\mu)E_{\lambda\mu}.$$

Thus, if we set $\alpha_{\lambda\mu} = (f_\lambda, T_a f_\mu)$ for any $a \in \mathfrak{A}$, then $e_{\lambda\lambda}ae_{\mu\mu} = \alpha_{\lambda\mu}e_{\lambda\mu}$. Now, by Lemma (4.10.12), it follows that

$$\mathfrak{A} = \overline{\sum e_{\lambda\lambda}\mathfrak{A}e_{\mu\mu}}.$$

Therefore, finite linear combinations of elements of the form $e_{\lambda\lambda}ae_{\mu\mu}$

are dense in $\mathfrak{A}$. Since $e_{\lambda\lambda}ae_{\mu\mu}$ is a scalar multiple of $e_{\lambda\mu}$, property (iii) follows and the theorem is proved.

Notice that the mapping $\Sigma\xi_{\lambda\mu}e_{\lambda\mu} \to (\xi_{\lambda\mu})$ defines an isomorphism between a dense subalgebra of $\mathfrak{A}$ and the matrix algebra of all $\Lambda \times \Lambda$ matrices with at most a finite number of non-zero entries. In this sense, $\mathfrak{A}$ contains a dense matrix subalgebra. The family $\{e_{\lambda\mu} : \lambda, \mu \in \Lambda\}$ is called a COMPLETE SYSTEM OF MATRIX UNITS for $\mathfrak{A}$.

The next two theorems give the form of representations of $\mathfrak{A}$ on Hilbert space.

THEOREM (4.10.22). *Any two irreducible $\star$-representations of $\mathfrak{A}$ on Hilbert space are unitarily equivalent.*

PROOF. Let $a \to T_a$ and $a \to T'_a$ be two (topologically) irreducible $\star$-representations of $\mathfrak{A}$ on the Hilbert spaces $\mathfrak{H}$ and $\mathfrak{H}'$ respectively. Also, let $\{e_{\lambda\mu} : \lambda, \mu \in \Lambda\}$ be a complete system of matrix units for $\mathfrak{A}$ and denote by $E_{\lambda\mu}$ and $E'_{\lambda\mu}$ the images of $e_{\lambda\mu}$ under the two representations. Fix an index $\rho \in \Lambda$ and choose vectors $f_0 \in E_{\rho\rho}(\mathfrak{H})$ and $f'_0 \in E'_{\rho\rho}(\mathfrak{H}')$ such that $|f_0| = |f'_0| = 1$. Next define, for each $\lambda \in \Lambda$, the vectors $f_\lambda = E_{\lambda\rho}f_0$ and $f'_\lambda = E'_{\lambda\rho}f'_0$. Since

$$
\begin{aligned}
(f_\lambda, f_\mu) &= (E_{\lambda\rho}f_0, E_{\mu\rho}f_0) \\
&= (f_0, E_{\rho\lambda}E_{\mu\rho}f_0) = \delta_{\lambda\mu}(f_0, f_0),
\end{aligned}
$$

we see that $\{f_\lambda : \lambda \in \Lambda\}$ is an orthonormal system in $\mathfrak{H}$. Suppose that $(f, f_\lambda) = 0$ for all $\lambda \in \Lambda$. Then it follows that $(f, E_{\lambda\mu}f_0) = 0$ for all $\lambda, \mu \in \Lambda$. Since linear combinations of the elements $e_{\lambda\mu}$ are dense in $\mathfrak{A}$ and the representation $a \to T_a$ is continuous (Theorem (4.1.20)), we conclude that $(f, T_af_0) = 0$ for all $a \in \mathfrak{A}$. But the fact that the representation is irreducible implies that f_0 is a cyclic vector. Therefore it follows that $f = 0$, and hence, that the system $\{f_\lambda : \lambda \in \Lambda\}$ is also complete. Similarly, $\{f'_\lambda : \lambda \in \Lambda\}$ is a complete orthonormal system in $\mathfrak{H}'$. Now, let U be the unitary transformation of $\mathfrak{H}$ onto $\mathfrak{H}'$ defined by the relations $Uf_\lambda = f'_\lambda$, $\lambda \in \Lambda$. Then we have

$$
\begin{aligned}
UE_{\lambda\mu}f_\nu &= UE_{\lambda\mu}E_{\nu\rho}f_0 = \delta_{\mu\nu}UE_{\lambda\rho}f_0 \\
&= \delta_{\mu\nu}Uf_\lambda = \delta_{\mu\nu}f'_\lambda = E'_{\lambda\mu}f'_\nu.
\end{aligned}
$$

Therefore $UE_{\lambda\mu} = E'_{\lambda\mu}U$ for all $\lambda, \mu \in \Lambda$. Again, since linear combinations of the matrix units are dense in $\mathfrak{A}$ and the representations are continuous, we conclude that $UT_a = T'_aU$ for all $a \in \mathfrak{A}$. In other words the representations are unitarily equivalent.

Since the representation of $\mathfrak{A}$ constructed in Theorem (4.10.16) is strictly irreducible, we obtain the following result.

COROLLARY (4.10.23). *Every topologically irreducible $\star$-representation of $\mathfrak{A}$ on Hilbert space is strictly irreducible.*

THEOREM (4.10.24). *Every essential $\star$-representation of $\mathfrak{A}$ on Hilbert space is a direct sum of unitarily equivalent irreducible representations.*

PROOF. In view of the preceding theorem, we have only to show that the Hilbert space of any essential $\star$-representation decomposes into an orthogonal direct sum of irreducible invariant subspaces. This will follow from an application of Zorn's Lemma if we show that irreducible invariant subspaces always exist for essential representations. To this end, let $a \to T_a$ be any essential $\star$-representation of $\mathfrak{A}$ on a Hilbert space $\mathfrak{H}$ and again denote by $E_{\lambda\mu}$ the image of $e_{\lambda\mu}$ under the representation, where $\{e_{\lambda\mu} : \lambda, \mu \in \Lambda\}$ is a complete system of matrix units for $\mathfrak{A}$. Also, fix $\rho \in \Lambda$ and choose any $f_0 \in E_{\rho\rho}(\mathfrak{H})$ such that $|f_0| = 1$. Define $f_\lambda = E_{\lambda\rho} f_0$ and denote by $\mathfrak{H}_0$ the cyclic subspace of $\mathfrak{H}$ generated by f_0. Precisely as in the proof of the preceding theorem, we conclude that $\{f_\lambda : \lambda \in \Lambda\}$ is a complete orthonormal system for $\mathfrak{H}_0$. It only remains to show that $\mathfrak{H}_0$ is irreducible. Let f be any non-zero vector in $\mathfrak{H}_0$. Then $f = \Sigma \varphi_\lambda f_\lambda$, where not all φ_λ are zero. If $\varphi_\mu \neq 0$, then $f_0 = \varphi_\mu^{-1} E_{\rho\mu} f$. It follows that f is a cyclic vector in $\mathfrak{H}_0$. Therefore $\mathfrak{H}_0$ is irreducible and the theorem is proved.

For the next theorem, we specialize to B$\star$-algebras.

THEOREM (4.10.25). *Let $\{\mathfrak{A}_\lambda : \lambda \in \Lambda\}$ be a family of dual B$\star$-algebras. Then the B$\star$-algebra $\mathfrak{A} = (\Sigma\mathfrak{A}_\lambda)_0$ is also dual.*

PROOF. For any element $x \in \mathfrak{A}_\lambda$, let $\tilde{x}$ be the element of $\mathfrak{A}$ such that $\tilde{x}(\lambda) = x$ and $\tilde{x}(\mu) = 0$ for $\mu \neq \lambda$. Then $x \to \tilde{x}$ is obviously a $\star$-isomorphism of $\mathfrak{A}_\lambda$ into $\mathfrak{A}$. Since these are B$\star$-algebras, this isomorphism is also an isometry. In this way, we can (and do) identify $\mathfrak{A}_\lambda$ with a subalgebra (actually an ideal) of $\mathfrak{A}$. Now let $\mathfrak{L}$ be a closed left ideal in $\mathfrak{A}$ and denote by $\mathfrak{L}_\lambda$ the image of $\mathfrak{L}$ in $\mathfrak{A}_\lambda$ under the mapping $f \to f(\lambda)$ of $\mathfrak{A}$ onto $\mathfrak{A}_\lambda$. Then it is readily verified that $\mathfrak{L}_\lambda$ is a left ideal in $\mathfrak{A}$ and that $\mathfrak{A}\mathfrak{L}_\lambda \subseteq \mathfrak{L}$. Since $\mathfrak{L}$ is closed, it follows by Corollary (4.9.3) that $\mathfrak{L}_\lambda \subseteq \mathfrak{L}$. Hence $\mathfrak{L}_\lambda = \mathfrak{L} \cap \mathfrak{A}_\lambda$ and, in particular, $\mathfrak{L}_\lambda$ is a closed left ideal in $\mathfrak{A}_\lambda$. Next let $\mathscr{E}$ be an arbitrary subset of $\mathfrak{A}$ and denote by $\mathscr{E}_\lambda$ the image of $\mathscr{E}$ in $\mathfrak{A}_\lambda$ under the mapping $f \to f(\lambda)$. Denote the annihilator operations in $\mathfrak{A}$ by $\mathscr{A}_l$, $\mathscr{A}_r$ and in $\mathfrak{A}_\lambda$ by $\mathscr{A}'_l$, $\mathscr{A}'_r$. Then $(\mathscr{A}_l(\mathscr{E}))_\lambda = \mathscr{A}'_l(\mathscr{E}_\lambda)$ and $(\mathscr{A}_r(\mathscr{E}))_\lambda = \mathscr{A}'_r(\mathscr{E}_\lambda)$. Since $\mathfrak{A}_\lambda$ is dual, we obtain

$(\mathscr{A}_l(\mathscr{A}_r(\mathfrak{L})))_\lambda = \mathscr{A}'_l(\mathscr{A}'_r(\mathfrak{L}_\lambda)) = \mathfrak{L}_\lambda$. In particular, $(\mathscr{A}_l(\mathscr{A}_r(\mathfrak{L})))_\lambda \subseteq \mathfrak{L}$. Thus, $\mathfrak{L}$ contains the linear subspace of $\mathfrak{A}$ generated by the sets $(\mathscr{A}_l(\mathscr{A}_r(\mathfrak{L})))_\lambda$, $\lambda \in \Lambda$. But this subspace clearly is dense in $\mathscr{A}_l(\mathscr{A}_r(\mathfrak{L}))$. Therefore $\mathscr{A}_l(\mathscr{A}_r(\mathfrak{L})) = \mathfrak{L}$. Similarly, if $\mathfrak{R}$ is a closed right ideal in $\mathfrak{A}$, then $\mathscr{A}_r(\mathscr{A}_l(\mathfrak{R})) = \mathfrak{R}$. This completes the proof that $\mathfrak{A}$ is dual.

By Theorem (4.10.14) and Corollary (4.10.20), we have the following result.

COROLLARY (4.10.26). *Every annihilator $B^\star$-algebra is dual.*

We now specialize even further to a class of Banach algebras which were introduced by Ambrose [1] to generalize the L^2 algebra of a compact group. These algebras, which are called H*-algebras, admit essentially perfect generalization of the classical Wedderburn structure theorems for finite dimensional associative algebras.

An H*-ALGEBRA $\mathfrak{A}$ is a complex Hilbert space which is at the same time a Banach algebra relative to the inner product norm $|x| = (x, x)^{1/2}$. The algebra structure of $\mathfrak{A}$ is further related to the inner product through the condition that there exist, for each $u \in \mathfrak{A}$, at least one element $u^\star \in \mathfrak{A}$, called an ADJOINT of u, such that

$$(ux, y) = (x, u^\star y), \quad (xu, y) = (x, yu^\star)$$

for all $x, y \in \mathfrak{A}$. Throughout the remainder of this section, $\mathfrak{A}$ will denote an H*-algebra.

If u, x, y are arbitrary elements of $\mathfrak{A}$, then

$$(xu, y) = (uy^\star, x^\star).$$

It follows that $u\mathfrak{A} = (0)$ if and only if $\mathfrak{A}u = (0)$. In other words, the left and right annihilators of $\mathfrak{A}$ are identical. These annihilators constitute a closed 2-sided ideal in $\mathfrak{A}$ which we denote by $\mathfrak{Z}$. The condition $\mathfrak{Z} = (0)$ is necessary and sufficient that the adjoint of each element of $\mathfrak{A}$ be uniquely determined. In this case, the mapping $x \to x^\star$ is an involution in $\mathfrak{A}$ and the left regular representation of $\mathfrak{A}$ on itself is a faithful $\star$-representation. In particular, if $\mathfrak{Z} = (0)$, then $\mathfrak{A}$ is an A*-algebra and is hence semi-simple.

LEMMA (4.10.27). *Let $\mathfrak{L}$ be a closed left ideal in $\mathfrak{A}$. Then*

(*i*) *the orthogonal complement of $\mathfrak{L}$ in $\mathfrak{A}$ is also a closed left ideal in $\mathfrak{A}$;*

(*ii*) *If* $\mathfrak{Z} \subseteq \mathfrak{L}$, *then* $\mathfrak{A}x \subseteq \mathfrak{L}$ *implies* $x \in \mathfrak{L}$. *Similar statements hold for right ideals.*

PROOF. Let $\mathfrak{L}^{\perp}$ be the orthogonal complement of $\mathfrak{L}$ in $\mathfrak{A}$ and let $u \in \mathfrak{L}$, $v \in \mathfrak{L}^{\perp}$ and $x \in \mathfrak{A}$. Then

$$(xv, u) = (v, x^{\star}u) = 0.$$

Hence, $xv \in \mathfrak{L}^{\perp}$ and it follows that $\mathfrak{L}^{\perp}$ is a left ideal. This proves the first statement. For the proof of (ii), let x be any element of $\mathfrak{A}$ such that $\mathfrak{A}x \subseteq \mathfrak{L}$ and write $x = u+v$ where $u \in \mathfrak{L}$ and $v \in \mathfrak{L}^{\perp}$. For arbitrary $y \in \mathfrak{A}$, $yx \in \mathfrak{L}$ and $yu \in \mathfrak{L}$, so that $yv = 0$. Thus, $v \in \mathfrak{Z}$ and, since $\mathfrak{Z} \subseteq \mathfrak{L}$, it follows that $v \in \mathfrak{L}$. Therefore $v = 0$ and we obtain $x \in \mathfrak{L}$.

LEMMA (4.10.28). *If* $\mathfrak{I}$ *is a closed 2-sided ideal in* $\mathfrak{A}$ *which contains* $\mathfrak{Z}$, *then* $\mathfrak{I}^{\star} = \mathfrak{I}$ *and* $\mathfrak{I}$ *is itself an* $H^{\star}$*-algebra.*

PROOF. Let $\mathfrak{I}^{\perp}$ be the orthogonal complement of $\mathfrak{I}$. Consider any u in $\mathfrak{I}$ and let $u^{\star}$ be any adjoint of u. Since $\mathfrak{I}^{\perp}$ is also a 2-sided ideal in $\mathfrak{A}$ and $u \in \mathfrak{I}$, we have $\mathfrak{I}^{\perp}u \subseteq \mathfrak{I} \cap \mathfrak{I}^{\perp} = (0)$. Hence

$$(\mathfrak{A}u^{\star}, \mathfrak{I}^{\perp}) = (\mathfrak{A}, \mathfrak{I}^{\perp}u) = (0),$$

so that $\mathfrak{A}u^{\star} \subseteq \mathfrak{I}$. Therefore, by the above lemma, $u^{\star} \in \mathfrak{I}$. This implies $\mathfrak{I}^{\star} \subseteq \mathfrak{I}$. Since $u^{\star} \in \mathfrak{I}$ and u is an adjoint of $u^{\star}$, we have $u \in \mathfrak{I}^{\star}$. Therefore $\mathfrak{I} \subseteq \mathfrak{I}^{\star}$ and hence $\mathfrak{I} = \mathfrak{I}^{\star}$.

The following theorem is the first of the Wedderburn structure theorems extended to H⋆-algebras.

THEOREM (4.10.29). *The radical of* $\mathfrak{A}$ *is equal to the annihilator ideal* $\mathfrak{Z}$, *and* $\mathfrak{A} = \mathfrak{Z} \oplus \mathfrak{Z}^{\perp}$, *where the orthogonal complement,* $\mathfrak{Z}^{\perp}$, *is a closed 2-sided ideal in* $\mathfrak{A}$ *and is a semi-simple* $H^{\star}$*-algebra.*

PROOF. By the preceding two lemmas, $\mathfrak{Z}^{\perp}$ is a closed 2-sided ideal in $\mathfrak{A}$ and is an H⋆-algebra. Also, since any element of $\mathfrak{A}$ annihilates $\mathfrak{Z}$, an element which annihilates $\mathfrak{Z}^{\perp}$ must belong to $\mathfrak{Z}$. Therefore the annihilator ideal of $\mathfrak{Z}^{\perp}$ is equal to zero, so that $\mathfrak{Z}^{\perp}$ is semi-simple. Since $\mathfrak{Z}^{\perp}$ is isomorphic with $\mathfrak{A}/\mathfrak{Z}$, it follows that $\mathfrak{Z}$ must contain the radical of $\mathfrak{A}$. On the other hand, the annihilator ideal is always contained in the radical, and so the theorem is proved.

In the remainder of this section, the H⋆-algebra $\mathfrak{A}$ will be assumed to to be semi-simple.

THEOREM (4.10.30). *Let* $\mathfrak{L}$ *and* $\mathfrak{R}$ *be closed left and right ideals respectively in* $\mathfrak{A}$. *Then* $\mathscr{A}_r(\mathfrak{L}) = (\mathfrak{L}^{\perp})^{\star}$ *and* $\mathscr{A}_l(\mathfrak{R}) = (\mathfrak{R}^{\perp})^{\star}$. *In particular,* $\mathfrak{A}$ *is dual.*

PROOF. We make the proof for a left ideal $\mathfrak{L}$. For arbitrary $u \in \mathfrak{A}$, we have $(\mathfrak{L}u, \mathfrak{A}) = (\mathfrak{L}, \mathfrak{A}u^\star)$. It follows that $u \in \mathscr{A}_r(\mathfrak{L})$ if and only if $\mathfrak{A}u^\star \subseteq \mathfrak{L}^\perp$. Moreover, by Lemma (4.10.27) (ii), $\mathfrak{A}u^\star \subseteq \mathfrak{L}^\perp$ if and only if $u^\star \in \mathfrak{L}^\perp$. Therefore $\mathscr{A}_r(\mathfrak{L}) = (\mathfrak{L}^\perp)^\star$ and the theorem is proved.

The next theorem is the second Wedderburn structure theorem for H*-algebras.

THEOREM (4.10.31). *The algebra* $\mathfrak{A}$ *is equal to the orthogonal (Hilbert space) direct sum of its minimal-closed 2-sided ideals each of which is a simple H***-algebra.*

PROOF. That $\mathfrak{A}$ is equal to the topological direct sum of its minimal-closed 2-sided ideals is given by Theorem (2.8.15). It remains to show that the direct sum is actually an orthogonal direct sum. For this, it is clearly sufficient to prove that any two minimal-closed 2-sided ideals in $\mathfrak{A}$ are orthogonal as subspaces of $\mathfrak{A}$. We accordingly let $\mathfrak{J}_1$ and $\mathfrak{J}_2$ be two such ideals and note that each ideal is a $\star$-ideal and $\mathfrak{J}_1\mathfrak{J}_2 = (0)$. Now let $u \in \mathfrak{J}_2$, then also $u^\star \in \mathfrak{J}_2$ and hence $\mathfrak{J}_1 u^\star = (0)$. Therefore

$$(\mathfrak{J}_1, \mathfrak{A}u) = (\mathfrak{J}_1 u^\star, \mathfrak{A}) = (0).$$

In other words, $\mathfrak{A}u \subseteq \mathfrak{J}_1^\perp$. It follows, by Lemma (4.10.19) (ii), that $u \in \mathfrak{J}_1^\perp$ and thus $\mathfrak{J}_2 \subseteq \mathfrak{J}_1^\perp$. Similarly $\mathfrak{J}_1 \subseteq \mathfrak{J}_2^\perp$ and the proof is complete.

The problem now is to obtain the structure of the simple components of $\mathfrak{A}$. Therefore we add the condition that $\mathfrak{A}$ be (topologically) simple. It is perhaps worth noting that the semi-simplicity is practically redundant here, since simplicity of an H*-algebra clearly implies that the algebra is either semi-simple or is a one-dimensional zero algebra (all products equal to zero). The objective below is to represent $\mathfrak{A}$ as an appropriately defined "full matrix algebra", and thus establish the third and final Wedderburn structure theorem for these algebras. Before proceeding, we define the matrix algebras which are involved.

Let Λ be an index set of arbitrary cardinality, finite or infinite. Denote by $\mathscr{M}_\Lambda$ the collection of all doubly indexed sets $\{\xi_{\lambda\mu}\}$ of complex numbers $\xi_{\lambda\mu}$ $(\lambda, \mu \in \Lambda)$ such that

$$\sum_{\lambda, \mu} |\xi_{\lambda\mu}|^2 < \infty.$$

Let $x = \{\xi_{\lambda\mu}\}$ and $y = \{\eta_{\lambda\mu}\}$ be any two elements of $\mathscr{M}_\Lambda$ and define

$$\alpha x = \{\alpha\xi_{\lambda\mu}\}, \quad x+y = \{\xi_{\lambda\mu}+\eta_{\lambda\mu}\},$$

$$xy = \left\{\sum_{\nu}\xi_{\lambda\nu}\eta_{\nu\mu}\right\}, \quad (x, y) = \sum_{\lambda,\mu}\xi_{\lambda\mu}\bar{\eta}_{\lambda\mu}.$$

It is straightforward to verify that, under these operations and inner product (x, y), $\mathscr{M}_\Lambda$ becomes a simple H⋆-algebra. This is the desired FULL MATRIX ALGEBRA of order Λ over the complex field. Observe that $x^\star = \{\xi'_{\lambda\mu}\}$, where $\xi'_{\lambda\mu} = \bar{\xi}_{\mu\lambda}$.

THEOREM (4.10.32). *The simple H⋆-algebra $\mathfrak{A}$ is ⋆-isomorphic with a full matrix algebra $\mathscr{M}_\Lambda$. Except for a multiplicative constant, the isomorphism is also an isometry.*

PROOF. By Theorem (4.10.16), there exists a Hilbert space $\mathfrak{H}$ and a ⋆-isomorphism of $\mathfrak{A}$ into $\mathscr{B}(\mathfrak{H})$ such that the image of $\mathfrak{A}$ in $\mathscr{B}(\mathfrak{H})$ contains all elements of finite rank. We identify $\mathfrak{A}$ with its image on $\mathscr{B}(\mathfrak{H})$. As in the proof of Theorem (4.10.21), let $\{h_\lambda\}$ be a complete orthonormal set in $\mathfrak{H}$ and sets $E_{\lambda\mu} = h_\lambda \otimes h_\mu$. Then $E^\star_{\lambda\mu} = E_{\mu\lambda}$ and the operators $E_{\lambda\mu}$ constitute a system of matrix units in $\mathfrak{A}$. Furthermore,

$$\begin{aligned}(E_{\lambda\mu}, E_{\rho\sigma}) &= (E_{\lambda\lambda}, E_{\rho\sigma}E_{\mu\lambda}) = \delta_{\sigma\mu}(E_{\lambda\lambda}, E_{\rho\lambda}) \\ &= \delta_{\sigma\mu}(E_{\lambda\rho}E_{\lambda\lambda}, E_{\lambda\lambda}) = \delta_{\sigma\mu}\delta_{\rho\lambda}|E_{\lambda\lambda}|^2.\end{aligned}$$

Similarly,

$$(E_{\lambda\mu}, E_{\rho\sigma}) = \delta_{\rho\lambda}\delta_{\sigma\mu}|E_{\sigma\sigma}|^2.$$

It follows that the matrix units $E_{\lambda\mu}$ constitute an orthogonal system in $\mathfrak{A}$ relative to the inner product of $\mathfrak{A}$ and also that their norms are all equal to a constant β. We observe next that these matrix units constitute a complete orthogonal system in $\mathfrak{A}$. In fact, let T be any element of $\mathfrak{A}$ such that $(T, E_{\lambda\mu}) = 0$ for all λ, μ. Since

$$\begin{aligned}(T, E_{\lambda\mu}) &= (E_{\lambda\lambda}T\,E_{\mu\mu}, E_{\lambda\mu}) \\ &= ((h_\lambda \otimes h_\lambda)(Th_\mu \otimes h_\mu), E_{\lambda\mu}) \\ &= (Th_\mu, h_\lambda)(E_{\lambda\mu}, E_{\lambda\mu}) = \beta^2(Th_\mu, h_\lambda),\end{aligned}$$

it follows that $(Th_\mu, h_\lambda) = 0$ for all λ, μ. But $\{h_\lambda\}$ is a complete orthonormal system in $\mathfrak{H}$ and therefore T must be zero. This proves that

$\{E_{\lambda\mu}\}$ is a complete orthogonal system in $\mathfrak{A}$. Therefore each T in $\mathfrak{A}$ can be written in the form

$$T = \sum_{\lambda, \mu} \tau_{\lambda\mu} E_{\lambda\mu},$$

where

$$\sum_{\lambda, \mu} |\tau_{\lambda\mu}|^2 = \beta^2 |T|.$$

Since the $E_{\lambda\mu}$ are matrix units, it is readily verified that $T \to \{\tau_{\lambda\mu}\}$ defines the desired isomorphism between $\mathfrak{A}$ and a full matrix algebra.

Kaplansky [4], in his study of dual rings, generalizes the structure theorems for H*-algebras. Also, Smiley [1] extends these results to algebras which he calls RIGHT H*-ALGEBRAS. (See the remarks following Definition (2.8.1).)

APPENDIX

EXAMPLES AND APPLICATIONS

Introduction. In this appendix we present a variety of examples of Banach algebras which are intended primarily to motivate and illustrate the general theory which has been discussed in the preceding chapters. There is accordingly no claim made for completeness and it is certain that a number of readers will find their favorite Banach algebras missing. The omissions in some instances are deliberate and in others are no doubt oversights. However, it is hoped that enough examples have been included to show how the theory has been used in the past and perhaps to suggest further applications for the future.

A detailed analysis of many of the most important examples involves a great deal of special material out of the particular areas of mathematics from which the examples are taken. Therefore, because of space limitations, we must necessarily omit most of the details. On the other hand, the filling in of some of the missing details is a good source of exercises for the interested reader and perhaps will compensate in part for the absence of formal sets of exercises in the main text. In any case, an attempt has been made to give enough references to the literature to enable the reader to supply as much of the omitted material as he wishes.

The examples included fall into three main classes which may be described roughly as ALGEBRAS OF OPERATORS, ALGEBRAS OF FUNCTIONS, and GROUP ALGEBRAS.

§ **1. Algebras of operators.** We are concerned here with algebras of bounded operators on a Banach space. Since every Banach algebra can be so represented, this category of algebras includes all Banach algebras. However, the emphasis in this section is on certain special algebras associated with specific Banach spaces. Unless otherwise stated, the spaces can be either real or complex. We consider first some special properties of the algebras of all bounded operators on a Banach space and on a Hilbert space.

A.1.1. THE ALGEBRAS $\mathscr{B}(\mathfrak{X})$ AND $\mathscr{B}(\mathfrak{H})$. Let $\mathfrak{X}$ be an arbitrary Banach space. Then $\mathscr{B}(\mathfrak{X})$ is the algebra of all bounded linear operators on $\mathfrak{X}$ under the usual algebraic operations and the operator bound $|T|$ as norm. There is always an identity element and, if $\mathfrak{X}$ has dimension greater than one, then $\mathscr{B}(\mathfrak{X})$ is non-commutative. Since it contains all bounded operators of finite rank, $\mathscr{B}(\mathfrak{X})$ obviously operates irreducibly on $\mathfrak{X}$ and is therefore semi-simple. More precisely, it is a primitive algebra with minimal ideals, and, by Corollary (2.5.10), has a unique norm topology. More generally, by Theorem (2.4.17), any norm under which $\mathscr{B}(\mathfrak{X})$ is a normed algebra necessarily majorizes the operator bound. Its socle is the 2-sided ideal consisting of all bounded operators with finite rank. Since the socle is contained in every 2-sided ideal, the algebra $\mathscr{B}(\mathfrak{X})$ is never strongly semi-simple. According to Theorem (2.4.12), $\mathscr{B}(\mathfrak{X})$ associates with $\mathfrak{X}$ a dual Banach space $\mathfrak{Y}$ which obviously coincides with the conjugate space $\mathfrak{X}'$ consisting of all bounded linear functionals on $\mathfrak{X}$. If u is a non-zero element of $\mathfrak{X}$ and f is a non-zero element of $\mathfrak{X}'$ such that $(u, f) = 0$, then the operator $u \otimes f$ is clearly nilpotent with $(u \otimes f)^2 = 0$. Hence the set N of topologically nilpotent elements of $\mathscr{B}(\mathfrak{X})$ contains non-zero elements. Since $\mathscr{B}(\mathfrak{X})$ is semi-simple, we thus have a case in which N is not an ideal, a fact which is also easily verified directly. The closure of the socle in $\mathscr{B}(\mathfrak{X})$ is an annihilator algebra if and only if $\mathfrak{X}$ is reflexive (Theorem (2.8.23)).

If $\mathfrak{Y}$ is a second Banach space such that $\mathscr{B}(\mathfrak{Y})$ is algebraically isomorphic with $\mathscr{B}(\mathfrak{X})$ then, by the fundamental isomorphism theorem (Theorem (2.5.19)), the given isomorphism is implemented by a bicontinuous linear transformation between the two Banach spaces. This is the classical result of Eidelheit [2] who also proved, incidentally, that $\mathscr{B}(\mathfrak{X})$ has a unique norm topology.

We observe next that the set of singular elements of $\mathscr{B}(\mathfrak{X})$ may contain interior points. This can be proved as follows. First let S be any singular element of $\mathscr{B}(\mathfrak{X})$ which is a limit of regular elements. Then, by Theorem (1.5.4) (iii), S is both a left and a right topological divisor of zero. Let $\{Z_n\}$ be a sequence of elements of $\mathscr{B}(\mathfrak{X})$ such that $|Z_n| = 1$ and $SZ_n \to 0$. Choose elements $u_n \in \mathfrak{X}$, such that $|u_n| = 1$ and $|Z_n u_n| \geqslant \frac{1}{2}$, and set $z_n = |Z_n u_n|^{-1} Z_n u_n$. Then $|z_n| = 1$ and

$Sz_n \to 0$. It follows from this observation that any element of $\mathscr{B}(\mathfrak{X})$ which maps $\mathfrak{X}$ homeomorphically onto a proper closed subspace of $\mathfrak{X}$ is necessarily an interior point of the set of singular elements. Although such elements obviously exist in special cases (for example, if $\mathfrak{X}$ is an infinite dimensional Hilbert space), it is an open question whether or not they exist for every infinite dimensional Banach space.

Return now to the singular element S and assume that $Z_nS \to 0$ instead of $SZ_n \to 0$. Suppose further that $S(\mathfrak{X}) = \mathfrak{X}$ and let $\mathfrak{N} = \{x : Sx = 0\}$. Since S is singular, $\mathfrak{N}$ is a non-zero closed linear subspace of $\mathfrak{X}$. Let $\bar{\mathfrak{X}} = \mathfrak{X} - \mathfrak{N}$. Then $\bar{\mathfrak{X}}$ is a Banach space under the norm $|\bar{x}| = \inf|x+n|$, $n \in \mathfrak{N}$, where $\bar{x} = x + \mathfrak{N}$. Define $\bar{S}\bar{x} = \overline{Sx}$. Then $\bar{S}$ is a bounded one-to-one linear transformation of $\bar{\mathfrak{X}}$ onto $\bar{\mathfrak{X}}$ and accordingly has a bounded inverse. Now choose elements $v_n \in \mathfrak{X}$ such that $Sv_n = u_n$, where, as before, $|u_n| = 1$ and $|Z_nu_n| \geqslant \frac{1}{2}$. Since $\{u_n\}$ is bounded and $\bar{S}$ has a bounded inverse, we can assume $\{\bar{v}_n\}$, and hence $\{v_n\}$, bounded. It follows that $Z_nSv_n \to 0$. But this is a contradiction, since $|Z_nSv_n| = |Z_nu_n| \geqslant \frac{1}{2}$. Therefore $S(\mathfrak{X})$ must be a proper subspace of $\mathfrak{X}$. We have thus established that any operator S in $\mathscr{B}(\mathfrak{X})$ such that $S(\mathfrak{X}) = \mathfrak{X}$ is either regular or is an interior point of the set of singular elements.

Both of the above remarks on interior points of the set of singular elements of $\mathscr{B}(\mathfrak{X})$ are consequences of more general results which have been obtained by Yood [1] in the study of the Banach space $\mathscr{B}(\mathfrak{X}, \mathfrak{Y})$ of all bounded linear transformations of one Banach space $\mathfrak{X}$ into a second one $\mathfrak{Y}$.

We observe next that every singular element S in $\mathscr{B}(\mathfrak{X})$ is a topological divisor of zero. Note first that, $S(u \otimes f) = Su \otimes f$, where u is any element of $\mathfrak{X}$ and f is any element of $\mathfrak{X}'$. Hence $Su = 0$, for some $u \neq 0$, implies that S is even a divisor of zero. Therefore we can assume that S maps $\mathfrak{X}$ one-to-one into itself. Furthermore, since S is singular, we must have $S(\mathfrak{X}) \neq \mathfrak{X}$. Now suppose that $\overline{S(\mathfrak{X})} \neq \mathfrak{X}$ and choose $f \in \mathfrak{X}'$ such that $(S(\mathfrak{X}), f) = (0)$. Then, for any non-zero $u \in \mathfrak{X}$, we have $(u \otimes f)S = 0$ and S is again a divisor of zero. We are thus reduced to the case $\overline{S(\mathfrak{X})} = \mathfrak{X}$ and $S(\mathfrak{X}) \neq \mathfrak{X}$. Then there exists a sequence $\{u_n\} \subset \mathfrak{X}$ with $|u_n| = 1$ and $Su_n \to 0$. Choose any $f \in \mathfrak{X}'$ with $|f| = 1$ and define $Z_n = u_n \otimes f$. Then $|Z_n| = |u_n||f| = 1$ and $|SZ_n| = |Su_n \otimes f| = |Su_n|$. Therefore $SZ_n \to 0$ and hence S is a topological divisor of zero. Thus it is proved that all singular elements in $\mathscr{B}(\mathfrak{X})$ are topological divisors of zero. This result was also obtained by Yood [1].

Now consider an algebra $\mathscr{B}(\mathfrak{H})$ where $\mathfrak{H}$ is a complex Hilbert space. These algebras are characterized among the general algebras $\mathscr{B}(\mathfrak{X})$ by their possession of an involution. More precisely, if $\mathscr{B}(\mathfrak{X})$ admits an involution $T \to T^\star$ such that $T^\star T = 0$ implies $T = 0$, then an inner product norm $|x| = (x, x)^{1/2}$ can be introduced into $\mathfrak{X}$ which is equivalent to the given norm and such that $(Tx, y) = (x, T^\star y)$ for all $x, y \in \mathfrak{X}$ and $T \in \mathscr{B}(\mathfrak{X})$. This result, which is given in Corollary (4.10.8), is due to Kakutani and Mackey [1, 2] who also proved that the additivity property of the involution is not needed provided the space $\mathfrak{X}$ is assumed to be infinite dimensional. (See also Rickart [4].) Another characterization of $\mathscr{B}(\mathfrak{H})$ among all B*-algebras was obtained by Wolfson [1] who showed that a B*-algebra $\mathfrak{A}$ is *-isomorphic with an algebra $\mathscr{B}(\mathfrak{H})$ if and only if $\mathfrak{A}$ contains a minimal closed (non-zero) 2-sided ideal and, for any pair $\mathfrak{L}_1$, $\mathfrak{L}_2$ of left annihilator ideals such that $\mathfrak{L}_1\mathfrak{L}_2^\star = (0)$, the ideal $\mathfrak{L}_1 + \mathfrak{L}_2$ is also a left annihilator ideal.

It has already been observed that the set of singular elements of $\mathscr{B}(\mathfrak{H})$ contains interior points when $\mathfrak{H}$ is infinite dimensional, since $\mathscr{B}(\mathfrak{H})$ then contains operators which map $\mathfrak{H}$ isometrically onto a proper linear subspace of itself. A characterization of those singular elements of $\mathscr{B}(\mathfrak{H})$ which are limit points of regular elements has been obtained by Feldman and Kadison [1]. Halmos, Lumer and Schaffer [1] show that there exist regular elements in $\mathscr{B}(\mathfrak{H})$ which do not have square roots. It follows that not all regular elements have logarithms. An equivalent formulation of this property is that the mapping $T \to \exp(T)$ of $\mathscr{B}(\mathfrak{H})$ into the group of regular elements is not an onto map.

Kakutani has pointed out to us that the group of regular elements in $\mathscr{B}(\mathfrak{H})$ is connected. This follows from properties of the logarithm obtained *via* the spectral theorem. (See Wintner [1].) We sketch here a direct proof. The problem is to show that every regular element T in $\mathscr{B}(\mathfrak{H})$ is contained in a connected set of regular elements which contains the identity operator I. Define $H = (T^\star T)^{1/2}$ and $U = TH^{-1}$. Then H is a regular positive hermitian element, $U^\star U = UU^\star = I$, and $T = UH$. This is the polar decomposition of T. Let $\mathfrak{C}$ be a maximal commutative *-subalgebra of $\mathscr{B}(\mathfrak{H})$ which contains U, and observe that the carrier space $\Phi_{\mathfrak{C}}$ is totally disconnected (see A.2.1. below). Since U is unitary,

$$\hat{U}(\varphi) = \exp(i\theta_\varphi), \quad \varphi \in \Phi_{\mathfrak{C}},$$

where θ_φ is real and is determined only modulo 2π. However, for fixed $\varphi_0 \in \Phi_{\mathfrak{C}}$, it is not difficult to show that the numbers θ_φ can be so chosen that they define a function $f_{\varphi_0}(\varphi) = \theta_\varphi$ which is continuous in some neighborhood V_{φ_0} of φ_0. Now, since $\Phi_{\mathfrak{C}}$ is totally disconnected (and compact), the neighborhood V_{φ_0} can be taken to be both open and closed. Using the compactness of $\Phi_{\mathfrak{C}}$ again, we obtain a finite set $V_1, \cdots, V_n$ of disjoint open and closed sets, whose union is all of $\Phi_{\mathfrak{C}}$, and a finite set $f_1, \ldots, f_n$ of real functions such that f_k is continuous in V_k and

$$\hat{U}(\varphi) = \exp(if_k(\varphi)), \quad \varphi \in V_k, \quad k = 1, \cdots, n.$$

Now define

$$f(\varphi) = f_k(\varphi), \quad \varphi \in V_k, \quad k = 1, \cdots, n.$$

Then f is a continuous function on $\Phi_{\mathfrak{C}}$ and $\hat{U}(\varphi) = \exp(if(\varphi))$, for all φ. Since $\mathfrak{C} = C(\Phi_{\mathfrak{C}})$, there exists a hermitian operator $K \in \mathfrak{C}$ such that $\hat{K}(\varphi) = f(\varphi)$, for all φ. Thus $U = \exp(iK)$. Now define

$$U_\xi = \exp(i\xi K), \quad 0 \leqslant \xi \leqslant 1.$$

Then each U_ξ is unitary, $U_0 = I$, $U_1 = U$ and

$$|U_\xi - U_{\xi_0}| \leqslant |\xi - \xi_0||K|,$$

which shows that $\xi \to U_\xi$ is a continuous mapping of $[0, 1]$ into $\mathscr{B}(\mathfrak{H})$. Next define

$$T_\xi = U_\xi H_\xi, \quad 0 \leqslant \xi \leqslant 1,$$

where $H_\xi = \xi H + (1-\xi)I$. Since $H > 0$, each of the operators H_ξ is regular, so that each T_ξ is regular. Also $T_0 = I$, $T_1 = T$ and $\xi \to T_\xi$ is a continuous mapping of $[0, 1]$ into the regular elements of $\mathscr{B}(\mathfrak{H})$. Thus I and T are contained in a connected set of regular elements. This completes the proof that the group of regular elements in $\mathscr{B}(\mathfrak{H})$ is connected. Notice that the proof applies to any W*-algebra or, more generally, to any B*-algebra whose maximal commutative *-subalgebras are generated by projections. It also follows from the above proof that the group of unitary elements in any one of these algebras is connected. Although not every regular element of $\mathscr{B}(\mathfrak{H})$ admits a logarithm, Theorem (1.4.10) plus the fact that the group of regular elements is connected shows that every regular element is equal to the product of a finite number of elements with logarithms. Actually, in this case every regular element is equal to a product of at most two elements with logarithms. In fact, since $T = UH$ with U unitary and $H > 0$, and since, by the above proof, U has a logarithm, it only remains to show that H admits a logarithm. For this it is sufficient to consider the case $|H| < 1$. But then we have $\nu(I-H) < 1$ and it follows that H has a logarithm, by the remarks preceding Theorem (1.4.10).

We close the discussion of $\mathscr{B}(\mathfrak{H})$ by giving an example of a sequence of nilpotent operators on $\mathfrak{H}$ which converges in $\mathscr{B}(\mathfrak{H})$ to an operator which is not topologically nilpotent. This will show that the spectrum is not a continuous function in $\mathscr{B}(\mathfrak{H})$. The example is due to Kakutani and has not been published before. Assuming $\mathfrak{H}$ to be separable, we fix a complete orthonormal sequence of vectors $\{f_m\}$. Consider the sequence of scalars

$$\alpha_m = e^{-k}, \quad \text{for} \quad m = 2^k(2l+1),$$

where $k, l = 0, 1, 2, \cdots$, and define the operator A by the relations

$$Af_m = \alpha_m f_{m+1}, \quad m = 1, 2, \cdots.$$

The bound of such a "shift" operator is given by $|A| = \sup |\alpha_m|$. Observe also that

$$A^n f_m = \alpha_m \alpha_{m+1} \cdots \alpha_{m+n-1} f_{m+n}$$

and hence

$$|A^n| = \sup_m (\alpha_m \alpha_{m+1} \cdots \alpha_{m+n-1}).$$

Furthermore, from the definition of the α_m,

$$\alpha_1 \alpha_2 \cdots \alpha_{2^t-1} = \prod_{j=1}^{t-1} \exp(-j2^{t-j-1}).$$

Therefore

$$(\alpha_1 \alpha_2 \cdots \alpha_{2^t-1})^{1/2^{t-1}} > \left(\prod_{j=1}^{t-1} \exp[-(j/2^{j+1})]\right)^2$$

and, if we set

$$\sigma = \sum_{j=1}^{\infty} \frac{j}{2^{j+1}},$$

then

$$e^{-2\sigma} \leqslant \lim_{n\to\infty} |A^n|^{1/n}.$$

In particular, A is *not* topologically nilpotent. Next we define the operator A_k by the relations

$$A_k f_m = \begin{cases} 0, & \text{for } m = 2^k(2l+1) \\ \alpha_m f_{m+1}, & \text{for } m \neq 2^k(2l+1). \end{cases}$$

Then it is not difficult to see that A_k is nilpotent. On the other hand,

$$(A - A_k)f_m = \begin{cases} e^{-k}f_{m+1}, & \text{for } m = 2^k(2l+1) \\ 0 \quad , & \text{for } m \neq 2^k(2l+1). \end{cases}$$

Therefore $|A - A_k| = e^{-k}$, so that $\lim A_k = A$ in $\mathscr{B}(\mathfrak{H})$ and we have the desired example.

A.1.2. THE ALGEBRA $\mathfrak{F}_{\mathscr{C}}$ OF COMPACT OPERATORS. We consider first an arbitrary Banach space $\mathfrak{X}$. Recall that an operator T is said to be COMPACT (or COMPLETELY CONTINUOUS) if it maps bounded sets into conditionally compact sets. These operators form a closed 2-sided ideal $\mathfrak{F}_{\mathscr{C}}$ in $\mathscr{B}(\mathfrak{X})$ which includes the ideal $\mathfrak{F}$ of all operators in $\mathscr{B}(\mathfrak{X})$ having finite rank. It is an open question of long standing whether or not $\mathfrak{F}_{\mathscr{C}}$ is in general equal to the closure of $\mathfrak{F}$ in $\mathscr{B}(\mathfrak{X})$. In certain special cases the answer to the question is in the affirmative, so that $\mathfrak{F}_{\mathscr{C}}$ is a minimal closed 2-sided ideal in $\mathscr{B}(\mathfrak{X})$. This is true, in particular, when $\mathfrak{X}$ is a Hilbert space $\mathfrak{H}$. In this case $\mathfrak{F}_{\mathscr{C}}$ is a $\star$-ideal in $\mathscr{B}(\mathfrak{H})$. Furthermore, if $\mathfrak{H}$ is infinite dimensional but separable, then $\mathfrak{F}_{\mathscr{C}}$ is not only a minimal but is also a maximal closed 2-sided ideal in $\mathscr{B}(\mathfrak{H})$. It is therefore the only closed 2-sided ideal in $\mathscr{B}(\mathfrak{H})$ and must coincide with the strong radical of $\mathscr{B}(\mathfrak{H})$. If $\mathfrak{H}$ is not separable, then $\mathfrak{F}_{\mathscr{C}}$ is no longer a maximal ideal. These results for $\mathfrak{F}_{\mathscr{C}}$ were obtained by Calkin [1] who also showed that $\mathscr{B}(\mathfrak{H})/\mathfrak{F}_{\mathscr{C}}$ is a C*-algebra.

We turn now to an examination of $\mathfrak{F}_{\mathscr{C}}$ as an algebra in its own right, restricting attention to complex Hilbert space. Note first that $\mathfrak{F}_{\mathscr{C}}$ is a C*-algebra on its Hilbert space. Moreover, it is not difficult to show that $\mathfrak{F}_{\mathscr{C}}$ is topologically simple and dual. In fact, $\mathfrak{F}_{\mathscr{C}}$ is characterized by these properties, since, according to Corollary (4.10.20), every topologically simple dual B*-algebra is isometrically $\star$-isomorphic with an algebra $\mathfrak{F}_{\mathscr{C}}$. Actually a stronger result holds. Any closed subalgebra of $\mathscr{B}(\mathfrak{H})$ which is primitive and dual coincides with the algebra $\mathfrak{F}_{\mathscr{C}}$ on $\mathfrak{H}$. Notice that in this statement the subalgebra is not assumed to be a $\star$-subalgebra of $\mathscr{B}(\mathfrak{H})$. This result is due to Wolfson [1] who shows that it is not even necessary to assume the algebra to be closed under multiplication by scalars. (In other words, "subalgebra" can be replaced by "subring".) Since $\mathfrak{F}_{\mathscr{C}}$ is dual, we can apply Corollary (2.8.25) to obtain that every closed right ideal $\mathfrak{R}$ in $\mathfrak{F}_{\mathscr{C}}$ is of the form

$$\mathfrak{R} = \{T : T \in \mathfrak{F}_{\mathscr{C}}, \quad T(\mathfrak{H}) \subseteq \mathfrak{M}\},$$

where $\mathfrak{M}$ is a closed linear subspace of $\mathfrak{H}$. Also, if $\mathfrak{L}$ is a closed left ideal in $\mathfrak{F}_{\mathscr{C}}$, then the above representation for right ideals applied to $\mathfrak{L}^\star$ can be used to show that

$$\mathfrak{L} = \{T : T \in \mathfrak{F}_{\mathscr{C}}, \quad T(\mathfrak{N}) = (0)\},$$

where $\mathfrak{N}$ is a closed linear subspace of $\mathfrak{H}$ which is, in fact, equal to the orthogonal complement of the subspace associated with $\mathfrak{L}^\star$. (Kaplansky [9, Theorem 8.4].)

All topologically irreducible $\star$-representations of $\mathfrak{F}_{\mathscr{C}}$ on Hilbert space are unitarily equivalent to the given representation of $\mathfrak{F}_{\mathscr{C}}$ on its Hilbert space. This follows from Corollary (4.10.10) plus the fact that $\mathfrak{F}_{\mathscr{C}}$ is topologically simple, which forces non-zero $\star$-representations to be $\star$-isomorphisms. A stronger result is that every $\star$-representation of $\mathfrak{F}_{\mathscr{C}}$ on Hilbert space is unitarily equivalent to a direct sum of $\star$-representations, one of which is the zero representation and all of the remaining ones being unitarily equivalent to the given representation of $\mathfrak{F}_{\mathscr{C}}$ on its Hilbert space. (See Theorem (4.10.24).) A converse result is that any B*-algebra for which all irreducible $\star$-representations on Hilbert space are unitarily equivalent is $\star$-isomorphic to an algebra $\mathfrak{F}_{\mathscr{C}}$. (Rosenberg [1].)

A B*-algebra $\mathfrak{A}$, such that $\mathfrak{A}/\mathfrak{P}$ is an algebra $\mathfrak{F}_{\mathscr{C}}$ for each primitive ideal $\mathfrak{P}$, has been called a *CCR* algebra by Kaplansky [9] who obtains the following structure theorem for these algebras. First define a well-ordered ascending sequence of closed 2-sided ideals $\mathfrak{I}_\lambda$ in $\mathfrak{A}$ to be a COMPOSITION SERIES if it contains $\mathfrak{A}$ and, for each limiting ordinal λ, the ideal $\mathfrak{I}_\lambda$ is equal to the closure of the union of the preceding ideals in the sequence. Then every *CCR* algebra possesses a composition series $\{\mathfrak{I}_\lambda\}$ such that each of the algebras $\mathfrak{I}_{\lambda+1}/\mathfrak{I}_\lambda$ has a Hausdorff structure space. Kaplansky [9] also studies a more inclusive class of algebras which he calls *GCR* algebras. These are B*-algebras which have a composition series $\{\mathfrak{I}_\lambda\}$ such that each $\mathfrak{I}_{\lambda+1}/\mathfrak{I}_\lambda$ is a *CCR* algebra. The reader is referred to Kaplansky's paper for further properties of these algebras.

It is appropriate to call attention here to a very special class of Banach algebras which are called COMPLETELY CONTINUOUS. Such an algebra is, by definition, one whose left and right regular representations consist of compact operators. Kaplansky [5] shows that a complex completely continuous Banach algebra has a discrete structure space. The L^2 algebra of a compact group (see § 3 below) is completely continuous. The compact elements of a general Banach algebra (that is, elements whose images in the regular representations are compact) have been studied by M. Freundlich [1].

A.1.3. THE SCHMIDT-CLASS $\mathfrak{F}_{\mathscr{S}}$. This class of operators is also a 2-sided $\star$-ideal in $\mathscr{B}(\mathfrak{H})$, where $\mathfrak{H}$ is a Hilbert space. It contains, of course, the ideal $\mathfrak{F}$ of operators of finite rank. The definition requires a bit of preparation. Let $\{u_\lambda\}$ and $\{v_\lambda\}$ be any pair of complete orthonormal systems of vectors in $\mathfrak{H}$. For any $A \in \mathscr{B}(\mathfrak{H})$, consider the three sums

$$\sum_{\lambda} |Au_\lambda|^2, \quad \sum_{\lambda,\mu} |(Au_\lambda, v_\mu)|^2, \quad \sum_{\mu} |A^\star v_\mu|^2.$$

Using the Parseval equality, we obtain

$$|Au_\lambda|^2 = \sum_{\mu} |(Au_\lambda, v_\mu)|^2.$$

Therefore

$$\sum_{\lambda} |Au_\lambda|^2 = \sum_{\lambda,\mu} |(Au_\lambda, v_\mu)|^2 = \sum_{\lambda,\mu} |(A^\star v_\mu, u_\lambda)|^2 = \sum_{\mu} |A^\star v_\mu|^2.$$

It follows that the three sums written above are equal to one another (possibly to $+\infty$). Furthermore, since the two systems $\{u_\lambda\}$ and $\{v_\mu\}$ are independent of one another, the common value $|A|_{\mathscr{S}}^2$ of the sums is independent of the choice of $\{u_\lambda\}$ and $\{v_\mu\}$. The SCHMIDT-CLASS $\mathfrak{F}_{\mathscr{S}}$ consists of all those operators $A \in \mathscr{B}(\mathfrak{H})$ such that $|A|_{\mathscr{S}} < \infty$. These operators are abstract analogues of integral operators studied by Schmidt [1], who considered the Hilbert space $L^2(0, 1)$ and integral operators on $L^2(0, 1)$ of the form

$$Tf(\xi) = \int_0^1 \tau(\xi, \omega) f(\omega) d\omega, \quad f \in L^2(0, 1),$$

where $\tau \in L^2(\Delta)$, $\Delta = \{(\xi, \omega) : 0 \leqslant \xi \leqslant 1, 0 \leqslant \omega \leqslant 1\}$. This class of integral operators coincides with $\mathfrak{F}_{\mathscr{S}}$ in the case $\mathfrak{H} = L^2(0, 1)$. (See Stone [8, Ch III, §2].)

Returning to the general case, we observe that it is not very difficult to prove that the following properties hold for arbitrary A, B, X, Y in $\mathscr{B}(\mathfrak{H})$:

(1) $|A^\star|_{\mathscr{S}} = |A|_{\mathscr{S}}$.

(2) $0 \leqslant |A| \leqslant |A|_{\mathscr{S}} \leqslant \infty$.

(3) $|\alpha A|_{\mathscr{S}} = |\alpha||A|_{\mathscr{S}}$, α a scalar, where we take $|\alpha||A|_{\mathscr{S}} = 0$ if $\alpha = 0$ and $|A|_{\mathscr{S}} = \infty$.

(4) $|A+B|_{\mathscr{S}} \leqslant |A|_{\mathscr{S}}+|B|_{\mathscr{S}}$.

(5) $|AB|_{\mathscr{S}} \leqslant |A|_{\mathscr{S}}|B|_{\mathscr{S}}$.

(6) $|XAY|_{\mathscr{S}} \leqslant |X||A|_{\mathscr{S}}|Y|$.

(7) $|f\otimes g|_{\mathscr{S}} = |f||g| = |f\otimes g|$.

It follows immediately from these properties that $\mathfrak{F}_{\mathscr{S}}$ is a 2-sided $\star$-ideal in $\mathscr{B}(\mathfrak{H})$ which contains $\mathfrak{F}$. Furthermore, $\mathfrak{F}_{\mathscr{S}}$ is a Banach algebra under $|A|_{\mathscr{S}}$ as norm. In fact, properties (2)–(5) show that $\mathfrak{F}_{\mathscr{S}}$ is a normed algebra. In order to prove completeness, let $\{A_n\}$ be a Cauchy sequence in $\mathfrak{F}_{\mathscr{S}}$ relative to the norm $|A|_{\mathscr{S}}$. Then property (2) shows that $\{A_n\}$ is also a Cauchy sequence relative to the operator bound $|A|$. Therefore there exists $A_0 \in \mathscr{B}(\mathfrak{H})$ such that $\lim |A_n - A_0| = 0$. If $\{u_\lambda\}$ is any complete orthonormal system in $\mathfrak{H}$, then

$$|A_n|_{\mathscr{S}}^2 = \sum_\lambda |A_n u_\lambda|^2,$$

for all n. Since $\{|A_n|_{\mathscr{S}}\}$ is a Cauchy sequence it is bounded and there accordingly exists a constant β independent of n such that

$$\sum_\lambda |A_n u_\lambda|^2 \leqslant \beta, \quad \text{all } n.$$

Now let π denote any finite set of the indices λ. Then also

$$\sum_{\lambda\in\pi} |A_n u_\lambda|^2 \leqslant \beta, \quad \text{all } n.$$

Taking the limit as $n \to \infty$, we obtain

$$\sum_{\lambda\in\pi} |A_0 u_\lambda|^2 \leqslant \beta,$$

for all π. It follows that $A_0 \in \mathfrak{F}_{\mathscr{S}}$. Again, for arbitrary π, set

$$|A|_\pi = \Big(\sum_{\lambda\in\pi} |Au_\lambda|^2\Big)^{1/2}.$$

Then $|A|_\pi \leqslant |A|_{\mathscr{S}}$ and

$$|A_0 - A_n|_\pi \leqslant |A_0 - A_m|_\pi + |A_m - A_n|_{\mathscr{S}},$$

for all m, n. For arbitrary $\epsilon > 0$, choose n_ϵ such that $m, n \geqslant n_\epsilon$ implies $|A_m - A_n|_{\mathscr{S}} < \epsilon$. Fix $n \geqslant n_\epsilon$ in the above inequality and let $m \to \infty$. This gives

$$|A_0 - A_n|_\pi \leqslant \epsilon, \quad n \geqslant n_\epsilon.$$

Since this holds for all π, we obtain $|A_0 - A_n|_{\mathscr{S}} \leqslant \epsilon$ for $n \geqslant n_\epsilon$. This proves that $\mathfrak{F}_{\mathscr{S}}$ is complete and is therefore a Banach algebra under the norm $|A|_{\mathscr{S}}$.

Next let A by any element of $\mathfrak{F}_{\mathscr{S}}$ and $\{u_\lambda\}$ a complete orthonormal system in $\mathfrak{H}$. For any finite set π of the indices λ, define

$$A_\pi = \sum_{\mu \in \pi} Au_\mu \otimes u_\mu.$$

Then

$$A_\pi u_\lambda = \begin{cases} Au_\lambda, & \text{for } \lambda \in \pi \\ 0\ , & \text{for } \lambda \notin \pi. \end{cases}$$

Therefore

$$|A - A_\pi|_{\mathscr{S}} = (\sum_{\lambda \notin \pi} |Au_\lambda|^2)^{1/2}.$$

Since the sum on the right is small for "large" π, it follows that $\mathfrak{F}$ is dense in $\mathfrak{F}_{\mathscr{S}}$ relative to the norm $|A|_{\mathscr{S}}$. Thus $\mathfrak{F}_{\mathscr{S}}$ is a topologically simple annihilator Banach $\star$-algebra (Corollary (4.10.17)).

Again let $\{u_\lambda\}$ be any complete orthonormal system in $\mathfrak{H}$ and, for arbitrary operators A and B in $\mathfrak{F}_{\mathscr{S}}$, define

$$(A, B) = \sum_{\lambda} (Au_\lambda, Bu_\lambda).$$

Then (A, B) is clearly an inner product in $\mathfrak{F}_{\mathscr{S}}$ and $|A|_{\mathscr{S}}^2 = (A, A)$. In other words, $\mathfrak{F}_{\mathscr{S}}$ is a Hilbert space. From the fact that $|A^\star|_{\mathscr{S}} = |A|_{\mathscr{S}}$ and the polarization identity

$$4(A, B) = (|A+B|_{\mathscr{S}}^2 - |A-B|_{\mathscr{S}}^2) + i(|A+iB|_{\mathscr{S}}^2 - |A-iB|_{\mathscr{S}}^2),$$

it follows that $(A^\star, B^\star) = \overline{(A, B)}$. This observation, plus the definition of (A, B), leads easily to the result

$$(A, CB^\star) = (AB, C) = (B, A^\star C),$$

which holds for all A, B, C in $\mathfrak{F}_{\mathscr{S}}$. In other words, $\mathfrak{F}_{\mathscr{S}}$ is an H*-algebra and, being topologically simple, can be identified with an infinite matrix algebra (see Theorem (4.10.32)).

All of the results outlined above have been obtained by Schatten [1]. Schatten also studies the ideal $\mathfrak{F}_{\mathscr{C}}$ of compact operators and the trace-class of operators to be discussed in the next example. Note that property (7) of $|A|_{\mathscr{S}}$ says that this norm defines in $\mathfrak{F}$ a CROSS NORM in the sense of Schatten. In this connection, it is worth noting that the operator bound $|A|$ is itself a cross norm in $\mathfrak{F}$ so that $\mathfrak{F}_{\mathscr{C}}$ can also be regarded as the completion of $\mathfrak{F}$ relative to a cross norm. The completion of $\mathfrak{F}$ with respect to various cross norms is discussed systematically by Schatten [1], not only for Hilbert space but for general Banach spaces.

A.1.4. THE TRACE-CLASS $\mathfrak{F}_{\mathscr{T}}$. The TRACE-CLASS $\mathfrak{F}_{\mathscr{T}}$ of operators on a Hilbert space $\mathfrak{H}$ is equal to the collection of all operators of the form

$$T = \sum_{i=1}^{n} A_i B_i,$$

where A_i and B_i belong to the Schmidt-class $\mathfrak{F}_{\mathscr{S}}$. Evidently, $\mathfrak{F}_{\mathscr{T}}$ is a 2-sided $\star$-ideal in $\mathscr{B}(\mathfrak{H})$ which is contained in $\mathfrak{F}_{\mathscr{S}}$ and contains $\mathfrak{F}$. Actually, it turns out that every element of $\mathfrak{F}_{\mathscr{T}}$ is of the form $T = AB$, where A and B belong to $\mathfrak{F}_{\mathscr{S}}$. The name "trace-class" derives from the fact that $\mathfrak{F}_{\mathscr{T}}$ admits a complex-valued function $\tau(T)$ which has the characteristic properties of the trace for matrices. As a matter of fact, if $\mathfrak{F}_{\mathscr{S}}$ is realized as an algebra of infinite matrices, then $\tau(T)$ is actually the trace of the matrix associated with T. The trace function can be defined directly in $\mathfrak{F}_{\mathscr{T}}$ in terms of a complete orthonormal system $\{u_\lambda\}$ in $\mathfrak{H}$ as follows:

$$\tau(T) = \sum_{\lambda} (Tu_\lambda, u_\lambda) = \sum_{i=1}^{n} (B_i, A_i^\star),$$

where $T = \Sigma A_i B_i$, with $A_i, B_i \in \mathfrak{F}_{\mathscr{S}}$, and $(B_i, A_i^\star)$ is the inner product defined in $\mathfrak{F}_{\mathscr{S}}$. For all $A, B \in \mathfrak{F}_{\mathscr{S}}$ and $S, T \in \mathfrak{F}_{\mathscr{T}}$,

(1) $\tau(AB) = \tau(BA)$.

(2) $\tau(T^\star) = \overline{\tau(T)}$.

(3) $\tau(\alpha T) = \alpha\tau(T)$, α a scalar.

(4) $\tau(S+T) = \tau(S)+\tau(T)$.

(5) $\tau(f \otimes g) = (f, g)$, $\quad f, g \in \mathfrak{H}$.

The reader is referred to Schatten [1] for proofs of these properties of τ as well as the remarks which follow concerning the trace-class as a Banach algebra.

The trace-class $\mathfrak{F}_{\mathscr{T}}$ is a Banach $\star$-algebra under the norm

$$|T|_{\mathscr{T}} = \tau((T^\star T)^{1/2}), \quad T \in \mathfrak{F}_{\mathscr{T}}.$$

In addition to the usual norm properties, we also have the following properties for $|T|_{\mathscr{T}}$:

(1) $|T| \leqslant |T|_{\mathscr{T}} = |T^\star|_{\mathscr{T}}$, $T \in \mathfrak{F}_{\mathscr{T}}$.

(2) $|AT|_{\mathscr{T}} \leqslant |A||T|_{\mathscr{T}}$, $A \in \mathscr{B}(\mathfrak{H})$, $T \in \mathfrak{F}_{\mathscr{T}}$.

(3) $\tau(T) \leqslant |T|_{\mathscr{T}},\ T \in \mathfrak{F}_{\mathscr{T}}$.

(4) $|f \otimes g|_{\mathscr{T}} = |f||g| = |f \otimes g|$, for $f, g \in \mathfrak{H}$.

The last property says that $|T|_{\mathscr{T}}$ is a cross norm in $\mathfrak{F}$. The norm $|T|_{\mathscr{T}}$ is Schatten's "greatest cross norm" for $\mathfrak{F}$. It turns out that $\mathfrak{F}$ is dense in $\mathfrak{F}_{\mathscr{T}}$ so we see that $\mathfrak{F}_{\mathscr{T}}$, as well as $\mathfrak{F}_{\mathscr{C}}$ and $\mathfrak{F}_{\mathscr{S}}$, is obtained by completion of the algebra $\mathfrak{F}$ with respect to an appropriate norm which majorizes the operator bound. Therefore each of these algebras is an example of a (topologically) simple, semi-simple annihilator Banach ⋆-algebra. (Corollary (4.10.17).)

Schatten [1] also obtains the following interesting properties of the above classes of operators. As Banach spaces, $\mathfrak{F}_{\mathscr{T}}$ is equal to the conjugate space of $\mathfrak{F}_{\mathscr{C}}$ and $\mathscr{B}(\mathfrak{H})$ is equal to the conjugate space of $\mathfrak{F}_{\mathscr{T}}$. Furthermore, the algebra structure of $\mathscr{B}(\mathfrak{H})$ coincides with that assigned to it, as the second conjugate space of the algebra $\mathfrak{F}_{\mathscr{C}}$, by Arens [6]. The class $\mathfrak{F}_{\mathscr{C}}$ is not the conjugate space of any Banach space. (Schatten [1, 2].)

A.1.5. W⋆-ALGEBRAS AND AW⋆-ALGEBRAS. A W⋆-ALGEBRA is a ⋆-subalgebra of $\mathscr{B}(\mathfrak{H})$ ($\mathfrak{H}$ a Hilbert space) which is closed relative to the weak neighborhood topology for operators in $\mathscr{B}(\mathfrak{H})$. These algebras, which are also called RINGS OF OPERATORS and, more recently, VON NEUMANN ALGEBRAS, were introduced by von Neumann [1] and studied systematically by von Neumann [2, 6, 7, 8] himself and jointly by Murray and von Neumann [1, 2, 3]. There is an extensive literature concerned with this important class of Banach algebras (actually C⋆-algebras) culminating in a comprehensive book by Dixmier [15], to which the reader is referred for further information on the subject.

It is perhaps appropriate to call attention to a collection of papers devoted to an abstract treatment of those portions of the theory of W⋆-algebras not directly concerned with the representation of the algebras on Hilbert space. An early attempt along these lines is due to Steen [1, 2]. The present author made a start on such a treatment (see Rickart [1]) which was picked up by Kaplansky [1] who carried the study more or less to its completion in his series of papers on AW⋆-algebras. An AW⋆-algebra can be defined as a B⋆-algebra $\mathfrak{A}$ such that the (left or right) annihilator of an arbitrary subset of $\mathfrak{A}$ is a principal ideal generated by a projection (that is, a hermitian idempotent). Although much of the "non-spatial" theory of W⋆-algebras can be extended to AW⋆-algebras, additional conditions on an AW⋆-algebra are needed for it to be representable as a W⋆-algebra. That this is already the case for commutative algebras was proved by Dixmier [8] who gave a characterization of commutative W*-algebras among algebras $C(\Omega)$, Ω a compact Hausdorff space. (See A.2.1. below.) Characterizations of general W*-algebras have been obtained by Kadison [13] and Sakai [3]. The latter shows that a necessary and sufficient condition for a B*-algebra to admit a *-representation as a W*-algebra is that it be the conjugate space of some Banach space. The necessity had already been obtained by Dixmier [12].

The ultimate purely algebraic treatment of the W*-algebra theory is given by Kaplansky [16] in his Chicago notes on RINGS OF OPERATORS where he develops the theory of BAER RINGS. A substantial number of additional papers on AW*-algebras and related matters will be found in the Bibliography.

Wright [1] proves that AW*-algebras are weakly central. Hence these algebras are completely regular in the sense of § 7, Chapter II. (See Theorem (2.7.9).) The fact that W*-algebras are weakly central was proved by Misonou [1].

A.1.6. SPECTRAL OPERATORS. We now discuss very briefly an important class of operators on a Banach space $\mathfrak{X}$ which were introduced and have been studied extensively by N. Dunford [3, 4] and his collaborators. These operators lead to some interesting algebras of operators which will be described below. It will be necessary to omit all proofs. An exhaustive account of spectral operators and their applications will be found in the papers cited above and in Dunford and Schwartz [1]. We begin with some definitions.

Consider the σ-field $\mathscr{S}$ of all Borel subsets of the complex plane K and let $\mathfrak{X}$ be an arbitrary complex Banach space. A function $P(\cdot)$ defined on $\mathscr{S}$ to $\mathscr{B}(\mathfrak{X})$ is called a SPECTRAL MEASURE IN $\mathfrak{X}$ provided the following properties are satisfied for all Δ_1, Δ_2 and Δ in $\mathscr{S}$:

(1) $P(\Delta_1 \cap \Delta_2) = P(\Delta_1)P(\Delta_2)$.

(2) $P(\Delta_1 \cup \Delta_2) = P(\Delta_1)+P(\Delta_2)-P(\Delta_1)P(\Delta_2)$.

(3) $P(K-\Delta) = I-P(\Delta)$.

(4) There exists a constant β such that $|P(\Delta)| \leqslant \beta$ independently of Δ.

Observe that condition (1) implies $P(\Delta) = P(\Delta)^2$ for every $\Delta \in \mathscr{S}$, so that the function $P(\cdot)$ is projection valued. The range of a spectral measure is thus a bounded boolean algebra of projections. If Γ is a total subset of the conjugate space $\mathfrak{X}'$, that is, $(x, f) = 0$ for every

$f \in \Gamma$ implies $x = 0$, then the spectral measure $P(\cdot)$ is said to be Γ-COMPLETELY ADDITIVE if the following condition is satisfied:

(5) For any pairwise disjoint sequence $\{\Delta_k\}$ of elements of $\mathscr{S}$, let $\Delta = \bigcup \Delta_k$. Then, for all $x \in \mathfrak{X}$ and $f \in \Gamma$,

$$(P(\Delta)x, f) = \sum_{k=1}^{\infty} (P(\Delta_k)x, f).$$

A bounded linear operator T on $\mathfrak{X}$ is called a SPECTRAL OPERATOR, if there exists a Γ-completely additive spectral measure $P(\cdot)$ in $\mathfrak{X}$ such that the following conditions hold for all $\Delta \in \mathscr{S}$:

(6) T commutes with each $P(\Delta)$.

(7) If $\mathfrak{X}_\Delta = P(\Delta)\mathfrak{X}$ and $T_\Delta = P(\Delta)T$, then $Sp_{\mathscr{B}(\mathfrak{X}_\Delta)}(T_\Delta) \subseteq \bar{\Delta}$, where $\bar{\Delta}$ is the closure of Δ.

The spectral measure $P(\cdot)$ in this case is called a RESOLUTION OF THE IDENTITY for T. It turns out that $P(Sp_{\mathscr{B}(\mathfrak{X})}(T)) = I$. Also, any element of $\mathscr{B}(\mathfrak{X})$ which commutes with T commutes with each of the projections $P(\Delta)$. If T can be written in the form

$$T = \int_{Sp_{\mathscr{B}(\mathfrak{X})}(T)} \lambda P(d\lambda),$$

then T is said to be of SCALAR TYPE. The integral, which is an operator-valued integral of Riemann type, exists with respect to the norm topology in $\mathscr{B}(\mathfrak{X})$. A variety of examples of spectral operators which occur in analysis will be found in Dunford and Schwartz [1]. The motivating example is, of course, a normal operator on Hilbert space.

A fundamental result is that every spectral operator T is of the form $T = S+N$, where S is of scalar type and N is topologically nilpotent and commutes with S. The operators T and S have the same spectra and the same resolutions of the identity in $\mathfrak{X}$. Furthermore, this decomposition of T is unique. The operator S is called the SPECTRAL PART of T.

Next let $\mathscr{E}$ be any set of operators in $\mathscr{B}(\mathfrak{X})$. Then the smallest closed subalgebra of $\mathscr{B}(\mathfrak{X})$, which contains the inverses of any of its elements which are regular in $\mathscr{B}(\mathfrak{X})$ and also contains $\mathscr{E}$, is called the FULL SUBALGEBRA OF $\mathscr{B}(\mathfrak{X})$ GENERATED BY $\mathscr{E}$. The algebra results for spectral operators can now be stated. They provide some non-trivial instances of the first Wedderburn structure theorem. Proofs will be found in Dunford [4].

I. Let T be a spectral operator on $\mathfrak{X}$ and S its scalar part. Denote by

$\mathfrak{B}$ and $\mathfrak{B}_0$ the full subalgebras of $\mathscr{B}(\mathfrak{X})$ generated by the pair of elements T, S and the element S respectively. Also let $\mathfrak{R}$ be the radical of $\mathfrak{B}$. Then

$$\mathfrak{B} = \mathfrak{B}_0 \oplus \mathfrak{R},$$

where the sum is a direct vector space sum. Every operator in $\mathfrak{B}$ is of spectral type and $\mathfrak{B}_0$ is isomorphic with the algebra of all complex functions on $Sp_{\mathscr{B}(\mathfrak{X})}(T)$ which are uniform limits of rational functions on $Sp_{\mathscr{B}(\mathfrak{X})}(T)$.

II. Let $\mathscr{E}$ be a commutative family of spectral operators whose resolutions of the identity together generate a bounded boolean algebra of projections. Let $\mathfrak{B}$ denote the full subalgebra of $\mathscr{B}(\mathfrak{X})$ generated by the totality of elements in $\mathscr{E}$ and their resolutions of the identity and let $\mathfrak{R}$ denote the radical of $\mathfrak{B}$. Then

$$\mathfrak{B} = \mathfrak{C} \oplus \mathfrak{R},$$

where the sum is a direct vector space sum and $\mathfrak{C}$ is isomorphic with $C(\Phi_{\mathfrak{B}})$. Also, every operator in $\mathfrak{B}$ is of spectral type. If $\mathscr{E}$ contains only a single operator T, then $\mathfrak{C}$ is the full subalgebra of $\mathscr{B}(\mathfrak{X})$ generated by the resolution of the identity $P(\cdot)$ for T. Moreover, in this case, $\mathfrak{C}$ is isomorphic with the algebra of all $P(\cdot)$-essentially bounded Borel measurable complex functions on $Sp_{\mathscr{B}(\mathfrak{X})}(T)$. The norm of a $P(\cdot)$-essentially bounded function f is equal to its "essential bound",

$$|f| = \inf_{P(\Delta)=I} (\sup_{\lambda \in \Delta} |f(\lambda)|).$$

§ 2. **Algebras of functions.** Many classes of functions which arise naturally in the theory of functions are actually Banach algebras under appropriately defined algebraic operations and norm. Most of the examples described in the present section fall into this category. The operations of addition and multiplication by scalars are always the usual pointwise operations for functions while the product may or may not be the pointwise product. In any case, all of the algebras considered are commutative. Some non-commutative algebras of functions are discussed in the next section.

On being confronted with a commutative Banach algebra, one is obligated, from our point of view, to determine if possible the carrier space. It is significant that, in the case of the most important examples which arise in practice, the problems which are encountered in the determination of the carrier space and its properties are already important analysis problems.

A.2.1. THE ALGEBRA $C(\Omega)$, FOR CERTAIN SPECIAL Ω. Recall that $C(\Omega)$ is the algebra of all bounded complex-valued continuous functions on the topological space Ω. Only Hausdorff spaces are considered and, except for the case of a discrete space which is considered later, the space Ω is assumed to be compact.

General properties of the algebras $C(\Omega)$ were obtained in Chapter III, § 2 and Chapter IV, § 2. In particular, if Ω is compact, then its topological structure is completely determined by the algebraic structure of $C(\Omega)$. (See Corollary (3.2.9).) Therefore, at least in principle, there corresponds to each topological property of Ω an algebraic property of $C(\Omega)$. For example, closed sets in Ω are associated with closed ideals in $C(\Omega)$ so that points, in particular, are associated with maximal ideals. Also, Ω is connected if, and only if, 0 and 1 are the only idempotents in $C(\Omega)$. It is also possible to describe the property that Ω be a Cartesian product of two compact Hausdorff spaces in terms of reasonable algebraic properties of $C(\Omega)$. (See McDowell [1].) A systematic examination of the relationship between elementary topological properties of Ω and algebraic properties of $C(\Omega)$ has been carried out by Ahlberg [1]. The main problem obviously is to obtain natural algebraic descriptions for properties of $C(\Omega)$ corresponding to interesting topological properties of Ω. (See Myers [2].) Our objective here is less ambitious and is only concerned with describing some of the algebraic properties of $C(\Omega)$ for certain very special Ω.

Consider first a totally disconnected compact Hausdorff space Ω. In this case, $C(\Omega)$ is generated by its idempotents. In fact, if ω_1 and ω_2 are distinct points of Ω, then there exists a decomposition, $\Omega = \Omega_1 \cup \Omega_2$, of Ω into disjoint closed sets Ω_1 and Ω_2 such that $\omega_1 \in \Omega_1$ and $\omega_2 \in \Omega_2$. The function f which is equal to 1 on Ω_1 and to zero on Ω_2 is an idempotent in $C(\Omega)$ and separates the points ω_1, ω_2. Therefore, by the Stone–Weierstrass theorem, $C(\Omega)$ is generated by its idempotents. Conversely, if $C(\Omega)$ is generated by its idempotents, then Ω is easily seen to be totally disconnected.

If $C(\Omega)$ is generated by a countable set $\{e_n\}$ of idempotents, then it is already generated by a single real-valued function. In fact, define

$$h(\omega) = \sum_{n=1}^{\infty} \frac{2e_n(\omega) - 1}{3^n}, \quad \omega \in \Omega.$$

Since $2e_n(\omega)-1 = \pm 1$, for every ω, the series converges uniformly and therefore defines a real-valued function in $C(\Omega)$. Moreover, being generators of $C(\Omega)$, the idempotents will separate points of Ω. Hence, if ω_1 and ω_2 are any two distinct points of Ω, there exists a smallest integer k such that $e_k(\omega_1) \neq e_k(\omega_2)$. Then

$$|h(\omega_1)-h(\omega_2)| = 2\left|\sum_{n=k}^{\infty} \frac{e_n(\omega_1)-e_n(\omega_2)}{3^n}\right|$$

$$\geqslant \frac{2}{3^k} - 2\sum_{n=k+1}^{\infty} \frac{1}{3^n} = \frac{1}{3^k}.$$

This proves that h separates points of Ω. Therefore, since h is real, the Stone–Weierstrass theorem shows that h generates $C(\Omega)$. This result, for commutative W*-algebras was proved by von Neumann [1].

When $C(\Omega)$ is generated by its idempotents, so that Ω is totally disconnected, the discussion of $\mathscr{B}(\mathfrak{H})$ in A.1.1 shows that the group of regular elements in $C(\Omega)$ is connected. On the other hand, the group of regular elements in $C(\Omega)$ need not be connected if Ω is not totally disconnected. This is shown for Ω equal to the boundary of the unit circle in the plane. In this case the group of regular elements has a countable number of components, one for each of the unitary elements u_n, where

$$u_n(\omega) = e^{in\omega}, \quad n = 0, \pm 1, \pm 2, \cdots.$$

This example was called to our attention by Kakutani.

We next specialize Ω even further to an EXTREMELY DISCONNECTED compact Hausdorff space. By definition, this means that the closure of every open subset of Ω is also open. Thus Ω is *a fortiori* totally disconnected. An extremely disconnected space is also sometimes called a STONIAN space after M. H. Stone [5] who introduced them. These spaces are characterized by the fact that the algebra $C^R(\Omega)$ of real continuous functions on Ω is a BOUNDED COMPLETE LATTICE. In other words, every bounded subset of $C^R(\Omega)$ has a supremum in $C^R(\Omega)$ relative to the natural ordering for real functions. For a proof of this result, we refer to Stone [5]. The following result gives an abstract characterization of the algebras $C(\Omega)$ where Ω is an extremely disconnected space: In order for a commutative B*-algebra $\mathfrak{C}$ (with an identity) to be an AW*-algebra, it is necessary and sufficient that its carrier space $\Phi_{\mathfrak{C}}$ be extremely disconnected. In order for $\mathfrak{C}$ to be a W*-algebra, it must admit an abundance of positive functionals F which are NORMAL in the sense that

$$F(\sup_{\alpha} h_{\alpha}) = \sup_{\alpha} F(h_{\alpha}),$$

for any bounded directed set $\{h_{\alpha}\}$ of hermitian elements of $\mathfrak{C}$ (that is $\alpha \leqslant \beta$ implies $h_{\alpha} \leqslant h_{\beta}$). This was proved by Dixmier [8] who also exhibited an example of a commutative AW*-algebra which is not a W*-algebra by constructing an extremely disconnected space Ω such that $C(\Omega)$ carries no normal positive functionals whatsoever.

Now let Ω be a discrete space. Then $C(\Omega)$ coincides with the algebra $B(\Omega)$ of all bounded complex-valued functions on Ω. Note that Ω is completely regular, so that, by Theorem (3.2.11), the carrier space of $B(\Omega)$ is equal to the Stone–Čech compactification of Ω. Since $B(\Omega)$ contains the characteristic function of every subset of Ω, it is well-supplied with idempotents. In particular, $B(\Omega)$ is readily seen to be generated by its idempotents. With involution $x \to x^{\star}$ defined by the complex conjugate $x^{\star}(\omega) = \overline{x(\omega)}$, $B(\Omega)$ is a B*-algebra. Furthermore, it is not difficult to prove that $B(\Omega)$ is even an AW*-algebra, so that the Stone–Čech compactification of Ω is extremely disconnected. Wolfson [2] has given a characterization of the algebras $B(\Omega)$ among all B*-algebras which can be formulated as follows: A B*-algebra is isometrically $\star$-isomorphic with an algebra of type $B(\Omega)$ if and only if every non-zero closed ideal contains a minimal ideal and the sum of any two annihilator ideals is also an annihilator ideal. Heider [1] also gives the following characterization: A B*-algebra is isometrically $\star$-isomorphic with an algebra $B(\Omega)$ if and only if its carrier space Φ contains a dense open subset Ω such that every subset of Ω is the intersection of an open and closed subset of Φ with Ω. The isomorphism is defined between $C(\Phi)$ and $B(\Omega)$ by the restriction of functions in $C(\Phi)$ to the subset Ω.

Since $B(\Omega)$ is a B*-algebra, we know from Theorem (4.1.8) that each of its singular elements is a topological divisor of zero. This is also implied by the stronger result that regular elements are dense in $B(\Omega)$. (See Blum [2].) For the proof of this density property, let x be any element of $B(\Omega)$ and, for $\epsilon > 0$, define

$$u(\omega) = \begin{cases} x(\omega), & \text{if } |x(\omega)| \geqslant \epsilon, \\ \epsilon\ , & \text{if } |x(\omega)| < \epsilon. \end{cases}$$

Then $u \in B(\Omega)$ and $\|x-u\| \leqslant 2\epsilon$. Furthermore, $\inf |u(\omega)| > 0$, and this is necessary and sufficient for u to be regular in $B(\Omega)$.

Finally we take Ω as a special subset of the euclidean plane which can be described as follows. First let Γ be a circle and choose points A, B, C on Γ with A and C end-points of a diameter. Denote by Ω_0 the set in the plane of Γ consisting of Γ plus the region bounded by the diameter AC and the semi-circle ABC. We obtain the desired space Ω from Ω_0 by extending the radii through B and C to points B' and C' respectively outside of Γ. Now Ω has the "obvious" (but not so easily proved!) property that the only homeomorphism of Ω onto itself of period two is the identity mapping. (See Civin and Yood [3].) Thus, in view of the remarks at the beginning of § 2 of Chapter IV, it follows that $C(\Omega)$ admits only one involution; namely, its natural involution, $x \to x^\star$, where $x^\star(\omega) = \overline{x(\omega)}$. This space Ω will also be used later to exhibit a commutative Banach algebra which does not admit any involution. (See end of A.2.5.)

A.2.2. THE l^p-ALGEBRAS. Let Λ be an arbitrary index set and consider $B(\Lambda)$, the algebra of all bounded complex-valued functions on Λ. For $1 \leqslant p \leqslant \infty$, denote by $l^p(\Lambda)$ the subset of $B(\Lambda)$ consisting of all f such that

$$\|f\|_p = \left(\sum_{\lambda} |f(\lambda)|^p \right)^{1/p} < \infty,$$

where, in the case $p = \infty$, we take $\|f\|_\infty = \sup |f(\lambda)|$, so that $l^\infty(\Lambda) = B(\Lambda)$. That $l^p(\Lambda)$ is a linear subspace of $B(\Lambda)$ and is a Banach space with $\|f\|_p$ as norm, is a well-known fact in the theory of Banach spaces. We observe further that $l^p(\Lambda)$ is also a subalgebra of $B(\Lambda)$ and is a Banach algebra under $\|f\|_p$. The problem is to establish the inequality $\|fg\|_p \leqslant \|f\|_p\|g\|_p$. This inequality is obvious when $p = 1$ or $p = \infty$. Therefore we assume $1 < p < \infty$ and note that it will be sufficient to take $\|f\|_p = \|g\|_p = 1$, in which case $|f(\lambda)| \leqslant 1$ and $|g(\lambda)| \leqslant 1$ for all λ. Also set $q = p(p-1)^{-1}$. Then, by the Hölder inequality,

$$\sum |f(\lambda)g(\lambda)|^p \leqslant (\sum |f(\lambda)|^{p^2})^{1/p}(\sum |g(\lambda)|^{pq})^{1/q}.$$

Since $|f(\lambda)| \leqslant 1$ and $p > 1$, we have $|f(\lambda)|^{p^2} \leqslant |f(\lambda)|^p$. Similarly $|g(\lambda)|^{pq} \leqslant |g(\lambda)|^p$. Therefore it follows that $\|fg\|_p \leqslant 1$. This completes the proof that $l^p(\Lambda)$ is a subalgebra of $B(\Lambda)$ and is a Banach algebra under the norm $\|f\|_p$. From the fact that $l^q(\Lambda)$ is the conjugate space of $l^p(\Lambda)$, for $1 \leqslant p < \infty$, it is easily proved that the natural mapping of Λ into $\Phi_{l^p(\Lambda)}$ is one-to-one and onto. For $1 < p < \infty$, the algebra $l^p(\Lambda)$ is an example of a reflexive Banach algebra whose conjugate space is also a Banach algebra.

The Banach space $l^p(\Lambda)$ can be converted into a Banach algebra in another way. Let δ be a fixed real function on Λ such that $0 < \delta(\lambda) \leqslant 1$, $\lambda \in \Lambda$. Then, for any $f, g \in l^p(\Lambda)$, define

$$(f \cdot g)(\lambda) = \delta(\lambda)f(\lambda)g(\lambda), \quad \lambda \in \Lambda.$$

It is easy to verify that $l^p(\Lambda)$ becomes a Banach algebra with $f \cdot g$ as its operation of multiplication. We denote this algebra by $l^p(\Lambda, \delta)$. Note that $l^p(\Lambda, \delta)$ reduces to the previous algebra when $\delta(\lambda) \equiv 1$. A result of Keown [1] on reflexive Banach algebras amounts to an abstract characterization of the algebras $l^p(\Lambda, \delta)$.

We now exhibit an example of a Banach algebra $\mathfrak{A}$ which cannot be written in the form $\mathfrak{A} = \mathfrak{A}_1 \oplus \mathfrak{R}$, where $\mathfrak{R}$ is the radical of $\mathfrak{A}$, $\mathfrak{A}_1$ is homeomorphically isomorphic with $\mathfrak{A}/\mathfrak{R}$ and the sum is a vector space direct sum. First take Λ to be an infinite sequence $\{\lambda_n\}$ and denote by $l_0{}^2(\Lambda)$ the dense subalgebra of $l^2(\Lambda)$ consisting of those f which vanish outside a finite set. Next let $\mathfrak{A}_0$ be the algebra obtained by introducing in the vector space direct sum of $l_0{}^2(\Lambda)$ with the complex field the following definition of multiplication:

$$(f, \alpha)(g, \beta) = (fg, 0),$$

for $f, g \in l_0{}^2(\Lambda)$ and α, β scalars. Also define a norm in $\mathfrak{A}_0$ by the relation

$$\|(f, \alpha)\| = \max\left(\|f\|, |\alpha - \textstyle\sum f(\lambda)|\right).$$

The desired algebra $\mathfrak{A}$ is the completion of $\mathfrak{A}_0$ with respect to this norm. Observe that the radical $\mathfrak{R}$ of $\mathfrak{A}$ is one-dimensional and consists of all scalar multiples of the nilpotent element $q = (0, 1)$. Furthermore, if $(f, \alpha) \in \mathfrak{A}_0$ and $[f, \alpha]$ denotes the image of (f, α) in $\mathfrak{A}/\mathfrak{R}$, then it is easily proved that $[f, \alpha] \rightarrow f$ defines an isometric isomorphism of $\mathfrak{A}_0/\mathfrak{R}$ into $l_0{}^2(\Lambda)$. This isomorphism can now be extended to an isometric isomorphism of $\mathfrak{A}/\mathfrak{R}$ onto $l^2(\Lambda)$. Suppose that there exists a homeomorphic isomorphism of $l^2(\Lambda)$ with a subalgebra $\mathfrak{A}_1$ of $\mathfrak{A}$. Let u_k denote the element of $l^2(\Lambda)$ such that $u_k(\lambda_k) = 1$ while $u_k(\lambda) = 0$ for $\lambda \neq \lambda_k$ and denote by e_k the corresponding element of $\mathfrak{A}_1$. Choose $\{(f_n, \alpha_n)\}$ in $\mathfrak{A}_0$ such that $\lim(f_n, \alpha_n) = e_k$ in $\mathfrak{A}$. Since $e_k{}^2 = e_k$, we also have $\lim(f_n{}^2, 0) = e_k$. This implies that $\lim f_n(\lambda) = 0$ or 1, for each $\lambda \in \Lambda$, and also that $e_k \in l_0{}^2(\Lambda)$. Note that the elements e_k are pairwise orthogonal idempotents. Finally define

$$d_n = \sum_{k=1}^{n} \frac{e_k}{k}, \qquad t_n = \sum_{k=1}^{n} \frac{u_k}{k}.$$

Then, since $\Sigma\, k^{-2}$ is convergent, the sequence $\{t_n\}$ converges in $l^2(\Lambda)$. On the other hand, the sequence $\{d_n\}$ obviously does not converge in $\mathfrak{A}$. This proves that a decomposition $\mathfrak{A} = \mathfrak{A}_1 \oplus \mathfrak{R}$ with $\mathfrak{A}_1$ homeomorphically isomorphic with $\mathfrak{A}/\mathfrak{R}$ is impossible. (See C. Feldman [1].)

A.2.3. FUNCTIONS WITH ABSOLUTELY CONVERGENT FOURIER SERIES. Consider the class W of all complex-valued functions x, which are defined on the closed interval $[0, 1]$ and have absolutely convergent Fourier series on this interval. In other words, x has the form

$$x(\omega) = \sum_{-\infty}^{\infty} \xi_n \exp(2\pi i\omega), \quad 0 \leqslant \omega \leqslant 1,$$

where ξ_n is the nth Fourier coefficient of x and

$$\sum_{-\infty}^{\infty} |\xi_n| < \infty.$$

Since the series for x is uniformly convergent, it follows that W is contained in $C([0, 1])$. It is not difficult to verify that W is actually a $\star$-subalgebra of $C([0, 1])$ (containing the identity element). Furthermore, W is a Banach algebra under the norm

$$\|x\| = \sum_{-\infty}^{\infty} |\xi_n|.$$

We now obtain the carrier space of W.

Denote by z the element of W defined by $z(\omega) = \exp(2\pi i\omega)$. Then

$$x = \lim_{n\to\infty} \sum_{-n}^{+n} \xi_k z^k,$$

where the convergence is in the norm of W. Next let φ be any element of Φ_W. Since $\|z\| = \|z^{-1}\| = 1$, we must have $|\hat{z}(\varphi)| = 1$. Hence there exists a real number ω_φ with $0 \leqslant \omega_\varphi < 1$ such that $\hat{z}(\varphi) = \exp(2\pi i\omega_\varphi)$. Moreover,

$$\hat{x}(\varphi) = \lim_{n\to\infty} \sum_{-n}^{+n} \xi_k \hat{z}(\varphi)^k,$$

so that

$$\hat{x}(\varphi) = \sum_{-\infty}^{+\infty} \xi_n \exp(2\pi i\omega_\varphi) = \hat{x}(\omega_\varphi).$$

This means that the natural embedding of [0, 1] in Φ_W (see Chapter III § 3) exhausts Φ_W. It is obvious that this embedding is one-to-one except for 0 and 1 which map onto the same element of Φ_W. Furthermore, if 0 and 1 are identified in [0, 1], then the resulting compact Hausdorff space is homeomorphic with Φ_W.

As a consequence of this representation of Φ_W, we see that an element $x \in W$ has an inverse in W if and only if $x(\omega)$ is never zero on [0, 1]. In other words, if x is a non-vanishing function with an absolutely convergent Fourier series, then the reciprocal function $x(\omega)^{-1}$ also has an absolutely convergent Fourier series. This is the famous Wiener [1] lemma which was mentioned in the preface. The algebra W is also known as the WIENER ALGEBRA. A generalization of the Wiener lemma due to P. Levy [1] can also be obtained here by an application of Theorem (3.5.1). Let x be any element of W and let f be a complex function which is holomorphic on a domain of the complex plane which contains the range of the function x. Then the relation $y(\omega) = f(x(\omega))$, $\omega \in [0, 1]$, defines an element $y \in W$.

The algebra W admits a second natural involution defined by the relation

$$x^\star(\omega) = \sum_{-\infty}^{+\infty} \bar{\xi}_n \exp(2\pi i\omega),$$

where $\{\xi_n\}$ are, of course, the Fourier coefficients of x. This is an example of an involution which is not hermitian.

We now consider a class of subalgebras of W which includes W as a special case. Assume given a doubly infinite sequence $\{\alpha_n\}$ of real numbers which has the following properties: $\alpha_0 = 1$, $\alpha_{m+n} \leqslant \alpha_m\alpha_n$ and $1 \leqslant \alpha_n \leqslant \beta|n|^k$, where β is a constant and k is a fixed positive integer independent of n. Define $W_{<\alpha_n>}$ to be the class of all x in W such that

$$\|x\|_{<\alpha_n>} = \sum_{-\infty}^{\infty} |\xi_n|\alpha_n < \infty.$$

Then $W_{<\alpha_n>}$ is a $\star$-subalgebra of W (containing the identity element) and is a Banach algebra under $\|x\|_{<\alpha_n>}$ as norm. The same argument used to obtain the carrier space of W can be applied here to show that $W_{<\alpha_n>}$ and W have the same carrier space. In other words, the natural embedding of [0, 1], with 0 and 1 identified, is a homeomorphism onto $\Phi_{W_{<\alpha_n>}}$.

The condition

$$\liminf_{|n|\to\infty} \frac{\alpha_n}{|n|} = 0,$$

can be shown to be necessary and sufficient for the algebra $W_{<\alpha_n>}$ to be an N*-algebra in the sense of Šilov. In particular, W is an N*-algebra. In other words, a closed ideal whose hull reduces to a single point is automatically maximal. (See Chapter II, § 7.) These results are due to Šilov [5].

A.2.4. FUNCTIONS OF CLASS $C^{(n)}$. A complex-valued function x is of class $C^{(n)}$ on the interval [0, 1] if its derivative of order n is defined and continuous on [0, 1]. These functions obviously constitute a *-subalgebra of $C([0, 1])$. We denote it by $C^{(n)}(0, 1)$. With norm defined by

$$\|x\| = \max_{0 \leqslant \omega \leqslant 1} \sum_{k=0}^{n} \frac{|x^{(k)}(\omega)|}{k!},$$

$C^{(n)}(0, 1)$ is a commutative Banach *-algebra with identity element. The element z, defined by the relation $z(\omega) = \omega$, is a generator for $C^{(n)}(0, 1)$. Since the spectrum of z is obviously equal to [0, 1], it follows that the carrier space of $C^{(n)}(0, 1)$ is equal to [0, 1]. This also follows by Corollary (3.2.8), which shows that the natural embedding is a homeomorphism of [0, 1] onto the carrier space. It is not difficult to show that $C^{(n)}(0, 1)$ is completely regular. (See Corollary (3.7.2).)

Let ω_0 be a fixed point in [0, 1] and consider the ideal $J(\omega_0)$ in $C^{(n)}(0, 1)$ consisting of all x which vanish in some neighborhood of ω_0. Then the closure of $J(\omega_0)$ is equal to the collection of all $x \in C^{(n)}(0, 1)$ such that $x^{(k)}(\omega_0) = 0$ for $k = 0, 1, \cdots, n$. In proving this assertion, we note first that, if $x_m \to x$ in $C^{(n)}(0, 1)$, then clearly $x_m{}^{(k)}(\omega) \to x^{(k)}(\omega)$ uniformly on [0, 1], for each $k = 0, 1, \cdots, n$. Therefore it is immediate that elements of $\overline{J(\omega_0)}$ satisfy the stated condition. On the other hand, let x be any element of $C^{(n)}(0, 1)$ with $x^{(k)}(\omega_0) = 0$, for $k = 0, 1, \cdots, n$. Given $\epsilon > 0$, define the function

$$x_\epsilon(\omega) = \begin{cases} x(\omega+\epsilon), & \text{for } 0 \leqslant \omega < \omega_0 - \epsilon \\ 0, & \text{for } \omega_0 - \epsilon \leqslant \omega \leqslant \omega_0 + \epsilon \\ x(\omega-\epsilon), & \text{for } \omega_0 + \epsilon < \omega \leqslant 1. \end{cases}$$

Then x_ϵ clearly belongs to $J(\omega_0)$. Moreover, since each of the functions $x^{(k)}$ is uniformly continuous on [0, 1], it follows that x_ϵ converges in the norm of $C^{(n)}(0, 1)$ to x as $\epsilon \to 0$. In other words $x \in \overline{J(\omega_0)}$ and the assertion is established.

Let x be an arbitrary element of $C^{(n)}(0, 1)$ and consider a fixed $\omega \in [0, 1]$. If y is any element such that $x - y \in \overline{J(\omega)}$, then $x^{(k)}(\omega) = y^{(k)}(\omega)$, for each k, so that

$$\sum_{k=0}^{n} \frac{|x^{(k)}(\omega)|}{k!} = \sum_{k=0}^{n} \frac{|y^{(k)}(\omega)|}{k!}.$$

Set $\|x\|_\omega = \inf \|y\|$, for $x - y \in \overline{J(\omega)}$, then

$$\sum_{k=0}^{n} \frac{|x^{(k)}(\omega)|}{k!} = \|x\|_\omega.$$

It follows that

$$\|x\| = \max_{0 \leqslant \omega \leqslant 1} \|x\|_\omega.$$

This proves that $C^{(n)}(0, 1)$ is an algebra of type C in the sense of Šilov [5, 7, 8]. (See Chapter III, § 7.) Therefore the Šilov structure theorem obtained in Chapter III, § 7 applies to $C^{(n)}(0, 1)$.

We now determine the "primary components" of $C^{(n)}(0, 1)$, namely, the difference algebras $C^{(n)}(0, 1)/\overline{J(\omega)}$, which will be denoted by $\mathfrak{Q}_\omega$. Fix $\omega_0 \in [0, 1]$ and define $u(\omega) = \omega - \omega_0$, $0 \leqslant \omega \leqslant 1$. Then $u = z - \omega_0$ and, since z is a generator for $C^{(n)}(0, 1)$, the element u is also a generator. Let $\tilde{x}$ denote the image of x in $\mathfrak{Q}_{\omega_0}$. Then $\tilde{u}$ is a generator for $\mathfrak{Q}_{\omega_0}$. Furthermore, since $u^{n+1} \in \overline{J(\omega_0)}$, it follows that $\mathfrak{Q}_{\omega_0}$ is isomorphic with the algebra P_n of all polynomials

$$\tilde{x} = \sum_{k=0}^{n} \xi_k \tilde{\ }^k,$$

with the usual algebraic operations for polynomials, plus the condition $\tilde{u}^{n+1} = 0$, and norm

$$\|\tilde{\ }\| = \sum_{k=0}^{n} |\xi_k|.$$

Consider the maximal ideal $\mathfrak{M}_{\omega_0}$ in $C^{(n)}(0, 1)$, with $n \geqslant 1$, associated with the fixed point $\omega_0 \in [0, 1]$; that is, $\mathfrak{M}_{\omega_0}$ consists of all x such that $x(\omega_0) = 0$. Then $\overline{J(\omega_0)} \subseteq \mathfrak{M}_{\omega_0}$. Since $\mathfrak{M}_{\omega_0}$ obviously contains elements x such that $x'(\omega_0) = 1$, it follows that $\overline{J(\omega_0)}$ is properly contained in $\mathfrak{M}_{\omega_0}$. Thus $C^{(n)}(0, 1)$ does not have the N*-property, since

$\overline{J(\omega_0)}$ is a closed primary ideal which is contained in only one maximal ideal but is not maximal. In particular there are closed ideals in $C^{(n)}(0, 1)$ which are not intersections of maximal ideals.

The algebra $C^{(n)}(0, 1)$ has the property that each of its closed ideals is an intersection of closed primary ideals. A similar result holds for n-times differentiable functions of k-variables. (Whitney [1].)

Most of the above properties of $C^{(n)}(0, 1)$ were obtained by Šilov [5]. For additional results along these lines for other special algebras, see Šilov [5, 7, 8, 9, 12, 14]. For some generalizations, see Mirkil [1], Mirkil and de Leeuw [1], and Willcox [1].

A.2.5. Continuous functions of bounded variation. The class $BVC(0, 1)$, consisting of all complex-valued continuous functions on $[0, 1]$ which are of bounded variation, is easily seen to be a $\star$-subalgebra of $C([0, 1])$. It is also a Banach algebra under the norm

$$\|x\| = \max_{0 \leqslant \omega \leqslant 1} |x(\omega)| + \text{Var}\, x,$$

where Var x is the total variation of x on $[0, 1]$. The element z such that $z(\omega) \equiv \omega$ is a generator for $BVC(0, 1)$. The spectrum of z is clearly equal to $[0, 1]$ which is therefore equal to the carrier space. It is obvious that $BVC(0, 1)$ is completely regular.

The observation which we wish to emphasize here is that $BVC(0, 1)$ is an N-algebra. In other words, if F is any closed subset of $[0, 1]$ and $J(F)$ is the ideal of all elements of $BVC(0, 1)$ which vanish in some neighborhood of F, then

$$\overline{J(F)} = k(F) = \{x : x(F) = (0)\}.$$

For the proof of this, observe first that always $\overline{J(F)} \subseteq k(F)$. For the opposite inclusion, it will be sufficient to consider only real functions $x \in BVC(0, 1)$. Let $x \in k(F)$ and set

$$G_n = \{\omega : |x(\omega)| < n^{-1}\}.$$

Then $G_n \supset F$. Now define

$$x_n(\omega) = \begin{cases} -\dfrac{1}{n}, & \text{for } x(\omega) \leqslant -\dfrac{1}{n} \\ x(\omega), & \text{for } \omega \in G_n \\ \dfrac{1}{n}, & \text{for } x(\omega) \geqslant \dfrac{1}{n}. \end{cases}$$

Evidently $x_n \in BVC(0, 1)$ and

$$\|x_n\| \leqslant \frac{1}{n} + \operatorname{Var} x_n = \frac{1}{n} + \operatorname{Var}_{G_n} x,$$

where $\operatorname{Var}_{G_n} x$ denotes the total variation of x on the set G_n. Furthermore, $x_n \to 0$. Therefore, if $y_n = x - x_n$, then $y_n \in J(F)$ and $y_n \to x$. Thus $x \in \overline{J(F)}$ and the statement is proved.

Essentially the same proof used for $BVC(0, 1)$ can be used to prove that the following algebra is also an N-algebra. This is the *-subalgebra $AC^p(0, 1)$ of $C([0, 1])$ consisting of all complex-valued continuous functions whose derivative exists and is absolutely integrable to the pth power ($p \geqslant 1$) on [0, 1]. This is a Banach algebra under the norm

$$\|x\| = \max_{0 \leqslant \omega \leqslant 1} |x(\omega)| + \left(\int_0^1 |x'(\omega)|^p d\omega\right)^{1/p}.$$

The element z, such that $z(\omega) \equiv \omega$ is a generator. Again the natural mapping is a homeomorphism of [0, 1] onto the carrier space of $AC^p(0, 1)$ and the algebra is completely regular. (Šilov [5].)

A.2.6. HOLOMORPHIC FUNCTIONS OF ONE VARIABLE. Our main interest here is in the DISC ALGEBRA $\mathscr{A}(\Delta)$ of all complex-valued functions which are defined and continuous on the closed disc $\Delta = \{\zeta : |\zeta| \leqslant 1\}$ of the complex plane and which are holomorphic in the interior of the disc. It is obvious that $\mathscr{A}(\Delta)$ is a closed subalgebra of $C(\Delta)$. Denote by $\mathscr{A}_0$ the class of those functions each of which is holomorphic in some open set containing Δ. When its elements are restricted to Δ, $\mathscr{A}_0$ can be regarded as a subalgebra of $\mathscr{A}(\Delta)$. We show that $\mathscr{A}_0$ is dense in $\mathscr{A}(\Delta)$. For any $x \in \mathscr{A}(\Delta)$ and positive integer n, define

$$x_n(\zeta) = x\left(\frac{n\zeta}{n+1}\right).$$

Then x_n is holomorphic on the disc $\{\zeta : |\zeta| < (n+1)/n\}$ and hence belongs to $\mathscr{A}_0$. Furthermore, since x is uniformly continuous on Δ, it follows that $\lim x_n = x$ in the norm of $\mathscr{A}(\Delta)$. Thus $\mathscr{A}_0$ is dense in $\mathscr{A}(\Delta)$. Now, for any $x \in \mathscr{A}_0$, the power series expansion

$$x(\zeta) = \sum_{n=0}^{\infty} \xi_n \zeta^n$$

will converge uniformly on Δ. Therefore, the element z, defined by the relation $z(\zeta) \equiv \zeta$, is a generator for $\mathscr{A}(\Delta)$. Since the spectrum of z

is obviously equal to Δ, it follows that Δ is equal to the carrier space of $\mathscr{A}(\Delta)$.

If E is a subset of Δ which has a limit point in the interior of Δ, then any function which vanishes on E and is holomorphic in the interior of Δ must vanish identically in Δ. Therefore $\mathfrak{k}(E) = (0)$ so that $\mathfrak{h}(\mathfrak{k}(E)) = \Delta$. In other words, the set E is dense in Δ relative to the hull–kernel topology. We thus have an example in which the hull–kernel topology differs from the usual topology for the carrier space.

Denote by Γ the boundary, $\{\zeta : |\zeta| = 1\}$, of Δ. By the maximum modulus principle, it is immediate that Γ is the Šilov boundary of Δ relative to the algebra $\mathscr{A}(\Delta)$. If x_Γ denotes the restriction of a function $x \in \mathscr{A}(\Delta)$ to the boundary Γ, then the mapping $x \to x_\Gamma$ is an isometric isomorphism of $\mathscr{A}(\Delta)$ into $C(\Gamma)$. In this realization, $\mathscr{A}(\Delta)$ consists of those elements of $C(\Gamma)$ which are "boundary values" of holomorphic functions and is accordingly sometimes called a BOUNDARY VALUE ALGEBRA. Notice that the generator z is singular in $\mathscr{A}(\Delta)$ but does not vanish on Γ and so is not a topological divisor of zero. (See Corollary (3.3.7).) Hence z is an interior point of the singular elements. (See Theorem (1.5.4) (iii).)

The algebra $\mathscr{A}(\Delta)$ is not a $\star$-subalgebra of either $C(\Delta)$ or $C(\Gamma)$. In fact, both x and $x^\star$ will belong to $\mathscr{A}(\Delta)$ if and only if x is a constant function. A commutative Banach algebra with this property is called ANTISYMMETRIC. (Šilov [16].) Although $\mathscr{A}(\Delta)$ is not a $\star$-subalgebra of $C(\Delta)$, it is still possible to define an involution in $\mathscr{A}(\Delta)$. We have only to let $x^\star$ be the function defined by $x^\star(\zeta) = \overline{x(\bar{\zeta})}$. Then $x \to x^\star$ is an involution in $\mathscr{A}(\Delta)$ but is obviously not hermitian.

Next let I denote the closed interval $[-1, 1]$ and, for $x \in \mathscr{A}(\Delta)$, denote by x_I the function x restricted to I. Then $x \to x_I$ is an isomorphism of $\mathscr{A}(\Delta)$ into $C(I)$. Note that this embedding of $\mathscr{A}(\Delta)$ in $C(I)$ is continuous but is not a homeomorphism. On the other hand, $x \to x_I$ is a $\star$-isomorphism of $\mathscr{A}(\Delta)$ into $C(I)$, where the involution in $\mathscr{A}(\Delta)$ is the one defined above. In particular, $\mathscr{A}(\Delta)$ is self-adjoint on I and so, by Theorem (3.3.2), the $\mathscr{A}(\Delta)$-boundary of I is equal to I. Thus $\partial_{\mathscr{A}(\Delta)} I$ is larger than the intersection of I with $\partial_{\mathscr{A}(\Delta)}\Delta$. It is not difficult to see that the points of I are precisely those points of Δ which are fixed points under the homeomorphism $\varphi \to \varphi^\star$ induced in $\Phi_{\mathscr{A}(\Delta)}$ by the above involution (see § 2, Chapter IV); that is, $I = \Phi_{\mathscr{A}(\Delta)}^{(\star)}$.

Let ω_0 be a fixed point in Δ and define

$$F(x) = \tfrac{1}{2}[x(\omega_0) + \overline{x(\bar{\omega}_0)}],$$

for $x \in \mathscr{A}(\Delta)$. Then F is a hermitian functional on $\mathscr{A}(\Delta)$ where $\mathscr{A}(\Delta)$ is given the involution defined above. If $\omega_0 \in I$, then it is obvious that F is a positive functional. On the other hand, if $\omega_0 \notin I$, then Theorem (4.6.15) can be used to show that F is not even a linear combination of positive functionals. (See Naïmark [7, p. 247].)

The disc Δ in the first part of the above discussion can be replaced by any simple closed curve plus its interior. The crucial point for this is that polynomials are still dense in the algebra of functions which are holomorphic inside the simple closed curve and continuous on the curve plus its interior. (See Walsh [1].) More generally, we can start with an arbitrary compact set Ω in the plane and restrict attention to the subalgebra of $C(\Omega)$ consisting of all those complex-valued functions on Ω which are uniform limits on Ω of polynomials (allowing a constant term). We also denote this algebra by $\mathscr{A}(\Omega)$ as in the special case of the disc algebra. By the remarks following Theorem (3.4.5), we have $\Phi_{\mathscr{A}(\Omega)} = \Omega$ if and only if Ω does not separate the plane. In any case $\Phi_{\mathscr{A}(\Omega)}$ is a subset of the complex plane which contains Ω.

An important question which arises here concerns just what elements of $C(\Omega)$ belong to $\mathscr{A}(\Omega)$. It is obvious that every element of $\mathscr{A}(\Omega)$ is holomorphic at interior points of Ω. Furthermore, elements of $\mathscr{A}(\Omega)$ extend uniquely to $\Phi_{\mathscr{A}(\Omega)}$ where they are continuous and are holomorphic at interior points. A fundamental result due to Mergelyan [4] states that, if Ω does not separate the plane, then $\mathscr{A}(\Omega)$ consists precisely of those elements of $C(\Omega)$ which are holomorphic at interior points of Ω. In particular, if Ω has a vacuous interior and does not separate the plane, then $\mathscr{A}(\Omega) = C(\Omega)$. An analogous problem involves approximation by rational functions. (See Mergelyan [4].)

The algebra $\mathscr{A}(\Omega)$ can also be considered as a closed subalgebra of the algebra $C(\partial\Omega)$, where $\partial\Omega$ denotes the $\mathscr{A}(\Omega)$-boundary of Ω. Therefore one can also ask which elements of $C(\partial\Omega)$ belong to $\mathscr{A}(\Omega)$. In the case of the disc algebra, Wermer [3] has proved that $\mathscr{A}(\Delta)$ is a maximal subalgebra of $C(\Gamma)$ (here $\partial\Delta = \Gamma$). More precisely, $\mathscr{A}(\Delta)$ separates strongly the points of Γ and, if $\mathfrak{A}$ is any closed subalgebra of $C(\Gamma)$ which contains $\mathscr{A}(\Delta)$, then either $\mathfrak{A} = \mathscr{A}(\Delta)$ or $\mathfrak{A} = C(\Gamma)$. Wermer [7, 9] has obtained a large class of maximal subalgebras of $C(\Gamma)$ which are associated with a Riemann surface. Helson and Quigley [1, 2] show that, for an arbitrary compact Hausdorff space Ω, proper maximal subalgebras of $C(\Omega)$ tend to exhibit analytic-like behavior. For example, let $\mathfrak{A}$ be a closed maximal subalgebra of $C(\Omega)$ which contains the scalars, separates the points of Ω and is without zero divisors. Then any element of $\mathfrak{A}$ which vanishes on an open set must vanish identically and the only real functions in $\mathfrak{A}$ are constants. The restriction that $\mathfrak{A}$ be without zero divisors is natural and, as the authors show, involves no real loss of generality. Rudin [5] proves that, if Ω contains a Cantor set, then there always exists a maximal closed subalgebra of $C(\Omega)$ which separates strongly the points of Ω. A partial converse to this result asserts that no such maximal subalgebra of $C(\Omega)$ exists if Ω does not contain a perfect set. This follows from the fact that every closed subalgebra of $C(\Omega)$ in this case is self-adjoint. (See Rudin [5].) The special case in which Ω is countable was considered by Civin and Yood [2].

We consider next a class of subalgebras of $C(\Delta)$ each of which contains the algebra $\mathscr{A}(\Delta)$. Let δ be a real number such that $0 < \delta < 1$ and denote by $\mathscr{A}_\delta$ the class of all $f \in C(\Delta)$ which are holomorphic in the open disc $\{\zeta : |\zeta| < \delta\}$. It is obvious that $\mathscr{A}_\delta$ is a closed subalgebra of $C(\Delta)$. The discussion at the end of § 2, Chapter III, can be applied to $\mathscr{A}_\delta$ to show that the natural mapping is a homeomorphism of Δ onto the carrier space of $\mathscr{A}_\delta$. The Šilov boundary in this case is obviously equal to the annulus $\Gamma_\delta = \{\zeta : \delta \leqslant |\zeta| \leqslant 1\}$. This shows that the Šilov boundary can be a proper subset of the carrier space and at the same time contain interior points.

We construct next an example of a complex commutative Banach algebra which does not admit any involution. (See Civin and Yood [3].) Let Ω be the subset of the plane described at the end of A.2.1. Then the desired example is the subalgebra $\mathfrak{A}$ of $C(\Omega)$ consisting of all f which are holomorphic at interior points of the semi-circular region ABC in Ω. A straightforward application of the construction described at the end of § 2, Chapter III, shows that Ω is the carrier space of $\mathfrak{A}$. (See also Arens [13].). Now, since the identity mapping is the only homeomorphism of Ω onto itself with period two and since $\mathfrak{A}$ is obviously not self-adjoint on Ω, it follows that $\mathfrak{A}$ cannot have an involution (§ 2, Chapter IV).

In closing, we call attention to the important class of all complex-valued functions which are bounded and holomorphic in the open disc $\Delta_0 = \{\zeta : |\zeta| < 1\}$. This is a closed subalgebra of $C(\Delta_0)$, the algebra of all bounded continuous functions on Δ_0. The carrier space of this algebra is much larger than Δ_0, and has not as yet been described.

A.2.7. Holomorphic functions of several variables. Functions of several variables exhibit a number of properties which are quite different from any which occur for functions of a single variable. The purpose here is to indicate a few of these differences as they are reflected in certain algebras of holomorphic functions.

Let Ω be a compact subset of n-dimensional complex euclidean space K^n and denote by $\mathscr{A}(\Omega)$ the subalgebra of $C(\Omega)$ consisting of all complex-valued functions on Ω which are uniform limits on Ω of polynomials in n complex variables $(\zeta_1, \cdots, \zeta_n)$ (allowing a constant term). Then, as in the case of one variable ($n = 1$), functions belonging to $\mathscr{A}(\Omega)$ are holomorphic at each interior point of the set Ω. Also, since the maximum modulus principle applies, the $\mathscr{A}(\Omega)$-boundary of the set Ω is contained in the topological boundary of Ω. The algebra $\mathscr{A}(\Omega)$ is an algebra with n generators $z_1, \cdots, z_n$, where

$$z_k(\zeta_1, \cdots, \zeta_n) = \zeta_k, \quad (\zeta_1, \cdots, \zeta_n) \in \Omega.$$

Therefore its carrier space, *via* the canonical mapping (§ 1, Chapter III), is a subset of K^n. By the remarks following Theorem (3.4.5), the carrier space of $\mathscr{A}(\Omega)$ is given by

$$\Phi_{\mathscr{A}(\Omega)} = \bigcap_P \{(\zeta_1, \cdots, \zeta_n) : |P(\zeta_1, \cdots, \zeta_n)| \leqslant |P|_\Omega\},$$

where P is any polynomial in the n variables $\zeta_1, \cdots, \zeta_n$ and

$$|P|_\Omega = \max |P(\zeta_1, \cdots, \zeta_n)|,$$

for $(\zeta_1, \cdots, \zeta_n) \in \Omega$.

Note that, if $\{P_n\}$ is a sequence of polynomials which converges uniformly on Ω to an element $x \in \mathscr{A}(\Omega)$, then $\{P_n\}$ also converges uniformly on $\Phi_{\mathscr{A}(\Omega)}$. This means that every element of $\mathscr{A}(\Omega)$ has a unique extension to an element of $\mathscr{A}(\Phi_{\mathscr{A}(\Omega)})$. It follows that $\mathscr{A}(\Phi_{\mathscr{A}(\Omega)}) = \mathscr{A}(\Omega)$ in the sense that the restriction of elements of $\mathscr{A}(\Phi_{\mathscr{A}(\Omega)})$ to Ω defines an isometric isomorphism of $\mathscr{A}(\Phi_{\mathscr{A}(\Omega)})$ onto $\mathscr{A}(\Omega)$. The set $\Phi_{\mathscr{A}(\Omega)}$ is also maximal in the sense that any open set into which every element of $\mathscr{A}(\Omega)$ can be extended by analytic continuation is already contained in $\Phi_{\mathscr{A}(\Omega)}$. In fact, let V be such an open set and suppose that it contains a point $(\zeta_1^{(0)}, \cdots, \zeta_n^{(0)})$ which does not belong to $\Phi_{\mathscr{A}(\Omega)}$. Then there will exist a polynomial P such that

$$|P(\zeta_1^{(0)}, \cdots, \zeta_n^{(0)})| > |P|_\Omega.$$

Set $\lambda = P(\zeta_1^{(0)}, \cdots, \zeta_n^{(0)})$ and define $f = (\lambda - P)^{-1}$. Since the values of P on the set $\Phi_{\mathscr{A}(\Omega)}$ constitute the spectrum of P in $\mathscr{A}(\Omega)$, it follows that $f \in \mathscr{A}(\Omega)$. But f obviously cannot be continued analytically to $(\zeta_1^{(0)}, \cdots, \zeta_n^{(0)})$. Therefore V cannot exist and the asserted maximality property of $\Phi_{\mathscr{A}(\Omega)}$ is proved.

It has already been observed (see remark following Theorem (3.4.5)) that, since the maximum modulus principle holds for functions of several variables, the set $\Phi_{\mathscr{A}(\Omega)}$ does not separate the space K^n. We also know that, if $n = 1$ and Ω does not separate the plane, then $\Omega = \Phi_{\mathscr{A}(\Omega)}$. This result for $n = 1$ is no longer true in general for $n > 1$ and, in fact, fails already in the case $n = 2$. We construct an example to illustrate this fact.

Let α be a fixed real number such that $0 \leqslant \alpha \leqslant 1$ and define the following two subsets of K^2:

$$\Omega = \{(\zeta_1, \zeta_2) : |\zeta_1| \leqslant 1, \quad |\zeta_2| \leqslant 1\}$$

$$\Omega^\alpha = \{(\zeta_1, \zeta_2) : |\zeta_1| \leqslant 1, \quad |\zeta_2| \leqslant (1-\alpha)|\zeta_1| + \alpha\}.$$

Note that Ω^α is a proper subset of the bicylinder Ω and that Ω^α does not separate the space K^2. We prove that $\Phi_{\mathscr{A}(\Omega^\alpha)} = \Omega$. It is obvious that $\Phi_{\mathscr{A}(\Omega^\alpha)} \subseteq \Omega$. (Consider the two polynomials $P_1(\zeta_1, \zeta_2) \equiv \zeta_1$ and $P_2(\zeta_1, \zeta_2) \equiv \zeta_2$.) On the other hand, let (ζ_1^0, ζ_2^0) be an arbitrary point of Ω and, for P any polynomial in two variables, define $Q(\xi) = P(\xi, \zeta_1^0)$. Then Q is a polynomial in one variable ξ. By the maximum modulus principle (for a polynomial in one variable), there exists a complex number ξ_0 such that $|\xi_0| = 1$ and $|Q(\xi)| \leqslant |Q(\xi_0)|$ for $|\xi| \leqslant 1$. Since $|\xi_0| = 1$ implies $(\xi_0, \zeta_2^0) \in \Omega^\alpha$, it follows that

$$|P(\zeta_1^0, \zeta_2^0)| \leqslant |P(\xi_0, \zeta_2^0)| \leqslant \max |P(\zeta_1, \zeta_2)|$$

for $(\zeta_1, \zeta_2) \in \Omega^\alpha$. This proves that Ω is contained in $\Phi_{\mathscr{A}(\Omega^\alpha)}$ and hence that $\Omega = \Phi_{\mathscr{A}(\Omega^\alpha)}$. In particular we have $\mathscr{A}(\Omega) = \mathscr{A}(\Omega^\alpha)$.

It is interesting to determine the $\mathscr{A}(\Omega)$-boundary of the set Ω in the above example. Note first that, because of the maximum principle, $\partial_{\mathscr{A}(\Omega)}\Omega$ is obviously contained in the topological boundary of Ω. This means that either $|\zeta_1| = 1$ or $|\zeta_2| = 1$ for points of $\partial_{\mathscr{A}(\Omega)}\Omega$. Since $\mathscr{A}(\Omega) = \mathscr{A}(\Omega^\alpha)$, we also have $\partial_{\mathscr{A}(\Omega)}\Omega \subseteq \Omega^\alpha$, for every α such that $0 \leqslant \alpha \leqslant 1$. In particular, we conclude from the case $\alpha = 0$ that $|\zeta_2| \leqslant |\zeta_1|$ for points of $\partial_{\mathscr{A}(\Omega)}\Omega$. The reverse inequality must also hold by symmetry, so that $|\zeta_1| = |\zeta_2| = 1$ for all points of $\partial_{\mathscr{A}(\Omega)}\Omega$. Finally, let (ζ_1^0, ζ_2^0) be any point such that $|\zeta_1^0| = |\zeta_2^0| = 1$ and consider the polynomial $P(\zeta_1, \zeta_2) = (\zeta_1^0\zeta_1 + 1)(\zeta_2^0\zeta_2 + 1)$. This polynomial assumes its maximum value on Ω only at the point (ζ_1^0, ζ_2^0). Therefore $\partial_{\mathscr{A}(\Omega)}\Omega$ is precisely the set of points (ζ_1, ζ_2) such that $|\zeta_1| = |\zeta_2| = 1$. (See Gelfand, Raikov and Šilov [1, p. 215].)

Another interesting example is obtained by taking

$$\Omega = \{(\zeta_1, \zeta_2) : |\zeta_1| + |\zeta_2| \leqslant 1\}.$$

In this case $\Phi_{\mathscr{A}(\Omega)}$ can be shown to coincide with Ω. Furthermore, the $\mathscr{A}(\Omega)$-boundary of Ω coincides with the topological boundary and consists of those points (ζ_1, ζ_2) such that $|\zeta_1|+|\zeta_2| = 1$. The algebra $\mathscr{A}(\Omega)$ has the property that every singular element vanishes at some point on the boundary of Ω. (See Gelfand, Raikov and Šilov [1, p. 215].) Thus, by Corollary (3.3.7), every singular element of $\mathscr{A}(\Omega)$ is a topological divisor of zero. This property also implies that every value assumed by an element of $\mathscr{A}(\Omega)$ in the interior of Ω is also assumed on the boundary. These properties are shared by the algebra $\mathscr{A}(\Omega)$ when Ω is the unit sphere in K^2. (See Quigley [1, § 6.2].)

For $n > 1$, the problem of polynomial approximation becomes much more complicated than for $n = 1$. When $n = 1$, Mergelyan's [7] theorem provides a complete solution of the problem. In particular, if Γ is any arc in the plane, then $\mathscr{A}(\Gamma) = C(\Gamma)$. On the other hand, Wermer [7] has given an example of an arc Γ in K^3 such that $\mathscr{A}(\Gamma) \neq C(\Gamma)$. Rudin [9] gives such an example in K^2. It is conjectured that if the arc Γ is sufficiently smooth, then $\mathscr{A}(\Gamma) = C(\Gamma)$. Helson and Quigley [2] show that, if Γ is a differentiable arc or a closed curve in K^n, then either $\mathscr{A}(\Gamma) = C(\Gamma)$ or Γ is a proper subset of $\Phi_{\mathscr{A}(\Gamma)}$.

A.2.8. A NON-SELF-ADJOINT ALGEBRA WITH ŠILOV BOUNDARY EQUAL TO THE CARRIER SPACE. Consider the Cartesian product K^∞ of a sequence of complex planes and let Ω be the subset of this product consisting of all sequences $\{\zeta_n\}$ of complex numbers such that $\Sigma|\zeta_n| \leqslant 1$. Then, with the usual product space topology, Ω is a compact subset of the space K^∞. The desired example is $\mathscr{A}(\Omega)$; that is, the subalgebra of $C(\Omega)$ consisting of all uniform limits on Ω of polynomials in a sequence $\{\xi_n\}$ of indeterminants. (See § 4, Chapter III.)

We prove first that $\Phi_{\mathscr{A}(\Omega)} = \Omega$. By the remarks following Theorem (3.4.5),

$$\Phi_{\mathscr{A}(\Omega)} = \bigcap_P \{\{\zeta_n\} : |P(\{\zeta_n\})| \leqslant |P|_\Omega\},$$

where P is an arbitrary polynomial in the sequence of indeterminants $\{\xi_n\}$ and $|P|_\Omega$ is its supremum on Ω. Let $\{\zeta_n{}^0\}$ be an arbitrary point of $\Phi_{\mathscr{A}(\Omega)}$ and consider the polynomial

$$P(\{\xi_n\}) = \sum_{k=1}^{m} \frac{\bar{\zeta}_k{}^0}{|\zeta_k{}^0|}\, \xi_k.$$

Then

$$\sum_{k=1}^{m} |\zeta_k{}^0| = |P(\{\zeta_n{}^0\})| \leqslant |P(\{\zeta_n{}^1\})|,$$

for some $\{\zeta_n{}^1\} \in \Omega$. Since

$$|P(\{\zeta_n{}^1\})| \leqslant \sum_{k=1}^{m} |\zeta_k{}^1| \leqslant 1,$$

it follows that

$$\sum_{k=1}^{m} |\zeta_k{}^0| \leqslant 1.$$

This holds for all m and proves that $\{\zeta_n{}^0\} \in \Omega$. In other words, $\Phi_{\mathscr{A}(\Omega)} = \Omega$.

We prove that $\partial_{\mathscr{A}(\Omega)}\Omega = \Omega$. Let Ω_0 denote the subset of Ω consisting of those sequences $\{\zeta_n\}$ with at most a finite number of non-zero elements and such that $\Sigma|\zeta_n| = 1$. It is not difficult to show that Ω_0 is dense in Ω. Therefore, since $\partial_{\mathscr{A}(\Omega)}\Omega$ is closed, the desired result will follow if we prove that $\Omega_0 \subseteq \partial_{\mathscr{A}(\Omega)}\Omega$. To this end, let $\{\zeta_n{}^0\}$ be any element of Ω_0, with $\zeta_n{}^0 = 0$ for $n > m$, and set $\mu > \max |\zeta_n{}^0|$. Also set $\omega_k = \zeta_k{}^0/|\zeta_k{}^0|$ and define

$$\alpha_k = (\mu - |\zeta_k{}^0|)\omega_k, \quad k = 1, \cdots, m.$$

Next define the polynomial

$$P(\{\xi_n\}) = \prod_{k=1}^{m} (\xi_k + \alpha_k).$$

Let $\{\beta_n\}$ be any point of Ω where $|P(\{\xi_n\})|$ assumes its maximum value $|P|_\Omega$. We prove that $\{\beta_n\}$ must be identical with $\{\zeta_n{}^0\}$, and this will show that $\Omega_0 \subseteq \partial_{\mathscr{A}(\Omega)}\Omega$. In order for

$$\prod_{k=1}^{m} |\beta_k + \alpha_k| = |P|_\Omega,$$

it is necessary, by an elementary argument on complex numbers, that

$$|\beta_k + \alpha_k| = |\beta_k| + |\alpha_k|, \quad k = 1, \cdots, m,$$

and in addition that

$$\sum_{k=1}^{m} |\beta_k| = 1.$$

The first condition also implies

$$\beta_k = \frac{|\beta_k|\alpha_k}{|\alpha_k|} = |\beta_k|\omega_k, \quad k = 1, \cdots, m.$$

By the second condition, $\beta_n = 0$ for $n > m$ and

$$\sum_{k=1}^{m} |\beta_k+\alpha_k| = 1+\sum_{k=1}^{m} |\alpha_k| = m\mu.$$

Now, since $|P(\{\zeta_n{}^0\})| \leqslant |P|_\Omega$ and $|\zeta_k{}^0+\alpha_k| = \mu$, for each k, we obtain $\mu^m \leqslant |P|_\Omega$. Therefore

$$\mu \leqslant \left(\prod_{k=1}^{m} |\beta_k+\alpha_k|\right)^{1/m}.$$

But this says that the arithmetic mean of the numbers $|\beta_1+\alpha_1|, \cdots, |\beta_m+\alpha_m|$ is not greater than the geometric mean, a result which is possible only if $|\beta_k+\alpha_k| = \mu$ for each k. Since

$$|\beta_k+\alpha_k| = |\beta_k|+|\alpha_k| = |\beta_k|+\mu-|\zeta_k{}^0|,$$

it follows that $|\beta_k| = |\zeta_k{}^0|$ and therefore $\beta_k = \zeta_k{}^0$, for each k. This completes the proof that $\partial_{\mathscr{A}(\Omega)}\Omega = \Omega$.

We prove finally that $\mathscr{A}(\Omega)$ is anti-symmetric. Suppose both f and the conjugate function $\bar{f}$ belonged to $\mathscr{A}(\Omega)$. The problem is to show that f is a constant. Let $\{\zeta_n\}$ be an arbitrary fixed point of Ω and, for fixed k, define the function f_k of a single variable ζ by the relation $f_k(\zeta) = f(\{\zeta_n+\delta_{kn}(\zeta-\zeta_k)\})$, where $\delta_{kn} = 0$, if $n \neq k$, and $\delta_{kk} = 1$. Then f_k is holomorphic for $|\zeta| < |\zeta_k|$ and continuous for $|\zeta| \leqslant |\zeta_k|$. Since $\bar{f}_k$ has the same property, it follows that f_k is a constant. In particular, we obtain $f(\{\zeta_n\}) = f(\{\zeta_n-\delta_{kn}\zeta_n\})$. By repetition of this argument, we obtain $f(\{\zeta_n\}) = f(\{\zeta_n{}^{(k)}\})$, where

$$\zeta_n{}^{(k)} = \begin{cases} 0, & \text{for } n = 1, 2, \cdots, k \\ \zeta_n, & \text{for } n > k. \end{cases}$$

Since f is continuous and the origin $\{0\}$ is a limit point of the set of points $\{\zeta_n{}^{(k)}\}$, for $k = 1, 2, 3, \cdots$, it follows that $f(\{\zeta_n\}) = f(\{0\})$. This proves that $\mathscr{A}(\Omega)$ is anti-symmetric and shows, in particular, that $\mathscr{A}(\Omega)$ is not self-adjoint. (See Gelfand, Raikov and Šilov [1].)

A.2.9. NON-EXISTENCE OF THE ŠILOV BOUNDARY. Consider the class of all complex-valued continuous functions x defined on the closed interval $[0, 1]$ which satisfy the condition $x(\omega) = \overline{x(1-\omega)}$, $0 \leqslant \omega \leqslant 1$. These functions constitute a closed, self-adjoint, *real* subalgebra $\mathfrak{A}$ of $C([0, 1])$. The reason for this example is that the $\mathfrak{A}$-boundary of $[0, 1]$ does not exist. In fact, observe that each of the intervals $[0, \frac{1}{2}]$ and $[\frac{1}{2}, 1]$ is a maximizing set for $\mathfrak{A}$, but their intersection, the single point $\frac{1}{2}$ is obviously not a maximizing set. The carrier space is clearly the set $[0, 1]$.

A.2.10. ALGEBRAS OF SET FUNCTIONS ON THE LINE. These are commutative Banach algebras which are of particular importance in the theory of semi-groups. The first and most general of the algebras was studied by Phillips [1] and is analyzed in detail in Hille–Phillips [1, p. 141]. We sketch without proofs a few of its properties.

Consider first a real-valued Borel measurable point function μ defined on $[0, \infty)$ and possessing the properties, $\mu(0) = 1$ and $0 < \mu(\omega_1 + \omega_2) \leqslant \mu(\omega_1)\mu(\omega_2)$, for $\omega_1, \omega_2 \geqslant 0$. The function μ is called a WEIGHT FUNCTION. It can be shown that

$$-\infty \leqslant \mu_0 = \inf_{0<\omega} \omega^{-1} \log \mu(\omega) = \lim_{\omega\to\infty} \omega^{-1} \log \mu(\omega).$$

Define $S(\mu)$ to be the class of all complex-valued set functions x, defined and countably additive on all bounded Borel subsets of $[0, \infty)$, which satisfy the condition

$$\|x\| = \int_0^\infty \mu(\omega)|x|(d\omega) < \infty.$$

Here $|x|$ denotes the total variation of x and is defined by the relation

$$|x|(E) = \sup \sum |x(E_i)|,$$

where the supremum is taken over all subdivisions $\{E_i\}$ of the Borel set E into disjoint sequences of bounded Borel subsets of $[0, \infty)$. It turns out that $S(\mu)$ is a Banach space under the obvious algebraic operations for functions and $\|x\|$ as norm. Furthermore, with multiplication defined by the convolution

$$(x \star y)(E) = \int_0^\infty x(E-\omega)y(d\omega),$$

it can be shown that $S(\mu)$ is a commutative Banach algebra.

For a fixed $\omega \in [0, \infty)$, define the set function u_ω as follows

$$u_\omega(E) = \begin{cases} 1, & \text{if } \omega \in E \\ 0, & \text{if } \omega \notin E. \end{cases}$$

Then u_0 is an identity element for $S(\mu)$. We have $\|u_\omega\| = \mu(\omega)$ and $(u_\omega \star x)(E) = x(E-\omega)$. In particular, $u_{\omega_1} \star u_{\omega_2} = u_{\omega_1+\omega_2}$. Hence the elements $\{u_\omega : \omega \in [0, \infty)\}$ constitute a semi-group in $S(\mu)$.

If $L(\mu)$, $A(\mu)$ and $N(\mu)$ denote respectively the absolutely continuous (with respect to Lebesque measure), the atomic, and the non-atomic singular set functions respectively in $S(\mu)$, then each of these sets is a closed linear subspace of $S(\mu)$, and $S(\mu)$ is a vector-space direct sum of these subspaces. The subspaces $L(\mu)$ and $L(\mu)+N(\mu)$ are proper ideals in $S(\mu)$.

Assume for the moment that $-\infty < \mu_0$ and, for $x \in S(\mu)$, define

$$\tilde{x}(\zeta) = \int_0^\infty \exp(\zeta\omega)x(d\omega).$$

This integral converges for $\mathscr{Re}(\zeta) \leqslant \mu_0$ and defines a continuous function $\tilde{x}$ on the half-plane $\Omega_{\mu_0} = \{\zeta : \mathscr{Re}(\zeta) \leqslant \mu_0\}$. By the uniqueness theorem for Laplace–Stieltjes integrals, the correspondence $x \to \tilde{x}$ is one-to-one. In fact, $x \to \tilde{x}$ is an isomorphism of $S(\mu)$ with a subalgebra of $C(\Omega_{\mu_0})$. In particular, $S(\mu)$ is semi-simple. The elements u_ω map into the functions $\tilde{u}_\omega(\zeta) = \exp(\omega\zeta)$. The natural mapping is a homeomorphism of Ω_{μ_0} with an open subset of $\Phi_{S(\mu)}$. The image of Ω_{μ_0} in $\Phi_{S(\mu)}$ consists precisely of those elements of $\Phi_{S(\mu)}$ which do not map $L(\mu)$ into zero. Thus Ω_{μ_0} can be identified with $\Phi_{L(\mu)}$. Now denote by Φ_0 the hull of $L(\mu)$ in $\Phi_{S(\mu)}$; that is, Φ_0 consists of all those elements of $\Phi_{S(\mu)}$ which map $L(\mu)$ into zero. The set Φ_0 contains, in particular, the element φ_0 defined by the relation $\hat{x}(\varphi_0) = x(\{0\})$, where $\{0\}$ is the subset of $[0, \infty)$ consisting of the single point 0. Every element φ in Φ_0 different from φ_0 is of the form

$$\hat{u}_\omega(\varphi) = \chi(\omega)\exp(\alpha\omega),$$

where $\alpha \leqslant \mu_0$ and χ is a character of the (discrete) additive group of the real line. Conversely, every $\varphi \in \Phi_{S(\mu)}$ of this form belongs to Φ_0. Observe that, if $\mu_0 = -\infty$, then Φ_0 reduces to the single element φ_0 defined above.

In the above discussion, one can replace the half-line $[0, \infty)$ by the full line $(-\infty, \infty)$. The resulting algebra is denoted by $S_0(\mu)$ with $L_0(\mu)$, $A_0(\mu)$ and $N_0(\mu)$ as its absolutely continuous, atomic and non-atomic singular portions. In this case, the elements u_ω already constitute a multiplicative group in $S_0(\mu)$. The only essential change here is that the integral

$$\tilde{x}(\zeta) = \int_{-\infty}^\infty \exp(\zeta\omega)x(d\omega), \quad x \in S_0(\mu),$$

will converge for ζ in a strip instead of a half-plane. The strip is defined by

$$\Omega_{(\mu'_0, \mu_0)} = \{\zeta : \mu'_0 \leqslant \mathscr{Re}(\zeta) \leqslant \mu_0\}$$

where $\mu'_0 = \sup \omega^{-1} \log \mu(\omega)$, for $\omega < 0$, and μ_0 is the same as before.

If $-\infty < \mu_0$, then the group of regular elements in $S_0(\mu)$ has an uncountably infinite number of components. In fact, the elements u_ω belong to distinct components for distinct values of ω. To see this, observe first that, if u_α and u_β belong to the same component, then $u_{\alpha-\beta}$ belongs to the principal component. Therefore one only needs to prove that an element u_ω can belong to the principal component only if $\omega = 0$. If u_ω is in the principal component, then according to Theorem (1.4.12), it has a logarithm. Hence there exists $v \in S_0(\mu)$ such that $u_\omega = \exp v$. Passing over to the image of $S_0(\mu)$ in $C(\Omega_{(\mu'_0, \mu_0)})$, we obtain the relation $\exp(\omega\zeta) = \exp(\tilde{v}(\zeta))$, $\zeta \in \Omega_{(\mu'_0, \mu_0)}$. Therefore

$$\tilde{v}(\zeta) = \omega\zeta + 2n\pi i, \quad \zeta \in \Omega_{(\mu'_0, \mu_0)}.$$

Since $\Omega_{(\mu'_0, \mu_0)}$ is unbounded while $\tilde{v}(\zeta)$ is bounded, it follows that $\omega = 0$. This establishes the desired result. (See Hille–Phillips [1, p. 287].)

Denote by $S(-\infty, \infty)$, $L(-\infty, \infty)$, $A(-\infty, \infty)$ and $N(-\infty, \infty)$ respectively, the algebras $S_0(\mu)$, $L_0(\mu)$, $A_0(\mu)$ and $N_0(\mu)$ for the special weight function $\mu(\omega) \equiv 1$. Then $\mu'_0 = \mu_0 = 0$ so that $\Omega_{(\mu'_0, \mu_0)}$ reduces to the imaginary axis. Also denote by $LA(-\infty, \infty)$ the algebra $L(-\infty, \infty) + A(-\infty, \infty)$. We describe briefly the carrier space of $LA(-\infty, \infty)$. As in the case of $S(-\infty, \infty)$, the algebra $LA(-\infty, \infty)$ is isomorphic with a subalgebra of $C(-\infty, \infty)$ under the mapping $x \to \tilde{x}$, where

$$\tilde{x}(\lambda) = \int_{-\infty}^{\infty} \exp(i\lambda\omega) x(d\omega), \quad -\infty < \lambda < \infty.$$

In this case the natural mapping takes $(-\infty, \infty)$ homeomorphically onto an open dense subset of $\Phi_{LA(-\infty, \infty)}$ which consists of all those φ which do not map $L(-\infty, \infty)$ into zero. An element of $\Phi_{LA(-\infty, \infty)}$ which does map $L(-\infty, \infty)$ into zero is of the form

$$\hat{x}(\varphi) = \sum \chi(\omega) x(\{\omega\}),$$

where $\{\omega\}$ is the subset of $(-\infty, \infty)$ consisting of the single point ω and χ is a character of the additive (discrete) group of the real line.

The algebra $LA(-\infty, \infty)$ admits a natural involution $x \to x^\star$, defined, by the relation $x^\star(E) = \overline{x(-E)}$, where E is a Borel set and $-E = \{-\omega : \omega \in E\}$. Evidently, if $\tilde{x}^\star$ is the element of $C(-\infty, \infty)$ corresponding to $x^\star$, then $\tilde{x}^\star(\lambda) = \overline{\tilde{x}(\lambda)}$. This, along with the fact that the natural mapping takes $(-\infty, \infty)$ onto a dense subset of $\Phi_{LA(-\infty, \infty)}$, shows that the involution is real. (See Hille–Phillips [1, p. 155].)

The algebra $S(-\infty, \infty)$ can also be identified as an algebra of complex-valued point functions on $(-\infty, \infty)$. The isomorphism $x \to \check{x}$ is defined by the relation

$$\check{x}(\lambda) = x((-\alpha, \lambda]) = \int_{-\infty}^{\lambda} x(d\omega).$$

Then $\check{x}$ is of bounded variation on $(-\infty, \infty)$ and satisfies the conditions

$$\check{x}(-\infty) = \lim_{\lambda \to -\infty} \check{x}(\lambda) = 0, \quad \check{x}(\lambda) = \check{x}(\lambda + 0), \quad \lambda \in (-\infty, \infty).$$

On the other hand, let f be any complex function which is of bounded variation on $(-\infty, \infty)$. Then the right and left hand limits $f(\lambda \pm 0)$ exist for every $\lambda \in (-\infty, \infty)$. Also the limits $f(\pm\infty)$ exist. By a standard construction, one can associate with f an element $x \in S(-\infty, \infty)$ such that

$$x([\alpha, \beta]) = f(\beta + 0) - f(\alpha + 0), \quad \alpha < \beta.$$

If we define $BV(-\infty, \infty)$ as the class of all complex-valued point functions f which are of bounded variation on $(-\infty, \infty)$ and which satisfy the normalization conditions

$$f(-\infty) = 0, \quad f(\lambda) = f(\lambda + 0), \quad \lambda \in (-\infty, \infty),$$

then the correspondence $x \to \check{x}$ is one-to-one between $S(-\infty, \infty)$ and $BV(-\infty, \infty)$. The class $BV(-\infty, \infty)$ is a linear space under the usual algebraic operations for functions and is a Banach space under the norm

$$\|f\| = \mathrm{Var}(f) = \int_{-\infty}^{\infty} |f(d\lambda)|.$$

With these definitions, the mapping $x \to \check{x}$ is linear and isometric. Furthermore, under convolution multiplication,

$$(f \star g)(\lambda) = \int_{-\infty}^{\infty} f(\lambda - \nu) g(d\nu),$$

$BV(-\infty, \infty)$ becomes a commutative Banach algebra with identity element u defined by

$$u(\lambda) = \begin{cases} 0, & \text{for } \lambda < 0 \\ 1, & \text{for } 0 \leqslant \lambda, \end{cases}$$

and the mapping $x \to \check{x}$ is an isometric isomorphism between the two algebras $S(-\infty, \infty)$ and $BV(-\infty, \infty)$. Translation of the properties of the carrier spaces is left to the reader. (See Gelfand, Raikov, and Šilov [1] and also Šreider [2].)

A.2.11. Some radical algebras. The first example here is the disc algebra $\mathscr{A}(\Delta)$ under a different multiplication defined in terms of a convolution, *viz*

$$(x \star y)(\omega) = \int_0^{\omega} x(\omega - \zeta) y(\zeta) d\zeta,$$

where $|\omega| \leqslant 1$ and the integral is taken over any Jordan arc which (except possibly for ω) lies entirely within the interior of the disc Δ. The other algebraic operations remain the same as before. With this definition of multiplication, it is not difficult to prove that

$$\|x^n\| \leqslant \frac{\|x\|^n}{(n-1)!}.$$

This implies that $\lim \|x^n\|^{1/n} = 0$. Thus $\mathscr{A}(\Delta)$ is a radical algebra under convolution multiplication. (See Hille–Phillips [1, p. 701] or Hille [2, p. 478].)

The next example is the class $L(0, 1)$ of all complex-valued functions x which are absolutely continuous on $[0, 1]$. Under the ordinary definitions of addition and multiplication by scalars and the norm

$$\|x\| = \int_0^1 |x(\omega)| d\omega,$$

$L(0, 1)$ is a Banach space. It becomes a Banach algebra under the convolution multiplication,

$$(x \star y)(\omega) = \int_0^{\omega} x(\omega - \zeta) y(\zeta) d\zeta, \quad \omega \in [0, 1].$$

As in the preceding example, we have

$$\|x^n\| \leqslant \frac{\max |x(\omega)|^n}{n!},$$

so that $L(0, 1)$ is a radical algebra. With involution $x \to x^\star$ defined by the relation $x^\star(\omega) = \overline{x(\omega)}$, $L(0, 1)$ becomes a $\star$-algebra. (See Gelfand, Raikov, and Šilov [1, p. 118].)

A.2.12. ALGEBRAS OF POWER SERIES. Consider the class $K(\zeta)$ of all formal power series in the indeterminant ζ and with complex coefficients. For any two elements

$$x = \sum_{k=0}^{\infty} \xi_k \zeta^k, \qquad y = \sum_{k=0}^{\infty} \eta_k \zeta^k,$$

of $K(\zeta)$ and scalar α, define

$$x+y = \sum_{k=0}^{\infty} (\xi_k + \eta_k)\zeta^k, \qquad \alpha x = \sum_{k=0}^{\infty} (\alpha \xi_k)\zeta^k,$$

$$xy = \sum_{k=0}^{\infty} \left(\sum_{l=0}^{k} \xi_{k-l}\eta_l \right) \zeta^k.$$

Then $K(\zeta)$ becomes a complex commutative algebra with an identity element. Now let $\mathfrak{A}$ be a subalgebra of $K(\zeta)$ which is a Banach algebra under a given norm $\|x\|$. Then $\mathfrak{A}$ is called a BANACH ALGEBRA OF POWER SERIES provided it satisfies the following conditions: (1) If $z = \zeta$, then $z \in \mathfrak{A}$ and $\mathfrak{A}$ is generated by z plus the identity element. (2) Convergence in the norm of $\mathfrak{A}$ implies convergence of the coefficients in the power series. In other words, if $x = \Sigma \xi_k \zeta^k$, then each coefficient ξ_k is a continuous function of x with respect to the norm topology in $\mathfrak{A}$. (See Lorch [3] and Šilov [5].)

As an example of a Banach algebra of power series, consider the class $K_{<\alpha_n>}$ of all formal power series $x = \Sigma \xi_k \zeta^k$, subject to the condition

$$\|x\| = \sum_{k=0} |\xi_k| \alpha_k < \infty,$$

where $\{\alpha_n\}$ is a given sequence of positive numbers such that $\alpha_0 = 1$, $\alpha_{m+n} \leqslant \alpha_m \alpha_n$ and $\lim_{k\to\infty} \alpha_k^{1/k} = 0$. Then $K_{<\alpha_n>}$ is a subalgebra of $K(\zeta)$ and is a Banach algebra with $\|x\|$ as norm. The element $z = \zeta$ and the identity element obviously generate $K_{<\alpha_n>}$. Also $|\xi_k| \leqslant \alpha_k^{-1}\|x\|$, so that ξ_k is a continuous function of x. Therefore, $K_{<\alpha_n>}$ is a Banach algebra of power series. The algebra $K_{<\alpha_n>}$ is a primary algebra with its unique maximal ideal consisting of all x such that $\xi_0 = 0$; that is, all power series in $K_{<\alpha_n>}$ with constant term equal to zero. (Šilov [5].)

Now let $\mathfrak{A}$ be any complex commutative Banach algebra which is generated by an element z plus an identity element. For any $x \in \mathfrak{A}$, denote by (x) the closed principal ideal generated in $\mathfrak{A}$ by x. In particular, $(\zeta - z)$ is a maximal ideal in $\mathfrak{A}$ for every $\zeta \in Sp_{\mathfrak{A}}(z)$. Note that, for every positive integer n, $(z^{n+1}) \subseteq (z^n)$. Lorch [3] has called the ideal (z) an ECTO-, MESO-, or ENDO-IDEAL according as $(z^{n+1}) = (z^n)$, for all n, $(z^{n+1}) = (z^n)$ for all but a finite set of values of n, or $(z^{n+1}) \neq (z^n)$ for all n. Each of the three cases actually occurs. In fact, consider the algebra $C^{(n)}([0, 1])$ discussed in A.2.3. The element z, where $z(\omega) = \omega$ for $\omega \in [0, 1]$, is a generator for $C^{(n)}([0, 1])$. If $n = 0$ (that is, we have the algebra $C([0, 1])$) then (z) is an ecto-ideal. If $n > 0$, then (z) is a meso-ideal. In the case of the algebra $K_{<\alpha_n>}$ described above, (z) is an endo-ideal. In the general case, if zero is an interior point of $Sp_{\mathfrak{A}}(z)$, then (z) is an endo-ideal. When (z) is an endo-ideal, the following generalization of Taylor's theorem with remainder is valid: *For arbitrary positive integer n, each element $x \in \mathfrak{A}$ has a unique representation in the form.*

$$x = \sum_{k=0}^{n} \xi_k z^k + r_{n+1},$$

where $r_{n+1} \in (z^{n+1})$. If $\mathfrak{I}$ is the intersection of all of the ideals (z^n), then $\mathfrak{I}$ is a closed ideal in $\mathfrak{A}$ and the above Taylor's theorem implies that $\mathfrak{A}/\mathfrak{I}$ is a Banach algebra of power series, the power series associated with $\bar{x} = x + \mathfrak{I}$ being $\Sigma \xi_k \zeta^k$ with the natural norm in $\mathfrak{A}/\mathfrak{I}$. Thus, if $\mathfrak{I} = (0)$, then $\mathfrak{A}$ is already a Banach algebra of power series. If zero is an interior point of $Sp_{\mathfrak{A}}(z)$, then the function $\hat{x}$ on $Sp_{\mathfrak{A}}(z)$ associated with an element $x \in \mathfrak{A}$ is holomorphic in a neighborhood of zero. As might be expected, the kth coefficient in the MacLaurin expansion of $\hat{x}$ about zero is equal to ξ_k. If Δ_0 is the component of the interior of $Sp_{\mathfrak{A}}(z)$ which contains zero, then all of the ideals

$$\mathfrak{I}_\zeta = \bigcap_{n=1}^{\infty} ((\zeta - z)^n), \quad \zeta \in \Delta_0$$

are equal. These results are due to Lorch [3]. Lorch also shows, under certain conditions, that, if $Sp_{\mathfrak{A}}(z)$ contains an interval $[\alpha, \beta]$, then $\mathfrak{A}$ is isomorphic with a subalgebra of $C^\infty([\alpha, \beta])$.

§ **3. Group algebras.** In this section, we describe a number of important Banach algebras which are associated with locally compact topological groups. Before discussing the algebras, it is desirable to sketch a few properties of these groups which will be needed below. Proofs are omitted and will be found in Loomis [1] or other references which will be cited as needed.

Recall that a topological group $\mathfrak{G}$ is a Hausdorff space such that the mapping $(\gamma, \delta) \to \gamma\delta^{-1}$ of $\mathfrak{G} \times \mathfrak{G}$ onto $\mathfrak{G}$, defined by the group operations (which we write multiplicatively), is continuous. A locally compact topological group $\mathfrak{G}$ is automatically a completely regular space and accordingly admits an abundance of continuous functions. The class of all complex-valued continuous functions on $\mathfrak{G}$ with compact support (that is, vanish outside a compact set which depends on the function in question) will be denoted by $C_{(0)}(\mathfrak{G})$. Note that $C_{(0)}(\mathfrak{G})$ is a dense $\star$-subalgebra of the algebra $C_0(\mathfrak{G})$ of all continuous functions which vanish at infinity. For any function f defined on $\mathfrak{G}$ and fixed $\delta \in \mathfrak{G}$, we denote by f_δ and f^δ the two functions defined by the relations

$$f_\delta(\omega) = f(\delta^{-1}\omega), \quad f^\delta(\omega) = f(\omega\delta), \quad \omega \in \mathfrak{G}.$$

A collection $\mathscr{E}$ of functions on $\mathfrak{G}$ is called LEFT (or RIGHT) INVARIANT if $f \in \mathscr{E}$ implies $f_\delta \in \mathscr{E}$ (or $f^\delta \in \mathscr{E}$) for every $\delta \in \mathfrak{G}$. Clearly the algebra $C_{(0)}(\mathfrak{G})$ is both left and right invariant. A functional F on $C_{(0)}(\mathfrak{G})$ is said to be LEFT INVARIANT if $F(f_\delta) = F(f)$, for every $f \in C_{(0)}(\mathfrak{G})$ and $\delta \in \mathfrak{G}$. Similarly, if $F(f^\delta) = F(f)$, then F is RIGHT INVARIANT.

The fundamental property of a locally compact group $\mathfrak{G}$, which underlies virtually everything we have to say here, is the existence of a non-trivial left invariant positive linear functional I on $C_{(0)}(\mathfrak{G})$. This functional, which is called a LEFT INVARIANT INTEGRAL, is uniquely determined up to a multiplicative constant. It is straightforward to verify that

$$\|f\|_p = (I(|f|^p))^{1/p}, \quad 1 \leqslant p < \infty,$$

defines a norm in the linear space $C_{(0)}(\mathfrak{G})$. The Banach space obtained by completing $C_{(0)}(\mathfrak{G})$ with respect to this norm will be denoted by $L^p(\mathfrak{G})$. By a standard construction, there is associated with the integral I a measure function μ in $\mathfrak{G}$ such that

$$I(f) = \int f(\omega)\mu(d\omega), \quad f \in C_{(0)}(\mathfrak{G}).$$

The μ-measurable sets include all σ-compact (unions of a countable number of conditionally compact sets) Borel subsets of $\mathfrak{G}$. Every open μ-measurable set has non-zero μ-measure and every compact set has finite μ-measure. It follows from the left invariance of I that μ is a left invariant measure; that is, if E is μ-measurable and $\delta \in \mathfrak{G}$, then δE is μ-measurable and $\mu(\delta E) = \mu(E)$. The measure μ, which is uniquely determined up to a positive multiplicative constant, is the left invariant Haar measure on $\mathfrak{G}$. When $\mathfrak{G}$ is compact, μ is always assumed to be normalized so that $\mu(\mathfrak{G}) = 1$. The space $L^p(\mathfrak{G})$ can, in the usual way, be identified with a linear space of complex-valued functions f on $\mathfrak{G}$ with the norm given by

$$\|f\|_p = \left(\int |f(\omega)|^p \mu(d\omega)\right)^{1/p}.$$

In this identification, the space $C_{(0)}(\mathfrak{G})$ corresponds to itself. If $f \in L^p(\mathfrak{G})$, then f_δ and f^δ belong to $L^p(\mathfrak{G})$ and the mappings $\delta \to f_\delta$ and $\delta \to f^\delta$ of $\mathfrak{G}$ into $L^p(\mathfrak{G})$ are continuous.

Left invariant Haar measure need not be right invariant. However, for fixed $\delta \in \mathfrak{G}$, the relation $\mu^\delta(E) = \mu(E\delta)$ defines a second left invariant measure μ^δ which, by the uniqueness property of μ, must be of the form

$$\mu^\delta = \Delta(\delta)\mu,$$

where $\Delta(\delta) \geqslant 0$. It turns out that the mapping $\delta \to \Delta(\delta)$ is a continuous homomorphism of $\mathfrak{G}$ into the multiplicative group of the positive real numbers. The function Δ is called the MODULAR FUNCTION of $\mathfrak{G}$ and, if it happens that $\Delta(\delta) \equiv 1$, then $\mathfrak{G}$ is called UNIMODULAR. Thus $\mathfrak{G}$ is unimodular if and only if its Haar measure is both left and right invariant. Every compact group and every locally compact abelian group is unimodular. In terms of the modular function, we can express the μ-measure of a set of the form $E^{-1} = \{\delta^{-1} : \delta \in E\}$ as an integral; namely,

$$\mu(E^{-1}) = \int_E \Delta(\omega^{-1})\mu(d\omega)$$

or, equivalently,

$$\int f(\omega)\mu(d\omega) = \int f(\omega^{-1})\Delta(\omega^{-1})\mu(d\omega),$$

for all $f \in L^1(\mathfrak{G})$. Since we shall be concerned below only with integration relative to left invariant Haar measure μ, it is convenient to write simply $d\omega$ instead of $\mu(d\omega)$. Thus

$$\int f(\omega)d\omega = \int f(\omega)\mu(d\omega).$$

Moreover, since

$$\int f(\omega)d\omega = \int f(\omega^{-1})\Delta(\omega^{-1})d\omega = \int f(\omega)\Delta(\omega)d\omega^{-1},$$

we can also write symbolically $d\omega^{-1} = \Delta(\omega^{-1})d\omega$. It is worth noting that, in the case of concrete examples, the Haar measure is usually given by a naturally defined measure on the group. For example, if $\mathfrak{G}$ is the additive group of the real numbers, μ is the ordinary Lebesque measure.

We are now prepared to examine the group algebras associated with $\mathfrak{G}$. Each of these algebras reduces, in the case of a finite group, to the familiar group algebra consisting of all linear combinations of the group elements. Only properties of the algebras, which are more or less directly relevant to the theory of Banach algebras, will be discussed.

A.3.1. THE ALGEBRA $L^1(\mathfrak{G})$. This is the algebra to which the expression "group algebra" is usually applied. It is equal to the Banach space $L^1(\mathfrak{G})$ in which the product $x \star y$ of two elements is defined as their convolution:

$$(x \star y)(\gamma) = \int x(\gamma\omega)y(\omega^{-1})d\omega = \int x(\omega)y(\omega^{-1}\gamma)d\omega.$$

That $L^1(\mathfrak{G})$ is indeed a Banach algebra under this definition of multiplication follows from an application of the Fubini theorem. The spaces $L^p(\mathfrak{G})$, for $p > 1$, are in general not closed with respect to convolution.

The algebra $L^1(\mathfrak{G})$ is commutative if and only if the group $\mathfrak{G}$ is abelian, and it will have an identity element if and only if $\mathfrak{G}$ is discrete. Although $L^1(\mathfrak{G})$ thus does not ordinarily possess an identity element, it does always contain an approximate identity. This consists of the family $\{e_V : V \in \mathscr{V}\}$, where $\mathscr{V}$ is the set of all compact neighborhoods of the identity in $\mathfrak{G}$ and e_V is any non-negative real function on $\mathfrak{G}$ which vanishes outside V and for which $\int e_V(\omega)d\omega = 1$. The partial ordering $V_1 \leqslant V_2$ in $\mathscr{V}$ is defined by inclusion $V_2 \subseteq V_1$. We have then

$$\lim_V (e_V \star x) = \lim_V (x \star e_V) = x,$$

for every $x \in L^1(\mathfrak{G})$. Since $(e_V)_\delta \star x = (e_V \star x)_\delta$, it follows that

$$\lim_V (e_V)_\delta \star x = x_\delta, \quad \delta \in \mathfrak{G}.$$

Similarly,

$$\lim_V (e_V)^\delta \star x = x^\delta, \quad \delta \in \mathfrak{G}.$$

In particular we see that a closed linear subspace of $L^1(\mathfrak{G})$ is a left (right) ideal in $L^1(\mathfrak{G})$ if and only if it is left (right) invariant.

The extent to which the group algebra $L^1(\mathfrak{G})$ determines the group $\mathfrak{G}$ is indicated by the following result due to Wendel [1, 2]: If $\mathfrak{G}_1$ and

$\mathfrak{G}_2$ are locally compact topological groups and if T is a norm non-increasing isomorphism of $L^1(\mathfrak{G}_1)$ onto $L^1(\mathfrak{G}_2)$, then there exists a bi-continuous isomorphism $\gamma \to \gamma^\tau$ of $\mathfrak{G}_1$ onto $\mathfrak{G}_2$, a continuous character χ on $\mathfrak{G}_1$, and a constant β such that

$$(Tx)(\gamma^\tau) = \beta\chi(\gamma)x(\gamma), \quad \gamma \in \mathfrak{G}_1, \quad x \in L^1(\mathfrak{G}_1).$$

(See Helson [3] for the commutative case and Kawada [5] for a related result.) This result fails even in the commutative case if the norm condition is dropped. (See Wendel [1].)

If an involution $x \to x^\star$, is defined by the relation

$$x^\star(\gamma) = \Delta(\gamma^{-1})\overline{x(\gamma^{-1})}, \quad \gamma \in \mathfrak{G},$$

then $L^1(\mathfrak{G})$ becomes a $\star$-algebra. The involution is continuous and, in fact, $\|x^\star\|_1 = \|x\|_1$. There is an intimate relationship between $\star$-representations of $L^1(\mathfrak{G})$ and unitary representations of the group $\mathfrak{G}$ on a Hilbert space $\mathfrak{H}$. More precisely, there is a one-to-one correspondence between essential (Chapter IV, § 4) $\star$-representations $x \to T_x$ of $L^1(\mathfrak{G})$ on $\mathfrak{H}$ and strongly continuous unitary representations $\gamma \to U_\gamma$ of the group $\mathfrak{G}$ on $\mathfrak{H}$, which is given by the relation

$$(T_x f, g) = \int x(\omega)(U_\omega f, g)d\omega, \quad x \in L^1(\mathfrak{G}),$$

where f and g are any two elements of $\mathfrak{H}$. In terms of a vector-valued or operator-valued integral, this relationship may be written in the form

$$T_x f = \int x(\omega)U_\omega f d\omega \quad \text{or} \quad T_x = \int x(\omega)U_\omega d\omega.$$

This correspondence is such that a closed subspace of $\mathfrak{H}$ is invariant with respect to the unitary representation of $\mathfrak{G}$ if and only if it is invariant with respect to the associated representation of $L^1(\mathfrak{G})$. In particular, $\gamma \to U_\gamma$ is irreducible if and only if $x \to T_x$ is irreducible. Two unitary representations of $\mathfrak{G}$ are unitarily equivalent if and only if their associated representations of $L^1(\mathfrak{G})$ are unitarily equivalent. (See Naĭmark [7, p. 341].)

Now consider the special Hilbert space $L^2(\mathfrak{G})$. There exists a natural $\star$-representation of $L^1(\mathfrak{G})$ on $L^2(\mathfrak{G})$ which may be defined as follows. For $x \in L^1(\mathfrak{G})$ and $f \in C_{(0)}(\mathfrak{G})$ it can be shown that $x \star f \in L^2(\mathfrak{G})$ and furthermore $\|x \star f\|_2 \leqslant \|x\|_1\|f\|_2$. Hence the mapping $x \to x \star f$ is continuous relative to the norm in $L^2(\mathfrak{G})$. Since $C_{(0)}(\mathfrak{G})$ is dense in $L^2(\mathfrak{G})$, it follows that there is defined a bounded linear operator A_x on $L^2(\mathfrak{G})$ such that $A_x f = x \star f$ for $f \in C_{(0)}(\mathfrak{G})$. It is convenient to write $A_x f = x \star f$ for arbitrary $f \in L^2(\mathfrak{G})$. The mapping $x \to A_x$ is a one-to-one $\star$-representation of $L^1(\mathfrak{G})$ on $L^2(\mathfrak{G})$. Thus $L^1(\mathfrak{G})$ is an A*-algebra and hence, by Theorem (4.6.7), is $\star$-semi-simple and, *a fortiori*, is semi-simple. The semi-simplicity of $L^1(\mathfrak{G})$ was first proved by Segal [2] who also obtained many of the fundamental properties of these algebras. The strongly continuous unitary representation of $\mathfrak{G}$ determined by the representation $x \to A_x$ is the representation $\gamma \to U_\gamma$, where $(U_\gamma f)(\omega) = f(\gamma^{-1}\omega)$, for $\omega \in \mathfrak{G}$, $f \in L^2(\mathfrak{G})$. Thus

$$(x \star f)(\gamma) = \int x(\omega) f(\omega^{-1}\gamma) d\omega, \quad \gamma \in \mathfrak{G}.$$

Since $L^1(\mathfrak{G})$ is $\star$-semi-simple, its irreducible $\star$-representations constitute a total family. In other words, if x_0 is any non-zero element of $L^1(\mathfrak{G})$, then there exists an irreducible $\star$-representation $x \to T_x$ such that $T_{x_0} \neq 0$. It follows from this fact that $\mathfrak{G}$ admits a total family of irreducible unitary representations.

It is desirable to examine briefly a relationship which exists between strongly continuous unitary representations of $\mathfrak{G}$ and certain continuous functions on $\mathfrak{G}$, which parallels the relationship which exists between $\star$-representations of a Banach $\star$-algebra and positive functionals on the algebra. Consider any strongly continuous unitary representation $\gamma \to U_\gamma$ of $\mathfrak{G}$ on a Hilbert space $\mathfrak{H}$ and, for a fixed vector $f_0 \in \mathfrak{H}$, define

$$\Psi(\gamma) = (U_\gamma f_0, f_0), \quad \gamma \in \mathfrak{G}.$$

Then Ψ is a complex-valued continuous function on $\mathfrak{G}$ and is easily seen to be such that

$$\sum_{i,j} \xi_i \Psi(\omega_i^{-1}\omega_j)\bar{\xi}_j \geqslant 0$$

for every finite set $\omega_1, \cdots \omega_n$ of elements of $\mathfrak{G}$ and complex numbers $\xi_1, \cdots, \xi_n$. A continuous function on $\mathfrak{G}$ which has this property is called POSITIVE DEFINITE. Every positive definite function on $\mathfrak{G}$ can be represented in the above manner by a strongly continuous unitary representation of $\mathfrak{G}$. It can also be shown that a continuous complex-valued function Ψ on $\mathfrak{G}$ is positive definite if and only if

$$\iint \overline{x(\zeta)} \Psi(\zeta^{-1}\omega) x(\omega) d\zeta d\omega \geqslant 0$$

for every $x \in L^1(\mathfrak{G})$. An analysis of unitary representations of a group in terms of positive definite functions exists and is closely analogous to the analysis of $\star$-representations of an algebra in terms of positive functionals which we have discussed in Chapter IV, §§ 6, 7. There also exists a one-to-one correspondence $F \leftrightarrow \Psi$ between positive functionals on $L^1(\mathfrak{G})$ and positive definite functions on $\mathfrak{G}$ which is defined by the relation

$$F(x) = \int x(\omega)\Psi(\omega)d\omega, \quad x \in L^1(\mathfrak{G}).$$

If $x \to T_x$ is the cyclic $\star$-representation of $L^1(\mathfrak{G})$ with cyclic vector f_0 such that

$$F(x) = (T_x f_0, f_0), \quad x \in L^1(\mathfrak{G}),$$

then

$$\Psi(\gamma) = (U_\gamma f_0, f_0),$$

where $\gamma \to U_\gamma$ is the unitary representation of $\mathfrak{G}$ determined by $x \to T_x$.

Some of the above remarks concerning representations can be extended to representations on Banach spaces other than Hilbert space. In this connection it is worth pointing out that a representation $x \to A_x$ of $L^1(\mathfrak{G})$ on the space $L^p(\mathfrak{G})$ of the form $A_x f = x \star f$ can be obtained just as in the case of $L^2(\mathfrak{G})$ considered above.

We describe next an example of a group algebra which is not symmetric. It is due to Gelfand and Naĭmark [4]. Let $\mathfrak{G}_2$ be the group of all complex 2×2 matrices (α_{ij}) with determinant equal to one. This group is unimodular. For a detailed analysis of its representations, see Naĭmark [1, § 13 or 7, § 29]. Consider the subgroup $\mathfrak{U}$ consisting of all unitary matrices in $\mathfrak{G}_2$ and denote by $\mathfrak{C}$ the subalgebra of $L^1(\mathfrak{G}_2)$ consisting of all $x \in L^1(\mathfrak{G}_2)$ such that

$$x_\delta = x^\delta = x, \quad \delta \in \mathfrak{U}.$$

Then $\mathfrak{C}$ can be proved to be a closed, commutative, $\star$-subalgebra of $L^1(\mathfrak{G}_2)$. Furthermore, $\mathfrak{C}$ contains quasi-inverses; that is, if $x \in \mathfrak{C}$ and x is quasi-regular in $L^1(\mathfrak{G}_2)$, then x is also quasi-regular in $\mathfrak{C}$. On the other hand, the algebra $\mathfrak{C}$ can be proved to be non-symmetric. This obviously implies that $L^1(\mathfrak{G}_2)$ is not symmetric, so that we have the desired example. (See Naĭmark [1, § 13 or 7, § 29].) This, of course, also provides an example of an A*-algebra which is not symmetric. A similar result holds for the group $\mathfrak{G}_n$ of all complex $n \times n$ matrices with determinant one. (Gelfand and Naĭmark [5].)

A simpler example of a non-symmetric group algebra has recently been exhibited by R. Bonic [1]. The group which he considers is the discrete free group $\mathfrak{G}$ on two generators σ and δ with the single relation $\sigma^2 = 1$. Since $\mathfrak{G}$ is discrete, $L^1(\mathfrak{G})$ coincides with $l^1(\mathfrak{G})$ and multiplication is defined by the convolution

$$(f*g)(\gamma) = \sum_{\omega \in \mathfrak{G}} f(\omega)g(\omega^{-1}\gamma), \quad \gamma \in \mathfrak{G}.$$

Note that the involution $f \to f^*$ is defined by the relation $f^*(\gamma) = \overline{f(\gamma^{-1})}$, $\gamma \in \mathfrak{G}$. Denote by u_ω the element of $L^1(\mathfrak{G})$ which is equal to zero everywhere in $\mathfrak{G}$ except at ω where it takes the value 1. Then linear combinations of the elements u_ω, $\omega \in \mathfrak{G}$, are dense in $L^1(\mathfrak{G})$. Now let $h = u_\sigma + u_\delta + u_{\delta^{-1}}$ and observe that $h^* = h$. From the fact that $L^\infty(\mathfrak{G})$ is the conjugate space of $L^1(\mathfrak{G})$, it is not very difficult to construct a linear functional F on $L^1(\mathfrak{G})$ such that $F((h-i)*u_\omega) = 0$, for each $\omega \in \mathfrak{G}$. It follows that $h-i$, as a linear operator on $L^1(\mathfrak{G})$ defined by left multiplication, maps $L^1(\mathfrak{G})$ into a proper subspace of itself. In other words, $i \in Sp(h)$. Therefore the involution is not hermitian and, *a fortiori*, the group algebra $L^1(\mathfrak{G})$ is not symmetric. Bonic also obtains a number of other results concerning symmetry properties of group algebras.

A.3.2. Locally compact abelian groups. We specialize now to the group algebra $L^1(\mathfrak{G})$ of a locally compact abelian group $\mathfrak{G}$. In this case the relationship between algebra and group is especially intimate. Since $L^1(\mathfrak{G})$ is commutative, the first problem is to describe its carrier space.

It is already known from the general case that there is a one-to-one correspondence between irreducible $*$-representations of $L^1(\mathfrak{G})$ on Hilbert space and strongly continuous irreducible unitary representations of $\mathfrak{G}$. With commutativity the irreducible representations are in both instances one dimensional. Therefore we have to do with a one-to-one correspondence between homomorphisms of $L^1(\mathfrak{G})$ onto the complex field and continuous homomorphisms of $\mathfrak{G}$ into the multiplicative group of the complex numbers with modulus equal to one. The former homomorphisms are elements of the carrier space of $L^1(\mathfrak{G})$ and the latter are the continuous characters of $\mathfrak{G}$ and constitute the character group $\hat{\mathfrak{G}}$ of $\mathfrak{G}$.

Recall that the group operation in $\hat{\mathfrak{G}}$ is defined by the relation

$$(\chi_1\chi_2)(\gamma) = \chi_1(\gamma)\chi_2(\gamma), \quad \gamma \in \mathfrak{G},$$

where χ_1 and χ_2 are any two elements of $\hat{\mathfrak{G}}$. In particular, $\bar{\chi} = \chi^{-1}$.

The topology in $\hat{\mathfrak{G}}$ is that defined by uniform convergence on compact subsets of $\mathfrak{G}$. With these definitions, $\hat{\mathfrak{G}}$ is also a locally compact abelian group. The second character group $\hat{\hat{\mathfrak{G}}}$ of $\mathfrak{G}$ is equal to $\mathfrak{G}$ in the sense that all characters of $\hat{\mathfrak{G}}$ are of the form $\chi \to \hat{\chi}(\omega)$ and the implied isomorphism of $\mathfrak{G}$ with $\hat{\hat{\mathfrak{G}}}$ is a homeomorphism. This is the Pontrjagin duality theorem.

The one-to-one correspondence between $\Phi_{L^1(\mathfrak{G})}$ and $\hat{\mathfrak{G}}$ is defined by the relation

$$\hat{x}(\varphi) = \int x(\omega)\bar{\chi}(\omega)d\omega,$$

where $x \in L^1(\mathfrak{G})$, $\varphi \in \Phi_{L^1(\mathfrak{G})}$ and $\chi \in \hat{\mathfrak{G}}$. The choice of $\bar{\chi}$ rather than χ in this relation is made in order to conform more closely with the established notations for the classical case of the additive group on the real line. This correspondence $\varphi \leftrightarrow \chi$ between $\Phi_{L^1(\mathfrak{G})}$ and $\hat{\mathfrak{G}}$ is a homeomorphism. In the remainder of the discussion, we identify $\Phi_{L^1(\mathfrak{G})}$ with $\hat{\mathfrak{G}}$ and write

$$\hat{x}(\chi) = \int x(\omega)\bar{\chi}(\omega)d\omega, \quad x \in L^1(\mathfrak{G}).$$

This is the abstract Fourier transform of x and provides the basis for abstract Harmonic analysis. Since $L^1(\mathfrak{G})$ is semi-simple, the mapping $x \to \hat{x}$ is one-to-one and is, in fact, a $\star$-isomorphism of $L^1(\mathfrak{G})$ into $C_0(\hat{\mathfrak{G}})$.

An important result for a locally compact abelian group $\mathfrak{G}$ is that its group algebra $L^1(\mathfrak{G})$ is completely regular. Furthermore, the set of those elements $x \in L^1(\mathfrak{G})$ such that $\hat{x}$ vanishes outside some compact set in $\hat{\mathfrak{G}}$ (that is, $\hat{x} \in C_{(0)}(\hat{\mathfrak{G}})$) is dense in $L^1(\mathfrak{G})$. These facts, which were proved by Wiener [1] for the additive group of the real line and by Godement [1] in the general case, imply that every proper closed ideal in $L^1(\mathfrak{G})$ is contained in at least one maximal modular ideal. In other words every proper closed ideal has a non-vacuous hull. The Wiener Tauberian theorem follows from this property.

Kaplansky [6] has proved that, for an arbitrary locally compact abelian group $\mathfrak{G}$, the group algebra $L^1(\mathfrak{G})$ is an N*-algebra; that is, every closed primary ideal is maximal. (See also Helson [2].) On the other hand, if $\mathfrak{G}$ is not compact, then $L^1(\mathfrak{G})$ is never an N-algebra. In fact, Malliavin [2] has recently shown in this case that $L^1(\mathfrak{G})$ always contains a closed ideal which is not an intersection of maximal modular ideals. This result was obtained by L. Schwartz [1] for the special case in which $\mathfrak{G}$ is euclidean 3-space. The general problem of determining when a closed ideal in $L^1(\mathfrak{G})$ is an intersection of maximal modular ideals is important and difficult. It is equivalent to the problem of "spectral synthesis" first proposed by Beurling. Roughly speaking, this is the problem of approximating a bounded measurable function on $\mathfrak{G}$ by linear combinations of certain characters associated with the given function. The approximation is relative to the weak topology for functionals on $L^1(\mathfrak{G})$ and involves delicate questions of Fourier analysis. (See, for example, Beurling [1] and Helson [1].)

Since the above results reduce to well-known classical analysis results for certain special groups, it is perhaps worthwhile to describe briefly the situation for these groups. First let $\mathfrak{G}$ be the additive group of the real line. Then Haar measure is ordinary Lebesque measure and the character group is again the real line. The characters are given by the relation

$$\chi(\gamma) = \exp(i\xi\gamma), \quad -\infty < \xi < \infty,$$

the mapping $\xi \to \chi$ being a homeomorphism of $(-\infty, \infty)$ onto $\hat{\mathfrak{G}}$. The correspondence between $\Phi_{L^1(-\infty,\infty)}$ and $\hat{\mathfrak{G}}$ is given by the relation

$$\hat{x}(\xi) = \int_{-\infty}^{\infty} x(\omega)\exp(-i\xi\omega)d\omega, \quad x \in L^1(-\infty, \infty),$$

so that $\hat{x}$ is the ordinary Fourier transform of x.

Next let $\mathfrak{G}$ be the additive group of the reals modulo 2π. This group is compact and its Haar measure is again given by Lebesque measure on $[0, 2\pi)$. The character group of $\mathfrak{G}$ is the (discrete) additive group of the integers. Characters on $\mathfrak{G}$ are given by the relation

$$\chi_n(\gamma) = \exp(in\gamma), \quad \gamma \in \mathfrak{G}.$$

where $n = 0, \pm 1, \pm 2, \cdots$. The correspondence between $\Phi_{L^1(0,2\pi)}$ and $\hat{\mathfrak{G}}$ is defined by the relation

$$\hat{x}(n) = \int_0^{2\pi} x(\omega)\exp(-in\omega)d\omega.$$

Therefore $\hat{x}(n)$ is the nth Fourier coefficient of x.

Finally, let $\mathfrak{G}$ be the additive group of the integers. This group is discrete and the Haar measure of a set is equal to the number of elements in the set. The character group is the additive group of the reals modulo 2π and characters are of the form

$$\chi(n) = \exp(i\zeta n), \quad n \in \mathfrak{G},$$

where $0 \leqslant \zeta < 2\pi$. The group algebra $L^1(\mathfrak{G})$ in this case coincides with the space l^1 of all (doubly infinite) absolutely convergent sequences of complex numbers. Multiplication is defined by the relation $\{\alpha_n\}\{\beta_n\} = \{\gamma_n\}$, where

$$\gamma_n = \sum_{k=-\infty}^{\infty} \alpha_{n-k}\beta_k, \quad n = 0, \pm 1, \pm 2, \cdots.$$

The correspondence between $\Phi_{L^1(\mathfrak{G})}$ and $[0, 2\pi)$ is given by the relation

$$\hat{x}(\zeta) = \sum_{k=-\infty}^{\infty} \xi_k \exp(-i\zeta k), \quad 0 \leqslant \zeta < 2\pi,$$

where $x = \{\xi_n\} \in L^1(\mathfrak{G})$. The mapping $x \to \hat{x}$ is an isometric *-isomorphism of $L^1(\mathfrak{G})$ with the Wiener algebra W of absolutely convergent Fourier series (see A.2.3 above).

A.3.3. THE CONVOLUTION ALGEBRA OF MEASURES. Let $\mathfrak{G}$ be an arbitrary locally compact topological group and denote by $M(\mathfrak{G})$ the class of all complex-valued bounded regular measures m defined on Borel subsets of $\mathfrak{G}$. (See Halmos [2, p. 224] for definitions.) Under the ordinary function definitions of addition and multiplication by scalars and with norm $\|m\|$ equal to the total variation of m, the class $M(\mathfrak{G})$ is a Banach space. It becomes a Banach algebra under convolution multiplication:

$$(m \star n)(E) = \int_{\mathfrak{G}} m(E\omega^{-1})n(d\omega), \quad E \in \mathscr{B},$$

where $\mathscr{B}$ is the field of Borel subsets of $\mathfrak{G}$. This algebra is commutative if and only if $\mathfrak{G}$ is abelian. For fixed $\delta \in \mathfrak{G}$, define $u_\delta(E) = 1$ or 0 according as $\delta \in E$ or $\delta \notin E$. Then $u_\delta \in M(\mathfrak{G})$ and $(u_\delta \star m)(E) = m(\delta^{-1}E)$, $(m \star u_\delta)(E) = m(E\delta^{-1})$ for every $m \in M(\mathfrak{G})$. In particular, u_1 is an identity element for $M(\mathfrak{G})$. Since $u_{\delta\omega} = u_\delta \star u_\omega$ for all $\delta, \omega \in \mathfrak{G}$, the mapping $\delta \to u_\delta$ is an isomorphism of the group $\mathfrak{G}$ into the multiplicative group of regular elements of $M(\mathfrak{G})$. If for $f \in L^1(\mathfrak{G})$ we define

$$m_f(E) = \int_E f(\omega)d\omega, \quad E \in \mathscr{B},$$

then the mapping $f \to m_f$ is an isometric isomorphism of the algebra

$L^1(\mathfrak{G})$ into the algebra $M(\mathfrak{G})$. In this sense, $L^1(\mathfrak{G})$ may be regarded as a subalgebra of $M(\mathfrak{G})$ and, as such, coincides, by the Radon–Nikodym theorem, with the class of all elements of $M(\mathfrak{G})$ which are absolutely continuous with respect to Haar measure. Actually, $L^1(\mathfrak{G})$ is a right ideal in $M(\mathfrak{G})$. Notice that $L^1(\mathfrak{G}) = M(\mathfrak{G})$ if and only if $\mathfrak{G}$ is discrete. Wendel [2, Theorem 1] proves that any bounded linear operator A on the Banach space $L^1(\mathfrak{G})$ such that $A(f \star g) = f \star (Ag)$, for all $f, g \in L^1(\mathfrak{G})$, is of the form $Af = f \star m$ where $m \in M(\mathfrak{G})$.

Most of the study of $M(\mathfrak{G})$ has been confined to the commutative case. We accordingly assume for the remainder of our discussion that $\mathfrak{G}$ is abelian. In this case, Rudin [9, § 1.6] has made the interesting observation that an element $m \in M(\mathfrak{G})$ is absolutely continuous relative to Haar measure if and only if $m(E\omega^{-1})$ is a continuous function of $\omega \in \mathfrak{G}$ for each fixed $E \in \mathscr{B}$. This gives a characterization of $L^1(\mathfrak{G})$ in $M(\mathfrak{G})$ without reference to Haar measure. Now let $\hat{\mathfrak{G}}$ be the character group of $\mathfrak{G}$ and, for $\chi \in \hat{\mathfrak{G}}$ and $m \in M(\mathfrak{G})$, define

$$\hat{m}(\chi) = \int \overline{\chi(\omega)} m(d\omega).$$

This is the Fourier–Stieltjes transform of m. For fixed χ, the mapping $m \to \hat{m}(\chi)$ is a homomorphsm of $M(\mathfrak{G})$ onto the complex numbers and so defines an element φ_χ of the carrier space of $M(\mathfrak{G})$. The mapping $\chi \to \varphi_\chi$ is a homeomorphism of $\hat{\mathfrak{G}}$ into $\Phi_{M(\mathfrak{G})}$ by virtue of which we can regard $\hat{\mathfrak{G}}$ as a subset of $\Phi_{M(\mathfrak{G})}$. This embedding is obviously consistent with the embedding of $L^1(\mathfrak{G})$ in $M(\mathfrak{G})$ and the identification of $\hat{\mathfrak{G}}$ with the carrier space of $L^1(G)$ given in A.3.2. If $\mathfrak{G}$ is discrete, then $M(\mathfrak{G}) = L^1(\mathfrak{G})$ and hence $\hat{\mathfrak{G}} = \Phi_{M(\mathfrak{G})}$. If $\mathfrak{G}$ is not discrete, then the fact that $L^1(\mathfrak{G})$ does not have an identity element implies that $\hat{\mathfrak{G}}$ is not compact and so is a proper subset of $\Phi_{M(\mathfrak{G})}$. However, $\hat{\mathfrak{G}}$ is an open set in $\Phi_{M(\mathfrak{G})}$ and is "determining" in the sense that $\hat{m}(\chi) = 0$ for all $\chi \in \hat{\mathfrak{G}}$ implies $m = 0$. This is the uniqueness of the Fourier–Stieltjes transform and shows, in particular, that $M(\mathfrak{G})$ is semi-simple. Notice that the algebra of functions $\widehat{M(\mathfrak{G})}$ is always self-adjoint on $\hat{\mathfrak{G}}$. On the other hand, if $\mathfrak{G}$ is not discrete, then $\widehat{M(\mathfrak{G})}$ is never self-adjoint on $\Phi_{M(\mathfrak{G})}$. This is proved by Williamson [3], who also obtains the following properties of $\hat{\mathfrak{G}}$ as a subset of $\Phi_{M(\mathfrak{G})}$ in case $\mathfrak{G}$ is not discrete: The closure of $\hat{\mathfrak{G}}$ in $\Phi_{M(\mathfrak{G})}$ does *not* contain the Šilov boundary and there exists an element $m \in M(\mathfrak{G})$ such that $(\hat{m}(\chi))^{-1}$ is bounded on $\hat{\mathfrak{G}}$ but m is not regular in $M(\mathfrak{G})$. The latter result was obtained by Wiener and Pitt [1] for $\mathfrak{G}$ equal to the additive group of the real line. If $f \in L^1(\mathfrak{G})$, then $\hat{m}_f(\varphi) = 0$ for $\varphi \notin \hat{\mathfrak{G}}$. On the other hand, if $\mathfrak{G}$ is the circle group (complex numbers of absolute value one) there exists $m \in M(\mathfrak{G})$ such that $m \notin L^1(\mathfrak{G})$ but $\hat{m}(\varphi) = 0$ for $\varphi \in \hat{\mathfrak{G}}$. We refer the reader to Rudin [9] for these results as well as a discussion of a number of other properties and outstanding problems concerned with $M(\mathfrak{G})$. In conclusion we note that Šreider [2] has described the carrier space of $M(\mathfrak{G})$ in terms of what he calls "generalized characters". Also, the algebra $S(-\infty, \infty)$ which was discussed in A.2.10 is just the algebra $M(\mathfrak{G})$ for $\mathfrak{G}$ equal to the additive group of the real line.

A.3.4. GROUP ALGEBRAS OF A COMPACT GROUP. When $\mathfrak{G}$ is a compact topological group, each of the Banach spaces $L^p(\mathfrak{G})$ is a semi-simple dual Banach algebra under convolution multiplication. (Kaplansky [4, Theorem 15].) In particular, the algebra $L^2(\mathfrak{G})$ is a semi-simple H*-algebra. It was this example which motivated Ambrose's initial study of H*-algebras. It can be shown that every non-zero closed ideal in $L^2(\mathfrak{G})$ contains a non-zero element of the center of $L^2(\mathfrak{G})$. (See Segal [2] or Loomis [1, p. 157]). Therefore, by Corollary (4.10.17), every minimal 2-sided ideal $\mathfrak{J}$ in $L^2(\mathfrak{G})$ is finite dimensional and contains an identity element e. Since $\mathfrak{G}$ is unimodular and $e^\star = e$, we have $e(\delta^{-1}) = \overline{e(\delta)}$. The elements e are called the CHARACTERS of $\mathfrak{G}$ and, when $\mathfrak{G}$ is abelian, they reduce to the characters as defined previously for this case. Therefore, if $x \in \mathfrak{J}$, then

$$x(\delta) = (x \star e)(\delta) = \int x(\delta\omega)e(\omega^{-1})d\omega$$

$$= \int x_{\delta^{-1}}(\omega)\overline{e(\omega)}d\omega = (x_{\delta^{-1}}, e), \quad \delta \in \mathfrak{G}.$$

Moreover, since $\delta \to x_\delta$ is a continuous mapping of $\mathfrak{G}$ into $L^2(\mathfrak{G})$, it follows that x is a continuous function on $\mathfrak{G}$. In other words, the minimal 2-sided ideals in $L^2(\mathfrak{G})$ consist of continuous functions. Therefore, by the structure theorem for H*-algebras, $L^2(\mathfrak{G})$ is equal to a direct sum of mutually orthogonal subspaces of continuous functions.

Denote by $\mathfrak{J}$ the subset of $C(\mathfrak{G})$ consisting of all $f \in L^2(\mathfrak{G})$ such that the elements $f_\delta{}^\gamma$ generate a finite dimensional subspace of $L^2(\mathfrak{G})$. These elements are called ALMOST INVARIANT. The set $\mathfrak{J}$ is a 2-sided ideal in $L^2(\mathfrak{G})$ and is, in fact, equal to the algebraic sum of all minimal ideals in $L^2(\mathfrak{G})$. Also, $\mathfrak{J}$ is a $\star$-subalgebra of $C(\mathfrak{G})$ which contains 1 and separates the points of $\mathfrak{G}$. Therefore $\mathfrak{J}$ is dense in $C(\mathfrak{G})$, by the Stone–Weierstrass theorem. (See Loomis [1, p. 160].)

Application of the representation theorems for H*-algebras to the present case will be left to the reader. We only remark that the results obtained in this way contain a number of classical results for representations of compact groups. (See Loomis [1, § 40], Naĭmark [7, § 32], Ambrose [1], Segal [1, 2].)

A.3.5. ALMOST PERIODIC FUNCTIONS ON GROUPS. Let $\mathfrak{G}$ be any topological group and consider the algebra $C(\mathfrak{G})$ of all bounded complex-valued continuous functions on $\mathfrak{G}$. An element $f \in C(\mathfrak{G})$ is said to be LEFT ALMOST PERIODIC provided the closure in $C(\mathfrak{G})$ of its set of left translates, $\{f_\delta : \delta \in \mathfrak{G}\}$, is compact. A RIGHT ALMOST PERIODIC function is defined similarly in terms of right translates f^δ. It turns out that left and right almost periodicity for a function f are equivalent. Therefore we call f ALMOST PERIODIC in case it is either left or right almost periodic. The class of all almost periodic functions on $\mathfrak{G}$ will be denoted by $AP(\mathfrak{G})$. It is not difficult to show that $AP(\mathfrak{G})$ is a closed $\star$-subalgebra of $C(\mathfrak{G})$. Therefore $AP(\mathfrak{G})$ is isometrically $\star$-isomorphic with $C(\Phi_{AP(\mathfrak{G})})$. Let $\omega \to \tilde{\omega}$ denote the natural mapping of $\mathfrak{G}$ into $\Phi_{AP(\mathfrak{G})}$. This mapping is continuous and the image of $\mathfrak{G}$ is dense in $\Phi_{AP(\mathfrak{G})}$. Furthermore, the group operation in the image of $\mathfrak{G}$ can be extended to all of $\Phi_{AP(\mathfrak{G})}$ so that $\Phi_{AP(\mathfrak{G})}$ becomes a compact topological group. This group, which we denote by $\bar{\mathfrak{G}}$, is uniquely determined up to an isomorphism and is the BOHR COMPACTIFICATION of $\mathfrak{G}$. Since $\bar{\mathfrak{G}}$ is compact, we have

$$C_{(0)}(\bar{\mathfrak{G}}) = C(\bar{\mathfrak{G}}) = AP(\mathfrak{G}).$$

Therefore the invariant integral I on $C_{(0)}(\bar{\mathfrak{G}})$ defines an invariant integral on $AP(\mathfrak{G})$. This integral turns out to be the von Neumann mean for almost periodic functions. Defined intrinsically in $AP(\mathfrak{G})$, $I(f)$ is equal to the value of a uniquely determined constant function which belongs to the uniformly closed convex set of functions generated by the left translations of the function f. (See Loomis [1, § 41].)

A.3.6. GROUP ALGEBRAS OF OPERATORS. The group algebras which we now describe are obtained as algebras of operators on the Banach spaces $L^p(\mathfrak{G})$. Consider first any element $x \in L^1(\mathfrak{G})$. Then, for $f \in L^p(\mathfrak{G})$, we have

$$\|x \star f\|_p \leqslant \|x\|_1 \|f\|_p.$$

Thus the relation $T_x f = x \star f$ defines a bounded linear operator T_x on the space $L^p(\mathfrak{G})$. In fact, $x \to T_x$ is a faithful representation of $L^1(\mathfrak{G})$ on $L^p(\mathfrak{G})$. We denote the closure of the image of $L^1(\mathfrak{G})$ in $\mathscr{B}(L^p(\mathfrak{G}))$ by $\mathscr{O}^p(\mathfrak{G})$. For $p = 1$, $x \to T_x$ is the left regular representation of $L^1(\mathfrak{G})$. Since $L^1(\mathfrak{G})$ has an approximate identity, the mapping $x \to T_x$ is an isometry for $p = 1$ so that $\mathscr{O}^1(\mathfrak{G})$ can be identified with $L^1(\mathfrak{G})$. A case of special importance is $p = 2$. Here $\mathscr{O}^2(\mathfrak{G})$ is a C*-algebra since $x \to T_x$ is a *-representation of $L^1(\mathfrak{G})$ on $L^2(\mathfrak{G})$. The algebra $\mathscr{O}^2(\mathfrak{G})$, although it is less closely related with the group $\mathfrak{G}$ than is the algebra $L^1(\mathfrak{G})$, is better behaved than $L^1(\mathfrak{G})$ for certain purposes. Going one step further, we can obtain an even more tractable algebra, which is at the same time even less closely related to $\mathfrak{G}$, by taking the W*-algebra generated in $\mathscr{B}(L^2(\mathfrak{G}))$ by the image of $L^1(\mathfrak{G})$.

Another algebra of operators on $L^2(\mathfrak{G})$ which is associated with $\mathfrak{G}$ in a natural way is the C*-algebra generated in $\mathscr{B}(L^2(\mathfrak{G}))$ by the image of $\mathfrak{G}$ under the unitary representation $\gamma \to U_\gamma$, where $U_\gamma f = f_\gamma$, $f \in L^2(\mathfrak{G})$. Denote this algebra by $\mathscr{U}^2(\mathfrak{G})$. It is not difficult to see that the W*-algebras generated by $\mathscr{O}^2(\mathfrak{G})$ and $\mathscr{U}^2(\mathfrak{G})$ are equal. This C*-algebra has far less control of the group than does $L^1(\mathfrak{G})$. In fact, Kodaira and Kakutani [1] show that, if $\mathfrak{G}$ is commutative, then $\mathscr{U}^2(\mathfrak{G})$ is independent of the topology in $\mathfrak{G}$. More precisely, the authors show in this case that $\mathscr{U}^2(\mathfrak{G})$ is a commutative C*-algebra which is isometrically *-isomorphic with the algebra $C(\Omega)$, where Ω is the (compact) group of *all* characters of $\mathfrak{G}$. In other words, Ω is the character group of $\mathfrak{G}$ in its discrete topology. This shows that $\mathscr{U}^2(\mathfrak{G})$ is independent of the topology in $\mathfrak{G}$.

In the above discussion, one can replace the left regular representation on $L^1(\mathfrak{G})$ by the right regular representation and so obtain "right" as well as "left" algebras associated with $\mathfrak{G}$. When $\mathfrak{G}$ is separable and unimodular, the corresponding W*-algebras are centralizers of one another in $\mathscr{B}(L^2(\mathfrak{G}))$. This opens the way to a use of the von Neumann reduction theory to decompose the representations into "factor" representations. (See Godement [5], Mackey [4], Mautner [1] and Segal [7].)

BIBLIOGRAPHY

J. Abdelhay

[1] *On a theorem of representation*, Bull. Amer. Math. Soc. **55** (1949) 408–417

G. M. Adelson-Velskii

[1] *Spectral analysis of a ring of bounded linear operators on Hilbert space*, Dokl. Akad. Nauk S.S.S.R. **67** (1949) 957–959

N. I. Ahiezer

[1] *Lectures on the Theory of Approximation*, OGIZ, Moscow-Leningrad (1947) 323 pp.

J. Ahlberg

[1] *Algebraic properties of topological significance*, Ph.D. Dissertation Yale University (1956)

W. Ambrose

[1] *Structure theorems for a special class of Banach algebras*, Trans. Amer. Math. Soc. **57** (1945) 364–386

[2] *The L_2-system of a unimodular group*, I, Trans. Amer. Math. Soc. **65** (1949) 27–48

F. W. Anderson and R. L. Blair

[1] *Characterization of the algebra of all real-valued continuous functions on a completely regular space*, Ill. J. Math. **3** (1959) 121–133

R. Arens

[1] *On a theorem of Gelfand and Neumark*, Proc. Nat. Acad. Sci. U.S.A. **32** (1946) 237–239

[2] *The space L^ω and convex topological rings*, Bull. Amer. Math. Soc. **52** (1946) 931–935

[3] *Linear topological division algebras*, Bull. Amer. Math. Soc. **53** (1947) 623–630

[4] *Representation of *-algebras*, Duke Math. J. **14** (1947) 269–282

[5] *Approximation in, and representation of, certain Banach algebras*, Amer. J. Math. **71** (1949) 763–790

[6] *Operations induced in function classes*, Monatshefte für Math. u. Physik. **55** (1951) 1–19

[7] *The adjoint of a bilinear operation*, Proc. Amer. Math. Soc. **2** (1951) 839–848

[8] *A generalization of normed rings*, Pacific J. Math. **2** (1952) 455–471

[9] *A Banach algebra generalization of conformal mappings of the disc*, Trans. Amer. Math. Soc. **81** (1956) 501–513

[10] *Cauchy integral for functions of several variables*, Tôhoku Math. J. **8** No. 3 (1956) 268–272

[11] *The boundary integral of* log $|\varphi|$ *for generalized analytic functions*, Trans. Amer. Math. Soc. **86** (1957) 57–69

[12] *Inverse producing extensions of normed algebras*, Trans. Amer. Math. Soc. **88** (1958) 536–548

[13] *The maximal ideals of certain function algebras*, Pacific J. Math. **8** (1958) 641–648

[14] *Dense inverse limit rings*, Mich. Math. J. **5** (1958) 169–182

[15] *The closed maximal ideals of algebras of functions holomorphic on a Riemann surface*, Ren. Cir. Mat. di Palermo **7** (1958) 245–260

R. Arens and A. P. Calderón

[1] *Analytic functions of Fourier transforms*, De Segundos Symposium sobre algunos problemas matemáticos que se estan estudiando en Latino América (Julio, 1954) 39–52, Centro de Cooperación Científica de la UNESCO para América Latina, Montevideo, Uruguay (1954)

[2] *Analytic functions of several Banach algebra elements*, Ann. of Math. (2) **62** (1955) 204–216

R. Arens and K. Hoffman

[1] *Algebraic extensions of normed algebras*, Proc. Amer. Math. Soc. **7** (1956) 203–210

R. Arens and I. Kaplansky

[1] *Topological representation of algebras*, Trans. Amer. Math. Soc. **63** (1948) 457–481

R. Arens and I. M. Singer

[1] *Function values as boundary integrals*, Proc. Amer. Math. Soc. **5** (1954) 735–745

[2] *Generalized analytic functions*, Trans. Amer. Math. Soc. **81** (1956) 379–393

B. H. Arnold

[1] *Rings of operators on vector spaces*, Ann. of Math. **45** (1944) 24–49

G. I. Arsen'ev

[1] *Algebras of linear operators in Hilbert space*, Uč. Zap. Borisoglebsk, Gos. Ped. Inst. (1958) no. 5, 119–132

K. E. Aubert

[1] *Convex ideals in ordered group algebras and the uniqueness of Haar measure*, Math. Scand. **6** (1958) 181–188

[2] *A representation theorem for function algebras with application to almost periodic functions*, Math. Scand. **7** (1959) 202–210

S. Aurora

[1] *Multiplicative norms for metric rings*, Pacific J. Math. **7** (1957) 1279–1304

W. G. Bade

[1] *Weak and strong limits of spectral operators*, Pacific J. Math **4** (1954), 393–413

[2] *On Boolean algebras of projections and algebras of operators*, Trans. Amer. Math. Soc. **80** (1955) 345–360

[3] *A multiplicity theory for boolean algebras of projections in Banach spaces*, Trans. Amer. Math. Soc. **92** (1959) 508–530

W. G. Bade and P. C. Curtis

[1] *Homomorphisms of commutative Banach algebras.* (To appear in Amer. J. Math.)

[2] *The Wedderburn decomposition of commutative Banach algebras.* (To appear in Amer. J. Math.)

F. S. Baher

[1] *On a basis in the space of continuous functions defined on a compactum*, Dokl. Akad. Nauk S.S.S.R. **101** (1955) 589–592

B. Banaschewski

[1] *On the Weierstrass–Stone approximation theorem*, Fund. Math. **44** (1957) 249–252

[2] *On certain extensions of function rings*, Canad. J. Math. **11** (1959) 87–96

H. Bauer

[1] *Uber die Beziehungen einer abstrakten Theorie des Riemann-Integrals sur Radonsche Masse*, Math. Z. **65** (1956) 448–482

L. E. Baum

[1] *Note on a paper of Civin and Yood*, Proc. Amer. Math. Soc. **9** (1958) 207–208

H. S. Bear

[1] *Complex function algebras*, Trans. Amer. Math. Soc. **90** (1959) 383–393

[2] *A strong maximum modulus theorem for maximal function algebras*, Trans. Amer. Math. Soc. **92** (1959) 465–469

[3] *Some boundary properties of function algebras*, Proc. Amer. Math. Soc. **11** (1960) 1–4

S. K. Berberian

[1] *On the projection geometry of a finite AW⋆-algebra*, Trans. Amer. Math. Soc. **83** (1956) 493–509

[2] *The regular ring of a finite AW⋆-algebra*, Ann. of Math. (2) **65** (1957) 224–240

[3] *$N \times N$ matrices over an AW⋆-algebra*, Amer. J. Math. **80** (1958) 37–44

Y. M. Berezanskiı

[1] *On the center of the group ring of a compact group*, Dokl. Akad. Nauk S.S.S.R. **72** (1950) 825–828

[2] *On certain normed rings constructed from orthogonal polynomials*, Ukrain. Mat. Zurnal **3** (1951) 412–432

Y. M. Berezanskiĭ and S. G. Kreĭn

[1] *Continuous algebras*, Dokl. Akad. Nauk S.S.S.R. **72** (1950) 5–8

[2] *Some classes of continuous algebras*, Dokl. Akad. Nauk S.S.S.R. **72** (1950) 237–240

[3] *Hypercomplex systems with continual basis*, Uspehi Mat. Nauk (N.S.) **12** no. 1 (73) (1957) 147–152

F. A. Berezin, I. M. Gelfand, M. I. Graev, and M. A. Naĭmark

[1] *Representation of groups*, Uspehi Mat. Nauk (N.S.) **11** (1956) 13–40

L. Bers

[1] *On rings of analytic functions*, Bull. Amer. Math. Soc. **54** (1948) 311–315

A. Beurling

[1] *Sur les integrales de Fourier absolument convergentes*, Congrès des Math. Scand., Helsingfors (1938)

G. Birkhoff

[1] *Moyennes de fonctions bornées*, Algèbre et Théorie des Nombres, Coll. Int. de Centre Nat. de la Recherche Scientifique, No. **24** 143–153, Centre Nat. de la Recherche Scientifique, Paris (1950)

E. A. Bishop

[1] *The structure of certain measures*, Duke Math. J. **25** (1958) 283–290

[2] *Subalgebras of functions on a Riemann surface*, Pacific J. Math. **8** (1958) 29–50

[3] *Some theorems concerning function algebras*, Bull. Amer. Math. Soc. **65** (1959) 77–78

[4] *A minimal boundary for function algebras*, Pacific J. Math. **9** (1959) 629–642

A. Blair

[1] *Continuity of multiplication in operator algebras*, Proc. Amer. Math. Soc. **6** (1955) 209–210

R. J. Blattner

[1] *Automorphic group representations*, Pacific J. Math. **8** (1958) 665–677

E. K. Blum

[1] *The fundamental group of the principal component of a commutative Banach algebra*, Proc. Amer. Math. Soc. **4** (1953) 397–400

[2] *A theory of analytic functions in Banach algebras*, Trans. Amer. Math. Soc. **78** (1955) 343–370

S. Bochner and R. S. Phillips

[1] *Abslolutely convergent Fourier expansions for non-commutative normed rings*, Ann. of Math, **43** (1942) 409–418

H. F. Bohnenblust and S. Karlin

[1] *Geometrical properties of the unit sphere of Banach algebras*, Ann. of Math. (2) **62** (1955), 217–229.

R. Bonic

[1] *The involution in group algebras*, Ph.D. Dissertation Yale University (1960)

F. Bonsall

[1] *A minimal property of the norm in some Banach algebras*, J. London Math. Soc. **29** (1954) 156–164

[2] *Sublinear functionals and ideals in partially ordered vector spaces*, Proc. London Math. Soc. (3) **4** (1954) 402–418

[3] *Regular ideals of partially ordered vector spaces*, Proc. London Math. Soc. (3) **6** (1956) 626–640

F. Bonsall and A. W. Goldie

[1] *Algebras which represent their linear functionals*, Proc. Cambridge Philos. Soc. **49** (1953) 1–14

[2] *Annihilator algebras*, Proc. London Math. Soc. (3) **4** (1954) 154–167

D. G. Bourgin

[1] *Approximately isometric and multiplicative transformations on continuous function rings*, Duke Math. J. **16** (1949) 385–397

J. Braconnier

[1] *Les algèbres de groupes et leur représentations*, Ann. Univ. Lyon Sect. A (3) **15** (1952) 27–34

[2] *L'analyse harmonique dans les groupes abéliens*, II, Enseignement Math. (2) **2** (1956) 257–273

H. J. Bremerman

[1] *On a generalized Dirichlet problem for plurisubharmonic functions and pseudo-convex domains. Characterization of Šilov boundaries*, Trans. Amer. Math. Soc. **91** (1959) 246–276.

A. Brown

[1] *On a class of operators*, Proc. Amer. Math. Soc. **4** (1953) 723–728

B. Brown and N. H. McCoy

[1] *Radicals and subdirect sums*, Amer. J. Math. **69** (1947) 46–58

N. G. de Bruijn

[1] *Function theory in Banach algebras*, Ann. Acad. Sci. Fenn. Ser. A. I. no. 250/5 (1958) 13 pp.

R. C. Buck

[1] *Generalized group algebras*, Proc. Nat. Acad. Sci. U.S.A. **36** (1950) 747–749

[2] *Operator algebras and dual spaces*, Proc. Amer. Math. Soc. **3** (1952) 681–687

[3] *Bounded continuous functions on a locally compact space*, Mich. Math. J. **5** (1958) 95–104

A. P. Calderón

[1] *Singular integrals*, Segundo symposium sobre algunos problemos mathemáticos que se están estudiando en Latino América, (Julio, 1954) 319–328, Centro de Cooperación Científica de la UNESCO para América Latiná, Montevideo, Uruguay (1954)

A. P. Calderón and A. Zygmund

[1] *Algebras of certain singular operators*, Amer. J. Math. **78** (1956) 310–320

J. W. Calkin

[1] *Two-sided ideals and congruences in the ring of bounded operators in Hilbert space*, Ann. of Math. **42** (1941) 839–873

L. Carleson

[1] *On generators of normed rings*, 12 Skand. Math.-Kongr. Lund **1953** (1954) 16–17

E. Čech

[1] *On bicompact spaces*, Ann. of Math. **38** (1937) 823–844

B. Charles

[1] *Sur certaines anneaux commutatifs d'opérateurs linéaires*, C.R. Acad. Sci. Paris **236** (1953) 990

P. Civin

[1] *A maximum modulus property of maximal subalgebras*, Proc. Amer. Math. Soc. **10** (1959) 51–54

P. Civin and B. Yood

[1] *Ideals in multiplicative semi-groups of continuous functions*, Duke Math. J. **23** (1956) 325–334

[2] *Regular Banach algebras with a countable space of maximal regular ideals*, Proc. Amer. Math. Soc. **7** (1956) 1005–1010

[3] *Involutions on Banach algebras*, Pacific J. Math. **9** (1959) 415–436

E. A. Coddington

[1] *Some Banach algebras*, Proc. Amer. Math. Soc. **8** (1957) 258–261

P. J. Cohen

[1] *Factorization in group algebras*, Duke Math. J. **26** (1959) 199–205

E. Correll and M. Henriksen

[1] *On rings of bounded continuous functions with values in a division ring*, Proc. Amer. Math. Soc. **7** (1956) 194–198

M. Cotlar

[1] *On a theorem of Beurling and Kaplansky*, Pacific J. Math **4** (1954) 459–465

P. C. Curtis

[1] *Order and commutativity in Banach algebras*, Proc. Amer. Math. Soc. **9** (1958) 643–646

W. F. Darsow

[1] *Positive definite functions and states*, Ann. of Math. (2) **60** (1954) 447–453

C. Davis

[1] *Generators of the ring of bounded operators*, Proc. Amer. Math. Soc. **6** (1955) 970–972

M. M. Day

[1] *Amenable semigroups*, Ill. J. Math. **1** (1957) 509–544

N. G. De Bruijn

[1] *Function theory in Banach algebras*, Annales Accad. Scientiarum Fennicae, Series A. I. (1958) 13 pp.

J. Dieudonné

[1] *Sur le socle d'un anneau et les anneaux simples infinis*, Bull. Soc. Math. France **70** (1942) 46–75

[2] *Sur l'anneau des endomorphismes continus d'un espace normé*, C.R. Acad Sci. Paris **216** (1943) 713–715
[3] *Análise Harmônica*, Notes prepared by J. Abdelhay, Univ. Brasil Publ. no. 9 Ser. A, Rio de Janeiro (1952)
[4] *Sur la bicommutante d'une algèbre d'opérateurs*, Portugal Math. **14** (1955) 35–38
[5] *Sur la théorie spectrale*, J. Math. Pures Appl. (9) **35** (1956) 175–187

V. A. Ditkin
[1] *On the structure of ideals in certain normed rings*, Uchenye Zapiski Moskov. Gos. Univ. Matematika **30** (1939) 83–130
[2] *On a question about the formal multiplication of trigonometric series*, Dokl. Akad. Nauk S.S.S.R. **60** (1948) 1495–1498

J. Dixmier
[1] *Position relative de deux variétés linéaires fermées dans un espace de Hilbert*, Revue Sci. **86** (1948) 387–399
[2] *Fonctionelles linéaires sur l'ensemble des opérateurs bornés d'un espace hilbertien*, C.R. Acad. Sci. Paris **227** (1948) 948–950
[3] *Mesure de Haar et trace d'un opérateur*, C.R. Acad. Sci. Paris **228** (1949) 152–154
[4] *Les anneaus d'opérateurs de classe finie*, Ann. Sci. Ecole Norm. Sup. **66** (1949) 209–261
[5] *Les idéaux dans l'ensemble des variétés J d'un espace hilbertien*, Ann. Fac. Sci. Univ. Toulouse (4) **10** (1949) 91–114
[6] *Les fonctionelles linéaires sur l'ensemble des opérateurs bornés d'un espace de Hilbert*, Ann. of Math. **51** (1950) 387–408
[7] *Sur la reduction des anneaux d'opérateurs*, Ann. Sci. Ecole Norm. Sup. **68** (1951) 185–202
[8] *Sur certaines espaces considérés par M. H. Stone*, Summa Brasil Math. **2** (1951) 151–182
[9] *Applications* $\natural$ *dans les anneaux d'opérateurs*, Comp. Math. **10** (1952) 1–55
[10] *Algèbres quasi unitaires*, Comm. Math. Helv. **26** (1952) 275–322
[11] *Remarques sur les applications* $\natural$, Arch. Math. **3** (1952) 290–297
[12] *Formes linéaires sur un anneau d'opérateurs*, Bull. Soc. Math. de France **81** (1953) 9–39
[13] *Sus-anneaux abeliens maximaux dans les facteurs de type fini*, Ann. of Math. (2) **59** (1954) 279–286
[14] *Sur les anneaux d'opérateurs dans les espaces hilbertiens*, C.R. Acad. Sci. Paris **234** (1954) 439–441

[15] *Les algèbres d'opérateurs dans l'espace hilbertien* (*Algèbres de von Neumann*), Cahiers scientifique, Fas. XXV, Gauthier-Villars, Paris (1957)

[16] *Sur les représentations unitaires des groupes de Lie algèbriques*, Ann. Inst. Fourier, Grenoble **7** (1957) 315–328

Y. Domar

[1] *Harmonic analysis based on certain commutative Banach algebras*, Acta Math. **96** (1956) 1–66

[2] *Closed primary ideals in a class of Banach algebras*, Math. Scand. **7** (1959) 109–125

G. I. Domračeva

[1] *Ideals in normal subrings of a ring of continuous functions*, Leningrad Gos. Ped. Inst. Uč. Zap. **166** (1958) 29–38

W. F. Donaghue, Jr.

[1] *The Banach algebra l^1 with an application to linear transformations*, Duke Math. J. **23** (1956) 533–537

N. Dunford

[1] *Spectral theory, I. Convergence to projections*, Trans. Amer. Math. Soc. **54** (1943) 185–217

[2] *Resolutions of the identity for commutative B★-algebras of operators*, Acta Sci. Math. Szeged **12** (1950) 51–56

[3] *Spectral theory in abstract spaces and Banach algebras*, Proc. of Symposium on Spectral Theory and Differential Problems, pp. 1–65, Okla. Agri. and Mech. Coll., Stillwater Okla. (1951)

[4] *Spectral operators*, Pacific J. Math **4** (1954) 321–354

[5] *A survey of the theory of spectral operators*, Bull. Amer. Math. Soc. **64** (1958) 217–274

N. Dunford and J. Schwartz

[1] *Linear Operators*, Part I: General Theory, Interscience, New York (1958)

N. Dunford and I. E. Segal

[1] *Semi-groups of operators and the Weierstrass theorem*, Bull. Amer. Math. Soc. **52** (1946) 911–914

H. A. Dye

[1] *The Radon-Nikodym theorem for finite rings of operators*, Trans. Amer. Math. Soc. **72** (1952) 243–280

[2] *The unitary structure in finite rings of operators*, Duke Math. J. **20** (1953) 55–69

[3] *On the geometry of projections in certain operator algebras*, Ann. of Math. (2) **61** (1955) 73–89

W. F. Eberlein

[1] *Abstract ergdoic theorems and weak almost perodic functions*, Trans. Amer. Math. Soc. **67** (1949) 217–240

[2] *Spectral theory and harmonic analysis*, Proc. of Symposium on Spectral Theory and Differential Problems, pp. 209–219 Okla. Agri. and Mech. Coll., Stillwater Okla. (1955)

D. A. Edwards

[1] *On absolutely convergent Dirichlet series*, Proc. Amer. Math. Soc. **8** (1957) 1067–1074

D. A. Edwards and C. T. Ionescu Tulcea

[1] *Some remarks on commutative algebras of operators on Banach spaces*, Trans. Amer. Math. Soc. **93** (1959) 541–551

R. E. Edwards

[1] *Multiplicative norms on Banach algebras*, Proc. Cambridge Philos. Soc. **47** (1951) 473–474

[2] *On certain algebras of measures*, Pacific J. Math. **5** (1955) 379–389

[3] *Note on two theorems about function algebras*, Mathematika **4** (1957) 138–139

[4] *Algebras of holomorphic functions*, Proc. London Math. Soc. (3) **7** (1957) 510–517

L. Ehrenpreis and F. I. Mautner

[1] *Some properties of the Fourier transform on semi-simple Lie groups I*, Annals of Math. **61** (1955), 406–439; II. Trans. Amer. Math. Soc. **84** (1957) 1–55; III. Ibid. **90** (1959) 431–484

M. Eidelheit

[1] *Concerning rings of continuous functions*, Ann. of Math. **41** (1940) 391–393

[2] *On isomorphisms of rings of linear operators*, Studia Math. **9** (1940) 97–105

C. Feldman

[1] *The Wedderburn principal theorem in Banach algebras*, Proc. Amer. Math. Soc. **2** (1951) 771–777

J. Feldman

[1] *Embedding of $AW^\star$-algebras*, Duke Math. J. **23** (1956) 303–307

[2] *Isopmorphisms of finite type II rings of operators*, Ann. of Math (2) **63** (1956) 565–571

[3] *Nonseparability of certain finite factors*, Proc. Amer. Math. Soc. **7** (1956) 23–26

[4] *Some connections between topological and algebraic properties in rings of operators*, Duke Math. J. **23** (1956), 365–370

J. Feldman and J. M. G. Fell

[1] *Separable representations of rings of operators*, Ann. of Math. (2) **65** (1957) 241–249

J. Feldman and R. V. Kadison

[1] *The closure of the regular operators in a ring of operators*, Proc. Amer. Math. Soc. **5** (1954) 909–916

J. M. G. Fell

[1] *Representations of weakly closed algebras*, Math. Ann. **133** (1957) 118–126

J. M. G. Fell and J. L. Kelley

[1] *An algebra of unbounded operators*, Proc. Nat. Acad. Sci. U.S.A. **38** (1952) 592–598

S. R. Foguel

[1] *Normal operators of finite multiplicity*, Comm. Pure and Appl. Math. **11** (1958) 297–313

[2] *The relations between a spectral operator and its scalar part*, Pacific J. Math. **8** (1958) 51–65

[3] *Boolean algebras of projections of finite multiplicity*, Pacific J. Math. **9** (1959) 681–693

C. Foias

[1] *Elementi completamente continui e quasi completamente di un' algebra di Banach*, Atti Accad. Naz. Lincei Rend. Cl. Sci. Fis. Mat. Nat. (8) **20** (1956) 155–160

[2] *Sur certains théorèms de J. von Neumann concernant les ensembles spectraux*, Acta Sci. Math. Szeged **18** (1957) 15–20

[3] *On a commutative extension of a commutative Banach algebra*, Pacific J. Math. **8** (1958) 407–410

M. Freundlich

[1] *Completely continuous elements of a normed ring*, Duke Math. J. **16** (1949) 273–283

B. Fuglede and R. V. Kadison

[1] *On a conjecture of Murray and von Neumann*, Proc. Nat. Acad. Sci. U.S.A. **37** (1951) 420–425

[2] *Determinant theory in finite factors*, Ann. of Math. **55** (1952) 520–530

K. Fujiwara

[1] *Sur les anneaux des fonctions continues à support compact*, Math. J. Okayama Univ. **3** (1954) 175–184

M. Fukamiya

[1] *Topological method for Tauberian theorem*, Tôhoku Math. J. (1949) 77–87

[2] *On B*★*-algebras*, Proc. Jap. Acad. **27** (1951) 321–327

[3] *On a theorem of Gelfand and Neumark and the B*★*-algebra*, Kumamoto J. of Sci. Ser. A.1, no. 1 (1952) 17–22

M. Fukamiya, M. Misonou, and Z. Takeda

[1] *On order and commutativity of B*★*-algebras*, Tôhoku Math. J. (2) **6** (1954) 89–93

B. R. Gelbaum

[1] *Tensor products of Banach algebras*, Canad. J. Math. **11** (1929) 297–319

I. M. Gelfand

[1] *On normed rings*, Dokl. Akad. Nauk S.S.S.R. **23** (1939) 430–432

[2] *To the theory of normed rings II. On absolutely convergent trigonometric series and integrals*, Dokl. Akad. Nauk S.S.S.R. **25** (1939) 570–572

[3] *To the theory of normed rings III. On the ring of almost periodic functions*, Dokl. Akad. Nauk S.S.S.R. **25** (1939) 573–574

[4] *Normierte Ringe*, Mat. Sbornik **9** (1941) 3–24

[5] *Ideals and primäre Ideale in normierten Ringen*, Mat. Sbornik. **9** (1941) 41–48

[6] *Zur Theorie der Charactere der abelschen topologischen Gruppen*, Mat. Sbornik **9** (1941) 49–50

[7] *Über absolut konvergente trigonometrische Reihen und Integrale*, Mat. Sbornik **9** (1941) 51–66

[8] *On subrings of the ring of continuous functions*, Uspehi. Mat. Nauk (N.S.) **12** (1957), No. 1 (73) 249–251

I. M. Gelfand and A. Kolmogoroff

[1] *On rings of continuous functions in topological spaces*, Dokl. Akad. Nauk. S.S.S.R. **22** (1939) 11–15

I. M. Gelfand and M. A. Naĭmark

[1] *On the embedding of normed rings into the ring of operators in Hilbert space*, Mat. Sbornik **12** (1943) 197–213

[2] *Unitary representations of the Lorentz group*, Izvestiya Akad. Nauk. S.S.S.R. Ser. Mat. **11** (1947) 411–504

[3] *The trace in fundamental and supplementary series of representations of the complex unimodular group*, Dokl. Akad. Nauk S.S.S.R. **61** (1948) 9–11

[4] *Normed rings with their involution and their representations*, Izvestiya Akad. Nauk S.S.S.R. Ser. Mat. **12** (1948) 445–480

[5] *Unitäre Darstellungen der Klassischen Gruppen*, Akademie-Verlag, Berlin (1957)

I. M. Gelfand and D. A. Raikov

[1] *Irreducible unitary representations of locally bicompact groups*, Dokl. Akad. Nauk S.S.S.R. **42** (1944) 199–201; Mat. Sbornik **13** (1943) 301–316

I. M. Gelfand, D. A. Raikov, and G. E. Šilov

[1] *Commutative normed rings*, Uspehi Matem. Nauk **1** (1946) 48–146; Amer. Math. Soc. Transl. (2) **5** (1957) 115–220

I. M. Gelfand and G. E. Šilov

[1] *Über verschiedene Methoden der Einfuhrung der Topologie in die Menge der maximalen Ideale eines normierten Ringen*, Mat. Sbornik **9** (1941) 25–39

Al. Ghika

[1] *Algèbres de transformations linéaires continues d'un espace hilbertien dans un autre*, Com. Acad. R. P. Romîne **7** (1957) 831–834

[2] *Decompositions spectrales généralisées des transformations linéaire d'un espace hilbertien dans un autre*, Rev. Math. Pures Appl. **2** (1957) 61–109

L. Gillman

[1] *Rings with Hausdorff structure space*, Fund. Math. **45** (1957) 1–16

L. Gillman, M. Henriksen, and M. Jerison

[1] *On a theorem of Gelfand and Kolmogoroff concerning maximal ideals in rings of continuous functions*, Proc. Amer. Math. Soc. **5** (1954) 447–455

L. Gillman and M. Jerison

[1] *Rings of continuous functions*, Van Nostrand, Princeton (1960)

R. Godement

[1] *Extension à une groupe abélien quelconque des théorèmes tauberiens de N. Wiener et d'un théorème de A. Beurling*, C.R. Acad. Sci. Paris **223** (1946) 16–18

[2] *Théorèmes taubériens et théorie spectrals*, Ann. Sci. Ecole Norm. Sup. **64** (1948) 119–138

[3] *Théorie générale des sommes continues d'espaces de Banach*, C.R. Acad. Sci. Paris **228** (1949) 1321–1323

[4] *Sur la théorie des représentations unitaires*, Ann. of Math. **53** (1951) 68–124

[5] *Memoire sur la théorie des caractères dans les groupes localement compacts unimodulaires*, J. Math. Pures Appl. (9) **30** (1951) 1–110

[6] *A theory of spherical functions I*, Trans. Amer. Math. Soc. **73** (1952) 496–556

[7] *Théorie des characteres I, Algèbres unitaires*, Ann. of Math. **59** (1954) 47–62; *II, Définitions et propriétés générales des characteres*, Ibid. **59** (1954) 63–85

I. C. Gohberg

[1] *On an application of the theory of normed rings to singular integral equations*, Uspehi Matem. Nauk (N.S.) **7**, No. 2 (48) (1952) 149–156

J. K. Goldhaber and E. Wolk

[1] *Maximal ideals in rings of bounded continuous functions*, Duke Math. J. **21** (1954) 565–569

M. Goldman

[1] *Structure of $AW^\star$-algebras I*, Duke Maths. J. **23** (1956) 23–34

[2] *On subfactors of type II_1*, Mich. Math. J. **6** (1959) 167–172

H. Gonshor

[1] *Spectral theory for a class of non-normal operators II*, Canad. J. Math. **8** (1956) 449–461; *II.* Ibid. **10** (1958) 97–102

H. F. Green

[1] *Rings of infinite matrices*, Quart. J. Math. Oxford Ser. (2) **9** (1958) 73

E. L. Griffin

[1] *Some contributions to the theory of rings of operators*, Trans. Amer. Math. Soc. **75** (1953) 471–504; *II.* Ibid. **79** (1955) 389–400

A. Grothendieck

[1] *Un résultat sur les dual d'une $C^\star$-algebre*, J. Math. Pures Appl. (9) **36** (1957) 97–108

A. Guichardet

[1] *Une caractérisation des algèbres de von Neumann de type I* C.R. Acad. Sci. Paris **248** (1959) 3398–3403

[2] *Sur un problème posé par G. W. Mackey*, C. R. Paris **250** (1960) 962–963

Z. I. Halilov

[1] *Linear singular equations in a normed ring*, Izvestiya Akad. Nauk S.S.S.R. Ser. Mat. **13** (1949) 163–176

[2] *Linear singular equations in a unitary ring*, Mat. Sbornik **25** (1949) 169–188

P. R. Halmos

[1] *Introduction to Hilbert space and the theory of multiplicity*, Chelsea, New York (1951)

[2] *Measure Theory*, Van Nostrand, New York (1950)

P. R. Halmos and G. Lumer

[1] *Square roots of operators II*, Proc. Amer. Math. Soc. **5** (1954) 589–595

P. R. Halmos, G. Lumer and J. J. Schaffer

[1] *Square roots of operators*, Proc. Amer. Math. Soc. **4** (1953) 142–149

Harish-Chandra

[1] *Representations of a semi-simple Lie group on a Banach space I*, Trans. Amer. Math. Soc. **75** (1953) 185–243; *II*, *III*, Ibid. **76** (1954) 26–65, 234–253

S. Hartman

[1] *Quelques rémarques sur les expansions de Fourier*, Studia Math. **14** (1954) 200–208

P. Hartman

[1] *On Laurent operators on l_p*, Proc. Amer. Math. Soc. **8** (1957) 45–48

A. Hausner

[1] *Ideals in a certain Banach algebra*, Proc. Amer. Math. Soc. **8** (1957) 246–249

[2] *The Tauberian theorem for group algebras of vector-valued functions*, Pacific J. Math. **7** (1957) 1603–1610

[3] *A generalized Stone–Weierstrass theorem*, Archiv der Math. **10** (1959) 85–87

P. Hebroni

[1] *Über lineare Differentialgleichungen in Ringen*, Comp. Math. **5** (1938) 403–429

[2] *On L-functions in the abstract differential ring with application to integrodifferential equations I, II*, Riveon Lematematika **9** (1955) 54–69; **10** (1956) 49–67

L. J. Heider

[1] *A note on a theorem of K. G. Wolfson*, Proc. Amer. Math. Soc. **6** (1955) 305–308

[2] *Directed limits on rings of continuous functions*, Duke Math J. **23** (1956) 293–296

S. Helgason

[1] *The derived algebra of a Banach algebra*, Proc. Nat. Acad. Sci. U.S.A. **40** (1954) 994–995

[2] *A characterization of the intersection of L^1-spaces*, Math. Scand. **4** (1956) 5–8

[3] *Multipliers of Banach algebras*, Ann. of Math. (2) **64** (1956) 240–254

[4] *Topologies of group algebras and a theorem of Littlewood*, Trans. Amer. Math. Soc. **86** (1957) 269–283

H. Helson

[1] *Spectral synthesis of bounded functions*, Arkiv. f. Mat. **1** (1951) 497–502

[2] *On the ideal structure of group algebras*, Arkiv. f. Mat. **2** (1952) 83–86

[3] *Isomorphisms of abelien group algebras*, Arkiv. f. Mat. **3** (1953) 475–487

H. Helson et J.-P. Kahane

[1] *Sur les fonctions opérant dans les algèbres de transformées de Fourier de suites ou de fonctions sommables*, C.R. Acad. Sci. Paris **247** (1958) 626–628

H. Helson, J.-P. Kahane, Y. Katznelson and W. Rudin

[1] *The functions which operate on Fourier Transforms*, Acta Math. **102** (1959) 135–157

H. Helson and F. Quigley

[1] *Existence of maximal ideals in algebras of continuous functions*, Proc. Amer. Math. Soc. **8** (1957) 115–119

[2] *Maximal algebras of continuous functions*, Proc. Amer. Math. Soc. **8** (1957) 111–114

M. Henricksen

[1] *On the equivalence of the ring, lattice and semi-group of continuous functions*, Proc. Amer. Math. Soc. **7** (1956) 959–960

[2] *On minimal completely regular spaces associated with a given ring of continuous functions*, Mich. Math. J. **4** (1957) 61–64

C. S. Herz

[1] *Spectral synthesis for the Cantor set*, Proc. Nat. Acad. Sci. U.S.A. **42** (1956) 42–43

E. Hewitt

[1] *Certain generalizations of the Weierstrass approximation theorem*, Duke Math. J. **14** (1947) 419–427

[2] *On rings of continuous real valued functions I*, Trans. Amer. Math. Soc. **64** (1948) 45–99

[3] *A note on normed algebras*, Anais Acad. Brasil Ci. **22** (1950) 171–174

[4] *The asymmetry of certain algebras of Fourier-Stieltjes transforms*, Mich. Math. J. **5** (1958) 149–158

E. Hewitt and J. H. Williamson

[1] *Note on absolutely convergent Dirichlet series*, Proc. Amer. Math. Soc. **8** (1957) 863–868

E. Hewitt and H. S. Zuckerman

[1] *Finite dimensional convolution algebras*, Acta Math. **93** (1955) 67–119

[2] *Harmonic analysis for certain semi-groups*, Proc. Nat. Acad. Sci. U.S.A. **42** (1956) 253–255

[3] *The l_1-algebra of a commutative semi-group*, Trans. Amer. Math. Soc. **83** (1956) 70–97

[4] *Structure theory for a class of convolution algebras*, Pacific J. Math. **7** (1957) 913–941

G. Higman

[1] *The compacting of topological spaces*, Quart. J. Math. Oxford Ser. **19** (1948) 27–32

E. Hille

[1] *On the theory of characters of groups and semi-groups in normed vector-rings*, Proc. Nat. Acad. Sci. U.S.A. **30** (1944) 58–60

[2] *Functional analysis and semi-groups*, Amer. Math. Soc. Coll. Publ. **31**, New York (1948)

[3] *On roots and logarithms of elements of a complex Banach algebra* Math. Ann. **136** (1958) 46–57

[4] *Inverse function theorem in Banach algebras*, Bull. Calcutta Math. Soc. (To appear.)

E. Hille and R. S. Phillips

[1] *Functional analysis and semi-groups*, Amer. Math. Soc. Coll. Publ. **31**, Providence (1957)

R. Hirschfeld

[1] *Sur les semi-groupes de transformations de Reynolds*, C.R. Acad. Sci. Paris **245** (1957) 1493–1495

I. Hirschman

[1] *Sur les polynomes ultrasphériques*, C.R. Acad. Sci. Paris **242** (1956) 2212–2214

K. Hoffman

[1] *Boundary behavior of generalized analytic functions*, Trans. Amer. Math. Soc. **87** (1958) 447–466

K. Hoffman and I. M. Singer

[1] *Maximal subalgebras of $C(\Gamma)$*, Amer. J. Math. **79** (1957) 295–305

[2] *On some problems of Gelfand*, Uspehi Mat. Nauk **14** (1959) 99–114

[3] *Maximal algebras of continuous functions.* (To appear.)

J. C. Holladay

[1] *Boundary conditions for algebras of continuous functions*, Ph.D. Dissertation, Yale University (1953)

[2] *A note on the Stone–Weierstrass theorem for quaternions*, Proc. Amer. Math. Soc. **8** (1957) 656–657

E. Hongo

[1] *A note on the commutor of certain operator algebras*, Bull. Kyushu Inst. Tech. (Math. Nat. Sci.) no. 1 (1955) 19–22

[2] *On left rings of certain *-algebras*, Bull Kyushu Inst. Tech. (Math., Nat. Sci.) no. 2 (1956) 1–15

[3] *On quasi-unitary algebras with semi-finite left rings*, Bull. Kyushu Inst. Tech. (Math., Nat. Sci.) no. 3 (1957) 1–10

[4] *On some properties on quasi-unitary algebras*, Bull. Kyushu Inst. Tech. (Math., Nat. Sci.) no. 4 (1958) 1–6

[5] *On left multiplicative operators on a quasi-unitary algebra*, Bull. Kyushu Inst. Tech. (Math. Nat. Sci.) no. 5 (1959) 19–22

E. Hongo and M. Orihara

[1] *A remark on a quasi-unitary algebra*, Yokohama Math. J. **2** (1954) 69–72

Ya. I. Hurgin

[1] *On subrings of the ring of complex continuous functions*, Moskov Gos. Univ. Uč. Zap. 145, Mat. 3 (1949) 165–167

C. Ionescu Tulcea

[1] *Spectral representation of certain semi-groups of operators*, J. of Math. and Mech. **8** (1959) 95–109

K. Iseki

[1] *On B*-algebras*, Koninkl. Nederl. Akad. van Wetenschappen, Amsterdam **15** (1953) 12–14

[2] *Sur les anneaux normés de Hilbert I*, C.R. Acad. Sci. Paris **236** (1953) 1123–1125; *II*, Ibid. **237** (1953) 545–546

T. Ishii

[1] *On homomorphisms of the ring of continuous functions onto the real numbers*, Proc. Japan Acad. **33** (1957) 419–423

U. Isiwata

[1] *On the ring of all bounded continuous functions*, Sci. Rep. Tokyo Kyoika Daigaku Sect. A **5** (1957) 293–294

N. Iwahori

[1] *A proof of Tannaka duality theorem*, Sci. Papers Coll. Gen. Ed. Univ. Tokyo **8** (1958) 1–4

K. Iwasawa

[1] *On group rings of topological groups*, Proc. Imp. Acad. Tokyo **20** (1944) 67–70

N. Jacobson

[1] *Structure theory of simple rings without finiteness assumptions*, Trans. Amer. Math. Soc. **57** (1945) 228–245

[2] *The radical and semi-simplicity for arbitrary rings*, Amer. J. Math. **67** (1945) 300–320

[3] *A topology for the set of primitive ideals in an arbitrary ring*, Proc. Nat. Acad. Sci U.S.A. **31** (1945) 333–338

[4] *On the theory of primitive rings*, Ann. of Math. **48** (1947) 8–21

[5] *Structure of Rings*, Amer. Math. Soc. Colloq. Publ. no. 37, Providence (1956)

[6] *Structure theory for algebraic algebras*, Ann. of Math. **46** (1945) 695–767

H. Jerison

[1] *An algebra associated with a compact group*, Pacific J. Math. **5** (1955) 933–939

M. Jerison and G. Rabson

[1] *Convergence theorems obtained from induced homomorphisms of a group algebra*, Ann. of Math. **63** (1956) 176–190

G. P. Johnson

[1] *Spaces of functions with values in a Banach algebra*, Trans. Amer. Math. Soc. **92** (1959) 411–429

R. V. Kadison

[1] *A representation theory for commutative topological algebras*, Memoirs of Amer. Math. Soc. No. 7, New York (1951)

[2] *Order properties of bounded self-adjoint operators*, Proc. Amer. Math. Soc. **2** (1951) 505–510

[3] *Isometries of operator algebras*, Ann. of Math. **54** (1951) 325–338

[4] *A generalized Schwarz inequality and algebraic invariants for operator algebras*, Ann. of Math. **56** (1952) 494–503

[5] *Infinite unitary groups*, Trans. Amer. Math. Soc. **72** (1952) 386–399

[6] *Infinite general linear groups*, Trans. Amer. Math. Soc. **76** (1954) 66–91

[7] *On the general linear group of infinite factors*, Duke Math. J. **22** (1955) 119–122

[8] *On the additivity of the trace in finite factors*, Proc. Nat. Acad. Sci. U.S.A. **41** (1955) 385–387

[9] *Isomorphisms of factors of infinite type*, Canad. J. Math. **7** (1955) 322–327

[10] *On the orthogonalization of operator representations*, Amer. J. Math. **77** (1955) 600–620

[11] *Multiplicity theory for operator algebras*, Proc. Nat. Acad. Sci. U.S.A. **41** (1955) 169–173

[12] *Report on operator algebras*, Arden House Conference on Operator Theory and Group Representations, Publ. 3§7 Nat. Acad. Sci. N.R.C., Wash. D.C. (1955) pp. 4–10

[13] *Operator algebras with a faithful weakly-closed representation*, Ann. of Math **64** (1956) 175–181

[14] *Irreducible operator algebras*, Proc. Nat. Acad. Sci. U.S.A. **43** (1957) 273–276

[15] *Unitary invariants for representations of operator algebras*, Ann. of Math. **66** (1957) 304–379

[16] *Theory of operators II: Operator algebras*, Bull. Amer. Math. Soc. **64** (von Neumann supplement) (1958) 61–85

R. V. Kadison and I. M. Singer

[1] *Three test problems in operator theory*, Pacific J. Math. **7** (1957) 1101–1106

[2] *Extensions of pure states*, Amer. J. Math. **81** (1959) 383–400

J.-P Kahne and Y. Katznelson

[1] *Sur la réciproque du théorème de Wiener-Lévy*, C.R. Acad. Sci. Paris **248** (1959) 1279–1281

J.-P. Kahane and W. Rudin

[1] *Caractérisation de fonctions qui opèrent sur les coefficients de Fourier-Stieltjes*, C.R. Acad. Sci. Paris **247** (1958) 773–775

S. Kakutani

[1] *Simultaneous extension of continuous functions considered as a positive linear operation*, Jap. J. Math. **17** (1940) 1–4

[2] *Rings of analytic functions*, Lectures on functions of a complex variable, pp. 71–83, The Univ. of Mich. Press, Ann Arbor (1955)

S. Kakutani and G. W. Mackey

[1] *Two characterizations of real Hilbert space*, Ann. of Math. **45** (1944) 50–58

[2] *Ring and lattice characterizations of complex Hilbert space*, Bull. Amer. Math. Soc. **52** (1946) 727–733

G. K. Kalish

[1] *On uniform spaces and topological algebra*, Bull. Amer. Math. Soc. **52** (1946) 936–939

S. Kametani

[1] *An elementary proof of the fundamental theorem of normed fields*, J. Math. Soc. Japan **4** (1952) 96–99

I. Kaplansky

[1] *Topological rings*, Amer. J. Math. **69** (1947) 153–183

[2] *Topological rings*, Bull. Amer. Math. Soc. **54** (1948) 809–826

[3] *Regular Banach algebras*, J. Ind. Math. Soc. **12** (1948) 57–62

[4] *Dual rings*, Ann. of Math. **49** (1948) 689–701

[5] *Normed algebras*, Duke Math. J. **16** (1949) 399–418

[6] *Primary ideals in group algebras*, Proc. Nat. Acad. Sci. U.S.A. **35** (1949) 133–136

[7] *Quelsques résultats sur les anneaux des opérateurs*, C.R. Acad. Sci. Paris **231** (1950) 485–486

[8] *Projections in Banach algebras*, Ann. of Math. **53** (1951) 235–249

[9] *The structure of certain operator algebras*, Trans. Amer. Math. Soc. **70** (1951) 219–255

[10] *A theorem on rings of operators*, Pacific J. Math. **1** (1951) 227–232

[11] *Group algebras in the large*, Tôhoku Math. J. **3** (1951) 249–256

[12] *Algebras of type I*, Ann. of Math. **56** (1952) 460–472

[13] *Symmetry of Banach algebras*, Proc. Amer. Math. Soc. **3** (1952) 396–399

[14] *Modules over operator algebras*, Amer. J. Math. **75** (1953) 839–858

[15] *Ring isomorphisms of Banach algebras*, Canad. J. Math. **6** (1954) 374–381

[16] *Topological Algebra*, Univ. of Chi. Notes (1952)

[17] *Rings of Operators* (notes prepared by S. Berberian with an appendix by R. Blattner) Univ. of Chi. Notes (1955)

[18] *Functional analysis. Some aspects of analysis and probability*, pp. 1–34. Surveys in Applied Mathematics, vol. 4, John Wiley and Sons, New York 1958

S. Kasahara

[1] *Sur un théorème de Gelfand*, Proc. Japan Acad. **32** (1956) 131–134

Y. Katznelson

[1] *Sur les fonctions opérant sur l'algèbre des séries de Fourier absolument convergentes*, C.R. Acad. Sci. Paris **247** (1958) 404–406

[2] *Algèbras caractérisées par les fonctions que opèrant sur elles*, C.R. Acad. Sci. Paris **247** (1958) 903–905

Y. Kawada

[1] *Über den Dualitätsatz der charaktere nichtokommutativen Gruppen*, Proc. Phys.-Math. Soc. Japan (3) **24** (1942) 97–109

[2] *Bemerkungen über das Weilsche Mass auf einer Abelschen Gruppe*, Proc. Imp. Acad. Tokyo **19** (1943) 348–355

[3] *Über die Erweiterung der maximalen Ideals in normierten Ringen*, Proc. Imp. Acad. Tokyo **19** (1943) 267–268

[4] *Über der Operatorenring Banachscher Räume*, Proc. Imp. Acad. Tokyo **19** (1943) 616–621

[5] *On the group ring of a topological group*, Math. Japonicae **1** (1948) 1–5

J. L. Kelley

[1] *Commutative operator algebras*, Proc. Acad. Sci. U.S.A. **38** (1952) 598–605

[2] *Averaging operators on $C_\infty(X)$*, Ill. J. Math. **2** (1958) 214–223

J. L. Kelley and R. L. Vaught

[1] *The positive cone in Banach algebras*, Trans. Amer. Math. Soc. **74** (1953) 44–45

I. Kenkichi

[1] *On group rings of topological groups*, Proc. Imp. Acad. Tokyo **20** (1944) 67–70

E. R. Keown

[1] *Reflexive Banach algebras*, Proc. Amer. Math. Soc. **6** (1955) 252–259

J. Khourguine and N. Tschetnine

[1] *Sur les sus–anneaux fermés de l'anneau des fonctions à n derivées continués*, Dokl. Akad. Nauk S.S.S.R. **29** (1940) 288–291

M. Kimura

[1] *A note on normed rings*, Kodai Math. Sem. Rep. **3** (1949) 23

D. C. Kleiniecke

[1] *On operator commutators*, Proc. Amer. Math. Soc. **8** (1957) 535–536

K. Kodaira and S. Kakutani

[1] *Normed ring of a locally compact Abelian group*, Proc. Imp. Acad. Tokyo **19** (1943) 360–365

F. Koehler

[1] *Note on a theorem of Gelfand and Šilov*. Proc. Amer. Math. Soc. **2** (1951) 541–543

C. W. Kohls

[1] *Ideals in rings of continuous functions*, Fund. Math. **45** (1957) 28–50

M. Kondo

[1] *Les anneaux des opérateurs et les dimensions*, Proc. Imp. Acad. Tokyo **20** (1944) 389–398; *II*, Ibid. **20** (1944) 689–693

[2] *Sur les réductibilité des anneaux des opérateurs*, Proc. Imp. Acad. Tokyo **20** (1944) 432–438

B. O. Koopman

[1] *Exponential limiting products in Banach algebras*, Trans. Amer. Math. Soc. **70** (1951) 256–276

B. I. Korenblyum

[1] *On certain special commutative normed rings*, Dokl. Akad. Nauk S.S.S.R. **64** (1949) 281–284

[2] *Generalization of Wiener's Tauberian theorem and the spectrum of fast-growing functions*, Dokl. Akad. Nauk S.S.S.R. **111** (1956) 280–282

[3] *On a normed ring of functions with convolution*, Dokl. Akad. Nauk S.S.S.R. **115** (1957) 226–229

Sh. Koshi

[1] *On Weierstrass–Stone's theorem*, J. Math. Soc. Japan **5** (1953) 351–352

G. L. Krabbe

[1] *Abelian rings and spectra of operators on l_p*, Proc. Amer. Math. Soc. **7** (1956) 783–790

[2] *Spectral isomorphisms for some rings of infinite matrices on a Banach space*, Amer. J. Math. **78** (1956) 42–50

[3] *Spectra of convolution operators on L^p and rings of factor-sequences*, Quart. J. Math. Oxford Ser. (2) **8** (1957) 1–12

[4] *Convolution operators which are not of scalar type*, Math. Zeitschr. **69** (1958) 346–350

[5] *Vaguely normal operators on a Banach space*, Archive for Rational Mech. and Analysis **3** (1959) 51–59

[6] *Convolution operators that satisfy the spectral theorem*, Math. Zeitschr. **70** (1959) 446–462

[7] *On the logarithm of a uniformly bounded operator*, Trans. Amer. Math. Soc. **81** (1956) 155–166

M. Krein

[1] *A ring of functions on a topological group*, Dokl. Akad. Nauk S.S.S.R. **29** (1940) 275–280

[2] *On a special ring of functions*, Dokl. Akad. Nauk S.S.S.R. **29** (1940) 355–359

[3] *On almost periodic functions on a topological group*, Dokl. Akad. Nauk S.S.S.R. **30** (1941) 5–8

[4] *On positive functionals on almost periodic functions*, Dokl. Akad. Nauk S.S.S.R. **30** (1941) 9–12

[5] *Sur une généralisation du théorème de Plancherel au cas des intégrales de Fourier sur les groupes topologiques commutatifs*, Dokl. Akad. Nauk S.S.S.R. **30** (1941) 484–488

[6] *Hermitian positive kernels on homogeneous spaces I*, Ukrain. Mat. Zurnal **1** (1949) 64–98; *II*, Ibid. **2** (1950) 10–59

[7] *On positive additive functionals in linear normed spaces*, Comm. Inst. Sci. Math. Méc. Univ. Kharkoff [Zapiski Inst. Mat. Mech.] (4) **14** (1937) 227–237

W. Kundt

[1] *Bemerkung zu einer Satz über kommutative Banach-Algebren*, Archiv. der Math. **9** (1958) 436–438

R. A. Kunze

[1] *An operator theoretic approach to generalized Fourier transforms*, Ann. of Math. **69** (1959) 1–14

P. Lax

[1] *Symmetrizable linear transformations*, Comm. Pure Appl. Math. **7** (1954) 633–647

K. de Leeuw

[1] *Functions on circular subsets of the space of n complex variables*, Duke Math. J. **24** (1957) 415–431

[2] *Homogenous algebras on compact abelian groups*, Trans. Amer. Math. Soc. **87** (1958) 327–386

K. de Leeuw and H. Mirkil

[1] *Intrinsic algebras on the torus*, Trans. Amer. Math. Soc. **81** (1956) 320–330

Z. L. Leibenzon

[1] *On the ring of continuous functions on a circle*, Uspehi Matem. Nauk (N.S.) **7** (50) (1952) 163–164

[2] *On the ring of functions with absolutely convergent Fourier series* Uspehi Matem. Nauk (N.S.) **9**, no. 3 (61) (1954) 157–162

H. Leptin

[1] *Zur Reduktionstheorie Hilbertscher Räume*, Math. Z. **69** (1958) 40–58

[2] *Reduktion linearer Funktionale auf Operatorenringen*, Abh. Math. Sem. Univ. Hamburg **22** (1958) 98–113

P. Lévy

[1] *Sur la convergence absolue des séries de Fourier*, Comp. Math. **1** (1934) 1–14

B. Lewitan

[1] *Normed rings generated by the generalized operation of translation*, Dokl. Akad. Nauk S.S.S.R. **47** (1945) 3–6

[2] *Plancherel's theorem for the generalized translation operator*, Dokl. Akad. Nauk S.S.S.R. **47** (1945) 138–321

[3] *The theorem on the representation of positively definite functions for the generalized operation of translation*, Dokl. Akad. Nauk S.S.S.R. **47** (1945) 159–161

[4] *On the theory of unitary representations of locally compact groups* Mat. Sbornik **19** (1946) 407–427

[5] *Rings of operators and operations of generalized translation*, Dokl. Akad. Nauk S.S.S.R. **52** (1946) 99–101

T. Lezanski

[1] *Sur les fonctionnelles multiplicatives*, Studia Math. **14** (1953) 13–23

[2] *On a representation of the resolvent*, Studia Math. **15** (1956) 144–147

L. H. Loomis

[1] *An Introduction to Abstract Harmonic Analysis*, Van Nostrand, New York (1953)

[2] *The lattice theoretic background of the dimension theory of operator algebras*, Memoirs Amer. Math. Soc. no. 18, 36 pp. (1955)

E. R. Lorch

[1] *The spectrum of linear transformations*, Trans. Amer. Math. Soc. **52** (1942) 238–248

[2] *The theory of analytic functions in normed abelian vector rings*, Trans. Amer. Math. Soc. **54** (1943) 414–425

[3] *The structure of normed abelian rings*, Bull. Amer. Math. Soc. **50** (1944) 447–463

[4] *Normed rings—the first decade*, Proc. of Symposium on Spectral Theory and Differential Problems, pp. 249–258, Okla. Agri. and Mech. Coll., Stillwater, Okla. (1955)

D. B. Lowdenslager

[1] *On postulates for general quantum mechanics*, Proc. Amer. Math. Soc. **8** (1957) 88–91

E. H. Luchins

[1] *On strictly semi-simple Banach algebras*, Pacific J. Math. **9** (1959) 551–554

[2] *On radicals and continuity of homomorphisms into Banach algebras*, Pacific J. Math. **9** (1959) 755–758

G. Lumer

[1] *Fine structure and continuity of spectra in Banach algebras*, An. Acad. Brasil. Ci. **26** (1954) 229–233

[2] *The range of the exponential function*, Bol. Fac. Ingen. Agrimens. Montevideo 6 = Fac. Ingen. Agrimens. Montevideo. Publ. Inst. Mat. Estadist **3** (1957) 53–55

[3] *Commutators in Banach algebras*, Bol. Fac. Ingen. Agrimens. Montevideo 6 = Fac. Ingen. Agrimens. Montevideo Publ. Inst. Mat. Estadist **3** (1957) 57–63

R. MacDowell

[1] *Banach spaces and algebras of continuous functions*, Proc. Amer. Math. Soc. **6** (1955) 67–68

G. W. Mackey

[1] *Isomorphisms of normed linear spaces*, Ann. of Math. **43** (1942) 244–260

[2] *A theorem of Stone and von Neumann*, Duke Math. J. **16** (1949) 313–326

[3] *Imprimitivity for representations of locally compact groups*, I. Proc. Nat. Acad. Sci. U.S.A. **35** (1949) 537–545

[4] *Functions on locally compact groups*, Bull. Amer. Math. Soc. **56** (1950) 385–412

[5] *Commutative Banach algebras* (Edited by A. Blair), Harvard Univ. Lecture Notes (1952)

[6] *Borel structure in groups and their duals*, Trans. Amer. Math. Soc. **85** (1957) 134–165

J. S. MacNerny

[1] *Stieltjes integrals in linear spaces*, Ann. of Math. (2) **61** (1955) 354–367

C. A. McCarthy

[1] *On open mappings in Banach algebras*, J. of Math. and Mech. **8** (1959) 415–418

[2] *The nilpotent part of a spectral operator*, Pacific J. Math. **9** (1959) 1223–1231

F. Maeda

[1] *Relative dimensionality in operator rings*, J. of Sci. Hiroshima U. Ser. A **11** (1941) 1–6

[2] *Lengths of projections in rings of operators*, J. of Sci. Hiroshima Univ Ser. A. **20** (1956) 5–11

P. Malliavin

[1] *Sur l'impossibilité de la synthèse spectrale dans une algèbre de fonctions presque periodiques*, C.R. Acad. Sci. Paris **248** (1959) 1756–1759

[2] *Impossibilité de la synthèse spectrale sur les groupes abeliens non compact*, Faculte des Sciences de Paris, Seminaire d'analyse (P. Lelong) 1958–59

[3] *Calcul symbolique et sous-algebres de $L_1(G)$*, Bull. Soc. Math. France **87** (1959) 181–190

[4] *L'approximation polynomiale ponderee sur un espace localement compact*, Amer. J. Math. **81** (1959) 605–612

L. A. Markuševič

[1] *On rings of continuous functions on a circumference*, Uspehi Mat. Nauk **12**, no. 4 (1957) 327–334

V. Martchenko

[1] *Sur les fonctions dont les distances à certains ensembles dans l'espace des fonctions bornées sont égales*, Dokl. Akad. Nauk S.S.S.R. **51** (1946) 663–666

P. R. Masani

[1] *Multiplicative Riemann integration in normed rings*, Trans Amer. Math. Soc. **61** (1947) 147–192

[2] *The rational approximation of operator-valued functions*, Proc. London Math. Soc. (3) **6** (1956) 43–58

[3] *The Laurent factorization of operator-valued functions*, Proc. London Math. Soc. (3) **6** (1956) 59–69

P. Masani and T. Vijayaraghavan

[1] *An analogue of Laurent's theorem for a simply connected region*, J. Ind. Math. Soc. (N.S.) **16** (1952) 25–30

S. Matsushita

[1] *Positive linear functionals on self-adjoint Banach algebras*, Proc. Japan Acad. **29** (1953) 427–430

[2] *Sur quelques types des théorèmes de dualité dans les groupes topologique I*, Proc. Japan Acad. **30** (1954), 849–854; *II*, Ibid. **30** (1954) 957–962

[3] *Positive functionals and representation theory on Banach algebras*, I. J. Inst. Polytech. Osaka City Univ. Ser. A 6 (1955) 1–18

K. Matthes

[1] *Über eine Verallgameinerung eines Satzes von Gelfand und Kolmogoroff*, Math. Nachr. **15** (1956) 117–121

K. Mauren

[1] *Elementare Bemerkungen über kommutative C*-Algebren (Beweis einer Vermutang von Dirac)*, Studia Math. **16** (1957) 74–79

F. I. Mautner

[1] *Unitary representations of locally compact groups I*, Ann. of Math. **51** (1950) 1–25; *II*, Ibid. **52** (1950) 528–556

S. Mazur

[1] *Sur les anneaux linéaires*, C.R. Acad. Sci. Paris **207** (1938) 1025–1027

S. N. Mergelyan

[1] *On best approximation in adjacent regions*, Dokl. Akad. Nauk S.S.S.R. **61** (1948) 981–983

[2] *On best approximation in a complex region*, Dokl. Akad. Nauk S.S.S.R. **62** (1948) 23–26

[3] *On best approximation on closed sets*, Dokl. Akad. Nauk S.S.S.R. **62** (1948) 163–166; errata **63** (1948) 220

[4] *On the representation of functions by series of polynomials*, Dokl. Akad. Nauk S.S.S.R. **78** (1951) 405–408; Amer. Math. Soc. Transl. No. 85

Y. Mibu

[1] *On Baire functions on infinite product spaces*, Proc. Imp. Acad. Tokyo **20** (1944) 661–663

E. A. Michael

[1] *Locally multiplicatively-convex topological algebras*, Memoirs. Amer. Math. Soc. No. 11 (1952) 79 pp.

A. D. Michal

[1] *The total differential equation for the exponential function in non-commutative normed linear rings*, Proc. Nat. Acad. Sci. U.S.A. **31** (1945) 315–317

J. G.-Mikusinski

[1] *L'anneau algébrique et ses applications dans l'analyse fonctionnelle I* Ann. Univ. Mariae Curie-Sklodowska, Sect. A. **2** (1947) 1–48

D. Mil'man

[1] *On the normalibility of topological rings*, Dokl. Akad. Nauk S.S.S.R. **47** (1945) 162–164

[2] *Characteristics of extremal points of regularly convex sets*, Dokl. Akad. Nauk S.S.S.R. **57** (1947) 119–122

[3] *Accessible points of a functional compact set*, Dokl. Akad. Nauk S.S.S.R. **59** (1948) 1045–1048

[4] *On the theory of rings with involution*, Dokl. Akad. Nauk S.S.S.R. **76** (1951) 349–352

S. Minakshisundaram and M. Rajagopalan

[1] *H*-algebras* (To appear)

H. Mirkil

[1] *The work of Šilov on commutative Banach algebras*, mimeographed notes, Univ. of Chi.

Y. Misonou

[1] *On a weakly central operator algebra*, Tôhoku Math. J. (2) **4** (1952) 194–202

[2] *Operator algebras of type I*, Kodai Math. Sem. Rep. (1953) 87–90

[3] *Unitary equivalence of factors of type III*, Proc. Japan Acad. **29** (1953) 482–485

[4] *On the direct product of W*-algebras*, Tôhoku Math. J. (2) **6** (1954) 189–209

[5] *Generalized approximately finite W*-algebras*, Tôhoku Math. J. (2) **7** (1955) 192–205

[6] *On divisors of factors*, Tôhoku Math. J. (2) **8** (1956) 63–69

Y. Misonou and M. Nakamura

[1] *Centering of an operator algebra*, Tôhoku Math. J. **3** (1951) 243–248

Y. Miyanaga

[1] *A note on Banach algebras*, Proc. Japan Acad. **32** (1956) 176

S. Mrówka

[1] *Functionals on uniformly closed rings of continuous functions*, Fund. Math. **46** (1958) 81–87

F. J. Murray and J. von Neumann

[1] *On rings of operators*, Ann. of Math. **37** (1935) 116–229

[2] *On rings of operators II*, Amer. Math. Soc. **41** (1937) 208–248

[3] *On rings of operators IV*, Ann. of Math. **44** (1943) 716–808

S. B. Myers

[1] *Algebras of differentiable functions*, Proc. Amer. Math. Soc. **5** (1954) 917–922

[2] *Differentiation in Banach algebras.* Summary of Lectures and Seminars, Summer Institute on Set Theoretic Topology, Madison, Wisc. (1955) 135–137

L. Nachbin

[1] *Sur les algébres denses de fonctions différentiables sur une variété,* C.R. Acad. Sci. Paris **228** (1949) 1549–1551

[2] *A generalization of Whitney's theorem on ideals of differentiable functions*, Proc. Nat. Acad. Sci. U.S.A. **43** (1957) 935–937

[3] *On the operational calculus with differentiable functions*, Proc. Nat. Acad. Sci. U.S.A. **44** (1958) 698–700

M. Nagasawa

[1] *Isomorphisms between commutative Banach algebras with an application to rings of analytic functions*, Kodai Math. Sem. Rep. **11** (1959) 182–188

M. Nagumo

[1] *Einige analytische Untersuchungen in linearen metrischen Ringen,* Jap. J. Math. **13** (1936) 61–80

M. A. Naĭmark

[1] *Rings with involution*, Uspehi Mat. Nauk **3** (1948) 52–145; Amer. Math. Soc. Translation No. 25 (1950)

[2] *Rings of operators in Hilbert space*, Uspehi Mat. Nauk **4** (1949) 83–147

[3] *On a problem of the theory of rings with involution*, Uspehi Mat. Nauk **6** (1951) 160–164

[4] *On a continuous analogue of Schur's lemma*, Dokl. Akad. Nauk S.S.S.R. **98** (1954) 185–188

[5] *On the description of all unitary representations of the complex classical groups I*, Mat. Sbornik **35** (1954) 317–356; *II*, Ibid. **37** (1955) 121–140; Amer. Math. Soc. Translation (2) **9** (1958) 155–215

[6] *Continuous analogue of Schur's lemma and its application to Plancherel's formula for the complex classical groups*, Izvestiya Akad. Nauk S.S.S.R. Ser. Mat. **20** (1956) 3–16; Amer. Math. Soc. Translation (2) **9** (1958) 217–231

[7] *Normed Rings*, Gosudarstv. Izdat. Tehn.-Teor. Lit., Moscow (1956)

M. A. Naĭmark and S. V. Fomin

[1] *Continuous direct sums of Hilbert spaces and some of their applications*, Uspehi Mat. Nauk **10** (1955) 111–142; Amer. Math. Soc. Translation (2) **5** (1957) 35–65

M. Nakai

[1] *Some expectations in AW*-algebras*, Proc. Japan Acad. **34** (1958) 411–416

[2] *On a ring isomorphism induced by quasiconformal mappings*, Nagoya Math. J. **14** (1959) 201–221

[3] *A function algebra on Riemann surfaces*, Nagoya Math. J. **15** (1959) 1–17

M. Nakamura

[1] *Notes on Banach spaces VIII. A generalization of Šilov's theorem*, Tôhoku Math. J. **1** (1949) 66–68, *XII, A remark on the theorem of Gelfand and Neumark*, Ibid. **2** (1950) 182–187

[2] *The two-sided representations of an operator algebra*, Proc. Japan Acad. **27** (1951) 172–176

[3] *On the direct product of finite factors*, Tôhoku Math. J. **6** (1954) 205–207

[4] *A proof of a theorem of Takesaki*, Kodai Math. Sem. Rep. **10** (1958) 189–190

M. Nakamura and Z. Takeda

[1] *The Radon-Nikodym theorem of traces for a certain operator algebra*, Tôhoku Math. J. **4** (1952) 275–283

[2] *Normal states of commutative operator algebras*, Tôhoku Math. J. **5** (1953) 109–121

[3] *On the extensions of finite factors I, II*, Proc. Japan Acad. **35** (1959) 149–154, 215–220

[4] *On some elementary properties of the crossed products of von Neumann Algebras*, Proc. Japan Acad. **34** (1958) 489–494

M. Nakamura and T. Turumaru

[1] *Simple algebras of completely continuous operators*, Tôhoku Math. J. **4** (1952) 303–308

[2] *Expectations in an operator algebra*, Tôhoku Math. J. **6** (1954) 182–188

[3] *On extensions of pure states of an abelian operator algebra*, Tôhoku Math. J. **6** (1954) 253–257

M. Nakamura and H. Umegaki

[1] *A remark on theorems of Stone and Bochner*, Proc. Jap. Acad. **27** (1951) 506–507

[2] *On a proposition of von Neumann*, Kodai Math. Sem. Rep. **8** (1956) 142–144

H. Nakano

[1] *On the product of relative spectra*, Ann. of Math. (2) **49** (1948) 281–315

[2] *Modern Spectral Theory*, Maruzen Co. Ltd., Tokyo (1950)

E. Nelson

[1] *A functional calculus using singular Laplace integrals*, Trans. Amer. Math. Soc. **88** (1958) 400–413

J. von Neumann

[1] *Zur Algebra der Funktionaloperatoren und Theorie der normalen Operatoren*, Math. Annalen **102** (1929) 370–427

[2] *On a certain topology for rings of operators*, Ann. of Math. **37** (1936) 111–115

[3] *On an algebraic generalization of the quantum mechanical formalism I*, Mat. Sbornik **1** (1936) 415–484

[4] *On regular rings*, Proc. Nat. Acad. Sci. U.S.A. **22** (1936) 707–713

[5] *On infinite direct products*, Comp. Math. **6** (1938) 1–77

[6] *On rings of operators III*, Ann. of Math. **41** (1940) 94–161

[7] *On some algebraical properties of operator rings*, Ann. of Math. **44** (1943) 709–715

[8] *On rings of operators. Reduction theory*, Ann. of Math. **50** (1949) 401–485

[9] *The non-isomorphism of certain continuous rings*, Ann. of Math. **67** (1958) 485–496

J. D. Newburgh

[1] *The variation of spectra*, Duke Math. J. **18** (1951) 165–176

D. J. Newman

[1] *Some remarks on the maximal ideal structure of H^∞*, Ann. of Math. **70** (1959) 438–445

G. Nöbeling and H. Bauer

[1] *Über die Erweiterungen topologischer Räume*, Math. Ann. **130** (1955) 20–45

T. Ogasawara

[1] *Finite dimensionality of certain Banach algebras*, J. Sci. Hiroshima Univ. Ser. A. **17** (1954) 359–364

[2] *A theorem on operator algebras*, J. Sci. Hiroshima Univ. Ser. A. **18** (1955) 307–309

[3] *A structure theorem for complete quasi-unitary algebras*, J. Sci. Hiroshima Univ. Ser. A. **19** (1955) 79–85

[4] *Topologies on rings of operators*, J. Sci. Hiroshima Univ. Ser. A. **19** (1955) 255–272

T. Ogasawara and S. Maeda

[1] *A generalization of a theorem of Dye*, J. Sci. Hiroshima Univ. Ser. A. **20** (1956) 1–4

T. Ogasawara and K. Yoshinaga

[1] *Weakly completely continuous Banach* $\star$*-algebras*, J. Sci. Hiroshima Univ. Ser. A. **18** (1954) 15–36

[2] *A characterization of dual* $B^\star$*-algebras*, J. Sci. Hiroshima Univ. Ser. A. **18** (1954) 179–182

[3] *A non-commutative theory of integration for operators*, J. Sci. Hiroshima Univ. Ser. A. **18** (1955) 311–347

A. Olubummo

[1] *Left completely continuous* $B^\#$*-algebras*, J. London Math. Soc. **32** (1957) 270–276

T. Ono

[1] *Local theory of rings of operators I, II*, J. Math. Soc. Japan **10** (1958) 184–216, 438–458

[2] *Note on a* $B^\star$*-algebra*, J. Math. Soc. Japan **11** (1959) 146–158

M. Orihara

[1] *Sur les anneaux des opérateurs I, II*, Proc. Imp. Acad. Tokyo **20** (1944) 399–405, 545–553

[2] *Rings of operators and their traces*, Mem. Fac. Sci. Kyusyu Univ. A. **5** (1950) 107–138; *Correction*, Ibid. **8** (1953) 89–91

M. Orihara and T. Tsuda

[1] *The two-sided regular representation of a locally compact group*, Mem. Fac. Sci. Kyusyu Univ. A. **6** (1951), 21–29

R. Pallu de la Barrière

[1] *Algèbres auto-adjoints faiblement fermées et algèbres hilbertiennes de classe fini*, C.R. Acad. Sci. Paris **232** (1951) 1994–1995

[2] *Décomposition des opérateurs non bornés dans les sommes continués d'espace de Hilbert*, C.R. Acad. Sci. Paris **232** (1951) 2071–2073

[3] *Isomorphisms des* $\star$*-algèbres faiblement fermées d'opérateurs*, C.R. Acad. Sci. Paris **234** (1952) 795–797

[4] *Algèbres unitaires et espaces d'Ambrose*, Ann. Sci. Ecole Norm. Sup (3) **70** (1953) 381–401

[5] *Sur les algèbres d'opérateurs dans les espaces hilbertiens*, Bull. Soc. Math. France **82** (1954) 1–52

S. Perlis

[1] *A characterization of the radical of an algebra*, Bull. Amer. Math. Soc. **48** (1942) 128–132

R. S. Phillips

[1] *Spectral theory for semi-groups of linear operators*, Trans. Amer. Math. Soc. **71** (1951) 393–415

[2] *On the generation of semi-groups of linear operators*, Pacific J. Math. **2** (1952) 343–369

A. G. Pinsker

[1] *On representation of a K-space as a ring of self-adjoint operators*, Dokl. Akad. Nauk S.S.S.R. **106** (1956) 195–198

T. S. Pitcher

[1] *Positivity in H-systems and sufficient statistics*, Trans. Amer. Math. Soc. **85** (1957) 166–173

A. Plans

[1] *A system of axioms for the ring of real bounded infinite matrices*, Collect. Math. **9** (1957) 35–40

[2] *A lattice structure of the ring of real bounded infinite matrices*, Collect. Math. **9** (1957) 87–104

G. Pólya and G. Szegö

[1] *Aufgaben und Lehrsätze aus der Analysis*, I. Springer, Berlin (1925)

G. Porath

[1] *Störungstheorie für abgeschlossene lineare Transformationen in Banachschen Raum*, Math. Nachr. **17** (1958) 62–72

E. T. Poulsen

[1] *On the algebra generated by a continuous function*, Math. Scand. **6** (1958) 37–39

A. Povsner

[1] *On equations of the Sturm-Liouville type on a semi-axis*, Dokl. Akad. Nauk S.S.S.R. **53** (1946) 295–298

[2] *On some general inversion formulas of Plancherel type*, Dokl. Akad. Nauk S.S.S.R. **57** (1947) 123–125

[3] *On the spectrum of bounded functions*, Dokl. Akad. Nauk S.S.S.R. **57** (1947) 755–758

A. Prekopa

[1] *Extension of multiplicative set functions with values in a Banach algebra*, Acta Math. Acad. Sci. Hungar. **7** (1956) 201–213

L. Pukansky

[1] *On a theorem of Mautner*, Acta Sci. Math. Szegd. **15** (1954) 145–148

[2] *The theorem of Radon-Nikodym in operator rings*, Acta Sci. Math. Szegd. **15** (1954) 149–156

[3] *On the theory of quasi-unitary algebras*, Acta Sci. Math. Szegd. **16** (1955) 103–121

[4] *Some examples of factors*, Publ. Math. Debrecen **4** (1956) 135–156

F. Quigley

[1] *Approximation by algebras of function*, Math. Ann. **135** (1958) 81–92

T. Radc and J. W. T. Youngs

[1] *On upper semi-continuous collections*, Acta Litt. Sci. Szegd. **9** (1940) 239–243

D. A. Raikov

[1] *Harmonic analysis on commutative groups with the Haar measure and the theory of characters*, Trav. Inst. Math. Stekloff **14** (1945) 86 pp.

[2] *To the theory of normed rings with involution*, Dokl. Akad. Nauk S.S.S.R. **54** (1946) 387–390

M. Rajagopalan

[1] *Classification of algebras*, J. Ind. Math. Soc. **22** (1958) 109–116

V. Ramaswami

[1] *Normed algebras, isomorphism and the associative postulate*, J. Ind. Math. Soc. **14** (1950) 47–64

H. J. Reiter

[1] *Investigations in harmonic analysis*, Trans. Amer. Math. Soc. **73** (1952) 401–427

[2] *On a certain class of ideals in the L_1 algebra of a locally compact abelian group*, Trans. Amer. Math. Soc. **75** (1953) 505–509

[3] *Contributions to harmonic analysis*, Acta Math. **96** (1956) 253–263; *II*, Math. Ann. **133** (1957) 298–302; *III*, J. London Math. Soc. **32** (1957) 477–483

C. E. Rickart

[1] *Banach algebras with an adjoint operation*, Ann. of Math. **47** (1946) 528–550

[2] *The singular elements of a Banach algebra*, Duke Math. J. **14** (1947) 1063–1077

[3] *The uniqueness of norm problem in Banach algebras*, Ann. of Math. **51** (1950) 615–628

[4] *Representation of certain Banach algebras on Hilbert space*, Duke Math. J. **18** (1951) 27–39

[5] *Spectral permanence for certain Banach algebras*, Proc. Amer. Math. Soc. **4** (1953) 191–196

[6] *An elementary proof of a fundamental theorem in the theory of Banach algebras*, Mich. Math. J. **5** (1958) 75–78

F. Riesz and B. Sz.-Nagy

[1] *Functional Analysis*, Frederick Unger Pub. Co., New York (1955)

V. Rohlin

[1] *Unitary rings*, Dokl. Akad. Nauk S.S.S.R. **59** (1948) 643–646

A. Rosenberg

[1] *The number of irreducible representations of simple rings with no minimal ideals*, Amer. J. Math. **75** (1953) 523–530

[2] *Finite-dimensional simple subalgebras of the ring of all continuous linear transformations*, Math. Z. **61** (1954) 150–159

M. Rosenblum

[1] *On the operator equation* $BX-XA = Q$, Duke Math. J. **23** (1956) 263–269

[2] *On a theorem of Fuglede and Putnam*, J. London Math. Soc. **33** (1958) 376–377

H. Rossi

[1] *The local maximum modulus principle*, Report on research supported by the U.S. Air Force under Contract No. AF 49 (638) 692 Princeton University (1959)

W. Rudin

[1] *Boundary values of continuous analytic functions*, Proc. Amer. Math. Soc. **7** (1956) 808–811

[2] *The automorphisms and the endomorphisms of the group algebra of the unit circle*, Acta Math. **95** (1956) 39–55

[3] *Subalgebras of spaces of continuous functions*, Proc. Amer. Math. Soc. **7** (1956) 825–830

[4] *Les ideaux fermés dans un anneau de fonctions analytiques*, C.R. Acad. Sci. Paris **244** (1957) 997–998

[5] *Continuous functions on compact spaces without perfect subsets*, Proc. Amer. Math. Soc. **8** (1957) 39–42

[6] *Factorization in the group algebra of the real line*, Proc. Nat. Acad. Sci. U.S.A. **43** (1957) 339–340

[7] *The closed ideals in an algebra of analytic functions*, Canad. J. Math. **9** (1957) 426–434

[8] *Representation of functions by convolution*, J. of Math. and Mech. **7** (1958) 103–116

[9] *Independent perfect sets in groups*, Mich. Math. J. **5** (1958) 159–161

[10] *On the structure of maximum modulus algebras*, Proc. Amer. Math. Soc. **9** (1958) 708–712

[11] *On isomorphisms of group algebras*, Bull. Amer. Math. Soc. **64** (1958) 167–169

[12] *Weak almost periodic functions and Fourier-Stieltjes transforms*, Duke Math. J. **26** (1959) 215–220

[13] *Measure algebras on abelian groups*, Bull. Amer. Math. Soc. **65** (1959) 227–247

[14] *Algebras of analytic functions.* Summary of Lectures and Seminars, Summer Institute on Set-Theoretic Topology, Madison Wisc. (1955) 137–139

T. Saitô

[1] *On incomplete infinite direct products of W*⋆*-algebras*, Tôhoku Math. J. (2) **10** (1958) 165–171

[2] *The direct product and the crossed product of rings of operators*, Tôhoku Math. J. **11** (1959) 299–304

S. Sakai

[1] *On the group isomorphism of unitary groups in AW*⋆*-algebras*, Tôhoku Math. J. **7** (1955) 87–95

[2] *The absolute value of W*⋆*-algebras of finite type*, Tôhoku Math. J. **8** (1956) 70–85

[3] *A characterization of W*⋆*-algebras*, Pacific J. Math. **6** (1956) 763–773

[4] *On the σ-weak topology of W*⋆*-algebras*, Proc. Japan Acad. **32** (1956) 329–332

[5] *On topological properties of W*⋆*-algebras*, Proc. Japan Acad. **33** (1957) 439–444

[6] *On some problems of C*⋆*-algebras*, Tôhoku Math. J. **11** (1959) 453–455

S. Sasaki

[1] *A proof of the spectral theorem*, Kumamoto J. Sci. Ser. A. **1** (1953) 14–16

U. Sasaki

[1] *Lattice of projections in AW*⋆*-algebras*, J. Sci. Hiroshima Univ. Ser. A. **19** (1955) 1–30

P. P. Saworotnow

[1] *On a generalization of the notion of H*⋆*-algebra*, Proc. Amer. Math. Soc. **8** (1957) 49–55

[2] *On the embedding of a right complemented algebra into Ambrose's H*⋆*-algebra*, Proc. Amer. Math. Soc. **8** (1957) 56–62

J. Schäffer

[1] *On some problems concerning operators in Hilbert space*, Anais. Acad. Brasil Ci. **25** (1953) 87–90

R. Schatten

[1] *A Theory of Cross-Spaces*, Ann. of Math. Studies, no. 26, Princeton (1950)

[2] *The space of completely continuous operators on Hilbert space*, Math. Ann. **134** (1957) 47–49

J. A. Schatz

[1] *Representation of Banach algebras with an involution*, Canad. J. Math. **9** (1957) 435–442

E. Schmidt

[1] *Entwicklung willkürlicher Funktionen nach Systemen vorgeschriebener*, Math. Ann. **63** (1907) 433–476

M. Schreiber

[1] *A functional calculus for general operators in Hilbert space*, Trans. Amer. Math. Soc. **87** (1958) 108–118

L. Schwartz

[1] *Sur une propriété de synthèse spectrale dans les groups non compacts*, C.R. Acad. Sci. Paris **227** (1948) 424–426

I. E. Segal

[1] *The group ring of a locally compact group I*, Proc. Nat. Acad. Sci. U.S.A. **27** (1941) 348–352

[2] *The group algebra of a locally compact group*, Trans. Amer. Math. Soc. **61** (1947) 69–105

[3] *Irreducible representations of operator algebras*, Bull. Amer. Math. Soc. **53** (1947) 73–88

[4] *Postulates for general quantum mechanics*, Ann. of. Math. **48** (1947) 930–948

[5] *Two-sided ideals in operator algebras*, Ann. of Math. **50** (1949) 856–865

[6] *The class of functions which are absolutely convergent Fourier transforms*, Acta. Sci. Math. Szeged **12** (1950) 157–161

[7] *The two-sided regular representation of a unimodular locally compact group*, Ann. of Math. **51** (1950) 293–298

[8] *An extension of Plancherel's formula to separable unimodular groups*, Ann. of Math. **52** (1950) 272–292

[9] *A class of operator algebras which are determined by groups*, Duke Math. J. **18** (1951) 221–265

[10] *Decomposition of operator algebras I, II*, Memoirs of Amer. Math. Soc. no. 9, New York (1951)
[11] *Equivalence of measure spaces*, Amer. J. Math. **73** (1951) 275–313
[12] *A non-commutative extension of abstract integration*, Ann. of Math. **57** (1953) 401–457

Z. Semadeni
[1] *Spaces of continuous functions II*, Studia Math. **16** (1957) 193–199
[2] *A localization theorem for multiplicative linear functionals*, Bull. Acad. Polon. Sci. Ser. Sci. Math. Astr. Phys. **6** (1958) 289–292

I. Shafarevich
[1] *On the normalizability of topological fields*, Dokl. Akad. Nauk. S.S.S.R. **40** (1943) 133–135

S. Sherman
[1] *Order in operator algebras*, Amer. J. Math. **73** (1951) 227–232
[2] *Non-negative observables are squares*, Proc. Amer. Math. Soc. **2** (1951) 31–33

G. Šilov
[1] *Ideals and subrings of the ring of continuous functions*, Dokl. Akad. Nauk S.S.S.R. **22** (1939) 7–10
[2] *Sur la théorie des ideaux dans les anneaux normés de fonctions*, Dokl. Akad. Nauk S.S.S.R. **27** (1940) 900–903
[3] *On the extension of maximal ideals*, Dokl. Akad. Nauk S.S.S.R. **29** (1940) 83–84
[4] *On normed rings possessing one generator*, Mat. Sbornik **21** (1947) 25–47
[5] *On regular normed rings*, Trav. Inst. Math. Stekloff **21**, Moscow (1947)
[6] *On a property of rings of functions*, Dokl. Akad. Nauk S.S.S.R. **58** (1947) 985–988
[7] *Rings of type C*, Dokl. Akad. Nauk S.S.S.R. **66** (1949) 813–816
[8] *Rings of type C on the line and on the circumference*, Dokl. Akad. Nauk S.S.S.R. **66** (1949) 1063–1066
[9] *Description of a class of normed rings of functions*, Mat. Sbornik **26** (1950) 291–310
[10] *On a theorem of I. M. Gelfand and its generalizations*, Dokl. Akad. Nauk S.S.S.R. **72** (1950) 641–644
[11] *On continuous sums of finite dimensional rings*, Mat. Sbornik **27** (1950) 471–484
[12] *Homogeneous rings of functions*, Uspehi Mat. Nauk **6** (1951) 91–137; Amer. Math. Soc. Transl. no. 92

[13] *On rings of functions with uniform convergence*, Ukrain. Mat. Zurnal **3** (1951) 404–411

[14] *On homogeneous rings of functions on the torus*, Dokl. Akad. Nauk S.S.S.R. (1952) 681–684

[15] *On decomposition of a commutative normed ring in a direct sum of ideals*, Mat. Sbornik **32** (1954) 353–364; Amer. Math. Soc. Transl. (2) **1** (1955) 37–48

[16] *On certain problems of the general theory of commutative normed rings*, Uspehi Math. Nauk **12** (1957) no. 1, 246–249; *Letter to the editor*, Ibid. **12** (1957) no. 5, 270

J. Sebastião e Silva

[1] *Analytic functions and functional analysis*, Portugaliae Math. **9** (1950) 1–130

A. B. Simon

[1] *Vanishing algebras*, Trans. Amer. Math. Soc. **92** (1959) 154–167

[2] *On the maximality of vanishing algebras*, Amer. J. Math. **81** (1959) 613–616

I. M. Singer

[1] *Automorphisms of finite factors*, Amer. J. Math. **77** (1955) 117–133

I. M. Singer and J. Wermer

[1] *Derivations on commutative normed algebras*, Math. Ann. **129** (1955) 260–264

F. V. Širokov

[1] *Proof of a conjecture of Kaplansky*, Uspehi Mat. Nauk **11** (1956) no. 4 167–168

M. F. Smiley

[1] *Right $H^\star$-algebras*, Proc. Amer. Math. Soc. **4** (1953) 1–4

[2] *Right annihilator algebras*, Proc. Amer. Math. Soc. **6** (1955) 698–701

V.Šmulian

[1] *On multiplicative linear functionals in certain special normed rings*, Dokl. Akad. Nauk S.S.S.R. **26** (1940) 13–16

I. E. Šnol

[1] *The structure of ideals in rings R_α*, Mat. Sbornik **27** (1950) 143–146

[2] *Closed ideals in the ring of continuously differentiable functions*, Mat. Sbornik **27** (1950) 281–284

Y. A. Šreider

[1] *The structure of maximal ideals in rings of completely additive measures*, Dokl. Akad. Nauk S.S.S.R. **63** (1948) 359–361

[2] *The structure of maximal ideals in rings of measures with convolution*, Mat. Sbornik **27** (1950) 297–318; Amer. Math. Soc. Transl. no. 81

Č. V. Stanajevic

[1] *Note on regular elements in an extension Banach algebra without identity*, Bull. Soc. Math. Phys. Serbie **8** (1956) 183–190

S. W. P. Steen

[1] *An introduction to the theory of operators*, Proc. London Math. Soc. **41** (1936) 361–392; **43** (1937) 529–543; **44** (1938) 398–411

[2] *An introduction to the theory of operators*, Proc. Camb. Phil Soc. **35** (1939) 562–578; **36** (1940) 139–149

W. F. Steinspring

[1] *Positive functions on C⋆-algebras*, Proc. Amer. Math. Soc. **6** (1955) 211–216

[2] *Integration theorems for gages and duality for unimodular groups*, Trans. Amer. Math. Soc. **90** (1959) 15–56

M. H. Stone

[1] *Application of the theory of Boolean rings to general topology*, Trans. Amer. Math. Soc. **41** (1937) 375–481

[2] *A general theory of spectra I*, Proc. Nat. Acad. Sci. U.S.A. **26** (1940) 280–283

[3] *On a theorem of Polya*, J. Ind. Math. Soc. **12** (1948) 1–7

[4] *The generalized Weierstrass approximation theorem*, Math. Mag. **21** (1948) 167–184, 237–254

[5] *Boundedness properties in function-lattices*, Canad. J. Math. **1** (1949) 176–186

[6] *On unbounded operators in Hilbert space*, J. Ind. Math. Soc. **15** (1952) 155–192

[7] *On the theorem of Gelfand-Mazur*, Ann. Sci. Polon. Math. **25** (1953) 238–240

[8] *Linear Transformations in Hilbert Space*, Amer. Math. Colloq. Publ. no. 15, New York (1932)

H. Sunouchi

[1] *On rings of operators of infinite classes I, II*, Proc. Jap. Acad. **28** (1952) 9–13, 330–335

[2] *The irreducible decompositions of the maximal Hilbert algebras of the finite class*, Tôhoku Math. J. **4** (1952) 207–215

[3] *A characterization of the maximal ideal in a factor of the case* II_∞, Kodai Math. Sem. Rep. (1954) 7

[4] *A characterization of the maximal ideal in a factor II*, Kodai. Math. Sem. Rep. **7** (1955) 65–66

N. Suzuki

[1] *On the invariants of W⋆-algebras*, Tôhoku Math. J. **7** (1955) 177–185

[2] *On automorphisms of W⋆-algebras leaving the center elementwise invariant*, Tôhoku Math. J. **7** (1955) 186–191

[3] *Crossed products of rings of operators*, Tôhoku Math. J. **11** (1959) 113–124

[4] *Certain types of groups of automorphisms of a factor*, Tôhoku Math. J. **11** (1959) 314–320

D.-Š. Sya (Shah Dao-Shing)

[1] *Positive functionals on algebras*, Dokl. Akad. Nauk S.S.S.R. **121** (1958) 233–235

[2] *On semi-normed rings with involution*, Izvestiya Akad. Nauk S.S.S.R. Ser. Mat. **23** (1959) 509–528

R. Takahashi

[1] *Un théorème de commutation*, C.R. Acad Sci. Paris **242** (1956) 1103–1106

Z. Takeda

[1] *On a theorem of R. Pallu de la Barrière*, Proc. Jap. Acad. **28** (1952) 558–563

[2] *Conjugate spaces of operator algebras*, Proc. Jap. Acad. **30** (1954) 90–95

[3] *On the representation of operator algebras*, Proc. Jap. Acad. **30** (1954) 299–304

[4] *On the representations of operator algebras II*, Tôhoku Math. J. **6** (1954) 212–219

[5] *Inductive limit and infinite direct product of operator algebras*, Tôhoku Math. J. **7** (1955) 67–86

[6] *Perfection of measure spaces and W⋆-algebras*, Kodai Math. Sem. Rep. (1953) 23–26

Z. Takeda and T. Turumaru

[1] *On the property "position p"*, Math. Jap. **11** (1952) 195–197

M. Takesaki

[1] *On the direct product of W⋆-factors*, Tôhoku Math. J. (2) **10** (1958) 116–119

[2] *On the conjugate space of an operator algebra*, Tôhoku Math. J. (2) **10** (1958) 194–203

[3] *A note on the cross-norm of the direct product of operator algebras*, Kodai Math. Sem. Rep. **10** (1958) 137–140

[4] *A note on the direct product of operator algebras*, Kodai Math. Sem. Rep. **11** (1959) 178–181

S. Teleman

[1] *Sur les algèbres de von Neumann*, Bull. Sci. Math. **82** (1958) 117–126

E. Thoma

[1] *Zur Reduktionstheorie in allgemeinen Hilbert-Raumen*, Math. Z. **68** (1957) 153–188

A. F. Timan

[1] *Generalization of a theorem of Stone*, Dokl. Akad. Nauk S.S.S.R **111** (1956) 955–958

M. Tomita

[1] *On rings of operators in non-separable Hilbert spaces*, Mem. Fac. Sci. Kyusyu Univ. A. **7** (1953) 129–168.

[2] *Representations of operator algebras*, Math. J. Okayama Univ. **3** (1954) 147–173

[3] *Banach algebras generated by a bounded linear operator*, Math. J. Okayama Univ. **4** (1955) 97–102

[4] *Harmonic anlysis on locally compact groups*, Math. J. Okayama Univ. **5** (1956) 133–193

J. Tomiyama

[1] *On the projection of norm one in W*-algebras*, Proc. Japan Acad. **33** (1957) 608–612; *II*, Tôhoku Math. J. **10** (1958) 204–209; *III*, Ibid. (2) **11** (1959) 125–129

[2] *A remark on the invariants of W*-algebras*, Tôhoku Math. J. **10** (1958) 37–41

[3] *Generalized dimension function for W*-algebras of infinite type*, Tôhoku Math. J. **10** (1958) 121–129

[4] *On the product projection of norm one in the direct product of operator algebras*, Tôhoku Math. J. **11** (1959) 305–313

Hing Tong

[1] *On ideals of certain topologized rings of continuous mappings associated with topological spaces*, Ann. of Math. **50** (1949) 329–340

L. Tornheim

[1] *Normed fields over the real and complex fields*, Mich. Math. J. **1** (1952) 61–68

K. Tsuji

[1] *$N^\star$-algebras and finite class groups*, Bull. Kyushu Inst. Tech. (Math., Nat. Sci.) no. 1 (1955) 1–9

[2] *Representation theorems of operator algebras and their applications*, Proc. Japan Acad. **31** (1955) 272–277

[3] *Harmonic analysis on locally compact groups*, Bull. Kyushu Inst. Tech. no. 2 (1956) 16–32

[4] *$W^\star$-algebras and abstract (L)-spaces*, Bull. Kyushu Inst. Tech. no. 3 (1957) 11–13

A. Turowicz

[1] *Sur les fonctionnelles continues et multiplicatives*, Ann. Soc. Polon. Math. **20** (1948) 135–156

T. Turumaru

[1] *On the commutativity of the $C^\star$-algebras*, Kodai. Math. Sem. Rep. (1951) 51

[2] *On the direct product of operator algebras I*, Tôhoku Math. J. **4** (1952) 242–251; *II*, Ibid. **5** (1953) 1–7; *III*, Ibid. **6** (1954) 208–211; *IV*, Ibid. **8** (1956) 281–285

[3] *Crossed product of operator algebra*, Tôhoku Math. J. **10** (1958) 355–365

H. Umegaki

[1] *On some representation theorems in an operator algebra I, II*, Proc. Jap. Acad. **27** (1951) 328–333, 501–505; *III*, Ibid. **28** (1952) 29–31

[2] *Operator algebra of finite class*, Kodai Math. Sem. Rep. (1952) 123–129; *II*, Ibid. (1953) 61–63

[3] *Decomposition theorems of operator algebra and their applications*, Jap. J. Math **22** (1953) 27–50

[4] *Note on irreducible decompositions of a positive linear functional*, Kodai Math. Sem. Rep. (1954) 25–32

[5] *Conditional expectation in an operator algebra*, Tôhoku Math. J. **6** (1954) 177–181; *II*, Ibid. **8** (1956) 86–100; *III*, Kodai Math. Sem. Rep. **11** (1959) 51–64

[6] *Positive definite function and direct product Hilbert spaces*, Tôhoku Math. J. **7** (1955) 206–211

[7] *Weak compactness in an operator space*, Kodai Math. Sem. Rep. **8** (1956) 145–151

I. Vernikoff, S. Krein and A. Tovbin

[1] *Sur les anneaux semi-ordonnés*, Dokl. Akad. Nauk S.S.S.R. **30** (1941) 785–787

I. Vidav

[1] *Über eine Vermutung von Kaplansky*, Math. Z. **62** (1955) 330

[2] *Quelques propriétés de la norme dans les algèbres de Banach*, Acad. Serbe. Sci. Publ. Inst. Math. **10** (1956) 53–58

[3] *Eine metrische Kennzeichnung der selbstadjungierten Operatoren*, Math. Z. **66** (1956) 121–128

[4] *Le spectre du produit $a^\star a$ deux éléments a et $a^\star$ verifiant la relation $aa^\star - a^\star a = e$*, Glasnik Mat. Fiz. Astr. Drustvo Mat. Fiz. Hrvalske Ser. II **12** (1957) 3–7

[5] *Über die darstellung der positiven Funktionale*, Math. Z. **68** (1958) 362–366

B. Z. Vulich

[1] *The product in linear partially ordered spaces and its application to the theory of operations I, II*, Mat. Sbornik **22** (1948) 27–78, 267–317

L. Waelbroeck

[1] *Le Calcul symbolique dans les algèbres commutatives*, J. Math. Pures Appl. **33** (1954) 147–186; C.R. Acad. Sci. Paris **238** (1954) 556–558

[2] *Les algèbres à inverse continu*, C.R. Acad. Sci. Paris **238** (1954) 640–641

[3] *Structure des algèbres à inverse continu*, C.R. Acad. Sci. Paris **238** (1954) 762–764

[4] *Algèbres commutatives: éléments réguliers*, Bull. Soc. Math. Belg. **9** (1957) 42–49

[5] *Note sur les algèbres du calcul symbolique*, J. Math. Pures Appl. (9) **37** (1958) 41–44

J. L. Walsh

[1] *Über die Entwicklung einer analytischen Funktion nach Polynomen*, Math. Ann. **96** (1927) 430–436

S. Warner

[1] *Polynomial completeness in locally multiplicatively-convex algebras* Duke Math. J. **23** (1956) 1–11

[2] *Inductive limits of normed algebras*, Trans. Amer. Math. Soc. **82** (1956) 190–216

[3] *Weakly topologized algebras*, Proc. Amer. Math. Soc. **8** (1957) 314–316

[4] *Weak locally multiplicatively-convex algebras*, Pacific J. Math. **5**, Suppl. 2 (1955) 1025–1032

A. Weil

[1] *L'integrale de Cauchy et les fonctions de plusieurs variables*, Math. Ann. **111** (1935) 178–182

J. G. Wendel

[1] *On isometric isomorphism of group algebras*, Pacific J. Math. **1** (1951) 305–311

[2] *Left centralizers and isomorphisms of group algebras*, Pacific J. Math. **2** (1952) 251–261

[3] *Haar measure and the semi-group of measures on a compact group*, Proc. Amer. Math. Soc. **5** (1954) 923–929

C. Wenjen

[1] *On semi-normed *-algebras*, Pacific J. Math **8** (1958) 177–186

J. Wermer

[1] *Harmonic analysis of groups and semi-groups of operators*, Dissertation, Harvard Univ. (1951)

[2] *Ideals in a class of commutative Banach algebras*, Duke Math. J. **20** (1953) 273–278

[3] *On algebras of continuous functions*, Proc. Amer. Math. Soc. **4** (1953) 866–869

[4] *On a class of normed rings*, Ark. Mat. **2** (1954) 537–551

[5] *Algebras with two generators*, Amer. J. Math. **76** (1954) 853–859

[6] *Maximal subalgebras of group-algebras*, Proc. Amer. Math. Soc. **6** (1955) 692–694

[7] *Polynomial approximation on an arc in* C^3, Ann. of Math. **62** (1955) 269–270

[8] *Subalgebras of the algebra of all complex-valued continuous functions on the circle*, Amer. J. Math. **78** (1956) 225–242

[9] *Function rings on the circle*, Proc. Nat. Acad. Sci. U.S.A. **43** (1957) 173–175

[10] *Function rings and Riemann surfaces*, Ann. of Math. **67** (1958) 45–71

[11] *Rings of analytic functions*, Ann. of Math. **67** (1958) 497–516

[12] *The hull of a curve in* C^n, Ann. of Math. **68** (1958) 550–561

[13] *The maximum principle for bounded functions*, Ann. of Math. **69** (1959) 598–604

H. Whitney

[1] *On ideals of differentiable functions*, Amer. J. Math. **70** (1948) 635–658

H. Widom

[1] *Embedding in algebras of type I*, Duke Math. J. **23** (1956) 309–324

[2] *Approximately finite algebras*, Trans. Amer. Math. Soc. **83** (1956) 170–178

[3] *Nonisomorphic approximately finite factors*, Proc. Amer. Math. Soc. **8** (1957) 537–540

N. Wiener

[1] *Tauberian theorems*, Ann. of Math. (2) **33** (1932) 1–100

N. Wiener and R. H. Pitt

[1] *On absolutely convergent Fourier-Stieltjes transforms*, Duke Math. J. **4** (1938) 420–436

A. Wilansky and K. Zeller

[1] *Banach algebra and summability*, Illinois J. Math. **2** (1958) 378–385. *Correction*, Ibid. **3** (1959) 468

A. B. Willcox

[1] *Some structure theorems for a class of Banach algebras*, Pacific J. Math. **6** (1956) 177–192

[2] *Note on certain group algebras*, Proc. Amer. Math. Soc. **7** (1956) 874–879

[3] *Šilov type C algebras over a connected locally compact abelian group*, Pacific J. Math. **9** (1959) 1279–1294

J. H. Williamson

[1] *Two conditions equivalent to normability*, J. London Math. Soc. **31** (1956) 111–113

[2] *On the functional representation of certain algebraic systems*, Pacific J. Math. **7** (1957) 1251–1277

[3] *On constructions of Wiener–Pitt and Šreider*, Comm. Int. Cong. Math. Edinburgh (1958)

[4] *On theorems of Kawada and Wendel*, Proc. Edinburgh Math. Soc. **11** (1958/59) 71–77

[5] *A theorem on algebras of measures on topological groups*, Proc. Edinburgh Math. Soc. **11** (1958/59) 195–206

A. Wintner

[1] *On the logarithm of bounded matrices*, Amer. J. Math. **74** (1952) 360–364

K. G. Wolfson

[1] *The algebra of bounded operators on Hilbert space*, Duke Math. J. **20** (1953) 533–538

[2] *The algebra of bounded functions*, Proc. Amer. Math. Soc. **5** (1954) 10–14

[3] *Anti-isomorphisms of the ring and lattice of a normed linear space*, Portugal Math. **14** (1955) 1–7

[4] *A class of primitive rings*, Duke Math. J. **22** (1955) 157–163
[5] *Annihilator rings*, J. London Math. Soc. **31** (1956) 94–104
[6] *A note on the algebra of bounded functions II*, Proc. Amer. Math. Soc. **7** (1956) 852–855

F. B. Wright
[1] *A reduction for algebras of finite type*, Ann. of Math. **60** (1954) 560–570
[2] *The ideals in a factor*, Ann. of Math. **68** (1958) 475–483

T. Yen
[1] *Trace on finite AW**-*algebras*, Duke Math. J. **22** (1955) 207–222
[2] *Quotient algebra of a finite AW**-*algebra*, Pacific J. Math. **6** (1956) 389–395
[3] *Isomorphism of unitary groups in AW**-*algebras*, Tôhoku Math. J. **8** (1956) 275–280
[4] *Isomorphism of AW**-*algebras*, Proc. Amer. Math. Soc. **8** (1957) 345–349

B. Yood
[1] *Transformations between Banach spaces in the uniform topology*, Ann. of Math. **50** (1949) 486–503
[2] *Additive groups and linear manifolds of transformations between Banach spaces*, Amer. J. Math. **71** (1949) 663–677
[3] *Banach algebras of bounded functions*, Duke Math. J. **16** (1949) 151–163
[4] *Banach algebras of continuous functions*, Amer. J. Math. **73** (1951) 30–42
[5] *Topological properties of homomorphisms between Banach algebras*, Amer. J. Math. **76** (1954) 155–167
[6] *Difference algebras of linear transformations on a Banach space*, Pacific J. Math **4** (1954), 615–636
[7] *Multiplicative semi-groups of continuous functions on a compact space*, Duke Math. J. **22** (1955) 383–392
[8] *Periodic mappings on Banach algebras*, Amer. J. Math. **77** (1955) 17–28; *Corrections to . . .*, Ibid. **78** (1956) 222–223
[9] *Seminar on Banach algebras*, Univ. of California Notes, Berkeley, 1956–57
[10] *Homomorphisms on normed algebras*, Pacific J. Math **8** (1958) 373–381

H. Yoshizawa
[1] *On simultaneous extensions of continuous functions*, Proc. Imp. Acad. Tokyo **20** (1944) 653–654

[2] *A proof of the Plancherel theorem*, Proc. Jap. Acad. **30** (1954) 276–281

K. Yosida

[1] *On the group embedded in the metrical complete ring*, Jap. J. Math. **13** (1936) 459–472

[2] *Normed rings and spectral theorems*, Proc. Imp. Acad. Tokyo **19** (1943) 356–359, 466–470; **20** (1944) 71–73, 183–185, 269–273, 580–583

[3] *Iso-kaiseki* [*Topological analysis I*], Iwanami Shoten, Tokyo (1951)

K. Yosida and T. Nakayama

[1] *On the semi-ordered ring and its application to the spectral theorem I*, Proc. Imp. Acad. Tokyo **18** (1942) 555–560; *II*, Ibid. **19** (1943) 144–147

W. Zelazko

[1] *On the divisors of zero of the group algebra*, Fund. Math. **45** (1957) 99–102

LIST OF SYMBOLS

The numbers indicate the pages on which the symbols are introduced.

INDEX

Except for section and paragraph numbers, which are enclosed in parentheses, the numbers given refer to pages where the item in question is mentioned.